BALI &
LOMBOK

CHANTAE REDEN

Contents

Baluran
National Park

Badjulmati

Wangsaredja

JAVA

Bali Barat
National Park

Kubutambahan

Singaraja

Tedjakula

Bubunan

Banjar

Danau
Buyan

Mount Batur

Danau
Tamblingan

Danau
Beratan

Mount Abang
2,153m

Kubu

Banjuwangi

Mount Lesung

Mount
Sengayang

Auman

Mount Agung
3,142m

Belimbingsari

Mount Batukaru
2,276m

BALI

Negara

Mendaja

Penebel

Pajangan

Susut

Tembuku

Selat

Bali Strait

Tegallalang

Bangli

Manggis

Badjera

Selemadeg

Ubud

Padangbai

Klungkung

Krambitan

Tabanan

Mengwi

Gianyar

Kusamba

Sukawati

Alas Purwo
National Park

Tandjung Slokah

Denpasar

Sanur

Jungutbatu

Nusa
Lembongan

Toyapakeh

Kuta Bay

Kuta

Nusa
Ceningan

Nusa
Penida

BALI INTERNATIONAL
AIRPORT

Jimbaran Bay

Jimbaran

Nusa Dua

NUSA
ISLANDS

Tandjung Mebulu

Petjatu

Tandjung Gagar

Badung Strait

Medan

MALAYSIA

BRUNEI

INDONESIA

Manado

HALMAHERA

Pontianak

BORNEO
(KALIMANTAN)

Palu

SUMATRA

Jambi

Balikpapan

SULAWESI
(CELEBES)

SERAM

Jayapura

Palembang

Bali Sea

Ambon

BURU

NEW
GUINEA
(PAPUA)

JAKARTA

Makassar

BALI

INDIAN

JAVA

Mataram

Denpasar

FLORES

TIMOR-LESTE

OCEAN

LOMBOK

SUMBA

TIMOR

SUMBAWA

Kupang

BALI SEA

Gili
Islands

Tjulik

Karangasen

Tandjung Bugbug

Strait of Lombok

Tandjung Abah

Tandjung Batugendang

Desa Anjar

Salangan

Lepeloang

Sembelie

Tandjung

Pamenang

Segara
Anak
Lake

Mount Rinjani
3,726m

Gunang
Rinjani
National Park

Senggigi

LOMBOK

Lombok

Mataram

Pringgabaja

Tapir Beru

LOMBOK
INTERNATIONAL
AIRPORT

Kopang

Selong

Strait of Alas

Gerung

Praya

Taliwang

Lembar

Genti

Sengkol

Djareweh

Buwun Mas

Balai Desa

Kuta

Repoksampih

SUMBAWA

Tandjung Sara

Tandjung Amat

Tandjung Bangkdulan

INDIAN OCEAN

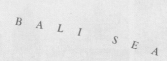

0   10 mi

0   10 km

© MOON.COM

DISCOVER

Bali & Lombok

The islands of Bali and Lombok are all about balance. Wherever you find one extreme, you're sure to find its counterpart close by. You'll find peace and energy, pop culture and tradition, modern luxury resorts and ancient temples, crowds and solitude, fresh coconut water and Bintang beer, barren beaches and rice terraces, volcanic peaks and a deep ocean.

Yet amid these contrasts, there is stability.

Bali has maintained its unique nickname, "The Island of the Gods," because of its connection to Hinduism in everyday life. Nearly every shop, car, and home is adorned with *canang sari,* an offering to appease the demons and please the gods. Chiming bells from local ceremonies set the tone for daily life and the sweet smell of incense lingers in the air. These rituals that stem from ancient traditions can still be seen even in Bali's most modern and glamorous towns, where the beer is cheap and parties are never-ending.

Venture to Bali's coastline for sandy beaches, sunsets, relaxation, surfing, and scuba diving. Inland, you'll discover miles of trails, emerald rice paddies, flowing rivers, and spiritual sanctuaries. There are temples, art museums, handicraft shops, welcoming guesthouses, and spas in-between.

Clockwise from top left: Tegenungan Waterfall; Pura Besakih; Gunung Rinjani; statue in Garuda Wisnu Kencana Cultural Park; Pura Ulun Danu Beratan; Bongkas surf point.

Once you cross the ocean to Lombok, the scenery changes again. The intimidating peak of Gunung Rinjani can be seen from the laid back, sandy shores of Lombok's tiny Gili Islands, where you can find your perfect balance of activity and relaxation. Surrounding the waterfall-dense forests of Gunung Rinjani are uncrowded beaches with world-class waves, stretches of desert, and sleepy villages.

The Sasak people of Lombok embrace creativity and celebration, and they welcome you to do the same. You can try handweaving a multicolored sarong on a complex wooden loom, collecting worms (for luck, of course) at the Bau Nyale Festival, and swapping stories over a thick cup of coffee.

There is truly an experience for everyone in Bali and Lombok, where no two trips are alike.

Clockwise from top left: sunset at Bingin Beach; Sanur Beach; snorkeling off Nusa Penida; Pura Masceti.

10 TOP
EXPERIENCES

1 Visiting one of Bali's most sacred temples at the dramatic cliff of **Uluwatu** (page 115).

2 Experiencing life like a local on **Nusa Penida,** an island where tiny villages and dramatic vistas are found around almost every turn (page 184).

3 Shopping in Ubud, where the markets and boutiques offer a colorful mix of traditional handicrafts and trendy souvenirs (page 216).

4 Learning how ancient cultivation techniques join the spiritual world to the natural one at the stunning **Jatiluwih Rice Terraces** (page 298).

>>>

5 Trekking to the crater rim of Indonesia's second highest volcano, **Gunung Rinjani,** to watch the sun rise over the caldera (page 451).

>>>

6 **Scuba diving** among shipwrecks and coral reefs, diving with manta rays, *mola-molas*, sea turtles, and reef sharks (page 30).

7 Escaping the crowds and finding a patch of soft sand all to yourself at one of **Lombok's southern beaches** like Selong Belanak, Tanjung Aan, Mawun, or Mawi (page 415).

8 Feeling the pulse of **nightlife in Kuta and Seminyak,** Bali's trendiest towns, where beach clubs turn effortlessly into nightclubs (page 75).

9 Relaxing on **Gili Trawangan,** the liveliest of a trio of little islands off Lombok, a beach escape from urban civilization with sea turtles, coral reefs, and technicolor fish galore (page 356).

10 **Surfing** some of Bali and Lombok's spectacular waves, no matter your ability level (page 28).

Planning Your Trip

Where to Go

Bali

KUTA, SEMINYAK, AND THE SOUTHERN BEACHES

Bali's international tourism scene first started in Kuta, and it reigns as the most-visited region today. The strip of umbrella-covered **beaches** hosts an array of **nightclubs, art performance venues, boutiques,** kitschy souvenir shops, and **hotels** ranging from budget to ultra-luxury. Each beach along this stretch of ocean has its own personality. Venture to **Kuta** for a bit of free-spirited debauchery, **Canggu** for a bohemian art scene, and **Seminyak** for boutique shops and innovative restaurants. Many of the world's best surfers caught their first wave in this region, where there's no shortage of beginner **surf spots.**

THE BUKIT PENINSULA

The Bukit Peninsula is awash with **cultural sights, beaches,** and **near-perfect waves.** More than 200 feet above the water, the **Pura Luhur Uluwatu** temple guards the region against malevolent spirits. Traditional *kecak* dancers gather at Uluwatu Temple to tell stories of ancient Hindu legends using elaborate costumes and movement. At sea level, the iconic waves called **Uluwatu, Dreamland,** and **Padang Padang** break along the Bukit Peninsula, where professional surf competitions take place throughout the year. Days are spent on the sand or in the water, while sunsets are enjoyed from a cliffside vista. Though the Bukit Peninsula has quickly become a hotspot for tourists, it holds tightly to its mysticism and charm.

Dreamland Surf Break

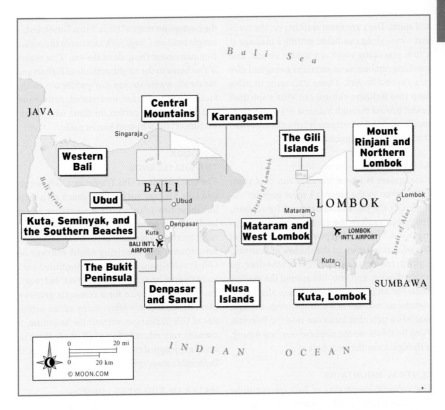

JAVA

Bali Sea

Singaraja

Central Mountains

Karangasem

Western Bali

The Gili Islands

Mount Rinjani and Northern Lombok

BALI

Ubud

Ubud

Strait of Lombok

Lombok

LOMBOK

Mataram

Bali Strait

Kuta, Seminyak, and the Southern Beaches

Kuta

Denpasar

BALI INT'L AIRPORT

Mataram and West Lombok

LOMBOK INT'L AIRPORT

Strait of Alas

The Bukit Peninsula

Kuta

SUMBAWA

Denpasar and Sanur

Nusa Islands

Kuta, Lombok

0   20 mi
0   20 km

INDIAN   OCEAN

© MOON.COM

DENPASAR AND SANUR

Denpasar, the island's capital, is a sprawling concrete metropolis where flowers and incense offerings are placed in the middle of major intersections and ceremonial attire intermixes with business suits. The **Bajra Sandhi Monument** punctuates the city, along with its surrounding grass lawns, where locals go to play sports or jog after work. On Denpasar's eastern end is the beach town of **Sanur,** a mellow area where you can stroll along the shoreline, stopping for **fresh food** or a **seaside massage.**

THE NUSA ISLANDS

Nusa Lembongan, Nusa Penida, and Nusa Ceningan offer many of the same benefits of Bali's southern mainland without the crowds. **Nusa Lembongan** is a playground for **cycling,**

beachside relaxing, kayaking, stand-up paddling, snorkeling, and **surfing** (there are waves for every ability). With plenty of scuba diving schools to choose from, students can earn their open water certification or enroll in a specialized course. Some of Indonesia's best **scuba diving** can be found off the coastline of **Nusa Penida,** where you might get lucky and catch a glimpse of a rare *mola-mola* fish or witness manta rays glide by. In **Nusa Ceningan,** travelers will find **beautiful vistas, snorkeling bays,** and **charming villages** that have yet to be touched by mass tourism.

UBUD

Surrounded by **rice terraces** that use ancient cultivation techniques, Ubud is an alluring place where travelers can focus on the mind, body, and spirit. Days are spent walking on the trails that weave along rice fields, getting a massage at a spa, practicing yoga at a hidden retreat, and watching rambunctious monkeys swing and play in a sacred forest. Those who want to delve deep into Balinese culture can visit a spiritual healer, browse through Balinese art museums, tour temples, and witness Hindu ceremonies that take place throughout the city.

KARANGASEM

Karangasem is where travelers can find tranquility even in the regency's most popular villages. Off the black sand beach of Tulamben, divers can explore the accessible and intriguing U.S.A.T. *Liberty* shipwreck. In the waters of Amed, a small town in the shadow of Gunung Agung, travelers can learn how to freedive, go muck diving, and snorkel around the shallow reefs. For an inside look at Balinese Hinduism, visit the incredible Pura Lempuyang, a temple that has a gate that looks out into the heavens. Pura Besakih, on the slopes of Gunung Agung, is thought to be the most holy of all.

CENTRAL MOUNTAINS

The volcanic mountains of Bali are not to be missed by travelers with a penchant for exploration. Trek to the summit of Gunung Batur to watch the sunrise. Then, soothe aching muscles in the healing waters of a nearby hot spring. There are plenty of cycling paths to explore in this region, as well. The cool climate at higher elevations offers respite from the tropical heat.

WESTERN BALI

The road weaving across Bali's northern end is lined with quiet villages, rice terraces, and waterfalls. The scuba diving, snorkeling, and boating are vastly underrated in this region, where visitors will be hard-pressed to find a crowd outside of Lovina—even in the high season.

The western peninsula of Bali includes Pulau Menjangan, an island surrounded by a thriving coral reef. Above the water, stroll along the trails of West Bali National Park and search

the treetops for tropical birds. Pura Tanah Lot, a temple built on a large rock cast out in the ocean, commemorates the gods of the sea. This region is also home to the neighborhoods of Balian and Medewi, where surfers can paddle out to the local waves. Quiet and underrated, Jembrana and Tabanan are perfect for those who love to venture off the well-trod tourist path.

Lombok

THE GILI ISLANDS

The Gili Islands of Gili Trawangan, Gili Meno, and Gili Air may not look like much on a map, but these tiny islands offer a sanctuary where landlocked worries won't follow. Discover all-night parties, a plethora of dive schools, little boutiques, and a thriving night market on Gili Trawangan. Gili Meno is outlined with sugar sand beaches and couples' retreats, and is the top choice for a romantic getaway. Meanwhile, Gili Air offers many of the activities of Gili Trawangan without the hedonism; it remains very relaxed. Best of all, these three islands are plopped right in the middle of some of Indonesia's most spectacular coral reefs.

MATARAM AND WEST LOMBOK

On the coastline of West Lombok is Senggigi, a sleepy beach town where you can relax in an upscale resort without the hefty price tag or battling crowds. Mataram, Lombok's capital, may not be as beach-blessed as the rest of the island, but it is still worth a visit for its many festivals, museums, impressive mosques, and cultural activities. Little islands colloquially called the "Secret Gilis" offshore of the southwestern peninsula offer some of the best snorkeling and beach lounging in all of the islands. Experienced surfers venture to the dangerously remote tip of the Tanjung Desert in hopes of getting barreled by one of the world's best left-hand waves.

KUTA, LOMBOK

Ten years ago, Kuta, Lombok, was a haven for surfers in search of unridden waves. Today, surf schools have sprung up in this bohemian beach town, and local fishermen have taken up a lucrative side gig of shuttling surfers out to waves on their fishing boats. On Kuta's main road, tourists can sample a variety of different foods, shop for **locally made textiles,** and dance the night away in a handful of **barefoot bars.** Outside of Kuta, tourists can beach-hop all along the coastline from one hidden enclave to the next; there are plenty of uncrowded waves still to be found.

MOUNT RINJANI AND NORTHERN LOMBOK

Lombok's most impressive feature is undoubtedly **Gunung Rinjani** (Mount Rinjani), Indonesia's second-highest volcano. A look at the turquoise waters of **Danau Segara Anak,** the lake inside of Gunung Rinjani's caldera, is reserved for those who make the trek up to its crater rim. Multiday treks in the reserve take hikers through a variety of different landscapes, ranging from dense rainforest to wide grasslands. Around the small towns of **Senaru** and **Sembalun Valley,** travelers can trek to **waterfalls** and snack on **fresh produce** grown throughout the region. In the tiny town of **Tetebatu,** rice terraces, plantations, and a sense of stillness await.

When to Go

Bali and Lombok are warm and worth visiting **all year round,** with an average temperature that ranges from **26-28°C** (79-82°F) no matter when you visit, though there are **two distinct seasons.**

DRY SEASON

The dry season takes place from **May** to **October,** when temperatures hover around 31-33°C (88-91°F) in the day and 22-23°C (71-73°F) at night. **July** and **August** are the driest months, with just 40 mm (1.5 inches) of rainfall on average. These are also Bali and Lombok's busiest months, considered to be the **high season,** with spiked accommodation prices. The period from the **end of September** to **early October** also sees an increase in tourists, as Australian families head over for the school holidays. Visit during **May, June,** or **early September** to beat the crowds and enjoy good weather.

WET SEASON

Bali and Lombok's **wet season** runs from **November** to **April,** with an uptick in crowds between **mid-December** and **mid-January.** The wet season is more humid than the dry season, often with overcast skies. Temperatures range from 29-31°C (84-87°F) during the day and 22-23°C (71-73°F) at night. **Storms** tend to be brief and heavy, affecting little in terms of sightseeing, though many major treks, like the one to **Gunung Rinjani,** are canceled. The rainiest months are from **December** to **March,** all with more than 230 mm (9 inches) of average monthly rainfall.

The wet season is a great time to visit if you want to see the islands' major sights without having to worry about elbowing your way through the crowds that inevitably gather during the dry season. Sadly, the beaches of Bali and Lombok are more **polluted** during the rainy season, as trash washes inland from the rivers to the shoreline; do not expect beaches like Kuta or Seminyak in Bali to be pristine. A current wrapping along Bali's eastern coastline pulls rubbish along the shoreline as well.

ONE WEEK

Spend your first day and night adjusting to island time in **Seminyak**, enjoying the sunset with a drink in hand at the beach. Then, venture south to the **Bukit Peninsula**, staying two nights at a boutique hotel in **Bingin** or **Padang Padang**, or near **Uluwatu**. Witness the *kecak* **fire dance** performance at **Pura Luhur Uluwatu** at night and **surf** one of the many waves in the region by day. Or, simply watch others paddle for waves from a cliffside warung (café). End your trip in the central town of **Ubud**, an artist's haven surrounded by **rice terraces** and **temples**. Don't miss the sunrise trek up **Gunung Batur**.

TWO WEEKS

From Ubud, venture along Bali's eastern coastline to the small town of **Sidemen**, a prime place to walk among the **rice fields** and experience local daily life. Then, spend two nights in **Amed**, a home base for **snorkeling** or **diving** around the **U.S.A.T.** *Liberty* **wreck** and seeing **Pura Tirta Gangga**, a palace with pools and fountains. Drive along Bali's eastern coastline and catch a boat from **Padangbai** to **Gili Trawangan**, **Gili Meno**, or **Gili Air**, where you can enjoy beachside bliss and snorkel with sea turtles.

THREE WEEKS

Take a boat from the Gili Islands to **mainland Lombok** and drive along the scenic coastal road to **Senggigi** for one night. Take a day trip to **Mataram** and explore the island's largest city

rice fields

and home of the **Islamic Center Mosque**, with an incredible rooftop view of Mataram. From Senggigi, head inland to **Tetebatu**, a little village surrounded by **rice terraces**. If the trails are open, ask your trek organizer to pick you up from Tetebatu and take you to the trailhead of **Gunung Rinjani** to spend the night on the volcano's crater rim. For some time spent in the sun, head south to **Kuta**, which makes a fine home base to **surf**, relax, and venture on day trips to some of Lombok's lesser known **bays** and **islands**.

Know Before You Go

Getting There
BALI

Most tourists arrive by **air** into **Ngurah Rai International Airport** (DPS) in Denpasar, Bali. Typical flight times, including layovers, are:

- U.S. (Los Angeles): 20-25 hours
- U.K. (London): 17-20 hours
- Australia (Sydney): 6.5 hours
- South Africa (Johannesburg): 15-22 hours

It is also possible to arrive by **ferry** into Gilimanuk, Bali, from Java. Boats also arrive into **Padangbai** and **Sanur, Bali,** from **Lombok.**

LOMBOK

International and domestic flights arrive in **Praya,** Lombok, at the **Zainuddin Abdul Madjid International Airport,** colloquially called Lombok International Airport (LOP). **Ferries** also connect Bali to Lombok in **Lembar, Bangsal,** and the **northern Gili Islands.**

Getting Around

BOAT AND FERRY

Boats and ferries connect Bali and Lombok as well as their outer islands. You can find routes connecting **Sanur, Padangbai,** and **Serangan** on Bali to **the northern Gili Islands, Bangsal, Senggigi,** and **Lembar** on Lombok. The Nusa Islands of **Nusa Penida** and **Nusa Lembongan** can be stopped at midway between Bali and Lombok. Public ferries and private fast boats are available for most routes.

BUS AND *BEMO*

Buses and *bemos* (minivans) connect some of Bali and Lombok's main towns but are largely unreliable. Expect to pay about 10,000 Rp per 10-minute ride on either bus or *bemo.* **Shared tourist shuttles** are much more efficient and often have room for luggage. The most efficient shuttle service is offered by **Perama** (peramatour. com) and **Kura-Kura** (kura2bus.com).

CAR

The most convenient way to get around Bali and Lombok is with a **private driver** or **rental car.** There are many private drivers in Bali who happily double as tour guides, suggesting itineraries and offering insider advice as they transport you from one place to the next. They can be found promoting their services in any major tourist area or arranged through your accommodation. To see the islands with your own set of wheels, arrange your rental in **Denpasar** or **Mataram.** If driving

on your own, you'll need a valid **international driver's license.**

MOTORBIKE

Motorbikes are the most common form of transportation among locals, and one of the only forms of transportation in some of Bali and Lombok's rural areas. Motorbikes can typically be **rented from accommodations** and **rental stands** in areas that are frequented by tourists. Because of chaotic and potentially unsafe road conditions, it is best to have previous motorbike driving experience before driving a motorbike in Bali and Lombok. **Travel insurance** that is valid for motorbike accidents is essential as well. Hopping on the back of a motorbike taxi, locally called an *ojek,* is also affordable and an easy way to move between short distances.

TAXI/RIDESHARE APPS

Metered taxis are commonly available in the **major tourist areas** of Bali and Lombok. **Rideshare apps** are becoming more popular, but it can be a challenge to get an app driver to commit to picking up in areas where there is a strong taxi presence—conflicts between taxi drivers and rideshare app drivers occur regularly.

Passports and Visas

For travelers from Australia, New Zealand, Canada, the United States, the U.K., and South Africa, no visa is needed for stays of 30 days or fewer. For visits longer than 30 days, purchase a **visa-on-arrival** ($35 USD), which grants you your first 30 days and can be extended for another 30 days while you are inside the country. Both the date of arrival and your date of departure count as full days toward your stay.

Your passport must be valid for six months from the date you intend to leave Indonesia. Your passport also must have two blank passport pages. Some airlines require you to show **proof of onward travel** before letting you board the aircraft, though this is inconsistently enforced. If you are unsure of your departure details, it's best to arrive early at the airport and prepare to book a flexible or refundable flight out of Indonesia.

Vaccinations

Some areas on Bali and Lombok are at higher risk than others for disease exposure. Consult a travel doctor to find out if you need any vaccinations or boosters before you travel. The following is a list of recommended vaccines, many of which you may have received in childhood.

- Measles, Mumps, and Rubella (MMR)
- Polio
- Hepatitis A
- Hepatitis B
- Typhoid
- Japanese Encephalitis (if you're staying in Indonesia for more than one month or participating in many rural outdoor activities)
- Rabies (if you're staying where you could be at risk for animal bites in Bali)
- Tetanus
- Yellow Fever

What to Pack

TOILETRIES AND MEDICATION

In addition to the usual toiletries you might pack on a trip (shampoo, toothbrush, etc.), it's a good idea to pack some **insect repellent reef-safe sunscreen** that does not contain oxybenzone. Some recommended reef-safe brands are Stream2Sea, Raw Elements, and Avasol. For women, it's a good idea to stock up on **menstrual products** before your trip.

Finally, remember to pack any **medications** or **prescriptions** that you take regularly, as these may be hard to find in Bali and Lombok.

CLOTHING

Pack **lightweight, quick-dry shirts** and **dresses,** along with **shorts** and **trousers.** A **sarong** is often necessary to visit some of Bali and Lombok's spiritual sights, and it will save you a lot of grief from vendors selling them at the entrance if you bring your own. If you're planning on doing any lengthy hikes in the sun, pack a **UPF 50+ lightweight long-sleeved shirt.** A **waterproof jacket,** comfortable **sandals, sturdy hiking shoes, swimwear,** and a **rashguard** are all good ideas. On rural beaches in Lombok, women will likely feel more comfortable covering up with a rashguard and leggings while swimming. Men should stick to shorts rather than brief-type swimwear.

ELECTRONICS AND ACCESSORIES

You'll want your **phone, camera** (don't forget a **memory card!**), and chargers, and it's a good idea to bring a small **padlock** if you're going to be staying in a hostel or visiting a hot spring. Bring a **reusable water bottle:** there are water bottle filling stations throughout Bali. Bali and Lombok have type C and F 240 V power sockets, which are compatible with **two-pin round plugs** (like the ones in continental Europe). If coming from Australia, the United States, the U.K., Canada, or South Africa, you will need an adapter.

Island-Hopping around Bali, Lombok, and the Gili Islands

There are more than 15,000 islands in the Indonesian Archipelago, ranging from small to large, jagged and mountainous to soft and flat, crowded to deserted. Which island will you fall in love with? There's only one way to find out. This itinerary is ideal for travelers who don't mind traveling by boat, moving at a quick pace, and exploring the diverse island experiences that Bali and Lombok have to offer. Be forewarned: it's not unheard of for travelers to find an island that feels like home, stay there, and chuck any semblance of a planned itinerary into the water.

With this itinerary, travelers can experience life on 11 of Indonesia's thousands of islands. However, those who want to relax can slow down by sticking to the main five areas that this itinerary suggests as a base: Sanur, Nusa Lembongan, Gili Trawangan, Senggigi, and Lombok's Kuta.

Day 1

Start your journey in the relaxed beach area of Sanur, a relatively quiet and convenient base for Bali, only half an hour from Ngurah Rai International Airport. Acclimate yourself on the sandy shoreline with a cold drink, massage, and lunch at Soul on the Beach. If you're up for a small excursion, take a taxi or *ojek* to Denpasar and visit the Bajra Sandhi Monument. Or, visit the beach towns of Kuta, Seminyak, or Canggu for sunset views before coming back to sleep in Sanur.

Day 2

Take a day trip to Ubud, about an hour's drive north of Sanur, either on a bicycle tour, taxi, or your own set of wheels. Visit the Sacred Monkey Forest, walk along Campuhan Ridge, visit the Tegallalang Rice Terraces, or stroll along the

Barja Sandhi Monument

Surfin' Safari: The Best Surf Spots

BALI

Bali's surf season tends to run parallel to the dry season: Waves are best from **April** to **September**. You'll find the best waves along the **western coastline**, though there are also some on **Nusa Lembongan** and **Nusa Ceningan**, as well. Bali's **eastern coastline** is more finnicky when it comes to waves, though you can occasionally score during the wet season.

Bali's Best Surf Spots

- **Balian:** A swell magnet with a long left and mediocre right. Stay close by to catch waves by yourself before surfers from the south make the drive up the coast (page 345).

- **The Bukit Peninsula:** This is Bali's powerhouse wave region, with incredible waves like **Padang Padang** (page 109), **Uluwatu** (page 117), **Impossibles** (page 108), **Bingin** (page 106), and many more. Beginners can still find a spot in the lineup at the lesser-sought friendly waves.

- **Keramas:** Testy surfers sit on the lineup at this high-performance right, now a part of the professional surfing circuit (page 251).

- **Kuta Area:** The beaches of **Kuta** (page 50), **Legian** (page 51), and **Seminyak** (page 51) are home to surf camps and peaky beach breaks. Waves breaking near the airport are some of the best around. At **Canggu** (page 52), there's a handful of beach and reef breaks peeling left and right.

- **Medewi:** Here, there's a left that goes on and on with the right south-southwesterly swell (page 341).

- **Nusa Lembongan:** Offshore of this little island are waves that range from fat and crumbling to fast, hollow barrels (page 168).

- **Sanur:** This spot is home to shallow reef breaks that range from mellow to merciless (page 147).

LOMBOK

Lombok's southwest peninsula is a wave powerhouse with its pinnacle wave, **Desert Point**, working from **May** to **September**. Elsewhere,

surfing off Pantai Mawi

Lombok is worth surfing year round. During the dry season, clean swells come in **before 9am**—before the trade winds blow through and chop them up. In the wet season, waves tend to be glassy and clean.

Lombok's Best Surf Spots

- **Ekas: Inside Ekas** is attractive for everyone, while **Outside Ekas** breaks heavy and is reserved for those with experience and paddle power (page 434).

- **Desert Point:** One of the best lefthand barrels in the world breaks at the edge of a remote peninsula (page 406).

- **Gerupuk:** There's a wave for every level of surfer inside the bay alongside a traditional fishing village (page 432).

- **Mawi:** A fast and shallow reef break peels into a quaint and quiet bay (page 431).

- **Selong Belanak:** Welcoming waves break along a picturesque beach (page 429).

- **Senggigi:** This is a friendly reef break where you can learn to stand and turn. Intermediates will have fun here as well (page 388).

Nusa Lembongan

rice fields to enjoy a meal at **Sari Organik.** You can easily spend a day visiting **waterfalls,** taking a **yoga** or **meditation** class, or visiting with a **traditional healer.**

Day 3

From Sanur, take the hourlong drive south to the Bukit Peninsula for the day, stopping at beaches like **Bingin, Padang Padang,** and **Uluwatu.** Pay a visit to **Pura Luhur Uluwatu,** one of the most iconic temples in Bali, home to dozens of macaque monkeys. For a beach with a local vibe, check out **Pantai Pandawa,** where intricate Hindu statues are carved into the cliffs. On the way back to Sanur, stop in **Jimbaran** for a dinner of fresh seafood on the sand.

Day 4

Check out of your hotel in Sanur and catch an early, 30-minute fast boat to **Nusa Lembongan,** a small island known for its diving, surfing, and beaches. Spend the rest of the day relaxing, taking **surf lessons,** or doing **yoga.** Or, **bike** around the island, stopping at **Devil's Tear** and crossing

the bridge to **Nusa Ceningan.** Many activities rely on the tides. For dinner, head to the cliffs of **Lembongan** for the best views and dinner at **Thai Pantry.**

Day 5

Sign up for a **snorkeling** or **scuba diving trip** ahead of time to see manta rays offshore of the neighboring island of **Nusa Penida.** Admire manta rays as they enter the cleaning station, where small fish clean their skin of algae and parasites. Look out into the blue and you might see the rare *mola-mola* fish. In the afternoon, relax at **Pantai Mushroom** or listen to music at **Sandy Bay Beach Club.**

Day 6

Across the channel from Nusa Lembongan and Nusa Ceningan is the largely uninhabited island of Nusa Penida. Check into a Nusa Penida hotel and **hire a driver** to see Nusa Penida's west coast, where you can visit **Kelingking Beach, Angel's Billabong,** and **Crystal Bay,** or venture to **Tembeling Forest.** Nusa Penida can also

See the Seas

The ocean surrounding Bali and Lombok is home to sea creatures big and small. Squint to see macro life like nudibranchs, pygmy seahorses, and tiny crabs hiding amid a coral reef. Out in the open water, manta rays, sea turtles, and *mola-mola*—the heaviest fish in the world—can be found. Snorkelers, freedivers, and scuba divers, here's where to go to make the most of the underwater world.

BALI

- **Amed and Tulamben:** A freediving hub and home of the U.S.A.T. *Liberty* wreck dive site. There are thriving reefs and a muck diver's delight (page 274).

- **Menjangan Island:** Dive or snorkel along a 30-meter (100-foot) wall accented by large sea fans (page 338).

- **Nusa Penida:** This is one of the best places in the world to spot manta rays and *mola-mola* (page 190). For mellow snorkeling, the mangroves off **Nusa Lembongan** provide a chilled-out spot with little current (page 168).

- **Pemuteran:** One of the island's most underrated dive sites with coral reefs and underwater coral encrusted statues, this spot offers depth and visibility for freedivers (page 333).

LOMBOK

- **Belongas Bay:** Scuba divers can swim alongside toothy hammerhead sharks outside the bay (page 429).

You can spot sea turtles off the Gili Islands.

- **The Gili Islands:** This trio of islands has rightfully earned its reputation as the sea turtle capital of the world from scuba divers, snorkelers, and freedivers (page 360).

- **Southwest Peninsula:** A cluster of islands off Lombok's southwestern peninsula invite snorkelers to take a peek at their healthy reefs (page 406).

be done as a day trip from Nusa Lembongan; if you're heading back, you'll want to leave Nusa Penida before sunset.

Day 7

To see more of Nusa Penida, explore the western coastline to find **Diamond Beach, Atuh Beach,** and the **Thousand Island** viewpoint. **Pura Goa Giri Putri** temple cave is another sight worth visiting. Roads can be difficult to navigate for novice

motorbike drivers; hiring a professional is recommended. For dinner, enjoy drinks and ocean views at **Penida Colada.**

Day 8

From Nusa Penida or Nusa Lembongan, take an early boat to the three little islands of **Gili Trawangan, Gili Meno,** and **Gili Air.** The ride takes 1.5 to 2 hours. Check into your hotel on Gili Trawangan and head to the coastline for a cold

With thousands of temples on Bali and mosques on Lombok, you won't go far before witnessing—or getting roped into—a ceremonial precession. Though each is unique and important, these are the cultural sites worth going out of your way for.

- **Pura Besakih:** Commonly called the "Mother Temple," this temple guards the slopes of active Gunung Agung (page 280).

- **Pura Lempuyang Luhur:** This is an ancient temple with gates that open out to the summit of Gunung Agung. A 1,700-step pilgrimage brings you to the top (page 282).

- **Pura Tanah Lot:** Protecting Bali's southwestern coastline, this island temple is open only to locals but can be admired by travelers from Bali's shoreline (page 344).

- **Pura Luhur Uluwatu:** Witness a *kecak* fire dance performance in a cliffside temple overtaken by cheeky monkeys (page 115).

- **Pura Tirta Empul:** This temple's fountains are known for their healing properties (page 236).

- **Brahmavihara-Arama:** This solitary Buddhist monastery hosts a replica of Borobudur (page 323).

- **Pura Ulun Danu Beratan:** This lakeside

Pura Tirta Empul

temple almost always has a ceremony taking place within its grounds (page 310).

- **Islamic Center Mosque:** Take a tour of the interior of the largest mosque on Lombok, and then look out over Mataram from the top (page 397).

drink and lunch at **Pituq Co.** Spend the afternoon **snorkeling, stand-up paddling,** doing **yoga,** or **lounging on the beach.** Sink your toes into the sand for dinner at **Casa Vintage** on the beach.

Day 9
In the morning, sign up for a **snorkel tour** or **scuba dive trip** of the Gili Islands. Alternatively, hop on the **public boat** over to **Gili Meno** with your own snorkel gear. Sea turtles are found close to the shoreline at spots like **Turtle Heaven.** Cruise around Gili Meno by **bike** for the rest of the day to see traditional

Sasak villages and the island's **interior lake.** Then, hop on the boat back to Gili Trawangan for a casual dinner at the **Trawangan Night Market.** If you still have the energy, join the island's famous **pub crawl.**

Day 10
After breakfast, hop on the **public boat** to **Gili Air,** the most romantic island of the trio. **Beach bars** and **warungs** line the coastline and welcome guests to sit and stay awhile. Take a **yoga class** at **H2O Yoga** or **Flowers and Fire Yoga Garden,** learn to cook at **Gili Cooking Classes,** or release travel tension with a **massage** at **Slow**

Spa. Don't relax too much or you might miss your boat back to Gili Trawangan.

Day 11

Check out of your hotel and take the boat to **Bangsal Harbor,** where you can catch a scenic ride to **Senggigi.** If with a private driver, ask to stop at the viewpoint of **Bukit Malimbu** along the way. Check into your Senggigi hotel. Spend the rest of the day exploring Senggigi on foot and visiting the **Senggigi Art Market.**

Day 12

While based in Senggigi, spend a day relaxing on the nearby beaches. If you'd rather venture out into the city, hire a driver or motorbike for a day trip into **Mataram,** Lombok's capital. The port town of **Ampenan** is a remnant of Dutch and Chinese influence, and the rooftop at the **Islamic Center Mosque** affords incredible views of the city below. Head back to Senggigi before dusk to admire the sunset at **Coco Loco** with a drink in hand. For dinner, go to **Asmara.**

Day 13

Drive from Senggigi and check into a hotel based in **Kuta, Lombok.** For a convenient beach hangout, enjoy **Pantai Kuta. Pantai Tanjung Aan** and its vantage point, **Bukit Merese,** are worth the short journey to get there. Stroll along the streets of Kuta and if you're hungry, enjoy restaurants like **Terra, Warung Flora,** or **El Bazar.**

Day 14

Wake up early for a day trip and **snorkel tour** to the southwestern Lombok islands of **Gili Nanngu, Gili Sudak,** and **Gili Kedis** with **Mimpi Manis Snorkel Tours.** Lunch will be had on one of the tiny islands. Back in Kuta, relax for the evening at the local treehouse bar, **Juice and Booze Bar.** The **Zainuddin Abdul Madjid International Airport** in Praya is a half-hour flight from the **Ngurah Rai International Airport** in Denpasar, Bali. Flights connecting Bali and Lombok depart regularly.

Islamic Center Mosque

Spiritual Wellness

With fresh produce, peaceful scenery, and retreats that range from fitness-focused to spiritual journeys, Bali and Lombok have plenty of places where you can arrive stressed and leave feeling revived.

- **Ubud:** If you're looking for yoga classes, guided meditations, detox programs, and spa pampering sessions, you'll find it all—and more—in Ubud (page 195).

- **Sanur:** This idyllic beach town hosts spas, yoga classes, and luxury resorts famous for their organic food (page 144).

- **Gili Air:** Seek solitude on the quiet island of Gili Air, where you can spend your days unwinding on the beach between yoga classes and healthy meals (page 374).

woman meditating on Sanur Beach

The Best of Bali

Bali has an overwhelming number of places that are worthy of your time. Fortunately, because of Bali's size, the southern beach towns of Kuta, Seminyak, Sanur, and Canggu make for great bases to embark on day trips. Towns like Pemuteran, Munduk, and Amed merit a night or two each once you arrive after a long drive. This itinerary covers the major highlights on the Island of the Gods.

Day 1

Most travelers will arrive at Bali's **international airport** in Denpasar. Check into your hotel or villa in **Seminyak,** a trendy town where boutique shops, restaurants, and clubs line the main roads. Have lunch at **Old Man's** in **Canggu,** a happening beach town. Go for a short swim or surf before venturing north to arrive at sunset at **Pura Tanah Lot,** a temple on its own island. Drive back to Seminyak for an upscale dinner at **Bambu.**

Day 2

From Seminyak, take a day trip to the **Bukit Peninsula,** spending the day **surfing** and **sunbathing** at the beaches of **Bingin, Padang Padang,** or **Balangan.** For a beach club experience, reserve a spot at **Oneeighty°** day club. In the afternoon, get a drink at **Single Fin,** an iconic bar on the cliffs of **Uluwatu** and a prime place to watch some of the region's best surfers catch waves. Before sunset, find a seat at **Pura Luhur Uluwatu** to watch the *kecak* **fire dance performance**—just remember to hold your belongings close to keep them away from thieving monkeys.

Day 3

Drive from Seminyak to the artistic town of **Ubud,** where the scene changes from chaotic to tranquil, beach to lush jungle. In the morning, wander through **Sacred Monkey Forest Sanctuary** and then drive a short way to **Pura**

Goa Gajah, a temple with an elephant cave. Release stress and tension with a **Balinese massage** at a local traditional spa. Have dinner locally and go to sleep early to prepare for an early wake-up the next day.

Day 4

Wake up at 2am for pickup and transportation to the trailhead of **Gunung Batur.** The hike starts around 3am and allows you to watch as the sun rises over **Gunung Agung** in the distance. On your return to Ubud, stop at **Tegallalang Rice Terraces** or **Pura Tirta Empul.** Relax back at your hotel and dine at **Locavore.**

Day 5

From Ubud, drive to **Sanur** via the coastal road from **Pantai Keramas,** stopping at the waterfalls of **Air Terjun Kanto Lampo** and **Air Terjun Tegenungan.** Spend the afternoon watching surfers catch waves from the comforts of a beachside warung and dine on fresh food at **Komune Resort and Beach Club.** Then, head to the white sand beach of Sanur, a perfect place to get a **beachside massage.**

Day 6

From Sanur, take a day trip to **Nusa Penida** by boat. You will want a **private driver** in Nusa Penida, as roads are poorly marked and can be stressful to drive in some parts. Stick to the island's west coast and see points like **Kelingking Beach, Broken Beach,** and **Crystal Bay.** Then, take the boat back to Sanur for dinner at **Three Monkeys.**

Day 7

Wind down your week on the sandy shoreline of **Sanur,** where days are dictated by the incoming and outgoing tides. This is an ideal spot to lounge, practice **yoga,** sip seaside cocktails, and laze the day away. If you're feeling ambitious, you can go into central Denpasar to check out the **Bajra Sandhi Monument** and shop at **Kumbasari Market** before heading back to Ngurah Rai International Airport for your flight home.

Tegallalang Rice Terraces

Hiking and Adventure

BEST TREKS

- **Gunung Batur, Bali:** Hike through the early morning and be rewarded with spectacular views of the sun rising over Gunung Agung (page 292).

- **Gunung Batukaru, Bali:** Your chances of seeing wildlife are high on treks up Gunung Batukaru, a seldom-trekked volcano with small temples along its trails (page 299).

- **Danau Tamblingan and Danau Buyan, Bali:** Trek over the headland that separates Bali's twin lakes (page 308).

- **Campuhan Ridge, Bali:** Stroll along a ridgeline that splits two valleys while watching for the elusive Bali Starling, the island's rare and beautiful bird (page 211).

- **Gunung Rinjani, Lombok:** Camp on the crater rim that overlooks a bright blue lake below (page 451).

- **Air Terjun Sendang Gile, Lombok:** A jungle trail leads to a unique waterfall, prime for cooling off in its spray (page 442).

Gunung Rinjani

BEST CYCLING TRIPS

- **From Sanur to Ubud, Bali:** Cycle from the sea to the center of Ubud, stopping at the waterfall of Air Terjun Tengenungan along the way (page 212).

- **Ubud, Bali:** Cycle along rivers and rice terraces in Ubud's outskirts (page 212).

- **Gili Islands, Lombok:** With no motorized transportation on the islands of Gili Trawangan, Gili Meno, and Gili Air, the best way to explore is with a bike (page 348).

BEST ADRENALINE THRILLS

- **Bali Treetop Adventure Park, Bali:** Ziplines and rope walks challenge your fear of heights (page 310).

- **White-Water Rafting along the Ayung River, Bali:** Hang on tight as you raft down rapids that range from mellow to white-knuckle-inducing (page 212).

Extend Your Stay

Though this itinerary is ideal for first-time visitors to Bali, there are also towns farther from the island's busy center that are certainly worth a visit. To escape fellow travelers, consider heading to **Amed,** a village famous for its **scuba diving** on Bali's east coast. **Sidemen,** near Semarapura, is where you'll find peace among rice terraces. The little village of **Munduk** near Bali's **twin lakes** is home to **waterfalls** and impeccable views. To the west, **Pemuteran,** one of the island's best-kept secrets, is where you'll find **pristine diving conditions** and a base for exploring **Menjangan Island.** Finally, the **Jatiluwih Rice Terraces** are worth the extra kilometers in the car.

The Best of Lombok

Whether you're seeking deep relaxation or non-stop adventure, you'll find it on the island of Lombok. Uncrowded beaches are the status quo, often with swaths of white sand. Coconut groves are the dividing lines between rice terraces and desert, as the terrain changes quickly from one kilometer to the next. Though this itinerary is packed with activities, you can always default to relaxing in a hammock alongside a rice field or throwing a sarong down on the beach. If you want to island-hop, experience bohemian beach life, trek to the crater rim of one of Indonesia's most spectacular volcanoes, and explore some sights rarely seen, this itinerary is for you.

If you are flying into Lombok's international airport, you may consider doing this itinerary in reverse. Getting to the islands of Gili Trawangan, Gili Meno, and Gili Air from Bali is easy via boat or by driving from the international airport to Bangsal Harbor, then taking a small boat to your island of choice.

Day 1

Get your trip to Lombok off on a relaxing start by making your way to **Gili Trawangan, Gili Meno,** or **Gili Air.** Gili Trawangan and Gili Air offer more accommodations, activities, and restaurant options than Gili Meno, where you can experience life like a local by staying in a boutique hotel alongside a traditional Sasak neighborhood. The islands are within a 10-minute boat ride from one another, and are all easily explored **on foot** or **bicycle.** Get acquainted with the island by walking or biking one lap around the coastline, stopping at a beachside warung for a midday treat. Recuperate from a day of travel, but make sure to be on your chosen island's western coastline to watch the **sunset over Bali,** just across the Lombok Strait.

Day 2

Embark on a **snorkel tour** around the Gili Islands or opt for a series of **fun dives.** Snorkelers

a hiker on Bukit Merese

Gunung Rinjani

will love looking down at the lazy sea turtles lounging at **Turtle Heaven** at **Gili Meno** and admiring the beautiful sculptures at **The Nest.** Scuba divers can search for reef sharks under reef crags at sites like **Shark Point.** After a morning of diving, head to the shoreline for lunch. Then, attend a **yoga class** in the afternoon—usually accompanied by a sunset. For dinner, enjoy sampling local fare at the **Gili Trawangan Night Market.** Then, it's time to **bar-hop** along **Jalan Gili Trawangan,** the island's most boisterous road. If you're sleeping on Gili Air or Gili Meno, expect a quiet night with a chilled coconut or cocktail in hand.

Day 3

In the morning, catch the **public boat** to **mainland Lombok.** With a **private driver,** venture to the slopes of **Gunung Rinjani,** staying in one of the smaller towns of **Tetebatu, Senaru,** or **Sembalun. Rinjani Lodge** in Senaru is a prime choice for a home base to hike Gunung Rinjani, with an infinity pool that overlooks a lush rainforest valley. If there is time,

venture to the waterfalls of **Air Terjun Sendang Gile** and **Air Terjun Tiu Kelep.**

Day 4

Plan a trek up to Gunung Rinjani's crater rim and spend the night on the rim under the stars. Treks are best arranged with **Green Rinjani.** Your legs will be put to the test as they take you through a variety of steep terrain with short breaks along the way. From the top, enjoy views of the **lake** and **smaller volcano** in its interior. Porters double as skilled chefs, cooking a warm meal after a long day's hike. Don't forget to peek out of your tent at the stars.

Day 5

Wake up just before **sunrise** to watch the sky change color over the caldera. Enjoy a hearty breakfast and cup of hot coffee or tea before your **return trek.** Trek for a few hours, arriving back at your base by midday. Then, drive to **Kuta, Lombok,** on Lombok's southern coast to check into your hotel. Spend the rest of the day recuperating at **Pantai Kuta,** the town's main beach. If you arrive before sunset, enjoy an incredible sky show and dinner at **Horizon at Ashtari,** a restaurant that overlooks Kuta.

As an alternative to the Gunung Rinjani, there are many treks in **Tetebatu** that lead to waterfalls and around rice fields. Hiking to the top of **Bukit Pergasingan** in **Sembalun** can also be done in one day.

Day 6

Do nothing but relax on the beautiful beaches of **Lombok's southern coastline;** most are best reached by **car** or **motorbike. Tanjung Aan** is an easy place to while away a day and have a meal at **Warung Turtle.** Its bordering hill of **Bukit Merese** provides an incredible view no matter the hour. If you can't sit still, explore other local beaches like **Mawun** or **Selong Belanak.** Kuta is a prime spot for enrolling in **surf lessons.** For dinner, head to **El Bazar** or **Lotus Mandalika.**

Day 7

In the morning, join a **surf lesson** or go for a surf at one of the many waves surrounding Kuta. **Selong Belanak** is best for beginners while **Gerupuk, Mawi,** and **Ekas** will call to intermediate and experienced surfers. After a morning in the water, venture back to Kuta and enjoy a filling lunch at **Warung Flora.** Then, witness how local crafts are made at the nearby village of **Ende,** famous for its colorful textiles. For dinner, wander along Kuta's main roads in search of a decent dinner and happy hour special, then head to the **Bus Bar** for a party. Head back to Zainuddin Abdul Madjid International Airport the next morning for your flight home.

Extend Your Stay

With so many things to do on Lombok, it's best to move at a slow pace and take advantage of day trips. **Senggigi** makes for a great base to enjoy uncrowded beaches or as a hub to explore nearby **Mataram** and the port of **Ampenan.**

From Kuta, **Mimpi Manis Snorkel Tours** offers a day trip to Lombok's southwestern tiny islands of **Gili Kedis** and **Gili Nanggu,** where you can **snorkel,** lounge on the beach, and enjoy a local lunch on the shoreline. Surfers will want to make the most of **Ekas, Gerupuk,** and potentially **Desert Point** (for experienced surfers only). **Pantai Tangsi,** a low-key beach with pink sand, is also a day trip away from Kuta.

Kuta, Seminyak, and the Southern Beaches

Few tourists pass through Bali without experi-

encing Kuta, Seminyak, and the southern beaches in some way. This region's proximity to the airport and its vast selection of restaurants, hotels, and activities make it an alluring and convenient place to explore. Sitting on the northern side of the isthmus that connects mainland Bali to the Bukit Peninsula, these towns are economic powerhouses for the island where venues follow global fashion and culinary trends (as opposed to Bali's other towns, which tend to cling to tradition). Each neighborhood has a slightly different personality and crowd. After a few days in the area, travelers tend to filter into the one that suits them best.

Seminyak steals the limelight, as it is the most sophisticated

Highlights

Look for ★ to find recommended sights, activities, dining, and lodging.

★ **Kuta Beach:** This is the beach where it all began. Surfers flock to the water, sunbathers bask under wide umbrellas, and vendors go from lounge chair to lounge chair trying to sell souvenirs (page 50).

★ **Legian Beach:** Kuta's crowds thin out a bit by the time you reach Legian Beach. Chill on the sand, then walk inland to dance and party (page 51).

★ **Waterbom Bali Water Park:** Waterbom Park offers thrills and spills with its range of waterslides and lazy rivers. It's fun for all ages—not just the kids (page 56).

★ **Learning to Surf:** Many famous surfers caught their first wave in Kuta's beginner-friendly, warm waters (page 56).

★ **Balinese Cooking:** Learn to cook Balinese classics at one of Seminyak's culinary classes. Go home with a recipe to remember (page 58).

★ **Street Art in Canggu:** Emerald-green rice paddies set a stunning foreground to some of Bali's best murals (page 59).

★ **Clubbing in Legian:** Dance the night away at Legian's clubs (page 74).

© MOON.COM

Top Restaurants

★ **Fat Chow:** Dine on experimental Asian fusion dishes in this restaurant with funky decor (page 65).

★ **Crumb & Coaster:** Come for brunch to enjoy the area's best cup of coffee and a hearty meal (page 65).

★ **Bali Pearl:** Here you'll find fine dining French cuisine with hints of Balinese influence (page 68).

★ **On the Juice:** Sweet juices and smoothie bowls are served from a converted Volkswagen bus on the beach (page 68).

★ **Bambu:** Upscale Indonesian dining where the service is top tier (page 69).

★ **MyWarung Pasar Petitenget:** Fresh seafood is served in a casual open-air wooden *joglo*, a traditional Javanese structure, accented with chic chandeliers (page 69).

neighborhood of the bunch, with award-winning restaurants, boutique hotels and villas, and galleries galore. There is competition to be better than the rest in Seminyak, and mediocre venues don't hang around for long. Seminyak rewards innovation in many forms. From art to culinary exploration, the culture embraces trends, and then works hard to create its own.

In Kuta and Legian, the party never stops. Socialize all day long on their wide, sandy beaches, then head to the streets after sunset for a night of bar-hopping and electronic dance music. Kuta itself is probably the most polarizing beach in the area: With tacky shops selling offensive souvenirs, street touts, and a culture of tourists who get drunk and behave rudely, Kuta has been pegged as abrasive and inauthentic. Despite this, Kuta also draws devoted visitors, some of whom grew up building sandcastles on its shoreline and have gone on to bring their own children to Kuta. There is good, clean fun to be had, if only you know where to look.

If you want to escape the imbibement and debauchery, you'll find vegan cafés, surf hostels, meditation centers, yoga retreats, and wellness workshops in Canggu. Canggu (known affectionately as "The 'gu") attracts talented artists and musicians who find their inspiration amid the quiet neighborhood's rice paddies, gray sand beaches, and mural-covered buildings.

The borders between each neighborhood are blurred. If you wander aimlessly through the area—as it's so easy to do—you're likely to stumble out of one neighborhood and into another. The main neighborhoods of Tuban, Kuta, Legian, Seminyak, Kerobokan, and Canggu all have sandy beaches with no shortage of lounge space. Surfers will find waves to suit all skill levels, from beginner to experts-only, with plenty of peaks to go around. Once you sink your toes into the Indian Ocean and feel the sun warming your skin, you'll forget all about the frenetic activity taking place in the clubs and on the neighborhoods' main roads.

The best thing about Kuta, Seminyak, and the southern beaches is that they offer non-stop energy when you want it and prime places to relax when you don't.

Previous: Plumeria tree; Kuta Beach; Legian Beach.

Top Accommodations

★ **Poppies Bali:** At this serene guesthouse, you can escape the chaos from the streets outside (page 78).

★ **Dash:** This funky industrial hotel is known for its colorful decor and stand-alone bathtubs (page 79).

★ **The Seminyak Beach Resort:** You might have trouble leaving the infinity pool at this chic beachside resort (page 81).

★ **The Oberoi:** This property's traditional villas with garden and ocean views are the epitome of Balinese luxury (page 81).

★ **The Chillhouse:** Let your worries wash away at this laid-back surf and yoga retreat (page 81).

★ **Desa Seni:** This wellness retreat offers yoga classes, spa treatments, and a restaurant with organic fare (page 83).

ORIENTATION

Kuta, Seminyak, and the southern beaches are located on the thin neck of Bali's **Bukit Peninsula.** They all host west-facing beaches, ideal for watching the sun set over the Indian Ocean. Inland, the neighborhoods are bordered by downtown Denpasar and its tightly packed suburbs. Each neighborhood is loosely linked by **Jalan By Pass Ngurah Rai, Jalan Sunset Road,** and **Jalan Raya Legian.**

The neighborhoods of Tuban, Kuta, Legian, Seminyak, Kerobokan, and Canggu are listed from south to north. You can reach them in succession by traveling north from the **Ngurah Rai International Airport,** just south of the area.

Tuban

Tuban is so small, it's often simply lumped into Central Kuta. It surrounds the Ngurah Rai International Airport and hosts **Jerman Beach,** a ribbon of sand that's typically visited by older tourists from nearby resorts and surfers using it as an access point to the waves. You know you're in Tuban when you see the gargantuan **Satria Gatotkaca Statue,** the neighborhood's most impressive fixture.

Central Kuta

Marked by busy Kuta Beach, Central Kuta (also known as Kuta Town) is fenced in by **Jalan Pantai Kuta** and **Jalan Sunset Road.** In its loose borders, you'll find **Lippo Mall** and **Circus Water Park** near Tuban. **Waterbom Park** and **Discovery Shopping Mall** lie in its center. Two of the main shopping roads, **Jalan Poppies I** and **Jalan Poppies II,** signal Central Kuta's border with Legian. On these funky roads, you'll find a swath of run-down bars, souvenir shops, and warungs. After dark, partygoers flock to the intersection of Jalan Poppies II and **Jalan Raya Legian** for their big night out.

Legian

Kuta's neighbor to the north, Legian is a lively neighborhood that attracts tourists who love to intermix the luxe life with merrymaking. Everything starts at **Legian Beach** and moves inland, where big-name resorts and restaurants are set up along **Jalan Raya Legian.** Signaling the border between Legian and Kuta is the **Ground Zero Monument** memorial, a large white statue engraved with Hindu deities and plaque with the names of those who lost their lives. For nonstop nighttime dancing,

Kuta, Seminyak, and the Southern Beaches

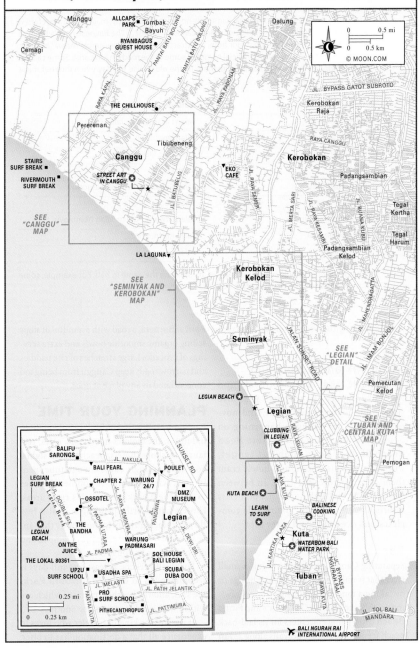

A Road By Any Other Name...

A road's official name and its colloquial name may not be the same. Most major roads are referred to as a **"jalan,"** while a smaller alley or road is called a **"gang."** The Balinese have a habit of calling roads by the name of the major hotel or attraction that's on it—simply throw "Jalan" in front. These are the official and unofficial names of some of the roads in Kuta area. Some call the roads by their new names, and others call them by the old. Praise the day when Internet maps catch up with all usages.

Official	Colloquial
Jalan Kaya Aya	Jalan Laksmana or Jalan Oberoi
Jalan Arjuna	Jalan Double Six
Jalan Pantai Arjuna	Jalan Blue Ocean Beach
Jalan Yudistira	Jalan Padma
Jalan Bakung Sari	Jalan Singo Sari or Jalan Singosari
Jalan Werk Udara	Jalan Bagus Taruna
Jalan Camplung Tanduk	Jalan Dhyana Pura or Jalan Abimanyu
Jalan Dewi Sartika	Jalan Kartika Plaza
Jalan Jenggala	Jalan Segara

If you're having trouble with street names, try splitting the name in half. For example, some venues use Jalan Bene Sari while others use Jalan Benesari.

head to the **Engine Room** and bar-hop from there.

Seminyak and Kerobokan

Fashionable and fun, Seminyak and Kerobokan appeal to travelers who love style, high-quality experiences, and novelty. Almost everything is happening on **Seminyak Beach** that hosts **Potato Head Beach Club** or along **Jalan Petitenget,** where restaurants, shops, and hotels cram themselves wherever they can. In between **Jalan Petitenget** and the ocean, world-class resorts like **The Oberoi,** luxury villa complexes, and rice paddies fill in the gaps.

Canggu

Separating Canggu from Seminyak is a small river that is only crossed via a small bridge or by taking a long detour. Canggu is a sprawling neighborhood, with **Old Man's** and **Finns Beach Club** being epicenters for its laid-back beach scene. Café culture prevails along Jalan

Pantai Berawa, a road with a handful of stops selling organic smoothie bowls and extra servings of avocado. Large stretches of rice paddies and narrow roads keep Canggu from being too concentrated in any place at once.

PLANNING YOUR TIME

For some, a month wouldn't be adequate to indulge in the region's many bars, cafés, restaurants, shops, hotels, beaches, and sights. For others, a single day is enough time spent in Kuta, Seminyak, and the southern beaches to send them packing for Bali's rural areas. However, it's worth spending at least **a few days** exploring the neighborhoods that appeal to you most. You can always jump in and out of the aspects you love.

For thrill-seekers, at least two full days is recommended to enjoy **Waterbom Park,** the surf, and the beaches, many of which are within walking distance of one another.

If you are the kind of traveler who loves to experience all that a destination has to offer, budget at least **three to five days:** Spend three days in Seminyak and Kuta enjoying the galleries, shops, beaches, and clubs before heading to **Canggu** for a two-day DIY wellness retreat. If you've come on holiday to relax, you can do that in any of the neighborhoods and will want at least two full days to recuperate from any lingering real-life stress.

Itinerary Ideas

DAY 1: MAKING THE MOST OF KUTA AND SEMINYAK

1 Enjoy breakfast at **Crumb & Coaster,** one of the town's best coffee and brunch spots.

2 Grab your swimwear and hop in a taxi to **Waterbom Bali Water Park,** where you can splash around in the sunshine.

3 After a morning of thrills, it's time to take a taxi to the coastline. Sip on a hydrating coconut at **Seminyak Beach.**

4 Walk or take a taxi to **Made's Warung,** where you can have dinner and enjoy a cultural performance.

5 Still have energy? End the night with a cocktail in hand at **Potato Head Beach Club.** Get there via taxi.

DAY 2: CHILLIN' IN CANGGU

1 Start your morning right. Get your caffeine and food fix at **Sprout.**

2 Rent a motorbike for the day and head toward the coastline. Surf, wade in the water, and sunbathe at **Echo Beach.**

the rice terraces of Canggu

Itinerary Ideas

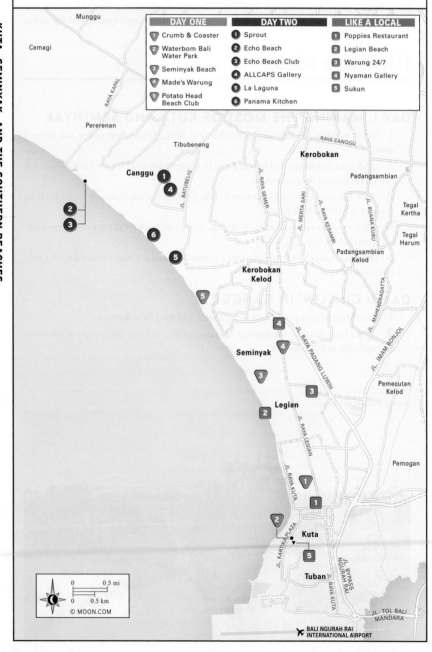

DAY ONE	DAY TWO	LIKE A LOCAL
1 Crumb & Coaster	1 Sprout	1 Poppies Restaurant
2 Waterbom Bali Water Park	2 Echo Beach	2 Legian Beach
3 Seminyak Beach	3 Echo Beach Club	3 Warung 24/7
4 Made's Warung	4 ALLCAPS Gallery	4 Nyaman Gallery
5 Potato Head Beach Club	5 La Laguna	5 Sukun
	6 Panama Kitchen	

Munggu

Cemagi

RAYA KAPAL

Pererenan

Tibubeneng

Canggu

JL. BATUBELIG

RAYA CANGGU

Kerobokan

Padangsambian

JL. RAYA SEMER

JL. MERTA SARI

JL. RAYA KESAMBI

JL. BUANA KUBU

Tegal Kertha

Tegal Harum

Padangsambian Kelod

Kerobokan Kelod

JL. MAHENDRADATTA

Seminyak

JL. RAYA PADANG LUWIH

JL. IMAM BONJOL

Pemecutan Kelod

Legian

JL. RAYA LEGIAN

JL. RAYA KUTA

Pemogan

JL. KARTIKA PLAZA

Kuta

JL. BYPASS NGURAH RAI

JL. RAYA KUTA

Tuban

0   0.5 mi
0   0.5 km
© MOON.COM

JL. TOL BALI MANDARA

✈ BALI NGURAH RAI INTERNATIONAL AIRPORT

3 On the shore, you can have lunch and a cold Bintang at **Echo Beach Club.**

4 Hop back on your motorbike and venture on a DIY street art tour around Canggu, starting at **ALLCAPS Gallery.**

5 Soak up the beautiful sunset and good vibrations at **La Laguna.**

6 End the day with a hearty meal from **Panama Kitchen.**

KUTA LIKE A LOCAL

1 Balinese locals eat *nasi goreng* (fried rice) for breakfast, lunch, and dinner, so you'd be remiss not to try it for the first meal of the day at least once from **Poppies Restaurant.**

2 Escape the tourists by venturing up to **Legian Beach**'s northern end for some undisturbed beach time. Traffic can be heavy in the area, so it's best to take a taxi rather than a motorbike.

3 When your stomach growls for lunch, walk, taxi, or *ojek* (hopping on the back of a motorbike) to get lunch at **Warung 24/7.**

4 Admire the artwork of Indonesian artists at **Nyaman Gallery.** Get there with a taxi or *ojek*. Then, refresh back at your hotel.

5 Dress in your finest lace and enjoy dinner at **Sukun** for Balinese fine dining.

Sights

TUBAN
Satria Gatotkaca Statue
Jalan Raya Tuban No. 1; daily 24 hours; free
Every traveler to Bali will see the Satria Gatotkaca Statue that shows the Hindu god Gatotkaca standing on a carriage of horses, as well as other Hindu entities. Gatotkaca is believed to be the god of flight, and the statue was built to protect all flights passing through the international airport. A well-kept footpath and garden area weave around the statue, forming a small park that's perfect for short pre- or post-flight walks.

CENTRAL KUTA
Vihara Dharmayana Kuta
Jalan Blambangan; tel. 361/762362; daily 9am-8pm; donation
Vihara Dharmayana Kuta is a Chinese Buddhist temple that is equal parts bold and peaceful, with its striking red and yellow paint, ornate lanterns, and manicured gardens. The smell of burning incense and joss paper lingers throughout the temple. When Tibet's 14th Dalai Lama, Tenzin Gyatso, visited Bali in 1982, Vihara Dharmayana Kuta was a stop on his tour.

St. Francis Xavier Catholic Church
Jalan Kartika Plaza No. 107; tel. 361/750043; www. kutafx.com; daily 6am-8pm, unless closed for events, English mass Sun. 6pm; donation
The St. Francis Xavier Catholic Church is one of the largest Catholic churches in Bali, with spacious white walls and ivory-colored statues of saints placed throughout the building. The main podium features the body of Jesus of Christ on the cross, surrounded by angels and white doves.

Dewa Ruci Statue
Jalan By Pass Ngurah Rai No. 120A; daily 24 hours; free
At a major roundabout connecting along the Jalan By Pass Ngurah Rai, you'll see

Tuban and Central Kuta

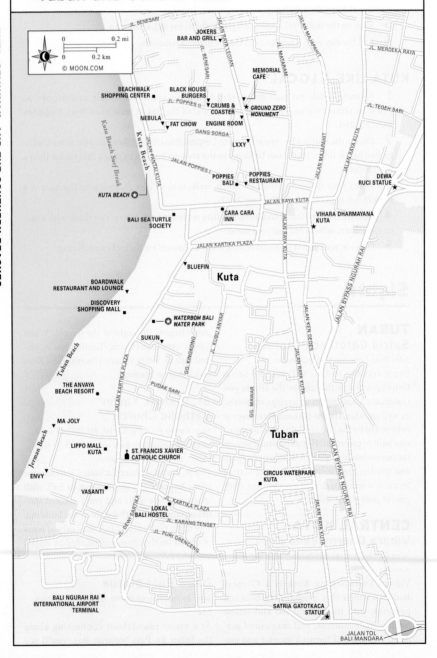

0   0.2 mi

0   0.2 km

© MOON.COM

JL. BENESARI

JL. BENESARI

JL. POPPIES II

GANG SORGA

JALAN POPPIES I

JALAN PANTAI KUTA

Kuta Beach Surf Break

Kuta Beach

JL. RAYA LEGIAN

JL. MATARAM

JL. MAJAPAHIT

JL. MERDEKA RAYA

JL. TEGEH SARI

JALAN MAJAPAHIT

JALAN RAYA KUTA

JOKERS
BAR AND GRILL

MEMORIAL
CAFE

BEACHWALK
SHOPPING CENTER ■

BLACK HOUSE
BURGERS

CRUMB &
COASTER

★ GROUND ZERO
MONUMENT

NEBULA ▼

▼ FAT CHOW

ENGINE ROOM

LXXY ▼

POPPIES
BALI ●

POPPIES
RESTAURANT

JALAN RAYA KUTA

DEWA
RUCI STATUE ★

KUTA BEACH ✪

BALI SEA TURTLE
SOCIETY ■

▼ CARA CARA
INN

VIHARA DHARMAYANA
KUTA

JALAN KARTIKA PLAZA

JALAN RAYA KUTA

JALAN BYPASS NGURAH RAI

▼ BLUEFIN

Kuta

BOARDWALK
RESTAURANT AND LOUNGE ▼

DISCOVERY
SHOPPING MALL ■

WATERBOM BALI
✪ WATER PARK

JL. KUBU ANYAR

JALAN KEN DEDES

JALAN RAYA KUTA

Tuban Beach

SUKUN ▼

GG. KINGKONG

JALAN KARTIKA PLAZA

PUDAK SARI

GG. MAWAR

THE ANVAYA
BEACH RESORT ●

MA JOLY ▼

LIPPO MALL
KUTA ■

Tuban

Jerman Beach

ENVY ▼

✝ ST. FRANCIS XAVIER
CATHOLIC CHURCH

CIRCUS WATERPARK
KUTA ■

JALAN BYPASS NGURAH RAI

VASANTI ●

JL. DEWI SARTIKA

JL. KARTIKA PLAZA

LOKAL
BALI HOSTEL

JL. KARANG TENGET

JL. PURI GRENCENG

BALI NGURAH RAI ■
INTERNATIONAL AIRPORT
TERMINAL

SATRIA GATOTKACA
STATUE ★

JALAN RAYA KUTA

JALAN TOL
BALI MANDARA

Inside Hotel K

The **Kerobokan Prison** is one of Indonesia's most famous prisons, as it has a long history of incarcerating high-profile foreign inmates, such as the "Bali Nine," a ring of nine Australians who were convicted of drug trafficking (two of whom were executed in Bali), as well as the Indonesians responsible for the Bali Bombings. In this prison, inmates are often housed together regardless of the relative severity of their crimes. Kerobokan Prison hosts a diverse crowd primarily because of Indonesia's strict no-drugs laws: Tourists who have been arrested for possessing marijuana often sit in the same cells as murderers and sex offenders. Trafficking is a crime punishable by death, and illegally consuming drugs in Bali can be penalized with a long jail sentence. The facility was built to house 300 inmates, though it usually is filled with more than 1,300.

An exposé book titled *Hotel K: The Shocking Inside Story of Bali's Most Notorious Jail* by Kathryn Bonella revealed the dramatic happenings inside "Hotel K" and sparked an interest among tourists who want to visit Bali's seedier side.

Tourists who visit Kerobokan Prison (Jalan Tangkuban Perahu; visiting hours 9am-2pm; free) often do so with the hopes of talking with a person jailed from their own country. The intention is to let the prisoner know that they have not been forgotten. Inmates from countries where English or Bahasa is not people's first language are especially prone to isolation. If you plan to visit Kerobokan Prison, you must dress conservatively, bring a passport, and list the name of the person you plan to see. Charity organizations can help connect tourists to inmates.

gargantuan Dewa Ruci statue, the partner deity to Raden Bima, a god that signifies strength. The sculpture tells the story of Raden Bima fighting and defeating a powerful sea dragon. Stretch your legs on the small walking path that goes around the statue or lounge in the manicured grassy area.

Bali Sea Turtle Society

Pantai Grand Inna Kuta; tel. 8113882683; www. baliseaturtle.org; hours depend on turtle hatchlings; donation

The olive ridley sea turtle is native to Bali, and populations are consistently threatened due to pollution, illegal sea turtle trade, rising sea temperatures, predation, and development. At Bali Sea Turtle Society, a nonprofit conservation organization, staff and volunteers work to gather sea turtle eggs, incubate them, and release the hatchlings back into the ocean. Visitors can watch the hatchlings be released and learn about the interesting life cycle of olive ridley sea turtles. Release times are typically announced on the Bali Sea Turtle Society Facebook page. Nesting takes place from March to September, and hatching happens from April to October.

LEGIAN
Ground Zero Monument

Jalan Raya Legian No. 38; tel. 361/9009270; daily 24 hours; free

This commemorative wall honors the 202 people who were killed during the 2002 bombing at Sari Club and Paddy's Irish Bar, two popular bars at the time. A large plaque surrounded by stone Hindu carvings lists the names of the deceased, hailing from a total of 21 countries. Visit before 10am to experience the monument in solitude.

SEMINYAK
Petitenget Temple
(Pura Petitenget)

Jalan Petitenget; 50,000 Rp admission includes sarong

Worth a wander if you're already in the area, Pura Petitenget is one of the major sea-facing temples in Bali. Its three main intricately carved doors welcome Balinese Hindus and non-Hindu visitors into a spacious prayer area. The temple is often used for traditional ceremonies that tourists can admire from a short distance.

Beaches and Surf Breaks

Most travelers come to Kuta for the beaches. The salty air, the sound of crashing waves, the long swaths of sand, the dreamlike sunsets all merge together to create a place to indulge and relax. And while the beaches tend to be somewhat uniform in their physical features, there is a beach to suit every type of traveler in the area. Some are lively and crowded while others resemble a deserted isle. The beaches on the southern end sport golden sand, and as you venture north the color desaturates to dark gray.

Many travel articles about Bali don't mention the trash problem that occurs during rainy season. Because of the ocean currents and an improper waste management system, plastic waste often washes ashore and cloaks Kuta's soft sand. The beaches tend to be much cleaner from May to October than they are from November to April.

TUBAN
Jerman Beach
(Pantai Jerman)

Jalan Wana Segara

Jerman Beach, also called Pasih Perahu Beach, was once a major trading port for fishermen and overseas merchants. Today, it is a peaceful hangout area lined with umbrellas and freshly painted wooden boats. Surfers can hire these fishing boats to drive them out to nearby waves, and the beach is a prime spot to watch planes take off and land at the nearby international airport.

AIRPORT REEF SURF BREAK

2/3 mile (about 1 km) offshore from Jerman Beach;
50,000-100,000 Rp boat ride per person round-trip

Airport Reef exists just off the international airport's runway and is divided into two breaks: Airport Rights and Airport Lefts. Both are a long paddle offshore, so it's best to hire a fishing boat to shuttle you between the breaks. Both breaks work best with a

southwesterly swell, easterly winds, and mid-to high tide. Airport Rights is finnicky, heavy, and shallow, and it can draw a crowd of aggressive surfers. Airport Lefts is a bit friendlier, with a larger takeoff area and mellower lineup.

Tuban Beach
(Pantai Tuban)

Jalan Kartika Plaza

Tuban Beach attracts families and locals who want the Bali beach experience without the crowds of Kuta. Warungs that have been here since the 1980s and earlier line the shore, and you'll find vendors selling hot corn, coconuts, and other island treats wandering about. You'll walk among a mix of sand and stone.

CENTRAL KUTA
★ Kuta Beach
(Pantai Kuta)

Jalan Pantai Kuta

Kuta Beach itself is little more than a wide, sandy beach with thumping waves. Being in the heart of Bali's tourism scene, it's developed into so much more. Most travelers find themselves walking along the tan brown sand at some point, regardless of whether they're on a tight budget or won't settle for less than luxury. Australian travelers specifically have an affinity for Kuta Beach. It's where many of them went on holiday as children and take their own families today. The surf is great for everyone here.

Beachside vendors selling food, trinkets, sarongs, surf lessons, beach chair rentals, and massages make their living wandering up and down Kuta Beach in search of customers. In the high season, it's mayhem. Embrace the scene and don't expect any alone time.

KUTA BEACH SURF BREAK

Paddle out from Kuta Beach

Kuta Beach offers fun times for all. Beginners

can catch waves in the whitewash while those with a little more experience paddle out. No matter the weather or conditions, you're guaranteed to see surfers having a good time. It works at almost every size (though large swells will overwhelm beginners), is wipeout-friendly with a sandy bottom, and has plenty of peaks to choose from. Look for southwesterly swells and northwesterly winds, but really, it's fine to go out whenever.

KUTA REEF SURF BREAK

800 meters (2,624 feet) offshore from Kuta Beach; paddle 15+ minutes, or 50,000-100,000 Rp boat ride per person round-trip

Kuta Reef is no stranger to surfers, being one of the original surf breaks that sparked mass surf tourism into Bali. You'll need strong arms or a boat to reach this lefthander that barrels in ideal conditions. Look for southwesterly swells with easterly winds. Rarely works at low tide.

LEGIAN
★ Legian Beach
(Pantai Legian)

Jalan Pantai Legian

Legian Beach attracts calmer crowds and offers plenty of hangout space. The typical routine is to lounge out all day in the sea, then head to Legian's shoreline for the nightlife once the sun goes down. Like Kuta Beach, this spot has plenty of beach chairs to rent and umbrellas for shade. The chaos is just a bit more controlled.

LEGIAN SURF BREAK

Paddle out from Legian Beach

While Kuta Beach's surfers are carefree and friendly, Legian attracts a more serious crowd. Bigger waves and stronger currents make Legian a beach that's better for intermediate surfers, unless you are supervised in a lesson. The wave maxes out at about 12 feet and works best with southwesterly swells and northwesterly winds. Don't be fooled by surfers clustered at a certain peak; they're often just following the pack.

SEMINYAK AND KEROBOKAN
Double Six Beach
(Pantai Double Six)

Jalan Arjuna

Double Six Beach is where you'll find people playing acoustic guitars, jogging, reading, surfing, and playing bocce ball in the sand. Small stands sell coconuts, cold drinks, and snacks, and rent beanbag chairs by the hour. The youthful vibe at Double Six is one even old souls can get behind.

Seminyak Beach
(Pantai Seminyak)

Jalan Raya Seminyak

It's almost impossible to tell when Double Six Beach ends and Seminyak Beach begins—and it really doesn't matter. Seminyak has established itself as being one of the more refined beaches around, leaving the debauchery to its neighbors in the south. Competition for space on the sand is almost nil, as large resorts block many day-trippers from conveniently reaching the beach.

SEMINYAK SURF BREAK

Paddle out from Seminyak Beach (no consistent spot)

Seminyak is a mixed bag when it comes to wave quality and consistency. One morning you'll have peaky A-frames, and the next you'll be battling walls of close-outs. If a southwesterly swell any bigger than 10 feet rolls through, the water will feel like a washing machine. Beginners can fare well if they stay in the whitewash. If Kuta is too small, check Seminyak.

Kerobokan Beach
(Pantai Kerobokan)

Jalan Petitenget

Walking onto Kerobokan Beach can be a challenge, as road access is monopolized by private villas and resorts. You can reach it via Potato Head Beach Club (and let's be real, you'll probably be spending some time there anyway). The journey is worth it for undisturbed

Seminyak and Kerobokan

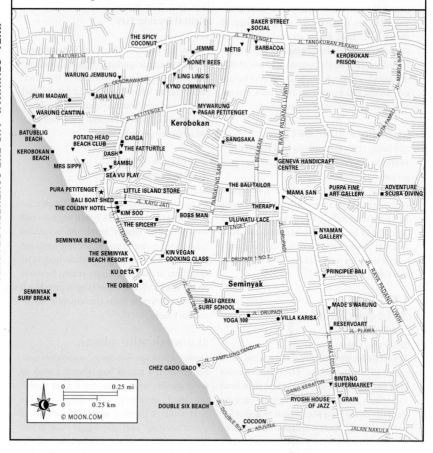

time on the sand. Opt for calmer waters elsewhere if you plan to swim.

Batubelig Beach
(Pantai Batubelig)

Jalan Batubelig

Intrepid travelers like Batubelig Beach for its semi-remoteness and the friendly warungs stationed on its shore. The water is wonderful for experienced surfers, but it's often too rough for swimmers. If you do plan to go for a dip, mind the flags and strong currents.

CANGGU
Berawa Beach
(Pantai Berawa)

Jalan Pantai Berawa; 5,000 Rp parking

A popular hangout for serious surfers and expats, Berawa Beach is a mellow, gray-sand beach set in front of Finns Beach Club. Enjoy the chilled-out ambiance there or walk a few minutes north to escape the crowd. Cold Bintang beers and coconuts seem permanently affixed to beachgoers' hands here.

1: Seminyak Beach 2: Petitenget Beach

Canggu

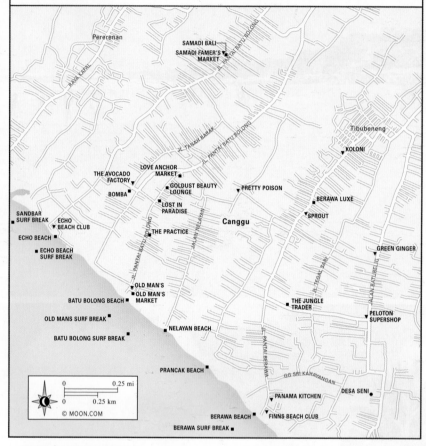

BERAWA SURF BREAK

Paddle out from Berawa Beach

Some breaks in the area seem to cater to only beginners or only the experts. Fortunately, Berawa is a safe space for intermediates with good surf manners wanting to progress. The wave sees a mix of rights and lefts thanks to its rocky bottom. Look for southwesterly swells and northeasterly winds in the forecast.

Prancak Beach
(Pantai Prancak)

Jalan Pemelisan Agung

Boldly guarding those who visit is Pura Dalem Prancak, a small Hindu temple at the base of Prancak Beach. It's worth the stop if you're exploring the area by motorbike, or if you want to walk from Berawa Beach. The beach itself is small and simple, and has a handful of merchants selling snacks perched at its entrance (though they're not always around).

Nelayan Beach
(Pantai Nelayan)

Jalan Nelayan

Canggu has boomed during the past 10 years, bringing a new vitality to its shoreline that it did not have before. At Nelayan Beach, you can see a glimpse of Canggu's calmer times, as it's where the fishermen bring in their catch. Locals looking to relax tend to venture here with their families, leaving the other beaches to the tourists.

Batu Bolong Beach
(Pantai Batu Bolong)
Jalan Pantai Batu Bolong

If tourists tell you that they're heading to Canggu Beach, they often mean Batu Bolong. This quirky volcanic ash beach is an ideal place to surf, lounge, and swim. The crowd is lively and active, but somehow rarely manages to get too boisterous. Surf lessons are offered here, but due to the crowded conditions and lack of surf etiquette, it's not the most peaceful experience.

OLD MAN'S SURF BREAK
Paddle out from Batu Bolong Beach

Fat and fun, this mellow wave can handle some size, and its wide shoulder helps it manage a crowd. It's a great wave for longboarders wanting to go right. The crowd is typically mellow, unless a stand-up paddler catches a few too many. Like all the other breaks along this stretch, you want southwesterly swells and northeasterly winds. There are also a handful of peaks nearby if Old Man's isn't your scene.

Echo Beach
(Pantai Echo)
Jalan Pura Batu Mejan; 5,000 Rp parking

Echo Beach has been popular for years among surfers because of the consistent waves that roll through. Venture here to enjoy beachside barbecued seafood, plush beanbag chairs, laid-back lounges, and people-watching from the little beach bars. The sound of the crashing surf combined with the contrast of sand and sky make Echo Beach one of the best spots to watch the sunset. Because of strong currents, it's not the best beach for families and swimmers.

ECHO BEACH SURF BREAK
Paddle out from Echo Beach

Echo Beach has a powerful left that breaks over shallow, rocky reef. Surfers from all over the region will flock here if it starts to barrel. During its mellower moments, it attracts aggressive crowds and athletes in search of sponsors. It's arguably one of the best waves around. At low and midtide, a southerly swell, northerly winds, and a decent size will give the wave serious power. This break is currently at risk of disappearing due to construction of a new jetty. Surfers are protesting, but the future is uncertain.

Water Sports

SURF SCHOOLS
PRO SURF SCHOOL
Jalan Raya Pantai; tel. 361/751200; , weather/tide permitting; 650,000 Rp or more, depending on ability and lesson

Pro Surf School offers classes for surfers of all abilities. Complete beginners will learn to surf on friendly waves, and more experienced surfers can get coached at the local reef breaks by former pro surfers. The school guarantees that every student will catch a wave, or the next lesson is free. Pro Surf School also offers surf excursions, board rental, and an overnight surf camp just a short walk away from the sea. Pro Surf School is sponsored by Billabong, one of the biggest brands in the surf industry.

BALI GREEN SURF SCHOOL
Jalan Drupadi 2 No. 9; tel. 81999344122; www. baligreensurf.net; 7am-sunset, weather/tide permitting; 650,000 Rp per lesson

Bali Green is a community-focused surf school in Seminyak that hosts 2.5-hour lessons, surf trips, and weeklong surf camps. Instructors tend to be locals who grew up in the area and know the variety of breaks very

★ Tips for Beginning Surfers

Kuta is one of the best places in the world to catch your first wave. Warm water, friendly waves, soft sand, and experienced instructors create an ideal atmosphere for beginners. If you've thought about surfing but haven't given it a go, here are a few tips to help boost your skills and confidence.

- **Take a lesson:** Bali is home to many experienced surf coaches who teach surf lessons all year. They'll show you how to stay safe, what to look for in a wave, how to paddle, and how to stand up. Some coaches also explain how to read a wave forecast so that you can feel confident surfing on your own afterward. Learn the proper technique from the beginning by investing in a few hours of surf coaching.

- **Rent a beginner-friendly board:** Don't make the mistake of renting a fiberglass short-board that you don't know how to ride. Instead, rent a soft board with foam on the top. It should be at least 7 feet long and 30 inches wide. The bigger your board is, the easier it will be for you to balance. Choosing a foam board over a hard board will also be safer when you wipe out.

- **Point your board toward the horizon when paddling out:** Most beginner surf injuries happen when the surfer holds the board parallel to the horizon. When a wave comes, it picks up the board—knocking the surfer back to shore with it. When you're standing in the water or paddling out, think of slicing your board through the wave by keeping it perpendicular to the horizon or shoreline.

- **Plant your feet and squat low:** When you pop up, spring into a squat with your feet a little more than hip distance apart. One foot should be on the back of the board with your front foot 45-degrees turned toward the front. If your feet are too close together, it will be difficult to balance.

- **Be patient:** Surfing takes dedication and patience to progress. Only about 10 percent of a surf session is spent surfing, while the rest of the time is spent waiting and paddling—even for professional athletes. Don't stress if you haven't caught a wave on your first day of lessons: it's a sport that is more challenging than it looks. A surfing proverb says, "The best surfer in the lineup is the one having the most fun!"

well. Part of the surf school's proceeds go toward charity events and surf lessons for local children.

UP2U SURF SCHOOL

Jalan Pantai Kuta; tel. 81384345408; www.up2usurfschool.com; 7:30am-5:30pm weather/tide permitting; 350,000 Rp per lesson

UP2U Surf School is one of the most comprehensive surf schools in Bali. Students learn in-depth about all things surfing over the course of five lessons. While many surf schools teach the basics of paddling out and catching a wave, UP2U also teaches surfers how to read a surf report, safety tips for surfing, how to turn, and the differences between surf breaks. Each lesson comes with surf gear,

drinking water, Wi-Fi, and access to lockers and showers.

WATER PARKS

★ WATERBOM BALI WATER PARK

Jalan Kartika Plaza Tuban; tel. 361/755676; www.waterbom-bali.com; 9am-6pm; 355,000 Rp 1 day, 620,000 Rp 2 days

Waterbom Bali is the best water park on the island, with experiences ranging from stomach-churning, almost-vertical rides to lazy rivers weaving about. There are nearly 20 rides, a bungy bounce area, a flow rider, and areas where families can have old-fashioned fun blasting one another with water cannons. Daredevils can duel on the Twin Racer slides, a ride where you're dropped head-first down a steep waterslide. The rides are placed among indigenous trees, serving as a constant reminder that you're still in Bali. Waterbom is a crowd pleaser for people of all ages and interests.

SCUBA DIVING

There are no worthwhile dive sites in the immediate area. Dive shops collect divers from their hotels and transport them to dive sites of their choice.

SCUBA DUBA DOO

Jalan Legian Kelod/Gang Melani No. 3B; tel.
361/750724; www.divecenterbali.com; 7am-3pm;
1,200,000-1,700,000 Rp for 2 fun dives

Scuba Duba Doo is a PADI (Professional Association of Diving Instructors) 5-Star Dive Center that runs scuba day trips to locations all around Bali, including Amed, Tulamben, Menhangan Island, Nusa Penida, and the Gili Islands. Day trips are either two or three tank dives and include transportation, lunch, drinks, gear, entrance fees, insurance, and a guide. The dive center also runs frequent snorkeling trips and PADI programs, ranging from Discover Scuba to Dive Master courses.

ADVENTURE SCUBA DIVING

Jalan Dewi Saraswati No. 50; tel. 87760102000;
www.adventure-scuba-diving.com; 1,800,000-
2,000,000 Rp for 2 fun dives

Many scuba divers get their start at Adventure Scuba Diving, a small dive center with a reputation for being beginner-friendly and accommodating to nervous divers. They keep groups small and tend to offer a more personal experience than many of the larger dive centers in Bali. Aside from running day trips to Amed, Tulamben, Padang Bai, and Nusa Penida, the dive center offers PADI training and specialty courses.

MANTA MANTA DIVING

Hotel pickup and drop-off only (no central location);
tel. 81237870200; https://mantamanta-diving.com;
2,000,000 Rp for 2 fun dives

Manta Manta Diving is an efficiently run remote dive center that picks up guests and takes them directly to the dive boat, where rental gear is already loaded. Choose to go on a snorkel safari or multiple fun dives or take a PADI course. Most trips run to Nusa Penida, where you're likely to see manta rays.

Other Sports and Recreation

SPAS
USADHA SPA

Jalan Melasti; tel. 361/751711; www.legianbeachbali.
com; daily 9am-9pm; 500,000 Rp and up for
60-minute treatment

The massage therapists at Usadha Spa take a unique approach to massage. Each morning from 8:30am to 9:00am, the massage therapists practice a combination of tai chi and kung fu (guests are welcome to join). This movement is to create energy and focus that they will then pass to their guests during treatment. Their best value package uses a blend of acupressure, hot stones, and massage to bring energy into the body. Revitalize in a private massage room or outside in an open garden area.

GOLDUST BEAUTY LOUNGE

Jalan Pantai Batu Bolong No. 66; tel. 811383721;
www.goldustbali.com; Mon. 10am-8pm, Tues.-Sun.
9am-8pm; 260,000 Rp and up for a 60-minute
treatment

Chic, trendy, and modern, Goldust Beauty Lounge is a spa where you can get a multitude of pampering treatments, including manicures, pedicures, waxing, hair treatments, and massages. Their signature gold facials involve the application of a 24K gold dust mask, believed to reduce wrinkles and to firm skin. Does it work? Who knows, but you'll certainly feel like royalty when gold dust is rubbed into your skin, and that alone makes the facial worth it. The spa also offers spa parties for those wanting to get pampered as a group.

THERAPY

Jalan Kayu Ayu No. 1A; tel. 81933011325; www. therapy.co.id; daily 10am-8pm; 270,000 Rp and up for 60-minute treatment

Therapy is a contemporary spa where only organic, cruelty-free products are used during treatment. Choose between massages, cream baths, scrubs, facials, waxing, manicures, and pedicures. Their deep tissue "Panel Beat" massage is a popular choice among surfers, athletes, and travelers wanting to work out some knots after a long-haul flight. Splurge and finish your treatment with a scrub; your skin will appreciate the extra attention after braving Bali's humidity.

YOGA
THE PRACTICE

Jalan Pantai Batu Bolong No. 94A; tel. 81236702160; www.thepracticebali.com; daily 7am-9pm; 140,000 Rp per class

Set among rice paddies, The Practice is a spacious yoga studio built from bamboo that hosts an array of yoga classes daily. Most classes are designated for a certain skill level or will be specifically noted when they suit all abilities. Multiple types of Hatha, Yin, Pranayama, and meditation classes take place throughout the day.

SAMADI BALI

Jalan Padang Linjong No. 39; tel. 81238312505; www. samadibali.com; Mon.-Sat. 7am-9pm, Sun. 7am-5pm; 140,000 Rp per class

Samadi Bali is a yoga *shala* where you can come for a single class or stay on-site in one of their private rooms for a yoga retreat. Samada Bali schedules Mysore, Ashtanga, flow, Yin, and Hatha classes. Most classes are suitable for all abilities, or beginners can take an intro to Ashtanga course before joining the main classes. After your practice, head to Samada Bali's on-site vegetarian restaurant.

YOGA 108

Jalan Drupadi No. 108; tel. 8170007108; www. yoga108bali.com; classes Mon.-Sat. at 7:45am, 9:30am, 11:30am, 5:30pm, closed Sun.; 100,000 Rp per class

While the exterior of Yoga 108's studio may not seem like much, inside, you'll find quality yoga classes offered about four times per day. The style of teaching is focused more on posture and breathing, leading it to be more intense than many expect. Arrive early, as the studio is on the smaller side and classes book up quickly. Expect there to be a parade of regulars.

★ COOKING CLASSES
THE SPICERY

Jalan Kayu Aya No. 1; tel. 81246552549; www. thespicerydeli.com; classes Tues.-Fri. 8am-4pm; 750,000-1,000,000 Rp for a half-day class, 1,300,000-1,500,000 Rp for a full-day class, alcohol 150,000 Rp per class

At The Spicery, a Balinese cooking class begins at a local market where you'll learn about the in-season produce, spices, and staples of local cuisine. Then students head to The Spicery Deli, where they'll chop, spice, and cook staple dishes that change with the season. The school is known for perfecting fragrant dishes like spiced duck *(bebek betutu)*, chili sauce *(sambal)*, and fried rice. Class admission includes transportation to and from set pickup points, drinks, snacks, lunch, and a recipe book.

KIN VEGAN COOKING CLASS

Jalan Kaya Ayu No. 17; tel. 81999975588; https:// kinvegancookingclass.com; daily 3pm-7pm; 500,000 Rp per class

On an island bountiful with fresh produce, spices, and skilled chefs, it's no wonder that Bali has quickly become one of the vegan capitals of Asia. At Kin Vegan Cooking Class, chefs and wannabe chefs will learn how to create Balinese vegan dishes like tempeh curry, vegetables steamed in banana leaves, satay, fritters, sauces like peanut sauce and *sambal,* and cakes. Classes are taught in a spacious, open-air kitchen.

The Best Street Art in Bali

It's easy to see why artists from all around the globe feel inspired to capture Bali's stunning scenery. And though street art hasn't taken off island-wide, there are a few neighborhoods where you can wander and enjoy murals painted on buildings surrounded by jungle backdrops.

★ CANGGU

Artists from all over the globe take inspiration from the tranquility of Canggu, and have moved to splashing their artwork onto hostel, restaurant, and stone brick walls. If you want to see some of Canggu's best art pieces for yourself, **Nelayan Beach, Jalan Pantai Berawa, Gang Nyepi, ALLCAPS gallery,** and **Jalan Pantai Batu Mejan** host stunning pieces painted by Indonesian artists who go by the artist names of Darbotz, Sleeck, and Quint.

ULUWATU

The cliffs of Uluwatu feature street art with a message. Paintings of waves, nature, and Balinese Hindu gods grace the concrete and urge people to keep Uluwatu clean. Many works demand that tourists cut down their single-use plastic consumption. Start at **Single Fin** and wander down the steps to see the murals—some are hidden.

SANUR

For 10,000 Rp, you can enter an abandoned theme park called **Taman Festival Bali** that's been taken over by street artists and jungle vines. Beautiful and bold murals cover the inside of dilapidated buildings and old carnival rides.

DENPASAR

The artists who use Denpasar as their canvas often have political and social messages to convey. Wander down roads like **Gang Rajawali, Jalan Sulawesi,** and **Jalan Gaja Mada** for intriguing artwork.

Entertainment and Events

THE ARTS

DMZ MUSEUM

Jalan Nakula No. 33X; tel. 361/8496220; www. dmzbali.com; daily 9am-10pm; 90,000 Rp per person

Unusual and quirky, the DMZ Museum's artists have mastered optical illusions to create murals that make visitors feel as though they're in the middle of the scene themselves. There are more than 120 murals to interact with, and a team of photographers who are always happy to take a picture of you standing near Egyptian pyramids, a French bistro, Cambodian temples, and more. It's a feast for the imagination. Bring your camera.

PURPA FINE ART GALLERY

Jalan Mertanadi No. 22B; tel. 81999408804; https:// purpagallerybali.com; Mon.-Sat. 10am-6pm, closed Sun.; free

Purpa Fine Art Gallery is a boutique gallery that features the art of contemporary artists, including works by Hans Snell, Gusti Nyoman Lempad, Arie Smit, and many more. The owners also show works from emerging local artists, and they are happy to share the backgrounds of pieces on exhibit.

NYAMAN GALLERY

Jalan Basangkasa No. 88; tel. 361/736226; www. nyamangroup.com; daily 9am-9pm; free

Nyaman Gallery features contemporary work from predominantly Indonesian artists over two floors. The atmosphere inside the gallery is anything but pretentious, making it an ideal place to spend some time admiring and learning about the pieces from all throughout the archipelago. An interesting blend of modern and traditional art is displayed in the cozy studio.

RESERVOART

Jalan Raya Seminyak No. 54; tel. 81236111693; www. reservo-art.com; daily 9am-9pm; free

Exhibiting work from more than 30 Asian artists, Reservoart is a spacious gallery with figurative, abstract, modern, and pop art on display. The curators tend to favor bold, bright pieces over traditional Balinese works. The gallery posts current pieces on its website to peruse before you visit in person. International shipping is included with each purchase.

MÉTIS

Jalan Petitenget No. 6; tel. 81805670588; www. metisbali.com; Mon.-Sat. 11am-2am, closed Sun.; free admission to gallery, 150,000-400,000 Rp mains in restaurant

Combining fine dining and fine arts, Métis serves French Mediterranean cuisine in a regal dining area alongside immaculately crafted sculptures, paintings, ancient Asian artifacts, furniture, and jewelry. Their finest pieces are protected behind glass cases. If you are looking for opulence and novelty, Métis is an upscale venue that stimulates all the senses. The outdoor dining area is set with white tablecloths and hanging plants.

ALLCAPS PARK

Jalan Tumbak Bayuh; tel. 81239693889; allcapsbali@ gmail.com; Mon.-Sat. 11am-8pm, Sun. 10am-5pm; free

Canggu is the most innovative neighborhood in Bali's street art scene, and ALLCAPS Park was founded by local street artists as a creative space to paint and purchase art supplies. The paint-covered property has a gallery, shop, and a large outdoor space with murals from artists hailing from all over the globe. The gallery also hosts private street art tours, graffiti workshops, and other art-centered events.

FESTIVALS AND CEREMONIES

KUTA BEACH FESTIVAL

Pantai Kuta; kutabeachfestival@gmail.com; usually happens in October; free entry

The Kuta Beach Festival welcomes tens of thousands of participants over the course of five days. The festival typically starts with an opening ceremony that showcases traditional dancers and live music, and is followed by events like kite flying, Balinese martial arts demonstrations, art exhibitions, sand sculpture competitions, surf contests, a turtle hatchling release, movies and plays, and more. However, the highlight tends to be Kuta Beach Festival's food stalls, which sell a variety of international and Indonesian street food dishes. The festival usually takes place in October each year. Updates can be found on the Kuta Beach Festival Instagram and Facebook page (@kutabeachfestival).

MELASTI PILGRIMAGE

Multiple beaches; free to watch

Three days before Nyepi, Bali's Day of Silence, Balinese Hindus from all over the island make a pilgrimage to the sea while wearing white ceremonial attire and carrying effigies. Once the pilgrims reach the ocean, they partake in a purification ceremony to cleanse evil spirits from their bodies and communities. Travelers are welcome to watch the processions from the distance, though formal ceremonial attire is required to participate. Most major beaches in the region (often marked by a large Hindu gate) are sites where the Melasti pilgrimage will occur.

Sightseeing Clues: Balinese Words to Know

Many attractions, shops, restaurants, and hotels will have signs printed in English, especially in tourist-heavy areas. However, there are a handful of Bahasa and Balinese words that you'll see consistently as you travel through this magical island.

- **Warung:** Restaurant—typically serving local food

- **Pura:** Temple

- **Dewa, Dewi:** God, Goddess—usually noting a statue

- **Toko:** Store

- **Nusa:** Island

- **Pantai:** Beach

- **Taman:** Garden

- **Jalan, Gang:** Road, Street

- **Buka:** Open

- **Tutup:** Closed

- **Dekat:** Near

- **Jauh:** Far

Shopping

CENTRAL KUTA
Malls
DISCOVERY SHOPPING MALL
Kartika Plaza; tel. 361/769572; www.discoveryshoppingmall.com; daily 10am-10pm

Discovery Shopping Mall is a large beachside shopping center packed with shops selling Balinese souvenirs, clothing, housewares, shoes, and accessories, as well as a handful of chain restaurants. Featured stores include Nike, Ripcurl, Billabong, Converse, and La Senza. This mall occasionally hosts outdoor movies under the the stars on their big screen.

BEACHWALK SHOPPING CENTER
Jalan Pantai Kuta; tel. 361/8464888; www.beachwalkbali.com; Sun.-Thurs. 10:30am-10:30pm, Fri.-Sat. 10:00am-midnight

A clean and modern shopping plaza, Beachwalk Shopping Center borders the beach and hosts shops selling luxury goods, clothing, souvenirs, jewelry, books, beauty, sweets, and more. There's a selection of restaurants and spas on-site as well. It's a great place to escape the sun for a few hours as you duck in and out of the air-conditioned shops.

LEGIAN
Specialty Goods
PITHECANTHROPUS
Jalan Raya Legian; tel. 82146498865; www.pithecanthropusbali.com; daily 9am-11pm

Pithecanthropus is a large boutique that sources its high-quality handmade batik and ikat textiles, clothing, sculptures, artwork, jewelry, and home goods from all over Indonesia. The boutique is divided into different sections ranging from traditional to more modern batik patterns and objects.

BALIFU SARONGS

Jalan Arjuna Block B No. 1; tel. 361/737169; https:// balifusarongs.com; daily 9am-6pm

Few travelers leave Bali without a sarong: a thin piece of fabric that quickly becomes a beachside staple. Balifu Sarongs has one of the largest selections of sarongs, batik fabrics, towels, and other textiles.

SEMINYAK
Clothing and Accessories
LITTLE ISLAND STORE

Jalan Kayu Aya; tel. 82145156040; daily 9am-9pm

The Little Island Store is stocked with tropical island-style women's clothing, home goods, and jewelry. Think feminine ruffles, artistic embroidery, T-shirts with sassy sayings, and palm leaf everything.

BALI BOAT SHED

Jalan Kayu Aya 23A; tel. 85700000000; https:// baliboatshed.com; daily 8am-10pm

A funky boutique with an exterior as colorful as the clothing inside, Bali Boat Shed sells men's and women's clothing made by local designers. Most of the women's dress prints tend to be tropical and flirty. Shop here for bathing suits, resort wear, formal wear, and matching outfit sets that you won't find anywhere else.

ULUWATU LACE

Jalan Laksamana No. 56; tel. 361/755342; https:// uluwatu.co.id; daily 8am-10pm

Balinese Hindu women wear intricate lace shirts to religious ceremonies and temple visits. The designers at Uluwatu Lace have combined the craft of *krawang* (cutwork) with today's fashion to create stunning pieces of men's and women's clothing, bedding, and home decor. Each item sold at Uluwatu Lace is handmade. Though there are other Uluwatu Lace shops in Bali, the Seminyak shop has the largest selection.

THE BALI TAILOR

Jalan Beraban No. 67; tel. 8179703408; https:// thebalitailor.com; Mon.-Sat. 9am-6pm, Sun. 10am-4pm

The Bali Tailor sells custom-made leather ensembles and staple items like leather shoes, jackets, boots, hats, and belts. Their items favor quality, classic looks rather than following trends. Special requests are encouraged, and they sell a separate vegan line of clothing as well.

Bali Boat Shed

Home Goods
GENEVA HANDICRAFT CENTRE
Jalan Raya Kerobokan No. 100; tel. 361/733542;
www.genevahandicraft.com; daily 9am-8pm

Geneva Handicraft Centre is one of the largest and most popular souvenir and handicraft shops in Bali. Prices are fixed—meaning you can purchase that market item you've been eyeing without hassle—and there are plenty of options to choose from. Visit early in the morning to beat the crowds who arrive via tour bus.

KIM SOO
Jalan Kaya Ayu No. 21; tel. 8214578043; https://
kimsoo.com; shop daily 9am-10pm, café daily
7:30am-5:30pm

Kim Soo has embraced minimalism and comfort with their Scandinavian, African, and Indonesian-influenced home decor. The shop itself is stylishly black and white, with enough space to browse in peace. Most items have a bold, geometric element to them. There is also a café on-site that serves cakes, coffee, and decadent meals.

CARGA
Jalan Petitenget No. 886; tel. 361/8478180; www.
cargabali.com; daily 9am-9pm

A cheerful shop in the heart of Seminyak, Carga sells fun and colorful home decor, ceramics, paper goods, children's clothing, accessories, and knick-knacks typically sourced from all throughout Indonesia. Most items are surprisingly well priced and decent quality, making it one of the best-value shops around.

Jewelry
TRIBALI: RABIA JEWELLERY BALI
Jalan Petitenget No. 12B; tel. 361/2168255; daily
9am-9pm

Tribali offers accessories for travelers who are drawn to healing crystals, Sanskrit letters, raw materials, and tribal-inspired patterns. Browse for necklaces, earrings, bracelets, anklets, watches, and clutch purses in their small, cozy shop. Lead designer Rabia

Bullough is often in the shop ready to answer questions.

JEMME
Jalan Petitenget No. 28; tel. 361/4733508; www.
jemmebali.com; 10am-10pm

Selling diamonds and other gems set in gold and silver, Jemme is a fine jewelry store where you can browse the array of intricate gem pieces and watch jewelers at work. Their styles range from bold and colorful to simple, and from haute couture to vintage.

CANGGU
Markets
LOVE ANCHOR MARKET
Jalan Pantai Batu Bolong No. 56; www.
loveanchorcanggu.com; Sat.-Sun. 9am-5pm

Undoubtedly one of the most hip and upbeat markets in Bali, Love Anchor Market is a bazaar held under a traditional Javanese wooden roof. You'll find a crowd of smiling faces enjoying the live music and browsing the stalls filled with trendy clothing, accessories, sarongs, souvenirs, and hand-crafted condiments. Many visitors come with the intent to socialize rather than shop.

OLD MAN'S MARKET
Jalan Pantai Batu Bolong; last Sat. each month
8am-3pm

Many Baliese startups and boutique labels got their start at Old Man's Market, a popular market that attracts tourists and expats from all over the Bukit Peninsula. You'll find designers selling clothing and jewelry, handcrafted soaps, sarongs, beauty products, and food cooked for the health-conscious.

Clothing and Boutiques
BERAWA LUXE
Jalan Raya Semat No. 185; tel. 817353586;
berawaluxe.com; daily 9am-5pm

Staying true to the free-spirited atmosphere that surrounds Canggu, Berawa Luxe is a women's boutique selling loose-fitting kimonos and clothing, as well as jewelry, shoes, purses, and accessories. The shop sources items that are comfortable and lightweight, making it an ideal place to look for sightseeing outfits.

LOST IN PARADISE
Jalan Pantai Batu Bolong No. 85; tel. 361/8469160; www.lostinparadisestore.com; daily 9:30am-9:30pm
Lost in Paradise was made for the surf-all-day, party-all-night lifestyle that many come to Bali to enjoy. The store's three in-house brands—Lost in Paradise, Veritas et Liberte, and CTZNS—are ready to equip both men and women with functional, stylish bathing suits and clothing made for days spent in the tropical heat.

Home Goods
THE JUNGLE TRADER
Jalan Pantai Berawa No. 46X; tel. 81353611112; www.thejungletrader.com; daily 9am-7pm

The Jungle Trader boutique offers intriguing, authentic home decor and art pieces from all over Indonesia. Most objects for sale are made from natural materials and complement Bali's tropical surroundings; there are no mass-produced plastic pieces in sight. Here, you can find Balinese masks, woven baskets, batik textiles, and other handmade items.

BOMBA
Jalan Batu Mejan No. 33A; tel. 81339199015; daily 9am-10pm
Bomba is a home goods shop that has embraced surf culture completely. You'll find bold throw pillows, surf movie posters, '70s-style prints, Bomba-branded textiles, and a decent selection of bikinis. Groovy.

Food

TUBAN
European
BOARDWALK RESTAURANT AND LOUNGE
Jalan Kartika; tel. 361/752725; www.boardwalk-restaurant.com; daily 11am-11pm; 40,000-100,000 Rp
Boardwalk Restaurant and Lounge is a venue where the ambiance is just as important as the food. The restaurant is on the beach and has a large bar that's perfect for sitting and making new friends. Most evenings, Boardwalk hosts entertainment shows ranging from fire dancing to traditional dance to acrobatics. The menu is made up of mostly Mediterranean-style soups, salads, tapas, seafood, and pastas. Their bartenders are skilled at making decent tropical cocktails.

MA JOLY
Jalan Wana Segara; tel. 361/753780; www.ma-joly.com; daily 7am-11pm; 100,000-300,000 Rp
A romantic place for a date, Ma Joly is a fine dining restaurant and bar set on the beach.

There is a main dining area with candlelit seating under a vast canopy accented with paper lanterns. For an intimate experience, book a private gazebo on the sand. Staff set candles in front of the table, illuminating a path to the sea. The restaurant serves grilled meats like lamb, beef, tuna, and chicken, as well as a variety of pastas.

American
ENVY
Jalan Wana Segara No. 33; tel. 361/755577; holidayinnresortbarunabali@ihg.com; daily 11am-11pm; 70,000-150,000 Rp
Envy has a casual cool vibe about it and it's the ideal spot to go for drinks and snacks, especially during the evening, when live music typically plays and the sun sparkles over the Indian Ocean. This beachside lounge restaurant is connected to the Holiday Inn. It has a basic lunch and dinner menu that serves simple salads, sandwiches, wraps, fish and chips, and tacos. Though it may not be the most experimental food option around, a daily

two-for-one happy hour special (5pm-6pm) makes Envy worth a sunset visit.

CENTRAL KUTA
Indonesian
WARUNG 24/7

Jalan Nakula Night; tel. 818491510; daily 10am-midnight; 40,000-270,000 Rp

This no-frills, family-run restaurant serves grilled seafood spiced to perfection along with Balinese classic dishes (*nasi campur, mie goreng, nasi goreng*). What the venue lacks in ambiance, it makes up for in personality and taste. The staff are cheerful and often remember repeat customers. The chefs tend to be heavy handed with the chili, so speak up if you don't want your meal too spicy.

POPPIES RESTAURANT

Poppies Lane I; tel. 361/751059; poppiesbali.com; 8am-11pm daily; 50,000-170,000 Rp

Once you step inside Poppies Restaurant, you'll quickly forget that you're in Bali's busiest area, thanks to the intimate garden. This family-run restaurant serves local dishes that haven't left the menu since the restaurant opened in 1973. A handful of pasta-based dishes is featured as well. The piña colada is a must.

★ FAT CHOW

Poppies Lane II No. 7C; tel. 87761330661; www. fatchowbali.com; daily 9am-11pm; 60,000-150,000 Rp

Fat Chow is not your average Indonesian and Asian fusion restaurant. Its quirky mix of industrial and cute decor, friendly service, and interesting flavor combos give it a fun vibe. Each dish is thoughtfully presented, and portions cater to the very hungry. A variety of soups, curries, salads, fried rice, and stir-fries grace the menu. Fat Chow is unfortunately no longer a well-kept secret; expect long wait times if you haven't reserved in advance.

SUKUN

Jalan Kartika Plaza, Gang Puspa Ayu No. 99; tel. 361/755380; www.amnayahotels.com; daily 6:30am-11pm; 250,000 Rp

Step away from the concrete streets of Kuta and into the tranquil garden at Sukun, an upscale restaurant serving fine Indonesian food. For the full experience, order the megibung, a five-course meal that includes *sambal* and crackers, soup, an array of traditional dishes like beef *rendang* (spicy red curry), fried noodles, grilled fish, and a local dessert. Meals are artfully presented on trays made from banana leaves.

Australian
★ CRUMB & COASTER

Jalan Benesari No. 2E; tel. 81999596319; daily 7:30am-11pm; 40,000-95,000 Rp

Crumb & Coaster is a spacious café with trendy decor that gives it a warehouse-meets-greenhouse vibe. Don't be surprised to see wannabe food bloggers staging a mini photo shoot over their meals. Crumb & Coaster takes coffee seriously and serves a mix of sandwiches, burgers, salads, and smoothie bowls. Their hearty Australian-style breakfasts are served all day long.

JOKERS BAR AND GRILL

Jalan Legian No. 153; tel. 361/761554; jokers. bar.grill.bali@gmail.com; daily 9am-11:30pm; 50,000-80,000 Rp

Jokers Bar and Grill is a jovial Australian pub with smiling, attentive staff who serve a mix of baguettes, wraps, grilled meat, and cold beers. Guests tend to stay awhile to play darts, sing karaoke, listen to live music, and watch whatever sporting match is being featured on TV at the time. Aussies will appreciate the pub's love for a sausage sizzle.

American
BLACK HOUSE BURGERS

Jalan Benesari No. 2; tel. 81547233775; www. blackhouseburgers.com; daily 12:30pm-10pm; 25,000-60,000 Rp

Indonesian Food 101

mie goreng (fried noodles)

Kerobokan and Seminyak are one of the food capitals of Southeast Asia, where chefs aren't afraid to shake up traditional foods with new recipes and flavors. Jalan Petitenget in Seminyak has earned the nickname "Eat Street." When you find yourself walking down this exciting road packed with restaurants and cooking schools, here are the local foods you must sample for yourself.

MIE GORENG

This dish can be found at nearly every food stand or warung. Noodles are fried in a sweet soy sauce and mixed with grilled meat, shallots, onions, and seasonal vegetables. It's often topped with a fried egg and served with a side of prawn crackers. The same dish is often made with rice *(nasi goreng)* in lieu of noodles.

NASI CAMPUR

Nasi campur is a serving of rice accompanied by a handful of sides of different types of vegetables and meat. If you enjoy variety, *nasi campur* will let you sample miniature portions of regional specialties at each meal.

SATAY

Satay is the top choice for a quick snack. The chef marinates skewered meat in a spiced coconut milk and chili sauce, then cooks it on a grill.

GADO-GADO

Gado-gado is a simple dish made from fresh, seasonal vegetables, stir-fried in a spicy and sweet peanut sauce.

BABI GULING

No special occasion is complete in Bali without a suckling pig stuffed with spices like lemongrass, black pepper, chili, and garlic. The suckling pig is then slow roasted. Fortunately, every day in Bali is a special occasion, and you can order *babi guling* at many places around the island.

SAMBAL

Every dish is served with a hearty spoonful of *sambal,* Bali's signature crushed chili sauce.

Black House Burgers is a simple, counter service food stop with a simple menu of chicken, beef, pork, vegetarian, and vegan burgers. Their famous "Nuclear" burger is not for timid taste buds, as it comes with chili paste, fresh chilis, and chili sauce. All burgers come with fries and mineral water, and you can choose between a white or black charcoal bun.

Asian
BLUEFIN
Jalan Kartika Plaza; tel. 361/764100; bluefin. ramarestaurantsbali.com; 11am-midnight daily; 50,000-100,000 Rp

Bluefin is an ultracool Japanese fusion restaurant and bar. Sit and be entertained as you eat at one of the teppanyaki tables, where skilled chefs prepare fresh meals over an iron hotplate, impressing guests with their bold knife and fire skills. Seating is limited at the teppanyaki tables, so book in advance. Enjoy dining on fresh sushi and sashimi, soups, and beef *tataki* (marinated and seared) in a modern atmosphere of glass fixtures and blue lighting.

NEBULA
Jalan Poppies Lane II No. 8; tel. 361/764502; book@ nebulagroupid.com; daily 7am-late; 70,000-195,000 Rp

Thoughtfully decorated, Nebula is a spacious restaurant with retro color combinations that give it a strong hipster feel. For a little variety, eat your meals on the main floor and then head to the rooftop area (complete with faux grass and beanbag chairs) for a drink. The menu features seafood, pork, Southeast Asian classics, salads, and curries. If you're feeling spontaneous, say "feed me" to receive a surprise medley of dishes (195,000 Rp/person).

Cafés
MEMORIAL CAFÉ
Jalan Legian; tel. 81246755076; daily 8am-midnight; 50,000-160,000 Rp

The interior of Memorial Café is spotless and bright, and its wagon-wheel tables are an interesting novelty. The coffees, juices, gelatos, milkshakes, and big breakfasts make it the type of spot where you can easily tuck away with a book or your laptop (free Wi-Fi). They serve lunch and dinner as well. Friendly staff will direct you to the air-conditioned or fan-only section of the café, depending on your preference.

LEGIAN
Indonesian
WARUNG PADMASARI
Jalan Padma No. 14; tel. 81236109808; daily 9am-11pm; 40,000-100,000 Rp

Warung Padmasari is a top spot for people watching, as it is located on a busy road. This casual restaurant serves large portions of fresh Indonesian fare that's a great value for the price. You may have to wait to get a table, but once you're seated, the service tends to be quick. If you ask the servers what they recommend, they're quick to suggest the beef *rendang* and the fried wontons. There's plenty for vegetarians to choose from as well.

CHAPTER 2
Jalan Werkudara; tel. 81338812998; daily 8am-11pm; 40,000-150,000 Rp

Chapter 2 is a lively and intimate venue known for its strong cocktails and thriving karaoke nights. The bartenders are always open to special requests, and their generous happy hour sells cocktails for 45,000 Rp from noon to 8pm daily. The menu features a mix of salads, Indonesian and Southeast Asian dishes, pizzas, steaks, and seafood.

THE LOKAL 80361
Jalan Sahadewa No. 13D; tel. 81999003339; daily 7am-10:30pm; 60,000-100,000 Rp

The Lokal 80361 is a nod to international café culture in Legian. This Instagram-friendly venue serves hot coffee (and they take it seriously), fresh smoothies, burgers, big breakfasts, quesadillas, and Indonesian staples. It's typically crowded with a mix of tourists and expats meeting over lattes or beers, depending on the time of day. During happy hour (4pm-7pm), visitors enjoy 20,000-rupiah beers and 20 percent off select cocktails.

European

POULET

Jalan Nakula No. 168; tel. 361/8475691; www. pouletbali.com; daily 8:30am-11:30pm; 45,000-80,000 Rp

Craving chicken? Poulet is a bright and joyfully decorated restaurant famous for its chicken dishes. Their breakfast menu has eggs, smoothie bowls, and pancakes. Lunch and dinner feature chicken just about every way imaginable, as well as a handful of beef and vegetarian items. Request a table on the second floor, where you can feel the ocean breeze in their open patio.

★ BALI PEARL

Jalan Arjuna Double Six; tel. 81934334060; www.balihotel-pearl.com; daily 6pm-midnight; 190,000-330,000 Rp

Led by Jeremy Blanchet, a renowned French chef, Bali Pearl is an authentic French fine dining restaurant that offers a unique dining experience. Inside, you'll find a formal seating area. However, request a table outside in the manicured gardens where the ambience is more romantic, as each table is illuminated by fairy lights. Bali Pearl's signature meal includes a gourmet tasting plate with samples of the chef's choice followed by confit salmon cooked with fennel, artichoke, snow peas, shiitake risotto, and kaffir lime. Come hungry—no dinner here is complete without a dessert.

Cafés

★ ON THE JUICE

Jalan Padma; tel. 81936093690; daily 8am-10pm; 40,000-85,000 Rp

By day, On the Juice serves healthy juices and smoothies out of an old Volkswagen bus. Come sunset, it turns into a lively bar with live music and sunset cocktail specials. Technicolor cushions, beanbag chairs, throw rugs, and small tables made from yellowed surfboards create a cozy, hippie vibe that perfectly encapsulates what Bali's beach scene is all about. On the Juice occasionally hosts movie nights on the sand, weather permitting.

SEMINYAK
Indonesian

MADE'S WARUNG

Jalan Raya Seminyak; tel. 361/732130; www. madeswarung.com; daily 10am-midnight; 30,000-90,000 Rp

On Seminyak's main stretch, Made's Warung serves a mix of Indonesian, Western, Japanese, and Italian fare. Locals often order the simple but fragrant dish of fresh fish grilled in homemade *sambal* chili sauce. While the food is delicious, the main draw of Made's Warung is the live entertainment, as Balinese cultural performances delight guests during dinnertime each evening. Decked out in elaborate costumes, dramatic makeup, and gold accessories, dancers of all ages tell stories of vivid Balinese legends through movement and sound. Reserve a table with a view of the stage in advance.

HONEY BEES

Jalan Peitienget No. 18X; tel. 361/4731444; daily 8am-10pm; 40,000-70,000 Rp

Honey Bees is a simple, clean restaurant with minimal decor that lets its food do the heavy lifting when it comes to building a reputation. It serves Indonesian staples, Indochinese fusion dishes, and a handful of pasta dishes. This is one of the best value places in Seminyak, so come hungry and order more than one item off the menu. Their friendly staff always seem to be up for a quick chat.

GRAIN

Jalan Raya Seminyak No. 16B; tel. 81353279966; www.grainbali.com; daily 7:30am-10pm; 60,000-100,000 Rp

Grain is an urban bistro that serves all-day breakfasts, Indonesian dishes, an extensive drinks menu that includes local wines, and a mix of Australian-influenced meals. Sit upstairs to enjoy their open-air terrace or dine downstairs in their air-conditioned al fresco section. Their Indonesian plates adhere to traditional recipes while their international menu items tend to feature more modern mixes. Their single-origin coffee is some of the best in Bali—even the most discerning coffee connoisseurs can't fault it.

★ BAMBU
Jalan Petitenget No. 198; tel. 361/8469797; www.banyantree.com; daily 6pm-11pm; 80,000-250,000 Rp

Once you're led behind the tall stone walls surrounding Bambu, it will seem as though you've stepped into an exclusive oasis. This fine dining venue is both indoors and outdoors, with tables set on a large covered patio area surrounded by water. The service is formal yet friendly, thanks to attentive staff, who are happy to explain each dish in depth or give recommendations based on your preferences. Their simple menu specifies the Indonesian island where each dish originated; guest favorites tend to be the soft-shell crab, crispy duck, and bamboo-baked barramundi.

★ MYWARUNG PASAR PETITENGET
Jalan Lebak Sari No. 18A; tel. 82235005718; daily 6pm-midnight; 100,000-200,000 Rp

One of the most stunning restaurants in Seminyak, MyWarung Pasar Petitenget serves Indonesian and Thai food in a seating area that's surrounded by greenery and lit by an array of vintage chandeliers. Ingredients are sourced locally whenever possible, and the restaurant has a strong reputation for serving delicious papaya salad and grilled fish. Plates are served family-style; visit with a group to sample as many things as possible.

BINTANG SUPERMARKET
Jalan Raya Seminyak No. 17; tel. 361/730552; bintangsupermarket.com; 7:30am-10:30pm

Bintang Supermarket has become somewhat of a Seminyak staple, a gathering point that people seem to wander into whenever they're unsure of what they want to eat. It's one of the largest supermarkets in the area, where you can stock up on Balinese snacks and staples like cold beers, fresh produce, cheese, baked goods, meat, spices, and ready-made meals.

Vegan/Vegetarian
THE SPICY COCONUT
Jalan Batu Belig No. 81; tel. 81246458250; www.thespicycoconut.com; daily 9am-4pm; 45,000-70,000 Rp

The Spicy Coconut has nailed on-trend dishes within the green community. The menu features a mix of vegan, vegetarian, and raw vegan dishes, and the restaurant's DIY salad is a popular choice among guests. Come for breakfast to enjoy plates of intricately cut fresh fruit and rainbow-colored smoothie bowls. Who knew that food could be so photogenic?

KYND COMMUNITY
Jalan Petitenget No. 12x; tel. 85931120209; www.kyndcommunity.com; daily 6am-5pm; 53,000-82,000 Rp

Kynd Community is a vegan café decked out in pastel pink and palm leaf paintings. Choose between three different plant-based milks for your coffee, or sample one of their specialty hot drinks like their matcha, beetroot, or turmeric lattes. They serve tofu scrambles, big salads, over-the-top toasts, waffles, burgers, nachos, and sandwiches. In the morning, the café gets crowded with people wanting to sample their famous smoothie bowl, which has fun phrases like "Bali Vibes" made from cut fruit and spelled out across the top.

American
THE FAT TURTLE
Jalan Raya Petitenget No. 886A; tel. 8998912127; daily 8am-6pm; 40,000-80,000 Rp

If you think breakfast is the most important meal of the day, The Fat Turtle agrees. Their all-day brunch menu aims to please with grilled cheese sandwiches, waffles, eggs many different ways, smashed avocado, breakfast pastas, fresh juices, kombuchas, and coffees. The red velvet pancakes will have you eating dessert for breakfast. The atmsophere is cheerful, with wooden signs featuring quirky quotes sprinkled throughout the small café.

BOSS MAN
*Jalan Kayu Cendana No. 8; tel. 81239167070; https://
bossmanbali.com; daily 11am-4am; 95,000 Rp*

What you see is what you get at Boss Man, a burger joint with six types of burgers and staff who have little patience for picky eaters. From its short menu to its black-and-white minimalist interior, everything is kept simple. Choose between a beef, pork, chicken, or veggie burger, and then add a side of fries, mac and cheese balls, or jalapeño poppers. Wash it all down with a cold drink.

European
PRINCIPLE BALI
*Jalan Raya Basangkasa No. 25; tel. 81241628203;
https://eatcompany.co; daily 8am-10pm;
90,000-130,000 Rp*

Charming with a vintage interior design, Principle Bali is a farm-to-table-style restaurant serving European delicacies. Organic ingredients are used whenever possible, and while there is a wide range of healthy plant-based offerings on its brunch and dinner menus, most people come for their dishes featuring the restaurant's homemade pastrami, sausages, and cured fish. The pulled lamb tagliatelle and truffle pappardelle are also guest favorites.

CHEZ GADO GADO
*Jalan Camplung Tanduk No. 99; tel. 361/736966;
https://gadogadorestaurant.com; daily 8am-11pm;
100,000-200,000 Rp*

Chez Gado Gado is a beachside fine dining restaurant without any pretentiousness. Inside, the white tablecloths, intricate wooden carvings, and glass chandeliers create an elegant and romantic ambiance. Outside, meals are served on a large platform overlooking the sea. Friendly staff serve tapas plates, seafood dishes, steak, pastas, and grilled chicken, and there are plenty of choices for vegetarians. The three-course lunch special is a decent value at 250,000 Rp per person, and their happy hour runs from 4pm-7pm daily, when every

two cocktails ordered come with free tapas. If you're coming to watch the sunset, book a table in advance.

Asian
LING LING'S
*Jalan Petitenget No. 43X; tel. 81916417867; www.
linglingsbali.com; noon-1am; 60,000-110,000 Rp*

As you walk into Ling Ling's, you'll be greeted by a gargantuan teal robot with a peace sign emblazoned across its chest. The funky style continues across its walls and menus, where huge cartoons, splashes of color, and nods to 1970s comic book characters seem to be the norm. The playful restaurant's chefs cook up interesting Japanese and Korean classic dishes like *gyoza* (pan-fried dumplings), sushi rolls, *banh mi* pork sandwiches, and more. There are also oddball menu items like cheeseburger spring rolls, jackfruit sushi rolls, and tuna nachos topped with wasabi mayonnaise—weird, but it works.

KEROBOKAN
Indonesian
WARUNG JEMBUNG
*Jalan Cendrawashih 14; tel. 81246291332; daily
8am-9pm; 22,000-32,000 Rp*

Warung Jembung is a small hut squeezed between villa complexes with tables that overlook a tranquil rice terrace. The menu lists simple Indonesian dishes, and you'll be encouraged to order the chef's plate of the day. Choose the private table with a thatched roof in the grassy area and listen to the grass blow in the breeze. Juices are made fresh.

WARUNG CANTINA
*Pantai Batu Belig; tel. 81237452606; daily
10am-10pm; 30,000-70,000 Rp*

Warung Cantina is a casual beachside restaurant doling out fresh fish and Indonesian dishes along with cold Bintang beers. Come just before sunset for spectacular views, or plop yourself in one of their beanbag chairs during the day for prime people watching. It's one of the few places along this stretch of beach that's both affordable and delicious.

1: Boss Man 2: Warung Jembung 3: Bambu

SANGSAKA

Jalan Pangkung Sari No. 100X; tel. 81236959895;
www.sangsakabali.com; daily 6pm-11pm;
80,000-200,000 Rp

Sangsaka is an intimate fine dining venue that serves delectable modern Balinese food. The menu features a variety of seafood, chicken, and beef marinated and cooked in Indonesian spices. It's common for the staff to give complimentary plates while you look over the menu, or during your meal just because. The best way to enjoy Sangsaka is to relinquish control and hand over 550,000 Rp per person to experience the tasting menu, which consists of nine dishes over five courses. Request a table near the kitchen to watch the chefs work their magic.

American

BARBACOA

Jalan Petitenget No. 14; tel. 361/739233;
barbacoa-bali.com; noon-midnight; 150,000 Rp

Barbacoa caters to carnivores with a variety of meats smoked over a wood-fire barbeque. The venue itself is a high-ceilinged converted warehouse with dim lights and warm, rustic decor. An aroma of smoke and spices wafts in the air. Out back, the restaurant opens out to rice terraces. Their Latin American-style pork, ribeye, and chicken are popular picks. While the restaurant boldly favors its meat dishes, vegetarian guests won't go hungry.

Cafés

EKO CAFE

Jalan Bumbak No. 89X; tel. 81237709989;
ekocafebali.com; daily 7:30am-7pm; 35,000-75,000
Rp

This bright and cheerful café serves healthy smoothie bowls, chia seed concoctions, and big breakfasts. Their lunch menu focuses on burgers, sandwiches, salads, and stir-fried vegetables. Each meal is colorful, fresh, and thoughtfully plated, making it a foodie favorite when it comes to taking pictures. Service can be a bit slow but it's worth the wait.

Asian

MAMA SAN

Jalan Raya Kerobokan No. 135; tel. 81339423033;
https://mamasanbali.com; daily noon-3:30pm and
6pm-11pm; 160,000-300,000 Rp

With a stunning mural of "Mama San" accenting the back wall, plush leather couches, and weathered portraits on the wall, Mama San is one of the most stylish restaurants around. The venue is divided into two floors, both featuring vintage decorations and romantic lighting. Dine on Chinese dumplings, Hainanese chicken, Vietnamese pho, Singaporean chili prawns, and other Asian delicacies. A smart-casual dress code (no flip-flop sandals or singlets) is loosely enforced after 5pm.

CANGGU

Indonesian

ECHO BEACH CLUB

Jalan Pura Batu Mejan; tel. 85100474604;
www.echobeachclub.com; daily 8am-11pm;
50,000-180,000 Rp

By day, Echo Beach Club is a popular breakfast and lunch spot for surfers and beachgoers looking for a place to relax with prime views of the surf. Come sunset, the chefs ignite the barbecue and serve fresh seafood and meats fresh off the grill. Pizzas, Indonesian meals, salads, and sandwiches also grace the menu. At nighttime, the beach club transforms once again into a popular party spot for Canggu residents and tourists.

European

LA LAGUNA

Jalan Pantai Kayu Putih; tel. 81999015777;
https://lalagunabali.com; daily 11am-midnight;
80,000-120,000 Rp

Once you step onto the stone footpaths of La Laguna, you'll feel as if you're in a fairy tale. The beachside hangout spot has twinkle lights, ramshackle wooden caravans, and colorful cushions sprawled across a soft grass lawn. You can dine on grilled meats, seafood, and Mediterranean fare. Unfortunately, the food quality doesn't seem to match the price point, so it's best to eat elsewhere and come to La Laguna for drinks and tapas. La Laguna also hosts a Sunday market that sells organic produce, crystals, and handcrafted goods from 3pm onward.

American
PANAMA KITCHEN

Jalan Pantai Berawa No. 13; tel. 361/9064715; www. sunofpanama.com; Mon.-Thurs. 8am-10pm, Fri. 8:45am-11pm, Sat.-Sun. 8am-11pm; 70,000-110,000 Rp

Hidden away from the main road, Panama Kitchen is a quirky 1960s-style restaurant with nostalgic backyard pool-party vibes and happy staff. The menu offers North American comfort foods with a few shakes of chili on top here and there. A fair selection of breakfasts, pastas, burgers, tacos, and grilled meats are on the menu. Their chia seed puddings and smoothie bowls make a refreshing treat on a hot day.

Cafés
KOLONI

Jalan Raya Semat No. 1; tel. 81338946085; https://koloni.business.site; daily 8am-10pm; 60,000-90,000 Rp

Quickly becoming a favorite stop among Canggu regulars, Koloni is a small café serving healthy and hearty meals in a rustic, chic ambiance. On-trend meals like falafel bowls, smoothie bowls, *shakshuka* (eggs poached in tomato sauce), burgers with charcoal buns, and raw energy balls grace the menu alongside go-to classics like grilled meat and vegetable combos. Coffee snobs are welcome.

Vegan and Vegetarian
PELOTON SUPERSHOP

Jalan Raya Pantai Berawa No. 46; tel. 81337619335; www.pelotonsupershop.com; daily 7:30am-10pm; 60,000-70,000 Rp

Peloton Supership is part hipster café and part boutique, with an ethos that centers around environmental conservation. It was established by a group of cyclists who decided to create a plant-based menu of smoothie bowls, salads, burgers, and pastries. Connected to the café is a sustainable goods shop where you can purchase reusable water bottles, metal straws, takeaway containers, and sustainably sourced clothing.

THE AVOCADO FACTORY

Jalan Batu Mejan; tel. 82144111148; www. theavocadofactory.com; daily 7am-11:30pm; 60,000-85,000 Rp

Go crazy for avocado at The Avocado Factory, where nearly every menu item features this creamy fruit. Savory dishes include avocado benedict, avocado salad bowls, avocado and fried rice, guacamole tacos, salads, and much more. For a sweeter fix, there are avocado smoothies and chia seed puddings. The café itself is simple and overlooks rice paddies. By the time you leave, you'll be seeing green.

GREEN GINGER

Jalan Pantai Berawa No. 46; tel. 87862112729; www. elephantbali.com/green-ginger; daily 8am-10:30pm; 60,000-100,000 Rp

With a shabby-chic interior and a tranquil garden out back, Green Ginger creates a calm environment where you can dine on fragrant Asian noodle dishes and dumplings in peace. Most menu items are Thai-inspired, with a handful of Singaporean, Vietnamese, and Indonesian classics making an appearance as well. Green Ginger takes conservation to heart, offering a water station where you can refill a reusable water bottle. Almost any vegetarian dish can be turned vegan by request.

SPROUT

Jalan Raya Semat No. 18A; tel. 81236653165; www. sproutbali.com; daily 7am-6pm; 70,000 Rp

The building that houses Sprout looks as though it's growing out of the ground, thanks to a carpet of plants that cloaks the entrance. Inside, stunning murals of palm leaves and colorful birds cover the walls. The restaurant is part bakery, part vegetarian café, serving the usual Canggu offerings of avocado toast, smoothie bowls, eggs many ways, salads, grilled chicken, and more. Most are vegetarian, and there are plenty of options for vegan and gluten-free diners as well. Sprout also hosts a kids club where children can explore the restaurant's on-site garden, learn to cook, and create crafts.

Markets

SAMADI FARMERS MARKET

Jalan Padang Linjong No. 39; tel. 81238312505; www. samadibali.com; Sun. 9am-2pm; 10,000 Rp and up

Samadi, a yoga retreat and organic café, hosts a market each Sunday where local farmers and artists gather and sell their goods. You'll discover the freshest in-season produce, often including exotic fruits and vegetables not commonly found in restaurants or overseas. There are also a variety of handmade cosmetics, clothing items, artworks, and secondhand treasures on display. The market often has live acoustic music, and you'll see a diverse crowd of tourists and locals coming to browse around or shop for their weekly produce.

Bars and Nightlife

★ LEGIAN

ENGINE ROOM

Jalan Raya Legian No. 66; tel. 361/755121; www. engineroombali.com; daily 6pm-4am; no cover, 45,000-160,000 Rp drinks

Engine Room is one of the most popular nightclubs among locals, who come to listen to the array of hip-hop, techno, house, and rock music played among its four DJ booths. Crowds tend to gravitate toward different rooms each night. It's a no-frills club that looks better with the lights on low, but it makes up for it with its drink specials and friendly staff.

LXXY

Jalan Raya Legian No. 71; tel. 361/4753488; www. lxxybali.com; daily 10am-late; 85,000-150,000 Rp mains, 50,000-150,000 Rp drinks

One of the newest nightclubs in Bali, LXXY is quickly becoming one of the best to listen and groove to EDM. There are three tiers of entertainment areas in the venue, with a restaurant, dance area, and rooftop bar and pool. The lighting and sound system are top of the line. The crowd can be a bit hit or miss, so check the DJ schedule on their Facebook page before you go.

SEMINYAK AND KEROBOKAN

POTATO HEAD BEACH CLUB

Jalan Petitenget No. 51B; tel. 361/4737979; www. ptthead.com; daily 10am-2am; no cover, 500,000 Rp minimum for poolside daybed, 800,000 Rp minimum for beachside cabana

Potato Head Beach Club is the original beach club of Bali. Directly on the sand, its three restaurants, three bars, infinity pool, and stage area are impossible to resist for Seminyak regulars. Daybeds are first come, first served. Just about any big-name artist coming through the island will stop and play at Potato Head, and a mix of DJs and musicians perform most days. There is always a crowd and it gets rambunctious come sunset. If you plan to eat here, book a table on their website in advance.

MRS SIPPY

Jalan Taman Ganesha Gang Gagak No. 8; tel. 361/3351079; www.mrssippybali.com; 10am-9pm; 100,000 Rp entry fee toward food, drinks, daybeds, towels

Nostalgic for the days when pool parties were the norm? Mrs Sippy is a day club where blow-up pool floats, tropical music, and poolside cocktails are available every day. Time here is spent alternating between the saltwater

Where to Find the Best Nightlife in Kuta and Seminyak

No matter the day of the week or time of the year, there are plenty of places to party in Kuta and Seminyak. With beach clubs that seamlessly turn into night clubs after dark, dance clubs with multiple DJ stands, and swanky cocktail bars that suit casual conversation, there's enough space in the nest no matter what type of night owl you are.

Because the scene is so saturated with clubs competing for your attention (and rupiah), there are frequent specials and events created to lure patrons. With careful planning, you can bar-hop on a budget and put your money toward a post-party meal.

JALAN RAYA LEGIAN

The intersection of Jalan Raya Legian and Jalan Poppies II is the epicenter of Kuta's party scene. Bounce from bar to bar and wander in wherever the music sounds best. Popular haunts like **Engine Room** (page 74) and **LXXY** (page 74) are all within a few steps from one another. This is where you'll find Bali's most boisterous crowd.

JALAN PETITENGET

Seminyak has a stylish reputation to uphold, and its swanky clubs follow suit. Throw on something slightly more formal than jean shorts and a tank top and wander along Jalan Petitenget for trendy bars and clubs like Sea Vu Play, MRS SIPPY, and Ryoshi House of Jazz. Here are some of the best clubs and bars.

- For lounging: **Sea Vu Play** (page 76)

- For cocktails: **Baker Street Social** (page 76)

- For music: **Ryoshi House of Jazz** (page 75)

- For beach vibes: **Potato Head Beach Club** (page 74)

pool, the dining area, and the daybeds. Check the What's On section of the venue's website for special events. The food menu is mainly made up of fresh seafood and Mediterranean dishes. Children welcome.

RYOSHI HOUSE OF JAZZ

Jalan Seminyak No. 17; tel. 361/731152; www. ryoshibali.com; daily noon-midnight, jazz on Mon., Wed., Fri.; no cover, 40,000-170,000 Rp drinks, 70,000-120,000 Rp mains

Jazz and Japanese food may not seem like a popular combination, but it works well at Ryoshi House of Jazz. Three nights per week, talented jazz artists come to play their tunes on an open-air stage that is set so close to the guests, you almost feel as though you can join in any time. Arrive early, before

the music starts, for the best seats and food service—it tends to get busy once the music begins.

KU DE TA

Jalan Kayu Aua No. 9; tel. 361/736969; www.kudeta. com; daily 8am-late; no cover, 50,000-200,000 Rp drinks, 120,000-330,000 Rp mains

One of the best beach lounges in Seminyak, Ku De Ta is a beachside bar and restaurant with an infinity pool that overlooks the sea. The atmosphere is more upscale than many other venues in the area, and travelers often dress to impress. Book a table in advance for prime sunset seating. The venue also hosts regular music performances and runs its own weekly radio program on one of Bali's most popular stations.

★ SEA VU PLAY

Jalan Petitenget; 361/4736579; www.seavuplaybali.
com; 11am-1am; 85,000-175,000 Rp mains,
60,000-200,000 Rp drinks

Whimsical and fun, Sea Vu Play is a nautical-themed day club with a carefree vibe carried across its pool, shaded lounges, and open-air dining areas. There are frequent music performances, drag shows, and special events (find them on their Facebook page). They have a variety of refreshing fruit cocktails on the drinks menu. The food menu includes paella, pizzas, burgers, and seafood. The venue is family-friendly; kids will love the pirate motif.

COCOON

Jalan Double Six (Blue Ocean Blvd.); tel. 361/731266;
www.cocoon-beach.com; daily 10am-midnight; no
cover, 300,000 Rp minimum daybeds and lounges,
500,000 Rp minimum cabanas, 50,000-200,000 Rp
drinks, 150,000-300,000 Rp mains

One of the most stylish beach clubs in Seminyak, Cocoon is a place to enjoy drinks, tapas, steak dinners, salads, and pizzas alongside a well-kept pool area with plush daybeds placed around it. After a few minutes, it's easy to forget that you're in one of Seminyak's busiest areas. The club also hosts the Positive Negative Visual Gallery, a boutique art gallery featuring bold and beautiful works from local artists.

★ BAKER STREET SOCIAL

Jalan Petitenget No. 17C; tel. 8113973073;
Mon.-Thurs. 8pm-2am, Fri.-Sat. 8pm-3am;
120,000-200,000 Rp drinks

You might be hard pressed to find a true speakeasy in Bali; Baker Street Social is as close as it gets. Tucked behind Tiffin Indian Restaurant, this moody bar serves specialty cocktails with friendly bartenders who won't shy away from creating the most demanding concoctions. Its yellow lighting, checkered bar, and display of specialty alcohols create an atmosphere that's perfect for drinking and good conversation. A list of 10 house rules are posted on the venue, one of them being, "If

your drink isn't strong enough ... quit ordering lychee martinis and get a whiskey." It's one of the best respites from the crowds and chaos, especially in high season.

CANGGU

FINNS BEACH CLUB

Jalan Pantai Berawa; tel. 361/8446327; www.
finnsbeachclub.com; daily 9am-11pm; no cover,
500,000 Rp minimum daybed/general, 750,000 Rp
minimum VIP, 2,000,000 minimum for a booth for up
to 6 people, depending on selected food, drinks, and
spa treatments

Finns Beach Club is set on the ashy shoreline of Canggu and divided into two sections: the VIP club and the general club. The general beach club offers an infinity pool and swim-up bar, overshadowed by a funky bamboo dining and dancing area. The VIP section has a dedicated pool, lawn, rooftop bar, and changing rooms with complimentary toiletries. You'll find great music, laid-back vibes, and plenty of mingling opportunities at both.

★ PRETTY POISON

Jalan Subak Canggu; tel. 81246229540;
https://prettypoisonbar.com; daily 4pm-late;
50,000-80,000 Rp drinks

Yet to become a mainstream spot in Canggu, Pretty Poison is part bar, part boutique, with a very 1970s *Lords of Dogtown* feel. Skateboarders take turns dropping in and ripping around the concrete skate bowl while others watch with a cold beer in hand. The busiest nights are Tuesday, Thursday, and Saturday, when live music and DJs stop in to play. Service is friendly, and the crowd doesn't take themselves too seriously.

★ OLD MAN'S

Jalan Batu Bolong Beach; tel. 361 84159;
www.oldmans.net; daily 7am-1am; no cover,
25,000-85,000 Rp drinks, 70,000-130,000 Rp mains

Old Man's is set on Batu Bolong Beach and hosts live musicians and DJs nearly every night. It's a meeting ground for surfers and expats, and you can tell it's busy when motorbikes with surf racks crowd the parking

How Bintang Came to Rule Bali's Beer Scene

The word *bintang* means "star" in Bahasa, and Bir Bintang beer certainly is the star of Bali's alcohol industry. When ordering a beer, most people simply request a Bintang and then specify which brand they'd like after. (That is, on the rare occasion that they order something else.) As a 4.7 percent Pilsner, the pale lager is a refreshing drink to combat thirst in the thick Indonesian heat. Locals and tourists enjoy it so much, it holds a majority share of the market.

HISTORY

If Bintang's red star and logo font type look somewhat familiar, it's because Bintang is owned by popular Dutch beer brand Heineken. The brewery that would eventually make Bintang was built in 1929, when Indonesia was still under colonial rule of the Netherlands. Heineken introduced its namesake beer to Indonesians in the late 1930s. Then, following Indonesian independence, World War II, and political strife within Indonesia, the Heineken company ceased selling Heineken in Indonesia for more than a decade. Finally, in the late 1960s, Heineken resumed beer production in Indonesia, but this time under the Bintang brand.

BINTANG TODAY

Because Bintang was held to European brewing standards, it quickly became the beer of choice for Indonesians and tourists. Its light taste, low alcohol content, and cheap price (around 20,000 Rp per bottle) make it easy to have more than one. Seeing as Indonesia is a Muslim-majority country and has high tax rates, competing companies are hesitant to enter the market.

Bintang has become an icon in Bali for tourists, especially with Australian travelers, who consider shopping for singlets with the word "Bintang" emblazoned across the front an absolute must-do during their time in Bali. Today, Bintang is such a Balinese staple, most beer drinkers wouldn't think of ordering anything else.

---

area. The bar serves a mix of simple cocktails, beer, and wine while their food menu features fish and chips, burgers, nasi goreng, and ice cream. If you want to dance in the tropical heat, come on Wednesday, their biggest night of the week, when you can listen to music and test your aiming skills during their beer pong competition.

Accommodations

Though the Kuta region is being developed by chain hotels at an alarming rate, there are plenty of boutique hotels, homestays, hostels, and luxury villas. The competition among them makes stays relatively affordable, and the caliber of service is at an all-time high. It may be difficult to nab a beachside room that doesn't belong to a large hotel, but if you head just a few streets inland, you'll find a wide range of stylish stays. If you visit during the shoulder months—from February to April or September to November—rates can drop by 50 percent.

TUBAN
Under 1,000,000 Rp
LOKAL BALI HOSTEL
Jalan Kediri No. 93; tel. 361/4753707; www. lokalbalihostel.com; 200,000 Rp
A 20-minute walk from the international airport, Lokal Bali Hostel is a clean and casual hostel with double rooms and bunk bed dorm

rooms that sleep from four to eight people. Each bed has a private locker, curtain, power outlet, free Wi-Fi access, and reading light. The pool area is ideal for socializing, with plenty of space to lounge and make friends.

CENTRAL KUTA
Under 1,000,000 Rp
CARA CARA INN

Jalan Kahyangan Suci; www.caracarainn.com; 300,000-500,000 Rp

Bright and cheerful, Cara Cara Inn is a hostel and hotel with eight different room options and a social atmosphere around its tropical café and bar area. The small but fun splash pool is often filled with inflatable pool toys, and it has an overwater hammock and a miniature waterslide. There are also multiple hangout areas, including a den with a ping pong table and board games. This property is a popular pick among solo travelers and groups of friends keen to meet more.

VASANTI

Jalan Wana Segara No. 25; tel. 361/4753111; https://vasantikutahotel.com; 500,000 Rp

Vasanti is a mid-range boutique hotel near the international airport. Clean, modern rooms are decorated with wood, stone, and batik-accented furniture. Enjoy a pampering session at the spa, Balinese meals at the on-site restaurant, and ice-cold drinks at the hotel's rooftop bar and pool area. The superior room with a balcony offers the best value of the five room options.

Over 1,000,000 Rp
THE ANVAYA BEACH RESORT

Jalan Kartika Plaza; tel. 361/759991; http://theanvayabali.com; 1,200,000-3,000,000 Rp

In the heart of Kuta's beach scene is The Anvaya Beach Resort, an elegant five-star hotel with nearly 500 spacious rooms, some with direct pool access. The interior design is modern with traditional Balinese elements throughout the property. There are restaurants on-site, lounges, a well-kept grassy area, a large pool, and a spa. Guests tend to be couples on a romantic getaway, or families with kids thanks to the hotel's popular kids' club. If you stay, don't skip the breakfast by the beach; it is one of the best around.

★ POPPIES BALI

Jalan Legian; tel. 361/751059; www.poppiesbali.com; 1,500,000 Rp

If you didn't know better, you might not believe that this quaint property made of 20 traditional thatched-roof bungalows set amid dense gardens could exist in Kuta's urban area. Ornate wooden doors open into rooms that are spacious and charming. The natural smell of the thatched roofing, incense, and flowers lingers in the air. The pool area and restaurant are ideal for recharging after you've experienced the touts and hasslers of Kuta's center. Poppies Bali has hosted guests since the 1970s, and it shows through their hospitality.

LEGIAN
Under 1,000,000 Rp
SOL HOUSE BALI LEGIAN

Jalan Sriwijaya No. 16; tel. 361/4752999; www.sol-hotels.com; 600,000 Rp

Sol House Bali Legian is one of the hottest party hotels in the area, with clean, modern rooms. There is a restaurant inside the hotel serving a mix of Indonesian and international dishes, and their breakfast buffet spread changes daily. Guests tend to sleep in more than the average traveler, so breakfast is served until late. The main attractions are the rooftop pool, massive Jacuzzi, and bar area where they serve cocktails and frequently have DJ music sets and live music. Staff monitor their social media accounts around the clock, so you can make a room service request via a tweet.

Over 1,000,000 Rp
OSSOTEL

Jalan Padma Utara; tel. 361/754122; www.ossotel.com; 1,300,000 Rp

Ossotel is in Legian's Padma neighborhood, just a short walk to the beach and Legian's main restaurant and bar area. Rooms are simple, clean, and modern, and many of them have a glass door that opens out onto the hotel's 290-foot (88-meter) lap pool. The attached restaurant is popular with non-guests; it serves a variety of grilled meats and often hosts live music. One perk of the Ossotel is that guests have access to a handful of lounge chairs on the beach—no bartering with the beach chair mafia needed.

THE BANDHA

Jalan Padma Utara; tel. 361/757150; www.thebandha. com; 2,000,000 Rp

If you're after the beachside luxe lifestyle, The Bandha is an upscale hotel with seven accommodation options across its 90 rooms. Each room is simple, clean, and spacious—relaxing but lacking personality. Because The Bandha offers access to Legian Beach, a casual on-site restaurant, two pools with swim-up bars, a spa, and a gym, many guests use The Bandha as an excuse for a romantic staycation inside the hotel.

SEMINYAK AND KEROBOKAN
Under 1,000,000 Rp
★ DASH

Jalan Petitenget No. 148; tel. 361/3004667; www. dash-hotels.com; 600,000 Rp

Dash is a bold industrial-style hotel that doesn't shy away from giving hyper-sensual vibes; there are cheeky innuendos sprinkled all throughout the property. Hotel rooms surround a red-tiled swimming pool, and there is a small rooftop bar that looks out onto one of Seminyak's busiest roads. Once you swipe your key card, lounging around is encouraged thanks to the huge bathtub in the middle of the room and Dash's signature neon-yellow bathrobes hanging on the clothing rack. Details like the property's unique pop art, the included a la carte breakfast, and a card where you fill out your pillow preferences make Dash one of the most likable properties in town.

VILLA KARISA

Jalan Drupadi No. 100X; tel. 361/739395; www. villakarisabali.com; 600,000-1,000,000 Rp

Villa Karisa is a boutique homestay-style hotel in one of the most prime parts of Seminyak. Each of the hotel's shabby-chic rooms is unique, and there are strong traditional Balinese and Javanese elements throughout. Accommodation options include premium, standard, and deluxe double rooms, a stand-alone *joglo* with a spacious porch, or a two-bedroom apartment. All guests have access to the swimming pool, homey lounge area in the lobby, and restaurant.

Over 1,000,000 Rp
PURI MADAWI

Jalan Cendrawasih 68; www.madawi.com; tel. 361/4739363; 1,200,000 Rp

Consisting of just 16 *lumbung*-style rooms that resemble traditional rice barns, Puri Madawi is an intimate boutique hotel removed from Seminyak's main stretch. The hotel is just a few minutes away from Batu Belig Beach, one of the lesser-visited beaches in the area. Each room has a darling patio area that's perfect for sipping cocktails or tea in between adventures. Most rooms are centered around the pool, and there is a covered dining area where simple local meals are served. The rooms themselves are clean, and each of the main bed blankets was likely handmade in Lombok, the next island over.

THE COLONY HOTEL

Jalan Laksmana No. 22; tel. 361/736160; www. thecolonyhotelbali.com; 2,000,000-5,000,000 Rp

The Colony Hotel is a sophisticated boutique hotel with impressive colonial-style architecture. It's just a short walk from the beach, popular clubs, restaurants, and a shopping area. Choose from five room options, all featuring views of the pool, desks, and minibars. The Colony Hotel is strictly for guests aged 16 and up, so you can enjoy the 50-foot (16-meter) swimming pool without worrying about shrieking and splashing.

ARIA VILLA

Jalan Cendrawasih; tel. 361/4734133; www.
ariaexclusivevillas.com; 2,700,000-4,000,000 Rp
Everything about Aria's 19 villas is elegant.
From the dark wood and white color combination to the plush canopy bed, each villa was
thoughtfully designed. The bedroom opens
out to a private pool, and there is a large terrace where you can lounge in solitude. Each
villa has a kitchenette, dining area, fridge,
microwave, and mini bar. You can choose
between showering in the ensuite bathroom
or the private garden, surrounded by native
plants. In the communal area, you'll find a
spa, pool, and dining area. The villas are a few
minutes away from Seminyak's main area by
car, making it one of the more secluded spots.

★ THE SEMINYAK BEACH RESORT

Jalan Kaya Ayu; tel. 361/730814; www.theseminyak.
com; 3,500,000-4,000,000 Rp
An exquisite five-star resort, The Seminyak
Beach Resort offers a relaxing luxury experience, thanks to its beautiful grounds and
proximity to the sea. Enjoy sipping cocktails
at the infinity pool, getting pampered at the
spa with ocean views, dining at one of the on-
site restaurants, and sipping whiskey at the
1920s-style jazz bar. There's a range of double
rooms and villas to choose from, all sporting a
chic dark wood and white aesthetic. The one-
bedroom pool villa with ocean views is worth
the splurge with its private pool, Jacuzzi, flat-
screen TV, and background sound of the
ocean. Service at The Seminyak Beach Resort
is friendly and professional, with staff often
going out of their way to ensure your stay is
going smoothly.

★ THE OBEROI

Jalan Kayu Ayu; tel. 361/730361; www.oberoihotels.
com; 5,000,000 Rp
The Oberoi has set the standard for luxury
hotels in Bali. The property covers 15 acres of
land along Seminyak Beach and has not relin-
quished its Balinese charm and friendliness as
so many other hotels of this size have. Hindu
statues and shrines highlight the footpaths.
There are multiple accommodation choices
available, where you can enjoy ocean or garden views out of the large windows, stay inside
a thatched roof villa, and watch shows on a 32-
inch flat screen TV. The Oberoi also has multiple pools, restaurants, a spa, a tennis court,
plenty of open-air dining areas, and staff who
go above what's expected to ensure you have
a pleasant stay. While The Oberoi is on the
pricier side of accommodations, it strives to
meet high expectations.

CANGGU
Under 1,000,000
RYANBAGUS GUEST HOUSE

Jalan Tumbak Bayuh No. 13; tel. 81236455566;
300,000 Rp
Run by a friendly Balinese family, Ryanbagus
Guest House is a homestay in a quiet area of
Canggu, with the main center being about 10
minutes away by motorbike—available for
rent from the property. Rooms are simple,
clean, and spacious, and you can choose between a double room that is part of the main
block or stay in one of the traditional wooden
bungalows. The pool is surrounded by tropical gardens, and guests have access to an outdoor rainwater shower.

★ THE CHILLHOUSE

Jalan Kubu Manyar No. 22; tel. 361/8445463; www.
thechillhouse.com; 990,000-2,000,000 Rp
The Chillhouse, a laid-back surf and yoga
retreat, has managed to capture the health-
conscious Canggu lifestyle within its well-
kept property. The design embraces all
things beachy, and it's a popular pick among
solo travelers who often find new friends and
travel partners. There's a variety of single,
double, and villa options to choose from, and
no two are decorated exactly alike. Rates include breakfast and dinner made from ingredients sourced from Indonesia, as well as one
yoga class. Surf lessons and board rental are
available for additional fees. Your stay also

Things to Do on a Rainy Day

a rainy day in Seminyak

The wet season in Bali lasts from November to April, with December to February being the rainiest months. Rain showers typically only last for a few hours at a time and come during the mid to late afternoon. Many travelers prefer to visit Bali during the wet season because it means cheaper hotel rooms, minimal crowds, and verdant jungles, and it's easier to travel spontaneously because you don't need to book accommodation in advance.

Despite its perks, rain can put a damper on your trip if you've planned for days of lounging on the beach. Here are the top things to do on a rainy day.

- **Take a cooking class:** One of the best souvenirs you can take home is a recipe from a local chef. Learn to cook Balinese classic recipes at **The Spicery** or with **Kin Vegan Cooking Class.**

- **Get a spa treatment:** If you can't relax on the beach, you might as well relax in a spa. Consider getting pampered while the clouds blow over.

- **Attend a yoga class:** Most yoga and fitness classes take place under a covered area. Stretch to the meditative sound of raindrops.

- **Go diving:** If it's going to rain, you might as well get wet. If the rain is light and the wind is calm, visibility and safety shouldn't be affected.

- **Tour the galleries:** Kuta and Seminyak are among the few places in Bali where you can go from gallery to gallery and admire the works of local and Asian artists. **Nyamen Art Gallery** is a good place to start.

- **Curl up in a café with a book:** It's a challenge to catch up on reading if you're out exploring all day. Find a cozy café or sheltered hammock and let the printed word take your imagination elsewhere.

includes access to a small calisthenics gym, bicycles, and two pools.

Over 1,000,000 Rp
★ DESA SENI
Jalan Kayu Putih No. 13; tel. 361/8446394; www. desaseni.com; 3,000,000 Rp

It's obvious that the interior designers paid attention to detail at Desa Seni, where rooms are decorated with meticulously chosen furniture and art pieces sourced from throughout Indonesia. The hotel operates like a small community, attracting yogis from all over the globe who come to practice yoga and relax around Desa Seni's calming pool area. There are also wellness workshops and chakra healing therapists, who strive to help with any ailments you have. Each eco-luxury room and bungalow has a private bathroom with rainwater shower heads. Rates include breakfast, yoga, and meditation classes, water, Wi-Fi, and a *canang sari* (small Hindu offering) placed at your doorstep.

Information and Services

TOURIST INFORMATION

There are frequent informal **tourist stands** along beach boardwalks and busy roads. They are almost always advertising transport or private tours and are covered in activity brochures. These stands are not run by official tourism bureau representatives, and workers will most likely push the activities that will kick back the most commission to them. It is worth having a look at what activities are available and asking for a price—often negotiable. However, ask around before committing to a price or activity.

TOURIST INFORMATION CENTRE INDONESIA
Jalan Raya Kuta 2; tel. 361/766188; https:// balitourismboard.or.id; daily 8am-10pm

The **Bali Government Tourist Information Centre** is a place where you can sift through brochures and booklets, learn about upcoming events, and ask questions. They offer helpful suggestions and itineraries for those wanting to see other islands in the archipelago after exploring Bali. There is a small souvenir shop and a gallery here as well.

LOCAL NEWSPAPERS AND WEBSITES

Kuta Weekly (free) reports on worldwide news, pop culture, health, science, and sports, rather than local happenings. The ads, however, are local and are worth browsing for specials and upcoming events. You can get the weekly newspaper outside major cafés and shopping centers. *The Seminyak Times* is an online outlet that publishes stories related to Bali and other nearby islands. There are features specifically devoted to tourism, as well as local and investigative news.

HEALTH AND SAFETY
Pharmacies

There are three major pharmacy chains in the Kuta region: **Guardian** (Jalan Raya Legian No. 2; tel. 361 761907), **Watsons** (Jalan Raya Seminyak No. 71; tel. 361 9348257), and **Apotek Kimia Farma** (Jalan Raya Kerobokan No. 15; tel. 361 735860). They all typically stock first aid kits, antibiotics, antidiarrheals, sunscreen, over-the-counter painkillers, contraception, and treatments for general illnesses.

Hospital
BIMC KUTA
Jalan By Pass Ngurah Rai No. 100X; tel. 361/761263; www.bimcbali.com; daily 24 hours

BIMC Kuta is one of the largest hospitals in the Kuta area and should be a first consideration for treatment if illness or an emergency occurs. It has a 24-hour emergency department, an intensive care unit, isolation rooms, and an operating room. Ambulances and paramedic motorbikes are on standby round the clock.

COMMUNICATIONS

There are a handful of telecommunications companies that sell phone calling and data packages. On nearly every major road, you will find small booths or shops selling SIM cards with *pulsa,* or data. Many convenience shops sell them as well (Circle K and Indomart). The most reliable phone companies are **Telkomsel** and **XL.**

You must register your SIM card to your passport at an official store. There are Telkomsel and XL booths at the international airport, where prices for data are inflated.

GRAPARI KUTA (TELKOMSEL)

Galeria Mall, Jalan By Pass Ngurah Rai; tel. 8071811811; www.telkomsel.com; Mon.-Fri. 10am-9pm, Sat.-Sun. 10am-8pm

This is an official retailer where you can purchase and register a SIM card, activate a wireless device, and top up data. Visit early in the day to avoid long lines.

XL CENTER

Jalan Sunset Road No. 818; www.xl.co.id; Mon.-Fri. 8am-6pm, Sat.-Sun. 9am-5pm

In this usually uncrowded phone center, you can purchase and activate your SIM card and top up data.

BANKING AND MONEY CHANGING

The safest way to retrieve cash is through an ATM. There are also a handful of convenience stores that change money, like Circle K and Minimart, which are affiliated with trustworthy money changing companies. However, don't fall for handwritten signs with too-good-to-be-true rates. ATM card skimming is common in tourist areas, with many criminals being from outside of Indonesia. Give the ATM card reader a tug before you insert your card. Some skimmers place a plastic covering that easily comes off.

CENTRAL KUTA

Jalan Sunset Road No. 168; tel. 361/4741940; www. centralkutabali.com; daily 7:30am-9:30pm

A reputable money changing chain with over 50 locations in Bali, Central Kuta offers decently competitive rates and no commission.

BMC LEGIAN

Jalan Sriwijaya No. 18; tel. 361/756968; www. balimaspintjinra.com; daily 8am-midnight

This no-hassle money changing chain has multiple shops around Bali. There are no fees or hidden commissions, and security guards are stationed inside and outside the shop.

LAUNDRY SERVICES

Most hotels offer laundry services. There are also roadside laundromats all around the area where staff wash, fold, and iron your clothing. Laundry is typically weighed and charged per kilogram (around 20,000 Rp for 1 kg/2.2 lbs).

Cuciyu (Jalan Dewi Sri VIII Block B No. 9; tel. 816691884; www.m.cuciyu.com; daily 8am-8pm; 10,000 Rp for 1 kg/2.2 lbs) is a reliable laundromat that offers washing, pressing, and folding services as well as DIY coin-operated washing machines and dryers. You can contact them via phone to arrange laundry pickup and drop-off from your hotel. Pickup and delivery is free within 4 km (2.5 mi) of the hotel, or for bags of clothing weighing more than 11 lbs (5 kg).

POST OFFICES

Post offices are common. Look for bright orange signs with "Pos Indonesia" or "Kantor Pos" written across the top. Two post offices familiar with international shipping are **Kuta Post Office** (Jalan Selamet; tel. 361 754012; www.posindonesia.co.id; Mon.-Thurs. 7am-2pm, Fri. 7am-11am, Sat. 7am-1pm, closed Sun.) and **Kerobokan Post Office** (Jalan Raya Anyar No. 24; tel. 361/4714420; Mon.-Sat. 8am-6pm, closed Sun.).

Transportation

GETTING THERE

Fortunately, the Kuta region is easy to get to from just about any major point in Bali as it's along the main highways and is just beside Bali's only international airport.

By Air

All international and domestic flights coming into Bali arrive at the **Ngurah Rai International Airport** (Jalan Raya Gusti Ngurah Rai) in Tuban, just 10 minutes away by car from **Kuta.** Cars can be hired from the airport through **Avis** (www.avis.com), **Eazy** (www.eazyrent.co.id), or **TRAC Astra** (www.trac.astra.co.id), which hosts a meet-and-greet service. Tourists must have a valid **international driver's license** to rent a car. Typically, it's best to rent a driver and provide them with an itinerary. **Private drivers** can be arranged through your hotel and charge similar fares to Bluebird Taxis. Assume it will cost about 70,000-100,000 per hour for a private driver. Reputable local drivers can be contacted via WhatsApp and include **Edy Hoolley** (tel. 81999095864), Niwayan Artini from **Pink Lady Tours** (tel. 82144115973), and drivers arranged through **Ricky Bali Transport** (tel. 87800671983).

Taxi prices from the Ngurah Rai International Airport are higher than metered fares. Expect to pay at least 50,000 Rp to **Tuban,** 90,000 Rp to **Kuta,** 110,000 Rp to **Seminyak** and **Kerobokan,** 120,000 Rp to **Legian,** and 170,000 to **Canggu.**

Bluebird taxis (tel. 361/701111) are reliable and metered, and operate all around the island. Look for the Bluebird logo, as there are many imposters, especially around Kuta and Seminyak. Fares start at 7,000 Rp and run 6,500-10,000 Rp per km (.6 mi) with a minimum charge of 30,000 Rp. Estimate about 80,000-100,000 Rp for every 10 km (6 mi) traveled. You can request Bluebird taxis via the **Bluebird app.**

Grab and **Go-Jek** are the most popular rideshare apps in Bali. You can meet your Grab or Go-Jek driver in the departures terminal. Fares tend to be 20,000 Rp to **Tuban,** 30,000 Rp to **Kuta,** 50,000 Rp to **Seminyak** and **Kerobokan,** 60,000 Rp to **Legian,** and 70,000 Rp to **Canggu.** Double these prices if there is heavy traffic.

By Bus

Perama (Jalan Legian No. 39; tel. 361/750808; www.peramatour.com; daily 7am-10pm) is the most reliable bus that serves Kuta from main towns around the island. Tickets cost 35,000 Rp from **Sanur** (15 km/9.3 mi; 45 minutes), 60,000 Rp from **Ubud** (30 km/18.6 mi; 1.5 hours), 125,000 Rp from **Lovina** (85 km/53 mi; 4-4.5 hours), 75,000 from **Padang Bai** (50 km/31 mi; 3 hours) and **Candidasa** (60 km/62 mi; 3.5 hours), and 127,000 from **Amed** (95 km/59 mi; 4 hours). Note that travel times can vary greatly; the bus often runs behind schedule.

The **Trans Sarbagita** bus and minibus line runs air-conditioned buses between Kuta (Jalan Raya Kuta behind Kuta Galeria) and **Denpasar** (15 km/9.3 mi; 45 minutes), **Nusa Dua** (15 km/9.3 mi; 45 minutes), **Sanur** (15 km/9.3 mi; 45 minutes), and **Jimbaran** (7 km/4.3 mi; 30 minutes). Buses are supposed to leave every 20 minutes, though hour-long waits or more are not unheard of. Stops are at **Jalan Raya Kuta Kantor Terminal, Jalan Sunset Road** near Hypermarket, and the airport. Large buses cost 3,500 Rp per trip, and minibuses cost 3,000 Rp per trip; tickets are purchased onboard.

Kura Kura (www.kura2bus.com; 20,000-80,000 Rp) runs from **Ubud** (80,000 Rp, 40 km/25 mi; 2 hours) and **Sanur** (80,000 Rp, 12 km/7 mi; 30 minutes). Routes between Tuban, Kuta, Seminyak, and Legian cost 20,000 Rp per trip. Rides from **Nusa Dua** (13 km/8 mi; 15 minutes) and **Jimbaran** (7 km/4.3 mi; 15

minutes) also cost 20,000 Rp. If you're using this line regularly, opt for a 1/3/7-day pass (100,000/150,000/250,000 Rp). The main station of Kura Kura is at Galleria Mall DFS Bus Bay (Jalan By Pass Ngurah Rai).

GETTING AROUND

The Kuta region is notorious for its terrible traffic and chaotic driving. If you're traversing short distances, it's often faster to **walk** from place to place. Fortunately, most restaurants, shops, and bars tend to be clustered together, so it's easy to see a lot in just a short stretch of road. As the locals say, "Jalan jalan!" which translates to, "Let's go for a walk!" The **Bali Mandara Road** (tolls 4,500 Rp for a motorbike, 11,000 Rp for a car) is worth using to avoid traffic on Jalan By Pass Ngurah Rai. The road connects Nusa Dua to the Ngurah Rai International Airport.

By Bus and *Bemo*

Barely running *bemos,* dark blue and green minibuses, run from the airport to Kuta, and then around. Though they're cheap, they're unreliable and getting more challenging to flag down. Trips tend to cost around 3,000 Rp, and their routes run along **Jalan Pantai Kuta, Jalan Melasti, Jalan Legian,** and **Jalan Padma.** They don a mustard-colored license plate, which signals that they're licensed for public transport.

The **Kura Kura** (www.kura2bus.com) bus has three routes (lines 2, 3, 4) that shuttle people from most major resorts and shopping centers like **Lippo Mall, Waterbom,** the **Ground Zero Monument,** and **Bintang Supermarket.** Line 2 runs every 2 hours while lines 3 and 4 run every 30 minutes. Each trip costs 20,000 Rp.

By Car

Because of the congestion, getting around by car is not recommended unless your hotel offers **parking.** On the streets, parking spaces are limited and will cost you 2,000 Rp minimum to have a guard help guide you in and out of cramped spaces. Traffic laws are often not obeyed, and it can be a challenge to compete with the hundreds of motorbikes for tarmac. It's less stressful to hire a **private driver** for around 500,000-700,000 Rp per day or per trip.

Reputable local drivers can be contacted via WhatsApp and include **Edy Hoolley** (tel. 81999095864), Niwayan Artini from **Pink Lady Tours** (tel. 821 44115973), and drivers arranged through **Ricky Bali Transport** (tel. 87800671983).

motorbikes in Seminyak

By Motorbike

Most accommodations can arrange a motorbike rental, which costs around 50,000 Rp per day. Confident drivers may find driving a motorbike to be more convenient than walking—but beware of traffic.

By Taxi and Rideshare Apps

Bluebird taxis frequent the area, and it's rare to go more than a few minutes without seeing one drive along the main roads. They are quick to pick up when called in advance, and fares start at 7,000 Rp plus 6,500-10,000 Rp per km after; the minimum fare is 30,000-40,000 Rp. Grab and Go-Jek cars are less common and can be a hassle to get, due to the local taxi *banjars* (cooperatives that hold a monopoly system over rides). Grab and Go-Jek motorbike rides, however, are easy to get and are an economical way to get around. Most rides within the area will cost less than 30,000 Rp.

The Bukit Peninsula

The Bukit Peninsula is awash with cultural sites, beaches, and near-perfect waves. More than 200 feet above the water, Uluwatu Temple guards the region against malevolent spirits. Traditional *kecak* dancers gather at Uluwatu Temple to tell stories of ancient Hindu legends using elaborate costumes and movement. At sea level, waves like Uluwatu's, Bingin, and Padang Padang break along the Bukit Peninsula, calling like sirens to surfers who visit from around the globe.

Many Balinese people would tell you that they're surprised by the Bukit Peninsula's quick development. Being one of the most arid and hottest regions of the island, it remained mostly untouched for centuries. Only fishermen and sustenance farmers who could cope with

Highlights

Look for ★ to find recommended sights, activities, dining, and lodging.

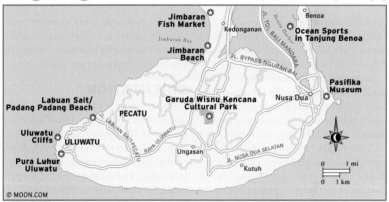

★ **Garuda Wisnu Kencana Cultural Park:** Prepare to be impressed by the size of the Garuda Wisnu Kencana Statue in one of Bali's liveliest cultural parks (page 95).

★ **Jimbaran Beach:** Throw down a sarong and feel the sun warm your skin on one of the island's longest stretches of golden sand (page 96).

★ **Jimbaran Fish Market:** Take your pick of fresh fish and give it to a nearby seafood restaurant to grill, in view of the wooden boats and fishermen who brought the catch in just hours before (page 99).

★ **Labuan Sait/Padang Padang Beach:** The trek between eerie 8-meter-high (26-foot) walls and down a steep staircase is worth the effort to reach a beach that's ideal for surfing and sunbathing (page 106).

★ **Pura Luhur Uluwatu:** Meander the grounds of this spectacular temple and learn the story of Ramayana by watching a traditional *kecak* dance performance (page 115).

★ **Uluwatu Cliffs:** Meander through paint-splashed walkways that open to views of Uluwatu's, Bali's most famous wave. Consider this the soul of Bali's surf scene (page 116).

★ **Pasifika Museum:** See the Pacific Islands depicted in more than 400 different ways at this underrated museum (page 124).

★ **Ocean Sports in Tanjung Benoa:** Thrill-seekers can get their adrenaline fix in the exciting waters of Tanjung Benoa (page 125).

Top Restaurants

★ **Cuca:** Share delicious tapas among friends in a casual atmosphere that serves fine food (page 98).

★ **Drifter Café and Surf Shop:** This part surf shop, part café serves hearty and healthy burritos to those looking to refuel before they paddle out again (page 112).

★ **Roosterfish:** Wood-fired pizzas, grilled seafood, and salads are served on the shore of Pantai Pandawa (page 120).

★ **Single Fin:** An Uluwatu icon, the cliffside bar serves cold drinks, pizzas, burgers, and incredible views (page 120).

★ **OneEighty°:** Reservations are essential at this modern beach club known for its seafood (page 122).

the dry landscape seemed to thrive. Tourists, mostly domestic, visited to pay homage to the temple Pura Luhur Uluwatu, but rarely did they venture farther.

In the 1960s, foreign surfers began to study maps of Bali's coastline. By the early 1970s, their suspicions were proven correct after watching Uluwatu's wave break along the reef. Then, a video of the wave was featured in a 1972 movie called *Morning of the Earth,* and surfers worldwide really took notice. Airlines had to set new rules to accommodate the plethora of surfboards flying in weekly. In 1980, the still-quiet town of Uluwatu hosted Bali's first surf contest called the Om Bali Pro, hosted by famous surfer Stephen Palmer. Shortly after, paved roads leading to Uluwatu and other surf breaks made the waves accessible to all—not only the intrepid. Surfers continue to make up a large percentage of the Bukit Peninsula's visitors, but it's also developed to cater to those seeking luxury, health-focused, and family-friendly getaways as well.

Days are spent on the sand or in the water while sunsets are enjoyed from a cliffside vista. Simple warungs share street names with five-star resorts. Family-run homestays offer the same panoramic views as luxury beach clubs. Though the Bukit Peninsula has quickly become a hotspot for tourists, it continues to have an air of mysticism and allure.

ORIENTATION

The Bukit Peninsula is the wing-shaped southern peninsula of Bali's main island. It stretches south from the **Ngurah Rai International Airport.** The area is made up of dry, shrub-covered hills; "Bukit" means "hill" in Bahasa Indonesian. The narrowest part of the peninsula, **Jimbaran** and **Tanjung Benoa,** has fewer elevation changes, making the beaches accessible, sandy, and spacious. On the Bukit Peninsula's southernmost points, like **Uluwatu, Bingin, Dreamland,** and **Padang Padang,** beaches are typically found at the bottom of limestone cliffs and are rockier than their northern counterparts.

Two main roads lead into the Bukit Peninsula. The most efficient way to access the peninsula is via the **Bali Mandara Toll Road,** which begins near the airport. This toll road runs overwater alongside Tanjung Benoa, connecting with **Jalan By Pass Ngurah Rai** near **Nusa Dua.** Jalan By Pass Ngurah Rai is

Previous: fishermen on Padang Padang Beach; Jimbaran Fish Market; Uluwatu Cliffs.

Top Accommodations

★ **Balquisse Heritage Hotel:** A serene luxury property that uses antique decor and traditional architecture to make you feel as though you've stepped back in time (page 102).

★ **Ayana:** This upscale retreat in Jimbaran offers beach access, multiple pools, restaurants, and a spa—you won't want to leave (page 102).

★ **The Temple Lodge:** Every room is unique at this bohemian lodge overlooking Pantai Bingin (page 114).

★ **Renaissance Bali:** Immaculate rooms and one of the region's best breakfasts await at this secluded retreat that looks out to the peninsula (page 122).

★ **Uluwatu Surf Villas:** This boutique hotel with 10 cliffside villas is the ideal retreat for yogis and surfers (page 122).

the other main road that leads into the heart of the Bukit Peninsula and connects to **Jalan Raya Uluwatu.** Roads are typically named after the beaches that they connect to; for example, **Jalan Labuan Sait** will connect to Labuan Sait Beach (Padang Padang), Jalan Raya Uluwatu will connect to Uluwatu, **Jalan Pantai Bingin** will connect to Bingin Beach, and so on. The map may look like a tangled web of streets, but the main roads are well paved and marked.

The west side of the peninsula is where you'll find the best sunsets, along with the neighborhoods of Jimbaran, Dreamland, Bingin, Labuan Sait (Padang Padang), and Uluwatu. The south side of the peninsula is less developed but hosts **Green Bowl** and **Pandawa Beach.** In the east you'll find glamourous Nusa Dua and Tanjung Benoa. The middle of the peninsula is marked by the impressive **Garuda Wisnu Kencana Statue,** which can be seen from many parts of the region.

PLANNING YOUR TIME

Most activities in the Bukit Peninsula revolve around the sand and the sea. Before you venture out, pack **sunscreen, water,** a **hat, sarong,** and a fresh **change of clothes.** Many of the peninsula's beaches like **Labuan Sait (Padang Padang), Bingin, Suluban,** Balangan, and **Green Bowl Beach** demand a tiring walk down sandy, uneven stairs. If you have limited mobility or are traveling as a family, it's best to center your time around the peninsula's more accessible beaches like **Jimbaran, Dreamland, Pandawa, Nusa Dua,** and **Tanjung Benoa.** The latter beaches tend to have more lifeguards and safer swimming areas as well.

This region is known for having some of the country's heaviest waves, attracting professional surfers, who pour in on last-minute flights whenever a decent swell arrives. Strong currents, large or barreling waves, crowds, and sharp reef are hazards that only experienced surfers know how to navigate. When in doubt, hire a **surf guide** who can show you the best waves for your skill set safely. If you are visiting as a surfer, keep a flexible itinerary just in case conditions change. You'll want plenty of time to relax, so budget at least three days in the region. Beaches and waves tend to be most crowded from late June to the end of August, but not so crowded that it should deter a visit.

It's easiest to get around with **your own car** or **motorbike.** Or, consider arranging transportation through your **accommodation.** Taxis and rideshare apps like Grab and GoJek are not common.

Itinerary Ideas

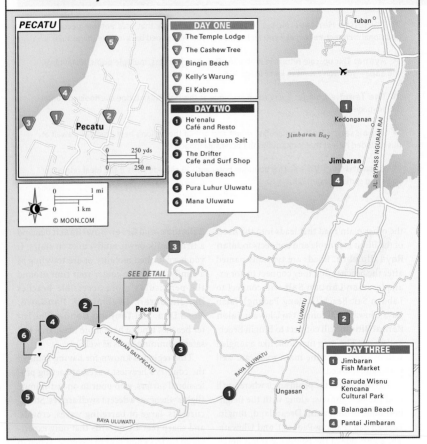

PECATU

Pecatu

0   250 yds
0   250 m

0   1 mi
0   1 km

© MOON.COM

DAY ONE
1. The Temple Lodge
2. The Cashew Tree
3. Bingin Beach
4. Kelly's Warung
5. El Kabron

DAY TWO
1. He'enalu Café and Resto
2. Pantai Labuan Sait
3. The Drifter Cafe and Surf Shop
4. Suluban Beach
5. Pura Luhur Uluwatu
6. Mana Uluwatu

DAY THREE
1. Jimbaran Fish Market
2. Garuda Wisnu Kencana Cultural Park
3. Balangan Beach
4. Pantai Jimbaran

Tuban

Kedonganan

Jimbaran Bay

Jimbaran

JL. BYPASS NGURAH RAI

SEE DETAIL

Pecatu

JL. LABUAN SAIT-PECATU

JL. ULUWATU

RAYA ULUWATU

Ungasan

RAYA ULUWATU

Itinerary Ideas

Navigating this region is easily done with your own rental car or motorbike, though private drivers can be arranged through your accommodation for around 500,000-700,000 Rp per day.

DAY 1: BEACHES AND VIEWS

1 Start your day off with a yoga class at **The Temple Lodge,** a yoga studio that overlooks Pantai Bingin.

2 Follow up with a healthy brunch at **The Cashew Tree,** a 700-meter (2,300-foot) walk or motorbike ride away.

3 Head back toward The Temple Lodge to spend the middle of the day relaxing on the sandy shores of **Bingin Beach.**

4 If hunger strikes, grab a snack at **Kelly's Warung,** right on the beach.

5 Keep your bathing suit on and drive to **El Kabron** for dinner, drinks, and a dip in their cliffside infinity pool.

DAY 2: SURF SAFARI

1 Drive along Jalan Uluwatu, stopping at **He'enalu Café and Resto.** Order a smoothie bowl bigger than you can handle to power you through a day at the beach.

2 Before lunch, drive to **Labuan Sait** (also known as Padang Padang Beach). Take a surf lesson with Rapture Surf Camp Padang. Beginners can learn at Baby Padang Padang Right, while experienced surfers can (fingers crossed) get barreled at Padang Padang.

3 Keep the surfer vibe going for lunch by driving to **the Drifter Café and Surf Shop.**

4 Drive to Uluwatu and park your motorbike at the main parking lot. Follow the main cliffside path to **Suluban Beach,** a small beach lined with caves to explore.

5 A short dive away, visit the **Pura Luhur Uluwatu** temple before sunset and watch the entertaining *kecak* dance.

6 Finish your day with dinner at **Mana Uluwatu,** a five-minute drive from the temple.

DAY 3: BUKIT PENINSULA LIKE A LOCAL

1 Drive early to Jimbaran to watch fishermen come to shore, and shop for fresh seafood at the **Jimbaran Fish Market.**

2 Learn about Balinese culture at the **Garuda Wisnu Kencana Cultural Park** and admire the grandiosity of Indonesia's largest statue, a 20-minute drive from Jimbaran.

3 Have lunch and hang out at **Balangan Beach,** still untouched by mainstream tourism. If you surf, strap your board to your set of wheels.

4 Back in Jimbaran, head to **Pantai Jimbaran** to enjoy a seafood dinner on the sand. Each seaside warung offers similar options; choose one of the busier ones to ensure your meal is cooked fresh.

Bukit Peninsula

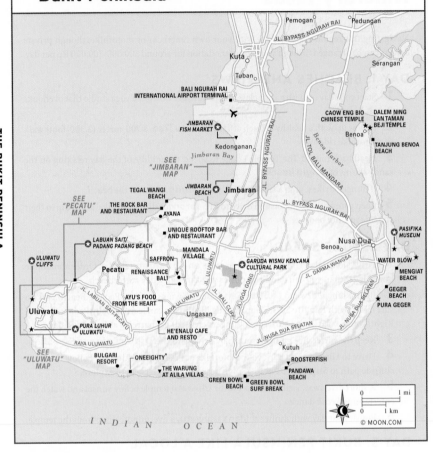

Jimbaran

Until the 1980s tourism boom, Jimbaran was little more than a small fishing village that supplied central Denpasar and bordering towns with fresh seafood. While many neighborhoods throughout Southern Bali have traded centuries-old traditions and professions for roles in hospitality, Jimbaran is one place where you'll still find remnants of Bali life from before mega resorts developed the coastline. Locals shop at the morning markets set up in between luxury resorts and fine dining venues. Fishermen launch and land their vibrantly painted double-outrigger fishing boats and sort their catch just steps away from morning sunbathers. People can choose to eat fresh seafood served to them on the sand or inside a world-class restaurant.

When it comes to spending time in the sun, Jimbaran offers ample space for everyone. Beachcombers and joggers can traipse the long stretch of sand from Jimbaran Bay to the northern end near the airport undisturbed. Beginner surfers can catch their first wave with one of the local surf schools, while those with more experience can paddle out back. It's easy to spend a day switching between the sand, the shade, and the water, drinking fresh coconuts in between.

Sleepy by day, Jimbaran comes alive at sunset. Locals and tourists crowd to the shoreline to admire the bubblegum pink sky and watch the sun drop below the water. Restaurants get busy preparing candlelit tables for hungry customers, vendors park their carts of spiced corn on the sand, and other merchants walk through the crowds offering sarongs, toys, and whatever else they can pile onto their arms and shoulders. Once darkness comes, traditional Balinese dancers and cultural performers step into the limelight. Restaurants host their own entertainment in hopes of enticing tourists to sit and eat.

ORIENTATION

Jimbaran is the narrow neck of the Bukit Peninsula that covers the neighborhoods of **Kedonganan, Jimbaran,** and **Balangan.** It is only a 10- to 20-minute **taxi ride** from **Ngurah Rai International Airport.** The west side hosts **Jimbaran Beach,** the

sandy shores that meet with **Jimbaran Bay.** The east is marked with dense mangroves. The fish market is up toward the northern Kedonganan side of Jimbaran, while **Tegal Wangi Beach, Balangan Beach,** and the famous **Ayana** resort lie to the south. The southern inland point of Jimbaran is marked by the **Garuda Wisnu Kencana Cultural Park. Jalan Raya Uluwatu** and **Jalan Bypass Ngurah Rai** are the main roads running north and south along Jimbaran. Short, smaller roads head east and west.

SIGHTS
Ulun Siwi Temple
(Pura Ulun Siwi)
Jalan Raya Uluwatu; tel. 8579266888; 7am-7pm

Pura Ulun Siwi is a small temple in the heart of Jimbaran dedicated to the Hindu gods of protection and agriculture. Built in the 1700s, the temple is still used daily as ceremonial and prayer grounds among Balinese Hindus. Prayers tend to center around the 11-tiered pagoda, making it the highlight of the temple. The morning market takes place daily near the entrance of Pura Ulun Siwi.

★ Garuda Wisnu Kencana Cultural Park
Jalan Raya Uluwatu, tel. 361/700808; www.gwkbali. com; daily 8am-9pm; 110,000 Rp per adult (tourist), 80,000 Rp per adult (local), children free

The Garuda Wisnu Kencana Cultural Park makes for a great stop while traveling through the Bukit Peninsula for those who want to know more about Hinduism and Balinese culture. Live theater and musical shows take place from mid-morning to early evening. The park's main **amphitheater** inside the grounds can accommodate more than 800 guests to watch barong and *kecak* dances, traditional performances that are part of Bali's cultural heritage. Through these dances, you'll learn stories of Hindu and Indonesian legends. Performances take place daily, and the timetable and performance location can be found online, with many events happening around other areas of the park, like the lotus

Jimbaran

PURA ULUN SIWI ★

JL. ULUWATU

Jimbaran Bay

CUCA KAYUMANIS RESTO

JIMBARAN BEACH

JIMBARAN MARKET

Jimbaran

BALQUISSE HERITAGE HOTEL

BEEKINI BOWL

JL. ULUWATU

JALAN ULUWATU 2

SUNDARA

JL. BUKIT PERMAI

ABOVE ELEVEN BALI

1,000 ft
250 m

© MOON.COM

pond and main plaza. The price of admission includes viewing of the performances.

Adventurous spirits can see the park from the wheels of a Segway, while those who prefer to explore on foot can stroll between the **gardens** and **viewpoints** around the 60-hectare (148-acre) park. Between enjoying performances and walking around, it's easy to spend half a day inside the cultural center. If you want a unique memento of your stay, get your picture taken while wearing a traditional Balinese outfit. There are multiple restaurants on site, though **Jendela Bali Restaurant** (Jalan Raya Uluwatu; tel. 361/703603; www.gwkbali.com; daily 10am-8pm; 60,000-90,000 Rp) offers the best view.

Overlooking the cultural park is the **Garuda Wisnu Kencana** statue. At 120 meters (394 feet) tall, it is the tallest statue in Indonesia and one of the largest religious monuments in the world (larger than Brazil's Christ the Redeemer). The statue depicts the Hindu god Wisnu riding his half-man and half-bird companion, Garuda. Stories of Garuda and Visnu are engraved in the limestone cliffs that surround the park. Kids will love watching *Garuda Cilik Adventure,* an animated film about Garuda as a young boy that plays eight times per day from 11am to 6pm in the **Garuda Cinema;** exact showtimes are updated on the park's website. The movie viewing is included in your entrance ticket, and children under 100 cm (3.3 feet) tall can enter the park for free.

If you're on a budget, it's possible to see the carvings in the cliffs and admire the Garuda Wisnu Kencana statue from the park's parking lot without paying the entrance fee.

Dalem Balangan Temple
(Pura Dalem Balangan)

Jalan Pantai Balangan, South Kuta; sunrise-sunset
This small temple is tucked in a cave on Balangan's cliffside and guards the northern end of Balangan Beach. From the temple, you can look out over the ocean and onto the beach below. Though it's not as busy as many

other temples in the region, you'll occasionally see locals visit and place their offerings.

BEACHES AND SURF BREAKS
★ Jimbaran Beach
(Pantai Jimbaran)

Access via Jalan Pantai Kedonganan (North end); parking along Jalan Pantai Kedonganan (5,000 Rp motorbike, 10,000 Rp car) and at Jalan Bukit Permai (5,000 Rp motorbike, 10,000 car), car parking is very limited while motorbike parking is easy to find
At about 4 km (2.5 mi) long, Jimbaran Beach is one of the largest stretches of sand on the Bukit Peninsula. While the sun is shining, you can watch fishing boats come in with their catch of the morning, ride a friendly wave during a surf lesson, build sand castles, dine at one of the many beachside restaurants, enjoy lounging in their beanbag chairs, swim, and be mesmerized by the constant take-offs and landings from the international airport. Because the beach is so spacious, there's no shortage of quiet places to throw down a towel.

The northern end of Jimbaran Beach is home to the **Jimbaran Fish Market.** The middle of the beach is largely untouched, and you can sunbathe without worrying about getting targeted by a vendor. Jimbaran Beach's southern end is where most of the action happens, where you can step around half-built sandcastles, surf, eat, and shop.

JIMBARAN SURF BREAK

Starts from the southern end of Jimbaran Beach
This is a friendly surf break for longboarders, stand-up paddlers, and beginner surfers. This gentle wave breaks over sand and offers plenty of space for mistakes. It works best up to 2 meters (7 feet). After that, the outside section will be too big for beginners, who will do better sticking to the whitewash. If a large southwest swell comes through, playful, peaky waves pop up across the bay.

1: Garuda Wisnu Kencana Cultural Park **2:** Jimbaran Beach **3:** Balangan Beach **4:** Balangan Surf Break

Tegal Wangi Beach
(Pantai Tegal Wangi)

Jalan Tegal Wangi, parking lot along road, path to beach is not well-marked but is well-worn (5,000 Rp motorbike, 10,000 Rp car, irregularly staffed)

Hidden from the crowds, this sandy beach is surrounded by cliffs and small, bat-inhabited caves. Head to the shore while the sun is shining and walk to the top of the cliffs for prime sunset views. While Tegal Wangi Beach is not ideal for swimming because of dangerous waves and currents, there are a handful of calm, natural pools to relax in that feel like tepid Jacuzzis. Visit during low tide when there will be more beach area to explore.

Balangan Beach
(Pantai Balangan)

Jalan Pantai Balangan, 2,000 Rp parking, 10,000 Rp beach access

Balangan Beach stokes a sense of adventure, as getting there is a journey itself. The pot-holed, bumpy road of Jalan Pantai Balangan eventually leads to an open parking area. A long walk down the path (made of plenty of uneven stairs) weaves along Pura Dalem Balangan temple and drops you on beach made of sand and stone. Surprisingly, the beach itself is mostly untouched by the tourism industry, aside from the handful of shacks serving heaping plates of *mie goreng* (spicy fried noodles) for 25,000 Rp to satiate surfers' appetites. Let's hope it stays this way.

BALANGAN SURF BREAK

Starts from the southern end of Jimbaran Beach

Surfers can paddle out at all tides to the left-hand reef break that works best during a southwesterly swell from five to 15 feet. Intermediate surfers will have fun on smaller days but should leave the bigger waves to the experts who can handle the close-out sections and strong currents.

FOOD
Indonesian
BEEKINI BOWL

Jalan Bukit Permai No. 5A; tel. 87881817505; https:// beekinibowl.business.site; 9am-11pm; 40,000-90,000 Rp

Beekini Bowl is the epitome of beachside bliss, with colorful beanbag chairs and sun-faded umbrellas lined along the sand. Watch Jimbaran's waves roll in and people walk by while you enjoy a Balinese lunch and dinner. For breakfast, opt for a bowl of granola and a fresh fruit smoothie. After 11am, drinks are never served warmer than ice-cold.

KAYUMANIS RESTO

Jalan Yoga Perkanthi, South Kuta; tel. 361/705777; www.kayumanis.com; 7am-10pm; 80,000-200,000 Rp

One of the most romantic spots in Jimbaran, Kayumanis Resto hosts candlelit dinners in a garden surrounded by coconut trees. The menu features authentic Indonesian meals that match the restaurant's Javanese decor and architecture. For the full experience, order the *babek,* a traditional dish made of crispy smoked duck served with rice.

SUNDARA

Jalan Kawasan Bukit Permai (Four Seasons Resort), South Kuta; tel. 361/708333; www.sundarabali. com; Sun.-Thurs. 11am-1am, Fri.-Sat. 11am-3am; 150,000-575,000 Rp

Sundara is a beach club and tapas-style restaurant that serves light Balinese and Indonesian dishes in a kick-your-shoes-off atmosphere. Spend the day moving between the 57-meter (187-foot) infinity pool, the daybeds, Jimbaran Beach, and the lounge chairs. Kids can make new friends at Sundara's free kids club. Happy hour takes place 5pm-7pm daily.

Tapas
★ CUCA

Jalan Yoga Perkanthi, South Kuta; tel. 361/708066; www.cucaflavor.com; daily noon-midnight; 80,000-190,000 Rp

Cuca is a no-frills tapas restaurant with

minimalist decor and exceptional food. Think fine dining without the pretentiousness. Nearly every ingredient is sourced within Indonesia and used to create a blend of international dishes. Choose seats in the garden or opt for a table with curtains for privacy. Chef Kevin Cherkas, also the owner of Cuca, has developed somewhat of a cult following that expands every time a plate of tapas is served.

International
SAFFRON

Jalan Pantai Balangan, South Kuta; tel. 81238391110; mandalavillagebali.com/dining/saffron; daily 5:30pm-10:30pm; 60,000-120,000 Rp

In one of the region's quieter neighborhoods is Saffron, an open-air restaurant that serves seafood and vegetarian food. Meals are healthy and thoughtfully presented. Vegetarians will love the variety of mock meat dishes on the menu (a rarity in the region), and all breads, pastas, and cheeses are made in house. The decor is a mishmash of objects from around the globe, giving the space an eccentric, international feel.

Markets
★ JIMBARAN FISH MARKET

Pantai Kedonganan/Pantai Jimbaran, South Kuta; daily 6am-3pm

Have you ever wondered where your meal came from? Before daybreak each morning, fishermen venture out to sea on wooden traditional *jukung* boats. On the northern side of Jimbaran Beach, in Kedonganan, travelers can watch the fisherman arrive just after sunrise with their daily catch. The boats are so heavy, it often takes at least eight people plus a trolley to pull the boats onto shore. Once the boat is safely on the sand, the fisherman hurry to sort the catch and wrap up their nets before the next boat arrives. The seafood is then sorted and sold in the market.

The market is divided into separate areas. One area caters to the local restaurants and wholesale buyers, while another is specifically for public sale. Haggling is not common inside the market unless the seafood is purchased in bulk. For the best deal, purchase seafood directly from the fishermen, who sometimes sell their seafood directly on the beach. Take your prized catch to one of the many beachside restaurants, where a skilled chef will fillet and grill it over dried coconut husks for a cooking fee of 20,000 Rp per kg (2.2 lbs) of seafood. Squid (70,000 Rp per kg/2.2 lbs), giant prawns (200,000 Rp per kg/2.2 lbs), crab (250,000 per kg/2.2 lbs), red and white snapper (120,000 per kg/2.2 lbs), and lobster (300,000 Rp per kg/2.2 lbs) are regular catches. Market rates vary, and bargaining is expected.

JIMBARAN MORNING MARKET

Pantai Muaya/Pantai Jimbaran, South Kuta; daily 6am-11am

Many Jimbaran locals spend their morning at the Jimbaran Morning Market, where seasonal fruit and vegetables are piled onto small tables and truck beds and sold. The market has a fragrant, floral smell often mixed with the sweet scent of burning incense. Large bags packed with flower petals and foliage are sold in the market alongside bundles of incense (*dupa*) and small woven baskets. These supplies will be carefully crafted into offerings (*canang sari*) and placed all around living spaces, road intersections, and temples. You can purchase an already-assembled offering to place yourself for around 3,000 Rp per small basket.

BARS AND NIGHTLIFE
THE ROCK BAR AND RESTAURANT

Jalan Karang Mas Sejahtera (Ayana Resort), South Kuta; tel. 361/702222; www.ayana.com; Mon.-Fri. 4pm-midnight, Sat.-Sun. 4pm-1am; 120,000-250,000 Rp

The Rock Bar offers ocean views, international food, and trendy music from the island's top DJs, who play from a booth etched into the cliffs. In between sets, you can often hear the wind whistling over stone. Most guests arrive just before sunset and stay for dinner and drinks. The service is surprisingly efficient and friendly, even though this is such

Catch of the Day: Choosing Sustainable Fish at the Market

The seafood sold at the Jimbaran Fish Market reflects the marine life that lives beyond Indonesia's shorelines. Unfortunately, many species of fish and other marine life populations are under major threat, and because most forms of fishing involve large nets, there's little discrepancy as to what seafood is caught and what isn't. This means threatened species and animals that have yet to mature are often caught and sold in the market. The average size of most fish species in the Indonesian archipelago is shrinking, and local fishermen will often attest to this.

Arrive early at the market and watch the fishermen come into shore to see precisely how the fish were caught. **Spearfishing** and **handline fishing** are more sustainable than large area nets or trawl nets. Note that large predatory fish like barracuda, all species of tuna, marlin, and king mackerel are more likely to contain traces of mercury, and thus are unhealthier to eat than prey fish.

According to the World Wildlife Fund (worldwildlife.org), you should **avoid** any species of shark (*hiu*), turtle (*penyu*), Napoleon wrasse (*maming*), bluefin tuna (*tuna biru*), tiger shrimp (*udang windu*), or fish eggs (*ikan telur*). More **sustainable options** include:

- **squid** (*cumi cumi*)
- **dolphinfish** (*mahi-mahi*)
- **anchovies** (*teri*)
- **rainbow runner** (*salem*)
- **Indian mackerel** (*kembung banjar*)

a popular venue. Skip the long line by reserving a table in advance.

UNIQUE ROOFTOP BAR AND RESTAURANT

Jalan Karang Mas Sejahtera (Rimba Resort), South Kuta; tel. 361/8468468; www.ayana.com; Mon.-Fri. 11am-midnight, Sat.-Sun. 11am-1am; 90,000-240,000 Rp

With sights that stretch over treetops and out to the ocean, UNIQUE Rooftop Bar and Restaurant serves Mexican food in a chic atmosphere. Their infinity pool makes for a prime margarita-sipping spot, while shrimp tacos are best eaten from the comforts of a poolside lounge chair. Visit on Sunday for live acoustic performances that take place from 11am-3pm, followed by a pool party and DJ.

ABOVE ELEVEN BALI

Jalan Wanagiri No. 1 (Mövenpick Resort), South Kuta; tel. 8113860402; www.aboveeleven.com; daily 4pm-1am; 125,000-305,000 Rp

Above Eleven Bali serves Nikkei cuisine, a fusion of Peruvian and Japanese meals. The bar's design was inspired by NYC's Central Park, giving it an urban-meets-nature ambiance that's well-executed. Guests first walk through a short maze before reaching the rooftop, where you can listen to the venue's DJ and enjoy views that stretch to the sea. The bar offers a varied selection of cocktails, and their wine list is longer than most. Bring the little ones, too; the staff will entertain them with a movie in the kids-only garden area.

1: Beekini Bowl **2:** Snakefruit **3:** Jimbaran Morning Market

ACCOMMODATIONS
Under 1,000,000 Rp
FLOWER BUD BUNGALOW BALANGAN

Jalan Pantai Balangan; tel. 8164722310; www. flowerbudbalangan.com; 700,000-800,000 Rp

Flower Bud Bungalow Balangan has 22 cozy bungalows built from wood and bamboo and placed in two separate locations; travelers will want to specify which one they want when making a reservation. Flower Bud 1 bungalows are on Balangan Beach and offer a choice between hot and cold-water showers. Flower Bud 2 bungalows are a 3-minute walk from the beach and tend to be larger and better for families. Both areas have a pool and restaurant. All rooms have an outdoor freshwater shower, patio area, fan, and mosquito net, and include breakfast. Some rooms also include a fridge.

Over 1,000,000 Rp
MANDALA VILLAGE

Jalan Pantai Balangan; tel. 361/4725462; mandalavillagebali.com; 1,500,000-2,000,000 Rp

Mandala Village is a community made up of a handful of hillside bungalows away from the main tourist areas. Each bungalow offers stunning ocean views seen from a spacious veranda and sports a minimalist, shabby-chic aesthetic. Each bungalow has hot water, a fan, mosquito net, and a large drinking-water tank. If you're looking for a wellness retreat, you'll find little reason to venture out; the village also has a spacious yoga studio with a covered outdoor platform, spa, and café known for its unique coffee concoctions.

★ BALQUISSE HERITAGE HOTEL

Jalan Uluwatu No. 18X; tel. 361/701695; www. balquisse.com; 2,200,000-3,000,000 Rp

Balquisse Heritage Hotel presents a unique take on vintage luxury with its blend of bohemian, antique, and Balinese decor, making the interior design its main draw. No two of the 16 rooms at Balquisse Heritage Hotel are alike. The owner of the hotel has a background in interior design and it's obvious that she has had a hand in each room's aesthetic. Some rooms have a bathtub in addition to a shower. The hotel is about a 10-minute walk from Jimbaran Beach and there are two pools, a restaurant, and a spa on the property.

★ AYANA

Jalan Karang Mas Sejahtera; tel. 361/702222; www. ayana.com; 3,500,000 Rp

Ayana is a five-star luxury resort set on the cliffs of Jimbaran Bay. The property offers 12 swimming pools, an 18-hole putting course, and 19 dining venues, so some guests find little reason to leave. The wood decor, infinity pools, lotus ponds, gardens, and ocean views create a feeling of tropical opulence. There are 294 rooms and 78 private villas with multiple types to choose from. Each option comes with a flat screen TV, bathtub, and access to the stretch of sand below the resort. A buffet breakfast is included with each stay, and guests can opt to have this breakfast at Rimba, Ayana's sister property that's also in Jimbaran.

GETTING THERE
By Rental Car or Motorbike

The main roads leading into Jimbaran are well-paved and marked for those driving a **rental car,** available for rent at the **international airport,** or **motorbike,** available for rent through your **accommodation** for around 50,000-70,000 Rp per day. Jimbaran is best reached by taking **Jalan By Pass Ngurah Rai** from the Ngurah Rai International Airport and **Kuta** (7 km/4.3 mi; 15 minutes). If coming from **Ubud,** drive one hour south to Denpasar and connect to Jalan By Pass Ngurah Rai, following Jalan By Pass Ngurah Rai to Jimbaran (total trip 40 km/25 mi; 1.5 hours).

By Taxi and Private Driver

Most taxis and private drivers will connect tourists from the **Kuta** area for around

---

1: Flower Bud Bungalow Balangan 2: Mandala Village

100,000-150,000 Rp. **Grab/GoJek** drivers will also connect tourists to Jimbaran for 80,000-130,000 Rp.

By Bus

Tourists can take the green and yellow **Kura-Kura shuttle bus** (tel. 361/3700244; www.kura2bus.com; Jimbaran-Kuta daily every 75 mins, 8:30am-10pm; 20,000 one-way, single and multiday passes available, children under 2 free) from **DFS Bus Bay** at Kuta's **Galleria Mall** (Jalan By Pass Ngurah Rai) and stop at hubs like **Jimbaran Beach, AYANA,** and **RIMBA**.

GETTING AROUND
By Rental Car or Motorbike

The area is easy to navigate with a motorbike or car—but mind the narrow side roads. The roads around Balangan specifically are pocked with potholes and gravel patches. **Motorbikes** are typically available for rent through your accommodation. You can also rent a car or motorbike at **Jimbaran Scooter Rental** (www.jimbaranscooterrental.com; tel. 81338763197; 50,000-150,000 Rp per day), which will deliver a motorbike to your accommodation in Jimbaran.

By Taxi and Private Driver

Bluebird taxis wait at the beachfront throughout the day. Some upscale restaurants offer free pickup and drop-off around the Jimbaran area for customers. Transport apps like **Grab** and **GoJek** can be hit or miss, as the taxi industry has intimidated most drivers in the area from operating, though you may have luck if you're requesting a ride from a private area.

Pecatu (Bingin, Dreamland, Padang Padang)

Every bend in Pecatu's windy roads leads to exciting discoveries, including boutiques, surf shops, homestays, motorbike rental stands, and tattoo parlors. Smaller roads connecting the coastline to the main road often reveal ocean views, small homes with chickens scampering out front, casual cafés, and tucked-away temples. While longtime visitors may have a "You should have been here yesterday!" mentality when it comes to traveling through Pecatu's beachside neighborhoods, the wild landscape and the intensity of the ocean have preserved the region's rawness and beauty.

The different areas of Pecatu proudly cling to their distinct personalities and reputations. In Dreamland, the mega-resorts offer hundreds of rooms and function as mini-metropolises, with guests congregating on Dreamland Beach all day long. One of the calmer and sandier beaches in the region, it tends to attract families, tour groups, beginner surfers, and couples craving a no-fuss holiday.

Meanwhile, Bingin is a bohemian beachside town with rickety warungs, shabby-chic boutique homestays, and bikini shops speckled along the face of its cliff. There simply isn't enough space to accommodate mega resorts, and it appears that Bingin's community has no desire to do so, either. To get to the cliffside neighborhood, you must first wander down a narrow alleyway that then opens to a fork of staircases. While some shops and homestays have made a point to guide you in the right direction with hand-painted signs, most assume that you'll find your way somehow. And it's true: Eventually, you'll wander through the maze of steps to the beach or your desired destination. The clear views and rolling waves have a way of making you forget all about the strenuous walk back up the cliff face. Inland from the cliff, you'll find yoga studios, organic cafés, and surf shops.

Pecatu

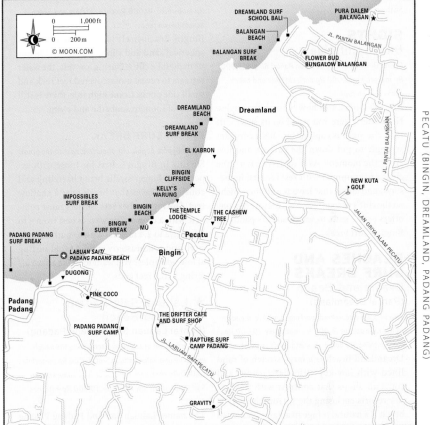

The bulk of Padang Padang's shops and restaurants are dotted along the main road of Jalan Labuan Sait. Each morning, just after the roosters crow, you might hear the revving of board-strapped motorbikes as surfers drive to catch waves at the famous break of Padang Padang. Take your pick of surf camps, homestays, and luxury hotels hidden away on Jalan Labuan Sait's side roads.

ORIENTATION

From north to south, the three towns of **Dreamland, Bingin,** and **Padang Padang** are named after their beaches and wedge into the center of the peninsula to form the greater area of Pecatu. On the main roads of **Jalan Labuan Sait, Jalan Raya Uluwatu, Jalan Uluwatu Pecatu,** and **Jalan Pecatu Indah Raya** you'll find a wide variety of cafés, boutiques, surf shops, homestays, motorbike rental stands, and tattoo parlors. These roads are well-paved but tend to get congested from 4pm to 5pm.

Dreamland and its surroundings consist mostly of large mid-range to luxury resorts. Bingin, however, hosts many of its best homestays and warungs directly on its cliffs. Padang Padang's surroundings consist of accommodations, shops, and restaurants on the road leading away from **Labuan Sait (Padang Padang) Beach** on Jalan Labuan Sait.

SIGHTS
Bingin Cliffside

Pantai Bingin, parking at Jalan Pantai Bingin (5,000 Rp motorbike, 10,000 Rp car), cliffside and beach accessible on foot

Bingin's cliffs know how to work the angles. No matter where you stand on its sheer cliff face, the sight is captivating. It's a constant struggle to put down the camera and just enjoy the moment. As if to defy gravity, the cliffs are crammed with restaurants, home-stays, and shops that have found their niche on the cliff's porous face. Nearly every balcony offers prime seats to watch surfers paddle at Bingin's surf break.

BEACHES AND SURF BREAKS
Dreamland Beach
(Pantai Dreamland)

Jalan Pantai Dreamland; parking available at end of the roundabout (5,000 Rp motorbike, 10,000 Rp car); entrance to beach downstairs off roundabout

Dreamland Beach is a large stretch of sand lined with low-key cliffside warungs and souvenir shops that contrast with the luxury resorts enclosing the surroundings. The beach is a natural refuge in an area blanketed in asphalt and concrete. There are usually lifeguards on duty, and they have no qualms about calling swimmers away from dangerous areas. To escape the crowd, walk north away from the beach's entrance.

DREAMLAND SURF BREAK

Dreamland Beach; paddle out from the beach

The break at Dreamland can handle a large crowd across its A-frame peak. The left is longer than the right, but both are decent in a southwesterly swell up to 8 feet (2.4 meters) with easterly winds. On larger days, the wave turns into a close-out and isn't worth the paddle.

Bingin Beach
(Pantai Bingin)

Pantai Bingin, Parking at Jalan Pantai Bingin (5,000 Rp motorbike, 10,000 Rp car), cliffside and beach accessible on foot

Bingin Beach itself is a narrow ribbon of spherical sand and slippery rocks just below its namesake cliffs. During low tide, the water retreats to reveal moss-covered reef rock and small tide pools. Come high tide, there is still plenty of room to sunbathe and swim.

BINGIN SURF BREAK

Bingin Beach; paddle out at current next to the break

Surfing in Bingin is best for those with experience. Bigger swells bring barreling and consistent waves that break over a shallow reef. During smaller sets, surfers must compete with a crowd. The wave is best from 4 to 8 feet (1.2 to 2.4 meters) with a southwesterly swell and southeasterly winds. Avoid surfing at low tide unless you want to make a skin offering to the reef gods.

★ Labuan Sait/Padang Padang Beach
(Pantai Labuan Sait/Padang Padang)

Secure parking at the road intersecting the beach entrance and Jalan Labuan Sait (5,000 Rp motorbike, 10,000 Rp car); beach entrance is at Jalan Labuan Sait, down a narrow staircase; 10,000 Rp entrance fee

The names Labuan Sait and Padang Padang are used interchangeably when talking about this beach, which is famous for having one of Bali's perfect barrels, the wave of **Padang Padang.** On the reef, you'll find fishermen casting a line, while the golden sand is accessorized with floppy hats, sunglasses, and towels belonging to Labuan Sait beachgoers. A cluster of small food and souvenir shops crowd the back of the beach, searching for shade under the cliff's shrubs. The beach suits swimmers and surfers, some of whom might recognize it from the film *Eat, Pray, Love.*

1: Bingin Cliffside 2: Dreamland Beach 3: Bingin Beach 4: Pura Labuan Sait

It's On When It's On: The Rip Curl Cup

Padang Padang surf break

Big-wave surfers all over the globe keep a watchful eye on Bali's surf forecast. The Rip Curl Cup is one of the most famous surf contests that *only* takes place when the waves are large and powerful enough. Organizers take the conditions extremely seriously, and won't run the contest for years if there isn't a swell worthy enough for it.

The motto of the contest is "It's on when it's on." Surfers looking to take home a title (and paycheck) must be ready to travel as soon as the contest is announced.

Anyone can watch the surf contest take place, and admission is free aside from the daily 10,000 Rp beach entrance fee. Visit during the contest, and you'll be lucky enough to see surfers and the ocean's power all working to their full potential. During the surf contest, surf celebrities cause a ruckus and tend to congregate at the local restaurants of Pecatu. Surfers who are still in the contest will disappear after sunset, craving a full night of sleep. Meanwhile, those who've been knocked out are often found sipping Bintangs in the cliffside warungs of Bingin. After the contest is over, everyone parties on the sand of Labaun Sait Beach.

To take the more interesting pathway down to the sand, walk past the temple of **Pura Labaun Sait** (closed to tourists), an 8-meter (26-foot) high, narrow passageway. If you get claustrophobic or don't prefer to walk single file, there's a second set of open stairs behind the toll booth and bathrooms.

Every Saturday night and during the full moon, a **beach party** congregates on the sand. Live DJs often perform in hopes of piquing the interest of those in the peninsula's glitzy clubs. Carry or hide your shoes before you dance barefoot on the sand—unattended shoes are known to "walk off" with someone else.

IMPOSSIBLES SURF BREAK

Labuan Sait or Bingin Beach; paddle out from deep water channel at Labuan Sait

Impossibles is a wave that you'll have to work hard to reach. The paddle out is long no matter where you're coming from. The wave is finnicky, needing a medium southerly swell to work. The three-sectioned wave is very fast but rarely crowded, giving surfers the opportunity to choose wisely. Impossibles works at all tides with a long southerly swell but becomes incredibly shallow when it's low.

PADANG PADANG SURF BREAK

Labuan Sait Beach; paddle out at the beach in the deep-water channel

If a painter was asked to paint a perfect wave, Padang Padang would no doubt be a muse. The barreling wave is famous among all surfers and needs very specific conditions to truly work. Look for a large swell from the south-southwest and south-easterly winds in the forecast. Mid- to low tide is best, as too much water makes it wobble. When it's working, every decent surfer in the area will be vying for a ride. It is not a wave for beginners, however; they should stick to the friendly wave breaking north of Padang Padang, dubbed "Baby Padang Padang."

WATER SPORTS
Surf Schools
RAPTURE SURF CAMP PADANG

Jalan Labuan Sait, Padang Padang; tel. 81337578261; www.rapturecamps.com; from 750,000 Rp per day

Learn to surf or simply advance your skills by checking into Rapture Surf Camp Padang. During the day, the camp will shuttle surfers to the region's best beginner surf spots. In between surf sessions, surfers like to lounge at the pool. The vibe is laid-back and social; this is a top spot for solo travelers wanting to make friends. For the best value, opt for their package that includes a bed, breakfast, dinner (weekdays only), surf lessons (two per day), video analysis of your surfing, transport between surf spots, yoga classes, and airport pickup. Dorm rooms and private rooms are available.

PADANG PADANG SURF CAMP

Jalan Labuan Sait, Padang Padang; tel. 81999283549; www.balisurfingcamp.com; rooms 300,000-600,000 Rp per day, surf lessons from 500,000 per day

This surf camp and school is walking distance from Dreamland, Bingin, Impossibles, and Padang Padang. The camp has an on-site yoga studio that hosts classes catered to surfers. There are also lounge areas with plenty of hammocks, a pool, a tennis court, and a spacious dining area. Padang Padang Surf Camp tends to attract health-conscious surfers rather than the party crowd. Their week-long surf camp package includes a private room with bathroom, two meals per day, rides between surf spots, and a surf guide. Lessons are extra.

Padang Padang Beach

DREAMLAND SURF SCHOOL BALI

*Jalan New Kuta Beach; tel. 85738704974; www.
dreamlandsurfschool.com; 400,000 Rp per 2-hour
lesson*

Dreamland Surf School Bali is set directly on Dreamland Beach, just after the stretch of warungs and souvenir shops. The school rents stable, soft-top surfboards and offers lessons to anyone interested in catching their first wave. More advanced surfers and those who want coaching can also rent fiberglass boards. Dreamland Beach is one of the best places to learn in the area, thanks to its sandy bottom and reputation for having consistent, beginner-friendly waves. Lesson times are dependent on tide, swell, and weather.

OTHER SPORTS AND RECREATION
Golf
NEW KUTA GOLF

*Jalan Raya Uluwatu, Dreamland; tel. 361/8481333;
www.newkutagolf.com; daily 6:30am-7:30pm;
2,100,000 Rp for 18 holes, 1,100,000 Rp for half
day/9 holes*

New Kuta Golf has an 18-hole course that spans 85 hectares (210 acres) and overlooks Dreamland and Balangan. Public golfers are welcome and can choose between full-day and half-day admission. Because of the Bukit Peninsula's dry climate and water shortage, the course can be patchy and varies between having fast and slow greens. The caddies are known for their friendliness and are happy to offer valuable advice when asked. A collared shirt is mandatory for admittance.

FOOD
Indonesian
KELLY'S WARUNG

*Jalan Pantai Bingin, Bingin; kellyswarung@gmail.
com; daily 8am-9pm; 40,000-80,000 Rp*

Kelly's Warung is a casual beachside restaurant that serves simple and healthy Indonesian staples along with fresh juices. All seats come with prime views of Bingin beach. It's a hot spot for surfers who want to skip trekking up and down Bingin's steep staircase and would rather rest at the warung instead. Kelly's Warung also offers basic dorm rooms for those who love lounging so much, they fancy spending the night.

DUGONG

*Jalan Pantai Labuan Sait, Padang Padang;
tel. 361/4725088; dugong@suarga.com; daily
7:30am-10pm; 170,000-280,000 Rp*

Dugong has some of the most interesting decor and architecture in an area that reflects Indonesian traditional luxury. The building is artfully constructed with bamboo, wood, and thatch in a way that merges with its natural surroundings. Meals are served on fine dinnerware, and most tables offer panoramic ocean views. Service can be slow, so it's best to get a drink order in as soon as you arrive and plan to stay awhile. Dugong's menu features freshly caught seafood, sauteed duck, and Southeast Asian dishes.

International
EL KABRON

*Jalan Pantai Cemongkak, Dreamland; tel.
82144370139; https://elkabron.com; daily
11:30am-11:30pm; 50,000-370,000 Rp*

Balanced on the top of a cliff and overlooking Dreamland and Bingin Beach, El Kabron is a swanky day club and European tapas restaurant serving cured Spanish ham, paella, and croquetas. Their cinnamon ice cream is a must on hot days. While the beach calls for Bintangs, a chic venue like this might have you ordering a drink that's a little more refined. Dining in the restaurant requires no minimum spend, but guests will need to purchase 400,000 Rp worth of food and drinks per person plus pay a 50,000 Rp entrance fee to take a dip in El Kabron's turquoise infinity pool. Reserve a space online in advance if you plan to visit during sunset.

Get the Shot: Surf Photography

Dreamland Beach

You might notice surf photographers parked with their tripods all along the cliff ledges, snapping shots of surfers. If you're a surfer and want a shot of yourself, walk up to a photographer before you paddle out and let them know that you're interested. This way, they'll prioritize capturing your waves over others who may not be up for buying a picture (about 50,000 Rp for a single photo, 200,000 Rp series).

If you're a photographer yourself, here are some tips to help you leave with a *Surfer's Journal*-inspired surf shot.

- **Shoot at sunrise and sunset:** The ocean tends to be glassiest at sunrise and sunset, making the waves smoother and more picturesque. Too much sun can cause glare in the photo.

- **Offshore wind:** When the wind is blowing from the shore to the sea, this not only makes for better surfing conditions but also for better photos. The spray from the wave will be wafting into the sky, adding extra movement and texture to your picture.

- **Position the surfer in 1/3 of the shot:** Position the surfer on one side of the frame, about one third into the picture. The other 2/3 of the picture should show the face of the wave so that the viewer can imagine where the surfer will be going next.

- **Shutter speed:** Because surfers will be moving fast, you'll need a fast shutter to avoid taking a blurry photo. A general rule is to keep the shutter about 1/640s. For a creative shot, slow down your shutter speed and physically move your camera in the same direction as the surfer. This will create an effect where the surfer is in focus and the wave is blurred.

- **Zoom:** Surfers tend to be far away from the shoreline. Pack a zoom lens or use your camera's zoom function to capture the surfer's posture and expression.

- **Mind the horizon:** Keep your camera level with the horizon. It's very obvious when a surf photo is crooked because of the clear divide between sea and sky.

Bukit's Best Breakfasts

Start your beach day with a meal that's satiating and delicious. Here are the Bukit Peninsula's best breakfasts (and where to find them).

- **Quinoa Bowl** (The Cashew Tree, page 112): A heaping pile of red quinoa is mixed with spinach and kale cooked in coconut oil and topped with grilled halloumi (cheese), poached eggs, and chopped almonds.

- **Bingin Breakfast Burrito** (Drifter Café and Surf Shop, page 112): A large tortilla stuffed with spiced refried beans, scrambled eggs, paprika-roasted potatoes, guacamole, cheese, and lettuce is served with a side of sour cream and salsa.

- **Supreme Avocado** (He'enalu, page 120): Smashed avocado on steroids: two slices of bread are covered with falafel balls, hummus, avocado, tomato, red onion, and a sprinkle of chili flakes.

- **Smoothie Bowl** (Ayu's Food from the Heart, page 120): A large wooden bowl is filled with blended dragon fruit and topped with seasonal fresh fruit, shredded coconut, seeds, and granola.

Healthy and Vegetarian-Friendly

★ DRIFTER CAFÉ AND SURF SHOP

Jalan Labuan Sait No. 52, Padang Padang; tel. 87777550001; www.driftersurf.com; daily 8am-10pm; 50,000-90,000 Rp

The Drifter Café and Surf Shop embodies the region's health-conscious, surfer lifestyle. At the front of the property, travelers can shop for surfboards, backpacks, clothes, books, surf-themed knick-knacks, wetsuits, and bathing suits. Out back, you can peruse the shop's small art gallery. Their outdoor restaurant serves some of the best coffee in the area, brewed from beans grown in Sumatra. The menu features vegetarian or pescatarian poke bowls, burritos, pastas, and curries.

THE CASHEW TREE

Jalan Pantai Bingin, Bingin; tel. 85953789675; daily 8am-10pm; 60,000-85,000 Rp

The Cashew Tree is a bohemian café and restaurant that is beloved among Bingin regulars for its hearty rice and vegetable bowls, fresh juices, and heaping salads. When in doubt, opt for the signature Soul Bowl with brown rice, many kinds of vegetables, hummus, sunflower seeds, and tahini dressing. The restaurant also hosts daily fitness classes and live musical performances. Shop for reusable straws, water bottles, clothes, and handmade soaps in the café's little boutique.

ACCOMMODATIONS

1,000,000-2,000,000 Rp

PINK COCO

Jalan Labuan Sait, Padang Padang; tel. 361/8957371; www.pnkhotels.com; 1,100,000 Rp

When you walk into Pink Coco, you might feel as though you've stepped onto a Wes Anderson film set. The bubblegum-pink motif (including a pink pool) sets an upbeat, whimsical, and tropical mood. The boutique hotel is within walking distance of Padang Padang Beach and many restaurants along Jalan Labuan Sait. There are 25 rooms, with five different types available. All rooms are very spacious and equipped with Wi-Fi, hot showers, and flat-screen TV. Spend your time at one of the three pools on-site (one is adults-only), the Italian restaurant, or the spa.

1: Kelly's Warung **2:** The Drifter Café and Surf Shop **3:** The Cashew Tree **4:** The Temple Lodge

GRAVITY

Jalan Labuan Sait, Padang Padang; tel. 85847435728; www.gravitybalihotel.com; 1,600,000 Rp

Gravity is an eco-friendly boutique resort that looks as though it was inspired by the white and cobalt architecture of Santorini, Greece. The open-air bathrooms, private balconies, and bright rooms lead to a strong feeling of tranquility. At night, guests can hear the peaceful sounds of nature outside like leaves blowing in the wind, frogs croaking, and birds singing (and on the flip side, crowing roosters at daybreak). Gravity has three pools, a restaurant with a simple but delicious menu, and a spa. Because Gravity is tucked away from the main road, a motorbike or bicycle is essential for getting around. Both fan-only and air-conditioned rooms are available.

★ THE TEMPLE LODGE

Jalan Pantai Bingin, Bingin; tel. 85739011572; www. thetemplelodge.com; 1,700,000 Rp

If it's relaxation you're after, check into The Temple Lodge. The boutique hotel sits atop Bingin's cliffs and overlooks the ocean. None of the 10 rooms are decorated exactly alike, though each incorporates elements of shabby-chic furniture, bright swaths of color, and natural materials like stone and bamboo. The Temple Lodge offers yoga classes each morning (8am-9:30am; 120,000 Rp per class), and most meals are eaten in an open-air communal dining area. Those desiring a bit of romance and privacy can request the Coral Cave Suite, which is carved into the cliff and comes with a spacious, cushioned balcony that overlooks the sea. One of the most unique rooms is the Driftwood Room that is built primarily out of wood found along Bingin's beaches. Rooms come with a fan, private bathrooms with hot showers, and mosquito nets.

Over 2,000,000 Rp

MÛ

Jalan Pantai Bingin, Bingin; tel. 361/8957442; mu-bali.com; 2,400,000 Rp

Mû is a quiet boutique resort with unique bungalows and villas set at the top of Bingin Cliff. Each structure was built out of natural materials that complements Bingin's natural environment. All bungalows come with air-conditioning or fans, hot water showers, and a mosquito net. The Isha and Cliff bungalows offer the best views of the sea. Mû's villas are ideal for groups and feature a private saltwater pool. Yoga classes take place every morning (9:30am-11am; 120,000 Rp per class) at their open-air thatched roof yoga platform. Meals are served family style each night, and the resort only buys enough ingredients to serve those who R.S.V.P.

GETTING THERE

The Pecatu area is about a 45-minute drive from Kuta and a **taxi** costs 150,000 Rp and up. From **Kuta,** take Jalan By Pass Ngurah Rai to Jalan Raya Uluwatu (18 km/11.2 mi). The area is easy to reach via **Jalan Raya Uluwatu** with your own **rental car** or **motorbike.**

GETTING AROUND

Taxis can be a challenge to flag down without help from your hotel. The area is too sparsely populated for Grab and GoJek to be reliable. Some travelers opt to stay somewhere **walking** distance from the main road and the beach. For this, the **Padang Padang area** is best.

By Private Driver or Motorbike

The easiest way to get around is with a **private driver** or **motorbike,** though car **parking** in Bingin is limited. Motorbikes are available at little shops along **Jalan Labaun Sait** or from a **homestay** (50,000-80,000 Rp per day). Rental cars are not easily found in the region. Private drivers are available through your accommodation.

Uluwatu

Uluwatu is the ever-beating heart of Bali's surf scene. Its namesake wave, Uluwatu's or "Ulu's," is what made Bali one of the world's most iconic surf destinations. A single video of it breaking is often cited as the catalyst for mainstream tourism in Bali. And while surfers come for the wave, they linger around even on days with no swell. The stunning sunsets, cold drinks served on the cliffs, relaxed atmosphere, and days that revolve around the weather have created a lifestyle that non-surfers have also come to crave. The definition of Uluwatu embodies its landscape. *Ulu* means land's end and *watu* means stone in Balinese.

Some companies in Uluwatu have tried to capitalize on its reputation and scenic vistas by developing glamorous day clubs and luxury villas. Many travelers make a day trip to listen to the island's hottest DJs bump music to a backdrop of Indo paradise before returning to Kuta or Seminyak.

But if you're looking for Uluwatu's more authentic and adventurous spirit, you'll find that all along the roads weaving the area together. Delightfully constraining Uluwatu's quick development are the chickens that always dart across the road in unpredictable patterns, the eternal protection of Pura Luhur Uluwatu, and a generally friendly, laid-back vibe.

ORIENTATION

"Uluwatu" is often used to describe the entire Bukit Peninsula (aside from Nusa Dua and Jimbaran). Locals seem to believe that if you want people to visit your business, simply tag "Uluwatu" on the end of your name. It creates confusion when venues with "Uluwatu" in their name are based outside of the vaguely agreed upon area. Nonetheless, this small beach neighborhood is easy to navigate and is punctuated by the **Pura Luhur Uluwatu Temple** at the southwestmost point of the peninsula and **Uluwatu Cliffs** slightly to the north. **Pandawa Beach** stands on its own in the south. **Jalan Labuan Sait** connects with **Jalan Raya Uluwatu Pecatu** to form one distinct loop. Uluwatu itself is also in the Pecatu region but is often treated as a separate area.

SIGHTS

★ Uluwatu Temple
(Pura Luhur Uluwatu)

Jalan Raya Uluwatu; daily 8am-7pm; kecak dance performance daily 6pm-7pm; 30,000 Rp temple entrance, 100,000 Rp kecak dance

Pura Luhur Uluwatu is part of the *sad kahyangan jagad,* the six most sacred temples in Bali. It was built in the 11th century out of dark coral blocks and its tiered pagoda stands humbly more than 70 meters (230 feet) above the sea. The temple itself is reserved solely for practicing Hindus, while the temple grounds that overlook the foaming waves below are open to all.

Pura Luhur Uluwatu is inhabited by long-tailed macaque monkeys, who are revered as guardians of the temple. Throughout the temple grounds, you'll see intricate carvings celebrating these cheeky white monkeys, who have a penchant for petty theft and tend to help themselves to tourists' belongings. These master manipulators have learned that they can often give back stolen items in exchange for food. Keep everything secured in a bag or backpack.

Every evening, the temple hosts a traditional *kecak* dance performance. Dancers in elaborate Balinese costumes tell the love story of Ramayana through movement and fire. The sunset backdrop adds to the drama. Arrive 30 minutes to an hour before the show for the best seats.

Uluwatu

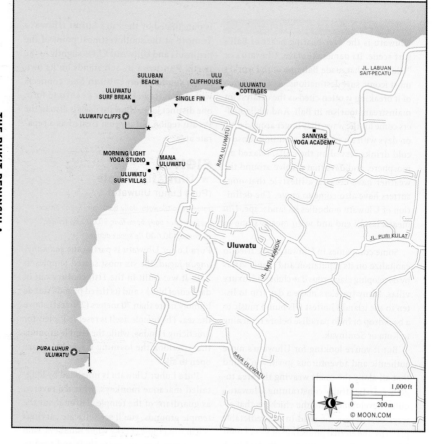

JL. LABUAN
SAIT-PECATU

SULUBAN
BEACH

ULU
CLIFFHOUSE

ULUWATU
COTTAGES

ULUWATU
SURF BREAK

SINGLE FIN

ULUWATU CLIFFS ⚙

RAYA ULUWATU

SANNYAS
YOGA ACADEMY

MORNING LIGHT
YOGA STUDIO

MANA
ULUWATU

ULUWATU
SURF VILLAS

JL. PURI KULAT

Uluwatu

JL. BATU KANDIK

PURA LUHUR
ULUWATU ⚙

RAYA ULUWATU

0   1,000 ft
0   200 m
© MOON.COM

★ Uluwatu Cliffs

Jalan Raya Uluwatu; 5,000 Rp parking fee

Warungs and souvenir shops have wriggled their way onto the cliffs of Uluwatu. Here, you can shop for custom board bags, bathing suits, surf clothes, and souvenirs. Nearly every warung serves similar variations of Balinese dishes, coconuts, and cold beers on their rickety balconies. Tropical-colored murals bring vibrancy to the cliffs and if you look closely, you'll notice they all convey a similar message: Keep Uluwatu clean. These murals were painted by the volunteers at **Project Clean**

Uluwatu, who work tirelessly to maintain the fragile balance of beauty and tourism around the cliffs.

BEACHES AND SURF BREAKS

Suluban Beach
(Pantai Suluban)

Jalan Raya Uluwatu (5,000 Rp motorbike, 10,000 Rp car); access via a path and steep stairs from Uluwatu Cliffs

At the bottom of Uluwatu Cliffs lies Suluban Beach, a sliver of sand wedged between

The Hindu Legend of Rama and the White Monkeys

kecak and fire dance at Uluwatu Temple

If you witness the traditional *kecak* and fire dance at Uluwatu Temple, you'll be told the Sanskrit epic *Ramayana*, a poem made up of nearly 24,000 verses.

Ramayana revolves around a young couple in love and an army of white monkeys. It begins when the protagonist, **Prince Rama**, is separated from his lover, **Princess Sita**. Sita was abducted by **Ravana**, a king with 10 heads and 20 arms who cannot be defeated easily. To overpower Ravana, Rama seeks help from **Sugriva**, the ruler over a kingdom of powerful monkeys. Through this alliance, Rama was able to rescue Sita. This triumph made Rama and Sita the king and queen of Ayodhya. King Rama, as a benevolent ruler, is credited by Hindus as introducing the golden age of mankind.

All throughout Bali, it's possible to see the story of Ramayana played out in many different forms. There are puppet shows, paintings, songs, books, and dances, all dedicated to this legend. While many details are interpreted differently, the theme of love and the message of good overpowering evil are always present.

sharp-edged limestone cliffs. Turquoise water flows in and out of the narrow passageway, and the surrounding caves stoke a sense of adventure in those who visit. A very steep set of stairs leads down to the sand, and if you follow it, you'll come to a cluster of cafés perched on one of the jutting limestone rocks. The setting is too rough to make for great swimming or sunbathing, but it's an ideal spot to watch surfers catch a wave at Uluwatu's, Bali's most famous surf break. Visit during mid- to low tide.

ULUWATU SURF BREAK

Suluban Beach; paddle out from the cave

Though other waves around Bali may be quickly gaining in popularity, they are merely flings in a complicated affair between surfers and the ocean. Uluwatu's wave consistency, ability to work in all tides and swell sizes, and sheer beauty make it marriage material. But don't expect to be the only suitor vying for its attention—the lineup is almost always crowded. It can handle a southwesterly swell of any size and works best with southeasterly winds. Paddle out at Suluban Beach and mind the current when you're paddling back in.

Green Bowl Beach
(Pantai Green Bowl)

Jalan Pantai Green Bowl; 5,000 Rp parking fee (inconsistently enforced); beach access down a steep, slippery staircase

It takes more than 320 steep steps to reach Green Bowl Beach, a remote stretch of sand that has yet to be developed by cafés or homestays. Visit during mid to low tide to enjoy the sand, crystal-clear water, caves, and small temple. Morning, specifically, will have you beating the heat, the tourist crowds, and consequentially, the persistent sarong sellers. Monkeys are present at all hours, though. Who knows when they rest? Pack a pair of reef shoes if you plan to swim or risk kicking a sharp rock as you wade through the water.

GREEN BOWL SURF BREAK
Green Bowl Beach

Green Bowl catches virtually any southwest swell that rolls along the peninsula. It works best up to 2.5 meters (8 feet). It's a fast right with some barrel sections. The challenging paddle alone in a strong current makes it a wave for experienced surfers only. The nearby left looks tempting but is often just a mirage.

Pandawa Beach
(Pantai Pandawa)

Jalan Pantai Pandawa; parking near beach entrance; 5,000 Rp parking fee

Pandawa Beach has a reputation for being more popular among Indonesian vacationers than with foreign tourists. The sandy beach is set against the backdrop of a perfectly vertical cliff with figures of Hindu gods, the five Pandawa brothers, embedded into it. Because of its religious importance, Pandawa Beach is the setting for many Balinese ceremonies and you might see precessions take place along the small beachwalk that's lined with warungs selling coconuts, roasted corn, and *nasi campur* (rice served with a variety of dishes). Outer reefs prevent waves from rolling in, making Pandawa Beach a decent spot for swimming and wading. For a fun souvenir photo, walk up the main road and take a picture standing next to the red Pantai Pandawa sign that overlooks the beach.

OTHER SPORTS AND RECREATION
Yoga
SANNYAS YOGA ACADEMY
Jalan Labuan Sait No. 8; tel. 81236258395; https://sannyasyogaacademy.com; 115,000 Rp per class

Sannyas Yoga Academy offers many different yoga classes throughout the day, including *yin, vinyasa, hatha,* acro yoga, and yoga for surfers. Visitors can also join guided meditations and sound healing sessions. For those wanting an immersive experience, Sannyas Yoga Academy hosts yoga and surf retreats, where yogis stay on-site in one of the academy's spacious, Mediterranean-influenced rooms. The retreats include all meals, a bed, Wi-Fi, yoga and meditation classes, surf lessons, and coconut water. Yoga teacher training is also available.

MORNING LIGHT YOGA STUDIO
Jalan Pantai Suluban; tel. 817555365; www.uluwatusurfvillas.com/yoga; 120,000 Rp per 90-minute class

Stretch to serene views of the ocean at Morning Light Yoga Studio's elevated yoga platform. Every day at 7:30am and 4pm, the yoga studio at Uluwatu Surf Villas offers a 90-minute class that varies depending on the teacher. Regulars seem to love savoring the post-savasna moment by enjoying a cold coconut on the property after class.

FOOD
Indonesian
THE WARUNG AT ALILA VILLAS
Jalan Belimbing Sari; tel. 361/8482166; www.the-warung.com; daily 11am-11pm; 80,000-250,000 Rp

---

1: Uluwatu Temple 2: monkeys at Uluwatu Temple 3: Pandawa Beach 4: yoga in Uluwatu

Hidden away from Uluwatu's main stretch, The Warung serves perfectly spiced Indonesian dishes in a casual atmosphere. Guests can order a la carte, but it's recommended to get the set menu that features a diverse spread of dishes made from locally sourced ingredients. Their *sambal* (chili sauce) sampling platter is also a hit among those who can handle the heat. If weather permits, choose a seat at one of their futuristic, cliffside table setups.

★ ROOSTERFISH

Jalan Pantai Pandawa; tel. 361/2003588; www. roosterfishbeachclub.com; daily 10am-8pm; 50,000-120,000 Rp

Located at the edge of Pandawa Beach, Roosterfish is a playful family-friendly restaurant and beach club with a seaside infinity pool that all who visit can access (free towel rental available). The menu features pizza, salads, ceviche, and fragrant Balinese staples. *Es campur* (shaved ice with sweet toppings) makes for a refreshing beachside snack and is large enough to share among friends. Cocktails and main dishes are served in generous portions, and the plush beach towels are oversized as well.

International
HE'ENALU CAFE AND RESTO

Jalan Raya Uluwatu No. 70X, South Kuta; tel. 81529101091; www.heenalu-bali.weebly.com; daily 9am-9pm; 35,000-60,000 Rp

He'enalu Café and Resto brings a little piece of the Pacific islands to Bali with its poke bowls and Hawaiian fried rice. Wraps, sandwiches, and pasta are also on offer. The vibe is casual and beachy inside the nautical-themed café, where many patrons walk in sporting wet hair from a recent dip in the sea.

MANA ULUWATU

Jalan Pantai Suluban; tel. 817555421 www. uluwatusurfvillas.com; daily 7am-10pm; 50,000-120,000 Rp

Mana Uluwatu is a new open-air restaurant that overlooks nearby bungalows and the

beach. The decor is surfer chic with smooth wooden furniture and surfboards mounted against the walls. Don't be afraid to try one of the interesting Latin-Asian fusion dishes on the menu, like jackfruit and cheese enchiladas, Balinese chorizo, or the brûlée trio made with matcha, ginger, and lemongrass.

Healthy and Vegetarian-Friendly
AYU'S FOOD FROM THE HEART

Jalan Raya Uluwatu; tel. 82237730163; daily 7am-5pm; 40,000-90,000 Rp

Ayu's Food from the Heart is the Bukit Peninsula's most cheerful café. The colorful furniture, motivational quotes hung all over the walls, and smiling staff make all who enter feel welcome. Come for breakfast to enjoy their large and delicious smoothie bowls. If you're in the mood for something warm, request the *gado-gado* (steamed vegetables with peanut sauce).

BARS AND NIGHTLIFE
★ SINGLE FIN

Jalan Mamo; tel. 361/769941; www.singlefinbali. com; Mon.-Tues. and Thurs.-Fri. 10am-10pm; Weds. 10am-midnight, Sun. 10am-1am; 60,000-170,000 Rp

Single Fin is the de facto icon for surf culture on the Bukit Peninsula. Surfers cluster on the balcony area to watch the waves roll through while those who are not-so-surf-obsessed congregate inside. When live music is playing, everyone mingles. Burgers and pizza are on the menu. The cucumber fling cocktail is equal parts hydrating and buzz-inducing—the right combo after a long day spent in the sun.

ULU CLIFFHOUSE

Jalan Labuan Sait No. 315; tel. 81338812502; www. uluccliffhouse.com; Sun.-Thurs. 11am-10pm, Fri.-Sat. 11am-midnight; no cover, minimum 1,000,000 daybed rental

Ulu Cliffhouse is a chic luxury day club that attracts a less Instagram-obsessed crowd than some of the other day clubs around. The menu

---

1: Single Fin 2: Renaissance Bali

of seafood, snacks, and grilled meat dishes is above par. Check the event page on the club website and plan a visit around the music calendar.

★ ONEEIGHTY°

Jalan Pura Goa Lempeh; tel. 361/8470700; www. oneeightybali.com; daily noon-10pm; 400,000 Rp general admission (350,000 Rp redeemable for food and drinks), 600,000 Rp VIP entrance (550,000 Rp redeemable for food and drinks)

Oneeighty° became famous for its glass-bottom pool, which juts off the edge of a cliff, making it one of the most unique pools in Bali. Expect friendly and efficient service. The drinks menu has a long list of wines and cocktails, while their food menu features seafood staples like ceviche and fish tacos. Because this club is becoming increasingly popular, reservations are essential. The VIP package is worth getting solely for the seating area.

ACCOMMODATIONS
Under 2,000,000 Rp
ULUWATU COTTAGES

Jalan Labaun Sait; tel. 361/8498715; www. uluwatucottages.com; 1,200,000-2,000,000 Rp

Uluwatu Cottages welcome guests with cozy, spacious, and clean rooms that have prime views of the ocean below. The property's gardens are well-kept and there is ample space to lounge around the infinity pool. Padang Padang beach and the warung area of Uluwatu are within walking distance from the cottages. If you're a light sleeper who likes to turn in early, note that the neighboring Ulu Cliffhouse often plays loud music late into the night.

★ RENAISSANCE BALI

Jalan Pantai Balangan 1 No. 1; tel. 361/2003588; www.marriott.com; 2,000,000-4,500,000 Rp

A few minutes inland from the coast, Renaissance Bali is a modern luxury resort with a large infinity pool and lounge area, spa, gym, ceramics studio, and multiple restaurants. There are more than 10 room types to choose from, ranging from double-occupancy to a three-bedroom villa. For the best value, choose the deluxe ocean room. It features a giant bathtub behind a massive window that overlooks the ocean. Pace yourself during breakfast (included), which has earned its well-deserved reputation of being the best buffet around. The Renaissance Bali runs a free shuttle service from the hotel to Pandawa Beach multiple times per day.

Over 2,000,000 Rp
★ ULUWATU SURF VILLAS

Jalan Pantai Suluban; tel. 817555365; www. uluwatusurfvillas.com; 2,000,000 Rp

Uluwatu Surf Villas embodies the healthy, laid-back, surfer lifestyle that so many travelers look for when they venture to Uluwatu. Rustic luxury villas cater to groups and families, while the bungalows are ideal for couples. The aesthetic of each room is simple and clean, blending Balinese fabrics with wood decor. Some rooms open out to the ocean or a pool. The property is peaceful and quiet, set on the edge of Uluwatu Cliffs. Uluwatu Surf Villas also hosts regular yoga classes and is walking distance from the beach.

BULGARI RESORT

Jalan Goa Lempeh; tel. 361/8471000; www. bulgarihotels.com; 15,000,000 Rp

Bulgari Resort is the pinnacle of luxury in Uluwatu. Every detail is right, and on the rare occasion that it isn't, a butler is available 24 hours to assist. The architecture of each of the 55 one-bedroom villas blends traditional Balinese thatch roofing and fabric patterns with Italian simplicity. Each of the villas has a private pool, open-air lounge area, and a plush, pillow-top bed. There are also six larger villas available for groups.

GETTING THERE

Uluwatu is about an hour away from **Ngurah Rai International Airport,** though the journey can be longer with traffic. **Taxis** cost 200,000 Rp and up each way between the airport and Uluwatu. Uluwatu is easily accessed by driving down Jalan Bypass Ngurah Rai to

The Perfect Beach For...

- Families: **Tanjung Benoa** (page 125)
- Lovers: **Suluban** (page 116)
- Adventurers: **Green Bowl** (page 118)
- Surfers: **Padang Padang** (page 106)
- Easy access: **Jimbaran** (page 96)
- Untouched beauty: **Balangan** (page 98)
- Sunset: **Bingin** (page 106)

Jalan Raya Uluwatu with your own **rental car** or **motorbike,** or with a private driver (500,000-700,000 Rp per day).

GETTING AROUND

A **motorbike** or **rental car** is by far the best way to get around Uluwatu.

It's often more convenient and economical to **hire a driver** for a few hours or for the day if you plan on seeing a handful of locations within the area, rather than worrying about finding multiple rides. **Ketut and Nico,** a team of local drivers (tel. 81239109620; www.uluwatubalidriver.com), offer day trips from 500,000 Rp per day and are best contacted via WhatsApp.

The day clubs and more upscale resorts in the area are notorious for having taxi monopolies where requesting a cab from the day club or resort can cost 5-10 times the usual fare in Bali. Instead, ask the driver who took you to the venue to return at a specific time. You may have to walk away from the venue to be picked up. The area also is not densely populated enough for Grab or GoJek to be reliable, so don't count on them as your plan A.

Nusa Dua and Tanjung Benoa

Nusa Dua means "Two Islands" in Balinese. And though they are not technically separate freestanding islands, Nusa Dua often seems as though it's an ocean away from Bali's mainland. Past its guarded gates and along its beaches are resorts, each with hundreds of rooms, luxury spas, and upscale restaurants. The area developed quickly in the 1970s to lure tourists away from their regular stays, as rumors of beautiful Southeast Asian beaches spread around the globe.

Today, Nusa Dua guarantees the simple yet luxurious beach-style holiday that so many travelers crave. Despite its somewhat sterile reputation, the resorts of Nusa Dua make a great effort to introduce guests to Balinese dance, live music, and cultural events.

To the north of Nusa Dua, Tanjung Benoa is a resort town with hotels dotted along a long, sandy beach. As you move away from Nusa Dua toward the tip of the peninsula, the town gets gradually less developed. High-adrenaline watersports activities are offered all along the shoreline to meet the demand of Tanjung Benoa's high-energy kids, teenagers, and other thrill-seekers. Punctuating the edge of Tanjung Benoa are seaweed farms, as well as a mosque, Chinese temple, and Hindu temple, creating an overall feeling of inclusiveness.

ORIENTATION

In the southern end of Nusa Dua, you'll find **Geger Beach, Pura Gegar,** and **Bali National Golf Club.** Along the coastline moving north is **Waterblow,** with the **Pasifika Museum** directly inland. **Nusa Dua** then merges with **Tanjung Benoa,** with mangroves on its inland edge and **Tanjung Benoa beach** on the sea.

SIGHTS

★ Pasifika Museum

BTDC Area Block P., Nusa Dua; tel. 361/774935; www. museum-pasifika.com; daily 10am-6pm; 100,000 Rp adult, free for children under 10

Travel around Asia Pacific through the eyes of international artists at the Pasifika Museum. More than 400 paintings, 200 sculptures, and a small collection of weavings are on exhibit throughout the museum's geographically themed 11 rooms. Occasionally, there are events and talks happening at the museum, but they are rarely advertised on the website. Call ahead to find out if there is anything scheduled while you're in Nusa Dua. This is one of the most underrated sights in the area, so you can view works by Romualdo Locatelli, Willem Gerard Hofker, Henri Matisse, and controversial Paul Gauguin without a crowd.

Geger Temple
(Pura Geger)

Jalan Pura Puget; walk from Geger Beach; 5,000 Rp parking and entrance fee

Overlooking Gegar Beach atop limestone cliffs, Pura Geger is a popular temple among locals, though it's less so with tourists. Visit to see intricate stonework and admire its elaborate gates. The temple itself is usually closed when ceremonies are not taking place, but it's still worth walking around outside.

Water Blow

Jalan Pantai Mengiat

Admire the power of the sea at Water Blow, a natural feature where waves crash into jagged limestone and spray saltwater high into the sky. For the most impressive explosions, visit when the wind is blowing and the tide is high. A dedicated walkway and lookout area lead out to the Water Blow. Simply take a seat, cover your camera to protect it from the splash, and enjoy.

Caow Eng Bio Chinese Temple

Jalan Seagara Lor, Tanjung Benoa; 6am-9pm daily; free, donation requested

Caow Eng Bio is a Chinese Taoist temple that is saturated with red, yellow, and green splashes of color. It was built by Chinese merchants who stopped at Tanjung Benoa on their trading routes. There are many deities represented within the temple area, all unique and ornate.

Dalem Ning Lan Taman Beji Temple
(Pura Dalem Ning Lan Taman Beji)

Jalan Seagara Lor, Tanjung Benoa; open only for ceremonies; free

Just a few steps away from the Chinese temple and Tanjuna Benoa's mosque is the Pura Dalem Ning Lan Taman Beji Hindu temple. The temple is made from white coral brick and accented with golden paint. The temple area itself is reserved primarily for practicing Hindus, thought the elaborate outside gates make it a worthy short stop.

BEACHES AND SURF BREAKS

Geger Beach
(Pantai Geger)

Jalan Nusa Dua Seletan, Nusa Dua; 3,000 Rp admission

Geger Beach is a quiet stretch of coastline that's backed by large resorts. The inland side of the beach is lined with water-sports vendors and massage tables, while the sand is lined with lounge chairs. Visit during mid to high tide to snorkel and swim over the reef.

NUSA DUA SURF BREAK

Offshore Nusa Dua, 100,000-200,000 Rp boat ride

The Nusa Dua surf break is a long right-hander about 500 meters (1,640 feet) offshore. It's one of Bali's swell magnets that works well, especially during the wet season. Currents can be quite strong during larger swells, so it's best for intermediate surfers and up. Beginner surfers shouldn't surf here without an instructor or a guide. Look for southerly swells and west-northwest winds in the forecast for the best experience. Though paddling out is possible for some, it's worth splurging on a boat ride out.

SRI LANKA SURF BREAK
Nusa Dua; paddle out in front of Club Med
Though it's rarely working well, Sri Lanka is a fast, right-hand barrel that's a favorite among locals. It's inconsistent and needs a large south-southwest swell to truly show its potential. The crowds, shallow reef, and quick take off make it a wave for more experienced surfers only.

Mengiat Beach
(Pantai Mengiat)
Jalan Pantai Mengiat, Nusa Dua
Calm and quiet, Mengiat Beach is one of the best places in Bali to watch the sunrise. The spacious beach hosts a lifeguard station with lifeguards who often close off any areas with dangerous currents, making it an ideal spot for families and swimmers. While resorts

have dominated part of the beach with their uniform lines of lounge chairs and raked sand, there is plenty of public space to run around as well. This is also called Nusa Dua Beach.

★ Tanjung Benoa Beach
(Pantai Tanjung Benoa)
Tanjung Benoa
Tanjung Benoa Beach is a long stretch of soft sand that extends along the Tanjung Benoa peninsula. Stalls selling water sports activities, restaurants, and hotels line its interior. If you're the type of beachgoer who likes to do an adrenaline activity one minute and nap in the shade the next, Tanjung Benoa Beach provides the ideal balance of action and relaxation.

WATER SPORTS
Diving and Snorkeling
LA MANTA
Jalan Nusa Dua, Nusa Dua; tel. 81238161828; www.lamantadivingbali.com; snorkel tour 1,000,000-1,300,000 Rp, scuba 2 tank dive 1,800,000-2,300,000 Rp, open water course 7,500,000 Rp
La Manta is a PADI-certified dive center that organizes dive courses and dive trips to Tulamben, Amed, Padang Bai, Candidasa, and Nusa Penida. All fun dives and courses include pickup and drop-off at your hotel in a private

parasailing at Tanjung Benoa Beach

car or van, a full set of rental equipment, snacks and lunch, and a knowledgeable guide.

BALI SCUBA MASTERS

Jalan Pratama No. 85, Tanjung Benoa; tel. 361/777156; www.baliscubamasters.com; open water certification 5,800,000 Rp, 2-tank dive 1,000,000-1,700,000 Rp

Bali Scuba Masters is a 5-star PADI dive center with a base in Tanjun Benoa. Bali Scuba Masters offers all PADI courses, ranging from Discover Scuba Diving to PADI divemaster certification levels, as well as all major specialty courses. Join a course, day trip, or multiday scuba safari to well-known dive sites like Nusa Penida, Amed, Tulamben, and Menjangan Island. Trips to more underrated and less-known sites like Nusa Dua, Seraya, Puri Jati, and Secret Bay are also available.

Wakeboarding
BALI WAKE PARK

Jalan Pelabuhan Benoa No. 7X; tel. 361/8468866; www.baliwakepark.com; Mon.-Thurs. 10am-6pm, Fri.-Sat. 10am-9pm; 700,000 Rp per day for cable park, 500,000 Rp per day for Aqua Land

Adrenaline junkies will love wakeboarding and water-skiing at Bali Wake Park, a 5-hectare (12-acre) lake with a cable system that's capable of pulling up to eight riders at a time. Beginners can simply do loops while more experienced riders can make use of the many obstacles and jib areas. New riders can learn to ride with the help of a coach. Bali Wake Park also hosts Aqualand, an inflatable park perfect for jumping, sliding, bouncing, and running around. If getting catapulted into the air is on your bucket list, plop yourself on the edge of the blob—an inflatable bubble—and have someone jump onto the other side.

OTHER SPORTS AND RECREATION
Spas
SEKAR JAGAT SPA

Jalan Bypass Ngurah Rai No. 96; tel. 361/770210; www.balinesespa.com; daily 9:30am-10pm; 650,000 for 2-hour Balinese massage

Get pampered at Sekar Jagat Spa, a traditional Balinese spa with more than 10 rooms set on a large, lush property. Sekar Jagat Spa is one of the only spas with charm in an area dense with impersonal resort chains. Choose between a hot stone massage, classic Balinese massage, couples' massage, or a package experience that features a massage, scrub, and flower bath. Semi-outdoor and air-conditioned rooms are available. Treatments include free pickup and drop-off from any neighboring towns, as well as the airport.

ZAHRA SPA

Jalan Nusa Dua No.1; tel. 81936018313; www.zahraspa.com; daily 9am-10pm; 180,000 Rp for 1-hour Balinese massage, 350,000 Rp for 2-hour Balinese massage

If you're looking for a great-value massage that focuses heavily on technique, Zahra Spa is a top pick. The spa itself is bright, clean, and spacious. Choose package deals or mix and match treatments. Families can enjoy the spa experience together thanks to a kids' treatment package that includes hair braiding, nail painting, and a body massage. Zahra Spa also offers free transport within Nusa Dua and surrounds—a bargain considering the prices.

Golf
BALI NATIONAL GOLF CLUB

Kawasan Wisata; tel. 361/771791; www.balinational. com; daily 6:30am-6:30pm; 1,800,000 Rp for 18 rounds, 1,300,000 Rp for 9 rounds, 900,000-1,300,000 late in the day (2pm-6:30pm)

Bali National Golf Club has a par 71 tournament 18-hole course that stretches along a sandy beach. Many areas feature views of Mount Agung as an added highlight. The grass is well-maintained and weaves through multiple types of natural terrain.

ENTERTAINMENT AND EVENTS
NUSA DUA THEATRE

BTDC Complex; tel. 361/770197; www.devdanshow. com; hours and price depend on show, Devdan show

Fun in the Water

Don't spend all your time on the sand, because there's plenty to do in the sea. All along Nusa Dua's beaches, you'll see vendors selling water-sports activities. Bargain for a package deal if you are planning to do more than one activity with the same vendor.

- **Stand-Up Paddling:** Explore the calm waters within the reef from a stand-up paddleboard. Board and paddle rental cost 80,000-100,000 Rp per hour.

- **Jet Skiing:** Adrenaline junkies will love speeding across the sea's surface. Jet Ski rentals cost 250,000 Rp and up per 15 minutes.

- **Parasailing:** Fly high above the water with a parachute and harness. The price is from 100,000 Rp per 5 minutes.

- **Jet packing/Jetovator/Flyboard:** Release your inner superhero! Get propelled into the air with a water jet pack. Price: 1,000,000 Rp per 15 minutes.

- **Banana Boat/Donut:** Hold on tight and bounce behind a boat while riding an inflatable. The cost is from 100,000 Rp per 15 minutes.

- **Snorkeling:** See the creatures that live just off the ocean surface. Snorkel set rental costs 50,000-100,000 per hour.

SAFETY TIPS

All water sports come with risks, but there are ways you can help stay safe:

- Do not swim or snorkel near Jet Ski areas. Many Jet Skis are driven by first-timers who don't understand that the ski won't stop simply because they let go of the throttle.

- Avoid parasailing if there is heavy boat traffic.

- Always wear a personal flotation device.

- The "flying fish" style of inner tubes have a poor safety record. Opt for the classic donut or banana-style inflatable ride instead.

300,000-500,000 Rp adults and 260,000-422,000 Rp children

Every Monday, Wednesday, Friday, and Saturday from 7:30pm-9pm, the Nusa Dua Theatre hosts the Devdan show. This colorful performance uses traditional Indonesian and contemporary dance, elaborate costumes, acrobatics, and special effects to tell the story of two children who discover something extraordinary. What is it? You'll have to see for yourself. Discounts are available for groups and those booking directly through the website.

FOOD
Seafood
SOLEIL

Jalan Raya Nusa Dua Selatan, Mulia; tel. 361/3017777; www.themulia.com; daily 11am-11pm; 80,000-425,000 Rp

Soleil is a beachfront restaurant with a long menu serving fine Asian and Mediterranean dishes. A highlight is the variety of different pastas. Their degustation options are carefully crafted and revolve around locally caught fish. Soleil is famous for its seafood and grilled meat brunch that's served each Sunday 11am-3pm. Otherwise, go for dinner.

International
TAVERN DE BALI SPORT BAR

BTDC Main Gate, Nusa Dua; tel. 361/4771469; www.
taverndebalirestaurant.com; daily 10am-10pm;
50,000-200,000 Rp

This humble, rustic tavern offers scuffed tables in a polished neighborhood. The laid-back sports bar serves a selection of cold beers and cocktails alongside Asian, Mexican, and European dishes. Stick to the Asian meals and take advantage of the tavern's free pickup and drop-off service within the Nusa Dua area.

MR. BOB BEACHFRONT BAR AND GRILL

Jalan Pratama, Tanjung Benoa; tel. 81238052366;
www.mrbobbarandgrill.com; daily noon-11pm;
60,000-180,000 Rp

Mr. Bob Beachfront Bar and Grill has brought a backyard barbecue vibe to a sandy beach of Tanjung Benoa. Travelers tend to ask Mr. Bob for one meal: 500 g (1 lb) of charcoal grilled ribs with a splash of sweet chili sauce (extra!). Eat with your hands (it's Bali!) and worry about the mess later. Free transport back to nearby hotels is provided upon request.

Healthy and Vegetarian-Friendly
VERDANT ORGANIC KITCHEN

BTDC Gate C; tel. 81239652693; daily 9am-10pm;
50,000-120,000 Rp

Verdant Organic Kitchen understands the type of traveler who sleeps through their hotel breakfast or simply wants pancakes for lunch. After all, breakfast is served until 5pm daily in this quiet, casual café. Dishes are fresh, healthy, and organic. If you are vegan or have dietary restrictions, you will be well cared for and you can be confident that they understand what you're requesting.

ACCOMMODATIONS
Under 1,000,000 Rp
KUBU GARDEN

Jalan Pratama; tel. 361/8498630; www.kubugarden.
com; 500,000 Rp

Kubu Garden is a cozy bed-and-breakfast run by friendly owners who are known to invite guests for dinner. They go out of their way to make guests feel comfortable and at home in an area rife with mega-resorts. The rooms have very soft beds and white and dark wood decor, and they are placed privately around a pool and garden area. The property is just a short walk from the main road and Tanjung Benoa Beach.

Over 2,000,000 Rp
INAYA PUTRI BALI

Kawasan Wisata; tel. 361/2002900; https://
inayaputribali.com; 2,500,000 Rp

Inaya Putri Bali offers 455 rooms and villas across its spacious and well-appointed private resort neighborhood. There are many accommodation types to choose from that cater to families, couples, and those looking for stays with poolside access or ocean views. This resort has a multitude of dining options and pool areas to spend time at, and many travelers use their time at Inaya Putri Bali as a semi-staycation.

SAMABE BALI

Jalan Pura Barong-Barong; tel. 361/8468633; www.
samabe.com; 7,600,000 Rp

Samabe Bali has mastered the combination of contemporary luxury and Balinese traditional decor. The 5-star resort offers 81 villas and suites along a sandy shoreline. Staff are attentive, friendly, and available thanks to a 24/7 butler service. The excellent meals served at Samabe Bali make the pricey all-inclusive package worth the splurge. One-bedroom suites and two-bedroom villas are available, all with pool or ocean views.

INFORMATION AND SERVICES
Tourist Information

Maps and tourist information is best sought through your accommodation or hotel. Unlike many of Bali's tourist-heavy areas, stalls of unofficial tour organizers are sparse in Nusa Dua and Tanjung Benoa.

Money

Multiple ATMs are found at Hardy's Nusa Dua (Jalan Nusa Dua).

Health and Medicine

BIMC SILOAM HOSPITAL NUSA DUA

Jalan Bypass Ngurah Rai No. 100X; tel. 361/2633303; www.bimcbali.com; 24 hours

BIMC Siloam Nusa Dua is one of Bali's most modern hospitals with an ambulance service, emergency center, intensive care unit, dental center, and dialysis center. The hospital is also equipped to handle emergency evacuation and repatriation. In a non-emergency situation, call ahead to make an appointment to avoid potentially long wait times. BIMC Siolam Hospital does not have an emergency hyperbaric chamber.

GETTING THERE

Reaching Nusa Dua and Tanjung Benoa is easy thanks to the **Bali Mandara Toll Road** (car 11,000 Rp, motorbike 4.5,000 Rp) that connects **Ngurah Rai International Airport** to **Sanur** and Nusa Dua. The area is about 40 minutes from **Kuta,** but travel time is heavily dependent on traffic. Budget at least 30 minutes extra if you must be somewhere at a specific time. It's not necessary to drive yourself in Nusa Dua, as everything is accessible via shuttle bus, taxi, or on foot. However, nearly all the larger resorts do have **parking.**

By Taxi or Private Driver

You can reach Nusa Dua from the **international airport** by **taxi** or **private driver** (15 km/9.3 mi, 30 minutes; 80,000-100,000 Rp). For taxi service, use the **Bluebird** app. Private drivers can be arranged through your accommodation. Lanus Nyoman, a reputable driver, is based in Nusa Dua and offers rides all throughout the region for short trips or 500,000 Rp per day (lanus. tour@gmail.com; tel. 8123762403).

By Bus

The **Kura-Kura bus** (kura2bus.com) also connects Nusa Dua to **Kuta** (20,000 Rp each way, single and multiday passes available; children under 2 free). It stops at Ayodya Resort Bali, Grand Hyatt Bali, Mercure Nusa Dua, and The Bale in Nusa Dua.

GETTING AROUND

Nusa Dua is very **walkable,** and many restaurants, hotels, and even spas will provide **free transport** within the area for customers. To venture around Nusa Dua and all the way up to Tanung Benoa, take the **free shuttle bus** that runs hourly from 9am-10pm daily. The shuttle bus stops at most major hotels and the **Bali Collection shopping center.** Contact a **private driver** like Lanus Nyoman (lanus.tour@gmail.com; tel. 8123762403) for custom trips around Nusa Dua.

Denpasar and Sanur

Though Denpasar's city center and the small

town of Sanur are both in the same city limits, these two areas are like yin and yang. Denpasar is rife with the buzz of motorbikes and the clashing scents of exhaust fumes and wet markets with produce, raw meat, and fish. Meanwhile, Sanur is tranquil and marked by the feeling of saltwater in the air.

Denpasar is Bali's business capital and home to nearly one fourth of the island's population. Concrete buildings with bold storefront signs have slowly spread out from the city center, turning what once were open rice paddies into small slivers of green. The word Denpasar itself means "market," of which there are plenty. In between work, prayer, shopping, and commuting, there is little time for leisure. Unfortunately,

Highlights

Look for ★ to find recommended sights, activities, dining, and lodging.

★ **Puputan Square:** Denpasar's largest park is always busy with sports, activities, and events (page 138).

★ **Barja Sandhi Monument:** This intricate statue stands as a tribute to Bali's tragic history (page 140).

★ **Kumbasari Market:** Artwork and items crafted all around the island are up for sale in this lively market (page 141).

★ **Jalan Sulawesi:** On a long road, you'll find rows and rows of intricate textiles (page 141).

★ **Big Garden Corner:** This peaceful sculpture garden has plenty of places to sit and enjoy the scenery (page 144).

★ **Sanur Beach:** Shops, restaurants, and hotels line the paved pathway of this seemingly endless ribbon of off-white sand (page 147).

★ **Rip Curl School of Surf:** Learn to surf, kite-surf, or stand-up paddleboard at Sanur's hub for ocean sports (page 147).

Top Restaurants

★ **Bodhi Leaf Eatery:** Enjoy veggie bowls, soups, and mountains of noodles in this bohemian all-vegan café (page 142).

★ **Three Monkeys:** Reservations are essential at this open-air restaurant known for its grazing plates and homemade pastas (page 154).

★ **The Glass House:** The best breakfast spot in town offers warm pastries and hot coffee inside a bright restaurant with antique decor (page 154).

★ **Soul on the Beach:** This trendy bistro serves healthy smoothie bowls and Mediterranean fare on Sanur's shoreline (page 155).

Denpasar is largely ignored by travelers, as most people walk out of the airport and onto a nearby beach. If you're one to stray from the main sites, Denpasar will reward you with cultural performances, museums rich in information, and a unique insight into Bali's take on a metropolis.

In Sanur, life moves at a slow pace. Most of this beach town is made up of modest homes turned into guesthouses, warungs, fine dining restaurants, spas, and shops. It's easy to spend a day rotating from the sea to a beachside massage table, with great dining only a short distance away. To the adrenaline addicted, Sanur has been nicknamed "Snore" and to this we say, "So what?" Sleeping under a shady tree on the beach is the ultimate form of relaxation, after all.

ORIENTATION

Denpasar is the sprawling city north of the **Bukit Peninsula,** directly east of Kuta and encompassing the beach town of Sanur. Sanur hosts the main beach of the city, **Pantai Sanur,** and is better suited for tourists. Roads weave like a labyrinth around the region with the **Bajra Sandhi Monument** marking one of central areas of Denpasar, 3.5 km (about 2 miles) inland from **Museum Le Mayeur** in Sanur. Near the **Kumbasari Market** and the

Bali Museum, found at Denpasar's northern end, you'll find the city's main sights. **Jalan By Pass Ngurah Rai** connects Kuta and the **international airport** to Denpasar and Sanur.

PLANNING YOUR TIME

Denpasar can be visited on a day trip, while you'll want to spend a little more time—at least two days—enjoying Sanur. Most of the best sights in Denpasar are centered around **Renon,** a local residential area with prominent government buildings. Compared to those in its neighboring beach towns, the hotels in Denpasar are lackluster. You'll find better quality and value if you head east to sleep in Sanur. Accommodations found around Sanur's main road, **Jalan Danau Tamblingan,** are ideal as bases for the whole region, as they are close to shops, restaurants, bars, the beach, and close enough to nearby Denpasar.

The region itself is easy to get around by **taxi, bus,** *ojek,* and **bicycle.** The main areas like Renon and **Jalan Gajah Mada** in Denpasar as well as Jalan Danau Tamblingan and the **beach boardwalk** in Sanur are easily **walkable.** Traffic in Denpasar can be chaotic and choked up, so leave plenty of time in between activities to get to and from each

---

Previous: *Jukung* on Sanur Beach; Barja Sandhi Monument; Sanur Beach.

Denpasar and Sanur

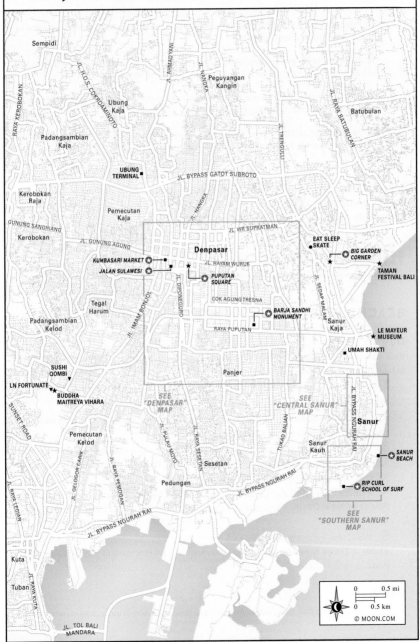

Sempidi

JL. H.O.S. COKROAMINOTO

JL. AHMAD YANI

JL. NANGKA

Peguyangan
Kangin

JL. RAYA BATUBULAN

Batubulan

RAYA KEROBOKAN

Ubung
Kaja

Padangsambian
Kaja

JL. TRENGGULI

Kerobokan
Raja

**UBUNG
TERMINAL**

JL. BYPASS GATOT SUBROTO

Pemecutan
Kaja

JL. NANGKA

JL. WR SUPRATMAN

GUNUNG SANGHIANG

Kerobokan

JL. GUNUNG AGUNG

Denpasar

**EAT SLEEP
SKATE**

**BIG GARDEN
CORNER**

KUMBASARI MARKET

JL. HAYAM WURUK

JALAN SULAWESI

**PUPUTAN
SQUARE**

JL. DIPONEGORO

JL. IMAM BONJOL

**TAMAN
FESTIVAL BALI**

JL. SEDAP MALAM

Tegal
Harum

COK AGUNG TRESNA

**BARJA SANDHI
MONUMENT**

Padangsambian
Kelod

RAYA PUPUTAN

Sanur
Kaja

**LE MAYEUR
MUSEUM**

UMAH SHAKTI

**SUSHI
QOMBI**

Panjer

LN FORTUNATE

**BUDDHA
MAITREYA VIHARA**

*SEE
"DENPASAR"
MAP*

*SEE
"CENTRAL SANUR"
MAP*

JL. BYPASS NGURAH RAI

Sanur

SUNSET ROAD

Pemecutan
Kelod

JL. PULAU MOTO

JL. RAYA SESETAN

TUKAD BALIAN

Sanur
Kauh

**SANUR
BEACH**

JL. GELOGOR CARIK

JL. RAYA PEMOGAN

Sesetan

**RIP CURL
SCHOOL OF SURF**

JL. RAYA LEGIAN

Pedungan

JL. BYPASS NGURAH RAI

*SEE
"SOUTHERN SANUR"
MAP*

Kuta

JL. RAYA KUTA

Tuban

JL. TOL BALI
MANDARA

0   0.5 mi

0   0.5 km

© MOON.COM

Top Accommodations

★ **Punyan Poh Bali Villas:** Live like a local in one of the clean and simple villas located in Denpasar's residential area (page 142).

★ **Artotel:** Sleep in a contemporary hotel next to the beach, where everything from the architecture to the paintings on the walls is inspired by local artists (page 156).

★ **Kejora Suites:** Each room is tastefully decorated with handcrafted wooden furniture in this luxury retreat with an infinity pool (page 156).

★ **Tandjung Sari:** One of the oldest hotels in Sanur, this beachside property has held on to the charm that made it famous in the first place (page 156).

place. The Denpasar workforce tends to clock in at 9 am and out at 5 pm; traffic congests accordingly. Plan your outdoor activities in the early morning or in the evening to **beat the heat and** leave the indoor experiences for midday.

Itinerary Ideas

BEACHSIDE BLISS IN SANUR

Day 1

Pack your swimsuit, sunglasses, hat, sunscreen, yoga leggings or shorts, water bottle, and towel to take advantage of a beach day.

1 Enjoy breakfast at **Genius Café,** located on the southern end of Sanur directly on Sanur beach.

2 After breakfast, walk to the **Rip Curl School of Surf** and spend the morning stand-up paddling or learning to surf, wakeboard, kitesurf, or windsurf.

3 Walk or rent a bicycle and continue north along Jalan Kusuma Sari for a scrumptious lunch at **Soul on the Beach.** If you're feeling parched, there are plenty of warungs selling ice-cold coconuts that are perfect for sipping in the sand.

4 Venture back south along Jalan Kusuma Sari and take an afternoon yoga class at the **Power of Now Oasis,** where you can stretch and *savasana* inside a large bamboo yoga *shala.*

5 Walk, taxi, cycle, or motorbike back to your hotel for a shower and freshen up. Reserve a table at **Three Monkeys** to end your day with a glass of wine and plate of homemade pasta.

Day 2

1 Today, pack a hat, sunglasses, sunscreen, sandals, book or Kindle, and sarong. Walk,

Itinerary Ideas

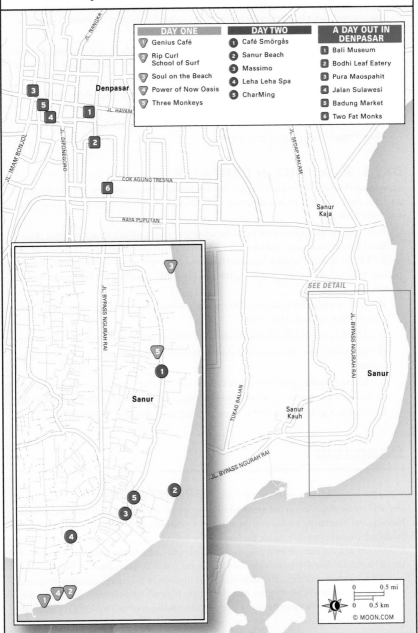

DAY ONE
1. Genius Café
2. Rip Curl School of Surf
3. Soul on the Beach
4. Power of Now Oasis
5. Three Monkeys

DAY TWO
1. Café Smörgås
2. Sanur Beach
3. Massimo
4. Leha Leha Spa
5. CharMing

A DAY OUT IN DENPASAR
1. Bali Museum
2. Bodhi Leaf Eatery
3. Pura Maospahit
4. Jalan Sulawesi
5. Badung Market
6. Two Fat Monks

© MOON.COM

taxi, or motorbike to **Café Smörgås** for breakfast and order whatever your barista recommends.

2   Walk from the café to **Sanur Beach.** Spend the morning forming a track in the sand that connects your lounge chair or towel to the water. For shade, park yourself under the canopy of a banyan tree.

3   Hungry yet? Walk to **Massimo** for an Italian meal where you're sure not to be rushed out of your table. The location on Jalan Danau Tamblingan is prime for people watching.

4   As an afternoon activity, walk or taxi to **Leha Leha Spa** for a well-deserved pampering treatment—the longer, the better.

5   Watch the sunset before dinner and change into clean clothes for a fine meal at **CharMing,** known for its marinated meats.

DAY 3: A DAY OUT IN DENPASAR

Experience Denpasar like a local on this day filled with cultural, culinary, and historical attractions. Pack clothes that are comfortable for walking, a sturdy pair of shoes, hat, sunglasses, and water bottle.

1   Enjoy breakfast near your hotel in Sanur and wait until just after rush hour (8am-9am) to venture by taxi, rideshare, or motorbike into Denpasar. Your first stop is the **Bali Museum** in Puputan Square. Here, you can learn about Bali's volatile history and witness locals playing sports games in the outdoor park. Pura Jagatnatha is also on-site.

2   Walk or taxi to **Bodhi Leaf Eatery,** an Indonesian café serving vegan delights located just over 600 meters (0.4 mi) away.

3   After lunch, walk to **Pura Maospahit,** one of the most important temples in Denpasar.

4   Cross back over the canal to **Jalan Sulawesi,** home to Denpasar's largest fabric market.

5   Nearby is **Badung Market,** where you can snack on fresh fruits available for sale. Look for snakefruit, mangosteen, or bananas—all fruits you can peel and eat without washing.

6   Walk or taxi 1.5 km (0.9 mi) to enjoy a scrumptious dinner at **Two Fat Monks.**

Denpasar

While the rest of Bali runs on island time, the city of Denpasar functions at full speed. Most tourism and hospitality workers in the surrounding coastal cities live inside the loose boundaries of Denpasar, contributing to the rise of its middle class. Denpasar's plethora of cultural performance centers, historical sites, public parks, markets, and warungs make it not only a livable city for locals but also a worthy place to visit as a tourist.

ORIENTATION

Denpasar is the capital of Bali, located on the southern end of the island, just above the Bukit Peninsula. Its border spans west to Kuta and includes the eastern beach town of Sanur. **Jalan Bypass Ngurah Rai,** the largest highway in the region, connects Denpasar to the **Ngurah Rai International Airport** in Kuta. The heart of the city—and arguably the most interesting area—stems from **Puputan**

Denpasar

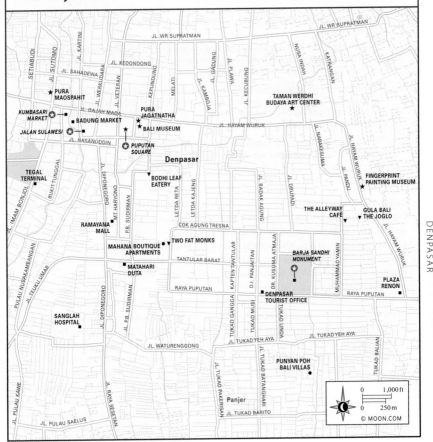

Square, where you'll find many of Denpasar's main attractions like **Badung Market, Kumbasari Market, Jalan Sulawesi,** the **Bali Museum,** and the **Barja Sandhi Monument,** all within a 5-km (3-mi) radius. The neighborhoods on the outer ring of Puputan Square are largely residential and consist of homes, small temples, and shops.

If you plan to shop during your trip, the major malls like **Plaza Renon, Ramayana Mall,** and **Matahari Duta** are also found within 5 km (3 mi) of one another near Jalan Raya Puputan in central Denpasar.

SIGHTS
Bali Museum

Jalan Mayor Wisnu No. 1; tel. 361/222680; www.museum.kemdikbud.go.id; Sat.-Thurs. 7:30am-3:30pm, Fri. 7:30am-3:30pm; 50,000 Rp adult, 25,000 Rp child

The Bali Museum was built in 1931 and modeled after the former Royal Palace, which was destroyed in 1906. Featuring 10,000 Indonesian artifacts, its unique architecture is one of the main highlights of the museum. Each of the four different sections of the museum represents a different region of

Strange Sights and Offbeat Attractions

If you're attracted to the odd, quirky, or offbeat aspects of a city, these interesting attractions are not to be missed.

- **Fingerprint Painting Museum:** Who needs paintbrushes when you have 10 fingers to do the job? This art gallery features one man's intriguing artworks, created using nothing but his own hands and a pallet of paint (page 140).

- **Taman Festival Bali:** This theme park was meant to be one of Indonesia's most profitable and famous attractions, complete with laser beam light shows and ponds filled with crocodiles. After a string of bad decisions, the theme park was abandoned. Now, it's an eerie spot that's quickly being overtaken by the jungle (page 144).

- **StrangeButCool:** This shop and museum is the lovechild of a woman and her collection of colorful and vintage handbags (page 151).

Bali and its unique building styles. One building houses historic artifacts like tools, coins, and ancient weaponry. The northern building displays costumes, masks, and other textiles related to Balinese Hinduism. The other two pavilions feature artwork by Balinese artists, as well as jewelry, textiles, and beauty items.

The exhibits themselves need a bit of a refresh, and many artifacts are missing the date that they were created. To see the highlights of the museum, choose a guided tour for an additional 50,000 Rp. Expect extra pressure for a tip at the end of the tour. Also, some tour guides can get aggressive when it comes to selling their services and may follow you around the premises in hopes of guiding you through the exhibits.

Jagatnatha Temple
(Pura Jagatnatha)
Jalan Surapati; 9am-sunset, may close for ceremonies; 20,000 Rp admission fee includes sarong

The Bali Museum borders the Pura Jagatnatha Temple, built in 1953 for the god that represents all Balinese Hindu gods, Sanghyang Widi. The temple is a popular site for two festivals that take place every new moon and full moon, where visitors can watch a traditional shadow puppet performance called *wayang*. The walls of the temple depict scenes from two Hindu epics, Ramayana and Mahabharata. Tour guides will offer you their services for

around 50,000 Rp but the temple can be easily explored on your own.

★ Puputan Square
Jalan Gajah Mada; open 24/7; free

The former site of the Royal Palace, before it was destroyed by Dutch forces in 1906, Puputan Square is a large garden area, with a statue that features a family starting *puputan*, a form of ritual suicide. The monument was built to commemorate the lives lost during the beginnings of Dutch occupation, when Dutch forces, armed with guns, met Balinese forces who were equipped with little more than spears and *krises* (daggers). The Balinese, dressed in white clothing typically reserved for burials, committed suicide rather than be killed by enemy fire. Women involved in the ritual held gold and other forms of jewelry, throwing it toward Dutch forces before dying.

Taman Werdhi Budaya Art Center
Jalan Nusa Indah; tel. 361/227176; Mon.-Thurs. 8am-3pm, Fri.-Sun. 8am-1pm; admission cost depends on event

Taman Werdhi Budaya Art Center is a

1: Denpasar city 2: Pura Jagatnatha
3: Taman Werdhi Budaya Art Center 4: Barja Sandhi Monument

cultural hub for art performances, festivals, plays, and markets in Denpasar. Sprawling nearly 14 acres, the complex is divided into four sections that revolve around an amphitheater capable of seating nearly 6,000. The art center tends to attract locals, meaning that most performances will take place in Bahasa or Balinese. However, many of the performances are easily understood through costume, music, and acting—even if you don't understand the words. It's recommended to visit during an event to see the different costumes, listen to music, and people watch. Most events take place during July and August.

Maospahit Temple
(Pura Maospahit)

Jalan Sutomo; daily 9am-5pm, may close for ceremonies; free

Pura Maospahit stands out from many of the other major temples in Bali because it is crafted from red brick and thatch roofing, while others are primarily made from limestone or coral. It is also the only temple in Bali to be built in a Panca Mandala formation, with the most sacred aspect of the temple in the center of the property. Pura Maospahit was built in the 13th century during the Majapahit dynasty, with Garuda and Batara Bayu for protection. The temple is split into five courtyards, each representing a different Hindu deity.

Fingerprint Painting Museum

Jalan Hayam Wuruk No. 175; tel. 361/235115; Mon.-Sat. 8am-4pm, closed Sun.; free

As children, we all created artwork crafted from nothing more than a paint palette and our own hands. Artist Ngurah Gede Pemucutan has created many works of art using fingerprints in lieu of paintbrushes or sponges. When viewed up close, the pieces look as though they're made up of circular pixels, but when you back away, it's easy to see clear and detailed images that emerge through the abstract form. At the Fingerprint Painting Museum, you can view more than 600 paintings and might even be lucky enough to get

a tour of the museum from Ngurah Gede Pemucutan himself.

★ Barja Sandhi Monument

Jalan Raya Puputan No. 142; daily 8:30am-5pm; 50,000 Rp adult, 5,000 Rp child

On any given day, the manicured grounds surrounding the Barja Sandhi Monument might host a festival, a school assembly, pickup games of soccer, picnics, group fitness sessions, or a combination of all the above. The monument itself symbolizes the struggles and darker history of Bali, with depictions of battles between Balinese *rajas* (kings) and Dutch forces. The architect, Ida Bagus Gede, made references to the date of Indonesia's independence, August 17, 1945, by designing 17 steps to the main rotunda of eight columns, and a tower that is 45 meters (147 feet) tall. Walking around the monument is free, though you can pay to enter the museum section of the Barja Sandhi Monument to learn more about Bali's history through paintings and informative plaques. Water fountains trickling sacred water into large ponds create a feeling of peace despite the disturbing historical paintings. Head up the stairs inside the monument for a panoramic view of Denpasar.

Buddha Maitreya Vihara

Jalan Laksamana Bintan; daily 10am-9pm; donation requested

Buddha Maitreya Vihara houses three Buddha statues in a large circular temple bordered by intricate columns. It is one of the largest Buddhist temples in Bali and houses an all-vegan restaurant, LN Fortunate, behind it. While the exterior of the temple is patterned and ornate, and can feel busy at first glance, the temple's stark white interior with three Buddhas placed at the front evokes a feeling of calmness and peace.

ENTERTAINMENT AND EVENTS
Bali Arts Festival

Taman Werdhi Budaya Arts Centre; Jalan Nusa Indah No. 1; tel. 361/222387; June-July; free

Bali Arts Festival is a yearly event that highlights Balinese culture through exciting parades, music, vivid dance performances, and art exhibitions. Local artists, including sculptors, fashion designers, writers, and musicians all work to portray their island as they know and love it. The biggest performances take place in the **Taman Werdhi Budaya amphitheater,** and fans of these performances often reserve seats hours in advance. The Bali Arts Festival is one of the largest celebrations on the island and is well worth braving the crowd to experience.

SHOPPING
Markets
★ KUMBASARI MARKET

Jalan Gajah Mada; tel. 361/264011; hours vary by shop

Kumbasari Market is one of the best places to find souvenirs and artwork at bargain or wholesale prices. It is a four-story building with more than 200 smaller shops inside. In the early morning, it's a traditional market with produce stands set up on the bottom floor. By 10am, most of the art shops open to welcome those in search of the perfect souvenir. The first floor sells household cleaning products and toiletries, while the second, third, and fourth floors sell artwork, batik, clothing, and home decor. Most of the artwork items are sourced from Bali's rural regions, making this a great place to compare the different types of handicrafts around the island. Come sunset, food stalls open to serve dinner. The haggling inside the market can get a bit aggressive, and occasionally someone will come by to offer their services as a mediator. Patience, persistence, and a bit of selective listening is necessary to score the best deals inside the market.

BADUNG MARKET

Jalan Sulawesi No. 1; open 24/7

One of the most popular markets in Denpasar, Badung Market is loud and crowded with people selling fresh produce, raw meat, spices, snacks, handicrafts, and textiles. You'll get a bargain at this newly built center—but you might have to fend off impromptu tour guides and touts to snag it.

★ JALAN SULAWESI

Jalan Sulawesi; daily 8am-6pm

If you're looking for Indonesian fabrics, you'll find rolls of technicolor textiles in the cluttered two-story shops that line Jalan Sulawesi. Many factory cut-outs and leftovers make their way to Denpasar and are sold at rock-bottom prices.

Malls
PLAZA RENON

Jalan Raya Puputan No. 210; tel. 361/4457615; plazarenon.com; Sun.-Thurs. 10am-10pm, Fri.-Sat. 10am-11pm

Escape the humidity and venture into Plaza Renon, a mall with four floors of coffee shops, small restaurants, chain clothing stores, boutiques, and a Cinemaxx movie theater. Head to the terrace on the top floor to enjoy views of the city.

MATAHARI DUTA

Jalan Dewi Sartika No. 4G; tel. 361/237365; matahari.com; daily 10am-9pm

Matahari Duta is a mid-range shopping mall known for its frequent sales, with chain stores selling clothes, swimwear, shoes, cosmetics, and fast food. If your accommodation comes with a kitchen, there is also a well-stocked supermarket on-site.

FOOD
Indonesian
GULA BALI THE JOGLO

Jalan Merdeka II No. 16; tel. 361/4745562; daily 9:30am-5pm; 12,000-35,000 Rp

If you're craving authentic Indonesian food in a relaxing atmosphere, Gula Bali the Joglo is a great pick. Seating is set inside a no-frills *joglo*-style building with traditional, hand-painted decor. Staff won't be quick to rush you out the door as you dine on spiced meats, salads, and soups. One plate won't be enough for a full meal, so choose two or three items to leave satisfied.

LN FORTUNATE

Jalan Gn. Soputan No. 98X; tel. 81999714182; daily 11am-10pm; 20,000-60,000 Rp

Behind the Buddha Maitreya Vihara temple is LN Fortunate, a vegan restaurant with an extensive menu that features coffee and plant-based milks, desserts like ice cream and cake, burgers, sandwiches, noodles, and salads. The decor is simple and clean, much like the Buddhist temple that houses this hard-to-find restaurant.

International
SUSHI QOMBI

Jalan Teuku Umar No. 255; tel. 361/237808; https://sushiqombi.business.site; daily 11am-11pm; 20,000-50,000 Rp

Sushi Qombi is a playful sushi restaurant with a lime-green Volkswagen Bus accenting the venue. Opt for hand rolls, nigiri, cut rolls, or noodle soup, all made fresh. Some of the rolls have a strong Indonesian flavor from a splash of *sambal,* if you are up for trying a fusion-style dish. Service is fast and their price is surprisingly good value.

THE ALLEYWAY CAFÉ

Jalan Merdeka No. 10B; tel. 8992816395; www.thealleywaycafe.com; daily 8am-11pm; 20,000-50,000 Rp

This industrial-style café has indoor air-conditioned and outdoor patio seating. The Alleyway Café is known for its coffee and brunch menu; you can nosh on scrambled eggs, Tex-Mex wraps stuffed with beef jalapeño sausages, and a duck omelet. For lunch and dinner, there's a choice of salads, sandwiches, pasta, and burgers. Though the food is rich, the juices are a bit watered-down, so opt for an iced caffe latte instead.

★ BODHI LEAF EATERY

Jalan Letda Made Putra; tel. 361/254307; daily 7am-8pm; 40,000-120,000 Rp

While Ubud reigns as the hub for healthy vegan restaurants, Bodhi Leaf Eatery offers similar dishes to what you'll find in Ubud for half the price. The clean and small restaurant is accented with a rainbow mandala and colorful couch cushions, and there's a small shop selling oils, cosmetics, and vegan treats. Choose between tempeh burgers, falafel wraps, salads, bibimbap, vegetable sushi rolls, and noodle bowls.

TWO FAT MONKS

Jalan Letda Tantular No 7; tel. 361/4456111; twofatmonks@gmail.com; daily 9am-11pm; 150,000-300,000 Rp

Spacious and stylish, Two Fat Monks is a restaurant that offers seating inside its raised-ceiling dining room or outside on the grass. The chefs take care in their presentation and serve a variety of curries and Asian noodle dishes. Most regulars opt for their pork belly dish that comes cooked in three different ways. While Two Fat Monks earned its popularity because of its photogenic plating, the taste lives up to its aesthetic.

ACCOMMODATIONS
MAHANA BOUTIQUE APARTMENTS

Jalan Letda Tantular No. 7; tel. 361/4456660; www.mahanabali.com; 360,000-600,000 Rp

A modern apartment building in central Denpasar, Mahana Boutique Apartment has 18 rooms with a balcony, TV and satellite channels, desk, Wi-Fi, and air-conditioning. All rooms open out to a cozy pool and lounge area. The ambience is bright and clean, and a hearty a la carte breakfast is included with each stay.

★ PUNYAN POH BALI VILLAS

Jalan Tukad Citarum No. A9; tel. 81246970250; www.punyanpoh.com; 650,000 Rp

Though the entrance to Punyan Poh Bali Villas can be a challenge to find and the neighborhood is primarily residential, this accommodation is a great option for those who want to experience a more authentic side of Bali's most-popular region without making compromises when it comes to hospitality.

The property offers spacious and clean one and two-bedroom villas, each of which comes with a private plunge pool, queen-size bed, LED TV, air-conditioning, Wi-Fi, and coffee maker.

INFORMATION AND SERVICES

Tourist Information

DENPASAR TOURIST OFFICE

Jalan Raya Puputan No. 41; tel. 361/235600; www. balitourismboard.org; Mon.-Sat. 9am-5pm, closed Sun.

The Denpasar Tourist Office is where you can learn about local events, exhibitions, and festivals, and pick up brochures, calendars, and a map of the Denpasar area. Though the office is dedicated to promoting Denpasar and Sanur, staff are surprisingly helpful when it comes to planning itineraries and highlighting other points of interest in Bali.

Health and Safety

SANGLAH HOSPITAL

Jalan Diponegoro; tel. 361/227912; www. sanglahhospitalbali.com; open 24/7

Being the largest hospital in Bali, Sanglah Hospital has more than 740 beds and 1,500 staff. The hospital has an emergency room and offers specialized care for cancer treatment, general surgery, delivery, and outpatient care. Should you need to go to Sanglah Hospital, request treatment at their Amertha Pavilion, which has English-speaking doctors and facilities that are up to international standards.

GETTING THERE

By Taxi and Rideshare

Central Denpasar is approximately 40 minutes' drive away from **Ngurah Rai International Airport.** It costs 80,000-150,000 Rp to get from the airport to Central Denpasar via **taxi,** or 100,000 Rp using a rideshare app like **Grab** or **GoJek.**

There are many roads connecting **Kuta** to Denpasar as they are neighbors, though the fastest way to get to Central Denpasar is via

Jalan Imam Bonjol, which runs north and south. If you want to venture to east Denpasar, take **Jalan By Pass Ngurah Rai** from Kuta.

By Bus and *Bemo*

Many locals use a bus or *bemo* (a minibus with benches on the inside—don't be surprised if chickens come along for the ride) to get to Denpasar from other regions.

Buses do not always follow a timetable, and instead wait until there are enough passengers on board before departing. Buses tend to stop less and take set routes. *Bemos* drive erratic routes, depending on the passengers, yet they do not need as many people to depart. Unless you are going to Java, it is not possible to purchase a bus ticket in advance.

TEGAL TERMINAL

Jalan Imam Bonjol; tel. 361/427172

If you are coming from **Kuta** (13,000 Rp), the **airport** (15,000 Rp), or **Jimbaran** (17,000 Rp), you will arrive at the Tegal Terminal, 1.5 km (0.9 mi) southwest of Puputan Square.

KERENENG TERMINAL

Jalan Hayam Wuruk; tel. 361/226906

If you are coming from **Sanur** (7,000 Rp), you can stop at the Kereneng Terminal, where you can request drop-off at or close to Puputan Square.

UBUNG TERMINAL

Jalan Cokroaminoto; tel. 361/427172

Buses coming from **northern** and **western Bali** (15,000-45,000 Rp) arrive at Ubung Terminal, 3.5 km (1.85 mi) north of Tegal Terminal.

GETTING AROUND

Due to congestion and lack of parking, it is not recommended to drive a motorbike in Denpasar.

By Taxi and Rideshare

Bluebird taxis frequent Denpasar, and the authentic cabs are outfitted with trustworthy meters. **Grab** and **GoJek** are commonly used rideshare apps and they frequent the Denpasar area.

By Bus and *Bemo*

There are multiple bus and *bemo* stops around Denpasar, with the major ones listed in the previous section. Because Denpasar largely caters to locals rather than tourists, some bus and *bemo* drivers may have limited English. The most convenient routes go along **Jalan Raya Puputan** for Puputan Square and the Bali Museum, and **Jalan Imam Bonjol** (get off at Tegal Terminal) to see the Kumbasari Market.

Sanur

Sanur is a sleepy town with more than 5 km (3 mi) of pristine coastline. It's nearly impossible to tell where one beach blends into another, as they're all connected, and all are protected by a coral reef that spans around 500 meters (1,640 feet) out to sea. Banyan trees, shops selling both antique and modern goods, hotels, guesthouses, impromptu markets, and massage tables are all wedged between the **boardwalk** and the sand in hopes of capturing your attention. At high tide, the ocean is perfect for swimming.

Those who stay in Sanur enjoy doing little more than swimming, sunbathing, shopping, and dining. It's what they came here for, after all.

ORIENTATION

Orienting yourself in Sanur is an easy task. **Jalan Ngurah Rai Bypass** marks the border between Sanur and Denpasar, with Sanur spanning all the way to the beach. In Sanur itself, there is one main road that runs along the length of the town, called **Jalan Danau Tamblingan.** Smaller roads lead from Jalan Danau Tamblingan to the beach, where you can walk almost the entire length of the sand on one single boardwalk named **Jalan Kusuma Sari. Mertasari Beach** marks the southernmost point of Sanur, while the fast boat terminal near **Jalan Hang Tuah** bookends this area in the north.

SIGHTS
★ Big Garden Corner
Jalan By Pass Ngurah Rai; tel. 361/9381543; daily 9am-9pm; 75,000 Rp adult, 30,000 Rp child (includes drink)

Big Garden Corner is a family-friendly garden and sculpture center that's ideal for expanding children's imaginations. Discover elephant statues made from aluminum cans, huts crafted from sticks and twigs, lifelike giraffe figures, fish ponds, Hindu stone statues, and much more. There are plenty of shaded spots to sit and enjoy a picnic, as well as a handful of places to grab food and a drink. For 100,000 Rp, you can rent a pedal car to drive around the park. To cool off, head to the splash pool, where admission is free for children and 100,000 Rp per adult.

Taman Festival Bali
Jalan Pandang Ganak; technically closed though locals usually monitor the entrance 9am-5pm; 10,000 Rp

If you're the type of traveler who seeks out offbeat and eerie tourist attractions, Taman Festival Bali might be just the place for you. Taman Festival Bali is an abandoned theme park in the process of being reclaimed by the jungle. Vines wrap around old carnival rides and leaves carpet the floor inside the park's dilapidated buildings. Graffiti artists use the abandoned walls as their canvas, with paint covering nearly every wall that's still standing. A handful of Balinese men guard the entrance to the park and demand about 10,000 Rp per person to enter, though this is often negotiable if you're in a group. It's not safe to enter any of the structures or buildings, so stick to the main pathways as you browse around.

Central Sanur

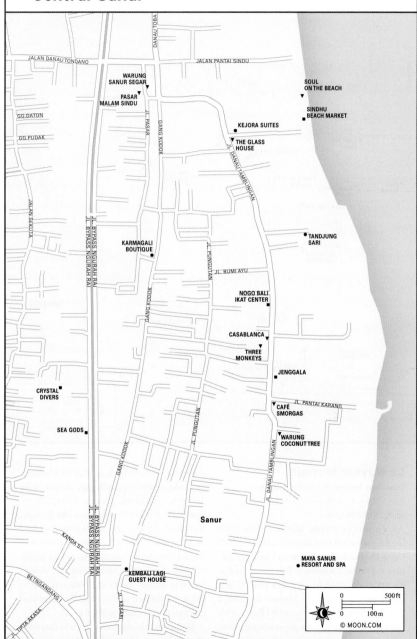

JALAN DANAU TONDANO

JALAN PANTAI SINDU

DANAU TOBA

WARUNG SANUR SEGAR

SOUL ON THE BEACH

PASAR MALAM SINDU

SINDHU BEACH MARKET

GG. DATON

KEJORA SUITES

JL. PASAR

GG. PUDAK

THE GLASS HOUSE

GANG KODOK

JL. DANAU TAMBLINGAN

JALAN SEKUTA

TANDJUNG SARI

KARMAGALI BOUTIQUE

JL. PUNGUTAN

JL. BUMI AYU

GANG KODOK

NOGO BALI IKAT CENTER

CASABLANCA

THREE MONKEYS

JENGGALA

CRYSTAL DIVERS

JL. PANTAI KARANG

SEA GODS

JL. PUNGUTAN

CAFÉ SMORGAS

WARUNG COCONUT TREE

JL. DANAU TAMBLINGAN

GANG KODOK

JL. BYPASS NGURAH RAI

JL. BYPASS NGURAH RAI

Sanur

KANDA ST.

MAYA SANUR RESORT AND SPA

BETNGANDANG I

JL. BYPASS NGURAH RAI

JL. BYPASS NGURAH RAI

KEMBALI LAGI GUEST HOUSE

JL. KESARI

TIRTA AKASA

0   500 ft
0   100 m

© MOON.COM

Southern Sanur

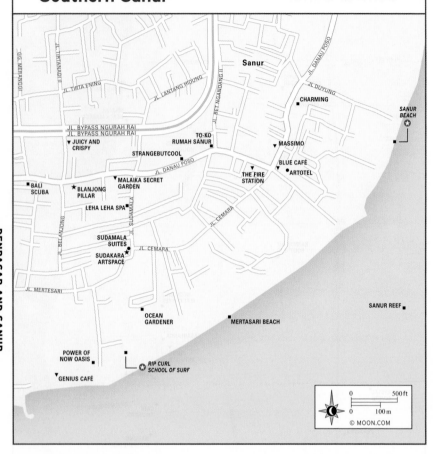

Le Mayeur Museum

Jalan Hang Tuah; tel. 361/286201; Sat.-Thurs.
8am-3:30pm, Fri. 8:30am-12:30pm; 50,000 Rp
adult, 25,000 Rp child

Adrien-Jean Le Mayeur Merpres (1880-1958) is a Belgian artist who arrived in Bali in 1932. Using the tropical landscape and Balinese culture as a muse, his home in Bali also served as his art studio until his death in 1958. While living on the island, Le Mayeur married a young Balinese Legong dancer, Ni Polok, with more than 40 years of age separating the two.

His home has since been turned into a museum, displaying dozens of Le Mayeur's artworks across two buildings. As you walk through each room, it's easy to see the influence that other destinations like Europe, Northern Africa, and Southeast Asia had on Le Mayeur's work. Le Mayeur eventually shifted from impressionistic to a more realistic style of painting, often using Ni Polok as his main subject. Busts of Le Mayeur and Ni Polok are housed under a small shelter that overlooks a lily-pad-speckled pond.

Unfortunately, the collection is in dire need of restoration. Many of Le Mayeur's early works have faded or are kept behind a dusty layer of glass.

Blanjong Pillar and Dalem Blanjong Temple

Jalan Danau Poso; daily 8am-5pm; free, sarong needed to enter

A nearly forgotten site in Sanur, the Blajong Pillar dates to the early 900s, from the first Balinese Warmadewa dynasty. Inscriptions written in Balinese and Sanskrit are wrapped around the pillar, relaying messages about military actions at the time. The pillar is significant in that it asserts Bali was independent from the rest of Indonesia at the time, and gives testament to the practice of both Hinduism and Buddhism during the Warmadewa dynasty. The pillar also mentions Sri Kesari Warmadewa, the first known king of Bali. The pillar was found in 1932 and left at the site of its initial discovery, with the **Dalem Blanjong Temple** beside it. Today, the pillar is enclosed in glass and protected by a fence.

The site is somewhat hard to find. Look for a sign that states its name in Indonesian, "Cagar Budaya Prasasti Blanjong," and walk down the alleyway to find the Blanjong Pillar and the Dalem Blanjong Temple.

Sudakara ArtSpace

Jalan Sudamala No. 20; tel. 361/288555; sudakaraartspace.com; daily 9am-6pm; free

The Sudakara ArtSpace is a small gallery in the center of Sudamala Resort. While many nearby galleries and resorts emphasize traditional Balinese artwork, Sudakara ArtSpace features the work of contemporary artists, with rotating exhibits of both foreign and local artists on display.

BEACHES AND SURF BREAKS
★ Sanur Beach
(Pantai Sanur)

Jalan Setapak; free

Sanur Beach is a narrow band of coarse white sand that edges 5 km (3 mi) along Sanur, from Jalan Matahari Terbit down to an estuary that runs along Jalan Pengembak. All along Sanur Beach, there are colorful fishing boats, fig trees, and lounge chairs. However, the shops, hotels, and restaurants that border the beach's inland end vary greatly. Shabby warungs built from scrap metal and driftwood serve coconuts just a few hundred meters from a ritzy bar. Guesthouses built in the mid-1970s see the same sunrise as the newly built five-star resort next door. The best way to experience Sanur Beach is to spend a day walking from one end to the other, taking note of which stretch of paradise you think is best. Even in high season, it's easy to find a spot for yourself.

SANUR REEF

Take boat out at northern end of Sanur Beach; 200,000-400,000 Rp return boat trip

Sanur Reef rarely breaks, but when it does, expect every surfer in Sanur to be in the lineup. Locals know how to work this punchy right-hand wave that breaks fast and hollow over shallow reef. Best conditions: 1.5-4.5-meter (5-15-foot) southwesterly swell, mid- to high tide, easterly winds.

HYATT REEF

Take boat out from Hyatt Regency Bali hotel; 200,000-400,000 Rp return boat trip

Here you'll find a finnicky right-hander, notorious for its strong current that gets heavy once swells top eight feet. When it works, everyone gets excited, paddles out, and disperses over its three peaks, and intermediate surfers will have fun sitting on the shoulder. Best conditions: 0.9-3.6-meter (3-12-foot) southwesterly swell, mid to high tide, northwesterly winds.

WATER SPORTS
Kitesurfing
★ RIP CURL SCHOOL OF SURF

Jalan Cemara (Prama Sanur Beach Hotel); tel. 85100038445; https://ripcurlschoolofsurf.com; hours depend on tide and weather; surf lesson packages from 700,000 Rp, kite-surf lessons from 1,500,000 Rp

Rip Curl School of Surf is a one-stop spot for

just about every ocean sport that Sanur has to offer. The school teaches lessons on how to surf, stand-up paddleboard, kayak, kitesurf, foil, scuba dive, wakeboard, and windsurf. Rental gear is also available for those who are confident and capable out on the sea. Many of these sports require specific tides and wind conditions, so you'll want to book your lesson at least a few days in advance. Lesson prices include all gear needed to learn, a rash guard, helmet, sunscreen, and life vests if needed. Rip Curl School of Surf is partnered with Blue Oasis Dive, a PADI dive center that runs scuba courses and dive trips to Padang Bai, Tulamben, Candi Dasa, and Nusa Penida.

Scuba Diving
BALI SCUBA

Jalan Danau Poso No. 46; tel. 85739292642; www. baliscuba.com; daily 7am-6pm; open water from 5,200,000 Rp, 2 fun dives from 1,300,000 Rp

Bali Scuba is a 5-Star PADI Career Development Center known for its friendly and accommodating staff. Like most of the dive centers in the area, Bali Scuba leads dives in Sanur, Tulamben, Nusa Penida, and Padang Bai. They also teach PADI courses ranging from Discover Scuba Diving to instructor and technical instructor level. Bali Scuba offers package deals and discounts for those who book multiple dives or courses with them. If you want to save even further, ask if there are discounts for booking on certain days.

CRYSTAL DIVERS

Jalan Bypass Ngurah Rai Gg. Griya No. 6; tel. 361/286737; www.crystal-divers.com; daily 6:30am-7pm; open water 5,500,000 Rp per course, 2 fun dives from 1,650,000 Rp and up

Crystal Divers is a 5-Star PADI Career Development Center that teaches everything from Discover Scuba Diving to instructor and technical diving courses. Crystal Divers offers day trips to Tulamben, Amed, Nusa Penida, and Padang Bai, as well as the Sanur channel. Crystal Divers has a strong reputation as a

career development center, and the guides and instructors have an abundance of experience and a strong focus on safety.

OCEAN GARDENER

Jalan Cemara (Prama Sanur Beach Hotel); info@ oceangardener.org; https://oceangardener.org; hours depend on tide, book tour in advance; from 500,000 Rp per tour

Because of pollution and rising sea temperatures, Bali's surrounding coral reefs are consistently under threat. Cue Ocean Gardener, an NGO that offers snorkeling workshops and tours to their coral gardens. Each 2-hour snorkel tour is led by a marine biologist who will teach budding conservationists what corals are and why they're so important. Then, you'll be trained on how to plant corals onto the coral gardens and will participate in the Ocean Gardener hands-on reef restoration program. Rashguards, booties, masks, and snorkels are provided. Avoid putting on sunscreen containing oxybenzone beforehand, as it damages the corals.

OTHER SPORTS AND RECREATION
Yoga
POWER OF NOW OASIS

Jalan Merta Sari; tel. 87861534535; https:// powerofnowoasis.com; daily 7am-7:30pm, class times vary; 120,000 Rp per class

Power of Now Oasis is a beachside yoga retreat for yogis of all abilities. Classes are taught on a spacious bamboo platform that overlooks the beach. Choose between *hatha, vinyasa, yin,* restorative, and Iyengar yoga classes. Classes are offered on a walk-in basis, and free meditation sessions take place from 6pm-6:30pm Monday through Friday. The studio also has an on-site spa where you can enjoy acupuncture, a *bokashi* treatment that uses herbs, and Ayurveda oil massages.

UMAH SHAKTI

Jalan Danau Beraton Gg. XI No. 14; tel. 81338584438; www.yogaumahshakti.com; Mon-Fri.

8:30am-7:30pm, Sat. 7am-10am, Sun. 8am-10am; 75,000 Rp per class

Umah Shakti is a small yoga studio that's more popular among Sanur residents than with tourists, and has a strong sense of community despite its size. Classes vary in levels, and the schedule will be clearly marked to show whether the class is suitable for all abilities, beginners, or advanced yogis only. A favorite class to try is their anti-gravity yoga class, where you'll use the help of a sling to stretch upside down. Because the studio is tucked in a residential neighborhood, it can be somewhat of a challenge to find. It's located behind Bali Island School.

Spas
LEHA LEHA SPA

Jalan Danau Poso No. 104; tel. 8113995510; www. balilehaleha.com; daily 9am-10pm; 150,000 Rp per 1-hour Balinese massage

If you're up for some pampering, the massage therapists at Leha Leha Spa offer facials, manicures and pedicures, body scrub treatments, and Balinese massages. Treatments take place in clean rooms with simple wooden and floral decor. The owner, Gusde, worked as a masseur in Dubai for years before bringing his skills and love of luxury treatments back home to Bali.

ENTERTAINMENT AND EVENTS
BALI KITE FESTIVAL

Padang Galak; July or Aug.; free

The Bali Kite Festival is one of the most colorful and exciting events of the year, drawing more than 50,000 visitors. People from all over Denpasar and the surrounding beaches pack up their kites and head to Sanur to participate, and teams of up to 80 people represent their town with their kite craftmanship and flying skills. This festival brings cultural performances, music, art exhibitions, and best of all, kite-flying competitions. Teams rally behind their kite and bang on drums, cheer, and fly smaller kites below the main kite as if to give the main kite an accessory.

Judges look at the appearance, altitude, stability, speed, sound, and construction before issuing a score. And while traditional-shaped kites dominate the sky, more modern ones are now welcome too. Those who are not flying the kites are easily mesmerized by the graceful way they dance across the sky. Some kites span over 200 meters (656 feet) in length and are flown in hopes of enticing the Hindu gods to ensure a fruitful harvest. To enjoy the festival, all you need to do is look up. Because the festival takes place during Bali's busiest months, you'll want to book your hotel at least two months in advance for the best options and rates.

SANUR VILLAGE FESTIVAL

tel. 361/286987; www.sanurvillagefestival.com; Aug.; free

Head to the beach to watch friendly, spirited sailing races, dance performances, culinary workshops, and art exhibitions at the Sanur Village Festival. Each year, the festival has a theme that highlights an aspect or item related to Bali's heritage.

SHOPPING
Markets
SINDHU BEACH MARKET

Jalan Segara Ayu; 9am-sunset

A narrow strip of shops that stretches inland from Sanur Beach, Sindhu Beach Market is one of the best places to buy souvenirs, clothes, decor, and snacks—if you don't mind a bit of haggling. Once you get past the swarm of touts near the market entrance, there's a handful of fixed-price shops where you can browse in relative peace.

Specialty Items
SEA GODS

Jalan By Pass Ngurah Rai No. 376; tel. 361/271199; www.seagodswetsuit.com; Mon.-Fri. 9am-6pm, Sat. 9am-4pm, closed Sun

Every surfer and diver knows the discomfort of trying to squeeze into an ill-fitting wetsuit. Sea Gods creates custom wetsuits, rashguards, bathing suits, and accessories on-site that are

Fly a Kite: The Meaning Behind Traditional Balinese Kites

Kite making and kite flying are Balinese traditions that have been passed down from generation to generation. As soon as leaves begin to rustle on trees, you can expect locals to take their kites to a nearby beach or rice paddy for launching. While kite flying is undeniably fun, it is also a way to honor the Hindu gods and ask them for a fruitful harvest. There is even a god dedicated to kite flying, called Rare Angon, who is often shown as a young boy with his face turned toward the sky, eyes fixed on his kite. Some Balinese Hindus believe that Shiva was a kite flyer himself.

What does a kite, or *layangan*, symbolize and what is it made from?

· **Colors:** Most kites are decorated in black, white, or red in striped or checkered patterns. These are like the sarongs and color themes you'll see in Hindu temples, especially on the guardian statue's (*bedogol*) sarongs.

· **Shapes:** There are three shapes that frequent the skies: The *bebean* kite is commonly seen, as it is the easiest and smallest to fly. It is shaped like a fish with an open mouth. The *pecukan* kite resembles a leaf and is typically the nimblest kite in the sky. The *janggan* kite is arguably the most impressive, with a long tail that can trail over 100 meters (328 feet) behind its lines. This kite can weigh over 400 kg (880 lbs.) and require more than 10 people to carry it. If you make a kite that doesn't fit this construct, it's called a *kreasi baru*, or "new creation."

· **Masks:** Kites are all fitted with a mask, which acts as the spiritual head of the kite while it's in the air.

· **Sound:** Some kites make a loud humming noise that stems from two strips of bamboo placed together. As the bamboo moves through the air, it vibrates to create a distinctive buzz.

tailored to your sport and your body measurements. Standard-size items also available.

Batik and Textiles
NOGO BALI IKAT CENTER
Jalan Danau Tamblingan No. 104; tel. 361/288765; www.nogobali.com; daily 10am-6pm

At the Nogo Bali Ikat Center, witness *ikat* textiles being woven on a wooden loom. *Ikat* is an intricate dyeing method that involves tying and binding threads and then dyeing them so that they create beautiful patterns. You can choose fabric and have a bespoke item tailored, or shop from the many clothing items off the rack. The quality of the textiles at this quaint shop is on par with the price.

Home Decor
JENGGALA
Jalan Danau Tamblingan No. 51; tel. 361/288147; https://jenggala.com; daily 9am-9pm

Jenggala is a housewares store where you can find Indonesian handmade ceramic items like glassware, dining sets, accessories, art, vases, and ceramic displays. Each item typically has something distinctly Indonesian, like plumeria, bamboo, or a banana leaf motif.

Clothing and Accessories
STRANGEBUTCOOL
Jalan Danau Poso No. 111; tel. 361/4720027; www.strangebutcool.com; Mon.-Sat. 11am-7pm, closed Sun.; 150,000 Rp museum admission (must be aged 16 and up to enter)

The shop name, StrangeButCool, speaks for itself. This funky boutique is part shop, and part museum that sells and features unique handbags. In their museum section, you can admire more than 450 vintage bags that date back to the 1920s. In the shop, you'll find totes and purses of varying sizes and bright colors.

TO-KO RUMAH SANUR
Jalan Danau Poso No. 51A; tel. 361/282477; https://rumahsanur.com; daily 8am-11pm

To-Ko Rumah Sanur is a boutique that stocks

home goods, furniture, accessories, clothing, and knickknacks, all created by independent designers. As you browse through the wide variety of displayed items, you'll find things you never knew you wanted (or needed). The curator tends to choose environmentally conscious items like handmade soaps and reusable products, making it a great stop for those who want to support local businesses in lieu of mega corporations or fast fashion. They also have a coffee shop, beer garden, and coworking space on-site.

FOOD
Markets
PASAR MALAM SINDU
Jalan Danau Toba; daily 6pm-1am; 15,000-50,000 Rp

If authentic Balinese dishes are what you're after, you'll find them at the Pasar Malam Sindu, a night market that offers a break from the large restaurants lining the main roads of Sanur. The ambience is lively, with local vendors selling the recipes that they know best. Hop from stall to stall and sample satay, *bakso* (meatball) soup, and duck egg *martabak* (stuffed fried bread). A fresh fruit smoothie is a refreshing dessert to wash it all down.

Indonesian
WARUNG COCONUT TREE
Jalan Danau Tamblingan No. 68; tel. 361/283851; 9am-11pm; 25,000-40,000 Rp

Warung Coconut Tree serves fresh Indonesian meals in a tiny shack with a reggae-themed motif. The energetic and chatty staff serve *mie goreng* (spicy fried noodles), *nasi goreng* (fried rice), and *cap cay* (stir-fried vegetables) with enthusiasm. It's also a great place to meet others as they host acoustic musician performances a few times per week—usually on Tuesdays, Wednesdays, and Fridays.

JUICY AND CRISPY
Jalan Tirta Nadi I; tel. 81236153336; https:// juicyandcrispy.com; daily noon-9pm; 25,000-85,000 Rp

Juicy and Crispy is a small and simple barbecue restaurant known for its chicken, which is the dish that earned the restaurant its name and a loyal following. Second to Juicy and Crispy's chicken are its ribs, served in hearty portions and spiced just right. Of course, it wouldn't be a true barbecue spot without a variety of mashed potatoes, potato salad, and coleslaw. The restaurant also offers delivery and pickup orders.

BLUE CAFÉ
Jalan Danau Tamblingan; tel. 361/270435; www. bluecafe-bali.com; daily 9am-1am; 30,000-80,000 Rp

No two meals are exactly alike at Blue Café, a small café decorated with quirky handmade signs with motivational messages. Each morning, the chef determines the day's menu based on what produce and meats they were able to gather from the market. There are typically both Indonesian and European-style dishes to choose from. The Blue Café has quite a social atmosphere, thanks to its buy-one-drink-get-one-free happy hour and live music. Herman, the owner, often stops from table to table to see how the food is tasting. The front patio makes for a prime people watching spot.

International
WARUNG SANUR SEGAR
Jalan Pantai Sindhu No. 2A; tel. 81237600256; 11am-8pm; 15,000-30,000 Rp

Some like it hot at Sanur Segar, where chilis and jalapeños make frequent appearances on their Mexican-themed menu. This four-table restaurant is more of a taqueria than a warung, with burritos, tacos, quesadillas, and chipotle salads on the menu. Warung Sanur Segar only stays open until their food is sold out, so get there before 2pm if you're hungry for lunch. If there's no room to sit, their food tastes just as good to-go.

1: Sea Gods 2: Sindhu Beach Market 3: Soul on the Beach

CAFÉ SMÖRGÅS

Jalan Danau Tamblingan No. 56; tel. 361/289361; cafesmorgas.com; 7am-11pm; 40,000-90,000 Rp

In 2006, a Swedish family left their home country to establish a quaint sandwich and coffee shop in Sanur. Inside the café, you'll find freshly baked breads with a variety of spreads, sandwiches, wraps, omelets, burgers, soups, and pasta dishes. Consider it a carb-lover's heaven. Though the shop has a strong reputation for its coffee, they also serve wine, beer, and cocktails. Visit from 5pm to 7pm to take advantage of their buy-two-get-one-free happy hour.

★ THREE MONKEYS

Jalan Danau Tamblingan No. 116; tel. 361/286002; www.threemonkeyscafebali.com; daily 11am-11pm; 40,000-150,000 Rp

Reservations during high season are essential at Three Monkeys, an upscale restaurant with outdoor shaded seating and bamboo decor indoors. The menu features a mix of Middle Eastern and Mediterranean dishes, with a bit of Indonesian flavor thrown in. Their three-dip meze platter is a great starter, while lamb kefte with tzatziki sauce tempts those with a bigger appetite. The espresso martini is one of the best cocktails in town.

MASSIMO

Jalan Danau Tamblingan No. 228; tel. 361/288942; www.massimobali.com; daily 11am-11pm; 60,000-120,000 Rp

Massimo, the head chef and owner of his namesake restaurant, hails from southern Italy, where he learned to master the art of Italian food made with simple ingredients. This no-frills restaurant serves large portions and offers no apologies for its extended wait times, as everything is made to order. Occasionally, Massimo hosts musicians. Reserve a table in advance if you plan to go for dinner. Save room for the gelato; it's the best in town.

CHARMING

Jalan Danau Tamblingan No. 97; tel. 361/288029; daily 6pm-11:30pm; 60,000-200,000 Rp

If an authentic Indonesian dining experience is what you're after, you'll find it at CharMing. Under the thatched-roof *joglo*-style building, the walls are decorated with hand-carved sculptures. Soft Balinese music plays in the background and the soft lighting adds a touch of sophistication. Try the prawns with local spices or the vegetable curry.

Cafés and Light Bites
MALAIKA SECRET GARDEN

Jalan Danau Poso No. 68; tel. 81238341000; malaikasecretgarden@gmail.com; daily 11am-10pm; 40,000-70,000 Rp

Malaika Secret Garden has an obsessive following among health-conscious foodies. The restaurant serves their food, raw and vegan, in a garden setting. This means that each item is only cooked on low heat—if it's cooked at all—with the belief that this retains each ingredient's nutrients. For a new take on a classic dish, try their raw lasagna with pesto, or the spicy carrot ginger soup. Malaika Secret Garden also offers a variety of *jamu*, a traditional Balinese elixir made with fresh herbs and spices.

★ THE GLASS HOUSE

Jalan Danau Tamblingan No. 25A; tel. 361/288696; www.kejoravillas-suites.com; daily 7am-10pm; 60,000-140,000 Rp

The Glass House is a rare architectural find in Sanur, with its tall glass windows and white shutters. Sit near The Glass House windows to feel a fresh breeze or tuck inside the small restaurant itself for air-conditioning. The personable staff and small eating space create an atmosphere that feels cozy. Many of the dishes at The Glass House feature some form of seafood, with the salt and pepper calamari being a top pick. Their baked goods and desserts are made fresh daily.

★ SOUL ON THE BEACH

Jalan Pantai Sindu; tel. 361/4720063; https://soulcafes.com; daily 8am-11pm; 70,000-190,000 Rp

With an upbeat vibe, attentive staff, and beachside dining tables, Soul on the Beach is a health-conscious restaurant that's quickly becoming one of the most popular spots in Sanur. The breakfast menu features a long list of juices and probiotic drinks, as well as smoothie bowls, pancakes, eggs, burritos, and more. You can create a D.I.Y. dish with eggs and toast as a base—simply add the sides. For lunch and dinner, choose from a mix of salads, pizzas, burgers, seafood, and Mediterranean fare. There are plenty of options for vegans and vegetarians as well. Soul on the Beach is a spot where you can easily come for breakfast and lounge until lunchtime rolls around. The staff won't judge.

Vegetarian/Vegan
GENIUS CAFÉ

Pantai Mertasari; tel. 8770477788; https://geniuscafebali.com; daily 7am-10pm; 50,000-90,000 Rp

If you want to reconnect with the online world, grab your laptop and head to Genius Café, a coworking café set on the beach. The long drinks menu features just about every fruity concoction you can think of—with or without alcohol. The plant-based menu offers hearty breakfasts, soups, salad and rice bowls, burgers, and a healthy kids menu. If you want to go offline and hang out, the café hosts frequent movie nights, talks, and music performances. Come for the sunset happy hour that takes place from 5pm to 7pm daily.

BARS AND NIGHTLIFE
THE FIRE STATION

Jalan Danau Poso No. 108; tel. 361/285675; www.tfsbali.com; Mon.-Sat. 4pm-1am, Sun. noon-1am; 80,000-200,000 Rp

An unpretentious bar with a lively atmosphere, The Fire Station serves a variety of pub-style food and ice-cold beers. Cocktails run strong, and you'll find all the classics on the menu as well as imported wines and spirits. Spend time perusing the photos hung around the bar as you enjoy the live music.

CASABLANCA

Jalan Danau Tamblingan No. 120; tel. 8113809939; www.casablancasanur.com; daily 10am-1am; 60,000-150,000 Rp

Sanur may have a laid-back reputation, but Casablanca strives to counter this with a live music area that can seat just more than 300 people. Each night, the bar hosts some sort of dance workshop, quiz, or music performance, with a different theme each day of the week. Expect Latin dance music one night and a 1970s cover band the next. Children are welcome, and the venue keeps performances family-friendly. The drinks are priced higher than other places, but the cost is worth it when you account for the free entertainment.

ACCOMMODATIONS
Under 1,000,000 Rp
EAT SLEEP SKATE

Jalan Sedap Malam, Gang Kwangen No. 13; tel. 82339536271; https://essbali.com; 300,000-600,000 Rp

About a five-minute drive outside of Sanur's main beach is a funky hostel with an on-site skate park that somehow blends in with the rest of the quiet Kesiman village. There are four traditionally built wooden homes that sleep two to four people and are decorated with simple, naturally crafted decor. There is also a large villa with two six-bed dorm rooms on the property for more social travelers. All rooms overlook the pool and garden area, while the dorm villa is connected to the skate park itself. Each Friday, Eat Sleep Skate hosts a wood-fired pizza and skate party that often draws a crowd of locals who love to skate.

KEMBALI LAGI GUEST HOUSE

Jalan Kesari No. 36; tel. 361/281766; www.kembalilagi.com; 600,000-1,000,000 Rp

Kembali Lagi Guest House is a cozy place to stay in the center of Sanur. An intricate wooden gate welcomes guests to a well-kept courtyard and pool area, surrounded by eight bright and spacious hotel rooms. Each room is thoughtfully decorated with traditional Balinese art pieces. Couples and solo travelers will enjoy the double rooms, while the family suite sleeps two adults and two children. All rooms come with air-conditioning, fan, hot water shower, and a TV. The guesthouse includes thoughtful details like mosquito repellent, cold drinks, travel adapters, and flashlights, reflecting the staff's high level of attention toward guests.

1,000,000-2,000,000 Rp
★ ARTOTEL

Jalan Kusuma Sari No. 1; tel. 361/4721000; www. artotelindonesia.com; 750,000-1,400,000 Rp

Artotel is stylishly decorated with works created by some of Indonesia's most talented contemporary artists. Each room is vibrant and there are three types to choose from, ranging in size and furniture choices. All rooms feature a 49-inch TV, coffee machine, and free Wi-Fi connection. Their rooftop infinity pool and bar area overlooks surrounding greenery, with views stretching to the sea. Live music plays regularly to create a fun, upbeat ambience. Some of the staff can seem a bit pretentious at times, but that's easy to ignore once you settle into the scene.

★ KEJORA SUITES

Jalan Danau Tamblingan No. 25; tel. 361/282199; https://kejorasuites.com; 1,700,000 Rp

Kejora Suites is an elegant and luxurious boutique hotel with rooms that overlook or open out to a quiet pool and garden area. Each room is clean and air-conditioned and comes with TV and cable access. Many of the art pieces throughout the property are available for purchase. The ambience is intimate and peaceful, while the action of Sanur is just a short walk away. Guests of Kejora Suites also have access to the facilities at Segara Village, a beachside hotel with a large pool, spa, restaurants, and Jacuzzi bar. Children under 12 years old are not permitted to stay at Kejora Suites.

KARMAGALI BOUTIQUE

Jalan Pungutan No. 24B; tel. 361/6200108; www. karmagaliboutiquesuites.com; 2,000,000 Rp

With just six unique suites available, Karmagali is an intimate and luxurious boutique hotel that offers highly personalized service for its guests. The hotel has a strong sustainability focus and reduces its environmental impact wherever possible. Each room surrounds a pool and garden area, and is equipped with a 32-inch TV, Wi-Fi, air-conditioning, and access to bicycles. Breakfast is included with each stay served on the room's balcony area. All meals are typically prepared with locally sourced ingredients.

Over 2,000,000 Rp
MAYA SANUR RESORT AND SPA

Jalan Danau Tamblingan No. 89M; tel. 361/8497800; www.mayaresorts.com; 2,000,000-3,000,000 Rp

Surrounded by tropical gardens and overlooking the beach, Maya Sanur is a luxury retreat for families and couples. The stylish resort offers four room types, all with pool access and ultramodern features like electric blinds, adapter outlets, and TV with an adjusting swivel. Enjoy the beach or main infinity pool if you want company; otherwise, the lagoon-style pool is rarely crowded. There is also an on-site spa, as well as a library, two restaurants, bar, and garden area. Free meditation and yoga classes take place regularly at Maya Sanur.

★ TANDJUNG SARI

Jalan Danau Tamblingan No. 41; tel. 361/288441; https://tandjungsarihotel.com; 3,000,000-4,000,000 Rp

One of the first major resorts built in Sanur, Tandjung Sari is worth visiting for its unique Balinese architecture and atmosphere alone. Built in the early 1960s, the property has a sense of nostalgia. Each of the thatched-roof bungalows was built by hand and is surrounded by frangipani-fringed gardens. Some bungalows offer views of the sea. Rooms include air-conditioning, a mini bar, Wi-Fi, and a safe. Spend time rotating between the

Choosing a Fast Boat: Tips for Getting the Safest Boat and Best Price

Indonesia does not have a strong history of watercraft safety. As more tourists show interest in traveling to the nearby **Nusa Islands** from Sanur, or to the **Gili Islands** from Padang Bai, new fast boats promising a safe, quick, and cheap journey are popping up weekly. With so many companies to choose from, it can be a challenge to know who is legitimate versus who is just trying to make an easy buck.

- **Do your research.** The first thing to do before booking a fast boat journey is to research the fast boat companies and any recent news surrounding them. Some fast boat companies offer cheap tickets to recoup the cost of a damaged reputation. Or, the company may not include hotel pickup and drop-off, leading you to pay extra in taxi fares. Most fast boat ticket prices are featured online.

- **Be wary of buying on the fly.** Do not purchase tickets from people you meet while you're out and about. Though these salespeople make it sound like a great deal, it is oftentimes a ticket to a boat owned by their friend or family member—which may not have the most stringent safety standards in place. The larger fast boat companies have safety plans (though some are loosely followed) and boat captains who are used to driving the same route day after day, making them more experienced in all weather conditions.

- **Look at the weather forecast.** Many times, hostile weather conditions will cause companies to cancel trips to and from the outer islands because of large swell conditions. If all other boats are grounded, yet yours is willing to make the journey, it's best to stay behind. The price of losing your ticket is simply not worth the risk.

- **Book through your accommodation.** In general, booking the journey through your homestay or hotel is best—especially if the hotel is a few years old. Hotel and homestay owners develop relationships with fast boat companies, and it's not a good look for them if the company they send you to is not reputable.

beach, the infinity pool, the library, and the gym. Come dinnertime, the hotel often hosts cultural dance and music performances.

SUDAMALA SUITES

Jalan Sudamala No. 20; tel. 361/288555; www. sudamalaresorts.com; 3,000,000-4,000,000 Rp
Sudamala Suites is a chic boutique resort where there is keen attention to detail. Each suite has a king-sized or two twin-sized beds, antique furniture and batik artwork, desk, balcony, air-conditioning, TV, and a large bathroom with rainwater shower. Fine touches at Sudamala Suites make it one of the most thoughtful properties in Sanur. Sweet treats and a bedtime story are left on the bed each evening, and guests can choose from a handful of different pillow types. Sudamala Suites is also in a convenient location—made even better with their free bicycle rental.

INFORMATION AND SERVICES

Money

ATMs are found along **Jalan Danau Tamblingan.** Card skimming is common in Bali's tourist areas; pull on the ATM card reader lightly to find out if a skimming device has been placed over the top. Money changers are not recommended.

Medical Services
SANUR MEDICAL CLINIC

Jalan By Pass Ngurah Rai No. 243; tel. 361/289116; www.sanurmedicalclinic.com; 8am-8pm clinic hours, 24-hour on-call service
This clinic offers basic medical care, dental care, vaccinations, and care for reef cuts. Doctors at the clinic can also give a physical to make sure you are fit to scuba dive.

GUARDIAN PHARMACY
Jalan Danau Tamblingan No. 45; daily 8am-10pm
The pharmacy sells over-the-counter medications and first-aid supplies.

GETTING THERE
Sanur is one of the main departure points for **boats to the Nusa Islands;** boats generally depart north of **Jalan Hang Tuah,** with each company hosting its own waiting area. You're best off booking a fast boat through a company that offers door-to-door service from your hotel. **Scoot** (tel. 361/285522; www.scootcruise.com), **Rocky Fast Cruise** (tel. 361/283624; rockyfastcruise.com), and **D'Camel Fast Ferry** (tel. 81338515837; dcamelfastferry.com) are generally safe options.

By Taxi
From **Ngurah Rai International Airport,** a taxi (found outside of the arrival terminal) costs 250,000 Rp and takes 20-30 minutes to reach Sanur. **Rideshare** services like Grab and GoJek are in the departure terminal and cost 100,000-180,000 Rp per trip; it takes 20-30 minutes to reach Sanur. Coming from Kuta, take Jalan By Pass Ngurah Rai, which runs alongside Sanur (13km/8 mi; 30min). Thirty km (18.5 mi) north of Sanur, Ubud is about one hour away by car and is best reached via Jalan Raya Sukawati, which then connects to Jalan By Pass Ngurah Rai.

By Bus
The lime green **Kuta-Kura Bus** (tel. 81139600777; www.kura2bus.com) runs on a set route and on a set schedule connecting Sanur with **Ubud** (40-60 minutes; 80,000 Rp) and **Kuta** (30 minutes; 40,000 Rp).

Bemos run regularly along **Jalan Danau Tambingan;** for 7,000 Rp, the *bemo* will take you from the **Kereneng Terminal** (Jalan Hayam Wuruk; tel. 361/226906) in **Denpasar.**

GETTING AROUND
On Foot
Sanur is very **walkable** with one main road, **Jalan Danau Tambingan,** running along the length of Sanur. You can walk along this road or along Sanur's **boardwalk,** located directly on the beach, to get to and from destinations within Sanur.

By *Bemo*
Bemos run regularly along **Jalan Danau Tambingan** and cost 3,500 Rp per ride, no matter where you get on or off. If you see one driving your way, simply flag it down and tell the driver your destination.

By Taxi and Rideshare App
Bluebird taxis frequent all of Sanur. Rideshare apps like **Grab** and **GoJek** typically only drop off, and do not pick up, in Sanur due to feuds with the taxi industry. If you're in a hurry, using one of these apps is not recommended—don't be surprised if your driver never shows up.

Nusa Islands

Decades after surf tourism hit Bali's mainland, the three Nusa Islands remained rarely visited afterthoughts. Today, if you talk to longtime travelers to Bali, you'll hear them describe the Nusa Islands as "Bali as it was 30 years ago." While the Bukit Peninsula became developed, the Nusa Islands were left undisturbed—partially due to their location, but also because of their reputation of being home to dark magic. At one point in their history, maritime maps marked the three islands with skulls and crossbones.

The Nusa Islands were autonomous until the late 17th century, when they were taken over by a Balinese kingdom, Klungkung. Mainland Bali used the three islands as an impromptu penal colony, often sending political prisoners to live as exiles in Penida's foothills. Left on

Highlights

Look for ★ to find recommended sights, activities, dining, and lodging.

★ **Devil's Tear:** Watch waves crash and swirl around a limestone punch bowl (page 168).

★ **Mushroom Bay:** Swim in this tranquil bay and lounge on its sandy beach, the color of eggshells (page 170).

★ **Nusa Islands Surf School:** Learn to surf or fine tune your skills with a passionate surf instructor (page 170).

★ **Yoga Shack:** Stretch out in a tranquil yoga *shala* (studio) built from bamboo (page 173).

★ **Tembeling Pools:** Visit small shrines and swim in freshwater pools tucked inside the Tembeling Forest (page 186).

★ **Thousand Island:** Admire Nusa Penida's incredible coastline, flecked with tiny islands (page 188).

★ **Nusa Penida's Beaches:** Explore the dramatic and vivid beaches of Nusa Penida; they're worth the effort it takes to get there (page 188).

★ **Scuba Diving off Nusa Penida:** Blow

bubbles with gigantic manta rays and *mola-molas*, the world's heaviest bony fish (page 190).

★ **Friends of National Parks Foundation:** Leave a lasting positive impact on Nusa Penida by volunteering at one of their varied wildlife, habitat, and community programs (page 192).

Best Restaurants

★ **Warung Putu:** Sit in a swing and dine on authentic Indonesian food at this sandy warung overlooking the ocean (page 174).

★ **Thai Pantry:** This funky cliffside bar serves piping hot Thai curries and cold drinks out of a converted Volkswagen Kombi (page 174).

★ **Green Garden Warung:** A haven for health-conscious travelers looking for fresh smoothies, salads, and burgers as a meal in between yoga classes (page 177).

★ **Sandy Bay Beach Club:** In this seaside beach club, you can enjoy cocktails, salads, and seafood by the pool or in the sand (page 177).

★ **Penida Colada:** Watch the tide rise and fall at this seaside café serving juices, coffee, cocktails, and sandwiches (page 192).

their own, the three islands earned an income through seaweed farming and became notorious for practicing their own variation of dark magic.

Despite the trepidation surrounding the Nusa Islands, a few travelers ventured there and recognized Nusa Lembongan for its surf. To accommodate surfers, rickety warungs and bamboo bungalows popped up along the shorelines of Jungubatu, the main hub of Nusa Lembongan, the closest island to the island of Bali. The area has been developing ever since. Today, tourism is the region's main source of income—and a different kind of magic can be seen at sunrise and sunset.

Each of the three islands—Nusa Lembongan, Nusa Ceningan, and Nusa Penida—is surrounded by a marine park, home to some of the world's most majestic sea creatures. Off the coastline of Nusa Penida, easily accessed from the other two islands and the largest of the three, divers and snorkelers can swim alongside manta rays and *mola-mola* fish, and admire thriving coral reefs. The ocean-obsessed can also surf, paddle, swim, and kayak along many of the region's stunning beaches.

On land, rugged landscapes of limestone cliffs, flat and sandy beaches, electric blue water, hidden temples, waterfalls, rolling green hills, and winding trails await. You could easily spend weeks traversing all of the unmarked roads, stopping wherever you see fit, without ever unearthing all that there is to see in the Nusa Islands.

ORIENTATION

Nusa Lembongan, Nusa Ceningan, and Nusa Penida are a cluster of three islands 30 minutes away by boat (12 km/7.5 mi) from Bali's mainland, along the same latitude as Kuta and Denpasar. It takes approximately 30 minutes by boat to get to **Jungutbatu** on Nusa Lembongan and 35 minutes to **Toyapakeh**, the main drop-off point for boats arriving in Nusa Penida from Sanur and Nusa Lembongan. Nusa Ceningan is accessible via a 5-minute boat ride from Nusa Lembongan or by driving over **Jembatan Cinta**, the Yellow Bridge connecting the two smaller islands.

One helpful point of reference is, if you can see **Mount Agung** in the distance from any of the three islands, this means that you

NUSA ISLANDS

Previous: Broken Beach; Devil's Tear; scuba diving off Nusa Penida.

Best Accommodations

★ **Krisna Homestay:** You'll find these family-run bungalows and suites just a short walk from the beach (page 177).

★ **Tigerlillys:** This shabby-chic boutique hotel was designed for relaxation (page 177).

★ **Ceningan Resort:** Scuba divers and yogis who want a hub to return home to after a day spent in saltwater and sunshine enjoy this eco-resort (page 183).

★ **La Roja Bungalows:** Picture-worthy red-roofed cottages are set among gardens and around a quaint pool (page 193).

★ **Penida Bambu Green:** A hidden retreat in Nusa Penida's green hills, this property offers bungalows that are built from bamboo with *alang-alang* (native grass) roofs; you won't want to leave (page 193).

are facing north. Nusa Penida is the largest of the three islands and the farthest east; Nusa Lembongan is the second-largest and westernmost, closest to mainland Bali; and Nusa Ceningan, in the middle, is the smallest.

PLANNING YOUR TIME

While tour companies offer day trips to the Nusa Islands, taking you on a snorkeling tour or to two or three major sights, it's best to spend a few days in the islands. Many of the islands' best features—the incredible beaches, natural pools, walking trails, and snorkeling sites—are meant to be enjoyed without a time constraint.

It's recommended to spend at least one day on **Nusa Lembongan,** half a day on **Nusa Ceningan,** and at least two days to truly experience **Nusa Penida.** With so many activities, accommodations, and sights, you won't be bored even if you budget a week to see all three islands.

If you have a **motorbike** (usually rented through your accommodation for 70,000 Rp per day), you can stay anywhere on Nusa Lembongan, using it as a home base for Nusa Lembongan and Nusa Ceningan. If you're **on foot,** pick a hotel in **Jungutbatu** or

Mushroom Bay. Many restaurants include free transport around the two islands with your meal or drinks, and you can easily use this to your strategic advantage.

In contrast to Nusa Lembongan and Nusa Ceningan, Nusa Penida is a challenge to negotiate. Many of the roads are unpaved, unmarked, and can be dangerous to drive on even for skilled motorcyclists. The most accessible parts of Nusa Penida are the neighborhoods of **Toyapakeh** and **Buyuk,** connected by a newly paved road called **Jalan Ped.** This area has a variety of accommodations, restaurants, dive centers, and sandy beaches. If you base yourself here, there are beaches and restaurants all within an easy drive or walking distance. To see the rest of the island, it's best to go with a **guide.** Budget one full day to see Nusa Penida's eastern attractions and another full day to enjoy the sights in the west. If you want to snorkel or scuba dive, this deserves an entire day as well. From place to place, you'll find that there are dozens of vistas and hidden beaches in between.

Many of the Nusa Islands' activities and sights are dependent on **swell size** and **tide.** Some surf breaks, beaches, and natural

Nusa Islands

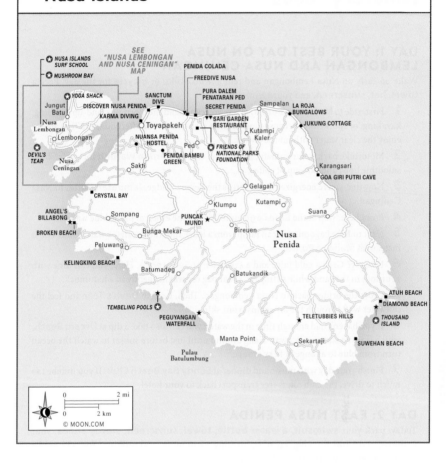

attractions need very specific tides to work. Use a wave and weather forecast like **Magic Seaweed** (www.magicseaweed.com) or **Surfline** (www.surfline.com) to plan your trip accordingly.

Boat cancellations are common during adverse weather and large swells, for safety reasons. Give yourself at least one extra day in between your visit to the Nusa Islands and your departure flight from Denpasar.

Itinerary Ideas

DAY 1: YOUR BEST DAY ON NUSA LEMBONGAN AND NUSA CENINGAN

Wake up early on Nusa Lembongan and rent a **motorbike** or **bicycle** for the day. Pack a **towel, hat, sunscreen,** and your **swimsuit.**

1 First, ride to **Mangrove Forest,** where you can spend the morning stand-up paddling, kayaking, or snorkeling. Because most tourists save this for the afternoon, you'll be able to enjoy the clear water without the crowd.

2 Motorbike back to Jungutbatu, stopping at **Green Garden Warung** for a refreshing smoothie bowl and hot cup of coffee.

3 Now that you're energized, head across the Yellow Bridge, **Jembatan Cinta,** to Nusa Ceningan.

4 From here, stop at the **Blue Lagoon** to admire the ethereal pastel blue water.

5 Next to Blue Lagoon, you can jump from a ledge into the ocean (or watch others do it instead) at **Mahana Point.**

6 Hungry? Grab a cold juice and a sandwich at **Seabreeze.** Here, you can dine with your toes in the sand while sitting on a beanbag or swaying gently in a hammock.

7 Cross the bridge back to Nusa Lembongan. Then, head to **Devil's Tear** and feel the saltwater waft through the air against your skin.

8 If you haven't had enough time in the water, you can also take a dip at **Dream Beach,** which is just a short walk away. Hang around until just before sunset to watch the ocean turn from blue to a range of fiery orange.

9 Finish your day with music and dinner at **Sandy Bay Beach Club.** If you imbibe too much to drive, the club offers free transport back to your hotel.

DAY 2: EAST NUSA PENIDA

Today, pack your **swimsuit, a water bottle, towel, sunscreen, sturdy shoes,** your **camera,** and a **hat** for a big day of sightseeing, swimming, and walking. You will need a **private driver** or **guide** for the day, which is best arranged in advance.

1 To start, grab a hearty breakfast of smashed avocado on toast at **Secret Penida.**

2 Drive to **Diamond Beach,** where you can admire the outlying gemstone-shaped formations from the top of a hill. If you're feeling ambitious, walk down the staircase onto the sand itself. (Ask your driver to park at the parking lot between Diamond Beach and Atuh Beach, so that you can enjoy both of these sites within one stop.)

3 Walk from Diamond Beach to **Atuh Beach** and go for a dip in the sea if the tide is right. Grab lunch and a cold coconut at one of the handful of warungs and relax for a while in a shaded lounge chair.

4 Trek back up the staircase, meet your driver, and head to **Thousand Island Viewpoint.** Again, it's a steep walk down more stairs to see Nusa Penida's beautiful coastline.

Itinerary Ideas

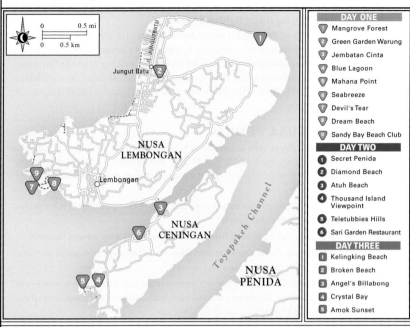

DAY ONE

1. Mangrove Forest
2. Green Garden Warung
3. Jembatan Cinta
4. Blue Lagoon
5. Mahana Point
6. Seabreeze
7. Devil's Tear
8. Dream Beach
9. Sandy Bay Beach Club

DAY TWO

1. Secret Penida
2. Diamond Beach
3. Atuh Beach
4. Thousand Island Viewpoint
5. Teletubbies Hills
6. Sari Garden Restaurant

DAY THREE

1. Kelingking Beach
2. Broken Beach
3. Angel's Billabong
4. Crystal Bay
5. Amok Sunset

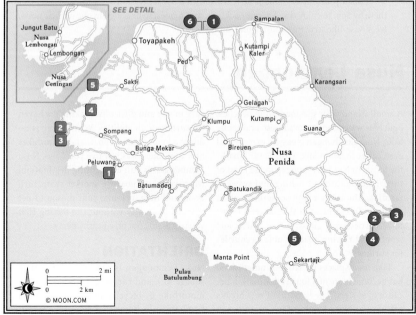

© MOON.COM

5 If time allows, drive to **Teletubbies Hills** and admire the emerald green countryside of Nusa Penida.

6 After all that walking, it's time for dinner. Drive to Buyuk and enjoy a heaping pile of *mie goreng* with a Bintang at **Sari Garden Restaurant.**

While it's possible to visit all these sights in one day, some travelers might find the constant trek up and down steep staircases too strenuous. You can enjoy the view at Diamond Beach and Atuh Beach from the pathway near the parking lot without walking down the full sets of stairs. At the top of the hill before going down to Atuh Beach, you can enjoy the view from a covered patio. Walking just a third of the way down to the tip of Thousand Island lookout will reveal stunning panoramas.

DAY 3: WEST NUSA PENIDA

You'll want to start your day as early as possible to beat the crowds in West Nusa Penida, the island's most popular region. Pack a **hat, sunscreen, sturdy shoes,** a **towel, swimsuit,** and **snorkel set.** It's best to see this area from a **private car** or on the back of a **guided motorbike.**

1 Eat an early breakfast at your hotel before driving to **Kelingking Beach** for golden hour, the magical time just after sunrise.

2 After Kelingking Beach, drive to **Broken Beach** and walk a lap around the cove.

3 The path then leads down a rocky trail to **Angel's Billabong,** a limestone pool that ebbs and flows with the changing tides.

4 Next stop is **Crystal Bay,** where you can feast on traditional Indonesian fare from one of the beachside warungs. Throw on your swimsuit and spend the afternoon snorkeling, swimming, lounging, and walking along the shoreline.

5 Finish your day of outdoor adventure with a sunset session at **Amok Sunset.** Get there by 5pm to enjoy two-for-one cocktails, and request to be seated in one of their nests, treehouse-like structures built from bamboo.

Nusa Lembongan

A small island with spacious white beaches, light blue water, a mangrove forest, and gentle hills, Nusa Lembongan is easy to explore and even easier to fall in love with. Traditionally, the locals in Nusa Lembongan made most of their income through fishing and seaweed farming, the latter being something of an artform. Today, most of the seaweed farms have turned into guesthouses and resort fronts, and fishing boats double as shuttles for surfers.

Like many places in Bali, this quiet island has become more of a tourist destination because of surfers. The handful of surf breaks offshore of Nusa Lembongan's main beach vary in size and difficulty, making it a haven for surfers of all abilities. While there is no doubt a louder buzz of boats and motorbikes now than there was just five years ago, Nusa Lembongan is still a charming destination, where you can scuba dive, snorkel, swim, surf, cycle, and then tuck into your mosquito-net covered bed early without the feeling that you're missing out on a nearby party.

ORIENTATION

Nusa Lembongan is only 8 square km (5 square mi), and can be quickly crossed by motorbike or bicycle. To the north, Nusa Lembongan is home to a mangrove forest.

Nusa Lembongan and Nusa Ceningan

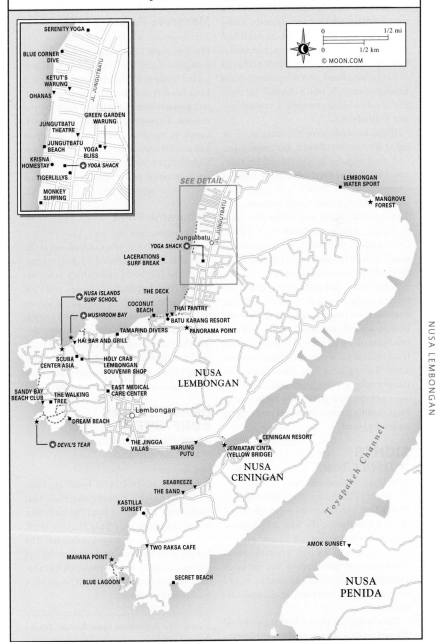

SERENITY YOGA ■

BLUE CORNER DIVE ■

KETUT'S WARUNG ▼

OHANAS ▼

JL. JUNGUTBATU

GREEN GARDEN WARUNG

JUNGUTBATU THEATRE ■

JUNGUTBATU BEACH ■

YOGA BLISS

KRISNA HOMESTAY ●

TIGERLILLYS ■

MONKEY SURFING ■

⊕ YOGA SHACK

0   1/2 mi
0   1/2 km
© MOON.COM

SEE DETAIL

LEMBONGAN WATER SPORT ■

★ MANGROVE FOREST

Jungutbatu ○

JL. JUNGUTBATU

YOGA SHACK ⊕

LACERATIONS SURF BREAK ■

THE DECK ■

⊕ NUSA ISLANDS SURF SCHOOL

COCONUT BEACH

⊕ MUSHROOM BAY

THAI PANTRY ■

TAMARIND DIVERS ▼

BATU KARANG RESORT ■

★ HAI BAR AND GRILL

★ PANORAMA POINT

SCUBA CENTER ASIA ★

HOLY CRAB LEMBONGAN SOUVENIR SHOP ■

EAST MEDICAL CARE CENTER ■

NUSA LEMBONGAN

SANDY BAY BEACH CLUB ■

THE WALKING TREE ■

Lembongan ○

★

DREAM BEACH ▼

⊕ DEVIL'S TEAR

THE JINGGA VILLAS ●

WARUNG PUTU ▼

CENINGAN RESORT ●

JEMBATAN CINTA (YELLOW BRIDGE) ■

NUSA CENINGAN

Toyapakeh Channel

SEABREEZE THE SAND ▼

KASTILLA SUNSET ■

TWO RAKSA CAFE ▼

AMOK SUNSET ▼

MAHANA POINT ★

BLUE LAGOON ■

SECRET BEACH ■

NUSA PENIDA

NUSA ISLANDS
NUSA LEMBONGAN

Running along the island's western coastline, the edge that faces mainland Bali, is **Jungutbatu Beach,** with the **Jungutbatu neighborhood** situated directly along **Jungutbatu road.** This is where you'll find the greatest density of shops, accommodations, restaurants, and dive centers. At the end of Jungutbatu Road, you'll encounter Nusa Lembongan's cliffs, which overlook the three surf breaks of **Playgrounds, Lacerations,** and **Shipwrecks.**

If you keep following the cliffs, you'll be led to **Mushroom Beach,** the island's second most popular neighborhood for tourists. The most western point of the island is where you'll find **Devil's Tear** and **Sandy Bay.** Traveling south, you'll encounter the **Ceningan channel** and bridge that leads to Nusa Ceningan, **Jembatan Cinta. Lembongan,** the town, is set alongside seaweed farms on the island's eastern end, which overlooks the estuarian channel.

Some hotels and restaurants, like those located along Nusa Lembongan's cliff that stretches from Jungutbatu Beach to **Coconut Beach,** are only accessible by foot and may involve walking up several flights of stairs. If accessibility is a concern, choose a venue situated along Jalan Jungutbatu. Your boat transfer ticket to Nusa Lembongan almost always includes pickup and drop-off from your hotel, making it easy to transport your luggage across the island.

SIGHTS
★ Devil's Tear

Pantai Dream; sunrise-sunset; free
The power of the ocean sprays and sloshes at Devil's Tear, a teardrop-shaped notch carved inside a limestone cliff. Sit a safe distance away and watch waves roll in and explode along the sides of the cliff, creating clouds of salty mist. At the waterline, you can catch a glimpse of deep caves and caverns etched over time. For the best experience, come during sunset.

The entrance to Devil's Tear is a dirt road that veers right when you head toward **Dream Beach.** The sea is rough here, so leave your swimsuit back at the hotel.

Mangrove Forest
Jalan Jungutbatu; daily 7am-7pm; 30,000 Rp
Much of Nusa Lembongan is made up of a mangrove forest with a clear-water estuary tucked inside of it. The labyrinth of roots and branches acts as a sanctuary for juvenile fish and protects Nusa Lembongan from coastal erosion. Explore the mangroves via boat, kayak, or stand-up paddleboard, or hop in and snorkel around. Gear can be rented from **Lembongan Water Sport** near the mangrove entrance, and it's best to allow at least two hours to enjoy the area.

Panorama Point
Desa Jungutbatu; open 24/7; free
At Panorama Point, you can look out at the red-roofed neighborhood of Jungutbatu, watch the fast boats and fishing boats arrive on Nusa Lembongan's shores, and view the tops of the mangrove trees all the way on the island's northern end. This vista point is easy to get to from Jungutbatu—simply follow the main road from Jalan Jungutbatu until you rumble up a windy hill. On a clear day, it's possible to see all the way across Nusa Lembongan and out to Mount Agung.

BEACHES AND SURF BREAKS
Jungutbatu Beach (Pantai Jungutbatu)
Gang Nusa Indah
Jungutbatu is the largest beach in Nusa Lembongan, with a sandy shoreline that spans about a mile long from the main boat arrival and departure area to Tanjung Ental, the northern point of Nusa Lembongan. The beach is ideal for throwing down a sarong and sipping coconuts. Most of the beach has a cement walkway and is lined with hotels, dive centers, and restaurants.

1: Devil's Tear **2:** Mangrove Forest **3:** Dream Beach **4:** Mushroom Bay

SHIPWRECKS

*Take a boat from Jangutbatu Beach; best at high
tide; best waves May-Sept.*

On large swells, Shipwrecks is a fun right-hander that can be tricky to time with the tide and current. The lineup is just beyond the rusted bow of a shipwreck. The current tends to be strong and fast at Shipwrecks, even when it's breaking small. This break is definitely best left to experienced surfers. Best conditions: southwesterly swell, easterly winds, 1-3 meters (4-10 feet), high tide.

Dream Beach
(Pantai Dream)

*Parking lot near Café Pandan, beach access is down
a staircase; sunrise-sunset; free admission, parking
5,000 Rp motorbike*

Walk down a steep set of stairs to Dream Beach, a family-friendly cove with restaurants and shops perched on the cliffs above. It's perfect for swimming during mid- to high tide and on low-swell days. The sandy beach is prime real estate for digging holes and building sand castles.

★ Mushroom Bay

*Pantai Mushroom Bay; motorbike parking can be
tricky with narrow roads, watch out for hot exhaust
pipes when parking*

Mushroom Beach is quickly becoming one of Nusa Lembongan's trendiest spots. Dive schools, homestays, restaurants, and boutique shops are blooming along the shoreline of this mushroom-shaped sandy bay. Its calm waters make it a great spot for stand-up paddleboarding and swimming.

Coconut Beach
(Pantai Coconut)

*Follow path along Nusa Lembongan's cliffs overlooking
Jangutbatu, or use trail from Tamarind Bay*

Coconut Beach is a tiny sliver of sand pockmarked with dog paw prints and crowded with ramshackle surfboard rental stands. Accessible only on foot, it's one of the most tucked away corners of Lembongan. Serious surfers use it as a paddle-out location for the surf breaks of Playgrounds and Lacerations, while beginners use the calm waters around it as a spot to test their balancing skills on a stand-up paddleboard (available for rent from beachside stands for 50,000 Rp per hour).

PLAYGROUNDS SURF BREAK

*Paddle out from Coconut Beach or take a boat from
Jangubatu Beach; best at mid- to high tide; best
waves May-Sept.*

If you can't tell from the name, Playgrounds is the friendliest wave in Nusa Lembongan. Its peaky A-frame breaks left and right along shallow reef. Because of its easy accessibility compared to the neighboring breaks, it tends to draw a crowd. Head out early if the tide allows, to have the break without the surf school students. Best conditions: southwest swell, easterly winds, 0.6-3 meters (2-10 feet), mid-high tide.

LACERATIONS SURF BREAK

*Paddle out from Coconut Beach or take a boat from
Jangutbatu Beach; best at mid- to high tide; best
waves May-Sept.*

Lacerations is a fast right-hand wave that barrels in the right conditions. Experienced surfers tend to sit deep and take off late though there are still plenty of waves to be had for intermediate surfers on smaller days. Lacerations earned its name from the cuts surfers get if they don't watch out for rusted poles and sharp corals hidden under the water's surface. To protect your skin, paddle out at mid- to high tide. Best conditions: southwesterly swell, easterly winds, 0.6-3 meters (2-10 feet) from mid- to high tide.

WATER SPORTS
Surfing
★ NUSA ISLANDS SURF SCHOOL

*Mushroom Bay; tel. 81805659124; www.
nusaislandsbali.com; daily 8am-6pm; lessons from
400,000 Rp*

1: Playgrounds Surf Break **2:** Lacerations Surf Break
3: Lembongan Snorkeling Trips **4:** Blue Corner Dive

Nusa Islands Surf School is a wooden rental stand on the far west side of Mushroom Bay. Here, you can learn to surf as a beginner and work on the basics of paddling and catching waves, advance your technique as an intermediate surfer, or go on a guided surf trip to the region's heavier breaks. Each lesson or guided trip comes with pickup and drop-off on Nusa Lembongan, gear rental, and access to the shop's shower afterward.

MONKEY SURFING

Gang Nusa Indah; tel. 82146147683; www.
monkeyactivities.com; daily 8am-6pm; lessons from
600,000 Rp

Monkey Surfing is one of the original surf schools on Nusa Lembongan. Beginner, intermediate, and advanced lessons are offered, all with a ratio of three students to one ISA-certified instructor. Your 2.5-hour lesson includes surfboard rental, a rashguard, reef booties (recommended for all surf breaks in Nusa Lembongan), and transfer to the surf spot.

Snorkeling, Scuba Diving, and Free Diving
LEMBONGAN SNORKELING TRIPS

Jalan Jungutbatu; tel. 82145426252; www.
lembongansnorkelingtrips.com; daily 8am-5:30pm;
tours from 500,000 Rp per person

Some of the Nusa Islands' best dive sites can be seen from the surface of the water. Join a snorkeling tour with Lembongan Snorkeling Trips. A local guide will take you to a few of the best snorkel sites, depending on the visibility, tide, swell, and current. Trips offer a good chance of seeing manta rays as well as the vibrant reef just along Nusa Lembongan's mangrove area. Each tour includes snorkeling equipment and a life vest.

BLUE CORNER DIVE

Jungutbatu Beach; tel. 82341308480; www.
bluecornerdive.com; daily 7am-9pm; 1,200,000 Rp
for 2 fun dives

One of the most established 5-Star PADI Career Development Centers in Nusa Lembongan, Blue Corner Dive has earned a reputation for hosting some of the most skilled instructors in Indonesia. Grab your gear and go for a fun dive or take one of their courses, which range from Discover Scuba to scuba instructor classes. For those who want to learn to dive without a tank, Blue Corner teaches PADI freediving classes as well. After your dive, enjoy sipping a cold Bintang from the comforts of their seaside pool, or from a beanbag chair on the beach. Blue Corner hosts a range of evening activities throughout the week; the most popular night is Friday.

TAMARIND DIVERS

Tamarind Beach; tel. 81238626677; www.
tamarinddivers.com; daily 7am-7pm; 1,150,000 Rp
for 2 fun dives

Being one of the smaller dive centers on the island, Tamarind Divers is ideal for divers who enjoy having a say in their diving sites or conditions. At this PADI dive center, you can enjoy fun diving, take a Discover Scuba course, or work your way up to a PADI divemaster certification.

SCUBA CENTER ASIA

Mushroom Bay; tel. 81246202085; www.
scubacenterasia.com; daily 7am-7pm; 1,150,000 Rp
for 2 fun dives

Scuba Center Asia is a 5-Star PADI Instructor Development Center founded by two Dutch divers, Kim and Bastiaan, who have created a welcoming and ocean-obsessed dive center just a short walk away from Mushroom Beach. Here, you can blow bubbles on a fun dive, take an introductory course, or work toward becoming a scuba instructor. This is an ideal center for nervous divers, as the instructors have a reputation for being understanding and patient. The bar attached to Scuba Center Asia is a great place to meet friends and chat about the creatures you've seen over a *broodje kroket*, a Dutch variation of a hot dog.

Kayaking

LEMBONGAN WATER SPORT

Mangrove Beach; tel. 8155773999; www.
lembonganwatersport.com; daily 8am-6pm; 150,000
Rp per kayak

Lembongan Water Sport is a catch-all tour and rental shop that offers snorkel trips and day tours around the Nusa Islands. One of their best tours takes place in the Mangrove Forest, where you can paddle over clear water and take a closer look at the vegetation from the comforts of a kayak. Each tour lasts about an hour and comes with transfer to and from your hotel on Nusa Lembongan, kayak rental, a locker, towel, and access to the on-site shower. You can also do the same tour with a stand-up paddleboard.

OTHER SPORTS AND RECREATION

Yoga

★ YOGA SHACK

Jalan Jungutbatu (Big Fish Diving); tel. 81353136861;
www.bigfishdiving.com; daily 8am-6pm; 100,000 Rp
per class

The Yoga Shack is a roomy yoga *shala* built from bamboo and topped with a large thatched roof. Because of how it's built, it lets you feel a slight breeze as you move through your practice. Yogis can come in on a drop-in basis and attend classes like *yin, hatha* flow, or *vinyasa,* or workshops that specialize in one category of postures, balances, or body part. Yoga mats and props are available with each class.

YOGA BLISS

Jungutbatu Neighborhood (behind Green
Garden Warung); tel. 81337801843; https://
yogablisslembongan.com; daily 7:30am-7:30pm;
100,000 Rp per class

Yoga Bliss is one of the best places for dedicated yogis to refine their practice with casual *vinyasa, yin,* restorative, *ashtanga,* and flow classes offered each week. Frequently, Yoga Bliss also hosts yoga teacher trainings

and yoga retreats, and it partners with local surf instructors for a surf-and-stretch-style retreat. The yoga area itself is peaceful, with a wooden platform under a huge open-air building. Mats, blocks, and props are included with class admission. Yoga Bliss invests 6 percent of its earnings into community and environmental programs that take place on Nusa Lembongan.

SERENITY YOGA

Jungutbatu Neighborhood; tel. 81238499141; www.
serenityyogalembongan.com; Sun.-Fri. 7:30am-7pm,
closed Sat.; 120,000 Rp per class

Surrounded by tropical gardens, the *shala* (yoga studio) at Serenity Yoga is where you can practice many variations of yoga like *yin,* flow, power yoga, and *ashtanga* yoga. The yoga centers welcomes beginners to most classes, and even offers a fundamentals class where new yogis can learn the basics of correct posture. Occasionally, Serenity Yoga hosts workshops, retreats, stand-up paddleboard yoga, and masterclasses for more advanced practicioners.

SHOPPING

THE WALKING TREE

Jalan Sandy Bay; tel. 87761417090; www.
thewalkingtree.com; daily 9am-7pm

The Walking Tree is part boutique, part deli, selling a mishmash of home goods, clothing, accessories, and specialty foods like imported wine and cheeses, as well as homemade chutneys. Its bright blue exterior and airy interior make it a pleasant place to browse around.

HOLY CRAB

Jalan Mushroom Bay; tel. 82147236993; daily
9am-10pm

Holy Crab is a small shop selling your typical Bali souvenirs as well as its own line of clothing. Here, you can buy shirts with manta rays and *mola-mola* fish printed on them—making it unique to the Nusa Islands. The staff will usually let you browse through the sarongs, accessories, and small decorations in peace.

FOOD
Indonesian and Asian
★ WARUNG PUTU

Jalan Jungutbatu (near the Yellow Bridge); tel. 81377454706; daily 10am-10pm; 20,000-60,000 Rp

Though it's rare to find great food in a restaurant that has great views, this fortunately isn't the case at Warung Putu. Feel the sand beneath your toes and dine while sitting in a swing at this warung set on the shoreline of Nusa Lembonga, looking across the channel to Nusa Ceningan. Dine on spiced meats, fried rice, noodle soups, or hamburgers. As a tip, it's best to stick to the Indonesian side rather than the American side of the menu.

KETUT'S WARUNG

Jalan Jungutbatu; tel. 82146358325; daily 10am-8pm; 20,000-80,000 Rp

Ketut's Warung is an unassuming little no-frills restaurant, hidden in an alleyway (turn at the green sign that says Saiko Mart). Their simple menu features Thai curries, *jaffles* (toasted sandwiches), *mie goreng, nasi goreng,* and *nasi campur,* and food is served in a covered dining area that extends as part of Ketut's home. This is a go-to spot for cheap, fresh, and authentic fare.

JUNGUTBATU THEATRE

Jalan Jungutbatu; tel. 8123619493; daily 7am-10pm; 30,000-100,000 Rp

Dinner and a movie go together like coconuts and Bali. At the Jungutbatu Theater along Nusa Lembongan's main road, you can watch a movie from the comforts of a beanbag chair. Anything goes when it comes to what's playing; you may see a 1980s rom-com one night and a horror flick the next. The menu features local fare like noodle soup, *nasi goreng, mie goreng,* and *gado-gado* (steamed vegetables with peanut sauce). If it's a rainy evening, get there early to snag the best seat.

★ THAI PANTRY

Cliffs near Coconut Beach; tel. 81353320568; https://thaipantrybali.com; daily 7:30am-9:30pm; 60,000-110,000 Rp

With an iconic Volkswagon Kombi that's been converted into a bar, Thai Pantry certainly is one of the more kitschy venues on the island. Dine on fresh Thai noodles, satay, and curries at this open-air restaurant set atop Nusa Lembongan's cliffs. Glass windows and an open floor plan create a relaxing ambience where it's easy to sit and watch the boats come and go below. Come for happy hour to enjoy the sunset and 25 percent off selected cocktails (4pm-6:30pm daily).

International
THE DECK

Batu Karang Lembongan Resort; tel. 8113869216; https://thedecklembongan.com; daily 7am-11pm; 60,000-130,000 Rp

The Deck is a cliffside bistro serving coffee, cocktails, Australian and European dishes, and an array of baked goods. The white wooden patio is accented with purple and pink foliage, giving it a tranquil and fresh vibe. Take a seat wherever you like and watch surfers catch waves at Lacerations surf break at sunset. It's best to stay for a drink and head elsewhere when it comes time to eat a full meal.

OHANA'S

Jungutbatu Beach; tel. 81139600787; www.ohanas.co; daily 7am-11:30pm; 70,000-280,000 Rp

Ohana's is a newly built beach club and restaurant set on the shores of Jungutbatu Beach. Dine on pizza, sandwiches, steaks, salads, or their signature bacon-and-egg breakfast, whether on a beach beanbag chair, at a table, or in a covered cabana by the pool. The restaurant offers free pickup at any Nusa Lembongan hotel for those who've made reservations. At sunset, Ohana's lights a bonfire on the beach and plays music. Friday nights are popular at Ohana's, thanks to their lineup of local and international DJs.

1: view from Warung Putu **2:** Thai Pantry

Vegetarian/Vegan
★ GREEN GARDEN WARUNG

Jangutbatu neighborhood, across from soccer field;
tel. 81337419282; greengardenlembongan@gmail.
com; daily 7am-9:30pm; 30,000-70,000 Rp

A hub for yogis and wellness gurus, Green Garden Warung is a health-conscious restaurant that serves Indonesian dishes, salads, burgers, pizza, pasta—all of which can be made vegan or vegetarian. For breakfast, choose between smoothie bowls, homemade granola, and eggs. Kombuchas, fresh juices, coffee, and tea grace the drinks menu. The dining area is set in a small garden with a yoga and eco goods boutique, bungalows, and yoga *shala*. Each week, the restaurant hosts a beach cleanup where you can make friends while keeping Nusa Lembongan beautiful.

NIGHTLIFE
HAI BAR AND GRILL

Mushroom Bay; tel. 361/720331; https://
haitidebeachresort.com; daily 7am-10pm;
60,000-160,000 Rp mains, 30,000-110,000 Rp drinks

Though Nusa Lembongan isn't known for its party scene, you can always find someone to chat with in the evenings at Hai Bar and Grill. This open-air beach club serves seafood and wood-fired pizzas in an expansive bamboo dining area, just steps away from the sandy beach of Mushroom Bay. For a chilled-out evening, come on Monday, Thursday, or Saturday around 7:30pm to watch a movie under the stars. All other evenings, you can expect tropical music and more upbeat vibes. There's free pickup and drop-off for those staying in Nusa Lembongan.

★ SANDY BAY BEACH CLUB

Jalan Sandy Bay; tel. 87862274780; https://
sandybaylembongan.com; daily 8am-11pm;
10,000-220,000 Rp mains, 30,000-115,000 Rp drinks

Sandy Bay Beach Club is set on a tiny beach, where you can sip a coconut or cocktail from one of their poolside lounge chairs. Dine on steak, burgers, sandwiches, salads, or seafood, and complement your meal with a glass of Australian wine or a cocktail. The music played over the pool area is upbeat, adding to the tropical ambience as you look out over the water. Come on Saturday evening to enjoy a live DJ. Sandy Bay Beach Club also offers fresh towels, and transportation to and from your hotel is included with each visit.

ACCOMMODATIONS
Under 1,000,000 Rp
★ KRISNA HOMESTAY

Br. Kaja Jungutbatu; krisnalembongan@gmail.com;
150,000-400,000 Rp

Run by Adil and his family, Krisna Homestay is a cozy, spotless property just a one-minute walk from Jungutbatu beach. The property is well-kept, with stone step pathways and manicured plants. Request to stay in the newly built wooden bungalows that come with air-conditioning, a desk, a mini fridge, and a patio area. If you need help arranging tours during your stay, Adil is happy to oblige.

THE JINGGA VILLAS

Jalan Laguna; tel. 81916626336; www.thejinggavillas.
com; 600,000-750,000 Rp

Owned and run by always-smiling Ketut and his family, the Jungga Villas is one of the best-value accommodation options on the island. Each bungalow is built from wood and bamboo, with a traditional thatch roof. The rooms are clean, spacious, traditionally decorated, and set among immaculately kept gardens. Most meals served at The Jingga Villas involve fresh seafood caught early each morning. The Jingga Villas is located along a bumpy road, so it is best to have your own motorbike to get there.

Over 1,000,000 Rp
★ TIGERLILLYS

Jalan Jungutbatu; tel. 87761741486; www.
tigerlillyslembongan.com; 900,000-1,500,000 Rp

Tigerlilly's might as well be a synonym for tranquility. Each of its eight lumbung-style bungalows with thatched roofing is surrounded by plumeria and palm trees. The shabby-chic-style restaurant with wicker and wooden furniture opens onto a small pool with stone statues. Each two-story bungalow is uniquely decorated and equipped with a reading nook, patio, semi-outdoor bathroom, hot water shower, air-conditioning, and mosquito net.

BATU KARANG RESORT

Jalan Jungut Batu; tel. 2665596377; https:// batukaranglembongan.com; 3,500-5,000,000 Rp

Batu Karang Resort is a five-star resort set on the cliffs of Nusa Lembongan, overlooking the ocean and set around an outdoor pool and open-air dining area. Room choices include a twin or double suite, one-bedroom villa, or three-bedroom villa—many with private plunge pools, stone bathtubs, and outdoor showers. Each room is airy and modern, featuring bright white linens with dark wooden decor. Request a room with a view of Mount Agung in the distance.

INFORMATION AND SERVICES

Stock up on cash before you arrive in Nusa Lembongan. There are only a handful of moody **ATMs** on the island, and they are often out of bills. On the off chance that a dive center or resort does accept credit card, the machine itself always seems to have trouble making a connection.

Health and Safety
EAST MEDICAL CARE CENTER

Jalan Mushroom Beach; tel. 81339555515; www. eastmedicalcarecenter.com; open 24/7; consultation starts at 500,000 Rp

East Medical Care Center is a modern medical clinic with English-speaking staff, an ambulance service, pharmacy, and an emergency room. They also offer hotel visits and doctor consultation appointments. Should you need to transfer to Denpasar, the medical center has an evacuation team on standby.

GETTING THERE
From Sanur

It usually takes 25-45 minutes to get from Sanur to Nusa Lembongan via a **fast boat.** These transfers tend to be door-to-door service, including pickup from your hotel in mainland Bali and drop-off at your accommodation in Nusa Lembongan. There is also a **public fast boat** run by local families that leaves regularly from 9am to 4pm daily

A motorbike is the best way to get around Nusa Lembongan.

(schedules irregular), costing 200,000 Rp per person; tickets are sold at the end of **Jalan Hang Tuah.**

For safety reasons, avoid getting on a small boat or one from an unnamed company. There are more than 15 reputable fast boat companies that service this route, so if one company is booked, you'll easily find another. Here are some of the most reliable:

- **Scoot** (www.scootcruise.com; tel. 361/285522): Includes hotel transfers; 280,000-325,000 Rp one way per adult, 650,000-800,000 Rp return per adult.

- **Rocky Fast Cruise** (https://rockyfastcruise.com; tel. 361/283624): Includes hotel transfers; 250,000 Rp one way per adult, 500,000 Rp return per adult.

- **D'Camel Fast Ferry** (https://dcamelfastferry.com; tel. 81338515837): Includes hotel transfers; 350,000 Rp one way per adult, 550,000 Rp return per adult.

Note that there is no pier in Nusa Lembongan, and you will be getting your feet wet. Boats from Bali drop off and depart at **Pantai Jungutbatu** on the shoreline. Boats coming from Nusa Penida arrive either at the **Mangrove Forest** or near the **Yellow Bridge.** Dress in shorts or pants that you can roll up and a pair of sandals. Before your journey, place your electronics in a dry bag to protect them from going into the water—it's not that rare for luggage to fall into the sea as staff offload baggage from the deck.

From Nusa Penida

You can also take a boat to and from one of the fishermen located in **Toyapakeh** on Nusa Penida (the largest island), which takes around 20 minutes and costs 50,000-60,000 Rp per person. These boats typically leave as soon as they are full. Public boats also run hourly from Toyapakeh and cost 50,000 Rp per person.

From Bangsal (Lombok)

Eka Jaya (www.ekajayafastboat.com; tel. 82266400678; 475,000 Rp per adult one way, 850,000 Rp per adult return, includes hotel pickup and drop-off) services the route between Bangsal and Nusa Lembongan. The journey takes roughly 1.5 hours.

GETTING AROUND

At just 4 km (2.5 mi) long, Nusa Lembongan is a small island that is easily accessible **on foot,** on **bicycle,** or on a **motorbike.** Most roads aside from the main road of **Jalan Jungutbatu** are unmarked, so it's best to use major landmarks like hotels and restaurants when asking for directions.

Motorbikes cost around 70,000 Rp per day to hire and include a helmet. You can also rent a **bicycle** and helmet for around 70,000 Rp per day through your **accommodation,** or from those offering them for rent on **Jalan Jungutbatu,** with decent bikes for rent at **The Coral Shop** (southern end of Pantai Jungutbatu; tel. 82236643261) for 80,000 Rp per day. If you crave exploration on four wheels, **golf carts** from **Ricky Raja** can be rented for 700,000 Rp per day (rickyraja7988@gmail.com; tel. 81338587988).

Many of the popular restaurants, dive centers, and beach clubs offer **free transport** around Nusa Lembongan. There are also small **trucks** that will shuttle you in the direction they're headed for about 20,000 Rp per ride.

Dive with the Locals: Marine Life You Can Expect to See

Scuba divers and snorkelers flock from all around the world to dive with some of the incredible marine animals that live along the Nusa Islands' coral reefs. On your dive, search for the following creatures:

- **Manta ray:** These gentle giants are filter feeders. They have a large brain to body ratio, and can grow up to 7 meters (23 feet) across. While you can spot them all year long, you'll have the best luck during April and May.

- *Mola-mola:* Perhaps one of the strangest looking fish in the sea, the gargantuan *mola-mola* is the world's heaviest bony fish and can weigh up to 1,000 kg (more than 1 ton). To spot them, dive from July to November, when the water is coldest.

- **Peacock mantis shrimp:** Flamboyantly colored and ferociously weaponized, this crustacean is quite the killer. The velocity of its punch is strong enough to shatter shells of its prey—and can easily crack glass. While humans have just three color receptors in our eyes, the peacock mantis shrimp has a whopping 12.

- **Moray eel:** Mouth agape, moray eels are often seen peering out of reef crevices. They're nocturnal creatures, so if you don't see one during the day, try again during a night dive.

- **Scorpionfish:** These highly venomous fish are masters of disguise and are usually spotted by experienced divers who know to look for their spiny backs and black eyes. Their patterned scales make them appear as though they're just another piece of the reef.

Nusa Ceningan

"Nusa Ceningan" means "small island," and it is the smallest of the three Nusa Islands. Most of the locals once farmed seaweed in the Ceningan channel separating Nusa Ceningan from Nusa Lembongan, and you can still see the checkerboard of seaweed farms today. Because of its manageable size, this island is easy to explore, and every month, more beach swings, hammocks, and coconut stands pop up to serve the travelers making their laps around the island.

ORIENTATION

Nusa Ceningan is wedged in between Nusa Lembongan and Nusa Penida, connected to Nusa Lembongan by a motorbike and the pedestrian-only Yellow Bridge, **Jembatan Cinta.** One road, **Jalan Nusa Ceningan,** circles the island. Sights like **Blue Lagoon** and **Mahana Point** are on the south side of the island, while Nusa Penida can be spotted in the west.

SIGHTS
Mahana Point

Jalan Sarang Burung; sunrise-9:30pm;
25,000-50,000 Rp supervised cliff jump

Natural Feature Mahana Point is a prime hangout spot for travelers looking to swim and cliff jump from a 5-meter (16-foot; 25,000 Rp) or 10-meter (32-foot; 50,000 Rp) platform. A little café on the point sells pizzas, sandwiches, and cold drinks in a shaded seating area. To swim without paying for the cliff jump, walk down the stairs and you'll find a ladder that leads into the water. If the waves on Lembongan aren't breaking, surfers come to Mahana Point in hopes of catching something at the left-hand point break.

1: Mahana Point **2:** Jembatan Cinta

Jembatan Cinta (Yellow Bridge)

Jalan Nusa Ceningan; 24 hours; free to cross

Connecting Nusa Lembongan to Nusa Ceningan, this bright yellow bridge is an icon of the area. The original suspension bridge collapsed as Balinese Hindus were walking to a local ceremony in 2016, killing nine people and injuring dozens. In the aftermath, the two islands were deeply affected due to the loss of their loved ones and the difficulty of getting to and from the two islands. The bridge was originally named Yellow Bridge (Jembatan Kuning) but renamed to what translates as "Bridge of Love," to commemorate the victims of the tragedy. Take care when crossing the bridge, as it is only wide enough across to fit two motorbikes at a time.

BEACHES
Blue Lagoon

Jalan Sarang Burung; daily 24/7; free

True to its name, Blue Lagoon's baby blue water fades to a deep cobalt as it spans out to sea. You can perch on one of the many rocks surrounding the lagoon itself. Visit at high tide to experience the blue hue at its brightest. While people do cliff jump here, it's not recommended, as the climb back up the cliff is tedious and needs to be timed strategically in between waves.

Secret Beach

Jalan Secret Beach; daily sunrise-10pm; free access with food or drink purchase from Villa Trevally

Secret Beach is a small sliver of sand wedged in between a shallow reef and a grassy area. Though the swimming here isn't ideal because of strong currents and a sharp reef, there's a good chance that you'll have this beach all to yourself. Because the beach access is near Villa Trevally, employees may nudge you to purchase something from the resort's restaurant if you want to hang out at Secret Beach undisturbed.

FOOD

The main restaurants and warungs are typically found in Toyapekeh and its surrounding areas. Smaller warungs and stands selling fresh produce and snacks can also be found on Nusa Penida's main beaches, as well as the side of the road.

Blue Lagoon

Indonesian
SEABREEZE
Jalan Nusa Ceningan; tel. 81239567407;
seabreezeceningan@gmail.com; daily 7:30am-11pm;
20,000-50,000 Rp

With brightly colored umbrellas, beanbag chairs, a beach pool, and a wooden deck, Seabreeze is an easygoing beach restaurant and bar with plenty of lounge options. Their menu has simple sandwiches with fries, *mie goreng, nasi goreng,* grilled fish served with *sambal,* and fresh juice. Come from 4pm to 8pm, when Seabreeze sells two cocktails for a mere 100,000 Rp. The drinks aren't the strongest, but the ocean views easily make up for the lack of alcoholic punch.

TWO RAKSA CAFÉ
Jalan Sarang Burung; tel. 8123651925; daily
8am-8pm; 30,000-60,000 Rp

Being barefoot is practically a given at Two Raksa Café, a restaurant where you can dine in a well-kept garden area with tables and hammocks spread throughout. Most locals and long-term expats come for a meal of fish grilled in banana leaf and a side of sweet corn fritters or spring rolls. The owner, Putu, often takes a moment to stop and chat with guests about what to do and see around the area. *Mie goreng, nasi goreng,* curry, and *gado-gado* are also winning items on the menu.

European
THE SAND
Jalan Nusa Ceningan; tel. 81337670983; daily
10am-midnight; 40,000-70,000 Rp

The Sand has become somewhat of an icon among Instagram influencers, thanks to its whimsical swings, hammocks, and seating area made from driftwood. The smoothie bowls served on patterned plates, stamped coconuts, and artfully decorated cocktails look as though they're made to be photographed. In between photo shoots, enjoy your pick of smashed avocado, *nasi goreng* or *mie goreng,* curry, burgers, sandwiches, pasta, salads, juices, and ice cream.

ACCOMMODATIONS

Most accommodations on Nusa Penida are found along the northern coastline of the island, especially clustered around Toyapekeh. Remote accommodations, like those found on the island's southern coastline or its interior, may require having a personal driver, as roads throughout these regions can be dangerous.

Under 1,000,000 Rp
KASTILLA SUNSET
Jalan Nusa Ceningan; tel. 81338071552;
800,000-1,500,000 Rp

Kastilla Sunset combines luxury and location in its newly built wooden huts with tiled roofs. Each hut is furnished with a desk, air-conditioning, mosquito net, crisp white linen, mini-fridge, safe, and modern bathroom. The property has an infinity and lounge chair area that overlooks the channel between Nusa Ceningan and Nusa Lembongan. To make a reservation, call the owner or use a booking platform like Booking.com or Agoda.com, as the resort has yet to set up a way to book a room with Kastilla Sunset directly.

★ CENINGAN RESORT
Jalan Nusa Ceningan, 500 meters (1,640 feet)
from Yellow Bridge; tel. 82145855934; https://
ceninganresort.com; 850,000 Rp

If you've come to the Nusa Islands to surf, dive, sleep, repeat, then Ceningan Resort is a top pick. This eco-resort has eight bungalows built from wood and topped with a traditional thatched roof. Each room comes with its own outdoor bathroom, air-conditioning, balcony, and hammock—all set among tropical gardens. Guests have access to a private jetty that juts out into the mangroves, a lounge area where you can smoke *shisha* (pipe) and order drinks, a pool, and an on-site restaurant. Ceningan Resort is also a 5-Star PADI dive resort, where you can save on scuba diving packages and lessons by combining them with your accommodation.

INFORMATION AND SERVICES

There are **no ATMs** on Nusa Ceningan, so you will need to come prepared with plenty of cash. Most accommodations and warungs do not accept credit or debit cards.

GETTING THERE

To reach Nusa Ceningan, you will need to first go to **Nusa Lembongan,** as most fast boat companies do not stop at Nusa Ceningan directly. From Nusa Lembongan, take a motorbike across the yellow suspension bridge, **Jembatan Cinta.** If you have a lot of luggage to transport and are in a **pickup truck,** you will need to offload it at the bridge, walk or motorbike it across, and then put your luggage in a separate pickup truck on Nusa Ceningan.

Alternatively, you can take a **boat** across from Nusa Lembongan to Nusa Ceningan at high tide for 30,000-50,000 Rp.

GETTING AROUND

Roam around Nusa Ceningan by **bicycle or motorbike,** or **on foot.** Though they're rarer than on Nusa Lembongan, you can also hail a ride in a **pickup truck** for about 20,000 Rp per trip.

Nusa Penida

TOP EXPERIENCE

Raw and dramatic, Nusa Penida's natural landscape commands attention. Unforgiving limestone cliffs intersect with sugar sand beaches that look like unpainted canvases from a distance, not yet accented with trails of footprints or the splash of multicolored sarongs. The ocean surrounding Nusa Penida ranges from light turquoise to deep blue, often within the same bay. Looking inland, dense bushland and palm trees give Nusa Penida its distinct green hue.

Five years ago, Nusa Penida was seen purely as an offbeat destination, and many of its most iconic vistas had yet to grace the hashtag galleries of Instagram. Balinese mainlanders stayed away from Nusa Penida, avoiding a land that they believe to be cursed. However, when social media-savvy travelers visited this untouched island and began revealing images of Nusa Penida's beaches on the internet, a wave of tourists arrived. Today, dozens more homestays and guesthouses appear each month, and restaurants are opening by the dozens.

Make no mistake, despite the fast-paced development of Nusa Penida, it's still an island for those who prefer to go down the road less traveled. The terrain is rugged, jagged, and untouched, and the best beaches, temples, and sights on the island are typically found at the end of a steep stairway or tucked between two precarious paths. In between these incredible sights, you'll find villages still functioning as if tourists never came at all.

When you feel the saltwater cool your skin or see the unfathomable view with your own eyes, you'll realize the journey, no matter how rough, was worth it.

ORIENTATION

Nusa Penida is the farthest island from Bali of the three Nusa Islands. **Toyapekeh** is the main area of Nusa Penida, where boats from other islands arrive at its harbor, which is directly across the northern part of the channel between Nusa Penida and Nusa Lembongan. Here, you can find a town that still predominantly caters to its residents, but there are also a handful of warungs, shops, and accommodations. **Jalan Ped** runs east and west of Toyapekeh all the way around the island, forming the island's main road.

East Nusa Penida hosts the sights of **Atuh Beach, Diamond Beach,** and **Suwehan**

1: Tembeling Pool 2: Angel's Billabong 3: Thousand Island

Beach. Angel's Billabong, Kelingking Beach, Tembeling Pools, and Crystal Bay are in West Nusa Penida. The highest point in the island, Bukit Mundi, is in the middle, slightly skewed toward the west.

SIGHTS
West Nusa Penida
DALEM PENATARAN PED TEMPLE
(Pura Dalem Penataran Ped)

Jalan Ped-Buyuk; sunrise-sunset (closes for ceremonies); free admission, 10,000 Rp sarong rental

Built from white limestone and embellished with intricate carvings, Pura Dalem Penataran Ped is one of the most sacred temples on Nusa Penida. This temple is home to Ratu Gede Macaling, one of the most powerful and malevolent gods in Balinese Hinduism. Visit with an offering of *canang sari* to appease Ratu Gede Macaling's spirit.

PUNCAK MUNDI

Jalan Puncak Mundi (Desa Klumpu); daily 9am-6pm; free

At over 500 meters (1,640 feet) above sea level, Puncak Mundi is the highest point on Nusa Penida. Puncak Mundi is a series of three Balinese Hindu temples called Pura Beji, Pura Krangkeng, and Pura Mundi. The air is noticeably cooler in this region, and the vegetation shifts from palm trees and shrublands to tall trees. Monkeys roam freely among the temple grounds, snatching food from offerings and helping themselves to whatever is in a visitor's bag. The journey up the windy road reveals an interesting perspective at nearly every turn.

PEGUYANGAN WATERFALL

Jalan Terta Bhuana Sari (Desa Batukandik); sunrise-sunset; free admission, 5,000 Rp parking, 10,000 Rp sarong rental

Like many of Nusa Penida's most stunning sites, Peguyangan Waterfall is both a natural feature and a space for Balinese Hindu religious ceremonies. To get to Peguyangan Waterfall, you'll first walk down a steep bright blue staircase that switchbacks and traces

Nusa Penida's coastline, offering panoramic views of the vegetation and ocean below. The walk down takes about 20 minutes at a brisk pace. The waterfall itself is truly more of a spring, where the water is diverted into three different spouts that come out of the mouths of Hindu statues and one larger spout just outside of the temple grounds. Balinese Hindus use these springs as a means of spiritual cleansing and to receive strength. Beyond the springs is a series of freshwater limestone pools that trickle down to the open ocean.

ANGEL'S BILLABONG

Desa Sakti; best at mid- to low tide; free

Angel's Billabong is a large pool of water carved into limestone cliff. On days with no wind or swell, the surface of the water flattens out to what resembles a sheet of glass, letting you peer clearly into the bottom. Along the cliff ledge, the billabong trickles into the sea, where manta rays are often spotted gliding just meters away from the cliff's edge. If the tide is low and the swell is small, Angel's Billabong doubles as a plunge pool.

★ TEMBELING POOLS

Desa Batumadeg; sunrise-sunset; free

Hidden in a dense forest are two freshwater pools with a signature teal hue. The Tembeling Pools are used as a religious site for water ceremonies, and marked by a small temple. The road leading to the Tembeling Pools is narrow and bumpy, with a steep cliff running along one side. Have a guide take you to the pools or walk from the top parking lot (30 minutes). You'll likely see kids jumping into the larger pool, taking care not to jump higher than the temple structure. The second pool is slightly smaller and acts as more of a natural Jacuzzi formed of smooth stones. Next to the pools, you can relax, picnic, or play music under a shady tree.

East Nusa Penida
GOA GIRI PUTRI CAVE

Desa Karang Sari; daily 9am-6pm; free admission, 10,000 Rp sarong rental

The Best Dive Sites in the Nusa Islands

Manta Point

MANTA POINT

Mantas galore can be found at Manta Point, where manta rays partake in their own form of a spa treatment. Manta Point has a gargantuan coral bommie that attracts many reef fish who feed on parasites attached to the manta rays' skin. This is why many divers also refer to Manta Point as the "cleaning station."

MANTA BAY

Manta Bay is the safe haven for Nusa Penida's juvenile manta rays, who take shelter in the shallow bay. This is a great spot to freedive and snorkel with mantas, as they tend to glide just a few meters below the surface. Occasionally, the surge can get strong in Manta Bay if there's a serious swell around, so it's best left to divers with a strong stomach.

TOYAPAKEH

Explore a ledge of reef covered in hard and soft corals, with animals like scorpionfish, moray eels, orangutan crabs, batfish, puffer fish, and nudibranchs taking shelter at the reef.

CRYSTAL BAY

Crystal Bay delivers what many people imagine when they think of diving in Indonesia. In Crystal Bay's shallower area, you'll find warm water, thriving coral bommies, sea turtles, peacock mantis shrimp, and reef fish galore. Don't forget to look out into the blue every once in a while, you might spot a *mola-mola*.

MANGROVE

Lazy divers will delight at this dive site where you drift along a vibrant coral reef made of soft and hard corals. Nudibranchs, anemones, clown fish, puffer fish, scorpion fish, box fish, Moray eels, and turtles all hang around this area.

At first glance, Goa Giri Putri Cave is unremarkable. After walking up 110 stairs, you're met with a small hole in a wall of piled rocks. However, once you weave your way through the entrance of Goa Giri Putri Cave, you'll find a large cave made of limestone, with stalagtites and stalagmites adorning its walls and ceiling. The air inside the cave is damp and smoky, thanks to the waft of incense and walls that never see daylight. Bats hang overhead, and Balinese Hindus kneel below.

All visitors must wear a sarong and sash into the temple cave, and will be blessed by a Hindu priest in exchange for their visit. It's rare to find the cave empty of practicing Hindus, as many believe that the water that flows through the cave has powerful healing properties. Though tourists are welcome to explore the cave, be mindful not to disturb any ceremonies that are taking place.

★ THOUSAND ISLAND

Desa Pejukutan; sunrise-sunset; free entrance, 10,000 Rp parking

The Thousand Island viewpoint is on a small peninsula that juts out into the ocean, where you can walk to the end and gaze at about 10 small islands along Nusa Penida's coastline (the name Thousand Island is quite the hyperbole). The viewpoint is located down a steep set of stairs that takes about 15 minutes to descend. Along the peninsula, you can stop and admire the view from a treehouse balcony or walk to the tip and admire the views from the respite of a shade shelter. Some locals refer to this spot as *Pulau Seribu*, which means "Thousand Island."

TELETUBBIES HILLS

Desa Tanglad; daily 24/7; free

Teletubbies Hills are a nod to the late-1990s children's show, which takes place in a fictional land made of bulbous rolling hills. Teletubbies Hills, also known as Gamal Hills, are made from smooth mounds of limestone carpeted in wild grass—an interesting contrast to Nusa Penida's sharp and jagged coastline.

★ BEACHES
West Nusa Penida
CRYSTAL BAY

Desa Sakti; 10,000 Rp parking

Crystal Bay is one of the most popular snorkeling and diving spots on Nusa Lembongan. A sandy beach spans across a valley and is marked by beach umbrellas, palm trees, and shabby warungs selling instant noodles, fried rice, and coconuts. Just a few hundred meters from shore is Crystal Bay's resident island, Batu Mejineng Island. Ease your way into the water and you'll find colorful coral bommies that are home to anemones, nudibranchs, sea turtles, and reef fish. If you're lucky, you might spot a rare *mola-mola* in the depths of Crystal Bay.

BROKEN BEACH
(Pantai Pasih Uug)

Desa Bunga Mekar; 5,000 Rp parking

Broken Beach, also called Pasih Uug Beach, is where you can see the power of water in action. Over centuries, saltwater has eroded the limestone cliff, forming an archway that opens to a rocky bay. Spend some time enjoying the waves roll in and out of the bay and take a short walk over the bridge-like archway.

KELINGKING BEACH
(Pantai Kelingking)

Desa Bunga Mekar; 10,000 Rp parking

In the past two years, Kelingking Beach has nearly become synonymous with Nusa Penida, gracing the covers of tour brochures and acting as the island's impromptu mascot, all in hopes of enticing people to visit their island. Kelingking Beach is on the western side of a peninsula that is vaguely shaped like a T-Rex. The white sand of Kelingking Beach brings out a turquoise hue to the water that deepens to a cobalt blue. This is a popular stop for most people who visit Nusa Penida, so visit as early in the morning as possible to beat the crowds.

1: Crystal Bay **2:** Atuh Beach **3:** Kelingking Beach **4:** Diamond Beach

Eastern Nusa Penida
ATUH BEACH
(Pantai Atuh)

Desa Pejukutan; 10,000 Rp parking

Atuh Beach is tucked between two green hills, often skipped by tourists due to the steep sets of stairs you need to walk down in order to get here. Inland, the beach is marked by thatched roof warungs and huts, with shaded lounge chairs available for rent toward the shore. The water itself is clear and idyllic for snorkeling around at high tide. From the beach, looking out toward the horizon, you can admire a jagged island that seems to point an arrow straight at you.

DIAMOND BEACH
(Pantai Diamond)

Desa Pejukutan; 10,000 Rp parking

Before late 2018, accessing Diamond Beach was nearly impossible. Now, a roped pathway that's been etched into the side of a cliff leads down to a sandy beach set beneath a limestone wall. The beach is bordered by a handful of diamond-shaped islands that make it look as though it's been accented by gemstones. The water is too tumultuous for swimming, but the beach itself makes for an idyllic sunbathing spot.

SUWEHAN BEACH
(Pantai Suwehan)

Desa Tanglad

For intrepid travelers, the journey to Suwehan Beach is certainly an adventurous one. The road leading to Suwehan Beach is poorly maintained and full of potholes. And like so many of Nusa Penida's best beaches, Suwehan Beach is found at the bottom of a cliff. To get here, you must walk down a steep staircase that's been partially destroyed by an earthquake. However, once you make it to the bottom, you're rewarded with a long stretch of white sand and clear water. If you're hesitant about heights, it's best to stick to the nearby beaches of Diamond Beach or Atuh Beach.

WATER SPORTS
★ Snorkeling, Scuba Diving, and Freediving
KARMA DIVING

Jalan Sanjaya; tel. 81238504880; www.karmadiving. fr; daily 8am-7pm; 1,100,000 Rp for 2 fun dives

Karma Diving is a new SSI dive center on Nusa Penida. It's owned by Raphael and Laura, a French diving duo with a passion for environmental conservation. The dive center itself is alive with colorful murals and is tucked inside a recently renovated building. Here, you can go on fun dives or progress your dive skills from complete novice to scuba instructor. The dive center hosts regular yoga classes as well. If you want to get involved with the Nusa Penida community, Karma Diving is a keen participant in beach cleanups and other environmental initiatives; just ask if you can come along.

SANCTUM DIVE

Jalan Ped-Buyuk; tel. 81285325669; www. sanctumdiveindonesia.com; daily 7am-10pm; 1,100,000 Rp for 2 fun dives

Sanctum Dive enables the travel to scuba lifestyle with its well-stocked dive school and open-air bar and restaurant on the beach. The vibe at Sanctum Dive is very casual, with hammocks, beanbag chairs, yoga mats, and tattered dive logs strewn throughout their open wooden deck. Come for a day of fun diving followed by drinks, or take a PADI dive course from open water to divemaster.

FREEDIVE NUSA

Jalan Ped-Buyuk; tel. 82147417679; https:// freedivenusa.com; daily 8am-7pm; 3,400,000 Rp for SSI Level 1 course, packages from 4,700,000 Rp

The only center on Nusa Penida dedicated solely to apnea, Freedive Nusa is where travelers can learn the basics of freediving or train with a master freediver to progress their skills. The school teaches both SSI and Molchanovs courses ranking from level one to instructor.

1: snorkeling off Nusa Penida 2: sea turtle 3: clown fish in anemone, Nusa Penida

Taking a holistic approach to freediving, Freedive Nusa also teaches regular yoga classes on their open-air yoga platform, and offers packages that include breakfast, accommodation, fun dives, and evening yoga.

DISCOVER NUSA PENIDA

Jalan Raya Toyapakeh; tel. 85737343308; www. discovernusapenida.com; 9am-3pm; 600,000 Rp per person for group tour

If you're not confident driving a motorbike, one of the best ways to enjoy Nusa Penida is on a tour. Discover Nusa Penida offers snorkeling tours to sites where you're likely to see manta rays, as well as day trips to Nusa Penida's main attractions. The North Island tour will take you to Atuh Beach, Thousand Island, and Teletubbies Hills. The South Island tour ventures to Kelingking Beach, Broken Beach, Angel's Billabong, and Crystal Bay. Each tour includes lunch, snacks, water, entrance fees, and a guide.

VOLUNTEERING

★ FRIENDS OF NATIONAL PARKS FOUNDATION

Banjar Bodong; tel. 361/4792286; www.fnpf.org; 180,000-325,000 Rp per night

Friends of National Parks Foundation is an organization that focuses on developing community programs and preserving Nusa Penida's wildlife and habitat. The wildlife protection program works to breed and release endangered bird species like the Bali starling, the Java sparrow, and the sulphur-crested cockatoo. There is also a program where you can work with locals to monitor the population of hawksbill sea turtles. The habitat project plants trees and mangroves and monitors sea turtle nesting sites. The community program collaborates with Nusa Penida residents and focuses on English coursework, environmental education, *ikat*-style weaving, and traditional dance. Volunteers typically complete 3-4 hours of work in the morning and enjoy free time in the afternoon. Accommodations are simple and range from twin-bed to dorm-style

bedrooms, all with a mosquito net, fan, and bedding.

FOOD

Indonesian

★ PENIDA COLADA

Jalan Ped-Buyuk; tel. 82146763627; daily 8am-11:30pm; 35,000-75,000 Rp

Sit and stare into the ocean at Penida Colada, a seashell-studded beach shack serving toasted sandwiches, seafood, and salads in its open-air dining area. There are also a variety of cold smoothies and juices to sip as you sway in a hammock or from a squishy beanbag chair. Ordering their signature drink, a Penida Colada, is a given. Service can be slow, but the food is worth the wait. As an environmental incentive, the restaurant offers guests a free coffee if they collect one bag of trash from the nearby beaches.

International

SARI GARDEN RESTAURANT

Jalan Ped-Buyuk; tel. 82146814810; sarigardencottages@gmail.com; daily 7am-10pm; 40,000-80,000 Rp

You'll know you're at Sari Garden Restaurant when you see its gigantic blue mural depicting two open wings painted on the side of the building. This open-air restaurant serves salads, burgers, pasta dishes, and crepes for dessert. The go-to is a chicken burger and a side of toast topped with avocado and feta. For breakfast, the restaurant serves eggs, toast, pancakes, and smoothie bowls.

AMOK SUNSET

Gamat Bay; tel. 82335555016; https://amoksunset. com; daily 11am-10pm; 100,000-250,000 Rp

Amok Sunset is one of the only places where you can climb up a wooden staircase and into a bamboo treehouse to watch the sun set behind Mount Agung. Amok Sunset uses traditional Balinese architecture, strategic location, and a freshwater pool to create one of the trendiest lounge spots on the island. The main eating area is under a large bamboo roof where you can dine on salads, seafood, meatloaf, Australian steak, or barbecue ribs. The drinks menu is extensive, with a mix of cocktails, spirits, juices, and imported wines. Reservations are essential during the high season (June-Aug.), especially if you want to take advantage of their two-for-one cocktail happy hour 5pm-6pm daily.

Vegetarian/Vegan
SECRET PENIDA

Jalan Ped-Buyuk; tel. 87861478222; https:// secretpenida.com; daily 7am-6pm; 50,000-55,000 Rp

Secret Penida has nailed the vacation aesthetic with its pastel pink and palm leaf motif, woven swing, and manicured garden area. Meals are served on an open-air deck, and their menu features healthy food options like bowls filled to the brim with vegetables, smoothies mixed with granola, and parfaits made with chia seed pudding and layered in between fresh fruit. For a heartier option, go for a burger, omelet, or smashed avocado on toast.

ACCOMMODATIONS
Under 1,000,000 Rp
NUANSA PENIDA HOSTEL

Jalan Banjar Anyar; tel. 85737314685; https:// nuansapenidahostel.com; 235,000 Rp for dorm

Nuansa Penida Hostel is an ideal option for solo travelers in search of travel partners. The hostel offers four-, six-, and eight-bed dormitories, each with a patio, locker, air-conditioning, and en suite bathroom with hot water shower. The price includes a buffet breakfast, and the owner, Wayan, is always happy to help arrange day tours around the island or snorkeling trips for his guests.

JUKUNG COTTAGE

Jalan Raya Batumylapan; tel. 3665582359; www. jukungcottage.com; 900,000 Rp

Jukung Cottage is a small resort built just a few steps away from a sandy beach where you can swim and enjoy the property's wooden over-water swings at high tide. The resort has a large clover-shaped pool set in front of

a patio bar and restaurant where guests can lounge the day away. Each stand-alone suite has its own covered gazebo, air conditioning, mini fridge, kettle, TV with satellite, en suite bathrooms, and desk. The on-site restaurant's food is not the best on the island but the Friday night live music performance is worth sticking around for.

Over 1,000,000 Rp
★ LA ROJA BUNGALOWS

Jalan Ped-Buyuk; 81999277424; book via Booking. com or Agoda.com; 1,200,000 Rp

La Roja Bungalows is a resort made of 16 charming, teardrop-shaped bungalows with a handful of them set around a small pool. The bungalows themselves are simply decorated and equipped with a spacious tiled bathroom, mini-fridge, TV, kettle, and wardrobe. A small breakfast is included with each stay. Since the rooms are not completely sealed and the resort is set in one of Nusa Penida's busier neighborhoods, light sleepers will want to bring a set of earplugs.

★ PENIDA BAMBU GREEN

Jalan Raya Adegan; tel. 81239172406; 1,200,000 Rp

Penida Bambu Green is a hidden retreat in the hills of Nusa Penida, surrounded by wildlife and dense bushland. Guests can choose between bamboo villas with sea or garden views. Each option comes with air-conditioning, Wi-Fi, private bathroom, balcony, and a hammock, and some of the villas come with a circular swing. The villas are set behind a large infinity pool that overlooks a green valley below. If you've had enough beach stays and are looking for somewhere remote and romantic, Penida Bambu Green is a top contender.

INFORMATION AND SERVICES

The most reliable **ATM** in Nusa Penida is in Toyapakeh at the intersection of Jalan Sanjaya and Jalan Ped-Toyapakeh. There are also two in Batununggul, though those tend to be very finnicky with foreign cards. Cash is essential.

GETTING THERE

The only way to get to Nusa Penida is by **boat.** Boats typically arrive at **Toyapekeh Harbor,** a wide stretch of beach where boats tie up to the shoreline. Passengers will likely need to wade through knee-deep water to board and disembark boats coming in. Many of the operators that offer fast boat trips to Lembongan also offer trips to Nusa Penida, stopping at Lembongan on the way.

From Sanur

From Sanur the ride takes approximately 30 minutes. There are several reputable operators:

- **Crown Fast Cruise** (tel. 81338377336; https://crownfastcruises.com) 400,000 Rp per adult one way, 800,000 Rp per adult return): Crown Fast Cruise offers three boats per day, including hotel transfer. Boat arrives in Toyapakeh.

From Bangsal (Lombok)

There are two companies that service the route between Nusa Penida and Bangsal. The journey takes roughly 1.5 hours.

- **Eka Jaya** (www.ekajayafastboat.com; tel. 82266400678): 475,000 Rp per adult one way, 850,000 Rp per adult return. Includes pickup and drop-off at hotel, arriving in Toyapakeh.

- **Golden Queen** (https://goldenqueen fastboat.com; tel. 361/283580): 500,000 Rp per adult one way, 1,000,000 Rp per adult return, 300,000 Rp per child one way, 550k/ per child return, arriving in Toyapakeh.

From Nusa Lembongan/ Nusa Ceningan

Public boats run every 30 minutes to an hour from the Yellow Bridge (**Jembatan Cinta**) to Toyapakeh and cost 50,000 Rp per person each way. You can also go on a **fishing boat,** which costs about 50,000 Rp each way, though they will wait until the boat is full to make the journey. The trip takes about 20 minutes.

GETTING AROUND

Motorbike accidents are very common on Nusa Penida because of steep hills, poor road conditions, and overly confident motorbike drivers. Even if you are comfortable driving motorbikes on Nusa Lembongan or Bali's mainland, it might be worth hiring a **private driver** and **car** for your excursions. The heat, dust, and relatively long distances between attractions make for a long day spent on a bike. If you are on a budget, hiring a **motorbike driver** and touring the island as a pillion is a safer option than driving one yourself, as locals have grown up driving these roads and know how to manage them better than an outsider. The family-owned tour agency **Dreaming About Penida** (https:// dreamingaboutbali.com; tel. 81952474042; best reached through Facebook @dreaming- aboutpenida) will customize itineraries for travelers—no matter how ambitious. Boats to snorkel spots can also be arranged through Dreaming About Penida.

A private driver and car costs about 700,000-1,000,000 Rp per day including fuel. A motorbike guide costs around 500,000 per day, including fuel. Renting a motorbike yourself will cost 70,000 Rp per day, not including fuel. Motorbikes can be rented at stands along **Jalan Toyapakeh,** but it's best to arrange them **through your accommodation.** If you want to go a short distance, you can usually hop on the back of a local's motorbike and pay 20,000-40,000 Rp.

Ubud

Ubud has been the cultural epicenter of Bali
since the late 1800s, when the Sukawati royal family established a base
within Ubud. During Dutch occupation of Bali, Ubud was given loose
autonomy, which allowed its arts and cultural scene—typically centered around Hinduism—to flourish. Today, Ubud draws in philoso-
phers, devout Hindus, artists, dancers, musicians, and others seeking
inspiration from all over the globe.

With religion and tradition as the overlays to Ubud's unique culture, it has begun attracting those in pursuit of enlightenment and op-
timal health. Yoga classes, health workshops, meditation sessions, and
wellness retreats are increasingly popular. It's common to see Balinese
dressed in ceremonial attire walking next to a tourist in yoga leggings.

Highlights

Look for ★ to find recommended sights, activities, dining, and lodging.

★ **Neka Art Museum:** This expansive museum features works by Bali's best artists over the centuries (page 207).

★ **Sacred Monkey Forest Sanctuary:** Monkeys call the shots in a vine-covered forest dedicated to protecting them (page 207).

★ **Goa Gajah Elephant Cave:** Explore a deep cave and temple built around the 11th century (page 210).

★ **Petulu White Heron Viewing:** Witness a natural phenomenon as hundreds of white herons fly into Petulu at sunset (page 211).

★ **Campuhan Ridge:** Walk along a ridge that splits two rivers (page 211).

★ **Dance Performances at Pura Dalem Ubud:** Witness the exciting story of *Ramayana* during a fire, chanting, and dance performance set on temple grounds (page 215).

★ **Festivals:** Food celebrations, cultural performances, and yoga festivals mean that Ubud's event calendar is always worth checking (page 216).

★ **Tegallalang Rice Terraces:** Listen to the sound of birds singing and water trickling as you walk among emerald green rice terraces (page 236).

★ **Pura Tirta Empul:** Devout Hindus perform rituals under dozens of water spouts in this sacred temple (page 236).

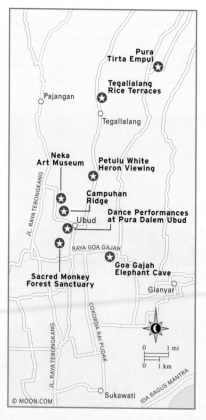

© MOON.COM

Top Restaurants

★ **Café Wayan:** Enjoy fragrant Balinese meals like a local, then learn to make them yourself (page 220).

★ **Sayuri Healing Food:** Sayuri is a master at creating delicious meals from raw and organic produce (page 220).

★ **Hujan Locale:** Traditional Asian street food meets its fine dining match in an elegant venue (page 222).

★ **Locavore:** The set course menus for vegetarians or omnivores are made from locally sourced ingredients (page 224).

★ **Swept Away:** Fine dining and a candlelit dinner on the banks of the Ayung River (page 224).

★ **Zest Ubud:** A cool—borderline hipster—restaurant with an innovative plant-based menu (page 225).

★ **Warung Enak:** Tasty Indonesian dishes with free tapas and sublime service (page 226).

★ **Room4Dessert:** Reservations are a must at this culinary experience that takes you on a journey through 9 different desserts (page 228).

As you stroll among the surrounding rice terraces and listen to the sounds of birds singing and water trickling downstream, a form of moving meditation is nearly forced upon you.

In stark contrast, the center of Ubud is marked by traffic and consumerism. Constant features in mainstream media mean that Ubud is certainly no longer the secret town it once was. Boutiques, cafés, tour stands, and homestays pile on top of each other. Tour groups led by guides holding flags can cause the sidewalks to come to a standstill. All the while, monkeys swing from telephone lines above.

Thankfully, the tranquil Ubud that has been a muse to so many can still be found just a short meander away from the main roads. Walk among Tegallalang Rice Terraces at sunrise and watch as the rice paddies glisten under the sun. Come sunset, white herons fly into the treetops of Petulu. In between,

explore temples, attend yoga classes, watch dance performances, and sample expertly made foods made from fresh produce harvested throughout the surrounding area.

ORIENTATION

Ubud is 35 km (22 mi) northeast of **Ngurah Rai International Airport,** about an hour away by car. Rivers, steep valleys covered in tropical plants, and rice paddies make up most of the terrain surrounding Ubud, and it is often a few degrees cooler than the coastlines. Since traffic is confined to set areas, it's very easy to walk or cycle along Ubud's outskirts.

Central Ubud

Ubud has a dense central area packed with shops, restaurants, and hotels all along one of the two main roads, **Jalan Monkey Forest.** Jalan Monkey Forest starts at Ubud's southern end at **Sacred Monkey Forest Sanctuary.**

Previous: Tegallalang Rice Terraces; Pura Tirta Empul; Sacred Monkey Forest Sanctuary.

Top Accommodations

★ **Adiwana Monkey Forest:** A haven for naturalists, with floral murals and expansive windows that look out onto a garden (page 229).

★ **Goya Boutique:** A retreat in the midst of Ubud's chaotic streets, with an infinity pool that overlooks treetops below (page 229).

★ **Zen Hideaway:** Sleep among the stars in an open-air treehouse and during the day, swing over the Ayung River (page 230).

★ **Wayan's Family House:** A hostel that feels like home thanks to the smiley family who lives onsite, with a spacious pool area that's perfect for forming a travel tribe of your own (page 230).

★ **Puri Garden Hotel and Hostel:** Glampackers get ready for this hostel offering clean rooms, a pool, free yoga classes, and visiting rescue puppies (page 231).

★ **Royal Kamuela Villas:** An adults-only ultra-luxe stay with highly personalized service (page 231).

★ **Glamping Sandat:** Safari tents and *lumbung* (barn) cottages that look as though they're one with the jungle around them (page 232).

★ **Viceroy:** This is an extravagant escape with over-the-top villas featuring private pools and full-time butler service (page 233).

It runs 1.5 km (0.9 mi) north until it connects to the other main road, **Jalan Raya Ubud.** Connecting the two roads, forming a rectangle, is **Jalan Hanoman.** You can explore a large part of Ubud by walking this circuit. **Jalan Cok Gede Rai** is the next major road east and sits within the city center, though it tends to be more residential. Central Ubud is home to sights like the **Ubud Palace** and **Pura Taman Saraswati.**

South of Ubud

Just southeast of the Sacred Monkey Forest Sanctuary (located in the village of **Padangtegal**), the neighboring eastern town of **Pengosekan** is quiet; tourists visit to admire art pieces at **Agung Rai Museum of Art** and take yoga classes at the **Yoga Barn.** **Celuk** is where silversmiths craft fine jewelry. Off in the outskirts, **Tegenungan** waterfall is worth a visit. Tack east to see **Pura Goa Gajah,** a cave devoted to elephants.

North of Ubud

Directly north of Ubud is **Petulu,** famous for its white herons. Venture further, and you'll reach the town of **Tegallalang,** an area rich in rice terraces and history. To the east, enjoy wandering the sacred grounds of **Pura Tirta Empul,** a holy water temple.

Northwest of Ubud are the quiet towns of **Campuhan** and **Sanggingan,** easily explored on foot as part of the **Campuhan Ridge Walk.** If walking the loop, you'll pass through Neka Art Gallery, arguably the best gallery on the island. This area was once home to German painter Walter Spies and third-culture raised artist Antonio Blanco.

PLANNING YOUR TIME

It's possible to see Ubud's central area within a day; walking from **Sacred Monkey Forest Sanctuary,** up to **Ubud Palace,** and back to Sacred Monkey Forest Sanctuary along **Jalan Hanoman** is only 3.5 km (2 mi) in total. This

Ubud and Vicinity

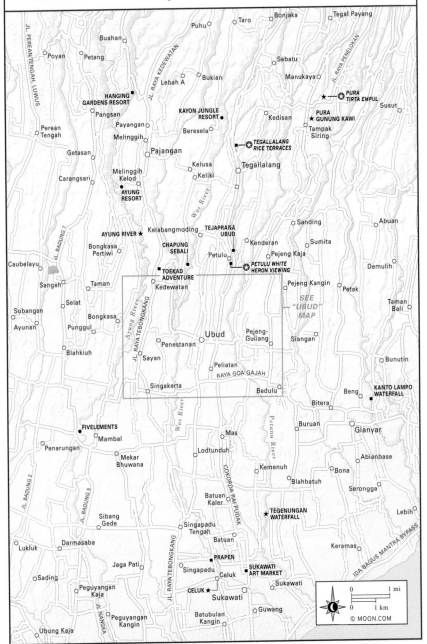

© MOON.COM

loop will show you many of the region's main **restaurants** and **shops.** Stopping for meals, shopping, and exploring the temples make for a full day.

To see Ubud's outer areas like **Tegallalang** and **Goa Gajah,** you will need an extra half day in each direction. Half-day **cooking classes, cycling tours, hikes,** and **river rafting excursions** are well worth your time. You'll find there's always something to do. You can spend hours immersing yourself in **museums,** wandering along **rice fields,** and discovering activities you didn't even know you liked.

While central Ubud makes a great base, as many places are walkable, many travelers find the constant buzz of motorbikes overwhelming. If you're comfortable driving a **motorbike,** consider staying slightly out of the center of Ubud in one of the nearby villages to experience the blend of tranquil rice paddies and accessibility of Ubud. Many resorts in the outskirts offer a **free shuttle service** to Ubud.

Itinerary Ideas

THREE DAYS IN UBUD

Day 1: Ubud Highlights

1 Just after sunrise, drive to the **Tegallalang Rice Terraces** to enjoy the rice paddies in a tranquil setting.

2 Head back to Ubud for lunch at **Café du Monyet.**

3 Next, take a stroll through **Sacred Monkey Forest Sanctuary.**

4 Walk and window shop along Jalan Monkey Forest, stopping at whatever place catches your eye. Stop at **Ubud Art Market,** where you can shop for souvenirs.

5 Wander around the tranquil lotus ponds of **Pura Taman Saraswati.**

6 After sunset, head to **Ubud Palace** to witness a cultural dance performance.

7 End the day with dinner at **Nia Ubud.** If you like the food, you can book an upcoming cooking class with the head chef.

Day 2: Health and Wellness

1 Motorbike or walk to **Sayuri Healing Food Café** for breakfast.

2 Take a yoga or guided meditation class at **Radiantly Alive.**

3 Stroll along rice fields toward **Sari Organik,** where you'll stop for a long and leisurely lunch overlooking the neighborhood.

4 In the afternoon, get a Balinese massage and sugar scrub at **Jaen's Spa.**

5 Dine on fresh salads, soups, or *gado-gado* made with fresh vegetables at **Warung Enak.**

Day 3: Learning About Ubud

1 Join the **Bali Bird Walk,** which takes you on a guided tour along Campuhan Ridge, to learn about the area's native wildlife and includes lunch at a nearby warung.

Itinerary Ideas

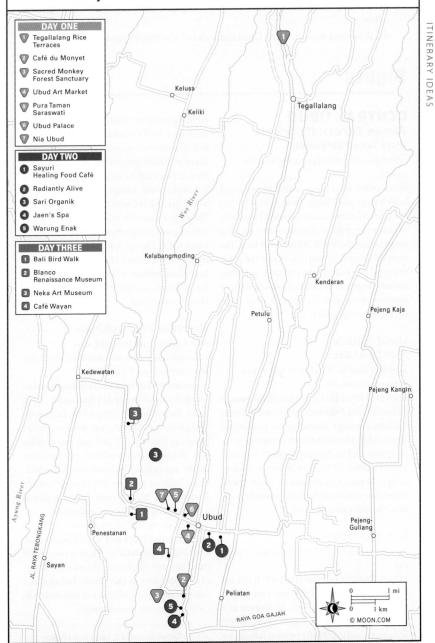

DAY ONE

1. Tegallalang Rice Terraces
2. Café du Monyet
3. Sacred Monkey Forest Sanctuary
4. Ubud Art Market
5. Pura Taman Saraswati
6. Ubud Palace
7. Nia Ubud

DAY TWO

1. Sayuri Healing Food Café
2. Radiantly Alive
3. Sari Organik
4. Jaen's Spa
5. Warung Enak

DAY THREE

1. Bali Bird Walk
2. Blanco Renaissance Museum
3. Neka Art Museum
4. Café Wayan

© MOON.COM

2 Stop by the **Blanco Renaissance Museum** to learn about eccentric artist Antonio Blanco.

3 *Bemo* up to the **Neka Art Museum** to admire the work of some of Ubud's greatest artists.

4 *Bemo* back toward central Ubud and walk to **Café Wayan** for dinner.

Sights

CENTRAL UBUD

Taman Saraswati Temple
(Pura Taman Saraswati)
Jalan Kajeng; daily 8am-6pm, usually closed to tourists

Surrounded by a pond with lily pads and bubblegum-pink lotus flowers blanketing the surface, Pura Taman Saraswati was built to honor the goddess of wisdom and learning sometime in the 1950s. Most of the time, the temple is closed to tourists. Inside the gold-accented *aling-aling*, the entrance guarding the temple grounds, a throne dedicated to the supreme Hindu gods sits among a series of intricate *merus* (pagodas).

Ubud Palace
(Puri Saren Ubud)
Jalan Raya Ubud No. 8; daily 8am-7pm, dances starting at 7:30pm; free

The Ubud Royal Palace was established under Cokorda Gede Sukawati, whose descendants still have a strong influence on the ongoings of Ubud today. One of the most masterful stone sculptors and architects, I Gusti Nyoman Lempad (1862-1978), was commissioned to design the palace's walls and entrance. Spend some time walking around the grounds to admire the intricate stonework.

Lempad House
Jalan Raya Ubud; tel. 361/975057; daily 8am-10pm; free

I Gusti Nyoman Lempad (1862-1978) did not fear expressing himself in a way that ranged outside of the norm for Bali. He worked as a sculptor and painter during a time of political instability, and eventually became famous for molding traditional Balinese styles into ways of his own. When other artists prioritized geometric patterns, Lempad painted soft curves. Many of Ubud's great structures and temples were influenced by Lempade. It's said that at 116 years old, Lempad chose what day he would die and did, with his family by his side. Today, you can view where Lempad lived at the Lempad House, where his family members reside today. Though some of his paintings are relegated to a corner, stacked in a somewhat haphazard fashion, others are hung for all to see, and there are sculptures available to gaze at in the courtyard.

Museum Puri Lukisan
Jalan Raya Ubud; tel. 361/971159; www. museumpurilukisan.com; daily 9am-6pm; 85,000 Rp adult, children under 15 free

Museum Puri Lukisan was a collaboration between the royal family of Ubud and a Dutch artist, Rudolf Bonnet (1895-1978). In its well-kept gardens and pond areas, you can admire paintings that depict Ubud as it was decades ago. Wooden statues and sculptures punctuate the museum. It also houses works from famous Balinese painters like I Gusti Nyoman Lempad and many others. Its collection is spread among four distinct galleries.

The Young Artists movement of Ubud started in the 1960s as a way to push social and religious boundaries. These artists would paint not only religious works—a main driver of artwork prior to the 1960s—but also as a colorful expression of emotion and daily life, outside of temple commitments.

1: Pura Taman Saraswati 2: Ubud Royal Palace

Ubud

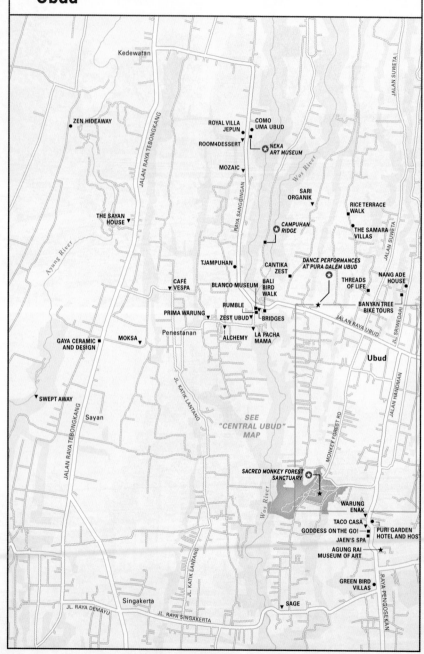

Kedewaten

ZEN HIDEAWAY

JALAN RAYA TEBONGKANG

ROYAL VILLA
JEPUN

COMO
UMA UBUD

ROOM4DESSERT

NEKA
ART MUSEUM

Wos River

MOZAIC

JALAN SUWETA

THE SAYAN
HOUSE

Raya Sanggingan

SARI
ORGANIK

RICE TERRACE
WALK

CAMPUHAN
RIDGE

THE SAMARA
VILLAS

Ayung River

TJAMPUHAN

CANTIKA
ZEST

DANCE PERFORMANCES
AT PURA DALEM UBUD

NANG ADE
HOUSE

JALAN SUWETA

CAFÉ
VESPA

BLANCO MUSEUM

BALI
BIRD
WALK

THREADS
OF LIFE

RUMBLE

PRIMA WARUNG

ZEST UBUD

BRIDGES

BANYAN TREE
BIKE TOURS

JALAN RAYA UBUD

JL. SRIWEDARI

ALCHEMY

LA PACHA
MAMA

GAYA CERAMIC
AND DESIGN

MOKSA

Penestanan

Ubud

JL. KATIK LANTANG

JALAN HANOMAN

SWEPT AWAY

Sayan

SEE
"CENTRAL UBUD"
MAP

MONKEY FOREST RD.

SACRED MONKEY FOREST
SANCTUARY

Wos River

WARUNG
ENAK

TACO CASA

GODDESS ON THE GO!

PURI GARDEN
HOTEL AND HOS

JAEN'S SPA

AGUNG RAI
MUSEUM OF ART

JL. KATIK LANTANG

Singakerta

GREEN BIRD
VILLAS

RAYA PENGOSEKAN

JL. RAYA DEMAYU

SAGE

JL. RAYA SINGAKERTA

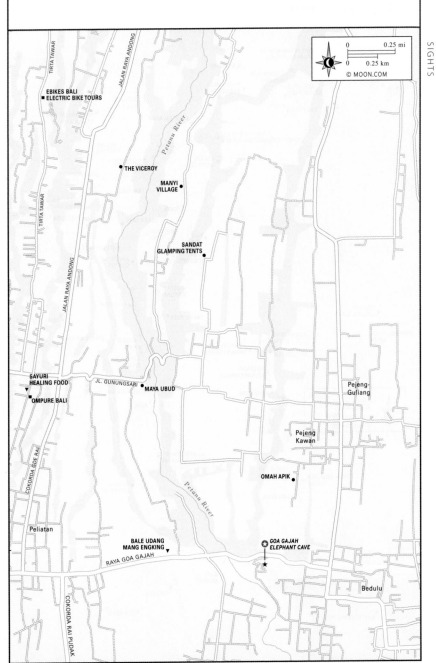

Central Ubud

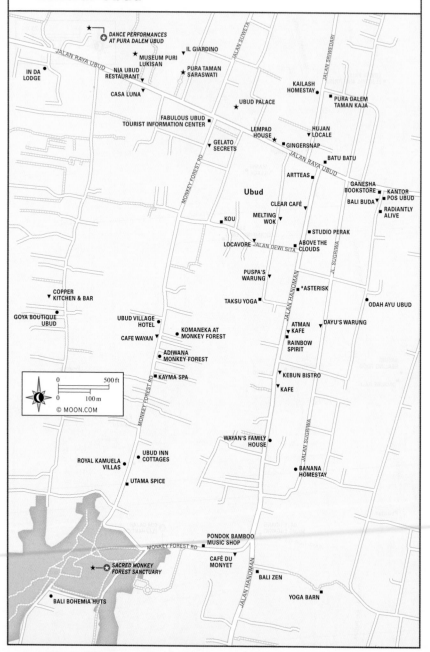

★ DANCE PERFORMANCES AT PURA DALEM UBUD

JALAN RAYA UBUD

IN DA LODGE

NIA UBUD RESTAURANT

★ MUSEUM PURI LUKISAN

IL GIARDINO

★ PURA TAMAN SARASWATI

CASA LUNA

UBUD PALACE

KAILASH HOMESTAY

PURA DALEM TAMAN KAJA

JALAN SUWETA

JALAN SRIWEDARI

FABULOUS UBUD TOURIST INFORMATION CENTER

LEMPAD HOUSE

HUJAN LOCALE

GELATO SECRETS

GINGERSNAP

JALAN RAYA UBUD

BATU BATU

MONKEY FOREST RD

Ubud

ARTTEAS

GANESHA BOOKSTORE

KANTOR POS UBUD

CLEAR CAFÉ

BALI BUDA

RADIANTLY ALIVE

KOU

MELTING WOK

LOCAVORE

JALAN DEWI SITA

STUDIO PERAK

ABOVE THE CLOUDS

IL SUGRIWA

PUSPA'S WARUNG

COPPER KITCHEN & BAR

*ASTERISK

TAKSU YOGA

ODAH AYU UBUD

JALAN HANOMAN

GOYA BOUTIQUE UBUD

UBUD VILLAGE HOTEL

KOMANEKA AT MONKEY FOREST

CAFE WAYAN

ATMAN KAFE

DAYU'S WARUNG

ADIWANA MONKEY FOREST

RAINBOW SPIRIT

KAYMA SPA

KEBUN BISTRO

KAFE

0   500 ft
0   100 m
© MOON.COM

WAYAN'S FAMILY HOUSE

ROYAL KAMUELA VILLAS

UBUD INN COTTAGES

JALAN SUGRIWA

BANANA HOMESTAY

UTAMA SPICE

MONKEY FOREST RD

PONDOK BAMBOO MUSIC SHOP

CAFÉ DU MONYET

JALAN HANOMAN

★ SACRED MONKEY FOREST SANCTUARY

BALI ZEN

BALI BOHEMIA HUTS

YOGA BARN

When viewing Balinese artwork, it's best to first step back and look at the entire painting. Then, move closer to inspect the details. You'll often find that looking at a work of art in Bali is like looking at a forest from above: it's only once you get close that you can see life and the details that make it distinctive.

WEST UBUD
★ Neka Art Museum

Jalan Raya Sangginggan; tel. 361/975074; www. museumneka.com; daily 9am-5pm; 75,000 Rp adult, children under 12 free

Neka Art Museum is one of the most impressive art museums in Bali, named after a passionate curator, Suteja Neka, who used Balinese artworks to teach about history and philosophy. The museum has both permanent and temporary exhibitions on display, with English descriptions underneath most of the artworks. The architecture of the museum itself is inviting, and it's the type of place you can easily spend a few hours in without noticing time pass by.

The museum is divided into six pavilions, each with a different focus, from traditional Balinese styles of artwork to photography and contemporary Indonesian art.

Blanco Museum

Jalan Raya Campuhan; tel. 361/975502; www. blancomuseum.com; daily 9am-5pm; 50,000 Rp admission

Antonio Blanco (1911-1999) was born in the Philippines to Spanish and American parents. He grew up moving from North America to the South Pacific until he landed in Southeast Asia, where he met his wife, Ni Ronji, a Balinese dancer. Blanco settled in Ubud, using the verdant jungles, his love, and Balinese Hinduism as inspiration for his art. His eccentric style is whimsical and ethereal, with women as the subjects. The Blanco Museum is a regal, expertly manicured building that honors his work and overlooks the Campuhan River. Each piece is given space to be viewed, and you can take a look at his studio, where everything has been left as it once was. Descendants of Antonio Blanco offer guided tours and share personal anecdotes about his life.

SOUTH UBUD
★ Sacred Monkey Forest Sanctuary

Jalan Monkey Forest; tel. 361/971304; www. monkeyforestubud.com; daily 8:30am-5:30pm; 80,000 Rp adult, 60,000 Rp child

People from all over the world come to Ubud just to see the long-tailed macaques swing from tree to tree, groom one another, and give piggyback rides to their young. The Sacred Monkey Forest Sanctuary is a dense 12.5-hectare (30-acre) jungle ruled by more than 700 monkeys, with more than 100 tree species growing within its borders. Ideally, the sanctuary strives to fulfill the *tri hita karana* (three causes of well-being) philosphy of connecting humans with nature and the spiritual realm. Locals perform ceremonies like *tempek kadang* to celebrate animals, in which locals offer fruits and nuts to the monkeys.

However, the monkeys likely follow a different philosophy. The three Cs of being a well-fed monkey: be cute, be clever, and be coordinated. Long-tailed macaques in Ubud have learned the fine arts of thievery and bribery. They are highly intelligent and can expertly steal a pair of sunglasses or work their way into backpacks to find something to use as a form of currency. The monkeys then scamper to a treetop and wait until a human offers them food in exchange for the item they stole. Unfortunately, the monkeys can and do bite. Only go in if you're holding the bare essentials—ideally with everything in your pockets. A first-aid booth is available inside the forest. Staff will tell you that the monkeys in Ubud do not have rabies, but the World Health Organization advises rabies post-exposure treatment and a tetanus shot following a monkey bite.

Inside Sacred Monkey Forest Sanctuary are three temples of **Pura Dalem Agung, Pura Beji,** and **Pura Prajapati;** the main one, Pura Dalem Agung, honors Shiva, the god of

Cheeky Monkeys

Monkeys swing from branch to branch, scamper across rooftops, and are notorious for helping themselves if they see something they like. In the area around Monkey Forest, monkeys seem to run the town. While monkeys overall in Bali are typically shy, those who are accustomed to human interaction—like in Uluwatu and Ubud—can be hostile and bite.

To keep yourself from becoming just another backpacker with a story about being bitten and robbed, here are a few ways to keep you and your belongings safe.

· **Bring the bare minimum:** Don't tempt monkeys to rummage through your bag—you'd be surprised at how quickly their agile fingers can work through a zipper. Avoid bringing food or having anything dangle from your backpack. Even sunglasses are a hot commodity among the more stylish primates, and it's not unheard of for monkeys to jump on a traveler's shoulders and snag them before swinging back into the treetops. The sound of a rustling bag or food wrapper is enough to prompt a curious primate to investigate.

· **Don't allow them to climb on you:** Many tourists encourage the monkeys to climb onto them, saying, "Their hands are so soft!" Their hands many be soft, but their teeth are sharp.

· **Don't feed the monkeys:** When monkeys associate food with humans, everyone loses. Monkeys venture closer to roads to get food from humans and are at risk of being struck by a car or attacked by dogs. Feeding monkeys can also cause aggression, an imbalanced diet, and the spread of disease as monkeys come closer to warungs and accommodations. Monkeys can be territorial, and if you use food to lure them close to you, you might be unwittingly offering yourself as a food source in a resource war.

· **Don't show threatening behavior:** Keep your distance from the monkeys and avoid staring into their eyes or baring your teeth. Hold your camera away from their face, where they might catch their reflection and react aggressively.

· **If you do get bitten, seek professional medical treatment:** First-aid care is simply not enough, as monkeys can carry diseases. Even if the monkey has a clean bill of health, wounds in tropical environments are at high risk of becoming infected.

destruction. Rangda, a demon goddess, is depicted eating a screaming child. You'll know it's her if you see a long tongue and bulging eyes.

Agung Rai Museum of Art (ARMA)

Jalan Raya Pengosekan; tel. 361/976659; www. armabali.com; daily 9am-6pm; 80,000 Rp admission, 155,000 Rp including evening performance and dinner

The Agung Rai Museum of Art was founded by Agung Rai, a passionate curator and entrepreneur with a penchant for Balinese artwork. It houses both prewar and contemporary works, and is the only place in Bali where you can admire the work of Walter Spies, a German artist who depicted Balinese workers tending to the rice terraces and other scenes of daily life, witnessed from his home in Campuhan. ARMA in combination with Neka Art Museum displays an impressive collection of artwork that spans across many styles and eras. As a bonus, the museum regularly hosts cultural performances, pop-up exhibits, artwork crafting workshops, and seminars.

The museum's tribute to Walter Spies lets you view his unique technique of using light and darkness to convey a mood. There is also a section devoted to Batuan-style artwork, a type that is believed to have formed without outside Western influence. Other notable artists on display include I Gusti Nyoman

1: Sacred Monkey Forest Sanctuary **2:** Goa Gajah Elephant Cave **3:** white herons in Petulu **4:** Campuhan Ridge

The *Eat, Pray, Love* Experience

Ubud's surge in popularity can be largely attributed to Elizabeth Gilbert's bestselling memoir *Eat, Pray, Love* (2006), which was adapted as a movie (2010) starring Julia Roberts. In the story, Elizabeth Gilbert leaves her comfortable job and marriage in pursuit of true love and self-discovery. Her journey leads her to Ubud, Bali, where she confides in a Balinese shaman, has her future told to her by a palm reader, cycles through rice paddies, and eventually finds love for herself with a handsome man whom she later marries (and divorces). Though the craze has slowly ebbed, for fans of the story, there are plenty of ways to have your own *Eat, Pray, Love* experience.

- *Eat, Pray, Love* **tour** (Get Your Guide; www.getyourguide.com; 1,300,000 Rp for full-day tour): Follow in the footsteps of Julia Roberts and tour the locations where the movie took place. As an aside, there is one beach scene in the movie that takes place in Padang Padang, not in Ubud (no beaches to be found here!). There are multiple highly rated tours that center around different themes like healing and location visits.

- **Palm Reading:** Elizabeth spent time with a Balinese medicine man named Ketut Liyer, who died in 2016. His son has carried on his father's tradition and now does palm readings and guided meditations at **Liyer House** (Jalan Raya Pengosekan; tel. 361/974092). The family now charges 300,000 Rp per reading. Consider trying another palm reader; it's still a reading in Ubud and will probably cost less than a third of the price.

- **Balian Healer:** Using herbs and juice concoctions, **Wayan Nuriasih** (Jalan Tirta No. 186; tel. 81933017155; 7,500,000 Rp treatment) was Elizabeth's go-to healer. Today, Wayan offers her knowledge and services for a steep price, and the quality of work has declined with popularity. Instead, try asking your hotel for a Balian recommendation. The experience will feel more personal and it will help avoid moonlighters.

Lempad, Ida Bagus Made, Widaya, and I Wayan Mardiana.

The museum hosts a **Legong** dance on Sunday at 7:30pm, **Topeng Jimat** on Wednesday at 7pm, **Barong** performances on Friday at 6pm, and **Legong Telek** on Tuesday at 7:30pm. Each new and full moon, a special show takes place at 7:30pm and costs 100,000 Rp for entrance or 175,000 Rp if you'd like to dine as well.

★ Goa Gajah Elephant Cave

Jalan Raya Goa Gajah; daily 8am-5pm; 15,000 Rp admission

Though Goa Gajah is believed to have been built in the 11th century, it was discovered in 1923 by archeologists. The baths around the caves were found in the 1950s, and much of the area remains unexplored. Carved into the front of the cave wall is an image that is thought to be the face of Bhoma, a protector against malevolent spirits (though some say

it could be a demon, Rangda). Once you walk through its narrow mouth, the cave opens out into smaller pockets. Dimly lit and stiflingly small, the cave belly hosts tributes to Ganesh on one side and Shiva on the other, represented by *lingam* and *yoni* (male and female genitalia) sculptures to depict Shiva's identity of both sexes.

The baths outside of the cave are equally as mysterious as the cave itself, though they may once have been a source of holy water. If you walk to the southern end of the area, you'll find a ravine rife with more shrines. Some relics are Shivite, which means the region could once have been an important area for Buddhists as well.

Sellers at the Goa Gajah parking lot may pressure you to purchase sarongs from their market stalls, claiming that none will be available for rent with your entry fee. This simply isn't true. Save yourself the hassle by bringing your own sarong.

NORTH UBUD
★ Petulu White Heron Viewing

Petulu Village; 24/7, birds fly in 1 hour before sunset;
20,000 Rp per person admission

Just before sunset, hundreds of white herons fly into the small village of Petulu. A blend of white feathers and bird droppings speckle the floor, and if you squint, it almost looks like snow. Many Balinese believe that the white herons hold the spirits of those who died in Bali's civil war in 1965, as many of those who lost their lives were buried nearby. In October of 1965, villagers held a large ceremony to rid the village of bad spirits. One week later, white herons began appearing in Petulu village by the dozens. It's thought that hunting the white herons could lead to bad luck. Today, villagers of Petulu protect them. Birders will enjoy discerning the different species of Java pond herons, cattle egrets, little egrets, and plumed egrets that visit the village.

Sports and Recreation

HIKING
BALI BIRD WALK

Jalan Raya Campuhan; tel. 361/975009; www.
balibirdwalk.com; Mon., Tues., Fri., Sat. 9am-12:30pm;
520,000 Rp guided walk, including lunch and
binocular rental

For bird nerds (or those who want to be), the Bali Bird Walk is a great way to spot and learn about Ubud's many bird species. This bird walk has been running for 25 years, with many repeat visitors, as no two walks are alike. The walk, hosted by expert guides Victor and Sumadi, starts at **Muri's Warung** at 9am. From there, you walk 5 km (3 mi) along rice paddies, villages, and the nesting sites of herons, black-winged starlings, Java sparrows, and more. Sumadi has such an enthusiastic way of guiding that by the end of the walk, you'll likely be as passionate about birds as she is. To discerning naturalists, spotting butterflies, plants, and herbs is also on the agenda. Ten percent of the proceeds go toward a conservation fund founded by the owners of the Bali Bird Walk. It's a great activity for kids.

RICE TERRACE WALK

Jalan Subak Soh Wayah; 24/7; free

Meander among rice paddies and watch ducks dutifully tend to the rice fields on an out-and-back walk that starts at **Jalan Subak Soh Wayah.** The ducks are used by Balinese rice farmers to rid the rice terraces of insects and budding weeds, all while dropping fresh fertilizer in the process.

To get to this walk, head from central Ubud toward Campuhan along Jalan Raya Ubud. Turn right at a small hill with a cluster of signs pointing toward **Ubud Yoga House,** just before the bridge. Walk up a small hill and turn left down a very narrow pathway with a cement wall on your right. If you see signs pointing toward Ubud Yoga House and **Sari Organik,** you're headed in the right direction. Continue on this path until it makes a sharp right turn where you'll find a field of rice paddies. Continue down this road for a leisurely and flat walk that creeps past cafés, tiny art galleries, and homes. Sari Organik is a good turnaround point for a 2.5-km (1.5-mi) round-trip walk from the main road. For a slightly more strenuous walk, continue on the road to **Café Wayan Wayan** (6 km/3.7 mi round-trip).

★ Campuhan Ridge

Jalan Raya Campuhan; 24/7; free

The Campuhan Ridge is the backbone of **Wos Barat Valley** and **Wos Timor Valley,** two valleys that converge at a temple called Pura Gunung Lebah, the trailhead of Campuhan Ridge. The valleys lead north of Ubud, made up of forest that cedes to rice terraces. On this walk, you can trek along a well-kept pathway and admire fields of alang alang grass, palm trees, and rice paddies as you stroll along.

The walk is a choose-your-own-adventure type of experience with multiple route options. All routes start at the Ibah Suites entrance, where you'll see a sign that says, "This way trekking Campuhan Ridge." Follow this path until you reach Pura Gunung Lebah, a temple made of dark stone. Veer right and you'll be led onto the Campuhan Ridge, an idyllic spot for birdwatching, thanks to its elevated vantage point. The trail is exposed with little shade, so it's best to go early in the morning and bring water.

OUT-AND-BACK TRAIL

Hiking Distance: 4-14 km (2.5-8.6 mi) round-trip

Hiking Time: 15 minutes per km/0.6 mi (1-3.5 hours, not including stops)

Information and Maps: Fabulous Ubud can assist with trail information

Two km (1.2 mi) along the Campuhan Ridge is Karsa Kafé and a handful of other cafés where you can stop for a drink and meal. Enjoy the sound of birds singing and the rush of water trickling down below. You can continue to the town of Keliki (7 km/4.3 mi from trailhead) for a longer trek that turns into a neighborhood walk rarely ventured to by other tourists. In between rice terraces, you'll pass warungs, spas, and family homes with motorbikes parked out front.

CAMPUHAN RIDGE LOOP TRAIL

Hiking Distance: 8 km (5 mi) loop

Hiking Time: 2.5-3 hours (not including stops)

Information and Maps: Fabulous Ubud can assist with trail information

If you want to continue and complete a loop, walk through the village of Bangkiang Sidem and turn left at the road of Jalan RSI Markandya II, before Jannata Resort. This will take you through the towns of Payogan, Lungsiakan, all the way to Jalan Raya Sanggingan, which leads back to Campuhan. Bemos often run along Jalan Raya Sanggingan if you want to catch a ride back into central Ubud.

CYCLING

EBIKES BALI ELECTRIC BIKE TOURS

Jalan Tirta Tawar; tel. 8123866408; www.ebikesbali. com; daily 8am-9pm; 590,000 Rp per person for 3-hour tour

One of the best ways to see the surroundings of Ubud is over the handlebars of an electric bike. EBikes Bali leads multiple tours from central Ubud. You can ride to the Tegallalang Rice Terraces, through a local village, and alongside a coffee plantation. One tour leads to the Tirta Empul Water Temple, one of the most sacred spaces in the region. For an offbeat trip, you can start in Sanur and cycle all the way to Ubud on paths that weave through towns and rice paddies. Your tour includes hotel pickup and drop-off, a Balinese lunch, bike, and helmet rental.

BANYAN TREE BIKE TOURS

Jalan Jambangan; tel. 81338798516; www. banyantreebiketours.com; daily 7:30am-4pm; 550,000 Rp adult, 350,000 Rp child under 5, 150,000 Rp child under 3 in child seat, 750,000 Rp adult for mountain biking tour

Banyan Tree Bike Tours hosts different cycling tours; one for all abilities, and another mountain biking tour for advanced cyclists. Their beginner-friendly three-hour tour ventures through Petang, a small village near Ubud, and goes along rice terraces, past a giant banyan tree, and local farms. The four-hour mountain biking tour spans 32 km (20 mi) and leads through valleys, over hills, around temples, and along rice paddies. All tours include equipment, lunch, and water. The company also leads guided hikes and river rafting excursions along the Telaga Waja River.

WHITE-WATER RAFTING

TOEKAD ADVENTURE

Jalan Raya Kedewatan No. 44; tel. 85100699923; www.balitoekadadventures.com; 950,000 Rp adult,

Yoga Classes

Ubud is one of the best places to branch out of your regular style and try something different. Typically, general yoga classes included with your hotel stay, or one-off yoga classes where all are welcome, will be led by a teacher who can scale each pose from beginner to advanced. For example, newcomers might only be able to touch their knees in a forward fold, while more flexible yogis can touch the ground. General yoga classes or classes that are advertised as **beginner-friendly** offer a great introduction into the world of moving meditation.

If you're new to the scene and find that the yoga schedules might as well be written in Sanskrit, here are some common terms you'll encounter.

- **Ashtanga:** Ashtanga is one of yoga's most ancient school of yoga teachings, where each pose sequence correlates to rhythmic breathing. In Ashtanga, a set of poses is done in the same order each time.

- *Restorative or yin:* Restorative yoga is a slow-moving class where postures are passive and held for a long time, allowing you to relax and work deep into each pose.

- *Hatha:* Most general yoga classes are *hatha* yoga classes. *Hatha* classes tend to be great introductory or intermediate classes because they feature accessible poses, and the teacher typically goes into detail on correct alignment.

- **Iyengar:** Iyengar classes center around proper alignment, and students of Iyengar will use props like blocks, straps, and bolsters to ensure that every body part is in the right place. Some studios require that you take a fundamentals course before joining an Iyengar yoga class, as its suited for moderately experienced yogis.

- **Vinyasa:** Vinyasa yoga classes focus on breathing strategically as you flow from one pose to the next, making it a very active class. Poses are typically not held for long, and no two classes are exactly alike.

650,000 Rp child, including hotel pickup/drop-off, insurance, equipment, buffet lunch

Get an adrenaline boost while white-water rafting or tubing down the Ayung River with Toekad Rafting. Though most of the journey is fairly tame, with class II rapids, the water can rush to a class IV during rainy season. Paddle together to navigate around rocks and rapids, or just sit in a tube and let the water take you in its own direction. Toekad Adventure also offers inflatable kayak tours and ATV rides around the area.

YOGA
RADIANTLY ALIVE

Jalan Jembawan No. 3; tel. 361/978055; www. radiantlyalive.com; daily 7am-8pm; 140,000 Rp per class

Radiantly Alive is a popular yoga studio among serious yogis—though there's no shortage of classes for inflexible newcomers

either. There are about 80 classes per week, all ranging in type and intensity, with acupuncture, massages, gemstone energy medicine, reiki, and astrology sessions taking place as well. You can dive as deep as you'd like into new age philosophies, or stick to the more physical aspects of the field. Yoga mats and props are included with class entry, and there is a vegan café on-site should you crave a post-yoga refuel.

TAKSU YOGA

Jalan Goutama Sel; tel. 361/4792525; www. taksuyoga.com; daily 9am-10pm; 130,000 Rp per class, 450,000 Rp 60-minute Balinese massage

If you crave small yoga classes with attentive teachers, venture to Taksu Spa and Yoga Center. There are classes for those who want to work on the fundamental poses for yoga, nailing the alignment and form, as well as more advanced classes for experienced yogis.

Wellness Bucket List

drink from a coconut

Going on vacation often means lounging as much as possible, imbibing sugar-laden cocktails, and eating deep-fried foods. In Ubud, however, you can indulge in pampering treatments for the body and mind that will help you to leave in a better condition than when you came. How often can you say that on vacation?

- **Balinese massage:** At just about every spa, you can get a full-body massage treatment that works on relaxing your muscles and mind. Massage therapists use scented oils, calming music, and a firm touch to relieve knotted muscles and tension.

- **Sugar scrub:** The humidity, dust, and sweat can irritate and clog pores as you travel. A sugar scrub exfoliates your skin, sloughing off old cells to make your skin silky and smooth.

- **Guided meditation:** Our minds run all day long, rarely getting a chance to rest. Join a guided meditation session to reduce stress and increase self-awareness.

- **Yoga:** Stretch and move to the rhythm of your breath in a yoga class. Your muscles will thank you.

- **Drink coconut:** Coconuts are available just about everywhere in Bali and provide a wonderful source of hydration, electrolytes, and nutrients. Swap out your soda or juice for coconut water and see how you feel.

Private classes are available. There is also an on-site spa where you can get facials, massages, scrubs, and reflexology treatments.

YOGA BARN

Jalan Hanoman; tel. 361/971236; www.theyogabarn. com; daily 7am-9pm; 130,000 Rp per class

Yoga Barn was once—and in many ways still is—the yoga capital of Ubud, with yoga classes, guided meditations, yoga teacher training, and retreats taking place inside of its spacious *shalas* that overlook a verdant jungle. When the sun is up, you can find yogis lounging around the garden and café area with a book in hand. Come sunset, many yogis make their way to participate in ecstatic dance. With its increasing popularity, Yoga Barn has lost some of its allure, with classes so packed you might find yourself dodging limbs rather than focusing on correctly placing your own.

SPAS AND WELLNESS

CANTIKA ZEST

Jalan Penestanan Kelod; tel. 85100944425; www. cantikazestbali.com; daily 10am-6pm; 175,000 Rp per 60-minute traditional Balinese massage

Cantika started in Ketut Jasi's home, where she experimented with plants and oils to create therapeutic massage and beauty treatments. Eventually, Jasi's reputation spread throughout Ubud, prompting her to train a team of masseuses, and to open a second spa and a place where she can teach workshops and sell handmade products. Cantika Zest is surrounded by well-tended gardens where you can learn to make your own products and massage techniques. You can also receive facials, scrubs, massages,

and aromatherapy treatments. All lotions, soaps, and oils used by Cantika Zest are made on-site.

KAYMA SPA

Jalan Monkey Forest No. 15; tel. 361/4792239; www. kaymaspa.com; daily 9am-9pm; 180,000 Rp per 60-minute traditional Balinese massage

Kayma Spa is an unassuming spa hidden behind Three Monkeys Café, where a stone pathway leads you to a spa that's practically hidden behind moss-covered trees. The staff at Kayma Spa pay keen attention to detail; each treatment is followed by a hot tea and baked treat. Massage rooms look out onto a rice terrace and are minimally decorated. Choose between body scrubs, massages, or wraps, or opt for the 3-hour Chanti Package, which includes a manicure, facial, scrub, and massage for 675,000 Rp.

Entertainment and Events

If there's a large-scale international event happening in Bali, chances are that it will take place in Ubud. With musical and cultural performances, festivals, and art exhibitions spread throughout the region, there are many ways to be entertained and inspired.

PERFORMING ARTS

★ DANCE PERFORMANCES AT PURA DALEM UBUD

Jalan Raya Ubud No. 23; shows Mon.-Sat. at 7pm or 7:30pm; 80,000 Rp adult, 40,000 Rp children under 10

Candles light the entrance at Pura Dalem Ubud, a temple where regular dance and musical performances take place inside an open courtyard. The most famous show, the *kecak* fire dance, takes place at 7:30pm on Monday and Friday. On Tuesday and Saturday at 7:30pm, you can witness a *legong* dance where young women in gold-plated costumes use facial expressions and dance to tell a story. On Wednesday at 7:30pm, bamboo gamelan

performers play music while dancers set the scene. On Thursday at 7pm, Barong dancers tell a popular tale of good and evil.

FIRE AND TRANCE KECAK DANCE AT PURA DALEM TAMAN KAJA

Jalan Sri Wedari No. 12; tel. 361/970508; Weds. and Sat. 7:30pm; 75,000 Rp adult

The Fire and Trance *Kecak* Dance tells a story of love, abduction, and war through the story of *Ramayana*. Dozens of men wearing checkered fabric chant in a circle around a fire. Intricately costumed main characters enter as the chanting continues to portray the story through movement. The chanting sets the tone for what's happening, lulling the audience and, seemingly, putting the performers into a trance. At the end of the show, dried coconut husks are lit on fire and piled in the center of the courtyard. A dancer kicks, stands on, and walks across the coconut husks, creating embers that burst like fireworks.

★ FESTIVALS

UBUD READERS AND WRITERS FESTIVAL

Jalan Raya Sanggingan; tel. 361/977408; www. ubudwritersfestival.com; Oct.-Nov.; 1,200,000 1-day pass; 4,000,000 4-day pass

The four-day Ubud Readers and Writers Festival is one of the most notable literary festivals in Southeast Asia. There are more than 50 sessions where writers can fine-tune their skills, listen to presentations, participate in contests, meet with publishers, and attend workshops. Each year has a theme that centers around an aspect of Balinese Hinduism. You can purchase a ticket for the entire festival, day passes, or one-off tickets to events.

UBUD FOOD FESTIVAL

Jl Raya Sanggingan No. 88X; tel. 361/977408; www. ubudfoodfestival.com; Apr.; 350,000 Rp 1-day pass, 850,000 Rp 3-day pass

Come hungry to the Ubud Food Festival, a three-day celebration of Indonesian food, where you can sample dishes from all over the archipelago; discover the different nuances of *sambals* and *nasi campur,* for example. Spend your time sampling different kinds of produce, attending culinary workshops, watching cooking demonstrations, and even enjoying movie nights. The dishes reflect everything from fine dining to popular street meals.

BALISPIRIT FESTIVAL

Jalan Ganung Abang (Purnati Center for the Arts, 15 minutes south of Ubud); tel. 361/970492; www. balispiritfestival.com; Mar.; 500,000 Rp 1-day pass; 2,200,000 8-day pass

BaliSpirit Festival is an eight-day yoga event that brings hundreds of people together to attend yoga classes ranging from relaxing and novice-friendly to specialized workshops for experienced yoga practitioners. Colorful decorations, beanbag chairs, live music stages, guided meditations, massage areas, dance sessions, sound healing, and an abundance of vegan food stalls are spread throughout the festival venue. Guests attend with the hopes of finding inner peace, making new friends, and connecting with their bodies.

UBUD JAZZ FESTIVAL

ARMA Museum, Jalan Raya Pengosekan; tel. 361/285196; www.ubudvillagejazzfestival.com; Aug.; 550,000 Rp 1-day pass, 850,000 Rp 2-day pass

Passionate musicians come together and play jazz music at the Ubud Jazz Festival, a two-day festival featuring local and international artists. More than 5,000 people usually attend the festival, coming from all over the island to listen to the different variations of jazz.

Shopping

TOP EXPERIENCE

Ubud is one of the best places in Bali to shop for boutique clothing, jewelry, yoga products, artworks, handcrafted soaps, and natural products. Shops open and close for business on a regular basis, with an equally interesting store reincarnating in its wake. A walk around Ubud will reveal a variety of items not found elsewhere in the world. Ubud and Seminyak are tied for being Bali's shopping hubs.

CENTRAL UBUD
Markets
UBUD ART MARKET
(Pasar Seni Ubud)

Jalan Raya Ubud No. 35 and Jalan Karna, across from Ubud Palace; sunrise-sunset daily

The Ubud Art Market is the most popular market in town to purchase handicrafts, textiles, purses, decor, and other souvenirs. This is where you'll see the effects of a capitalist economy and trendsetting in the works.

Most of the market spans along Jalan Karna, a pedestrian-only street packed with tourists starting at 10am. Explosions of color, cluttered stalls, and Hindu offerings create a feeling of excitement and awe. Here you can shop for on-trend items like woven purses, sarongs, crocheted clothing, and wooden sculptures. Items range from great finds to downright tacky.

Haggling is expected and done in good faith. Start at around 50 percent lower than the asking price and inch your way up to a price that makes both parties happy. Asking fellow tourists what they paid for items sets a good gauge of the going rates. Better deals are found in the mornings, when the first sale is considered lucky and there aren't as many potential customers to snag the shopkeeper's attention. Refreshingly, traders are not as pushy at this market as in stalls in Kuta, Seminyak, and Sanur.

JALAN RAYA ANDONG

Jalan Raya Andong; daily sunrise-sunset
Along Jalan Raya Andong, which spans from Ubud to Tegallalang, is a 2-km (1.2-mi) stretch of shops owned primarily by artists selling their work for wholesale prices. This is a popular spot to purchase ornate Balinese wooden furniture, stone sculptures, and wooden carvings. If you find a style you like, it doesn't hurt to inquire about commissioned work.

Bookstore
GANESHA BOOKSTORE

Jalan Raya Ubud; tel. 361/970320; www. ganeshabooksbali.com; daily 9am-6pm
Welcoming bookworms since 1986, Ganesha Bookstore sells a mishmash of new and used books that primarily feature stories and non-fiction works about Indonesia. Some books are in Bahasa Indonesian, though there are plenty of English texts to choose from as well. If you've just finished a book, trade it for a new one. This is also a great place to pick up postcards, maps, and posters. Nobody will hassle you if you choose to sit and read.

Jewelry
PRAPEN

Jalan Jagaraga 66; tel. 81339114877; https://prapen. com; daily 10am-8pm
Prapen is a large and sleek jewelry shop selling gold and silver items inspired by Bali's natural surroundings. Think bamboo wrapped in sterling silver, floral and seashell pendants, and metal woven together as though they're made from sisal or rattan.

Ubud Art Market

ASTERISK*

Jalan Monkey Forest; tel. 361/4792238; daily
9am-9pm

Asterisk* is a small jewelry boutique selling dainty and elegant necklaces, bracelets, and rings. Among their standout pieces are pendants that look like gamelan balls: sterling silver balls with chimes inside to resemble Balinese music. There are also beaded sets that look great paired with casual travel attire.

STUDIO PERAK

Jalan Hanoman No. 15; tel. 8123651809; daily
9am-8:30pm; 400,000 Rp per 3-hour class,
including 5 grams (.17 ounces) of silver, 15,000 Rp per
extra gram

If you've ever wanted to see a silversmith at work or try your hand at crafting yourself, enroll in a three-hour silver jewelry class at Studio Perak. The owner, Ketut, patiently teaches you how to craft a souvenir that you can take home, and the course is suitable for children. There is also a shop inside the studio where you can purchase sterling silver and gemstone jewelry.

RAINBOW SPIRIT

Jalan Hanoman No. 38; tel. 85100126053; www.
rainbowspiritbali.com; daily 9am-9pm

If you're in search of healing crystals, Rainbow Spirit is a small shop with birthstones, crystal pendants, and gemstone pendants. It's a fun place to browse and admire the colors of the different items, though the quality of the gold and silver is questionable.

BATU BATU

Jalan Raya Ubud No. 18; tel. 81337380359; www.
batubatubali.com; daily 9am-9pm

Batu-Batu is a two-story shop in Ubud where you can admire the many crystals, fossils, gemstones, and other mineral specimens on display. If you plan to make a gemstone piece at a jewelry workshop, it's a good idea to shop for the centerpiece here and bring that to your class, as Batu Batu offers a wonderful selection.

Art and Textiles
THREADS OF LIFE

Jalan Kajeng No. 24; tel. 361/972112; www.
threadsoflife.com; daily 10am-7pm

Threads of Life is one of the best places to shop for textiles in Bali. Textiles and woven goods are staples in Indonesian cultural heritage, and here is where you can browse through hundreds of different types of textiles gathered from 10 islands in Indonesia—each with its own unique style. Fabrics sold here are fair trade, high-quality, and priced higher than the mass-market textiles that you may find elsewhere. Each piece has the artist, origin, and information about the method used to create the textile on its label.

Threads of Life hosts weeklong themed **workshops,** where you can learn about the different designs, materials, and methods used to create woven and dyed fabrics for around 15,300,000 Rp. You'll learn to use a wooden loom and try crafting fabrics yourself using ikat and batik methods.

Clothing
GINGERSNAP

Jalan Raya Ubud No.14; tel. 361/970200; www.
gingersnapbali.com; daily 10am-9pm

A popular hub for fashionable expats, Gingersnap sells streetwear for men and women, with a dash of futuristic detail. The men's line strives to be polished yet casual while the women's line is focused on loose and lightweight fabrics. Most items are monochrome pieces of black or white.

ABOVE THE CLOUDS

Jalan Dewisita No.3; tel. 81353997798; https://
above-theclouds.com; daily 9am-9pm

Above the Clouds is a men's boutique selling casual and comfortable clothing made from cotton, hemp, and linen, and dyed with natural inks. It has a hippie-comfortable vibe without the use of kaleidoscope patterns. The shop collaborates with local factories and has a working culture that provides fair conditions to its employees.

OMPURE BALI
Jalan Sukma Kesuma No.5; tel. 85857430880; https://ompure.com; daily 10am-8pm

Flowy bohemian pieces and matching yoga sets are the key items at Ompure Bali, a shop selling leggings, shirts, tunics, dresses, cover-ups, and bras at its new location near Sayuri Healing Food Café.

Miscellaneous
KOU
Jalan Dewisita; tel. 361/971905; kou_soap@kou-bali.com; daily 10am-8pm

Take the pleasant scent of Bali with you whenever you shower. KOU sells natural soaps with scents like tuberose, frangipani, mango, vanilla, lemon tea, and other seasonal ingredients. You can shop in store or order over the phone to have products delivered directly to your hotel (200,000 Rp minimum order, 15,000-25,000 Rp delivery fee to hotels within Ubud area).

ARTTEAS
Jalan Hanoman No.1; tel. 83119942559; daily 10am-7pm

Artteas is a small tea house that sells teas and tisanes sourced from other islands in Indonesia, Japan, China, and India. You can purchase teapots and teacups, and sit down at a table to brew a cup of your own. Servers at Artteas are happy to talk about tea rituals and give brewing advice.

WEST UBUD
Art
GAYA CERAMIC AND DESIGN
Jalan Raya Sayan No.105; tel. 361/976220; www. gayaceramic.com; Mon.-Sat. 9am-5pm, drop-in class Thurs. 9am-noon, closed Sun.; 450,000 Rp per class, additional charge for bisque and glaze

Gaya Ceramic and Design has a studio and showroom across the street from one another. At the showroom, you can admire the hand-crafted ceramic pieces made by artists from all over the world. Dishes and decor range from detailed and gravity-defying to simple and practical. At the studio, you can learn to craft ceramic pieces by attending a two-week workshop or a drop-in 3-hour class Thursday at 9am.

Clothing
RUMBLE
Jalan Raya Campuhan; tel. 81337000074; www. xrmblx.co; daily 9am-9pm

This edgy shop sells clothing that pairs well with tattoos. Skull emblems, mechanic shop shirts, branded shirts, and raglan tees fill the racks. Most of the clothing is made for men, though there are a few items for women.

SOUTH UBUD
Clothing
GODDESS ON THE GO!
Jalan Raya Pengosekan; tel. 361/976084; www. goddessonthego.com.au; daily 9am-8pm

This on-trend clothing shop sells staple pieces for women who wear Australian sizes 12 to 22, with most of their items being made from modal, a comfortable and form-fitting fabric. Most of their pieces are designed with comfort and dressing up or down in mind, and there are yoga sets available for purchase as well.

Miscellaneous
BALI ZEN
Jalan Monkey Forest; tel. 361/976022; https:// balizenhome.com; daily 9am-7pm

Bright, Bali-inspired miniature umbrellas, bedding sets, rugs, bags, décor, and souvenirs are offered in this boutique. There is also a small clothing section with items featuring vibrant and bold print patterns. Many of their items are made in Indonesia using fair-trade practices.

UTAMA SPICE
Jalan Monkey Forest; tel. 361/975051; https:// utamaspicebali.com; daily 9am-8:30pm

The go-to shop for natural skincare and beauty products, Utama Spice has a range of soaps, bug repellents, aromatherapy oils, lotions, incense, hair oils, candles, and a pleasant-smelling lavender spray to mist onto your yoga mat.

PONDOK BAMBOO MUSIC SHOP
*Jalan Monkey Forest; tel. 361/974807; daily
9am-11pm*

Wherever you go in Bali, the calming sound of chimes follows. At Pondok Bamboo Music Shop, you can look for bamboo chimes and Balinese musical instruments and take classes on how to create music yourself inside the dingy shop. The real draw, however, are the *wayang kulit* shadow puppet show performances that take place (100,000 Rp per person); here, you can watch Hindu legends be re-created through the use of light and intricately cut puppets.

Food

CENTRAL UBUD
Indonesian
PUSPA'S WARUNG
*Jalan Gootama Selatan No. 22; tel. 85102643830;
daily 12:15pm-10pm; 20,000-40,000 Rp*

Puspa's Warung is the type of restaurant that lets its food do the heavy lifting when it comes to building a reputation. With limited seating and a makeshift menu made of handwriting on cardboard, the warung spends most of its energy creating Indonesian-meets-vegetarian meals like jackfruit *rendang*, veggie curry, and tempeh satay. Meat dishes are also available.

★ CAFÉ WAYAN
*Jalan Monkey Forest; tel. 361/975447; www.
alamindahbali.com; daily 8am-10:30pm;
40,000-100,000 Rp, 350,000 per 2-hour cooking class*

The owners of Café Wayan have been serving traditional Indonesian meals since 1980, when their restaurant was merely a small stand. Today, you can dine on Thai curries, satay, fried rice, and seafood at their dimly lit open-air restaurant surrounded by tropical plants. Café Wayan hosts a cooking class twice per day, at 10am and 4pm, teaching you how to cook your own Balinese meal. Cooking classes can be tailored to vegetarians. Don't skip the desserts section, and enjoy a range of baked goods like croissants and cakes.

NIA UBUD RESTAURANT
*Jalan Raya Ubud No. 24; tel. 87761556688; https://
niaubud.com; daily 7am-10pm; 50,000-150,000 Rp,
350,000 Rp cooking class, including hotel transport*

From the road, Ubud is an unassuming restaurant hidden behind an array of signs and posters. Inside, the café is picture-friendly, with pastel pink walls painted with palm leaves. The restaurant serves curries, ribs, and *gado-gado*, and is famous for its Balinese *rijstaffel*, a Dutch-Indonesian fusion of chicken curry and pork ribs served with rice and peanut sauce. Nia Ubud also hosts cooking classes where students visit a local market and then learn to make a handful of Balinese dishes (with suggestions on how to adapt the recipes to re-create them at home).

Vegetarian and Vegan-Friendly
DAYU'S WARUNG
*Jalan Sugriwa No. 28X; tel. 361/978965; daily
7:30am-10:30pm; 20,000-45,000*

Dayu's Warung is run by a friendly Balinese woman, Dayu, who is constantly experimenting with food and fine-tuning her health-conscious recipes. The interior is clean and simple, with a small ground-floor seating area and an upstairs area that overlooks the road. Healthy juices, Balinese dishes, salads, and sandwiches are available. Meals are mostly vegan, though there are a few traditional meat dishes as well. Portions are small, so hungry diners might want a side or an appetizer to go along with their main meal. Try their vegan cookies and fruit leathers as a snack.

★ SAYURI HEALING FOOD
*Jalan Sukma Kesuma No. 2; tel. 82240485154;
https://sayurihealingfood.com; daily 8am-11pm;
20,000-80,000 Rp*

Ubud's Best Cooking Schools

Ubud is home to some of the island's master chefs. Learn their culinary ways by enrolling in a cooking class. Most of the famous restaurants host some type of workshop or course, though these schools stand out above the rest.

- **Café Wayan:** Learn about the different herbs and spices that give Balinese fare their fragrant flavor. At Café Wayan, you'll learn to cook five different dishes over the course of two hours. There are seven different cooking courses to choose from, all with distinct menus. Vegetarian lessons are available upon request (350,000 Rp) (page 220).

- **Sayuri Healing Food:** Sayuri Healing Food hosts a range of un-cooking classes (food is served raw) that range from 4-day beginner-friendly courses where you learn to make many of the meals on the restaurant's menu (5,200,000 Rp) as well as more intensive courses that teach fermentation (14,000,000 Rp), raw chocolate making (13,000,000 Rp), dessert making (14,000,000 Rp), and more (page 220).

- **Moksa:** Moksa's cooking courses take place in a permaculture garden where you can craft vegan meals from produce harvested directly from the restaurant's property. Chef Made has an infectious passion for what he does, and you'll leave feeling as though you're a chef yourself (1,500,000 Rp, taught Weds. and Fri.) (page 225).

- **Copper Kitchen & Bar:** The mixologists at Copper Kitchen and Bar offer two workshops: one on the Indonesian medicinal drink of *jamu,* and another on cocktails. In the *jamu* workshop, you'll learn about the history and importance of *jamu* as well as how to craft this potent concoction from herbs (Sun. 4pm-5pm; 4 people maximum; 150,000 Rp per person). To learn how to make cocktails (and thus become every party's best asset), join a class on Saturday 3pm-4pm or 4pm-6pm (550,000 Rp per person for cocktails, 400,000 Rp per person for mocktails) (page 226).

Sayuri Healing Food is an impromptu meeting ground for yogis and health-conscious travelers in search of fresh juices, turmeric lattes, and fresh smoothies. Almost all food at Sayuri Healing Food is raw, and all meals are vegan. Dine on all-day breakfasts like burritos, smoothie bowls, omelets made with chickpea flour, or items from the afternoon side of the menu like the raw lasagna. You can also learn how to craft delicious raw meals from the menu, as well as how to craft vegan sushi.

ATMAN KAFE

Jalan Hanoman No. 38; tel. 85100620505; www. ptatman.com; daily 7am-10:30pm; 40,000-70,000 Rp

Atman Kafe knows that some diners can't handle the heat and serves most of their traditional Balinese dishes mild by default (extra chilis or jalapeños available upon request).

Tex-Mex burritos, quesadillas, and pasta make up the rest of the menu. The interior is cozy and rustic, and there is an area selling natural products, clothing, and home decor around the seating area. It feels like you're dining in a bohemian boutique.

BALI BUDA

Jalan Jembawan 1 No. 1; tel. 361/976324; www. balibuda.com; daily 7am-7pm; 40,000-80,000 Rp

The chefs at Bali Buda aren't shy about venturing away from traditional recipes, with the intent of serving something its guests haven't tasted before, like eggplant and almond enchiladas. The menu features on-trend items like smoothie bowls and charcoal burgers made from local produce, but you can also get a decent slice of pizza or bowl of gazpacho if you please. Bali Buda also works with local community programs like Say No to Plastic, eco-Bali, and a midwife program.

CLEAR CAFÉ

Jalan Hanoman No. 8; tel. 87862197585; www.
clearcafebali.com; daily 8am-11pm; 40,000-
90,000 Rp

Clear Café has some new-age influence with an interior that's upbeat and fun. Cozy couches, inspirational quotes spelled out in flower petals, and good music make this a place where you'll want to lounge around for a while. Almost all produce is sourced from farms in Bali to create breakfast burritos, Asian curries, tacos, pasta, and more. The Bali banana cake is a must.

KAFE

Jalan Hanoman No.44B; tel. 8111793455; http://
kafe-bali.com; daily 7:30am-11pm; 45,000-
90,000 Rp

KAFE is often packed and popular among ex-pats. The menu was built with yogis in mind, and it skews mostly vegetarian, with a minority of meat options on its menu. Most produce is sourced locally, and you can order hearty breakfasts like scrambled eggs served with freshly made bread or heaping super salads with vegetables, nuts, cheese, quinoa, and avocado. Pasta, soup, and sandwiches are also available.

CASA LUNA

Jalan Raya Ubud; tel. 361/977409; https://
casalunabali.com; daily 8am-11pm; 50,000-
130,000 Rp

Casa Luna is a stylish restaurant serving a blend of Balinese, Italian, and Spanish fare. Their Indonesian take on Spanish paella is a popular pick. Soups, salads, curries, and pasta dishes grace the menu. The chefs carefully plate each meal, and produce is sourced from around the island. Head over on Thursday or Sunday to enjoy a jazz performance. Delivery available to local hotels for orders over 50,000 Rp.

Asian
MELTING WOK

Jalan Gootama No. 13; tel. 82144174906; daily
10am-10pm; 30,000-60,000 Rp

You're going to want to make a reservation at Melting Wok, an understated restaurant with a small menu scribbled out onto a chalkboard that changes daily. From its basic exterior, it looks like just another warung in Ubud with only a handful of tables. Despite its humble size, this popular warung serves freshly made meals with personable service and a menu of curries and noodle dishes, typically cooked in a wok. The spot is also known for its sugary crepes, stuffed with fruit, caramel, chocolate, or coconut flakes.

★ HUJAN LOCALE

Jalan Sri Wedari No. 5; tel. 81339720306; https://
hujanlocale.com; Tues.-Sun. noon-11pm, Mon.
noon-3pm and 6pm-11pm; 80,000-250,000 Rp

Chef Will Meyrick experiments with traditional Asian dishes and turns them into a fine dining experience at Hujan Locale. Meals are served inside of a spacious and elegant two-story dining hall with open ceilings and ambient lighting. Dishes like tuna cooked with betel leaves and lemongrass, pork belly caramelized in soy sauce, lamb shank served with jackfruit and long beans, and other Indonesian-meets-modern dishes are featured; you won't see many of these dishes on any other menu. Separate vegetarian, nut-free, and gluten-free menus are available upon request.

International
IL GIARDINO

Jalan Kajeng No. 3; tel. 361/974271; www.
ilgiardinobali.com; daily 4pm-11pm; 50,000-
240,000 Rp

Handmade pasta, pizza, warm olives, risotto, bruschetta heaped with toppings, and fresh salads await at Il Giardino, an open-air Italian restaurant surrounded by a quaint garden and pond area. Service is prompt and friendly, with staff who seem genuinely happy to work there. White tablecloths and candles add a touch of elegance, though casual diners are welcome.

1: Café Wayan 2: Sari Organik

KEBUN BISTRO

*Jalan Hanoman No. 44; tel. 361/972490; https://
kebunbistro.com; daily lunch 11am-3pm, tapas
4pm-6pm, dinner 6pm-11pm; 70,000-250,000 Rp*

Kebun Bistro almost looks misplaced on the streets of Ubud with its Parisian shopfront and vintage European interior, marked by ornate chandeliers. Paintings of grape vines, solid Greek columns, and wine racks back against the walls. The menu suits the atmosphere, with cheese platters, duck confit, pastas, French onion soup, and classic Caesar salads. It's the type of place where you can dress up and treat it as an upscale experience, or walk in alone with a tattered book, ready to spend the afternoon reading with a glass of wine in hand. Each meal is flavorful and thoughtfully plated.

★ LOCAVORE

*Jalan Dewisita No. 10; tel. 361/977733; https://
locavore.co.id; Mon.-Sat. noon-2:30pm and
6:30pm-10pm, closed Sun.; 795,000-895,000 Rp
6-course meal; 1,100,000-1,200,000 Rp 9 courses,
drink pairings 500,000-650,000 Rp*

Reserve a table at Locavore at least two to three weeks in advance. There are two variations (omnivore and vegetarian), each with six or nine courses. Chefs Ray and Eelke work closely with nearby farmers (hence the name) to source most of their ingredients from Indonesia, and divert food waste to be used as animal feed or compost. Intriguing combinations like banana blossom curries, barbecued soursop fruit, cabbage roasted in bacon fat, and duck served with snails feature on the menu. For adventurous eaters, Locavore is a must.

Dessert
GELATO SECRETS

*Jalan Wenara Wana and Jalan Raya Ubud; tel.
82144011235; https://gelatosecrets.com; daily
10am-11:30pm; 33,000 Rp scoop*

Gelato Secrets is a fun gelato shop selling classic flavors along with more local takes like avocado, passionfruit, dragonfruit, and bamboo charcoal. Perfect for a hot day. Their flavor of the month is usually worth a try. There are three shops around town: one on Jalan Wenara Wana and two along Jalan Raya Ubud.

WEST UBUD
International
★ SWEPT AWAY

*Jalan Raya Sayan; tel. 361/973606; https://
thesamayabali.com; daily 11am-10pm;
100,000-500,000 Rp mains, 3,800,000 Rp per
couple for private table*

The regal Ayung river flows alongside Swept Away, a romantic restaurant that's worthy of anniversary and birthday celebrations. Even if all you're enjoying is the fact that you're in Ubud, Swept Away will be a memorable dining experience. Opting for their set-course menu is recommended; it features seafood, beef, duck, chicken, and dessert. To go all out, request a private dinner on the outdoor patio when you make your reservation. Staff can decorate the area with candles, twinkle lights, and flower petals for an extra charge and serve a 7-course tasting menu (1,900,000 Rp deposit).

Vegan and Vegetarian
ALCHEMY

*Jalan Penestanan No.75; tel. 81339457432; www.
alchemybali.com; daily 7am-9pm; 20,000-
120,000 Rp*

Vegans, get ready to cope with decision fatigue at this all-vegan, organic café famous for its raw creations of cakes, sandwiches, DIY smoothie bowls and salads, spring rolls, veggie sushi rolls, canneloni made from zucchini, and quiche with faux eggs made from cashew cream. All meals are served completely raw (cooked at a temperature no higher than 42°C), which the chef claims helps retain nutrients. The juice menu nearly overshadows the food—pair wisely.

PRIMA WARUNG

*Jalan Penestanan; tel. 87860986059; daily
noon-7pm; 35,000 Rp*

PriMa Warung is the place to go if you're

vegan or vegetarian and feeling left out when it comes to trying traditional Indonesian cuisine. This little warung owned by a bubbly chef, Prima, serves *nasi campur,* pumpkin soup, *cap cay, gado-gado,* and soy satay. Regulars snatch up the cakes early in the day, so if there is a slice leftover, get it. The venue can be hard to find as it's a tiny shack on a main road. Look for a big red wall. PriMa Warung is on the left.

MOKSA

Jalan Puskesmas Gang Damai; tel. 81339774787; www.moksaubud.com; daily 10am-9pm; 40,000-190,000 Rp

Moksa is a plant-based restaurant with lovely gazebos set amid a thriving permaculture garden. The restaurant has created a menu based on the season's harvest. Vegetable sushi rolls, zucchini pasta, tacos stuffed with vegetables, marinated jackfruit, and paella ensure that everyone leaves feeling content. For long-term visitors, Moksa also hosts a farmers market every Tuesday and Saturday 10am-2pm. The property also has an open space with scheduled yoga, martial arts, and meditation classes.

★ ZEST UBUD

Jalan Penestanan Kelod No. 8; tel. 82340065048; www.zestubud.com; daily 7:30am-11pm; 60,000-90,000 Rp

Colorful plates await at Zest Ubud. This cool dining venue with a tiered thatched roof uses words like badass, zesty AF, and copious amounts of the F word to describe the dishes served within its spacious and plant-laden dining room—though their food is a bit too healthy to be considered edgy. You can sit at a proper table or grab a fresh juice and let your body meld into one of the comfy sofas. Juicy mock-meats made from jackfruit, gargantuan veggie bowls, nibbles with dips, and wraps make up a majority of the menu. All meals are plant-based and made fresh.

Mexican
LA PACHA MAMA

Jalan Penestanen; tel. 361/9080225; daily 4pm-11pm; 80,000-150,000 Rp

La Pacha Mama is an airy Mexican-inspired restaurant that seems to have a goal of having all its dishes look like they're ready for a photoshoot—as does the funky horse statue placed in the middle of the venue. Tortilla chips with heaps of guacamole, tacos that need two hands, vegetable burritos, seafood, and quesadillas are on offer here. The food doesn't taste as though it came straight from Oaxaca, but it's a vibrant place to get a delicious and flavorful meal. Latin musicians often add a bit of life to an otherwise quiet atmosphere. Check the restaurant's Facebook page to see updated specials like margarita and taco combos.

Asian
THE SAYAN HOUSE

Jalan Raya Sayan No.70; tel. 82247370344; www.thesayanhouse.com; daily noon-10pm; 50,000-280,000 Rp

The Sayan House is an ambient and romantic restaurant surrounded by tropical greenery. The chefs serve an eclectic mix of Latin and Japanese dishes. The tuna *korokke* (croquettes) is a fine example of the blend, served with barbeque sauce, avocado salsa, cilantro, and wasabi mashed potatoes. Or, there are tempura tempeh tacos with salsa. Chicken, ribs, duck, beef, and prawns make up most of the protein portion of the dishes. Request a seat that overlooks the valley for a view with your meal.

International
BRIDGES

Jalan Raya Campuhan; tel. 361/970095; www. bridgesbali.com; daily 11am-11pm; 60,000-330,000 Rp

Bridges is one of Ubud's most in-demand dining venues, largely due to its incredible location, seven floors of views, and

Ubud's Best Chocolate Desserts

Despite Ubud's obsession with healthy living, there are plenty of places to dine on dessert. As a loophole, some restaurants will add "it's vegan" or "it's made with organic sugar" as a qualifier. We'll take it.

- **Death by Chocolate Cake** at Café Wayan (page 220): A devilish slice of chocolate cake is coated in a thick layer of chocolate frosting.

- **Rum and Chocolate Birthday Cake** at Sayuri Healing Food (page 220): Raw, dairy-free, gluten-free, and soy-free… If only it were calorie-free. Go for a scoop of vegan chocolate chip ice cream on the side.

- **Cacao and Cranberry Pit** at Atman Kafe (page 221): This wholesome pie is made with almond and date crust filled with raw cacao and cranberries.

- **Brownie a la Mode** at Clear Café (page 222): A brick of a brownie made from organic cacao, cashew milk, and walnuts is topped with a scoop of coconut ice cream. Ask for an extra handful of berries to toss over the top.

- **The 9 Course Experience** at Room4Dessert (page 228): Among nine courses of dessert at this culinary experience, there's bound to be chocolate.

fine-dining level of service. It's owned by Ubud's Sukawati royal family. Come for lunch, dinner, or tapas at the bar—one of the best places to get a decent glass of wine. For those who enjoy variety, order the Indonesian *rijsttafel*. The *rijsttafel* comes with six main dishes, six sides, and dessert. The variety of seating arrangements and swath of meal choices means that no two visits to Bridges are ever alike.

European
COPPER KITCHEN & BAR

Jalan Bisma; tel. 361/4792888; www.copperubud. com; daily 7am-11pm; 60,000-120,000 Rp

Copper Kitchen and Bar is an upscale restaurant with an elegant dining area furnished with dark wood and dim lighting. Upstairs, there's a rooftop area that feels slightly more casual with a cabana-style vibe. Dishes are mostly Mediterranean and Italian, with staff favorites being homemade gnocchi with pesto, eggplant parmigiana, and wild mushroom risotto. The Indonesian side of the menu is well worth a scan as well. If you like cocktails, imbibe here. Head over for happy hour every day from 4pm to 6pm to get two-for-one drinks at the bar.

Cafés and Light Bites
CAFÉ VESPA

Jalan Raya Penestanan; tel. 361/973034; www. cafe-vespa.com; daily 8am-10pm; 20,000-70,000 Rp

Café Vespa has a fitting name with a handful of patron's motorbikes parked haphazardly out front. It's earned somewhat of a reputation among expats as one of the quieter cafés in Ubud, and you'll hear the tapping of laptop keyboards as you dine. This little café serves hot coffee and a wide range of desserts displayed in a glass case. The menu is extensive, with plenty of Indian, Indonesian, and American dishes on offer, though they tend to be a bit underseasoned. For the best experience, keep it simple—stick to the coffee and cakes.

SOUTH UBUD
Indonesian
★ WARUNG ENAK

Jalan Raya Pengosekan; tel. 361/972911; www.warungenakbali.com; daily 11am-11pm; 60,000-120,000 Rp

Warung Enak is an eclectic Indonesian restaurant with a large bar area and funky posters. The servers pay keen attention to detail, offering cool washcloths, tea, and appetizers to diners who might be ready for a break after a long day in Ubud. Traditional Indonesian dishes like meat satays, stir-fries, crispy duck, and *nasi campurs* are the stars of the menu. There's a decent selection for vegetarians as well.

BALE UDANG MANG ENGKING

Jalan Raya Goa Gajah; tel. 361/978754; www. baleudang.com/ubud; daily 11am-10pm; 65,000-200,000 Rp

A *balé* in Bali is a thatched-roof gazebo built using wood and bamboo. Traditionally, they're used as prime napping and lounging spots in a Balinese household. At Balé Udang Mang Enging, dine in a traditional balé set over a calm pond, perfect for feeling a cool breeze as you dine. The restaurant serves Balinese fare like grilled fish, satay skewers, and *nasi campur*.

European
CAFÉ DU MONYET

Jalan Monkey Forest No. 9; tel. 82145381770; daily 8am-11:30pm; 70,000-125,000 Rp

If not for the view of a rice paddy at the back of the narrow dining area of Café du Monyet, it might feel as though you've transported to a small café in early 1900s Paris. Sepia pictures inside ornate frames hang on the aged brick walls of the café. Wooden rockers, vintage suitcases, Persian rugs, a gramophone, and leather armchairs add to the old-world feel. Choose between plates of pasta, baguette sandwiches, seafood, and tartes for dessert.

Vegetarian and Vegan
SAGE

Jalan Nyuh Bulan No. 1; tel. 361/976528; daily 8am-9:30pm; 40,000-70,000 Rp

This minimally decorated, bright café has colorful meals that act as statement pieces to Sage's decor. Enjoy cauliflower fritters, tempeh tacos, veggie burgers served with beetroot fries, smoky tofu burgers, heaped salads, and smoothie bowls. If you're feeling like trying something novel, craft a main meal from three plates of appetizers. For a pick-me-up, try a caffe latte made with coconut milk.

Mexican
TACO CASA

Jalan Raya Pengosekan; tel. 81224222357; www.tacocasabali.com; daily 10am-10pm; 50,000-100,000 Rp

Taco Casa serves flavorful Mexican dishes like enchiladas, tacos, burritos, fajitas, and quesadillas with handmade salsas and tortillas. Almost every dish pairs nicely with a margarita, cold beer, or sangria.

NORTH UBUD
Vegetarian and Vegan
SARI ORGANIK

Jalan Subak Sok Wayah; tel. 361/972087; daily 10am-8pm; 40,000-80,000 Rp

After a tranquil walk (or drive) along rice terraces, enjoy stopping at Sari Organik, an outdoor restaurant serving salads, soups, and Balinese and Thai dishes on a spacious platform that overlooks green paddies below. It's a calm retreat away from the crowded streets of Ubud, where the hum of a motorbike won't follow you. Juices are made fresh and you can also shop for homemade soaps, essential oils, and eco-friendly knickknacks like bamboo straws at the payment counter.

European
MOZAIC

Jalan Raya Sanggingan; tel. 361/975768; www. mozaic-bali.com; Mon.-Weds. 6pm-11pm; Thurs.-Sun. noon-2pm and 6pm-11pm; 600,000 Rp 5 courses, 900,000 Rp 7 courses, wine pairings 490,000-890,000 Rp

Mozaic is a luxurious dining venue that thoughtfully crafts each dish using a blend of seasonal produce and French cooking techniques. Arrive during set times for lunch or dinner, and enjoy a five- or seven-course meal featuring seafood, suckling pork, *waygu* beef, lamb, and fruit sorbets. One of the highlights of Mozaic is the Chef's Table, where you can watch the preparation and creation of each dish—an experience that quickly gets booked out in the high season, so reserve in advance.

Dessert

★ ROOM4DESSERT

Jalan Raya Sanggingan; tel. 81337050539; www.room4dessert.com; Tues.-Sun. 5pm-9pm; 120,000-150,000 Rp dessert, 580,000 Rp 9-course experience

Room4Dessert has earned somewhat of a cult following, with some guests booking their experiences at least a month in advance to try the delights created by master chef Will Goldfarb. It's a refreshing diversion from the sugar-free health scene of Ubud; you can sample sweet delights on their all-day dining menu or splurge on an experience where you are served nine courses of desserts—each one unique and heavily influenced by the seasonal produce of the island. To go all-out when it comes to vices, pair your desserts with nine cocktails or mocktails. Arrive early to get a seat at the front of the venue. As the menu is set in advance, Room4Dessert does not accommodate dietary requests. Children under 12 are not allowed.

Accommodations

CENTRAL UBUD

Under 1,000,000 Rp

ODAH AYU GUESTHOUSE

Jalan Jembawan No. 15; tel. 361/974845; 150,000-300,000 Rp

Odah Ayu's central location is the main draw to this feel-good homestay, which also has welcoming hosts, cozy rooms with air-conditioning, a small terrace, and private bathrooms with hot water showers. The garden area is immaculately maintained, and rooms are serviced daily. This is easily one of the best-value stays in Ubud.

NANG ADE HOUSE

Jalan Sri Wedari No. 39; tel. 81239094665; 200,000-350,000 Rp

Nang Ade House is a family-run homestay with clean, modern, light-filled rooms and a small patio out front, where your included breakfast is served. Each room has air-conditioning, Wi-Fi access, and a private bathroom. Tropical plants surround the rooms, and the homestay is within walking distance of Ubud's main drag. The family who manages the property are attentive without being overbearing. Tours and airport transfers can be arranged for an affordable price.

KAILASH HOMESTAY

Jalan Sri Wedari No.13; tel. 361/970601; www. kailashbali.com; 325,000-500,000 Rp

Kailash Homestay is a welcoming homestay with four different room types set around two pools, among tropical plants. Each room has access to free Wi-Fi, air-conditioning, a flat-screen TV with cable, and hot water bathrooms. The deluxe-style rooms are sleek and look out to the pool. The bale and junior suites are aesthetically pleasing, with ornate carvings, sun-kissed wooden furniture, Balinese decor, and a more traditional feel.

UBUD INN COTTAGES

Jalan Monkey Forest Road; tel. 361/975071; www. ubudinn.com; 500,000-900,000 Rp

Ubud Inn Cottages has 29 rooms that are surrounded by immaculately kept gardens. The exterior of the buildings are traditionally Balinese, with intricate designs and colorful artwork. Inside, rooms are clean, modern, and spacious. All guests are able to enjoy the on-site pool and spa, and its location is walking distance to most of Ubud's main sights.

Over 1,000,000 Rp
★ ADIWANA MONKEY FOREST

Jalan Monkey Forest; tel. 361/975231; www. adiwanamonkeyforest.com; 1,900,000-6,500,000 Rp

Adiwana Monkey Forest brings the foliage of Ubud's outskirts inside with hand-painted murals of rice terraces, rattan decorations, and light wooden furniture in its airy rooms. Each room has a floor-to-ceiling window that looks out onto the property's garden, plus air conditioning, high-end toiletries, and a TV. Some of the rooms have an open walk-in closet and stand-alone bathtub. This is one of the most unique stays in Ubud and worth it for those who are drawn to nature. Breakfast (included) with limited food options is served every morning at Watercress Restaurant next door.

UBUD VILLAGE HOTEL

Jalan Monkey Forest; tel. 361/975571; https:// theubudvillage.com; 2,000,000-3,000,000 Rp

From the road, Ubud Village Hotel looks like just another bland building along Jalan Monkey Forest. Once you walk onto the property, you'll find 62 rooms tucked behind drapes of tropical vines. Guests have access to two turquoise pools, free yoga classes twice per week, and tea served on the hotel's rooftop every afternoon—the perfect place to stop and rest before a sunset excursion. Get a massage at the on-site spa and dine at the hotel's accommodating restaurant, which serves a mix of Indonesian and European fare. Room options include a double suite with pool view, suite with patio, or a one-bedroom villa, all furnished with dark wooden features. Each stay comes with Wi-Fi access, refrigerator, minibar, and satellite TV.

★ GOYA BOUTIQUE

Jalan Bisma; tel. 361/9083368; www. goyaboutiqueresorts.com; 3,500,000-7,000,000 Rp

Goya Boutique is a luxury retreat in the middle of chaotic Ubud. Suites, one-bedroom, and two-bedroom villas have their own private plunge pool. Each room is decorated with a mix of contemporary and traditional Balinese decor. A large infinity pool overlooks a jungle of tropical plants and palm trees below. Each villa has its own outdoor lounge area and spacious bathroom equipped with a stand-alone bathtub looking out to a personal plunge pool. Staff also set up a texting service where you can request food, schedule tours, or ask questions without leaving the comforts of a poolside lounge chair. Book directly with the hotel

Ubud Inn Cottages

for the best price as well as meal discounts. The property also offers laundry service, minibar refill, shuttle service, and a choice between airport pickup or a massage for stays longer than four nights.

WEST UBUD
Under 1,000,000 Rp
IN DA LODGE
Jalan Ry. Ubud, Behind klinik Dharma Usada; tel. 361/975718; 50,000 Rp dorm bed

A centrally located hostel with bunk-bed dorm rooms, In Da Lodge is ideal for travelers who would rather spend their coin on the local food rather than where they sleep. Rooms are large and clean and have in-room bathrooms with hot water showers. Guests have access to a swimming pool, Wi-Fi, and bar area. It's a great place to make new friends over cheap drinks.

ROYAL VILLA JEPUN
Jalan Raya Sanggingan No.21; tel. 361/970012; https://royalvillajepun.com; 400,000-600,000 Rp

Royal Villa Jepun is a quaint hotel amid rice terraces and greenery. Rooms have updated amenities with four-poster beds and distressed wooden furniture. The atmosphere is simple only-in-Ubud luxury, with traditional Balinese decorative elements and a lagoon-style pool. Though the property is small, the rooms are spacious, with air-conditioning and outdoor bathrooms where you can shower with songbirds. Breakfast of fresh fruit, banana pancakes, and eggs is included.

Over 1,000,000 Rp
TJAMPUHAN
Jalan Raya Campuhan; tel. 361/975368; www. tjampuhan-bali.com; 1,500,000-2,000,000 Rp

Built in 1928 at the intersection of two rivers, Tjampuhan is a classic and regal hotel with rooms immaculately sculpted and decorated by Balinese artists. The superior rooms have private terraces and are built from local materials with a sauna-like devotion to wood. Each is equipped with a private bathroom, Wi-Fi, ceiling fan, and large balcony. The deluxe rooms have a spacious balcony area, large glass windows, Wi-Fi, and air-conditioning. Tjampuhan is also home to the former two-bedroom home of Walter Spies, a German painter who used the surroundings as his muse.

★ ZEN HIDEAWAY
Jalan Dewi Saraswati (30 minutes west of Ubud), Bongkasa; www.airbnb.com/users/show/21460517; 3,000,000-5,000,000 Rp

In the small village of Bongkasa, a 30-minute drive from Ubud, Zen Hideaway reached international fame thanks to its on-site swing that dangles guests over the gushing Ayung River. Staying inside Zen Hideaway is like sleeping in a 150-year-old teak treehouse. The building is open-air with cement and wooden pillars holding up the structure rather than conventional walls. There are three villas on the property (one three-bed villa and two two-bed villas), all with hammocks, open-air living spaces, kitchens, and plush beds cloaked in mosquito nets that are inviting no matter the hour.

COMO UMA UBUD
Jalan Raya Sanggingan; tel. 361/972 448; www. comohotels.com; 3,500,000-5,000,000 Rp

Elegant and chic, COMO Uma Ubud is a luxury stay with a range of rooms, suites, and villas. Each option is crisp-white with minimal decor and light wooden furniture. The stars of the resort are the pool villas, with infinity pool, that overlook a jungle valley. COMO Uma Ubud also has an on-site spa with four airy treatment rooms, an outdoor pool, and a small gym. Your stay includes breakfast, guided walks, yoga classes, a shuttle to and from Ubud's center, and a choice between airport pickup, a two-course lunch or dinner, or an hour-long massage per person.

SOUTH UBUD
Under 1,000,000 Rp
★ WAYAN'S FAMILY HOUSE
Jalan Hanoman No. 52; tel. 361/970345; 100,000 Rp dorm bed, 150,000 Rp double room

Centrally located, Wayan's Family House sleeps 22 guests in a mix of dorm and double rooms. The hostel attracts a young crowd of backpackers who use the small pool and shaded beanbag chairs to escape the midday heat. Wayan's family lives on-site, so there is someone available to assist no matter the time of day. Rooms are clean; they have air-conditioning, Wi-Fi access, and each bed has a reading light and locker access. Breakfast is included with your stay. The four-bed female dorm room has bunk beds that are made private by curtains.

BANANA HOMESTAY

Jalan Sugriwa No.59; tel. 361/8550723;
150,000-200,000 Rp

Walking distance from the Yoga Barn, Banana Homestay is a simple and clean guesthouse set on an intersection of shops and restaurants. The family that runs the homestay also owns the banana stand out front, where you'll likely have to step around bushels of bananas as you make your way to your room. Rooms are basic with spotty Wi-Fi access. Each stay includes breakfast, and most mornings you'll be served a meal made with the homestay's signature fruit. If you're a light sleeper, request a room at the back of the property as the street-facing rooms can be a bit loud.

★ PURI GARDEN HOTEL AND HOSTEL

Jalan Raya Pengosekan; tel. 361/973310; www.
purigardenhotel.com; 310,000-380,000 Rp dorm
bed, 980,000 Rp private room

Puri Garden Hotel and Hostel combines the best of the party traveler scene with those who just like to relax. In front of its mix of dorm and private rooms is a spacious yard with hammocks, beanbag chairs, massages, and a pool. Each stay includes lockers, spotty Wi-Fi access, air-conditioning, and breakfast. Staff host morning yoga classes, barbecue and movie nights, and cultural performances; they even bring puppies from the local shelter over as a form of canine therapy. At around 11pm each night, the hostel guides partying backpackers to a nearby bar, giving those who want to get an early start in the morning a chance to sleep.

GREEN BIRD VILLA

Jalan Raya Pengosekan No. 108; tel. 361/9081478;
greenbirdvillaubud.com; 750,000-1,200,000 Rp

This peaceful resort offers clean rooms, furnished with dark wood and a balcony that opens out to greenery or the pool area that looks as though it is part of a fairy tale. Each room has Wi-Fi, air-conditioning, minibar, TV, and hot water shower. Choose between double rooms or the family villa with a loft that can sleep four people inside. Included breakfast is served on the balcony each morning.

Over 1,000,000 Rp
BALI BOHEMIA HUTS

Jalan Nyuh Bojog; tel. 361/978631; www.balibohemia.
com; 1,000,000-2,000,000 Rp

Bali Bohemian Huts stay true to their name with splashes of paint inside each of their 10 unique double rooms, one-bedroom villa, and two-bedroom villa. The resort itself is a mishmash of primarily wooden bungalows with thatched roofs and free-spirited names like Passion and Dream. All rooms come with Wi-Fi access, a private bathroom, and a safe. All but two rooms have air-conditioning. Monkeys from nearby Monkey Forest often lurk in the treetops near the on-site Mediterranean restaurant, hoping to snag a dropped morsel from a meze plate.

★ ROYAL KAMUELA VILLAS

Jalan Monkey Forest; tel. 361/970099; www.
kamuelavillas.com; 3,000,000-5,000,000 Rp

Royal Kamuela Villas is an adults-only retreat with luxury villas, a private pool, and suites that have access to a 50-meter lap pool. Each accommodation has contemporary decor, with crisp white linen and dark wooden furniture. Service is personalized, and it's the type of place where staff members learn your name and serve tea each afternoon. Keeping your doors and windows shut is a must whenever you leave the complex, as the property is shared with curious monkeys. The resort also has a gym, spa, Jacuzzi, and a restaurant serving gourmet Indonesian fare.

KOMANEKA AT MONKEY FOREST

Jalan Monkey Forest; tel. 361/4792518; http:// monkeyforest.komaneka.com; 3,000,000-5,000,000 Rp

Komaneka at Monkey Forest has a reputation for being a hub for artists and writers, with bright rooms equipped with king or twin beds, minibars, air-conditioning, safe, hot water showers, and a TV. Though it's close to all the goings-on of Ubud, the property is set back from the road in a way that makes you feels outside of the fray. Service is five-star, and most rooms open out to rice terraces and tropical plants.

NORTH UBUD
Under 1,000,000 Rp
OMAH APIK

Jalan Kenyem Bulan; tel. 361/944324; www. omah-apik.com; 500,000-800,000 Rp

Omah Apik is a family-run bed and breakfast in the middle of rice paddies with 11 simple and serene rooms over two stories. The property is surrounded by tropical fruits, coconut trees, vegetable patches, and fresh herbs that the staff use to create meals. The rooms are modest with unreliable Wi-Fi access, a TV, tile floors, double bed, and stained-glass bathrooms. Green principles are used to reduce waste and conserve energy, making it a low-key retreat.

MANYI VILLAGE

Banjar Laplapan; tel. 361/8987889; www. manyivillageubud.com; 650,000-900,000 Rp

Escape the chaos of the city at Manyi Village, a small hotel set on lush green rice paddies. Rooms are simple and tasteful with wood floors and touches of batik textiles. All double rooms have a bathtub and shower, air-conditioning, TV, fridge, minibar, safety box, and hair dryer. Staff run a regular shuttle to

Ubud, making it ideal if you want both accessbility and escape.

Over 1,000,000 Rp
THE SAMARA VILLAS

Jalan Kajeng; tel. 81237727818; www.thesamara.com; 2,000,000-5,000,000 Rp

The Samara Villas is a luxury retreat offering six double rooms as well as a one-bedroom and two-bedroom villa. Rooms have a king-size bed, sofa, desk, minibar, large mirror, TV, safe, and air-conditioning. All rooms look out to rice paddies where you can fall asleep to the sounds of frogs, birds, and ducks without the disturbance of cars driving by. Spend your time at the Samara Villas relaxing, walking among the rice fields, lounging by the infinity pool, and dining on Italian dishes under dim candlelight with a glass of red wine in hand.

★ GLAMPING SANDAT

Jalan Subak Sala (GPS -8°29'58.02", +115°16'56.88"); tel. 361/9083222; www.glampingsandat.com; 3,500,000-6,500,000 Rp

Glamping Sandat is a resort that feels like a blend between camping under the stars and being treated at a luxury resort. It's safari meets Indonesian luxury. There are multiple options to choose from. The large safari tents can sleep up to four people and feature a fluffy, circular bed. The smaller tent sleeps from one to three people, while the lumbung cottages made from wood and bamboo can host up to five guests. All feature air-conditioning, Wi-Fi, and a minibar. All rooms are centered around a wooden yoga and meditation *shala.*

TEJAPRANA UBUD

Jalan Raya Tegallalang; tel. 361/9080939; www. tejaprana.com; 4,000,000-7,000,000 Rp

Tejaprana Ubud blends casual and comfortable with modern and sleek. All 28 hillside villas face east, revealing spectacular sunrises as the sun comes up over tropical vegetation. The villas on the bottom of the valley are private and are set alongside a tranquil river. Those up above have views of the sprawling valley below. All include a gazebo, infinity plunge pool, and outdoor standalone bathtub perfect for feeling one with your surroundings. Guests have access to the on-site spa and can relax in the dining area, where the smell of barbecue cooked next to a bamboo and thatched roofed seating area is a regular occurrence.

CHAPUNG SEBALI

Jalan Raya Sebali, Keliki, Kecamatan Ubud, Kabupaten Gianyar; tel. 361/8989102; www.chapung. com; 5,000,000-9,000,000 Rp

Chapung Sebali is a boutique resort on the ridge of a deep valley with palm trees to its front and rice paddies to its back. There are a variety of villas and rooms to choose from, all spacious and bright. The resort uses elements like brick, tile, hardwood, and stone paired with earthy tones to create an intriguing and unpretentious atmosphere. The resort restaurant serves a mix of Asian and Mediterranean fare, while the pool bar feels like it belongs in Seminyak—only it's trees that surround you rather than a sandy beach. After sunset, the jazz bar serves expertly crafted cocktails that you can sip on plush couches.

★ VICEROY

Jalan Lanyahan, Br. Nagi; tel. 361/971777; www. viceroybali.com; 9,000,000-22,000,000 Rp

Viceroy is one of the major players in Ubud when it comes to five-star extravagance and luxury. Its signature infinity pool overlooks tropical jungle, and there are spacious villas around the property (set back from its helicopter pad). Choose between one-bedroom suites with a private plunge pool, one-bedroom villas with a terrace and private infinity pool, or a two-bedroom villa with rooms that open out to a 15-meter-long outdoor pool and lawn. All stays include Wi-Fi access, 24-hour room service, breakfast, and a TV. For the best value, you can purchase packages centered around culinary delights, health and wellness, adventure activities, or romance. Many travelers who choose Viceroy treat it as a staycation, rarely leaving the resort.

UBUD OUTSKIRTS
Over 1,000,000 Rp
MAYA UBUD

Jalan Gn. Sari; tel. 361/977888; https://mayaresorts. com; 3,500,000-7,000,000 Rp

Uniform rows of copy and pasted palm trees lead the way to Maya Ubud, a resort hidden among 10 hectares (25 acres) of land that overlooks the Petanu River, a refuge for birds. You might not be tempted to leave the property, thanks to its on-site spa, well-equipped gym, tennis court, daily yoga classes, library, and two outdoor pools lined with shaded lounge chairs. Though the amenities are some you can find elsewhere, the decorations and attention to detail at this resort pay homage to Indonesia. Traditional architecture and upcycled objects like fish traps turned into lampshades act as reminders of where you are.

Information and Services

There are frequent ATMs in Ubud, and bank cards are accepted at many of the higher-end places. Like everywhere in Bali, card skimming is a risk, so choose ATMs that have a security guard nearby. Cash is still the preferred method of payment, even in modern Ubud.

FABULOUS UBUD TOURIST INFORMATION CENTER

Jalan Raya Ubud; tel. 361/973285; www. fabulousubud.com; daily 8am-9pm

The Fabulous Ubud Tourism Information Center is where you'll find maps and information about upcoming events, tours, accommodation, and transportation. Activities can be arranged at the information center, though prices might be higher here than what you will be quoted by booking direct or through your accommodation.

KANTOR POS UBUD (POST OFFICE)

Jalan Jembawan No. 1; tel. 361/975764; Mon.-Fri. 8am-6pm, Sat. 8am-2pm, Sun. 8am-noon

This post office handles international shipping. Staff are familiar with packing artwork and sculptures.

UBUD HEALTH CARE

Two sites: Jalan Sukma No. 37 and Jalan Raya Teges No. 8; tel. 8113977911; www.ubudcare.com; Jalan Sukma: Mon.-Sat. 7am-10pm, closed Sun.; Jalan Raya Teges open 24/7

Ubud Health Care has two locations with English-speaking physicians and modern medical facilities. If your hotel is within the Ubud area, Ubud Health Care can arrange home visits where doctors are dispatched within 20 minutes of calling. There is also free pickup and drop-off within the clinic if your illness or injury requires treatment in the facility.

Transportation

GETTING THERE
By Bus

The Kura-Kura Bus (www.kura2bus.com; 80,000 Rp per person one way, children under 2 free, 120,000 Rp round-trip) runs from Sanur and Denpasar, and its Line 5 route stops at Alaya Ubud Resort, Ubud Central Parking, and the Puri Lukisan Museum in Ubud four times daily. The journey takes about 2 hours.

Perama (Jalan Raya Pengosekan; tel. 361/750808; www.peramatour.com; daily 7am-9pm) offers shuttle bus service from multiple places like Amed (175,000 Rp), Candidasa (75,000 Rp), Kuta (60,000 Rp), Lovina (125,000 Rp), Padangbai (75,000 Rp), Sanur (50,000 Rp), and Tulamben (175,000 Rp). Prices are for one way.

By Car and Motorbike

If you're taking a car, Ubud is about 1.5 hours (35 km/22 mi) from Kuta and Ngurah Rai International Airport, 2 hours (55 km/34 mi) from Uluwatu, 1 hour from Sanur (30 km/18.5 mi), and 1 hour from Denpasar (25 km/15.5 mi). To get to Ubud from the south, connect to Jalan By Pass Nagurah Rai and follow Jalan Raya Batubulan north.

Ubud is 2.5 hours from Amed (70 km/43 mi) and is typically best reached via Bali's coastal road that links Jalan Prof. Dr. Ida Bagus Mantra to inland roads that weave through Gianyar to Ubud. From Lovina (70 km/43 mi; 2.5 hours), cut through Bali's Central Mountains, driving south of Danau Beratan. From Pemuteran (120 km/75 mi; 3.5 hours), drive west to Lovina and follow the Central Mountains south to Ubud.

Parking a car in central Ubud is nearly impossible, though you can typically find space at your accommodation if you're staying on Ubud's outskirts. Most central hotels will not have room for car parking. Motorbikes are crammed near the Ubud Art Market entrance or left at the venue you are visiting. Hotels usually have—or can create—space for motorbike parking.

By Taxi and Rideshare

BlueBird Taxis (www.bluebirdgroup.com) from Bali will take you to Ubud from **Kuta** (300,000 Rp), **Legian** (250,000 Rp), and the **Denpasar Airport** (350,000 Rp).

Grab and **GoJek** offer rides to Ubud from the **Kuta Area, Sanur,** and **Denpasar.** Prices depend on demand and range between 150,000 and 300,000 Rp from Bali's southern end to Ubud.

By Private Driver

Hiring a private driver is often the most convenient way to get to Ubud, especially if you are traveling with luggage. Prices start at around 50,000 Rp per hour; book through your accommodation.

GETTING AROUND

The streets of Ubud are traffic-choked and chaotic, with drivers disobeying the signs of one-way roads. You can get around the city center **on foot** or with a **rental motorbike** (50,000 Rp per day, not including fuel).

Take care when walking around Ubud, especially in condensed motorbike parking lots. Brushing your leg against a hot motorbike exhaust pipe can lead to serious burn injuries.

Many restaurants, spas, and accommodations provide **shuttle service** around the area with every purchase or booking.

By Private Driver

There is also no shortage of **private drivers** in Ubud, and you'll soon learn to tune out the constant touts of "Yes? Transport?" as you walk through the streets. Look around and you'll find drivers holding signs that say "Driver Available" or "Transport."

By Motorbike and *Ojek*

Motorbike rental stands are found along the main roads of **Jalan Hanoman.** For a bike with insurance, rent from **Ubud Scooter Rental** (Jalan Sri Wedari; tel. 87796997999; ubudscooterrental@gmail.com; Mon.-Sat.

getting around by motorbike or *ojek*

9am-5pm, closed Sun.; 50,000 Rp per day) who offer pickup and drop-off service. If you hop on the back of a motorbike, or *ojek,* rides around Ubud cost about 15,000 Rp from one end of town to the other.

For local day trips, consider going on a **guided motorbike tour,** where you follow your guide to and from different sites or simply sit on the back of the bike and enjoy the ride (400,000 Rp full day tour). **BEAT** (tel. 82245982688; www.beatbali.com; 300,000 day tour; pickup from hotel) is run by two charismatic English speaking guides who are happy to lead the way around Ubud.

LEAVING UBUD

The local private drivers of Ubud have banned taxis and rideshare app drivers like Grab and GoJek from picking up guests from Ubud. Transport away from Ubud is best arranged through your accommodation or a **private driver.** If you do use a rideshare app, request to be picked up somewhere inconspicuous to avoid being hassled by local drivers.

Around Ubud

NORTH OF UBUD
Sights
★ TEGALLALANG RICE TERRACES
Jalan Raya Tegallalang; 24 hours; 10,000 Rp gate entrance

The Tegallalang Rice Terraces are a set of emerald green rice terraces that weave across a steep valley in the small town of Tegallalang. *Subak,* the rice cultivation technique used at the Tegallalang Rice Terraces, dates to the 9th century and manifests *tri hita karana,* a philosophy that combines mankind with the spiritual and natural worlds. To make this connection, the water that feeds into the Tegallalang Rice Terraces must first pass through a temple before flowing into the rice paddies. Once the rice is grown, farmers harvest the crops by hand, using ancient techniques and tools rather than heavy machinery.

Though walking around the Tegallalang Rice Terraces is free, you will be asked to make a small donation (about 10,000 Rp) if you want to venture deeper into the fields, so carry a few small notes with you. Few tourists wander past the second donation station. If you do, you'll be rewarded with solitary surroundings where you can enjoy the soft sounds of water trickling from paddy to paddy and the rustling of palm leaves in the wind. While mindfully tiptoeing along the edge of a rice paddy, you might feel that connection of *tri hita karana* for yourself.

Enjoy a fresh coconut or cup of Balinese coffee from one of the many cafés perched alongside the valley. Nearly all of them offer incredible views of the Tegallalang Rice Terraces below. To beat the crowds and the heat, visit just after sunrise.

★ TIRTA EMPUL TEMPLE
(Pura Tirta Empul)
Jalan Tirta; daily 9am-5pm; 15,000 Rp per person

Pura Tirta Empul, a temple with sacred springs flowing within it, is where Balinese Hindus go to partake in purification rituals. The water is holy, and it is believed that health and property will bless those who visit. The temple was built in AD 962, and these rituals have taken place for more than 1,000 years. According to Hindu epics, the springs were created by Indra, the god of storms and war during a violent battle with a malevolent shapeshifter, Mayadenawa. Shrines to Shiva, Vishnu, and Brahma are spread throughout the temple grounds.

You enter the temple through a large gate known as *candi bentar,* used to protect the grounds against malevolent spirits. These gates lead to a courtyard that opens out to

---

1: Tegallalang Rice Terraces 2: Pura Tirta Empul

two bathing pools with 30 spouts of holy water flowing into them. Tourists can respectfully participate in the water purification ceremony called *melukat*. It's wise to be guided by a local, as there are certain protocols to follow. The goal is to move from one spout to the next. However, some spouts are reserved solely for the dead or priests, and it is disrespectful to bathe underneath them.

GUNUNG KAWI TEMPLE
(Pura Gunung Kawi)
Jalan Ganung Kawi, east of Jalan Raya Tampaksiring and down 315-step path; tel. 8563795229; daily 9am-5pm; 15,000 Rp per person

Pura Gunung Kawi is an 11th-century temple set in front of a large cliff with elaborate shrines carved into the cliff face. At 7 meters (23 feet) high, the shrines are a sight to behold. Five of the shrines sit on the eastern side of Pakerisan River, while another four sit on the western flank. The Tenth Shrine is found along a small pathway between the entrance staircase and the main *candi* (shrine) area; a short walk among rice paddies will take you there. The shrines are often mistaken for tombs, and it's thought that the reliefs were created to honor King Wungsu and his harem of queens. However, no bodies or ashes have been found within the shrines, so calling them tombs is somewhat of a misnomer. Relics and artifacts reveal that both Hindus and Buddhists have used this site as a place of worship, which explains the blend of architectural styles within the shrines.

Accommodations

Luxury accommodations are what make the outskirts of Ubud worth visiting. Get ready for great views, infinity pools, private villas, and jungle as far as the eye can see. The quiet and lush area of Payangan is an oasis in itself, so it's obvious why some of the region's best hotels have chosen it as the place to build their retreat.

AYUNG RESORT
Banjar Begawan, Payangan; tel. 361/9001333; www. ayungresortubud.com; 2,000,000-8,000,000 Rp

Devoted to maintaining Bali's captivating aesthetic, Ayung Resort is part luxury resort, part museum with its collection of Indonesian artwork and artifacts thoughout the property. Birds chirp overhead and frogs sing in the valley below. A range of room and villa options are available at the resort, with the standout pick being the Javanese wooden villas built from opulently carved dark wood and set next to a private infinity pool. Guests can access two restaurants, a spa, and gym.

KAYON JUNGLE RESORT
Banjar Beresela; tel. 361/978098; https:// thekayonjungleresort.com; 4,000,000-14,000,000 Rp

A romantic retreat surrounded by forest, Kayon Jungle Resort caters to couples looking for a romantic getaway, as children under 15 are not permitted. Villas are stylishly designed with plush beds and modern amenities. Choose between villas that have private pools, jungle views, or both. All guests have included breakfast, daily yoga classes, guided walks, and shuttle service to Ubud.

One of the main draws to this resort is its pool area that spans across three floors and is primed for relaxation with shaded lounge chairs, firepits, and a pool bar. There are also multiple restaurants, a five-star spa, gym, and art market, as well as a small museum revealing the life and work of I Gusti Nyoman Lempad.

HANGING GARDENS RESORT
Desa Buahan, Payangan; tel. 361/982700; https:// hanginggardensofbali.com; 9,000,000-11,000,000 Rp

If there is one resort with a pool that stands out above the rest, it has to be Hanging Gardens of Bali. Their infinity pool juts out over lush jungle below, and its spacious patio deck is ideal for lounging the day away. Each of its 44 private villas is surrounded by tall

Celuk: The Silver Capital of Bali

Many small towns around Ubud are known for their artwork. One town passes down the skill of stone sculpting while another is a community of bead makers. In Celuk, silversmiths and goldsmiths have been perfecting their craft for generations, and it's where you'll find great deals on expertly made pieces of jewelry.

WHERE TO BUY

In Celuk, shops selling silver and gold line the main road of Jalan Raya Celuk.

Because Celuk has become a stop for organized tour buses, it's lost some of its charm as vendors hike prices and use strong-arm sales tactics. However, if you venture here on your own and spend some time looking at the fixed-price shops like Prapen (Jalan Jagaraga No. 66; tel. 81339114877; https://prapen.com; daily 9am-5pm) and stalls hidden in alleyways, you can take your time and find a great deal without the hassle. Balinese homes double as shopfronts, with many displaying their family's artwork in a glass case on the patio.

CHOOSING CELUK SILVER

The traditional Celuk style is intricate, with many swirls and patterns weaving harmoniously together. Cutlery, trays, vases, statues, and home decor are also found among the shops. Silver varies in quality, which is often reflected in the price. Sterling silver (made of 92.5 percent silver, 7.5 percent other metals) jewelry is available for purchase, as are affordable pieces that are silver-plated or made with less than 80 percent silver. Discerning travelers can subtly test the piece to see if it is genuine sterling silver by holding it to a magnet (sterling silver is not magnetic), looking for flakes or lines that reveal it could be simply plated, or noticing a copper or sulfur-like smell, which means that the piece could be made of copper.

trees and comes with Wi-Fi, breakfast, afternoon tea, and a daily turndown service. The panoramic villa has floor-to-ceiling windows that overlook the area, while the riverside villa is more remote, just a short walk away from the Ayung River. All guests have access to the on-site spa, bar and restaurant, and a complimentary shuttle service to the center of Ubud.

Getting There and Around

The outskirts of Ubud are best accessed with your own car or motorbike rented from Central Ubud or through your accommodation, as there are few places to rent outside of the tourist centers. Many of the resorts offer free shuttles to and from Ubud, set on their schedule. Private drivers are recommended for sightseeing, as there are many hair-pin turns and unmarked roads within the area. Apps like Maps.me or Google Maps help when it comes to finding your way.

The Tegallalang Rice Terraces are 10 km (6 mi) north of Ubud along Jalan Raya Tegallalang, with Kayon Jungle Resort being 2 km (1.2 mi) north of the rice terraces. Puri Tirta Empul is 15 km (9 mi) north of Ubud, slightly east of the Tegallalang Rice Terraces. The town of Payangan, where all other resorts featured in this section are located, is 15 km (9 mi) north of Ubud, slightly west of Tegallalang.

SOUTH OF UBUD

Sights

TEGENUNGAN WATERFALL

Jalan Sutami; daily 6:30am-6:30pm; 20,000 Rp

Tegenungan Waterfall is an impressive single-sheet cascade flowing from a river into a large pool below. It's earned quite the reputation among selfie enthusiasts, to the point where Balinese entrepreneurs rent out signs, props, and nests to take pictures with the waterfall as a backdrop. Swings and cafés are perched at the top of the waterfall staircase.

Shopping
SUKAWATI ART MARKET
Jalan Raya Sukawati; daily 8am-7pm

Anything goes in the Sukawati Art Market, a labyrinth of cheap souvenirs mixed with high-quality local artwork. Shop for wood carvings, beaded jewelry, paintings, stone sculptures, and more. Many of the art stalls are manned by the artist, making it a great spot to learn more about the inspiration behind the work and place orders for great-value commissioned pieces. The pressure to buy can be intense—starting from when you enter the parking lot. Arm yourself with a number in mind for the things you'd like, and this place will be easier to handle if you're heavily caffeinated.

Accommodations
FIVELEMENTS
10km south of Ubud, Mambal, Abian; tel. 361/469206; https://fivelements.org; 4,000,000-8,000,000 Rp

The large bamboo buildings you see as soon as you enter Fivelements are breathtaking. Using a combination of wood, bamboo, and *aling-aling* (native grass) roofing, Fivelements is a sustainability-focused wellness retreat. The resort hosts a mix of imaginative suites, and one- and two-bedroom villas, all crafted in a way that combines the indoors with the lush vegetation outside. Rooms are set on the Ayung river, decorated with Balinese antiques, and all have air-conditioning, Internet access, and a safe. Guests have access to a spa, boutique, gorgeous dining area serving plant-based meals, medicinal herb gardens, and pool.

Getting There and Around

Because the southern region of Ubud tends to be sparsely populated in comparison to Ubud Central and Denpasar, public transportation is unreliable. You can see the region best with a **private driver, rental car,** or with your own **motorbike**, which is best arranged from Central Ubud. **Tegenungan Waterfall** is 10 km (6 mi) south of Ubud (20 minutes) and is best reached via **Jalan Goa Gajah,** turning south onto **Jalan Sutami.**

Karangasem

Wherever you go in Karangasem, which en- compasses most of the eastern tip of Bali, remnants of its intriguing past can be found. It once was home to powerful kings, who built extravagant palaces and temples in the shadow of Gunung Agung. Those who refused to conform to the kingdom's demands created reclusive villages of their own; their unique festivals can still be witnessed today. Stories of love, war, and betrayal are told through the region's architecture, craftwork, ceremonies, and monuments. It's the type of place where wandering along overgrown pathways is rewarded.

Karangasem's striking landscape is as interesting as its history. Jade-green rice terraces, untamed forests, and streaks of barren land created by Gunung Agung's previous eruptions cloak the region's mountains.

Highlights

Look for ★ to find recommended sights, activities, dining, and lodging.

Map labels:
- Danau Batur
- Mount Abang 2,153m
- ★ U.S.A.T. Liberty Wreck
- Pantai Jemeluk and Jemeluk Bay
- Pura Besakih ★
- Besakih-Gunung Agung
- Mt Agung 3,142m
- Pura Lempuyang Luhur ★
- Mount Lempuyang 1,058m
- Mount Seraya 1,175m
- Besakih
- Tirta Gangga ★
- Amlapura
- Bangli
- Bias Tugel Beach ★
- Taman Sukasada Ujung ★
- Ubud
- Taman Nusa Cultural Park ★
- Candidasa
- Gianyar
- Semarapura
- Padangbai
- 0   2 mi
- 0   2 km
- © MOON.COM

★ **Taman Nusa Cultural Park:** Admire Indonesian architecture and learn more about other cultures in the archipelago at this cultural park (page 249).

★ **Bias Tugel Beach:** This white sand beach is hard to find but is worth the journey (page 260).

★ **Taman Sukasada Ujung:** Remnants from Karangasem's last monarchy are revealed in this giant palace with ponds, gardens, and Bali-meets-Europe architecture (page 267).

★ **Tirta Gangga:** An ode to the Ganges—here you'll find koi fish ponds, community pools, statues, and views of rice terraces (page 267).

★ **Pantai Jemeluk and Jemeluk Bay:** Snorkel around this tranquil bay to find hidden statues, thriving coral bommies, and schools of fish (page 270).

★ **U.S.A.T. *Liberty* Wreck:** A US cargo ship, torpedoed during World War II, now sits under the sea, encrusted in corals and home to a variety of marine life (page 278).

★ **Pura Besakih:** Set on the slopes of Mount Agung, Pura Besakih is the holiest temple in Bali (page 280).

★ **Pura Lempuyang Luhur:** At this sacred temple, a gateway looks out to clouds below and the crater of active Gunung Agung (page 282).

Top Restaurants

★ **Pasar Gianyar:** The region is famous for its *babi guling,* pork, cooked over a spit-roast, and you can find it at the large market of Pasar Gianyar (page 252).

★ **Warung Lesehan:** Looks deceive at this no-frills warung serving fresh grilled fish with sides of spicy *sambal* (chili sauce) (page 261).

★ **Omang Omang:** Dine and enjoy live music in this bright and jovial restaurant, where it's easy to make friends (page 262).

★ **Vincent's:** Jazz music plays in the background at this fine dining venue with tables placed among gardens (page 265).

★ **The Cup Coffee Shop:** Peer over the shores of Amed as you feast on a heaping plate of spicy noodles (page 275).

★ **Bukit Segara:** This small farm-to-table restaurant offers flavorful Balinese fare (page 275).

Sugar-white beaches give way to glimmering black sand and jagged rock along the coastline, setting a dramatic scene. Offshore, thriving coral reefs, shipwrecks, and underwater sculpture gardens made from buddhas and nymphs beckon you to take a closer look.

ORIENTATION

Karangasem encompasses most of the eastern tip of Bali, with **Gunung Agung** as its highest point.

Moving from southwest to northeast, the artistic town of **Gianyar** is the southwestern-most town in the region, 15 km (9 mi) east of **Ubud** and 20 km (12 mi) from **Denpasar.** The town and coastline of Gianyar are in their own regency, which encompasses the popular black-sand beach town of **Keramas,** 5 km (3 mi) south of Gianyar town center. **Semarapura,** where you can learn about the history of Bali and view scars from its tumultuous past, is 13 km (8 mi) from the town of Gianyar and 20 km (12 mi) west of the coastal town of **Padangbai,** a laid-back beach town

with a **boat and ferry terminal** that links Bali to the Nusa Islands and Lombok.

The bucolic, small-town **Sidemen** is best accessed from Semarapura, located 10 km (6 mi) inland toward the slopes of Gunung Agung, Bali's holiest volcano. **Pura Besakih** is the region's farthest inland point, 20 km (12 mi) inland from Sidemen. The summit of Gunung Agung is closest to Pura Besakih but requires a steep and arduous hike to reach, on the off chance it's not on the brink of erupting.

Continuing along the coast, **Candidasa,** a beach town where you can relax and dive around nearby reefs, is 15 km (9 mi) west of **Amlapura,** a town famous for its gardens and architecture and the closest point to **Pura Luhur Lempuyang.** The quiet beach town of **Amed** is directly north of Amlapura on the northern flank of **Gunung Lempuyang,** Bali's easternmost mountain. The small town of **Tulamben,** home to the **U.S.A.T** *Liberty* **Wreck** dive site, is 12 km (7.5 mi) away from Amed.

Previous: Offering at Pura Lempuyang Luhur; Tirta Gangga; Pura Lempuyang Luhur.

Karangasem

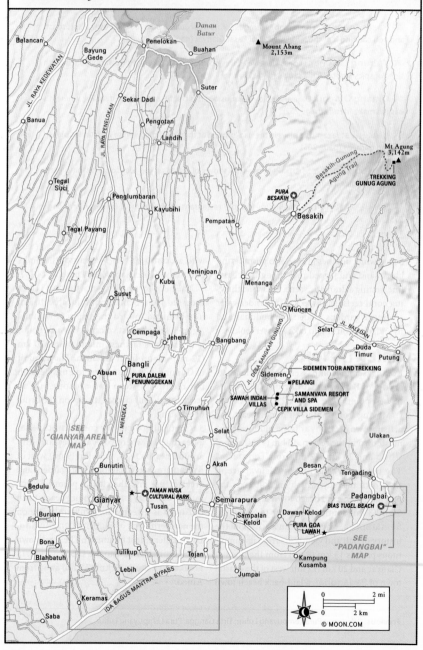

Danau Batur

Belancan

Bayung Gede

Penelokan

Buahan

▲ Mount Abang 2,153m

JL. RAYA KEDEWATAN

Banua

Sekar Dadi

Suter

JL. RAYA PENELOKAN

Pengotan

Landih

Mt Agung 3,142m ▲

TREKKING GUNUG AGUNG

Besakih-Gunung Agung Trail

PURA BESAKIH ⊛

Besakih

Tegal Suci

Penglumbaran

Kayubihi

Pempatan

Tegal Payang

Peninjoan

Menanga

Kubu

Susut

Muncan

Selat

JL. BALEDAN

Cempaga

Jehem

Bangbang

Duda Timur

Putung

Bangli

PURA DALEM PENUNGGEKAN ★

Abuan

JL. DESA BANGKAT GUNUNG

Sidemen

SIDEMEN TOUR AND TREKKING

■ PELANGI

SAWAH INDAH VILLAS ●

SAMANVAYA RESORT AND SPA

CEPIK VILLA SIDEMEN

Timuhun

Selat

JL. MERDEKA

SEE "GIANYAR AREA" MAP

Bunutin

Akah

Besan

Ulakan

Tengading

Bedulu

Buruan

Gianyar

★ TAMAN NUSA CULTURAL PARK

Tusan

Semarapura

Padangbai

BIAS TUGEL BEACH ⊛ ■

Bona

Sampalan Kelod

Dawan Kelod

PURA GOA LAWAH ★

SEE "PADANGBAI" MAP

Blahbatuh

Tulikup

Tojan

Lebih

Jumpai

Kampung Kusamba

Keramas

IDA BAGUS MANTRA BYPASS

Saba

0 ———— 2 mi
0 ———— 2 km

© MOON.COM

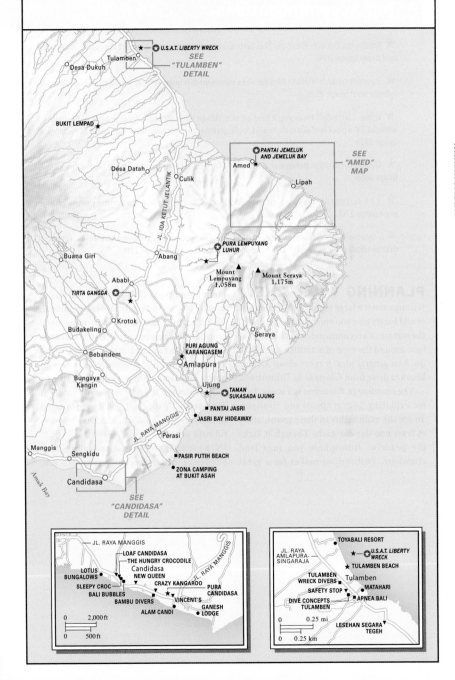

U.S.A.T. LIBERTY WRECK
SEE "TULAMBEN" DETAIL

Tulamben
Desa Dukuh

BUKIT LEMPAD

Desa Datah

PANTAI JEMELUK AND JEMELUK BAY
SEE "AMED" MAP

Culik
Amed
Lipah

JL. IDA KETUT JELANTIK

Buana Giri

Abang

PURA LEMPUYANG LUHUR

Ababi

Mount Lempuyang 1,058m

Mount Seraya 1,175m

TIRTA GANGGA

Krotok

Budakeling

Seraya

Bebandem

PURI AGUNG KARANGASEM

Bungaya Kangin

Amlapura

Ujung

TAMAN SUKASADA UJUNG

PANTAI JASRI

JL. RAYA MANGGIS

JASRI BAY HIDEAWAY

Manggis

Perasi

PASIR PUTIH BEACH

ZONA CAMPING AT BUKIT ASAH

Sengkidu

Candidasa

Amuk Bay

SEE "CANDIDASA" DETAIL

JL. RAYA MANGGIS

LOAF CANDIDASA
THE HUNGRY CROCODILE

LOTUS BUNGALOWS

Candidasa
NEW QUEEN

JL. RAYA MANGGIS

SLEEPY CROC

CRAZY KANGAROO

PURA CANDIDASA

BALI BUBBLES

BAMBU DIVERS

VINCENT'S

ALAM CANDI

GANESH LODGE

0   2,000ft
0   500ft

TOYABALI RESORT

JL. RAYA AMLAPURA-SINGARAJA

U.S.A.T. LIBERTY WRECK

TULAMBEN WRECK DIVERS

TULAMBEN BEACH

Tulamben

SAFETY STOP

MATAHARI

DIVE CONCEPTS TULAMBEN

APNEA BALI

LESEHAN SEGARA TEGEH

0   0.25 mi
0   0.25 km

Top Accommodations

★ **Komune Beach Resort:** This luxurious health and wellness resort looks out to Keramas surf break (page 254).

★ **Sawah Indah Villas:** Rice terraces surround this quiet retreat with a spacious lawn and infinity pool (page 257).

★ **Bloo Lagoon:** Here you'll find an eco-village with an organic farm, breezy bungalows without TV, a pool and waterslide, and rooftop restaurant set away from the noise of Padangbai (page 262).

★ **Ganesh Lodge:** Bohemian decor and a large pool are the main draws of this jungle stay (page 265).

★ **The Griya:** At this romantic property, each villa has ocean views and a private plunge pool (page 276).

★ **Toyabali Resort:** After a day of diving, reward yourself with views from the infinity pool that overlooks the ocean, or soak in your own private hot tub (page 279).

PLANNING YOUR TIME

Karangasem is a large region where one week would barely give you enough time to scratch the surface. It's recommended to choose your base around the type of activities you like to do. As a general idea, it takes about 2.5 to 3 hours to drive from **Gianyar** to **Tulamben.**

The coastline of **Keramas** is a scenic base for exploring **Semarapura** and **Gianyar.** To see the main sights in these towns, allow at least one day for each. Though it lacks the peaceful atmosphere you may find elsewhere, **Padangbai** makes for a great jumping-off point if you'd like a full day of **beach-hopping** or **scuba diving.** Inland, **Sidemen** is a tranquil retreat away from crowds where you can explore **rice terraces** and spend half a day visiting **Pura Besakih.** The seaside town of **Candidasa** is rife with hotels and restaurants; you'll want at least a day to enjoy it and the nearby town of **Tenganan.** Up the coast, you'll want to spend at least two days in **Amed,** which is a wonderful base to see **Tulamben, Tirta Gangga, Pura Lempuyang Luhur,** and all the **dive sites** just a short distance away from its beach.

Itinerary Ideas

THREE DAYS IN KARANGASEM

Day 1: Underwater Wonderland

1 Start your day with **Dive Concepts Tulamben** for a sunrise snorkel or scuba dive at the U.S.A.T. *Liberty*, a shipwreck where you're sure to see reef fish and possibly sea turtles.

2 Drive 7 km (4 mi) along Jalan Kubu, turning left at Jalan I Ketut Natih and continuing 4.5 km (2.75 mi) to Amed for a relaxing lunch with a view at **The Cup Coffee Shop.**

3 Keep your snorkel and bathing suit, then drive 1.3 km (0.8 mi) down Jalan I Ketut Natih to **Pantai Jemeluk,** known for its underwater sculptures and coral reefs. Walk up to the eastern headland at Jemeluk Bay for a snack and a cold drink.

4 For sunset, enjoy dinner at **Bukit Segara,** a seaside restaurant known for its friendly staff.

Day 2: Temples and Palaces

1 Hire a private driver for the day and visit **Pura Lempuyang Luhur** at sunrise to admire ornate temple gates and views of Gunung Agung. Arrive extra early if you plan to walk the stairs to other temples within the complex.

2 Then, drive 10 km (6 mi) west to **Tirta Gangga,** a garden with community pools and koi ponds. Food stands serve freshly cooked noodles and rice dishes on the road leading to Tirta Gangga; stop at any with a good view.

3 In the late afternoon, stroll around **Taman Sukasada Ujung,** reached by driving 11 km (7 mi) south along Jalan Abang-Amlapura. Here, you'll find a palace that's rarely crowded by international travelers—but is a popular place among locals.

4 For dinner, head 12 km (7.5 mi) along the coastal road of Jalan Raya Bugbug to **Vincent's** in Candidasa for seafood, steak, pasta, and jazz music.

Day 3: Sidemen Like a Local

1 Walk along quiet rice terraces of **Sidemen** and listen to the gentle sounds of chirping birds and trickling water.

2 Shop for Balinese textiles by driving a motorbike or walking along the main road of Jalan Semarapura-Karangasem. To see how the weaving is done, visit a shop called **Pelangi.**

3 Drive to **Pura Besakih** to pay homage to Bali's most sacred temple. Though you can't participate in ceremonies yourself, you can witness them from the outside. Bring a *canang sari* (an offering) along.

4 For dinner, enjoy a Balinese dish made from local ingredients at the restaurant at **Cepik Villa Sidemen.**

Itinerary Ideas

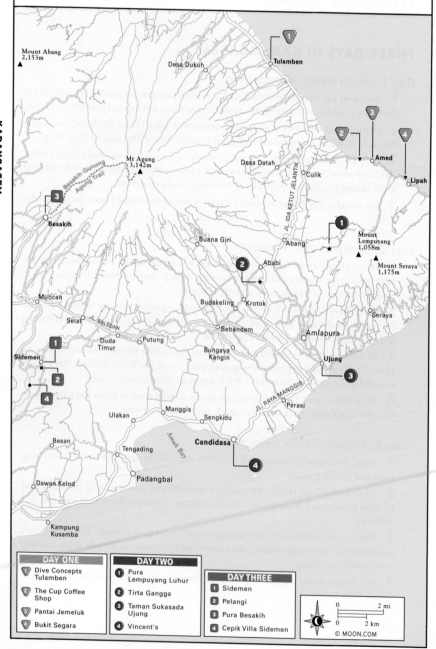

Mount Abang
2,153m ▲

Desa Dukuh

Tulamben ①

Mt Agung
3,142m ▲

Besakih-Gunung
Agung Trail

③ Besakih

Desa Datah

Culik

JL. IDA KETUT JELANTIK

② Amed

④ Lipah

③

④

Buana Giri

Abang ①

Mount
Lempuyang
1,058m ▲

Ababi ②
★

Mount Seraya
1,175m ▲

Muncan

Budakeling

Krotok

Seraya

Selat

JL. BALEDAN

Duda
Timur

Putung

Bebandem

Amlapura

Sidemen ①

Bungaya
Kangin

Ujung ③

②

④

Ulakan

Manggis

Sengkidu

JL. RAYA MANGGIS

Perasi

Besan

Tengading

Anuk Bay

Candidasa

④

Dawan Kelod

Padangbai

Kampung
Kusamba

DAY ONE	DAY TWO	DAY THREE
① Dive Concepts Tulamben	① Pura Lempuyang Luhur	① Sidemen
② The Cup Coffee Shop	② Tirta Gangga	② Pelangi
③ Pantai Jemeluk	③ Taman Sukasada Ujung	③ Pura Besakih
④ Bukit Segara	④ Vincent's	④ Cepik Villa Sidemen

0   2 mi
0   2 km

© MOON.COM

Gianyar Area

There's something about Gianyar that seems to spark creativity in all who visit. Of Bali's regencies, Gianyar is best known for its artists. Villages of woodworkers, painters, silversmiths, goldsmiths, and sculptors populate the area. Royal families in Ubud and Gianyar used artwork as status symbols, made easier once Gianyar received protectorate status from the Dutch during the early 1900s. This allowed the region to flourish in ways that those in other regencies were not able to. Once automobiles entered the royal scene, the Raja of Gianyar had a Garuda statue made from pure gold placed over the radiator of his Fiat Grand Phaeton. Inspiration seems to be taken from views of volcanoes, swaths of emerald-green rice paddies, palm trees that tickle the sky, and long stretches of black volcanic sand.

SIGHTS
★ Taman Nusa Cultural Park
Jalan Taman Bali; tel. 361/952952; www.taman-nusa. com; daily 9am-5pm; 410,000 Rp adult, 270,000 Rp child

Set over 10 hectares (25 acres) on the Melangit River, The Taman Nusa Cultural Park is an educational center that displays more than 60 traditionally built structures, dance and music performances, textile weaving workshops, art exhibitions, costumes, and a restaurant where you can sample different Indonesian dishes from throughout the archipelago. Also on-site is a replica of Borobudur Temple, which dates back to Indonesia's kingdom age. If anything, the park highlights how diverse each region in Indonesia is; distinct styles of clothing, architecture, and beliefs are all influenced by the specific environment and culture of the time. Some structures are built to protect against a constant battering of rain while others, like those from Nias, are set on earthquake-absorbing stilts. Many of the exhibits are interactive, making it an engaging stop to visit with kids. If you have limited mobility, there are carts to shuttle guests around the park. Book direct in advance for a small discount.

Dalem Sidan Temple
(Pura Dalem Sidan)
Jalan Raya Sidan; 50,000 Rp

Pura Dalem Sidan is dedicated to Durga, the goddess of death, and its gates are marked by long-tongued statues of Rangda, the widow witch. This temple compound is ornate with red-brick walls, gold accents, and odes to the afterlife. This temple is rarely open to outsiders. Much of it can be admired from the outside.

Masceti Temple
(Pura Masceti)
Jalan Prof Dr. Ida Bagus Mantra (Pantai Masceti); daily sunrise-sunset; 10,000 Rp parking

Pura Masceti is a seaside temple and an important site for the Melasti Pilgrimage that takes place just before Nyepi, the Saka New Year, when thousands of Balinese Hindus make their way to the coastline to partake in ceremonies revolving around the water. Though it isn't a popularly visited temple among travelers, it is one of the directional temples of Bali that protects Bali's southeastern coastline from evil intentions.

Watu Klotok Temple
(Pura Watu Klotok)
Pantai Klotok; sunrise-sunset; free

This is another site that is important during the Melasti Pilgrimage, when statues from the mother temple of Pura Besakih are brought to Pura Watu Klotok. This 10th-century compound has multiple courtyards, with one featuring a Hindu god standing atop a large turtle. Temple gates lead from its dual five-tiered merus to the sea.

Gianyar Area

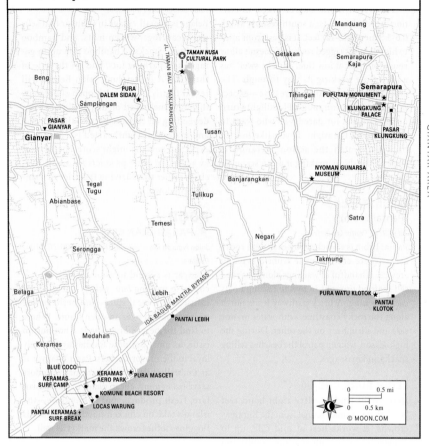

BEACHES AND SURF BREAKS
Keramas Beach
(Pantai Keramas)

Park along Jalan Pantai Keramas or on unnamed road north of Jalan Pantai Keramas with large green sign pointing to Keramas Surf Point and Car Park Surf Point; 10,000 Rp parking

Fields of rice lead the way to a beach of dazzling black volcanic sand. Pantai Keramas

---

1: Dalem Sidan Temple **2:** coastline by the Masceti Temple **3:** Keramas Beach **4:** Keramas Surf Break

looks like it belongs on another planet. When the waves aren't pumping, Keramas is mellow and ideal for beach strolls. A few warungs, hotels, and temples line its shore.

KERAMAS SURF BREAK
Northern end of Pantai Keramas

Keramas has been on the mainstream surf scene for a while, but its entrance into the WSL Pro Championship Tour solidified its status as one of the best waves in Bali. Couple this with the fact that recent contests have livestreamed near-perfect barrels, and you'll see why Keramas is a magnet for crowds.

The right-hand barrel likes north-northwesterly winds, a southwesterly swell, 0.6-3.5 meters (2-12) feet. It is best from mid- to high tide. Its jagged rock reef doesn't allow room for error at low tide, and the swell has a hard time working its way through. The crowds are notoriously aggressive—expect drop-ins and mean mugs. Floodlights turn on after sunset for daredevils who want to surf through the night. If you like to kick back and watch the action, Keramas is close to the shore, making it a fun scene for spectators.

Lebih Beach
(Pantai Lebih)

Jalan Raya Pantai Lebih; free

Pantai Lebih is a black sand beach with rocky areas where crabs scuttle from crevice to crevice. A handful of warungs along the road sell seafood brought in by the fishing boats each morning. A brick pathway leads north along the rocky coastline, with water on one side and shrubbery on the other. During the high season, women patrol the beaches selling snacks and massages.

LEBIH SURF BREAK

Here you'll find a shifty right-hand reef break that is a small refuge from the Keramas crowds. It works best at mid-tide, up to 3-meter (10-foot) south-southwest swells, and southerly winds. You'll need paddle strength thanks to strong currents, floating trash, and a challenging lineup.

Klotok Beach
(Pantai Klotok)

Jalan Pantai Klotok; free

Pantai Klotok is protected by Pura Watu Klotok, the temple set on its shoreline. The beach is a mix of fine black sand and large stones. It's okay for lounging but too tumultuous for swimming.

SHOPPING
BELAGA

Jalan Belaga; daily 9am-5pm

Belaga is a small village in Gianyar that sells wood carvings, woven mats, and bamboo furniture. Stacks of bamboo pile up in garages and parking lots, and on the side of the road. A drive along Jalan Belaga will reveal family homes with open shopfronts that have their craft on display. Prices vary, depending on the intricacy of the weaving and materials. Lighthearted bargaining is expected, and you might score a better deal by adding in other products for a bulk purchase rather than driving the price of a single item down.

FOOD
★ PASAR GIANYAR

Jalan Ngurah Rai; daily 7am-10pm; 10,000-30,000 Rp meal

Gianyar is second to none in Bali when it comes to making *babi guling,* a stuffed pig infused with local spices and herbs before it's spit-roasted over an open flame. Where to find the best *babi guling* is a hot button issue, as most Balinese foodies are fiercely loyal to their favorite chefs. Pasar Gianyar is an umbrella-filled place where many vendors serve *babi guling,* cheap plates of Indonesian fare, fresh produce, and *bakso ayam*—the island's take on chicken noodle soup. Stalls flogging clothes crowd the market as well.

LOCAS BEACHFRONT WAROENG

Pantai Keramas; tel. 81337520001; daily 11am-10pm daily; 30,000-70,000 Rp

Locas Waroeng is set on the black sand beach of Keramas and has an array of pizzas, burgers, and Balinese meals served inside a spacious open-air shack. It's the type of place where you can walk in sandy and barefoot and sit down for a cold beer. The owner, Locas, is chatty and inquisitive—especially if you're dining as a solo traveler. He also owns a smaller restaurant within walking distance

---

1: Keramas Aero Park 2: Locas Beachfront Waroeng

near the entrance of Komune Resort that serves plates of noodles and rice.

KERAMAS AERO PARK

Jalan Prof Dr. Ida Bagus Mantra; tel. 361/4791830; www.keramasaeropark.com; daily 10am-10pm; 40,000-100,000 Rp

File Keramas Aero Park under the bizzare finds category of restaurants. It's located inside a hollowed-out Boeing 737 and surrounded by rice paddies. Guests can sit in the cockpit and tinker with the buttons, or take a walk out onto the wing and look out to the ocean. The property has a large grassy area ideal for kids to run around while adults can hang back at the outdoor bar. Its menu of sandwiches, steaks, and pizzas could stand a bit of improvement, so go here for the novelty factor and not for the gourmet cuisine.

ACCOMMODATIONS

BLUE COCO

Jalan Prof Dr. Ida Bagus Mantra No. 300A; tel. 81239311018; https://bluecocobali.weebly.com; 350,000 Rp double room

Blue Coco is an upbeat and brightly colored surf school about a five-minute walk away from Pantai Keramas, with a small pool and lounge deck. All rooms come with air-conditioning, Wi-Fi, and a small patio. Breakfast is included with each stay. Think surf hostel vibes, but with the privacy of your own four walls. The hosts are happy to arrange surf lessons that include board and equipment rental for 700,000 Rp for a 2-hour class, or surf guiding for 800,000 Rp for an 8-hour guide.

KERAMAS SURF CAMP

Pantai Keramas; tel. 81999087070; book via booking. com or Agoda; 400,000 Rp double room

Keramas Surf Camp is a retreat among rice paddies. The beach is a short walk from the rooms, where guests can mingle at a beach bar. There are a variety of double-room bungalows with private cold-water showers, as well as single rooms in a hotel-style block with shared bathroom options. Each room has Wi-Fi access, air-conditioning, and a small patio area.

★ KOMUNE BEACH RESORT

Pantai Keramas; tel. 361/3018888; www. komuneresorts.com; 1,500,000 Rp suites, 2,500,000 Rp villas

Komune Beach Resort offers double rooms and one-, two-, and three-bedroom villas set behind a beachside pool. It has a strong wellness focus with a range of facilities like an on-site gym, spa, yoga studio, and health-conscious restaurant. It's the type of place where you can surf and play all day before checking in for a deep tissue massage. One of the main draws of Komune Beach Resort is its food. There are three top-notch restaurants on-site, one of them being a surfers' beach shack with tables in front of Keramas Surf Break. The poolside restaurant features a choice of burgers, seafood, pizzas, and an extensive vegan menu. Kids will love the trampoline, swing, and movie nights.

GETTING THERE AND AROUND

Unreliable *bemos* (7,000-10,000 Rp) run to Gianyar town from **Ubud** (12 km/7.5 mi; 30 min) and **Denpasar** (30 km/18.5 mi; 1.5 hours) and arrive at **Gianyar Terminal** (Jalan Kebo Iwa). Drivers might shout "'Nyar" to announce *bemos* headed to Gianyar. Otherwise, it is best accessible with your own **car**, **motorbike**, or **private driver**, arranged through your accommodation.

To reach Gianyar from **Ubud,** drive 2.5 km (1.5 mi) east along **Jalan Raya Goa Gajah,** turning right at **Jalan Raya Bedulu.** Follow this main road, veering south, which leads into Gianyar's central area. From **Denpasar,** drive 13.5 km (8.3 mi) east along **Jalan Prof Dr Ida Bagus Mantra,** turning left along **Jalan Raya Pantai Lebih** for 2.5 km (1.5 mi), which connects to **Jalan Sakura;** then it's another 2.5 km (1.5 mi) to Gianyar.

Keramas is located just off the main coastal road of **Jalan Prof. Dr. Ida Bagus**

Mantra. While **rideshare apps** aren't as common in this area, you might be able to use them if you're patient. Taking **Grab** from **Keramas** to Ubud costs 80,000 Rp and takes 1 hour. From Keramas to **Kuta** is 120,000 Rp and takes 1.5 hours. On all other routes, a **private driver, rental car,** or **motorbike** is the most convenient option. Jalan Prof. Dr. Ida Bagus Mantra, the road leading to Keramas, can be intimidating for novice motorbike drivers and cyclists. Expect speeding trucks and erratic traffic.

Semarapura (Klungkung)

Driving through the quiet town of Semarapura, you'll find the Kanda Pat Sari statue made up of four guardians protecting those traveling in all directions. Shops, monuments, and museums line the roads. What's not obvious about Semarapura is its interesting and dramatic history, as this area once hosted Bali's most powerful royal family, the kings and descendants of the Klungkung family. The family had a penchant for the arts, commissioning grand designs and works throughout the region. As a result, the area still fosters artists today.

Glimpses of Semarapura's interesting and tragic past can be seen in the remnants left behind at the Klungkung Royal Palace, Puri Agung Semarapura, as well as the heartbreaking Puputan Monument. Interesting works of art are easily found at the Nyoman Gunarsa Museum.

SIGHTS
Klungkung Palace
(Puri Agung Semarapura)
Jalan Untung Surapati; daily 8am-6pm; 12,000 Rp

Puri Agung Semarapura was once the palace of the Klungkung royal family. In 1908, Dutch colonial forces razed the palace before occupying the kingdom of Klungkung. The Klungkung royal family was Bali's most influential from the late 17th century until the date the Dutch sacked the Puri Agung Semarapura Palace. The Klungkung aristocrats lived a life of luxury, drawing thousands of followers from all around the island.

Today, you can see remnants of the palace and glimpse a small part of the detail it once held. The main features include two open-air meeting rooms with painted ceilings, its figures mimicking those used to create shadow puppets. The palace shows a time when Hinduism and Buddhism shared meeting spaces. Though Hindu figures adorn the area, some paintings in the Kerta Gosa building show tiers of tales that depict goings-on in the afterlife. Outside, a lily pond with a pavilion in the center illustrates tales of Sutasoma, a Buddist figure who stood for peace. Gardens surround. A museum at the back of the palace displays masks, *krises* (daggers), and costumes used in cultural performances.

Puputan Monument
Jalan Puputan; daily 8am-6pm; free

The Puputan Monument is a pillar that commemorates the death of about 400 Balinese defenders and the Klungkung royal family. In April 1908, Dutch forces stormed Klungkung after sacking Denpasar, where the Balinese committed mass suicide in a ritual called *puputan*. The Dutch then sent their troops and artillery to Klungkung. Dressed in all white and wearing their finest jewels, the royal family of Klungkung sacrificed themselves as a protest to the colonial army. Any high-ranking citizens of Klungkung who survived the invasion were sent to Lombok in exile. The intention of *puputan* is not widely understood. While some Balinese historians believe that it is a symbolic ritual that represents the choice of death by one's own hands rather than the hands of an enemy, more cynical historians claim that aristocrats would rather die than give up their lifestyle of opulence and wealth.

Nyoman Gunarsa Museum

The intersection of Jalan Raya Takmung and Jalan Raya Banda; tel. 366/22256; Mon.-Sat. 9am-4pm; 75,000 Rp adult, free children under 12

The Nyoman Gunarsa Museum is named after one of Bali's most prolific contemporary artists, Nyoman Gunarsa (1944-2017). His subjects often included Hindu legends, dancers, and musicians, painted in an expressionistic style. This three-story museum holds the work of Nyoman Gunarsa and was founded by the painter himself on his property, where you can take a look at his former studio. Gunarsa was also an art collector, and the building holds his personal collection of cloth paintings, *wayang kulit* puppets, wooden sculptures, and musical instruments. Sadly, a lack of funding and the absence of air-conditioning mean that many art pieces are exposed to heat and humidity, and some already show signs of damage.

SHOPPING

PASAR KLUNGKUNG

Jalan Puputan No. 7; daily 6am-6pm

At the textile market, Pasar Klungkung, you can shop for textiles crafted on a backstrap loom or on the more modern unmechanized loom. The area's specialty is endek, a fabric that usually has hues of red and orange and solid geometric designs. There are also stalls where you can purchase food, snacks, and many other types of sarongs or textiles. The market is divided into separate areas selling similar goods, so you can compare products easily by category.

GETTING THERE AND AROUND

Bemos arrive at the **Galiran Terminal** (Jalan Anyelir) from **Gianyar** (10 km/6 mi; 30 minutes; 20,000 Rp) and **Denpasar** (30 km/18.5 mi; 1.5 hours; 25,000 Rp). *Bemos* from **Padangbai** (15 km/9.3 mi; 45 minutes; 25,000 Rp) depart and arrive at the north side of **Pasar Klungkung.** However, it can be a scramble to know when or where the *bemos* are going unless you have an English-speaking driver. It's best to visit **Semarapura** with a private driver, arranged in advance through your accommodation, or with your own private car, rented from Denpasar.

To get to Semarapura from **Denpasar,** take Jalan **Prof Dr. Ida Bagus Mantra** 17 km (10.5 mi) to **Jalan Raya Tojan,** and follow it to **Jalan Puputan,** which leads into Semarapura. If coming from **Ubud** (22 km/13.5 mi; 45min) head west along **Jalan Goa Gajah to Gianyar** (11 km/7 mi; 20 minutes), following **Jalan Astina Timur** east to **Jalan Raya Banjarangkan** until you reach **Jalan Raya Takmung.** This road connects to **Jalan Puputan,** a main road of Semarapura.

Pasar Klungkung, Puputan Monument, and **Puri Agung Semarapura** are all within **walking** distance from one another. The **Nyoman Gunarsa Museum** is about 4 km (2.5 mi) or 10 minutes' drive southwest of the other sites.

Sidemen

Sidemen, a bucolic small town with views of Gunung Agung, is surrounded by waterlogged rice paddies, rolling hills, and forests of tropical fruit trees. Highly underrated, the scenery here trumps many of the more popular rice terraces. The scent of sweet and spicy cloves lingers in the air, with blankets of the aromatic flowers laid on the roads to dry. It's a place you can wander undisturbed in search of sweeping views of man-tamed greenery and wilderness beyond.

Locals produce stunning *kain songket* fabrics, a smooth silk with gold and silver threads glistening throughout the fabric—it was once highly sought by royals. The village also crafts *endek, ikat* weavings made on wooden looms where ties are used to craft patterns from cotton. Get a firsthand look at how these intricate fabrics are created at Pelangi, a workshop and store selling locally made products.

TREKKING

SIDEMEN TOUR AND TREKKING

Jalan Raya Sangkan Gunung-Sidemen; tel. 81933000775; www.sidementourandtrekking.com; 75,000 Rp per hour

Sidemen Tour and Trekking offers guided walks around the surrounding rice terraces, where a friendly guide explains how rice is grown. Tours start in the village and end at one of the village's most important temples. Tours can also be adapted to include workshop demonstrations of *songket* and *endek* weaving.

SHOPPING

The main road of Sidemen, Jalan Semarapura-Karangasem, is speckled with shops selling traditionally crafted fabrics. Some are simple and elegant while others are bold and visually hypnotic. Each craftsman has an individual take on what beauty looks like when it comes to creating a pattern. Look for shops with *ikat* displayed in the front; this means that there are fabrics inside. It's okay to negotiate if you're buying in bulk; prices tend to start at 150,000 Rp per meter of fabric and go up depending on material and pattern. For premium fabrics, expect to pay 1,000,000 Rp per meter.

PELANGI

The southern end of Sidemen's main road, Jalan Semarapura-Karangasem; tel. 8123923483; daily 9am-6pm

ACCOMMODATIONS

★ SAWAH INDAH VILLAS

Banjar Tebola Sidemen; tel. 366/5551109; www. sawahindahvilla.com; 400,000-600,000 Rp double room

A spectacular view of surrounding rice terraces is the main draw of Sawah Indah Villas, while its infinity pool comes in at a close second. Set below the pool's edge is a well-kept lawn and lounge chairs, ideal for relaxing the day away. The property has a mix of rooms within blocks, as well as more private standalone bungalows. All come with a terrace, Wi-Fi access, and private bathroom. If you're booking in advance, request a room with unblocked views.

CEPIK VILLA SIDEMEN

Banjar Tebola Sidemen; tel. 366/5551145; www. cepikvilla.com; 1,200,000 Rp double room

The quiet rooms and bungalows at Cepik Villa Sidemen are surrounded by gorgeous rice terraces and untamed foliage. Rooms are elegantly designed and furnished with touches of the textiles that Sidemen is famous for. Guests have access to a quaint pool and lounge area, and an on-site restaurant serving fresh Balinese and European fare. All rooms have a safe, Wi-Fi, air-conditioning, and outdoor seating area. Personable staff are happy to arrange tours around the region for extra cost.

SAMANVAYA RESORT AND SPA

*Banjar Tebola Sidemen; tel. 82147103884; www.
samanavaya-bali.com; 2,100,000 Rp deluxe lodge,
2,500,000 Rp 2-bedroom suite*

Samanvaya Resort and Spa has mastered the intermingling of nature and luxury, with one- and two-bedroom villas, and *lumbungs* (barns) built from bamboo and *aling-aling* grass. The decor is kept simple, allowing the scene of rice terraces outside the window to act as stand-in works of art. On-site, guests can make use of a bamboo and hardwood yoga *shala* (yoga studio), swim in the infinity pool, soak in the Jacuzzi, receive massages, and participate in chakra treatments from one of the village's renowned traditional healers. Guests must be 16 and older.

GETTING THERE AND AROUND

Bemos pick up and drop off along the main road of Sidemen (noted as **Jalan Raya Sinduwati/ Jalan Semarapura-Karangasem** on maps) for 7,000 Rp per ride and run to **Semarapura** (12 km/7.5 mi; 30 minutes), but the best way to get here is with a **private driver** (50,000 Rp per hour of driving). Sidemen is 45 km (28 mi; 1.5 hours) from **Denpasar;** 25 km (15.5 mi; 1 hour) from **Padangbai;** 40 km (25 mi; 1.5 hours) from **Ubud;** and 20 km (12.5; 40 minutes) from **Besakih.**

The town itself is easy to cruise around with your own **motorbike** (50,000 Rp rental per day), rented from your accommodation, as most everything is on one well-maintained stretch of road.

Padangbai

Most travelers who come through Padangbai rarely stay longer than what's needed to catch their boat to the next island over. Padangbai is home to a boat and ferry terminal that acts as a major link from Bali islands due east to the Nusa Islands, Lombok, and the Gili Islands. Because of this, it's a town that many people know of, but few people know well. Padangbai is unpretentious and laid-back, with hidden white sand beaches and a harbor that gives off a constant hum of buzzing motors from boats tethering up along its shoreline. Great-value accommodations and fun vibes are easily found in this quirky coastal community. As the locals might say, "Welcome to the Bay."

SIGHTS
Silayukti Temple
(Pura Silayukti)

Jalan Silayukti; free

This open and uncluttered temple features three courtyards ranging in significance. Rarely crowded with tourists, its open courtyards set the scene for meditation and deep thought.

Goa Lawah Temple
(Pura Goa Lawah)

Jalan Raya Goa Lawah; daily 8am-7pm; 30,000 Rp adult, 15,000 Rp child

Pura Goa Lawah, which translates into "Bat Cave Temple," marks the entrance of an expansive cave that is home to thousands of fruit bats. Legend says that at the back of the cave is a large dragon deity, Naga Basuki, that feeds on the fruit bats. This alone tends to discourage anyone from venturing too deep into the cave. The most sacred part of the temple holds three *merus* (shrines), with an eleven-tiered *meru* honoring Shiva, the god of destruction. *Candis* (temple gates) mark the entrance to the cave where you'll see the fruit bats hang until sunset, when they then leave to forage. Persistent hawkers might throw a necklace around your neck as a gift and then will expect payment as a thank you. Guides offer their services for

Padangbai

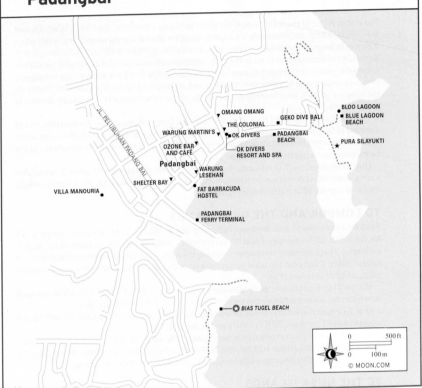

50,000 Rp, though it's a site you can explore within a half hour on your own.

BEACHES

As on Bali's southern beaches, trash can wash ashore onto Padangbai during strong swells and storms. These beaches are especially susceptible to pollution during rainy season.

BLUE LAGOON BEACH
(Pantai Blue Lagoon)

Pantai Blue Lagoon, entrance down a staircase on the south side of the lagoon; 10,000 Rp

Pantai Blue Lagoon is a thin 50-meter (164-foot) sandy enclave with a cluster of warungs toward the back that rent out lounge chairs and sell cheap bites. Snorkelers hit the

teal water in search of parrotfish, which can often be seen cruising around the rocky reef. *Jukung* boats float a few meters offshore, and green headlands protect the sand from wind. If coming from the south of Padangbai along Jalan Silayukti, follow a blue arrow that points to Blue Lagoon Eco Resort. When you get to the second sharp turn, veer right at a blue shack with a sign labeled Blue Lagoon Beach.

PADANGBAI BEACH
(Pantai Padangbai)

Pantai Padangbai, access along Jalan Silayukti; free

Padangbai is a wide stretch of white sand that hosts many of the inter-island fast boats, ferries, and fishing boats. It's one of the main harbors that connect Bali to Lombok. Because

Padangbai Ferry Terminal

Padangbai is one of the main harbors for boats servicing Lombok, the Nusa Islands, and the Gili Islands. Unfortunately, it's a guessing game of who is genuine and who is not when it comes to buying boat tickets, so you should purchase tickets directly through the provider or through your hotel. In the best-case scam scenario, you'll be overpaying for a ticket. Otherwise, you might be handing over cash for a counterfeit. Porters are available to help you load and unload your luggage onto the boat and will expect a tip for their services (10,000 Rp per luggage piece is recommended). Employees of the boat companies are usually dressed in logoed shirts.

Keep electronics and valuables in a small bag with you during the boat ride. It's not unheard of for checked luggage to get crushed by other bags or dropped into the water as it's loaded. Wear sandals and shorts or loose pants that you can roll up for the boat ride, as the boats arrive at the beach, not on a dock.

Due to weather, swell conditions, route changes, staff shortages, and other unscheduled events, many boats do not run on schedule and some may not run at all. Do not schedule a flight the same day as a boat trip to or from Padangbai.

TO LOMBOK AND THE GILI ISLANDS

Fast boats shuttle tourists between Padangbai and Lombok (Bangsal Harbor, Senggigi, Gili Air, Gili Meno, Gili Trawangan). Local hotel transfer within Padangbai is usually included with each price. There are many companies servicing the route, with varying degrees of comfort and safety history. A fast boat trip takes around one hour, though there may be extra stops between ports, which takes more time.

Bluewater Express (https://bluewater-express.com; tel. 81338418988; 650,000 Rp one way) runs boats between the Padangbai and Lombok/Gili Islands once per day.

Gili Gili runs twice daily service (www.giligilifastboat.com; tel. 361/763306; 550,000 Rp one way) between Lombok/Gili Islands and Padangbai.

The public ferry (ticket office Jalan Segara; 46,000 Rp adult, 29,000 Rp child) between Padangbai and Lombok (Lembar Harbor) runs 24/7 and is scheduled to leave every 90 minutes. The trip can take up to five or six hours (or longer), depending on weather conditions.

TO THE NUSA ISLANDS

A public ferry (tickets purchased onboard; 31,000 Rp adult, 26,000 Rp child) shuttles between Padangbai and Nusa Penida. The trip takes just over an hour and arrives at Sampalan.

of the frequent motor traffic and pollution, it's not an ideal place to swim or wade in the water past your waist. It is, however, a fun place to people watch, and there are swaths of sand where you can sit and relax. The main road of town, Jalan Sitayukti, runs alongside the beach, separating the sand from shops and restaurants.

★ BIAS TUGEL BEACH
(Pantai Bias Tugel)

Pantai Bias Tugel, South of Padangbai Ferry Terminal; 5,000 Rp parking, 10,000 Rp admission

Pantai Bias Tugel is often called "Secret Beach" among locals. Its soft white sand contrasts with the rocks of hardened lava on its edge, while bright blue water laps the shoreline. This beach is quirky and ideal for spending the day in the sun. Small warungs built from driftwood, bamboo, and corrugated metal sell cold drinks and plates of fried rice. Lounge chairs are available for rent. The road to the beach is narrow and windy. Follow Jalan Penataran Agung south of Padangbai Ferry Terminal. Turn left at the fork and follow white and blue signs indicating "White Sand Beach" or "Pantai Bias Tugel." Then, it's a narrow walk down.

WATER SPORTS
Scuba Diving

Padangbai is a surprisingly convenient home base for scuba divers. In front of town are a handful of interesting dive sites that range from gentle slopes to walls to reef and an abandoned old cruise ship jetty. Some sites are your go-to Balinese coral reefs while others are muck dives, revealing macro critters like frogfish, orangutan crabs, and seahorses in hard-to-see places. Moray eels, anemone fish, lionfish, octopus, green turtles, and reef sharks call the region home. Because most dive travelers opt to blow bubbles north of Padangbai, Padangbai's dive sites are often uncrowded.

OK DIVERS

Jalan Silayukti No. 6; tel. 8113858830; www. okdiversbali.com; daily 8am-7pm; 1,100,000-1,700,000 Rp for 2 fun dives

OK Divers is the type of place where people become regulars and stick around much longer than they planned. Aside from being a 5-Star PADI Resort and sticklers for safety, they also have a bar, spa, and rooms available for divers to spend their surface intervals. OK Divers offers dive courses ranging from Discover Scuba to Divemaster, as well as snorkeling tours of the area.

GEKO DIVE BALI

Jalan Silayukti No. 5; tel. 82121801997; https:// gekodivebali.com; daily 7am-7pm; 1,100,000 Rp-1,600,000 for 2 fun dives

A 5-Star PADI dive center that has been in operation for over 20 years, Geko Dive Bali has instructors who know the best sites and conditions for diving. Staff are friendly and accustomed to taking nervous divers underwater for the first time, though they also offer technical diving courses for divers who want to progress beyond recreational diving.

FOOD
WARUNG MARTINI'S

Jalan Silayukti; daily 11am-9pm; 10,000-50,000 Rp

If you take a seat at Warung Martini's, there's a strong chance that Martini, the friendly owner, will sit next to you. This family-run warung is an antidote to homesickness. Food options include fried or grilled fish served with *sambal*, soups, beef *rendang*, fried noodles, and rice. Vegans, vegetarians, and those with dietary restrictions will be well accommodated for if you give Martini a heads up.

OZONE BAR AND CAFÉ

Jalan Silayukti; tel. 8174708597; daily 8am-11pm; 20,000-50,000 Rp

With rasta colors and reggae music playing in the background, Ozone Bar and Café is a fun place to spend the evening. The snapper is a popular pick among regulars, with the menu offering a decent choice of other seafood, meat satay, *mie goreng*, and *nasi goreng*. Burgers and pasta are also featured options, though it's best to choose from the Indonesian side.

★ WARUNG LESEHAN

Jalan Segara; tel. 81805664587; daily 11am-9pm; 20,000-90,000 Rp

Warung Lesehan is a little warung with just eight tables inside that serves fresh fish with heaping sides of *sambal*. First, you pick the fish you want. Then, Wayan, the chef and owner, cooks it over the grill. Spiced fish grilled in banana leaves is the signature dish—get it if you can. The building itself looks like something you'd walk by without giving it a second thought, but the food more than makes up for it.

THE COLONIAL

Jalan Silayukti No. 6; tel. 8113978837; www. okdiversbali.com; daily 7am-11pm; 50,000-150,000 Rp

With a wide-open seating area and ambient lighting, The Colonial is a welcoming restaurant that serves soups, salads, ribs, curries, beef *rendang*, and creative takes on desserts. The banoffee pie—made from caramel, coffee cream, and mashed bananas—is one that will make you want seconds. There are many options for vegans and vegetarians, making it a top pick for mixed groups. Pair your meal with a cocktail or ice-cold Bintang—they have it on tap. Bring your bathing suit; diners have access to the site's pool.

BARS AND NIGHTLIFE

SHELTER BAY

Jalan Segara; tel. 87761535735; daily 10am-late; 20,000-80,000 Rp drinks

Drawing in a rambunctious bunch—usually in the form of drunk backpackers—Shelter Bay is a sports bar that serves a combination of cold drinks, gelato, and *shisha* (pipe). Loud music draws in a crowd, as do the two-for-one drink specials.

★ OMANG OMANG

Jalan Silayukti No. 12; tel. 363/4381251; daily 7:30am-11pm; 70,000-100,000 Rp

Omang Omang is one of Padangbai's most popular restaurants for a reason. Their casual setup includes dining on cushions and low tables (high tables also available), funky artworks on the walls, a fun music playlist, and a staff of friendly locals who love to joke around. Live music plays regularly, and you'll find a diverse menu of omelets, burgers, sandwiches, curries, meat skewers, and more. The vibe between breakfast and dinner changes drastically, so you'll want to come for both.

ACCOMMODATIONS

FAT BARRACUDA HOSTEL

Jalan Segara; tel. 82237971212; 100,000 Rp dorm bed, 250,000 Rp double room

Fat Barracuda Hostel gives off hippie vibes with its bright yellow paint, plethora of beanbag chairs, swirling mosaic decorations, and a large room furnished with bunk beds. The downstairs dorm room has solid bunk beds (more stable than their bamboo predecessors), each equipped with a power outlet and reading light. Noise from the road, a single hot water shower shared among 10 guests, and a rotating door of backpackers make it a stop you might consider just for one night. The double room upstairs is worth the splurge if you want privacy.

VILLA MANOURIA

Jalan Penataran; tel. 85237047122; 500,000 Rp double room

Set behind the scuffle of Padangbai, Villa Manouria is a hilltop guesthouse with stilted bungalows made from bamboo and wood. Rooms feel connected to nature, with views of the sea, outdoor bathrooms, and a surrounding garden area. It's easy to spend the day admiring Padangbai from above, watching boats shuttle in and out of the harbor. A lagoon-style pool adds to its appeal. All rooms have Wi-Fi access and breakfast included. Access to Villa Manouria requires a walk uphill and up stairs.

OK DIVERS RESORT AND SPA

Jalan Silayukti No. 6; tel. 8113978837; www. okdiversbali.com; 900,000-1,500,000 Rp double room

OK Divers Resort and Spa, set across the road from Padangbai's main beach, has become somewhat of a hub for divers. It has a spa, bar, restaurant, kid-friendly pool, and dive center all within a short distance of one another. Rooms are bright, clean, and minimally decorated. All 30 rooms have air-conditioning, Wi-Fi, a minibar, a small safe, and free refillable drinking water. Their best room, the Mola Mola Suite, has a queen bed, a daybed, and a spa with a stand-alone stone bathtub and massage table.

★ BLOO LAGOON

Jalan Silayukti; tel. 363/41211; https://bloolagoon. com; 1,500-3,000,000 Rp double room

Bloo Lagoon is designed to be an eco-village, made up of 25 one- to three-bedroom villas. The intention of the resort is to connect guests with nature through the use of open, airy windows, outdoor bathrooms, and wild surrounds that feature ponds and a permaculture farm. All stays come with breakfast, Wi-Fi, and an hour-long yoga class that takes place in their spacious yoga studio each morning. Kids are encouraged to participate in guided activities like weaving, dance, baking, and kite-flying workshops. Come sunset, head to the rooftop bar to enjoy views of the ocean from above.

INFORMATION AND SERVICES

ATMs are available along **Jalan Pelabuhan,** inland from the **ferry terminal.**

GETTING THERE
By Boat
Padangbai is one of the main harbors for boats servicing **Lombok,** the **Nusa Islands,** and the **Gili Islands.** See section on the Padang Ferry Terminal (page 260) for information on boats to and from these destinations.

By Private Driver and Taxi
A **private driver** can take you to Padangbai from **Denpasar** (45 km/28 mi; 1.5 hour), **Kuta** (55 km/34 mi; 2 hours), **Ubud** (40 km/25 mi; 1.5 hour), **Amed** (45 km/28 mi; 1.5 hour), and elsewhere in the region. Ride apps like Grab and GoJek are not popular in Padangbai. A **taxi** from the **Ngurah Rai**

International Airport will cost 350,000-400,000 Rp and takes 1.5 hours.

By Bus and *Bemo*
Bemos buzz between **Padangbai, Semarapura,** and **Candidasa** (10,000-30,000 Rp). From **Denpasar,** *bemos* leave from **Batubulan Terminal** (Jalan Pudak No. 21; tel. 361/298526) to Padangbai (1.5 hour; 30,000 Rp).

Perama (Jalan Pelabuhan; Peramatour. com; tel. 361/750808) offers air-conditioned tourist shuttles to Padangbai (and away) from **Amed** (100,000 Rp; 2.5 hours), **Bedugul** (150,000 Rp; 4 hours), **Candidasa** (35,000 Rp; 5 hours), **Kuta** (75,000 Rp; 2.5 hour), **Lovina** (175,000 Rp; 4.5 hours), **Sanur** (75,000 Rp; 1.5 hours), **Tulamben** (100,000 Rp; 3 hours), and **Ubud** (75,000 Rp; 2 hours).

GETTING AROUND
The town of Padangbai is very **walkable.** Follow the main **beach** and stroll along **Jalan Silayukti** and **Jalan Segara. Motorbike rentals** are readily available from your accommodation for 50,000 Rp per day.

Candidasa and Around

Candidasa was one of the most happening towns in Bali during the 1980s. Hotels and guesthouses sprung up with abandon, and divers set out to explore the local reefs. Today, it's a very relaxed area that attracts those who seek serenity and early nights. It's a place where you can find an idyllic hangout spot directly over the water.

SIGHTS
Candidasa Temple
(Pura Candidasa)
Jalan Raya Manggis; free
Pura Candidasa honors the goddess of fertility, Hariti. Women hoping to have children make pilgrimages to Pura Candidasa in hopes of receiving Hariti's blessing. The temple sits

across from a large lagoon blanketed in lily pads and lotus flowers; a sidewalk surrounds it. When you enter the temple, walk up a staircase that leads up to an upper level. Views of the pond and ocean await.

BEACHES
Candidasa's shoreline shows the tragic repercussions of unsustainable development. The reef in front of Candidasa was dredged up for construction materials, leading to an oceanographer's worst nightmare: As a result, beaches that once existed have eroded away and are now small patches of sand. A humble seawall and a series of rock jetties protect Candidasa from coastal inundation—a sad replacement for a reef.

PASIR PUTIH BEACH
(Pantai Pasir Putih)

Access road from Jalan Raya Pantura, or by boat, 9 km (5.5 mi) north of Candidasa; 10,000 Rp access road entrance

Pantai Pasir Putih is a 500-meter-long (1,640 feet) beach that goes by the moniker of "Virgin Beach." Streaks of black sand swirl along the white sand shoreline, giving it a gray hue from a distance. The back of the beach is lined with little warungs, palm trees, umbrellas perched over lounge chairs, and rows of white outrigger canoes. When the sea is calm, the gentle slope of the shoreline makes it great for sandcastle building, sunbathing, and swimming.

WATER SPORTS
Snorkeling and Scuba Diving
PONDOK BAMBU DIVERS

Jalan Raya Candidasa; tel. 363/41534; www. bambudivers.com; daily 8am-6pm; 1,300,000-1,900,000 Rp for 2 fun dives

Pondok Bambu Divers is a 5-Star PADI Dive Resort that runs dive trips all along Bali's eastern coastline, as well as over to Nusa Penida. Divers can join a course ranging from Discover Scuba up to Divemaster. Clean rooms placed along a garden pathway and a

seaside restaurant beckon those who are doing multiple days of diving.

BALI BUBBLES

Jalan Raya Candidasa; tel. 363/42196; www. bali-bubbles.com; daily 8am-7pm; 1,300,000-2,100,000 Rp for 2 fun dives

The instructors and dive guides at Bali Bubbles, a 5-Star PADI Dive Center, have a strong reputation for teaching beginners how to scuba dive in a way that's fun and informative. This little center hosts dives around Karangasem's coastline and Nusa Penida, and it offers courses from Discover Scuba to Divemaster. Book online for the best deals and check their specials for combo packages.

FOOD
LOAF CANDIDASA

Jalan Raya Candidasa; tel. 363/4381130; daily 8am-6pm; 30,000-70,000 Rp

LOAF Candidasa is a coffee shop and café that's a go-to place for breakfast, serving eggs benedict, English breakfast, cakes, and scones. For lunch, enjoy fresh sandwiches with thick slices of bread, as well as wraps and salads. The inside of the café is hip and modern, with chalkboard menus and tiny tables.

sea wall and rock jetties in Candidasa

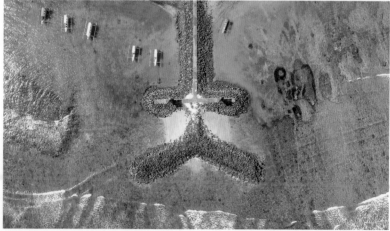

NEW QUEEN

Jalan Raya Candidasa; tel. 81236531832; daily 9am-midnight; 40,000-90,000 Rp

New Queen is a shabby warung marked with rasta-colored bunting flags on its outside. Inside, a mishmash of handwritten signs, colorful lights, and flags give it a jovial vibe. **Live music** plays on Monday, Tuesday, and Friday. If the mood is right, the crowd gets loose. Grilled fish, *nasi campur,* beef *rendang,* and meat skewers are the top picks of their menu.

THE HUNGRY CROCODILE

Jalan Raya Candidasa; tel. 363/4381003; daily 9am-10pm; 60,000-100,000

A wooden crocodile statue is the figurehead for The Hungry Crocodile, a casual restaurant serving seafood, steak, and Indonesian fare. They often host live world music, with Saturday being the most popular night of the week. Staff are friendly and happy to chat about menu recommendations.

★ VINCENT'S

Jalan Raya Candidasa; tel. 363/41368; www. vincentsbali.com; daily 10:30am-11:30pm; 60,000-150,000 Rp

With garden seating, Van Gogh replica paintings (the restaurant was named after the Dutch artist), and well-crafted meals, Vincent's treats dining as though it were a special occasion. Each option is thoughtfully plated, and their most popular dishes include grilled fish, steak, spinach rolls, and duck roasted in herbs. The atmosphere is upscale and romantic, with jazz musicians frequenting the restaurant's live music stage.

CRAZY KANGAROO

Jalan Raya Candidasa; tel. 363/41996; www. crazy-kangaroo.com; daily noon-midnight; 70,000-150,000 Rp

Watch chefs work at Crazy Kangaroo, a restaurant with wide windows that look into its large kitchen. The dining area is an open-air *bale* (pavilion) and garden area that hosts live music. Enjoy a range of pizza, pasta, seafood, and Indonesian dishes. The cocktail menu is

one of the most extensive in the area, and their bar has a first-come, first-play pool table.

ACCOMMODATIONS

SLEEPY CROC

Jalan Raya Candidasa; tel. 87762563736; 100,000 Rp dorm bed

Built in 2016, Sleepy Croc is a bright and upbeat hostel with clean, eight-bed mixed-gender and female-only dorm rooms. Each bunk bed is thoughtfully equipped with an overhead locker, storage area, private curtain (bottom bunk only), power outlet, and reading light. The property has a pool surrounded by cushy beanbag chairs, and it hosts live music at its on-site bar on a regular basis. Light sleepers will want to bring earplugs as the hostel is next to the main road.

ZONA CAMPING AT BUKIT ASAH

Access road from Jalan Raya Ulakan, town of Bugbug, 9 km (5.5 mi) north of Candidasa; tel. 87762094664; 150,000 Rp 4-person tent, plus 15,000 Rp admission to hill

On the southern end of the Pantai Pasir Putih, there is a grassy headland called Bukit Asah that's popular among locals for picnics and camping. Panoramic views look out to Lombok and along the Karangasem coastline. Your stay includes a pillow and mattress, a bundle of firewood, and a tent. Cooks are available to prepare simple meals on-site for extra cost. There are showers and toilets at the back of the campsite.

★ GANESH LODGE

Jalan Puri Bagus; tel. 81915600577; 750,000 Rp double room

In a jungle-meets-beach retreat, Ganesh Lodge is a boutique resort with an upscale free-spirited ambiance. It has a large lagoon-style pool surrounded by palm trees, lotus ponds, and an on-site restaurant that serves rightly spiced local and European fare. Each room is unique, with varying artworks displayed inside the room and around the property. All are equipped with air-conditioning, Wi-Fi, a semi-open bathroom, and desk.

LOTUS BUNGALOWS

*Jalan Raya Candidasa; tel. 363/41104; www.lotus
bungalows.com; 800,000-1,200,000 Rp double room*

Directly on the ocean with a pool that looks
out over the water, Lotus Bungalows has 20 elegant and bright bungalows with tile floors
and Balinese decor. Each comes with air-
conditioning, an outdoor bathroom, a safe, Wi-Fi
access in communal areas, and a patio. Some
rooms at the front of the property have sea views.
The resort is affiliated with Gangga Divers, who
can organize fun dives and scuba diving courses.

ALAM CANDI

*Jalan Raya Candidasa; tel. 363/4381343; www.
alamcandi.com; 900,000 Rp double room*

Alam Candi has a romantic appeal, with private, tastefully decorated rooms that have
touches of traditional Balinese wood carvings and decor. Rooms are set around a well-
kept garden area, and an open dining room
borders a tranquil pool. Each room has air-
conditioning, an outdoor bathroom, safe, a
small patio, and Wi-Fi access. If you stay, don't
miss the hotel's regular barbecue nights where
staff cook fresh-caught fish.

INFORMATION AND SERVICES

ATMs are found along **Jalan Raya
Candidasa.**

GETTING THERE

By Car

Candidasa is best accessed with a **private**

driver booked through your accommodation or a **rental car** arranged from Denpasar
if coming from areas like **Kuta** (60 km/37 mi;
2 hours), **Denpasar** (50 km/31 mi; 1.5 hours),
Sanur (50 km/31 mi; 1.5 hours), **Padangbai**
(10 km/6 mi; 20 minutes), **Ubud** (45 km/28
mi; 1.5 hours), and **Amed** (35 km/22 mi; 1
hour).

By Bus and *Bemo*

Bemos run between Candidasa to
Padangbai and **Semarapura**. From
Denpasar, *bemos* leave for Candidasa from
Batubulan Terminal (Jalan Pudak No. 21;
tel. 361/298526; 1 hour 45 minutes; 30,000
Rp).

Perama (Jalan Raya Candidasa;
Peramatour.com; tel. 361/750808) offers air-
conditioned tourist shuttles to **Padangbai**
(and away) from **Amed** (100,000 Rp; /2
hours), **Bedugul** (150,000 Rp; 4.5 hours),
Padangbai (35,000 Rp; .5 hour), **Kuta**
(75,000 Rp; 3 hours), **Lovina** (175,000
Rp; 5 hours), **Sanur** (75,000 Rp; 2 hours),
Tulamben (100,000 Rp; 2.5 hours), and
Ubud (75,000 Rp; 2.5 hours).

Getting Around

Bemos run along the main road of Candidasa,
Jalan Raya Candidasa, and can be flagged
down from the roadside for 10,000 Rp per
10-minute ride, though you may have to negotiate your fare in advance. Otherwise, driving
a **motorbike, walking,** or hiring a **private
driver** is the best option.

Amlapura Area

Until Mount Agung erupted in 1963, Amlapura was known as Karangasem. Following the aftermath of the eruption, the Balinese renamed the volcano as a symbol of rebirth. They hoped to rid the city of any negative spirits associated with the name Karangasem.

Karangasem (Amlapura) has a dramatic history that is tainted by a power-hungry royal family who sold slaves in exchange for opium, built and broke alliances, and once held control over Western Lombok. Today, Amlapura is a quiet town where remnants of its past stand in the forms of palaces, gardens, and Muslim influence from those moving from Lombok to Bali. The former kingdom's strong ties to China through trade can be seen in architectural details, and in the food. If you enjoy history, immaculate gardens, and architecture, Amlapura is well worth a stop.

SIGHTS
★ Taman Sukasada Ujung

Jalan Taman Ujung; 5 km (3 mi) north of Amlapura; tel. 363/4301870; daily 6am-7pm; 50,000 Rp admission, 5,000 Rp parking

Taman Suksada Ujung was designed and built from 1909-1921 by the last raja of Karangasem, I Gusti Bagus Djelantik, who remained in power until 1945, when the monarchy was dismantled by Indonesian independence from the Dutch. Some sections of Taman Sukasada Ujung required restoration following World World II, when Japanese forces pillaged the palace for iron. In 1979, following a magnitude 6.3 earthquake, the palace had to be rebuilt. Its architecture blends European and traditional Balinese styles, set around two large ponds with a third smaller pond toward the coast. The most impressive feature for many is a large, picturesque bridge that spans to a *bale gili* meeting house in its center. Stairs lead up the hillside to vantage points offering sweeping views of the palace below. Locals often come to walk, picnic, and admire the gardens.

★ Tirta Gangga

Jalan Abang-Amlapura; tel. 363/22503; daily 7am-7pm daily; 30,000 Rp admission, 5,000 Rp swimming pool, 2,000 Rp parking

Tiers of rice paddies and a winding road lead to Tirta Gangga, a water palace that honors Hinduism's most sacred river, the Ganges. Inside its grounds are a series of ponds, pools, and fountains, and koi fish who school inside the ponds, mouths agape and begging for food. There are two community pools inside the palace, one of which is often used by training freedivers who come from Amed. Mythical statues adorn the palace, referencing Hindu legends and honoring the sacred site of Bali. Plan your walk across the pond's steppingstones strategically. When it's crowded, lines form along the stones, making it a challenge to make your way back to solid ground without getting wet.

Agung Karangasem Temple
(Puri Agung Karangasem)

Jalan Teuku Umar; daily 8am-5pm; 10,000 Rp

Puri Agung Karangasem is a congregation of small palaces built around the center of Amlapura, with one central Puri Agung Karangasem palace in its center. The main guest house, Maskerdam, has antique furniture from the time as well as aged pictures of the royal family. Much of the palace is dilapidated, a shell of its former self. Views from the palace look over Amlapura and out to Lombok, making it an interesting perspective when you consider how large the Karangasem kingdom once was. A *bale kambang* surrounded by lotus flowers stands as the remaining highlight of the palace.

Tenganan and the Bali Aga

The village of Tenganan, inland of Candidasa, is a **Bali Aga** (also called the Bali Mula) community. It's widely said that the Bali Aga people are the indigenous people of Bali, though some evidence shows that other Balinese communities are just as old. Regardless, the Bali Aga communities like those at Tenganan and at **Trunyan** in the Central Mountains differ from the rest of Bali when it comes to culture and social structure. For example, those in Tenganan must marry within the village if they want to stay inside it.

The divide between the Bali Aga and the rest of Bali probably happened as a side effect of the 14th-century **Majapahit dynasty.** Some villages refused to conform to the new religious and social ideals, instead settling in the mountainous areas of Bali to develop in isolation. The most obvious differences between Bali Aga communities and the rest of Bali are their architectural style, artwork, and the lack of a caste system. It is the only place that produces *gerinsing* cloth, a double *ikat* weaving technique that is believed to fend off bad spirits.

Visitors can be led by a local guide through the main village of Tenganan (**Tenganan Pegrinsingan**) as well as the smaller community west of the main village (**Tenganan Dauh Tukad**). Entry is by donation, 50,000 Rp per person is recommended, and the tour always includes a visit to the local souvenir stalls. While outsiders are not privy to all the ongoing activities and rites of Tenganan, a blood-drawing festival that takes place called **Usaba Sambah** is open to tourists. Over the course of a month, animals are sacrificed, cocks fight, bachelors and bachelorettes swing from a ramshackle structure, and men slice one another's skin with the thorny edge of a pandanus leaf. The festival takes place during the fifth month of the Balinese year. An alternative festival is **Sabatan Biu,** in which adolescent boys must dodge bananas hurled at them while balancing stacks of coconuts on their backs.

BEACHES

JASRI BAY
(Pantai Jasri)
Follow Jalan Achmad Yani until it turns into an unnamed road and reaches the coastline

Boutique beach resorts and rice terraces surround Jasri Bay, a quiet haven also known as Turtle Bay. The bay is an important nesting site for Bali's sea turtles, which return year after year to lay clutches of eggs in the sand. For surfers, there's a decent right-hander that rarely draws a crowd.

UJUNG BEACH
(Pantai Ujung)
Access along Jalan Karangasem-Seraya

Glittering black sand and large stones back up against groves of palm trees at Pantai Ujung, an uncrowded beach that stretches along Ujung's coastline. Though it's not always great for swimming, it's a perfect place for a walk when the tide is low. *Jukung* boats teeter on the sand, and Taman Suksada Ujung is located on the beach's southern end. Pura Linggayoni, a temple with a phallic rock in its center, is also on the shoreline of Pantai Ujung and is thought to promote fertility.

FOOD AND ACCOMMODATIONS

PASAR AMLAPURA
Market in between Jalan Kesatrian and Jalan Gajamada; daily 5am-3pm

A maze of stalls selling produce, raw meat, food, clothing, offerings, and household staples weaves throughout the town's main market, Pasar Amlapura, with Chinese and halal dishes well represented. The inside of the market is humid and buzzing with locals trying to complete their errands for the day. Stop too long without purpose and you'll be gently pushed aside.

JASRI BAY HIDEAWAY
Jalan Pura Mascima; tel. 363/23611; www.jasribay. com; 1,500,000 Rp double room

1: Tirta Gangga 2: Tirta Gangga rice terraces

Jasri Bay Hideaway restores balance in a busy life, as represented by the huge yin/yang sign at the bottom of its beachfront pool. The resort offers unique one- and two-bedroom wooden villas with red-brick roofs. All rooms look out over the ocean and surrounding gardens, and all include pool access, Wi-Fi, and air-conditioning. Their Pandan Cottage is set on stilts with a lounge area set underneath it and a balcony above that overlooks the water and treetops.

GETTING THERE AND AROUND
By Bus and *Bemo*

Bemos run from Amlapura to **Padangbai** (30,000 Rp; /1 hour) and **Gianyar** (50,000 Rp; 1.5 hours) from the center of town (**Jalan Kesatrian,** across from Pasar Amlapura).

By Car

Like many parts of Karangasem, the best way to get to Amlapura is with your own **car** or **private driver.** If coming from **Kuta** (75 km/46 mi; 2.5 hours) or **Denpasar** (70 km/43 mi; 2 hours), take **Jalan By Pass Ngurah Rai** to **Jalan Prof. Dr. Ida Bagus Mantra** for 26 km (16 mi) passing through Padangbai until you reach Amlapura. The coastal road also leads to Amlapura from **Candidasa** (15 km/9.3 mi; 30 minutes) and **Amed** (20 km/12 mi; 40 minutes). If coming from **Ubud** (60 km/37 mi; 2 hours), pass through Gianyar until you reach the coastal road near Semarapura, then venture 40 km (25 mi) east along the coastline.

Amed Area

In the shadow of Gunung Agung, the Amed area is made up of a sleepy string of fishing villages along a black sand coastline. Amed is used colloquially to describe the 15-km (9-mi) stretch of villages that span from Culik to Aas, with Amed being the most popular among tourists. It's a tranquil place even in high season, and the crowds thin out the closer you get to Aas. Along this stretch, Jemeluk is where you'll find thriving reefs and a sculpture garden. Continue east to Lipah and Selang for more snorkeling and quaint beachside stays. If you look under the water's surface in Banyuning, you'll find a Japanese wreck encrusted with corals. All along you'll be met with peaceful bays to the east and hills of jungle and rice paddies to the west.

Amed appeals to divers and freedivers who come to make use of the warm water, coral reefs, and visibility. It's also an ideal base for trekking Gunung Agung whenever the volcano is not on an eruption alert. When the day's adventures are done, there are plenty of places to do nothing but relax.

BEACHES AND SIGHTS
Amed Beach
(Pantai Amed)
Jalan I Ketut Natih; free
Ashy sand mixed with large pebbles makes up Pantai Amed; fishing boats beached ashore come in and out with the tide. Calm, warm water makes it a prime spot for swimming, though it's not always easy to find shade. Guesthouses, villas, dive centers, and restaurants line the beach.

★ Pantai Jemeluk and Jemeluk Bay
Pantai Jemeluk; Jalan I Ketut Natih; free
Rent a set of snorkel gear and explore the thriving coral reef just offshore of Pantai Jemeluk, a bay with *jukung* outrigger canoes, warungs, and a modest temple on its shoreline. Beyond the reef, it's easy to reach depths of more than 50 meters (164 feet), making it an ideal spot for training freedivers. For sunset, head to the eastern headland to enjoy a view

1: Amed area 2: Pantai Jemeluk

Amed

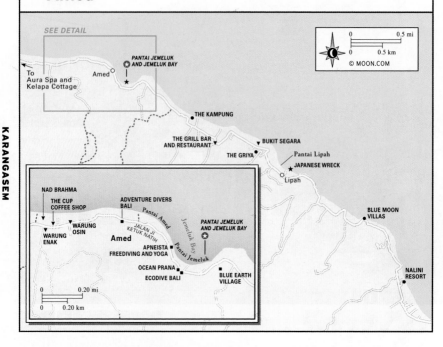

of the bay with a cold Bintang in hand, available from the hillside warung.

JEMELUK SUNKEN SCULPTURE GARDEN

Pantai Jemeluk; free

Offshore of Pantai Jemeluk, a garden of statues awaits. Most famous is an underwater mailbox that many travelers mistake for a shrine or temple. A buoy marks where the underwater mailbox should be. Statues of nymphs, a baby's head, sirens, and a barong are placed in the bay to stimulate coral growth while also encouraging tourism.

Lipah Beach
(Pantai Lipah)

Jalan Raya Amed; free

Hillside luxury retreats, guesthouses, and villas border the quiet beach of Pantai Lipah. Umbrellas and lounge chairs in a

ruler-straight row line one end of the beach while white fishing boats line the other. At high tide, it's an ideal spot for snorkeling, kayaking, and swimming.

JAPANESE WRECK

Village of Banyuning, Pantai Lipah, swim out in front of Baliku Dive Center; free

The origins of the Japanese Wreck, a small vessel that sits under 10 meters (33 feet) of water, is muddled. Some claim that there was a misunderstanding and that "Japanese" was actually "Javanese," which makes sense if a Javanese fishing boat wandered into the area in hopes of finding a score of fish. No matter, the Japanese Wreck is a wonderful snorkel site to spot macro life like nudibranchs, anemones, damselfish, pygmy seahorses, and seafans that cling to the wreck. Rays with electric blue spots often nestle into the sand under its hull.

WATER SPORTS
Scuba Diving and Freediving
ADVENTURE DIVERS BALI

Jalan Jemeluk; tel. 81353136113; www.
adventurediversbali.com; daily 8am-7pm;
850,000-1,000,000 Rp for 2 fun dives

Adventure Divers Bali is a family-friendly and welcoming SSI dive school that offers courses ranging from Discover Scuba to Divemaster. They focus on keeping groups small and taking the time to explain some of scuba diving's more challenging concepts to nervous divers.

ECODIVE BALI

Jalan I Ketut Natih; tel. 363/23482; https://
ecodivebali.com; daily 8am-7pm daily;
850,000-950,000 Rp for 2 fun dives

Ecodive Bali is a 5-Star PADI instructor development center that has been in operation on Pantai Jemeluk since 1997, welcoming more than 20,000 divers. Thanks to this experience, it's a well-oiled machine and its dive guides have explored just about every corner of the region. Take a refresher course if it's been awhile, or complete any course ranging from Discover Scuba to scuba diving instructor. Night dives and Nitrox diving also available.

APNEISTA FREEDIVING AND YOGA

Jalan I Ketut Natih; tel. 81338301158; www.apneista.
com; daily 9am-6pm

Apneista Freediving and Yoga is Amed's original freediving school that hosts freediving, yoga, and meditation classes. Former students can be found singing its praises from all over the world as the school has formed somewhat of a prideful following. Courses range from the SSI level 1 freediving course up to SSI freediving instructor. The business has a strong reputation of professionalism and organization.

OCEAN PRANA

Jalan I Ketut Natih; tel. 363/4301587; www.
oceanprana.com; daily 7am-8pm

Ocean Prana is a blissful freediving school that emphasizes using freediving skills in a practical sense. Courses are supervised by Yoram Zekri, a former record holder who has been freediving for more than 20 years. The school teaches AIDA level 1 to AIDA freediving instructor, with coaching also on offer. Hourlong yoga classes take place at 6:30pm daily (100,000 Rp per class).

freediving in Amed

Amed and Tulamben's Best Dive Sites

- **Gili Selang** (5-30+ meters/16-98+ feet): This spot offers the best chance to see pelagic fish like tuna, hammerhead sharks, *mola-mola*, barracuda, and more. When currents are strong, it's a site for experienced divers only.

- **Jemeluk Wall I and II** (10-45+ meters/32-147+ feet): A gentle drift dive takes you along a sloping reef where reef fish hide in the coral and bigger fish like groupers and *mahi-mahi* cruise in the blue.

- **Pyramids** (5-20 meters/16-65 feet): Named after concrete pyramids used to promote coral reefs, this site is great for snorkeling and spotting pufferfish, Harlequin sweet lips, pipefish, eels, turtles, mimic octopi, and rays.

- **Melasti** (5-25 meters/16-82 feet): This is a muck diver's delight, with long-horned cowfish, peacock mantis shrimp, frogfish, pygmy seahorses, and nudibranchs galore.

- **U.S.A.T.** *Liberty* (5-30 meters/16-98 feet): Sea turtles, groupers, parrotfish, barracuda, leaf fish, and many others live in this coral-encrusted shipwreck.

- **Drop Off** (10-30 meters/16-98 feet): This is a fun drift dive along a reef where juvenile and reef fish hide between corals on the wall. Look out into the blue for a chance to see reef sharks, rays, groupers, and elusive hammerheads.

- **Batu Niti** (10-30 meters/16-98 feet): A bizarre wall of basalt hides creatures that are just as strange looking, like frogfish, nudibranchs, and feather starfish.

- **Bunutan Point** (5-40+ meters/16-131 feet): Shy garden eels lead you to a gentle coral garden with sponges and sea fans accenting its appeal. Snapper, reef sharks, and pufferfish, groupers, and barracudas frequently seen.

OTHER SPORTS AND RECREATION

Yoga
BLUE EARTH VILLAGE
Pantai Jemeluk; tel. 82145543699; www. blueearthvillage.com; daily noon-8pm; 100,000 Rp for 90-minute class

A spacious, thatched-roof yoga deck built from bamboo is the ideal setting for yogis looking for inner peace and a good stretch. Blue Earth Village teaches yoga classes daily at 5:30pm, with occasional morning classes throughout the week. Classes include *yin, vinyasa, hatha,* and fly high yoga, where you stretch with the assistance of suspended straps. The space also hosts pub quiz sessions, guided meditations, and movie nights.

Spas
AURA SPA
Jalan Amed Celuk; tel. 85274030033; www. kelapacottage.com; daily 9am-6pm; 150,000 Rp 60-minute Balinese massage

Aura Spa is a peaceful retreat at the back of Kelapa Cottages. Talented massage therapists offer a range of massage treatments, scrubs, cream baths, facials, waxing, manicures, and pedicures. Ask for their loyalty card—it never expires, and you might go here enough to get a free massage.

FOOD
WARUNG ENAK
Jalan I Ketut Natih; tel. 81915679019; daily 8am-10pm; 20,000-70,000 Rp

A popular spot among expats and locals,

Warun Enak is known for its pizza. Grilled fish, satay, barbecue tempeh, soups, and salads are also on a diverse menu that'll please a picky crowd. Seating is open and limited, with only parts of it covered. Perhaps surprisingly, they also serve some of the best desserts in Amed.

WARUNG OSIN

Jalan Raya Amed; tel. 87863256991; daily 11am-9pm daily; 30,000-60,000 Rp

From outside, Warung Osin looks like an unremarkable restaurant with just a handful of tables inside its open storefront. However, this warung serves some of the best local food in town. Stick to classic dishes like *nasi campur, gado-gado,* or *mie goreng* for a meal that's flavorful and good value.

NAD BRAHMA

Jalan I Ketut Natih; tel. 81237310129; Tues.-Sun. 1pm-10pm, closed Mon.; 30,000-60,000 Rp

Nad Brahma is a rooftop restaurant that overlooks Amed's black sand beach. Well-spiced curries, dahl, samosas, roasted chickpeas, yogurt dressings, and chutneys are served on silver plates in this cramped but quirky space. Finishing your meal with a dessert and hot cup of chai is a must—though those who are still waiting for a table might glare if you enjoy your meal for too long. All dishes accommodate vegetarians.

★ THE CUP COFFEE SHOP

Jalan I Ketut Natih; tel. 81916141668; daily 7am-10pm; 30,000-100,000 Rp

The view from a rooftop table at The Cup Coffee Shop is one of the best in Amed. Over a cup of hot coffee, you can look out onto the black sand beaches and peek into the backyards of Balinese homes, where chickens peck and scamper. Come for breakfast to sample a stack of fluffy banana pancakes or stick around for lunch to twirl a spicy pile of fresh rice noodles around your fork. If you're looking to check in with the online world, the café also has power outlets and free Wi-Fi.

THE GRILL BAR AND RESTAURANT

Jalan Raya Amed; tel. 363/2787131; daily noon-10pm; 40,000-110,000 Rp

The Grill Bar and Restaurant is located inland of Amed's main drag. When you see a somewhat shabby building covered in bright blue and yellow paint, you're in the right place. The restaurant is known for its barbecued ribs, though grilled fish, steak, and burgers are also on the menu. Staff always seem to be smiling, and travelers on the road can swap out read books for new ones at their community bookshelf.

★ BUKIT SEGARA

Jalan Raya Bunutan; tel. 363/23012; www.villabukitsegara.com; daily 9am-9pm; 40,000-120,000 Rp

The open-air restaurant at Bukit Segara overlooks a two-tiered infinity pool that blends with the blue sea below. Chefs cook primarily Balinese and Indonesian fare like herb-roasted duck, *nasi campur,* meat satay, and beef *rendang.* It's a true farm-to-table experience, with many ingredients sourced from the property's small farm.

ACCOMMODATIONS

NALINI RESORT

Jalan Raya Amed; tel. 363/4301946; www.naliniresort.com; 800,000 Rp double room

Nalini Resort is a quaint family-run property set on a pebble-stone beach. The vibe is fun and carefree, with a pool that's small—but not too small to squeeze in a pool bar. A small dining area, lounge chairs, and beanbag chairs on the water's edge make Nalini Resort a prime spot to use as a relaxing base. Rooms are simple and clean, with air-conditioning, bright walls, and an outdoor bathroom. Snorkeling is right out front.

KELAPA COTTAGE

Jalan Celuke No. 36; tel. 82145710821; www.kelapacottage.com; 200,000 Rp dorm room, 1,000,000 Rp double room

Hidden away from the main road of Amed, Kelapa Cottage is a boutique resort with a central pool, on-site spa, restaurant, daily yoga classes, a six-bed dorm room, and bungalows that have an outdoor bathroom and patio. A mix of double rooms, three-person rooms with single beds, and family rooms that can accommodate up to four people make Kelapa Cottage a good option for families and traveling groups of friends.

BLUE MOON VILLAS

Jalan Karangasem; tel. 363/21428; www. bluemoonvillas.com; 1,000,000-2,000,000 Rp double room

Stacked along a headland and overlooking the water, Blue Moon Villas is a resort with garden lounge areas that rarely see a crowd. There are 17 accommodation options to choose from, ranging from one-room suites to four-bedroom villas, all with hot water showers, air-conditioning, safety deposit box, fridge and minibar, and Wi-Fi access. Each of the rooms is situated near one of the property's four infinity pools, creating a private, boutique hotel feel. In the evenings, live music and dance performances often take place at the resort's popular on-site restaurant, Komang John's Café.

THE KAMPUNG

Jalan Raya Amed; tel. 363/23058; www.thekampung. com; 1,500,000 Rp 2-bedroom villa

Traditional design and a commitment to wood make The Kampung one of Amed's most interesting stays. The property has two-, three-, and four-bedroom villas, each with access to its own dedicated pool. Inside, rooms are equipped with air-conditioning and Wi-Fi. Each villa is decorated with antique Balinese carvings and handmade textiles. Swimming and snorkeling are accessible directly in front of the property.

★ THE GRIYA

Jalan Raya Bunutan; tel. 363/23571; www.thegriya. com; 1,800,000 Rp double room

The Griya is where honeymooners go for a romantic stay. Each villa (one to three bedrooms) has its own outdoor lounge area,

private plunge pool, and ocean view. The decor is modern with dark wood furnishings and an outdoor bathroom with stone stand-alone tub. All guests can swim in the large communal infinity pool, dine at the on-site restaurant, and receive spa treatments. Though couples tend to make up the majority of guests, families with children are welcome as well.

INFORMATION AND SERVICES

ATMs are along the Jalan I Ketut Natih near Amed, but they become scarce to nonexistent as you head toward Aas. Many places only accept **cash.**

The **Internet** works well near Amed and Jemeluk, but it's spotty from Lipah to Aas, with some areas lacking phone coverage.

GETTING THERE

By Bus and *Bemo*

Bemos between **Amlapura** (30,000 Rp; 1 hour) and **Singaraja** (50,000 Rp; 2.5 hours) stop in **Culik,** where you can hop into another *bemo* and scoot over to Amed (10,000 Rp; 20 minutes).

Perama (www.peramatour.com; tel. 361/750808) buses run between the **Ngurah Rai International Airport** (175,000 Rp; 3 hours), **Candidasa** (100,000 Rp; 1.5 hours), **Kuta** (175,000 Rp; 3 hours), **Padangbai** (100,000 Rp; 2 hours), **Sanur** (175,000 Rp; 2.5 hours), **Tulamben** (35,000 Rp; .5 hours), and **Ubud** (175,000 Rp; 2.5 hours).

By Car

Many multiday scuba diving courses like **Adventure Scuba Diving** (www.adventure-scuba-diving.com) and **Scuba Duba Doo** (www.divecenterbali.com) include pickup from South Bali with your course admission. Before hiring a private driver, check to see if local dive centers or accommodations offer **discounted transport** in exchange for fun dives or stays.

A car or **private driver** is ideal if you're coming from **Kuta** (100 km/62 mi; 3 hours),

Denpasar (90 km/56 mi; 2 hours 45 minutes), Candidasa (35 km/22 mi; 1 hour), Ubud (70 km/43 mi; 2.5 hours), Tulamben (12 km/7.5 mi; 20 minutes), or Lovina (90 km/56 mi; 2.5 hours).

From Kuta, Denpasar, and Candidasa, follow Jalan Dr. Ida Bagus Mantra along the eastern coastline until you reach Amlapura. Then follow roads to Tirta Gangga and Culik, turning right on Jalan I Ketut Natih until you reach Amed. If you stick to the coastline all the way to Amed without cutting inland, expect to add about 10 km (6 mi) or 30 minutes to your journey. From Lovina,

follow the coastal road of Jalan Singaraja-Gilimanuk (90 km/56 mi; 2.5hrs) to Amed. Jalan Singaraja-Gilimanuk eventually turns into Jalan Kubu. In Culik, turn east onto Jalan I Ketut Natih, which leads into Amed.

Getting Around

A motorbike rented through your accommodation (50,000 Rp per day rental) is the easiest way to get around the area, though much of it is walkable if you stay in central Amed. Guided snorkeling tours and dives often include local transport between your hotel and the tour sites.

Tulamben

Most travelers who make it to Tulamben make a beeline for the water to explore the U.S.A.T. *Liberty* wreck, the village's only large attraction. Tulamben was in the lava flow of the 1963 Gunung Agung eruption, and its arid landscape has yet to fully recover. Though the village might look drab at first, explore the region on a motorbike and you'll be rewarded with sights of small-town life in Bali, interesting vistas, and decent side-of-the-road snacks.

BEACHES AND SIGHTS
Bukit Lempad

Found by searching "Romah Pohon" on Google maps; 10,000 Rp per person

Overlooking rice terraces, the town of Tulamben, and to the area between there and the ocean, is a quirky park where you can climb up bamboo treehouses, swing between the trees, take pictures inside of a nest made of sticks, lounge in a hammock, and roam

U.S.A.T. *Liberty* Wreck

Tulamben's Freediving Scene

Freediving is a niche sport, where divers explore the ocean on just a single breath. World record holders can hold their breath underwater for more than 11 minutes and swim to depths of over 100 meters (328 feet) without the help of fins. While freediving elsewhere in the world is a little-known sport, this lava-laden coastline is considered one of the best places in the world to dive as deep as you can.

WHAT TO EXPECT DURING A FREEDIVING COURSE

During a beginner freediving course, you will learn the theory behind safe breath holding, and the roles that oxygen and carbon dioxide play in our bodies. Then, you will learn how to hold your breath safely and what cues to look for during the breath hold. Your instructor may then take you to a pool where you try to hold your breath in water for the first time. Finally, you will swim out to the ocean and learn to dive along a rope that's attached to a buoy. Many beginners are able to hold their breath for more than two minutes and dive to depths of 15 meters (49 feet) within their first course.

IS FREEDIVING AN EXTREME SPORT?

Freediving is more comparable to meditation and yoga than it is to most extreme sports. Mindfulness, slow movements, and knowing your limits are all key aspects of freediving.

A FREEDIVER'S LIFESTYLE

Many of the best freedivers focus on physical flexibility, hydration, adequate sleep, and a healthy diet as a complementary lifestyle to freediving.

around a gigantic gumdrop-type structure. The owners are constantly building new features for people to climb up and around. File this attraction under "offbeat things to do."

Tulamben Beach
(Pantai Tulamben)

Jalan Raya Kubu; free

Pantai Tulamben is a narrow beach that'll work the arches of your feet as you hobble along its stones. At high tide, it nearly disappears.

★ U.S.A.T. *LIBERTY* WRECK

Pantai Tulamben, 30 meters (98 feet) offshore

In 1942, Japanese forces torpedoed the U.S.A.T. *Liberty,* a 120-meter-long (393-foot) U.S. cargo ship carrying livestock. It's found 30 meters (98 feet) offshore of Tulamben, with its shallowest point at 5 meters (16 feet) and deepest point at 30 meters (98 feet). Snorkelers, freedivers, and scuba divers all frequent the dive site, exploring its coral-coated hull to see sea turtles, reef sharks, pufferfish, damselfish, sweetlips, and giant barracudas. Most divers are coming from Bali's southern end and won't be in the water before 10am. Dive just after sunrise to see the fish while they're most active and check out the ship before it turns into an underwater zoo.

WATER SPORTS
Scuba Diving, Snorkeling, and Freediving
DIVE CONCEPTS TULAMBEN

Jalan Raya Singaraja; tel. 81236845440; www.diveconcepts.com; daily 7am-8pm; 600,000 Rp for 2 fun dives

Dive Concepts Tulamben offers fun dives to the U.S.A.T. *Liberty* wreck. Their dive center is less than 1 km (0.6 mi) from the wreck itself, as well as other local dive sites. Their school is SSI-certified, and divers can sign up to learn to scuba dive or progress all the way to divemaster. Free Nitrox is offered on all dives for certified Nitrox divers.

TULAMBEN WRECK DIVERS

Jalan Kubu; tel. 363/23400; www.
tulambenwreckdivers.com; daily 7am-8pm; 900,000
Rp for 2 fun dives

Tulamben Wreck Divers is a 5-Star PADI dive resort, offering dive courses and fun dives to the U.S.A.T. *Liberty* wreck and surroundings. Some of the divemasters have been diving around the area for more than a decade and will happily help you plan your dives according to the creatures you want to see.

APNEA BALI

Jalan Kubu; tel. 82266125814; https://apneabali.com;
daily 8am-6pm

Apnea Bali attracts serious freedivers chasing high numbers when it comes to depth, and those who want to fine-tune their skills through coaching. The school broke new ground in Bali when they set up a freediving platform that allows divers to dive 130 meters (426 feet) below the ocean surface. Courses include level 1 freediving up to instructor level. Specialty courses like static breath holding, surf survival, and depth training are also available on request.

FOOD

LESEHAN SEGARA TEGEH

Jalan Raya Tulamben; tel. 81936440849; daily
8am-10pm; 30,000-60,000 Rp

Lesehan Segara Tegeh is a restaurant with a rooftop dining area that serves grilled fish, curries, satay, fish ball soup, and a range of freshly made juices. Their most popular pick is a whole grilled snapper served with a heaping side of spicy *sambal*. Views of Gunung Agung help make up for any wait time.

SAFETY STOP

Jalan Kubu-Abang; tel. 8123881337; daily
10am-10pm; 40,000-110,000 Rp

Dine on German, English, and Asian dishes at Safety Stop. Surrounded by vines, this restaurant has a seating area outside, and a bar and pool table inside. Schnitzels, steaks, and fried chicken are done very well by these European owners, but the Asian meals could use a bit

more kick. Come in the evenings for a fun and social vibe.

ACCOMMODATIONS

MATAHARI

Jalan Kubu; tel. 363/22916; www.divetulamben.com;
200,000 Rp double room

Shoreside resort Matahari has been welcoming divers for more than 20 years. Rooms are modest with a cozy feel. Standard rooms come with a fan only, while all others are air-conditioned. The simple amenities, wholesome breakfast, friendly service, and dated decor create a feeling of nostalgia. In front of Matahari is "Suci Place," an underwater sculpture garden where concrete Buddhist and Hindu figures are placed for show and to encourage coral growth. The owner, Komang Suci, and her staff developed the project, accessible just steps away from the resort.

★ TOYABALI RESORT

Jalan Kubu; tel. 81228420514; www.toyabali-resort.
com; 1,200,000 Rp double room

With just five bungalows on the property, Toyabali Resort has a cobalt-blue infinity pool that overlooks the sea and never gets too crowded. Each bungalow is private, with a double bed, minibar, fridge, safe, and lounge area. One of the highlights is the spacious outdoor bathroom that has not only a small garden inside its walls but also a giant Jacuzzi. Small details like fresh flowers and fruit platters at breakfast add to the tropical luxury feel.

GETTING THERE

By Bus and *Bemo*

Bemos run from **Culik** to Tulamben semiregularly for 10,000 Rp; the trip takes 10 minutes.

Perama (www.peramatour.com; tel. 361/750808) buses run between the **Ngurah Rai International Airport** (175,000 Rp; 3.5 hours), **Candidasa** (100,000 Rp; 2 hours), **Kuta** (175,000 Rp; 3.5 hours), **Padangbai** (100,000 Rp; 2.5 hours), **Sanur** (175,000 Rp; 3 hours), **Amed** (35,000 Rp; .5 hour), and **Ubud** (175,000 Rp; 3 hour).

By Car

If you've booked a long stay, a scuba diving course, or fun diving package, transportation from South Bali to Tulamben may be included. Otherwise, the most efficient way to get to Tulamben is by car. From **Kuta** and **Denpasar** take **Jalan Dr. Ida Bagus Mantra** along the eastern coastline until you reach Amlapura. Then follow roads to Tirta Gangga and Culik, staying on Jalan **Ida Ketut Jelantik,** turning right onto **Jalan Kubu** until you reach Tulamben (90-100 km/56-62 mi; 2.5-3 hours).

GETTING AROUND

Motorbikes are available for rent along **Jalan Raya Tulamben** for the standard 50,000 Rp per day. If you're staying near the center, much of the area is **walkable.**

Gunung Agung Area

Gunung Agung is an area of extremes, seen as bringing both life and destruction to those who live in its lava path. When Gunung Agung is calm, the island feels a collective sense of relief. When it is active, conversations revolve around when the volcano will erupt. Gunung Agung is the most sacred mountain in Bali and it influences nearly every facet of life, including religion, architecture and home design, the weather, and tourism. It is home to Pura Besakih, the holiest temple on the island. At 3,142 meters (almost 2 mi) in elevation, Gunung Agung is also Bali's highest point. As there are very few warungs and accommodations on the slopes of Gunung Agung, it's best to spend your non-trekking time sleeping and dining in Sidemen.

SIGHTS

★ Besakih Temple
(Pura Besakih)

Jalan Raya Besakih Besakih; daily 7am-8pm; 60,000 Rp admission includes sash and sarong, 5,000 Rp parking

Pura Besakih is considered Bali's Mother Temple, housing ancestral spirits on the slopes of Gunung Agung. Twenty-three temples make up the complex, with **Pura Penataran Agung** and its 11-tiered *merus* (shrines) being the keystone of the temple. The main courtyard of the temple honors the supreme being of Sanghyang Widhi Wasa, comprised of the three gods of Brahma, Vishnu, and Shiva. Colorful offerings clutter the temple grounds and the smell of incense trails behind the many practitioners who come to Pura Besakih to worship. The temple itself is a mix of ornate stone carvings and statues in combination with simple, monolithic structures; religious significance rather than aesthetics is its main appeal.

Historians suspect that the foundation of Pura Besakih was built sometime during the 8th century, though it is unknown for exactly what purpose. It is theorized that under the kingdom of Gegel, the complex was turned into a Hindu temple. Earthquakes damaged a large part of the temple in 1917, and it had to be restored.

Only believers are allowed in most Pura Besakih's ceremonial areas, and proper temple attire is required throughout the complex, even for walking the outer grounds.

Like many temples in Bali, where foreigners come, aggressive souvenir peddlers follow. If you have a sarong and a sash, you are allowed to wander the main paths of the temple. Ceremonial areas are generally closed to tourists and marked with a sign. Purchasing an offering is optional. Your entrance ticket includes a **guide** who will request a tip at the end of your visit.

1: Besakih Temple 2: Pura Lempuyang Luhur

The 1963 Gunung Agung Eruption

In 1963, Gunung Agung erupted and killed nearly 1,500 people and decimated 62,000 hectares (239 square miles) of land.

In September 2017, Gunung Agung came back to life and more than 120,000 people living along its base were evacuated to safer areas. Throughout the rest of the year, Gunung Agung had minor eruptions, displacing villages and emitting plumes of ash that made it impossible for planes to fly into and away from the island. In 2018 there were more minor eruptions that spewed debris and ash from its crater.

Before your arrival and during your stay in Bali, check official government warnings (**magma. vsi.esdm.go.id**). Do not trek Gunung Agung even with minor warnings in place: This puts your life and the lives of potential rescuers at risk. A Facebook group called **Mount Agung Daily Report** posts regular updates and pictures of Gunung Agung (www.facebook.com/groups/415222448896889).

An eruption can happen any time. If a high-level warning or eruption does take place, evacuate as soon as possible from the region. Bali has narrow roads that are easily choked with traffic. Not all travel insurance companies cover **travel disruption** if there is an eruption warning in place. Flights can be delayed for weeks at a time if there is too much ash in the sky to take off and land.

★ Lempuyang Luhur Temple
(Pura Lempuyang Luhur)

Jalan Pura Lempuyang Luhur; 50,000 Rp admission, 5,000 Rp parking

Pura Lempuyang Luhur is a temple that hosts the "Gate to Heaven," an ethereal *candi bentar* gateway that frames Gunung Agung peaking above the clouds in the distance. The gateway sits at Penataran Tempuyang, the bottom of the complex. It protects Bali's eastern coastline from its high point on Gunung Lempuyang (1,058 meters/10,300 feet). Beyond the temple gate are 1,720 mossy steps that lead from the entrance of the temple grounds up to a series of temples above. The whole journey takes around four hours to complete. At the highest temple, you'll find a guard protecting the courtyard from monkeys. Guides offer their services and charge about 100,000 Rp per temple reached. Visit just after sunrise to beat the heat and the crowds.

Online, you might see that pictures of Pura Lempuyang Luhur make it look as though it is floating on a lake. This is purely an optical illusion. For a price, locals can take a picture while holding a mirror at the bottom of the frame, which then makes it look like the temple gates sit above water.

TREKKING GUNUNG AGUNG

Since mid-2017, Gunung Agung has been active with frequent minor eruptions. Hiking is not recommended while the volcano is active.

There are currently two major routes up Gunung Agung, though these paths may shift as volcanic activity causes the mountain to change shape. From its summit, you can admire a 360-degree view that spans across Bali and over the Lombok Strait to Lombok. Both routes require hikers to be fit and able to muster their way through steep and tedious sections.

Because Gunung Agung is considered a sacred place, it is important to dress conservatively during your hike. Trekking might also be closed during important ceremonies. Locals may act aggressively toward those hiking without a guide and the price paid for a guide is worth more than the stress of confrontation. **Guides** range from 600,000 to 1,000,000 Rp per trek. The trails are open from late April to October, when the trails are dry.

FROM PURA BESAKIH
Hiking Distance: *15 km (9 mi)*
Hiking Time: *8-10 hours round-trip*

Information and Maps: *Facebook Group: "Mount Agung Daily Report" (www.facebook.com/ groups/415222448896889), map on Alltrails.com*

This out-and-back route starts at Pura Besakih (950 meters/290 feet) and leads to the summit of Gunung Agung (3,142 meters/10,308 feet). Many sections of the trail are steep, with the last section of the trail requiring a hand-over-foot scramble. Plan to leave about 2:30am to see the sunrise across the crater of the volcano.

FROM PURA PASAR AGUNG

Hiking Distance: *8 km (5 mi)*
Hiking Time: *6-7 hours round-trip*
Information and Maps: *Visit the "Mount Agung Daily Report" Facebook Group (www. facebook.com/groups/415222448896889)*

The route from Gunung Agung's crater rim is also an out-and-back trail. It is slippery and steep, with many sections exposed, starting at 1,600 meters (5,250 feet) and climbing to nearly 3,000 meters (almost 10,000 feet) quickly. The trail leads to the crater rim, where it is not possible to safely reach Gunung Agung's summit. Start your ascent by 3am to score sunrise views.

GETTING THERE AND AROUND

The roads around Gunung Agung are relatively well maintained—unless you venture off the path. There is no reliable form of public transport that reaches this area, so you will need your own set of wheels. To reach Pura Besakih, the Gunung Agung's main temple, and the starting point for treks up to the summit, head north up **Jalan Raya Besakih.**

Central Mountains

In Bali's Central Mountains—a wild region

made of volcanoes, lakes, rivers, and calderas—nature takes center stage. Though the region's core threatens destruction with looming volcanic eruptions, the land itself is fertile and abundant. The volcanic soil and frequent rainfall make the area ideal for growing coffee, rice, and produce that feed not only the villages settled in the valleys between mountains but also the island's less-fruitful coastline. At 700 meters (2,300 feet) above sea level, The Jatiluwih Rice Terraces blanket the southern slopes of the Central Mountains, where you can wander without interruption and admire the beauty and precision that accompanies feeding Bali's growing population.

Balinese Hindus visit the temples tucked on the slopes of calderas and

Highlights

Look for ★ to find recommended sights, activities, dining, and lodging.

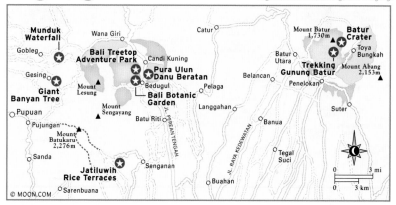

Munduk Waterfall · Wana Giri · Catur · Mount Batur 1,730 m · Batur Crater · Gobleg · Bali Treetop Adventure Park · Candi Kuning · Batur Utara · Toya Bungkah · Gesing · Bedugul · Pura Ulun Danu Beratan · Belancan · Trekking Gunung Batur · Mount Abang 2,153 m · Giant Banyan Tree · Mount Lesung · Bali Botanic Garden · Pelaga · Penelokan · Pupuan · Mount Sengayang · Batu Riti · Langgahan · JL. PEREAN TENGAH · Suter · Pujungan · Banua · Mount Batukaru 2,276 m · JL. RAYA KEDEWATAN · Sanda · Tegal Suci · Jatiluwih Rice Terraces · Senganan · Buahan · 0 3 mi · 0 3 km · Sarenbuana · © MOON.COM

★ **Trekking Gunung Batur and Batur Crater:** Spend the night trekking to the summit of Gunung Batur for the reward of a spectacular sunrise (page 292).

★ **Jatiluwih Rice Terraces:** Serenity is easily found among a sprawling land of rice terraces (page 298).

★ **Munduk Waterfall:** Feel the cool spray of a cascade that's surrounded by bright green leaves (page 303).

★ **Giant Banyan Tree:** Let your eyes trace the tangled roots of an ancient banyan tree that

was more than 700 years old before it collapsed in a storm (page 304).

★ **Bali Treetop Adventure Park:** In this eco-friendly park, you can climb, zipline, rope walk, and challenge yourself to reach new heights (page 310).

★ **Bali Botanic Garden:** Indonesia's largest botanic garden is home to more than 2,400 species of plant life (page 310).

★ **Pura Ulun Danu Beratan:** Honor the goddess of water, Dewi Danu, at a temple on Danau Beratan that looks as though it's floating (page 310).

Central Mountains

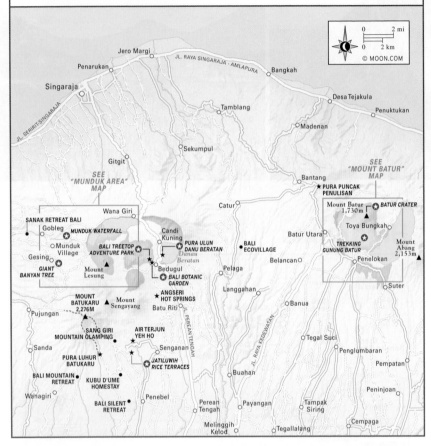

place offerings in hopes of placating the gods in charge of the lava below. In the past century, Gunung Batur has had at least 15 eruptions, keeping locals hyper-vigilant of any geothermal activity. The villages themselves are quiet, revolving around ceremonies and agriculture. Except for the motorbikes, printed signs, and cell phones, many villages likely look the same as they did 100 years ago. Wi-Fi is spotty at best, ATMs are rarely in working order, and this region's version of rush hour occurs daily

at three in the morning, when hikers crowd the trailheads of Gunung Batur to reach the summit by sunrise. Warungs serve traditional fare rather than hopping on the food trends of Bali's southern region, and accommodations are run by families rather than global franchises. But what the region lacks in glamour and amenities, it makes up for in 360-degree vistas and vibrant sunrises.

Winding trails and calm lakes make the area a playground for travelers on the hunt for

Previous: monkey eating fruit; trekking Gunung Batur and Batur Crater; Jatiluwih Rice Terraces.

Top Restaurants

★ **Kintamani Market:** The market is an early-morning hub for produce, handicrafts, and ingredients for temple offerings (page 296).

★ **Warung Classic:** This family-run warung has great *gado-gado,* strawberry juice, and sunset views (page 306).

★ **Kopi Bali Restaurant at Puri Lumbung Cottages:** Learn to cook a Balinese dish from the area's organically grown produce and spices (page 306).

adventure. Cycling, trekking, canoeing, and kayaking are all acceptable means of transportation. Trails lead through quiet communities, over crater rims, along shorelines, and under waterfalls, with the sounds of birds singing and leaves rustling in the background. Volcanic vents billow steam into the sky, making the terrain look like the workshop floor of a cloud factory.

ORIENTATION

The Central Mountain region is Bali's volcanic and mountainous core on the central-eastern side of the island. **Gunung Batur** is the focal point, along with **Danau Batur** inside of the **Batur Crater,** and the three lakes of **Danau Tamblingan, Danau Buyan,** and **Danau Beratan** to the east. **Gunung Batukaru** and the **Jatiluwih Rice Terraces** rest on the eastern border of the region. Distances between these major sites are not far as the crow flies, but serpentine roads make it tedious and time-consuming to get from one to the next. For example, though Gunung Batur and Gunung Batukaru are only about 35 km (22 mi) apart, the roads connecting these two points span nearly 100 km (62 mi). For practical purposes, distances in this chapter will be measured by road.

Gunung Batur is 40 km (25 mi) north of Ubud and 60 km (37 mi) north of Denpasar. **Jalan Kintamani,** the road that wraps around Gunung Batur's eastern side, is one of the most congested in Bali, as it connects the southern point of the island to the north. Danau Tamblingan, Danau Buyan, and Danau Beratan all reside within one large crater and

15 km (9.3 mi) of road connects the eastern edge of Danau Tamblingan to Danau Beratan. These lakes sit 55 km (34 mi) east of Gunung Batur, with Danau Batukaru 20 km (12 mi) southwest of Danau Tamblingan. Between Danau Tamblingan and Gunung Batukaru lies the quiet town of **Munduk,** which has the region's best accommodations and food.

PLANNING YOUR TIME

Bali's Central Mountains are worth visiting all year long, and it might be the only place on the island where you'll be thankful for packing a sweater. Clouds roll through on a moment's notice, oftentimes with rainstorms in their shadows. If you want to take advantage of the region's incredible **outdoor activities** like trekking, cycling, or paddling, plan to visit when the weather is clear—don't leave the sunrise trek for the last day of your trip. Expect to spend two days or more in the region to have at least one back-up trekking or outdoor day if your first day doesn't pan out. **AccuWeather** (www.accuweather.com) is a decent resource for checking the forecast.

The region experiences most of its rainfall from **October** to early **May.** Though you won't have the crowds that smother the Bukit Peninsula in July and August, the best accommodations might be snatched up if you try to book a room at the last minute. As a rule of thumb, **May** to **September** offer the most days with clear skies. To get around, it's best to have a **private driver.** Many trekking and activity tours include pickup and drop-off at your accommodation.

Top Accommodations

★ **Sang Giri Mountain Glamping:** Great views surround this retreat, where you sleep under the stars in safari tents outfitted with private bathrooms (page 302).

★ **Munduk Moding Plantation Resort:** Relax by the infinity pool with a hot cup of coffee made from the beans grown on the plantation itself (page 307).

★ **Sanak Retreat Bali:** Airy luxury bungalows are nestled between rice terraces, each with a private balcony (page 307).

Itinerary Ideas

DAY 1: SUNRISE TREK

1 Arrange a trekking tour of Gunung Batur at least one day in advance with **Bali Sunrise Tours.** Your day of hiking and exploring begins between 2am and 3:30am, when you'll start at the base of Gunung Batur. Your tour will arrange transportation to the trailhead.

2 Just before sunrise, find a comfortable spot to sit and watch the sun peek over Gunung Agung. You can purchase a coffee and snack at the **summit** (or in advance from your tour) if your stomach is rumbling.

3 After your trek, refuel with a hearty breakfast from one of the local warungs along the road near the trailhead to **Gunung Batur Natural Hot Springs,** where you can soak your sore muscles.

4 Drive to the **Batur Geopark Museum,** where you can learn more about the region's volcanic activity.

5 Walking distance from the museum is **Lakeview Restaurant,** a prime spot for dinner with a view.

DAY 2: WATERFALL WALK

1 Drive to the trailhead marked by **Munduk Waterfall,** where you can spend the morning exploring Munduk's three waterfalls of Munduk Waterfall, Golden Valley Waterfall, and if you still have energy, Melanting Waterfall.

2 Relax for lunch at **Puri Lumbung Cottages,** where you can enjoy a meal overlooking rice paddies (2 km/1.2 mi by car or foot).

3 In the afternoon, visit the **Giant Banyan Tree,** toppled in a storm but still impressive with its twisting roots.

4 Drive to **Warung Classic** just before sunset to watch the sun drop behind the mountains. Sip strawberry juice and order a hearty plate of noodles to end your day.

DAY 3: JATILUWIH

1 Drive to the **Jatiluwih Rice Terraces** for sunrise and walk among the rice paddies.

Itinerary Ideas

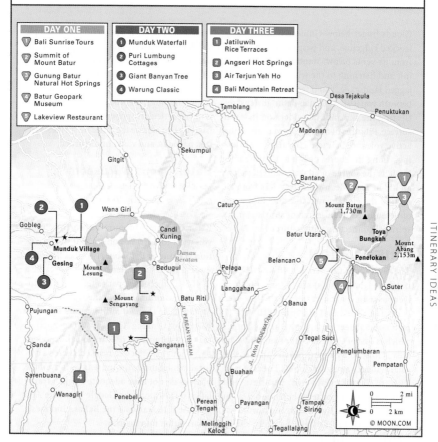

DAY ONE
1. Bali Sunrise Tours
2. Summit of Mount Batur
3. Gunung Batur Natural Hot Springs
4. Batur Geopark Museum
5. Lakeview Restaurant

DAY TWO
1. Munduk Waterfall
2. Puri Lumbung Cottages
3. Giant Banyan Tree
4. Warung Classic

DAY THREE
1. Jatiluwih Rice Terraces
2. Angseri Hot Springs
3. Air Terjun Yeh Ho
4. Bali Mountain Retreat

2 Refresh yourself at **Angseri Hot Springs,** where you can also get lunch at the small on-site warung.

3 Venture to **Air Terjun Yeh Ho** by car; you'll find a tranquil waterfall set behind a manicured garden and temple.

4 In the evening, check into **Bali Mountain Retreat,** where you'll have dinner sourced from local farmers.

Gunung Batur Area

Clouds linger below Gunung Batur's grass-frocked ridgeline, and wisps of steam bellow from its vents below. Standing atop its summit and listening to the wind whistle over a jagged landscape, you'll feel that the ground beneath you is alive. Danau Batur glistens, reflecting the sky and the caldera on its calm surface. Pilgrims of many types venture to the active volcano. Balinese Hindus place offerings along the shores of Danau Batur, viewing it as the source of all water and therefore all life in Bali. Meanwhile, travelers from all around the globe march like ants to the top of Gunung Batur in search of sunrises and a spiritual connection with nature.

ORIENTATION

The Gunung Batur Area is 40 km (25 mi) north of Ubud and 60 km (37 mi) north of Denpasar in central-eastern Bali. The area is distinguished by **Gunung Batur** (1,717 meters/5,633 feet high) and **Danau Batur,** which is east of Gunung Batur's summit. The area is formed by a gargantuan caldera with small villages along its slopes. The towns of **Kuban, Trunyan, Abang, Buahan,** and **Kedisan** sit on the eastern shoreline of Danau Batur, with **Toya Bungkah,** the town closest to Gunung Batur's trekking trails, sitting on the lake's western shoreline. One road, **Jalan Pendakian Gunung Batur,** traces Danau Batur. **Jalan Penelokan** is the main road that encircles Gunung Batur and hosts the **Batur Geopark Museum,** the town of **Batur,** and **Kintamani. Gunung Abang** (2,152 meters/7,060 feet high) is part of the Gunung Batur region and sits on Danau Batur's southeastern side.

SIGHTS

Bukit Mentik Temple
(Pura Bukit Mentik)

Jalan Tabu (Desa Adat Batur), sign for turnoff along Jalan Raya Penelokan; free

Pura Bukit Mentik is a peaceful Hindu temple that has earned a reputation as a place of refuge and protection from natural disasters. In 1974, Gunung Batur erupted and molten lava destroyed nearly everything in its path aside from Pura Bukit Mentik. Because this temple is not a particularly popular spot among tourists, you can admire the intricate shrines, statues, pagodas, and views undisturbed.

Batur Geopark Museum

Jalan Raya Penelokan; tel. 366/51186; www.baturglobalgeopark.com; Mon.-Fri. 8am-4pm, Sat.-Sun. 8am-2pm; free

Batur Geopark Museum is a worthy stop if you want to learn not only about the formation of Gunung Batur but also all of Bali. The museum was built after the region became a UNESCO Global Geopark site. You'll find interesting dioramas depicting the formation of Bali more than 20 million years ago. The volcano at Gunung Agung is still very active, making the museum relevant to Bali's modern day. Though it's not well marked, there's a cultural exhibit inside the museum. Many of the plaques do not have adequate English translations. Download the Google Translate App and use it to translate the Bahasa Indonesia information into English.

Puncak Penulisan Temple
(Pura Puncak Penulisan)

Jalan Raya Kintamani; free

Set 1,745 meters (5,725 feet) high, Pura Puncak Penulisan is the highest temple on the island, resting on the summit of Gunung Penulisan. Some sculptures and artifacts inside the temple's courtyard date back to the 11th-13th centuries, and the temple itself is one of the oldest in Bali (some say it is the oldest). Because of this, some of the detail of the sculptures has been worn over time, but they are interesting to admire nonetheless. Though you'll need to make your way up over a series

Mount Batur

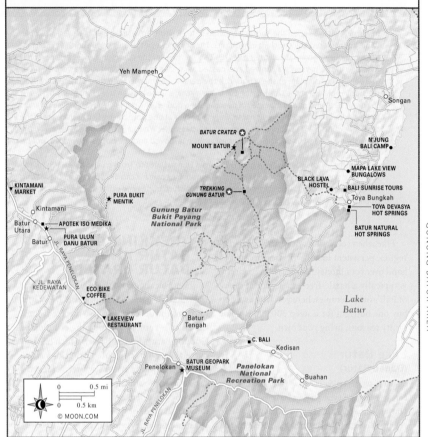

of steep moss-covered staircases, the views of Gunung Batur, Gunung Abang, and Gunung Agung are worth the effort—especially at sunrise. This temple is also called **Pura Tegeh Kahuripan.**

Ulun Danu Batur Temple
(Pura Ulun Danu Batur)

Jalan Raya Kintamani; tel. 81339587473; 35,000 Rp admission plus sarong rental

Pura Ulun Danu Batur is dedicated to Vishnu, the Hindu god of preservation, as well as the goddess Danu, the ruler of water. Because Danau Batur is essential to rice agriculture

and irrigation, many locals make regular offerings to Dewi Danu. Inside the temple compound, you'll find nine different temples with hundreds of shrines set among them. One of the main appeals of the temple is its gold-painted doors and the colorful *bedogol* statues, guardians placed at the temple gates that protect the area from evil. The original temple was nearly destroyed in a volcanic eruption in 1917, an event that snuffed over 2,000 temples in its lava path. For safekeeping, Balinese Hindus rebuilt the temple in a less threatened location in 1926, making it one of the island's newer major temples.

Trunyan Cemetery: Balinese Funerals under the Trunyan Tree

In a small village set on the shores of Danau Batur is Trunyan, a village of Bali Aga people, widely considered Bali's ancient inhabitants. Trunyan is one of the only communities in Bali that does not bury or cremate all their dead. Once a member of the community dies, the person is assessed. If the person was unwed and passed away due to an accident such as drowning or in a vehicle collision, he or she is buried. If the person was married and died of natural causes, the body is placed at the trunk of the *taru menyan,* a large banyan tree. Taru menyan means "fragrant tree" and masks the smell of decomposing bodies. The name "Trunyan" is also thought to be a derivative from the tree's name. Only 11 bodies at one time can be laid at the base of the tree, reflecting the 11 pagodas at Trunyan's main temple. When a 12th body passes away, the body that has been under the tree longest is then removed and the bones are placed around the cemetery.

Though it is possible to take a boat ride across Danau Batur to Trunyan and take a tour of the cemetery, we do not recommend visiting, as a tourist, because it can disrupt ceremonies taking place, and too much traffic into the cemetery can disturb bones and other offerings next to the bodies.

Like when you visit many other sites in this region, persistent locals will pressure you to hand over your money. While renting a sarong is typically a hassle-free experience at many of Bali's other temples, here you'll be asked to buy one outright for a steep 300,000 Rp. For sanity reasons, bring your own.

Lake Batur
(Danau Batur)

Danau Batur, accessible via Jalan Pendakian Guning Batu and Jalan Trunyan; free

Danau Batur is the tranquil body of water set inside Gunung Batur's giant crater, fed by rainwater and hot springs that flow into the lake from the crater's eastern side. With nearly a 16 square km (3,900 acres) of surface area, Danau Batur is the region's main source for agricultural irrigation and fish. It is considered to be holy, as the water that runs from Danau Batur into the rice terraces below follows the traditional *subak* system, a sacred irrigation method that involves water passing through temples before it reaches the rice. Tourists can rent a canoe (C. Bali offers guided tours) and paddle around the lake to discover small temples, villages, and wildlife along its shoreline.

★ TREKKING GUNUNG BATUR AND BATUR CRATER

Without volcanoes and their outbursts of lava, the island of Bali would not exist. Daily life, tourism, and development also revolve around the volatile rumble of a looming eruption of Gunung Batur (Mount Batur), which has had more than 20 documented eruptions since 1800. On Gunung Batur's western side, you can still see the aftermath of eruptions. Areas that were once dense with trees are now little more than fields of sparse shrubs.

Gunung Batur stands at 1,717 m (5,633 ft) and sits inside of a gargantuan caldera, with multiple smaller craters inside. To the west, you'll see Danau Batur, formed inside the crater walls at the eastern slope of Gunung Abang. Gunung Batur has a well-deserved reputation as being one of the best places to watch the sunrise. Views from its summit reveal the twinkle of village lights below and the soft landscape of steam vents, grasslands, Danau Batur, and a lineup of volcanoes in the distance. The shuffle of footsteps, whispers, and glare of flashlights can be distracting as you trek up the mountain, but as soon as the sun peeks over the clouds, the crowd falls still. Even the monkeys seem to be mesmerized.

Get the Shot: Sunrise Photography Tips

Gunung Batur sunrise

Anyone who has pointed a camera at a sunrise or sunset quickly realizes that the photo rarely reflects what we see with our eyes. Sunrise from a mountain's summit reveals dramatic shadows, illuminated foliage, and vibrant colors that range from pastel pink to bright orange. If you've hiked all the way to the top with a camera (or camera phone in hand) here are some tips for photographing stunning sunsets.

- **Keep Still:** For a crisp and clear picture, set your camera up on a tripod or still surface. Because sunrises are low light scenarios, any movement might cause the picture to be blurry. Even if you don't have a tripod, you can quickly make one with your backpack or a pile of rocks. Set your camera to take a picture one to two seconds after you press the shutter to prevent camera shake.

- **Camera Settings:** If your camera has manual settings, keep your ISO low (100-400), aperture of around f/4-11, and shutter speed 1/15-5 seconds. Think of ISO, aperture, and shutter speed as the three ingredients that create your picture. Take a few sample shots, then adjust each accordingly.

- **Composition:** It's tempting to point your camera directly at the sun and click the shutter. Look around at all the aspects of the scene that make it unique to Bali. Are there interesting shrines, trees, or ridgelines to set the scene?

- **Look Back:** Turn around and photograph the landscapes, people, and objects that are glowing from the natural light.

- **Practice Before:** Practice taking sunrise shots before your trek—even if the scene is a parking lot in front of your hotel. Sunrises don't last long, so you'll want to capture your images quickly and efficiently. This lets you enjoy the sunrise without wasting time fiddling around with the camera menu.

All trekkers must be accompanied by an **official trekking guide.** Some trekking fees include breakfast (typically eggs on toast with the eggs cooked over a piping-hot steam vent). Although it's possible to complete the trek yourself, there are many unmarked paths that may lead to another section of the crater rim, where you risk falling off a narrow trail with a steep drop on both sides. If you are caught hiking without a guide, you'll likely be hassled and berated by aggressive locals.

To see this sunrise from Gunung Batur for yourself, there are a few trekking main routes you can follow to Batur I crater rim, detailed below. You can also complete treks that loop around two of Gunung Batur's other craters (**Batur II** and **Batur III**) that take about eight hours at a moderate pace to complete. If you have a small group, it's best to **plan your route in advance with a guide.** Trails to Batur's other craters (such as **Batur IV**) often close due to volcanic activity. It's not wise to wander without purpose around the area, as cliffs and open vents can be deadly.

Packing list: Bring a light **windbreaker** or **sweater** to put on at the top of the trek to combat cool weather and wind chill. A warm layer will also be useful for evenings in the area. You'll also want **sturdy shoes,** a **small backpack** to carry **snacks** and **water,** and a **head torch** or **flashlight.** Don't forget to apply **sunscreen** to protect your skin post-sunrise.

FROM TOYAK BUNGKAH

Hiking Distance: *9 km (5.5 mi) round-trip, including crater rim*
Hiking Time: *3-4 hours*
Information and Maps: *www. baturglobalgeopark.com/map*

There are multiple trailheads from Toya Bungkah, one of the towns set on Danau Batur. This trail to Batur I crater rim starts flat and then forks into two separate trails. The **southern** (left) trail is easier while the **northern trail** (right) is steep and leads directly to the summit. Loose ash and gravel

make **solid footwear** essential. Allow 2-3 hours to reach the summit at a moderate pace.

FROM PURA JATI

Hiking Distance: *9 km (5.5 mi) round-trip, including crater rim*
Hiking Time: *3-4 hours*
Information and Maps: *www. baturglobalgeopark.com/map*

South of Toya Bungkah, off Jalan Pendakian Gunung Batur, you'll find the southern route to trek Gunung Batur, and to Batur I crater rim. This trail is slightly more challenging and less popular than the route from Toya Bungkah, thanks to the lack of shade, and will take fit hikers about 3 hours to complete.

FROM SERONGGA

Hiking Distance: *7 km (4.3 mi) round-trip, including crater rim*
Hiking Time: *3 hours*
Information and Maps: *www. baturglobalgeopark.com/map*

If you drive to Serongga, you'll find a **parking area** set off **Jalan Yehmampeh.** A steep trail leads to the top and takes 1-1.5 hours to complete. Though this trail is shorter, it tends to be more challenging than the two main routes, as the trail is less defined, much of it traversing steep volcanic rock.

Guides

ASSOCIATION OF MOUNT BATUR TREKKING GUIDES (PPPGB)

2 locations: Toya Bungkah, Jalan Pendakian Gunung Batur; tel. 366/52362; daily 3am-6pm; Pura Jati; daily 3am-3:30pm; 350,000-500,000 Rp sunrise trek to Batur Crater, 650,000 Rp per person for 8-hour tour of Batur I, II, and III

The local community around Gunung Batur requires that travelers trek Gunung Batur with an official trekking guide from the Association of Mount Batur Trekking Guides (PPPGB). All tours—even third-party tours—must include a PPPGB guide. Your fee includes a guided trek up to the summit, with the guide helping you set the pace and inform you about the natural environment (though some guides may take this latter skill less seriously than others). Some of these guides can be aggressive if you choose to hike without one, to a point where it's best to skip the stress and hand over your money for the trek. Before you climb, confirm what route you'll be taking and whether or not breakfast is included. You can also purchase breakfast at the top of the mountain for 50,000 Rp, should you choose to opt for it later. Sometimes, larger groups can push the price down to 300,000 Rp per person for the basic summit sunrise trek.

BALI SUNRISE TOURS

Jalan Songan; tel. 87730664336; www.
balisunrisetours.com; daily 3am-3:30pm; from
500,000 Rp sunrise trek

Bali Sunrise Tours offers stress-free tours up Gunung Batur and along the Batur Crater. They also host guided treks to the top of Gunung Abang—the third-highest volcano in Bali—which sits directly across from Gunung Batur. Trips are easily customizable in terms of difficulty level or terrain. Their waterfall-themed trek and rice terrace walk around Jatiluwih are highly recommended.

OTHER SPORTS AND RECREATION
Hot Springs

Though there are a few pricey hot springs (with a loose definition of the term) created for tourists, there are also smaller, Jacuzzi-sized natural hot springs found in between the villages. Though these hot springs are reserved for locals, it's worth asking a staff member of your hotel or homestay if they can arrange a visit for you. Be sure to clarify that you do not mean the hot springs listed below.

BATUR NATURAL HOT SPRINGS

Jalan Toya Bungkah; tel. 81338325552; daily
8am-6pm; 150,000-190,000 Rp adult, 75,000 Rp
child

The Batur Natural Hot Springs is a popular spot to soak sore muscles after a morning hike or bike ride. There are multiple package options that can include a towel, lunch, and entrance to the hot and cold water pools. You can pay an additional fee to rent an inner tube for the slides. Massages are also available on-site. Don't expect five-star service, and the amenities themselves are in dire need of a scrub-down—which is exasperating when you consider the steep price. The real draw to Batur Natural Hot Springs is its view of Danau Batur.

TOYA DEVASYA HOT SPRINGS

Jalan Puri Bening; tel. 81933094796; www.
toyadevasya.com; daily 8am-7pm; 180,000-
300,000 Rp

The Toya Devasya Hot Springs are part of a larger resort, where you can choose between eight different pools of varying temperatures, sizes, and views, with a motif of purple elephants around the place. The lakefront pool has a sunken bar and looks directly over Danau Batur. Though entrance to the pool is 180,000 Rp, the staff will pressure you to purchase the 300,000 Rp package that includes a buffet meal (you'll find better value and quality at a local warung). Once inside, you'll be asked to put a 100,000-Rp deposit on a card that goes toward drink purchases. Any excess funds will be returned at the end of your stay, though not without a bit of hassle. The pools and view are quite relaxing, but the resort's claims of its waters having healing properties warrant a side glance.

Cycling and Canoeing
C. BALI

Jalan Kedisan; tel. 81353420541; www.c-bali.com;
daily 8:30am-4:30pm daily; from 300,000 Rp canoe
tour, 400,000 Rp cycling tour, 50,000 Rp bike hire,
200,000 Rp canoe hire

Explore the region by bike on a cycling tour from C. Bali. One of the best-known providers in the area, C. Bali leads cycling tours that can be combined with trekking, canoeing, crafting classes, hot springs visit, and a tour of one of the nearby villages, where you might be invited onto someone's patio for a snack and a drink. The guides are friendly and informative, and there's a lot of room to tailor each tour to your own interests and abilities if you book as a private group. If you want to explore the roads and lake on your own, you can rent bicycles and canoes from C. Bali directly.

FOOD

This region is not really known for its food. Warungs shutter and reopen with different names, with many of them serving Indonesian fare for cheap. The large restaurants, where drivers and tour guides eat free in exchange for dropping off tourists, often have sub-par buffet meals that are served with incredible views.

Markets

★ KINTAMANI MARKET

Jalan Raya Kintamani; every three days 5am-2pm

Every three days, a sleepy market comes alive with piles of vegetables and fresh fruits, like mangosteens, snakefruit, tiny bananas, juicy oranges (which the region is known for), and other produce grown throughout the area. You can also shop for handicrafts and all the trappings to create a *canang sari,* a Hindu offering.

Indonesian

ECO BIKE COFFEE

Jalan Raya Penelokan; tel. 87861322552; daily 8am-7:30pm; 40,000-80,000 Rp

Eco Bike Coffee, a bright and cheerful new coffee shop, is a welcome relief among the buffet-style restaurants along Jalan Raya Penelokan. The café hosts coffee roasting workshops and uses beans sourced throughout the region. Enjoy pastries, fried bananas, pancakes, milkshakes, and coffee in a café that looks out to Bali's major mountains.

LAKEVIEW RESTAURANT

Jalan Raya Penelokan; tel. 366/51464; www. lakeviewbali.com; daily 8am-8pm; 88,000-150,000 Rp buffet

Request a table outside or by a window at Lakeview Restaurant to be rewarded with views of Danau Batur. They open for breakfast and lunch each day, with both meals served buffet-style. Most dishes are Indonesian with a handful of European plates as well—though the Indonesian plates tend to move quicker and are thus fresher. You might not remember the meal, but you'll certainly remember the view.

ACCOMMODATIONS

BLACK LAVA HOSTEL

Jalan Pendakian; tel. 81337558998; 130,000 Rp dorm bed, 300,000 Rp double room

Black Lava Hostel is a simple, clean, and sociable hostel that's set on a hill overlooking Danau Batur. There are two large dorm rooms decorated with traditional Indonesian textiles, each with 10 single beds inside and shared hot water showers. Double rooms with private bathrooms are also available. Guests have access to a newly built pool that is filled by waters from a local hot spring, and a small open-air dining area surrounded by manicured gardens. The on-site restaurant serves a simple menu of Indonesian meals. The real draw to Black Lava Hostel is its proximity to the trail entrance where guests summit Gunung Batur, making the morning wake-up a bit later and therefore a little less painful.

N'JUNG BALI CAMP

Jalan Banjar Dalem; tel. 87861527536; 320,000 Rp double tent

Sleep among the stars and admire the serene setting of Danau Batur at N'jung Bali Camp. This campsite has a spacious tent area as well as glamping cottages set on stilts over the water. The cottages are large enough to fit a double bed and an outlet, making it a cozy and quirky place to spend the night. Weather permitting, the staff light a communal campfire and the host is always happy to share stories about life in Bali. The accommodation itself is very basic and well-kept. Bathrooms are shared. Early risers will love N'jung Bali Camp because the sunrise here is spectacular.

MAPA LAKE VIEW BUNGALOWS

Jalan Bukit Selat; tel. 81338382096; 400,000 Rp double room

At the base of Gunung Batur, Mapa Lake

View Bungalows is a simple and clean home-stay with large suites that surround a garden area. Each room comes with a private bathroom and hot water shower. Though Wi-Fi is advertised, it's unreliable at best. The hosts are happy to arrange tours, answer questions, and serve breakfast on your patio each morning. The trail leading up to the summit of Gunung Batur is walking distance from the accommodation; because of this, the bungalows can get a bit noisy with the hum of cars and motorbikes if you're one to sleep in.

INFORMATION AND SERVICES

Tourist information is scarce in the Gunung Batur area, where your best bet for arranging drivers and excursions is through your hotel or a tour company.

ATMs are found in Kintamani and Penelokan, though they may not be working or well-stocked, so bring cash as a backup.

For serious **medical emergencies,** you will need to relocate to Denpasar or Kuta for treatment.

APOTEK ISO MEDIKA (PHARMACY)
Jalan Raya Kintamani; daily 9am-9pm
At this small family pharmacy, you can get basic first-aid supplies and over-the-counter medications.

GETTING THERE

For the best value, it's worth asking a tour company or accommodation to include pickup from the Bukit Peninsula in your package.

By Bus and *Bemo*
Buses and *bemos* from the **Batubulan Terminal** in **Gianyar** (Jalan Pudak No. 21; tel 361/298526) run in the mornings (irregular schedule) to **Penelokan** (25,000 Rp; 35 km/21.7 mi) and **Kintamani** (25,000 Rp; 37 km/23 mi). However, once you're in the Batur

region, it may be hard to find reliable transport to your accommodation.

By Private Driver
A private driver is the most comfortable way to get to Gunung Batur and will cost 400,000-800,000 Rp, as some drivers charge for a full day of driving. Rideshare apps like **GoJek** and **Grab** may offer rides from Denpasar to the region for around 350,000 Rp.

By Rental Car and Motorbike
If you are using a rental car or motorbike, beware of **sharp turns** and **loose gravel** on the roads—particularly around Penelokan. **Tolls** to enter Penelokan cost 30,000 Rp per vehicle and 5,000 Rp per person.

If you're coming from **Denpasar** and **Kuta,** take **Jalan By Pass Ngurah Rai** and follow signs to Ubung/Tabanan/Gilimanuk via **Jalan WR Supraman,** which turns into **Jalan Raya Batubulan;** follow for 6 km (3.7 mi). Take **Jalan A.A. Gede Rai,** where you can pass through Ubud to Batur. If coming from the south, there are many roads that connect to **Jalan Raya Penelokan,** with the road wrapping around southwestern Batur.

GETTING AROUND

Getting around the Gunung Batur area efficiently might be one of the most frustrating things about the region. There are *bemos* that run in the mornings between Penelokan to Kintamani (10,000 Rp) and from Penelokan to Toya Bungah (10,000 Rp). **Motorbikes** are available for rent for 50,000 Rp per day, typically arranged through your accommodation. Rideshare apps do not work in this region. Taxis are infrequent. **Having your own set of wheels** is an advantage here; otherwise, **make the most of your legs** and **pickup/drop-off that may be included with your tour or hotel.** One road connects the crater rim from Penelokan, where you'll find the Batur Geopark Museum, to Kintimani.

Gunung Batukaru Area

It's surprising that the Gunung Batukaru area hasn't received more attention when you consider its unique natural landscape and rich cultural history. Gunung Batukaru rewards travelers who venture off the well-trod trails of Central Bali, with the best chance at spotting wildlife living under a rainforest canopy like pangolins, small deer, and an array of birdlife.

Gunung Batukaru is a spiritual place. Every morning, locals make the trek along Gunung Batukaru's lush trails to set offerings at the many shrines and temples standing on its slopes. At its base, the Jatiluhwih Rice Terraces blanket the earth in emerald green. Best of all, those who visit the area can have much of it to themselves thanks to nearby Gunung Batur's popularity. A tip: Visit Gunung Batukaru while it's still a secret.

ORIENTATION

Gunung Batukaru is in the center of Bali in the **Tabanan regency.** This region includes the villages of **Penebel, Angseri,** and **Jatiluhwih.** Coming from Bali's southern end, Penebel is 30 km (18.5 mi) north of **Ubud** and 35 km (22 mi) north of **Denpasar.** Gunung Batukaru has one road that zigzags around its western side and one that cuts through the base of its southeastern side. However, most roads within Gunung Batukaru are unnamed, making it a destination that relies heavily on landmarks and **GPS coordinates.**

The **Jatiluhwih Rice Terraces** sit on the eastern base of Gunung Batukaru, 40 km (25 mi) north of Ubud. **Pura Luhur Batukaru,** the main temple in the area, is often used as a landmark and is located on Gunung Batukaru's southern edge. Because it can take up to 2 hours to drive from Gunung Batukaru's southern end to its northern end, it's essential to know your destination before driving to the region. Gunung Batukaru sits within a chain of volcanoes that sprawl from its northeastern end, with the lakes of **Danau Tamblingan, Danau Buyan,** and **Denau Beratan** acting as a top hat. Though Danau Beratan is only about 12 km (7.5 mi) northeast of Gunung Batukaru as the crow flies, it is a little over 30 km (18.5 mi) by road.

SIGHTS
Luhur Batukaru Temple
(Pura Luhur Batukaru)
Jalan Penatahan; tel. 81338236095; 20,000 Rp

Pura Luhur Batukaru is a temple that looks and feels as though it was built by the rainforest that surrounds it. Moss covers the intricate walls of the temple and the statues that guard it. A cool mist intermingles with incense in the air as Balinese Hindus orchestrate their ceremonies. The Pura Luhur Batukaru temple sits on the slopes of Gunung Batukaru, 1,300 meters (4,265 feet) above sea level, where it honors the gods that preside over the island's volcanoes.

TOP EXPERIENCE

★ Jatiluwih Rice Terraces
Jalan Jatiluwih; 20,000-40,000 Rp

Every shade of green exists at Jatiluwih Rice Terraces, a sprawling carpet of rice paddies that are irrigated using the UNESCO World Heritage-recognized *subak* system, in which the water that flows into the paddies must flow through a temple and is considered holy. The terraces are so uniform, Jatiluwih looks like a staircase created for the gods. Spend some time walking along the quiet pathways, watching birds burst out of the paddies as you tread near. Shadows drift by as clouds blow overhead, small streams trickle along the pathways. Workers quietly harvest the rice when it's ready. If you come for sunrise, you'll be rewarded with a peaceful experience all to yourself. It's almost eerie how calm the Jatiluwih Rice Terraces are when you consider the crowds that flock to Tegallalang Rice Terraces near Ubud. Consider Jatiluwih a synonym of serenity.

Air Terjun Yeh Ho

Jalan Gunungsari Umakayu; tel. 81237882856; daily 7am-6pm; 10,000 Rp

A narrow staircase leads you down into a bamboo forest where you'll first find one small waterfall trickling into a stream. Follow the path upstream and enjoy the garden and temple area to the left and the blissful sound of running water on the right. Air Terjun Yeh Ho is a 5-meter (16-foot) high waterfall at the end of the path that flows into a wading area.

TREKKING GUNUNG BATUKARU

Gunung Batukaru is the island's second-highest volcano at 2,276 meters (7,467 feet) high. Unlike Gunung Agung and Gunung Batur, Gunung Batukaru is dormant. Trails here are explored primarily by offbeat travelers who are interested in trekking through dense rainforests where the best views are reached on foot. If you tread lightly, you may have a chance to see barking deer, frogs, macaque monkeys, civets, and pangolins, one of Indonesia's most endangered species. Songbirds chirp in the treetops and the wall of green is accented with plumeria flowers, hibiscus, and other tropical flora. Small temples are tucked between trees for Hindu pilgrims who walk to place their offerings.

The trek from the trailhead to the top of Gunung Batukaru takes 3-4 hours with a guide (budget 8 hours round-trip). Should you make the journey, you'll be rewarded with views of Lombok to the east, Java to the west, Gunung Agung, and Bali's rugged coastline. Though it's possible to trek without a guide— yellow sashes mark the way—the path can be steep and slippery along some sections. A guide is recommended. Trek only during the dry season, from June to September.

There are multiple trails up Gunung Batukaru. The most popular is behind **Pura Luhur Batukaru,** where you'll be pressured to pay a local guide at least 500,000 Rp to accompany your journey. Otherwise, there is another trailhead on Gunung Batukaru's southeastern flank near the **Jatiluwih rice terraces,** where the trail starts at **Pura Luhur Bhujangga** in the small village of **Gunung Sari.** Wear long pants, long sleeves, and proper shoes to keep leeches from hitching a ride up the mountain.

Guides
BALI JUNGLE TREKKING

tel. 82236600967; www.balijungletrekking.com; daily 8am-6pm; 1,400,000 Rp per person, minimum 2 people, includes pickup, drop-off, and lunch

Bali Jungle Trekking is one of the main players in the hiking scene, offering licensed guides and tours all throughout the island, with one of their best offerings being a guided tour to the summit of Gunung Batukaru. Your tour includes pickup at your accommodation, guided tours of four temples encountered on the trail, lunch at the summit of Gunung Batukaru, and drop-off. The company also offers treks to other destinations in the area like Gunung Batur, Gunung Abang, Munduk, Danau Tamblingan, and walks along the rice terraces.

HOT SPRINGS
ANGSERI HOT SPRINGS

Desa Angseri; daily 8am-6pm; 45,000 Rp

Angseri Hot Springs is a small resort that is popular among locals and intrepid travelers who don't want the overhyped experience of Gunung Batur's hot springs. A steep staircase leads you to teal-colored pools that are surrounded by small waterfalls, rice terraces, and colorful foliage. The main area has a handful of private tubs and showers that can sit up to four people comfortably, as well as open-air Jacuzzis that fill with piping hot water. It's a simple spot that does the trick if you just want to soak without the pressure of being sold anything. A tiny warung on-site serves cheap Indonesian meals and cold drinks.

A Single Grain of Rice: How Rice Is Grown

Jatiluwih Rice Terraces

Rice is Bali's most important crop; it's eaten for breakfast, lunch, and dinner and is used as an of-fering to the Hindu gods and during holidays like **Galungan** and **Kuningan,** when rice is left out for ancestors to enjoy in the afterlife.

Bali has a unique method of growing and harvesting rice that is not found elsewhere in the world. Because rice is seen as a gift from the Hindu gods, growing rice is both a spiritual and practical process that involves the philosophy of *tri hita karana,* a belief that the human world, the natural world, and the spiritual world are all connected. The water irrigation part of the rice growing process is called *subak.*

To grow rice that adheres to the *tri hita karana* philosophy, water must flow from a Hindu temple devoted to water, like Pura Ulun Danu Batur. Water originating from these temples is considered blessed. A series of canals and dams channel the holy water to Bali's rice paddies, where it flows from terrace to terrace—a process that has been in effect since the 12th century. *Danau Batur* is believed to be the source of every spring and river in Bali and is therefore considered sacred. Rice seedlings are planted in the terrace and grown over 6-12 months. Before harvest, farmers consult spiritual leaders who let them know when to harvest the rice. The rice is harvested by hand, laid to dry, then threshed to remove the rice grains from the stalk. After this, the rice is set to dry again before it is ready for consumption.

The temples connect the spiritual world to the natural world, and by participating in ceremo-nies and rituals, humans connect their world as well, thus fulfilling the *tri hita karana* belief system. Rice terraces that follow *subak* must adhere to strict laws called *awig-awig.* This process has earned UNESCO World Heritage recognition and will likely continue long into the future.

ACCOMMODATIONS
KUBU D'UME HOMESTAY

Jalan Batu Luwih Kawan; 600,000 Rp double room

An accommodation like Kubu D'ume Homestay is a far cry from the large resorts you'll find in Bali's tourist hubs. This two-bedroom bungalow is newly built and set in the middle of rice paddies where you can lis-ten to frogs and birds sing as you fall asleep. The bedrooms have floor-to-ceiling windows that make it feel as though you're sleeping on

1: Jatiluwih Rice Terraces 2: trekking Gunung Batur
3: Air Terjun Yeh Ho 4: Angseri Hot Springs

the rice terrace itself. The property is within walking distance of Pura Luhur Batukaru, and rooms have air-conditioning. The host, Putu, and his family go out of their way to ensure guests are feeling welcome and well-fed (opt for the meal plan for an extra 150,000 Rp per person, per day). Don't miss Putu's walking tour where he shows you around the property and finds fruits for you to sample.

BALI MOUNTAIN RETREAT

tel. 8283602645; https://balimountainretreat.com; 700,000 Rp budget double room, 1,300,000 Rp deluxe double room

Bali Mountain Retreat truly is a quiet getaway in the foothills of Gunung Batukaru. Situated on a private and spacious property, the eco-friendly resort is ideal for travelers who enjoy a bit of relaxation mixed in with adventure. The rooms are built in a traditional style with wooden and tile roofing. Each room includes breakfast, Wi-Fi, and access to the retreat's restaurant, meditation platform, and garden area. It's well-situated with easy access to hiking trails, springs, rice terraces, coffee plantations, and cycling paths. Food is made from produce sourced from local farmers. The views of the jungle below alone make a stay here worth it.

Don't bother hiring a private driver to get to Bali Mountain Retreat; instead, arrange transport directly with the accommodation. The road to the retreat is unkept, hard to find, and most private drivers end up going to the wrong location near Pura Luhur Batukaru, which can be up to a 2-hour detour.

BALI SILENT RETREAT

Desa Mongan; tel. 85237347608; https:// balisilentretreat.com; 420,000 Rp single room, 850,000 Rp double room

Bali Silent Retreat is a secular meditation and prayer retreat as well as an off-grid getaway where guests can stay in airy dorm, single, and double rooms. While staying at Bali Silent Retreat, guests are encouraged to uphold silence by not talking except in specific authorized areas. Wi-Fi is nonexistent, and guests will have trouble establishing a basic phone connection. Guests are required to purchase an extra daily pass for 520,000 Rp that includes three vegetarian buffet meals daily, all yoga and meditation sessions, weekday trips to hot springs, and all extra events.

★ SANG GIRI MOUNTAIN GLAMPING

GPS Coordinates - 8.35874, 115.115574; tel. 361/4749086; https://sanggiri.com; 2,200,000 Rp double room

You'll feel like you're sleeping among the jungle wildlife at Sang Giri Glamping, a luxury retreat with safari-style glamping tents that all have private bathrooms, a spacious patio with a daybed, queen-sized beds, and hot water showers. Each of the tents overlooks the jungle below and is an ideal hub for trekking, cycling, and enjoying the scenery while being disconnected—Wi-Fi is only available during mealtimes. There are packages offered where you can combine your stay with tours, cooking classes, and candlelit meals.

Getting to Sang Giri Mountain Glamping is a challenge. First, navigate to the Jatiluwih Rice Terraces. Then, using Google Maps, input in a temple called "Pura Luhur Sri Rambut Sedana." Look for a blue sign along the road, as this temple is the best marker to help you find the turn-off for Sang Giri Glamping.

GETTING THERE

Gunung Batukaru is one of the most inaccessible parts of Bali unless you are strictly visiting the **Jatiluwih Rice Terraces.** This is what keeps the area so pristine. To get here, you will need a **private driver, motorbike,** or a **rental car.** However, a private driver will likely be the most convenient option. If coming from Kuta or Denpasar, take Jalan Dr. Ir. Sukarno/Jalan Raya Denpasar-Gilimanuk west for 20 km (12 mi), turning right on Jalan Antosari Puputan and following it inland to Gunung Batukaru's southern slope.

Mobile data coverage is not reliable in

the area. Download **offline maps** of Bali on the app **Maps.Me** or on **Google Maps**, and use GPS coordinates to aid with navigation. Otherwise, book a **tour** with Bali Jungle Trekking or transportation through your accommodation.

Locals navigate the area on **motorbike** or by **car.** You can **cycle** with a bike rented through your accommodation, take a **tour,** or use your own means of transportation, such as a motorbike or rental car, to get around.

Munduk and the Three Lakes

Three lakes, **Danau Buyan, Danau Tamblingan,** and **Danau Beratan,** sit within one giant caldera, with the town of **Munduk** located 8 km (5 mi) east of Danau Tamblingan. One main road, Jalan Kayu Putih-Munduk, starting on the eastern side of the region, connects Munduk, wraps along the northern side of Danau Tamblingan and Danau Buyan through the small town of **Pancasari** to **Bedugul,** and around Danau Beratan's eastern shoreline. Danau Beratan is 45 km (28 mi) north of **Ubud** and 80 km (50 mi) east of Danau Batur by road. Danau Tamblingan is 25 km (15.5 mi) south of **Singaraja.**

MUNDUK

A quiet village set on a windy road with vistas around every turn, Munduk is where you go when you want to get away from a city without missing any creature comforts. Senses are overloaded with the scent of oranges and vanilla grown along its slopes, and blankets of cloves sprawled out on the streets. Your eyes drift to the deep, lush valleys of jungle and coffee plantations below. Take a short walk to one of the town's waterfalls and feel the mist blow onto your skin. The air is cool and fresh.

During the Dutch invasion and occupation of Bali, the Dutch came to Munduk and built holiday homes, where they'd go to escape the heat of Bali's coastline. This has made Munduk an interesting place to see European architecture alongside traditional Balinese structures.

Sights

★ MUNDUK WATERFALL

Jalan Kayu Putih; 20,000 Rp admission, 5,000 Rp parking

Munduk Waterfall is the most accessible waterfall in Munduk, with a sign along Jalan Kayu Putih that marks its entrance. A large cascade about 15 meters (49 feet) high dumps into a gorge of tumultuous water. If you ask around, you'll find that this waterfall often goes by a handful of names (some correct, some not). Munduk Waterfall is also called Red Coral Waterfall and Tanah Barak Waterfall. In addition, it often adopts the names of the waterfalls around it. Oh well, a waterfall by any other name would look as beautiful! Just follow the path to a waterfall (any waterfall), and you're sure to be impressed. Note that none of the waterfalls are ideal for swimming, but it's worth bringing swimwear to stand near the waterfall and feel its cool spray.

GOLDEN VALLEY WATERFALL

Jalan Kayu Putih; included with Munduk Waterfall admission

A 20-minute walk along the path of Munduk Waterfall is Golden Valley Waterfall. A jagged wall of stone creates a multitiered waterfall into a shallow pool surrounded by wet rocks. You can enjoy feeling the cool mist against your skin without the hassle of vendors that you might encounter at some of Bali's equally impressive, yet more crowded, falls.

Munduk Area

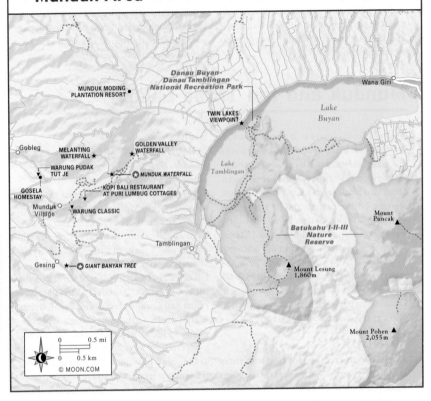

MELANTING WATERFALL

Jalan Air Terjun Melanting; 10,000 Rp

Melanting Waterfall is the third waterfall in Munduk's main waterfall area and the hardest to reach. About an hour's walk from Golden Valley Waterfall along a quadburning steep and moss-covered stair path is Melanting Waterfall. Wear a sturdy pair of shoes to avoid injury. At the end of the path, you'll find a narrow ribbon of white water pouring from a 25-meter (82-foot) high drop.

★ GIANT BANYAN TREE

Jalan Gesing, in village of Gesing; free

The Giant Banyan Tree in Gesing once could've been the scene in a fantasy film. At 700 years old, this tree played an important role during the Dutch occupation of Bali. When Dutch forces took over the region of Munduk, it's said that many locals took shelter and hid between the roots of the Giant Banyan Tree. Today, the tree is seen as having protective powers. The top half of the tree was destroyed in a storm, but visitors can still walk around the trunk to admire its roots and visit the two temples, Pura Subak and Pura Pecalang, on-site.

1: Munduk Waterfall 2: Melanting Waterfall
3: Munduk

Food
★ WARUNG CLASSIC

Jalan Pura Puseh; tel. 81999779750; daily 11am-10pm; 30,000-60,000 Rp

At Warung Classic, it feels as though you're dining among clouds. This family-run warung built from bamboo overlooks verdant rice fields with mist rolling along the hills below. The menu features Indonesian fare with satay meat skewers, spring rolls, and *tempeh manis* (sweet and salty tempeh)—all worth a try and served with a side of strawberry juice. The restaurant faces west, so head over for sunset. Thanks to glowing online reviews, it's no secret spot, so arrive early for your best chance at getting a good table.

WARUNG PUDAK TUT JE

Jalan Dinas Jembong; tel. 81236126578; daily 7am-11pm; 30,000-100,000 Rp

Warung Pudak Tut Je is a family-run warung at the back of a private home where you're treated like friends. To get to the warung, walk from the main road of Jalan Kayu Putih and turn at the large sign pointing to a small road. There, you'll find a manicured pathway that leads to the back of a private home. The family serves pizza, pasta, and sandwiches along with typical Indonesian fare. It's common for the owners to bring out extra appetizers and samples free of charge in exchange for feedback on how they can make their new dishes even better.

★ KOPI BALI RESTAURANT AT PURI LUMBUNG COTTAGES

Jalan Kayu Putih; www.purilumbung.com; tel. 8123874042; daily 11am-10pm; 60,000-200,000 Rp

Puri Lumbung Cottages is a hotel with traditional wooden cottages and villas set among rice fields. Its main appeal is its on-site restaurant, open to outside guests, where tastefully presented Indonesian meals are served on an open-air patio overlooking treetops below. Visitors can partake in a cooking class to learn how to make Balinese meals like satay, fried rice, and noodles using local organic ingredients.

Accommodations
GOSELA HOMESTAY

Jalan Kayu Putih; tel. 81239179698; 300,000 Rp double room

Gosela Homestay is one of the most welcoming homestays in the region. Its owners treat guests like family and often greet newcomers with a pile of fresh fruits harvested from the property. A hearty breakfast is included in

Warung Classic

every stay. Each room is outfitted with double beds, private bathrooms, and a spacious patio. The Wi-Fi isn't always reliable, and hot water is an even hotter commodity, but each room opens onto a garden area lined with passionfruit vines, and that helps to make up for the property's shortcomings.

★ MUNDUK MODING PLANTATION RESORT

Jalan Asah Gobleg; tel. 811385059; www. mundukmodingplantation.com; 2,200,000 Rp double room

Munduk Moding Plantation has an ambiance of old Indonesia, where stress can't reach you. It's well-known among luxury travelers, thanks to its 18-meter (59-foot) infinity pool that overlooks a never-ending forest. Munduk Moding Plantation Resort is a working coffee plantation that partners with nearby farms, serving luwak coffee—the world's most expensive coffee—made from coffee beans that have been digested by wild civets. However, unlike many other luwak coffee plantations, Munduk Moding Plantation only crafts luwak coffee from beans found on the plantation floor, keeping no animals in captivity.

Guests can choose between villas and suites, some with a heated Jacuzzi or stand-alone stone bathtub. Paintings and sculptures used to decorate the rooms are all crafted by Indonesian artists. The resort also has a heated pool, gym, restaurant and bar, lounge area, and fireplace that's lit each evening for socializing.

★ SANAK RETREAT BALI

Jalan Kayu Putih; tel. 811397758; https://sanakbali. com; 2,400,000 Rp double room

Sanak Retreat Bali is the type of luxury retreat where you can relax in privacy and listen to rice stalks rustle in the breeze. The hotel has 11 bungalows available with one, two, or three rooms, each with a balcony and traditional Indonesian decor. No two are exactly alike. Guests have access to a shared turquoise swimming pool, while the three-bedroom bungalow has its own. The resort overlooks

Munduk's mountains and offers yoga classes and massage treatments at its on-site spa. Meals are top-notch, and it's worth requesting the chef's surprise dinner, where you'll be treated to a meal made from the resort's garden vegetables and entertained with a traditional Balinese dance.

Getting There

Perama (tel. 361/751875; www.peramatour. com) offers shuttle bus service to **Bedegul** near Danau Beratan (Jalan Baturiti Bedugul) once daily from **Ubud** (departs 11:30am daily; 75,000 Rp), **Kuta** (departs 10am daily; 75,000 Rp), **Lovina** (departs 9am daily; 75,000 Rp), and **Padang Bai** (departs 9am daily; 150,000 Rp). **Public buses** connecting **Denpasar/ Kuta/Sanur** to **Singajara** on Bali's northern coastline stop at **Bedegul.** From there, you can take a *bemo* to Munduk (20,000 Rp).

Buses run from the **Ubung Terminal** in **Denpasar** (Jalan Coksoamindo; tel. 361/427172; 60,000 Rp).

From **Pemuteran,** you can hop on the **Pemuteran Shuttle** (tel. 81338575384; https://pemuteranshuttle.wordpress.com) that coasts between Pemuteran and Munduk for 150,000 Rp. The shuttle also connects to **Ubud, Kuta,** and **Sanur** for 150,000 Rp each.

Getting Around

It's easy to rent a **motorbike** in Munduk for 50,000 Rp per day, typically through your accommodation. **Private drivers** will take you around the area for 800,000 Rp per day (8 hours) and can be arranged through your accommodation or through **Gosela Homestay** (tel. 81239179698).

DANAU BUYAN AND DANAU TAMBLINGAN

Uncrowded trails and panoramic vistas await at Danau Buyan and Danau Tamblingan, two lakes that are often skipped over by travelers on their way to Bali's northern coastline or Gunung Batur. The view of both at once from a caldera ridgeline is worth the stop alone. Explore unfettered trails that lead to temples or plantations, along the shoreline, and up ridge ledges. Canoe from one end of the lake to the other. It's a choose-your-own-adventure region where you decide the next move; one-size-fits-all tours be gone.

Sights
TWIN LAKES VIEWPOINT
600 meters (1,968 feet) north of intersection of Jalan Raya Wanagiri and Jalan Asah Gobleg; free

Danau Tamblingan and Danau Buyan, inside of a volcanic caldera, are commonly known as the twin lakes. A 2-km (1.2-mi) stretch of forest splits the twin lakes apart, forming a panoramic viewpoint. Locals have built a cement platform where you can stand and admire views of both lakes at once; it's a prime spot to sit and watch the clouds roll over the ridgeline in the distance. Along Jalan Raya Wanagiri, there are plenty of other photo opportunities for travelers who want to spend 30,000-50,000 Rp per person to take a picture sitting on a swing or inside a nest that overlooks the twin lakes. Skip the opportunities to take a picture posing with a bat or a civet—the animals here are often kept in squalid conditions.

Lake Tamblingan
(Danau Tamblingan)
Access at Jalan Danau Tamblingan; free

Danau Tamblingan is the smallest of the three lakes inside the volcanic caldera. Viewed as sacred by Balinese Hindus, the lake is encircled by untouched forest hosting small shrines and temples between its trees. You can search for these temples yourself on foot and with the help of a canoe, as many things can only be seen from the water. Canoes accommodating up to four people are rented on the waterfront and cost 400,000 Rp per day. The lake's main temple, **Pura Dalem Tamblingan,** is thought to have been there since the 10th century, surviving floods and persistent rain.

Lake Buyan
(Danau Buyan)
Access at Jalan Pancasari, parking on lakefront; free

While the area around Danau Tamblingan is untouched and undeveloped, there is a large farming community that sits on the northern point of Danau Buyan that's famous in Bali for growing strawberries, coffee, cloves, and ceremonial flowers. Danau Buyan is the largest of the three lakes in the region, and an important food source thanks to its stock of freshwater fish. If you want to be shuttled from one end to the other, you can catch a ride from a fisherman for about 50,000 Rp.

TREKKING AROUND THE LAKES

The area surrounding Danau Tambingan, Danau Buyan, and Danau Bratan is a dream for hiking enthusiasts. With so many trails to choose from with varying inclines, terrains, and sceneries, you could easily spend a few weeks wandering the trails of the area without seeing it all.

ORGANISASI PRAMUWISATA BANGKIT BERSAMA
Jalan Danau Tamblingan; tel. 85238678092; daily 8:30am-4pm; 2-hour hikes 200,000 Rp, full-day hikes 800,000 Rp

The Organisasi Pramuwisata Bangkit Bersama is an organization of trekking guides who offer guided tours and walks around the region. They can lead canoe and walking tours, treks to the summit of nearby **Gunung Lesong,** waterfall treks, and other customizable trips. Guides tend to be a bit more hands-on and engaged than a lot of the hit-or-miss guides around the Gunung Batur area.

One popular trekking trail is a canoe and walking trip where you start from the village of **Gubung** on **Danau Tamblingan** and cross the lake by canoe until you reach the divide with **Danau Buyan.** You trek across the divide and catch a glimpse of Danau Buyan before returning and walking along Danau Tamblingan's southeastern end, home to a modest lakeside temple called **Pura Dalem Gubung.**

1: Lake Buyan 2: Lake Tamblingan 3: Pura Dalem Tamblingan 4: Pura Ulun Beratan

A walk to the summit of Gunung Lesong, south of Danau Tamblingan, is an adventure through dense forest up to a crater rim. There are also treks that venture to waterfalls in Munduk, mountainside temples, and vine-wrapped valleys.

Getting There and Around

The most convenient way to get to the lakes and around is with a **private driver,** available for 600,000-800,000 Rp per day, or with your own **car** or **motorbike.** One main road called **Jalan Munduk-Wanagiri/ Jalan Raya Wanagiri** runs along the lake's northern coastline. **Parking** is available at the shorefront of Danau Buyan and Danau Tamblingan. Motorbikes are typically available for rent through your accommodation for 50,000 Rp per day.

DANAU BERATAN

Danau Beratan is home to some of the most photogenic spots in Bali, with **Pura Ulun Beratan** being the main draw. Spend your time walking among botanic gardens, gliding along treetops in an adventure park, zooming across the lake in a fishing boat, sampling strawberries at one of the many cafés, or enjoying daily life like a local from **Bedugul,** its main village. Because Danau Beratan is the largest and most popular of the three lakes inside of its surrounding crater, it often seems like it is an only child. Come here to be a part of the action, then venture to the twin lakes up north for a self-imposed time out.

Sights

★ BALI TREETOP ADVENTURE PARK

Jalan Kebun Raya Eka Karya; tel. 361/9340009; www.balitreetop.com; daily 8:30am-6pm; 310,000 Rp adult, 200,000 Rp child for 2.5-hour admission block

Release your inner Tarzan or Jane at Bali Treetop Adventure Park, an outdoor park with more than 70 activities like tightropes, suspended bridges, swings, and a flying fox that spans 160 meters (525 feet) across the sky.

There are courses for children as young as four years old, and admission includes all circuits in the park as long as you meet the 140-cm (4 ft, 7 in) height requirement. Different courses vary in thrill levels, making it a great place to go no matter how adventurous you are. The park is inside of the Bali Botanic Garden.

★ BALI BOTANIC GARDEN

Jalan Kebun Raya Eka Karya; tel. 3682033211; www. kebunrayabali.com; daily 8am-6pm; 20,000 Rp admission, 6,000 Rp parking

Bali Botanic Garden is the largest botanic garden in Indonesia, and a sanctuary to more than 100 species of birds, as well as monkeys, and more than 2,000 species of plants, all living at 1,300 meters (4,265 feet) above the sea. Set aside a few hours to wander around the garden on foot, enjoying the giant ferns, orchids, and rasamala trees. Thanks to frequent rainfall and fertile soil, nearly everything that is planted in the Bali Botanic Garden thrives. Consider this garden the antidote to feeling stressed.

★ ULUN DANU BERATAN TEMPLE (Pura Ulun Danu Beratan)

Jalan Raya Bedugul; tel. 3682033050; www. ulundanuberatan.com; daily 8am-6pm; 50,000 Rp admission, 2,000-5,000 Rp parking

One of the most iconic temples in Bali is found in Pura Ulun Danu Beratan, where an 11-tiered pagoda looks as though it is floating on the mirror-flat water of Danau Beratan. Thanks to its size, the temple is almost always busy with Hindu ceremonies and cultural performances, and watching from a respectful distance is usually acceptable. The temple was built in 1633 and is dedicated to the god Shiva, with some *merus* honoring the goddess of water, Dewi Danu.

Because of its popularity among travelers and prevalence in glossy magazines, you might find locals asking for additional money to guide you once you're inside the temple area. Politely yet firmly decline any requests to pay more than your entrance fee. Ignore the tacky statue of Spongebob Squarepants holding an exit sign, and leave through the entrance where you came in to avoid being funneled into a cluster of pushy souvenir vendors.

Getting There and Around

Perama (tel. 361/751875; www.peramatour.com) offers shuttle bus service to **Bedegul** near Danau Beratan (Jalan Baturiti Bedugul) once daily from **Ubud** (departs 11:30 am daily; 75,000 Rp), **Kuta** (departs 10am daily; 75,000), **Lovina** (departs 9am daily; 75,000 Rp), and **Padang Bai** (departs 9am daily; 150k). **Public buses** connecting **Denpasar/Kuta/Sanur** to **Singajara** on Bali's northern coastline stop at **Bedegul.**

To get around, hire a **private driver** for 600,000-800,000 Rp per day through your accommodation, or use pickup and drop-off points included in a **tour. Motorbikes** are usually available from your accommodation for 50,000 Rp per day.

Western Bali

Diverse and largely uncrowded, West Bali is where you'll find waterfall treks, pumping surf, and technicolor coral reefs. Unassuming towns in the region often have the more spectacular temples. In Singaraja, the former capital and the island's second largest city, you can look through ancient books made from palm leaves at the Gedong Kirtya Library and learn about history at Museum Buleleng. Lovina, a laid-back beach town, was established by the Buleleng regency's former monarch as a holiday destination.

Along the coral reefs of West Bali National Park, scuba divers and snorkelers marvel at thriving corals, sea turtles, and schools of pelagic fish. Pemuteran, where you can wander the beaches without being hassled, makes an ideal base. When you've finished exploring what

Highlights

Look for ★ to find recommended sights, activities, dining, and lodging.

★ **Sekumpul Waterfall:** Multiple waterfalls flow from 80 meters (262 feet) high into a clear pool below (page 321).

★ **Brahmavihara-Arama:** Meditate inside Bali's largest Buddhist monument (page 323).

★ **Rama Lovina Tour:** Explore West Bali's hardest-to-reach places with Ketut, a trusted guide (page 323).

★ **Lovina Beach Festival:** Three days of cultural events and performances are set on the sandy shoreline of Lovina's main beach (page 327).

★ **Pura Pulaki:** This sacred seaside temple in Pemuteran is guarded by boisterous monkeys (page 331).

★ **Freediving off Pemuteran:** Corals and fish have taken residence on intriguing steel sculptures in this artificial reef (page 333).

★ **Menjangan Island:** The coral reefs that surround this small island are Bali's most pristine dive and snorkel site (page 338).

★ **Tanah Lot Temple:** A lonely temple 100 meters (328 feet) offshore guards Bali's coastline (page 344).

Western Bali

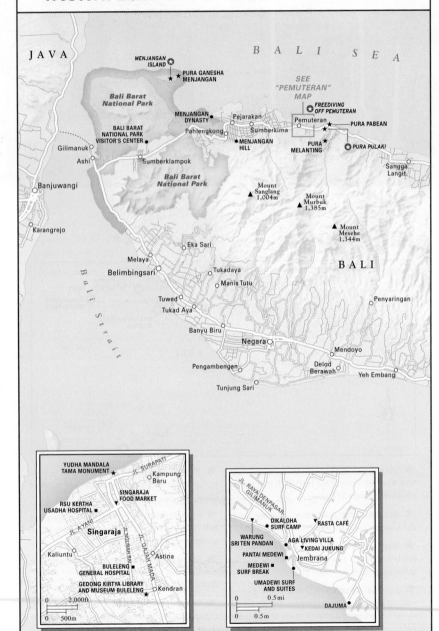

JAVA

B A L I   S E A

MENJANGAN
ISLAND ✪
★ PURA GANESHA
MENJANGAN

SEE
"PEMUTERAN"
MAP

Bali Barat
National Park

MENJANGAN ● Pejarakan
DYNASTY
Pahlengkong ● Sumberkima   Pemuteran
BALI BARAT
NATIONAL PARK
VISITOR'S CENTER ● MENJANGAN
● HILL   PURA
MELANTING ★
FREEDIVING
OFF PEMUTERAN
★ PURA PABEAN
★
✪ PURA PULAKI

Gilimanuk ○
Ashi ○
○ Sumberklampok   Sangga
Langit ○

Bali Barat
National Park

Banjuwangi ○

Karangrejo ○   Mount
Sanglang
▲ 1,004m   Mount
Murbuk
▲ 1,385m   BALI

Eka Sari ○   ▲ Mount
Mesehe
1,344m

Melaya ○
Belimbingsari ●   ○ Tukadaya
○ Manis Tutu   Penyaringan ○

Tuwed ○
Tukad Aya ○
Banyu Biru ○   Negara ○
Mendoyo ○
Pengambengan ○   Delod
Berawah ○   Yeh Embang ○
Tunjung Sari ○

Bali   Strait

Singaraja (inset)

YUDHA MANDALA
TAMA MONUMENT ★   JL. SURAPATI
Kampung
Baru ○
RSU KERTHA   SINGARAJA
USADHA HOSPITAL ■   FOOD MARKET

JL. A. YANI   Singaraja

Kaliuntu ○   Astina ○

BULELENG ■
GENERAL HOSPITAL
GEDONG KIRTYA LIBRARY
AND MUSEUM BULELENG ★   Kendran ○

0   2,000ft
0   500m

Jembrana (inset)

JL. RAYA DENPASAR-
GILIMANUK

▼ DIKALOHA
SURF CAMP   ▼ RASTA CAFÉ
WARUNG
SRI TEN PANDAN   ● AGA LIVING VILLA
PANTAI MEDEWI   ▼ KEDAI JUKUNG
● MEDEWI ■   Jembrana ○
SURF BREAK
UMADEWI SURF
AND SUITES

0   0.5mi
0   0.5m   ● DAJUMA

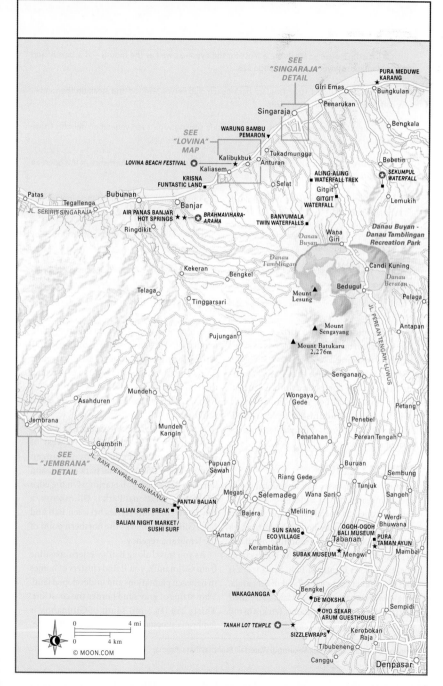

Top Restaurants

★ **Buda Bakery:** Meals are a feast for the eyes—as well as the mouth—at a bakery and restaurant set over two floors (page 328).

★ **Spice Beach Club:** This laid-back beach club serves seafood and steak on the sand—often with live music (page 328).

★ **Akar Café:** Green is the theme at this café serving vegan and vegetarian delights (page 328).

★ **Warung Tirta Sari:** Enjoy dinner with a dance or live music performance at this open-air restaurant (page 336).

★ **Warung D'Bucu:** An unassuming warung serves some of the freshest food in West Bali (page 336).

★ **Rasta Café:** Balinese classics are served inside a rasta-colored warung, surrounded by rice fields (page 341).

★ **Sizzlewraps:** Choose your own filling for a burrito, wrap, or quesadilla made to order (page 346).

WESTERN BALI

exists underneath the ocean surface, catch the waves at Balian or Medewi—all levels of experience are welcome.

When it comes time to turn inward, wander through the compounds of a beautiful temple. Pura Tanah Lot, Pura Taman Ayun, and the largest Buddhist temple in Bali, Brahmavihara-Arama, offer plenty of places to sit and meditate.

ORIENTATION

West Bali encompasses Bali's northern coastline, dominated by the **Buleleng regency,** and stretches to the west of the **Central Mountains.** It includes most of the **Jembrana** and **Tabanan** regencies, rounding out Bali's western point. Starting from the north coastline, the former capital of Bali, **Singaraja** is Bali's second largest city. Inland of Singaraja, jungle valleys marked by waterfalls make their way to Bali's Central Mountains. Ten km (6 mi) west of Singaraja along the coastline is **Lovina,** a popular beach town with a famous dolphin population. Farther west of Lovina (50 km/31 mi) is **Pemuteran,** an ideal base for scuba divers and snorkelers who want to explore the thriving coral reefs off **Menjangan Island** with a choice of fine hotels, restaurants, and activities.

West Bali National Park is Bali's westernmost point, 25 km (15.5 mi) west of Pemuteran and punctuated by Mejangan Island. It's the only national park on Bali and home to Bali's rare Bali Starling. On the edge of West Bali National Park is **Gilimanuk,** a tiny town that runs ferries between Bali and Java. Gilimanuk marks the northern point of the Jembrana regency.

As you travel along Bali's western coastline from Gilimanuk, you'll find clusters of homes in between plantations and undeveloped land. Thin strips of gray sand border the coastline. Thirty km (18.5 mi) south of Gilimanuk is Jembrana's capital, the small town of **Negara.**

Previous: Pantai Pemuteran; Sekumpul Waterfall; Brahmavihara-Arama.

Top Accommodations

★ **Lovina Loca:** Enjoy an affordable stay in this whimsical beach boutique hostel with colorful rooms (page 329).

★ **The Damai:** Savor the luxe life at this inland retreat with tasteful villas and ocean views (page 329).

★ **Pondok Sari:** This beachside retreat offers gardens, lotus ponds, and rooms that are distinctly Indonesian (page 336).

★ **Kinaara Resort:** Stay in a bamboo bungalow that's perched around a lagoon-style pool (page 337).

★ **Menjangan Dynasty:** Dive, snorkel, and swim during the day before retreating to your safari tent at night (page 340).

★ **Dajuma:** A family-friendly beach resort with multiple pools, Dajuma also offers daily yoga classes and a spa (page 343).

★ **WakaGangga:** Couples will like this romantic retreat with quirky conical bungalows, many with private pools (page 347).

The interior of West Bali is largely uninhabited, with small dirt roads spiderwebbing throughout. Continue 25 km (15.5 mi) along the coastline to find one of Bali's best waves at **Medewi Beach**, with a handful of surf camps and guesthouses clustered around the point. **Balian**, another neighborhood that's famous for its river-mouth wave, is 24 km (15 mi) away from Medewi in the regency of Tabanan. **Tabanan**, the capital town of its namesake regency, is about 30 km (18.5 mi) from Balian Beach, and 15 km (9 mi) from **Pura Tanah Lot**, a seaside temple that many travelers come to admire. Continue southbound, and within minutes you'll be in the outskirts of **Canggu**. All major towns are connected with Bali's **main coastal road, Jalan Singaraja-Gilimanuk**. West of **Bubunan** to the north and **Pulukan** to the south, there are no major roads venturing inland.

PLANNING YOUR TIME

If you travel west along the coastline, 200 km (124 mi) of road joins **Tabanan** to **Singaraja**. From north to south, 70 km (43 mi) separates the two towns. Although it's possible to do day trips to Tabanan and the southern edge of Jembrana, you will want to stay in the farther north and western regions of West Bali to truly make the most of it. It takes three days to see West Bali on a superficial level. If you spend at least a week in West Bali, you'll have time to scuba dive and snorkel, hike, go on side trips to its cultural sites, and still have time to relax.

Consider **Lovina** as a base to explore Singaraja and the **waterfalls** of the region. You can also take day trips to the **Central Mountains** from Lovina. To see the coral reefs of West Bali, sleep in **Pemuteran**, a small town where many dive centers run snorkeling and scuba diving trips to the nearby reefs and **Menjangan Island**. West Bali National Park is easily seen as a day tour from Pemuteran or from the scattered accommodations around the park. The beach towns of **Medewi** and **Balian** offer the Bali beach experience without the crowds you'd find in Kuta or Sanur. Public transportation and taxis are unreliable in the region, so it's best to get around with a private driver or with your own rental car or motorbike.

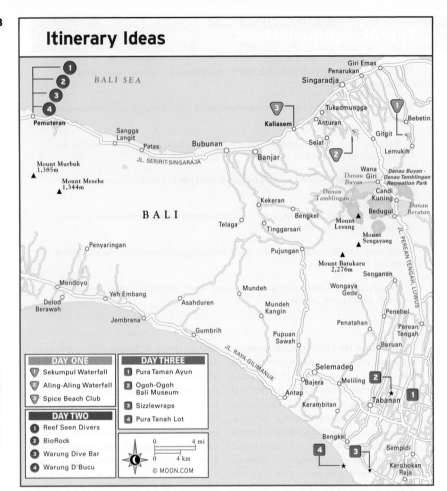

Itinerary Ideas

BALI SEA

Pemuteran

Mount Murbuk
1,385m

Mount Mesehe
1,344m

BALI

Sangga
Langit

Patas

JL. SERIRIT-SINGARAJA

Bubunan

Banjar

Giri Emas

Penarukan

Singaradja

Tukadmungga

Anturan

Selat

Bebetin

Gitgit

Lemukih

Kaliasem

Wana
Giri

Danau
Buyan

Danau Buyan -
Danau Tamblingan
Recreation Park

Danau
Tamblingan

Candi
Kuning

Bedugul

Danau
Beratan

Kekeran

Bengkel

Telaga

Tinggarsari

Penyaringan

Pujungan

Mount
Lesung

Mount
Sengayang

JL. PEREAN TENGAH, LUWUS

Mount Batukaru
2,276m

Senganan

Mendoyo

Yeh Embang

Asahduren

Mundeh

Mundeh
Kangin

Wongaya
Gede

Penebel

Penatahan

Perean
Tengah

Delod
Berawah

Jembrana

Gumbrih

Pupuan
Sawah

Buruan

JL. RAYA-GILIMANUK

Selemadeg

Bajera

Meliling

Antap

Tabanan

Kerambitan

Bengkel

Sempidi

Kerobokan
Raja

DAY ONE	
1	Sekumpul Waterfall
2	Aling-Aling Waterfall
3	Spice Beach Club

DAY TWO	
1	Reef Seen Divers
2	BioRock
3	Warung Dive Bar
4	Warung D'Bucu

DAY THREE	
1	Pura Taman Ayun
2	Ogoh-Ogoh Bali Museum
3	Sizzlewraps
4	Pura Tanah Lot

0   4 mi

0   4 km

© MOON.COM

Itinerary Ideas

THREE DAYS IN WESTERN BALI

Day 1: Wandering Around Waterfalls

1 Pack a sturdy pair of walking shoes and a bathing suit. Drive to **Sekumpul Waterfall** and admire the many cascades flowing from 80 meters (260 feet) above. Enjoy a picnic lunch, packed in advance, at the waterfall. Alternatively, you can stop at a roadside warung for a local experience.

2 Drive to **Aling-Aling Waterfall,** where you can swim and enjoy the rush of rumbling water. Alternatively (or additionally, for those who want a big day out), GitGit Waterfall is nearby.

3 Drive to Lovina for sunset and a relaxing dinner at **Spice Beach Club.**

Day 2: West Bali Underwater

1 In the early morning, head out by boat to Menjangan Island with **Reef Seen Divers** to admire Bali's thriving corals and marine life. Your trip will likely include a picnic lunch on the shores of Menjangan Island. Tours must be arranged at least one day in advance.

2 Back in Pemuteran, snorkel over the **Biorock,** an artificial reef that's working to encourage coral growth—a counterbalance to the region's lasting history of dynamite fishing.

3 Grab a sunset drink at **Warung Dive Bar.**

4 Have dinner at **Warung D'Bucu:** it's where many of the scuba dive guides go.

Day 3: Temples of Tabanan

The night before this day's itinerary, check the tide calendar for Tanah Lot (Search for "Tabanan" on Tideschart.com). Consider visiting Pura Tanah Lot during mid- to high tide, when the temple is surrounded by water. The temple is most crowded at sunset, but watching the sky change color over the water is a worthwhile experience even with the crowds.

1 Pack a sarong and sleeved shirt before driving to the town of Tabanan. Admire the many *merus* of **Pura Taman Ayun.** Stop for lunch at one of the local warungs along Jalan Ayoda.

2 Walk to the **Ogoh-Ogoh Bali Museum** near the temple to see a frightening display of Hindu demons.

3 Drive 20 minutes south to grab a burrito or quesadilla at **Sizzlewraps.**

4 Head to **Pura Tanah Lot** for sunset.

Singaraja Area

Singaraja was once the capital of Bali and a vital port for trade; it lost this title to Denpasar in 1958 and is now the capital of the Buleleng regency. Because of this legacy, you'll see Dutch colonial architecture as well as Chinese, Arab, and Javanese influence throughout the city. Today, Singaraja is the island's second most populous city, where locals work, study, and run errands without the obvious influence of tourism. One of Bali's most prestigious universities is in Singaraja, making it a hub for social progress and innovation. Singaraja is worth a visit if you're interested in Bali's more offbeat destinations. When you wander, keep an eye out for lions—the city's name stems from the word meaning "king of lions."

ORIENTATION

The city of Singaraja is condensed around the **harbor,** one of the longtime major trading ports of Bali. The **Yudha Mandala Tama Monument** is the harbor's central marker, with most of Singaraja clustered within a 2-km (1.2-mi) radius of the area like the **university** and the **Banyuasri bus terminal.** From the monument leading inland, the main road of **Jalan Imam Bonjol** intersects with **Jalan Durian,** where you'll find the **Singaraja Food Market.** Heading 2.5 km (1.5 mi) inland from the harbor along **Jalan Imam Bonjol,** you'll find the **Gedong Kirtya Library** and **Museum Buleleng.** The **Penarukan bus terminal** and **Pura Meduwe Karang** are on the eastern outskirts of the city.

The waterfalls of **Aling-Aling, Sekumpul, Gitgit,** and **Banyumala** are all at least 8 km (5 mi) inland from Singaraja, hidden between dense forest area and often found on unmarked roads; you'll want a **private driver** who is familiar with the area leading the way.

SIGHTS

Yudha Mandala Tama Monument

Jalan Pelabuhan; free

The Yudha Mandala Tama Monument honors I Ketut Merta, a revolutionary fighter who was shot and killed by a Dutch patrol boat for raising an Indonesian flag as an act of defiance. This statue of I Ketut Merta shows him on a platform with an Indonesian flag in hand. It's worth spending an hour walking around the monument and along the harbor wall.

Gedong Kirtya Library and Museum Buleleng

*Jalan Veteran; tel. 362/3303668; Mon.-Thurs.
8am-4pm, Fri.-Sun. 9am-4pm; free*

The Gedong Kirtya Library was founded in 1928 by the Dutch after a surge of Dutch interest in Balinese culture. Once coveted by Southeast Asian merchants, the library has thousands of manuscripts crafted from dried palm leaves, called *lontar*. Inside the books' wooden covers are stories of Balinese political strategies, history, philosophies, medicine, and legends. The more macabre pieces tell tales of black magic. Because of the fragile nature of *lontar* books, which are susceptible to being destroyed by heat and humidity, students in the community transcribe the text from older *lontar* books into new ones—a multi-step and tedious process. The library also has a collection of engraved metal plates.

Next to the Gedong Kirtya Library is the Museum Buleleng, a small and somewhat tired museum that hosts pictures and the typewriter of Anak Agung Panji Tisna (1908-1978), once the raja of the region. He was more interested in writing novels than reigning, and his stories took place in Singaraja. He is credited with founding Lovina, a place he used as a writing retreat. The museum also houses a handful of artifacts, paintings, and other interesting pieces gathered throughout the region. Also on-site is the Puri Agung Singaraja, the former palace of the Buleleng kingdom.

Meduwe Karang Temple
(Pura Meduwe Karang)

Jalan Raya Air Sanih, 12 km (7.5 mi) east of Singaraja; daily 8am-5pm; donation requested

Pura Meduwe Karang is one of the most unique temples in Bali and is dedicated to the gods of agriculture and earth. The entrance is guarded by three rows and 34 statues from the Hindu legend, Ramayana. The split gates open out to a courtyard that is used to host ceremonies. Beyond the farthest set of split gates, the temple has a main shrine where you can see figures of noblemen, Hindu priests, and scenes from everyday life, such as mothers tending to their children and village settings.

The most unique feature of the temple is a stone relief of a Dutch man, thought to be the Dutch artist W.O.J. Nieuwenkamp, who cycled around Bali with a paint pallet and a canvas in the early 1900s.

WATERFALLS

The Singaraja and Lovina area is known for its abundance of waterfalls. Some are large, crowded cascades, while others are trickles found in villages. Though the largest are arguably the most impressive waterfalls around, it's worth searching for the waterfalls rarely found by other travelers.

ALING-ALING WATERFALL
(Air Terjun Aling-Aling)

Jalan Raya Desa Sambangan; 125,000 Rp, 250,000 Rp, or 375,000 Rp per person for guided trek, depending on the length, guides hired at entrance, 10,000 Rp entrance, 2,000 Rp parking

Wander down a set of stairs to Aling-Aling Waterfall, a split waterfall that rises nearly 30 meters (90 feet) high, surrounded by jungle vines and rocks where water trickles over algae. Since the waterfall is considered sacred, swimming is not allowed. The trail starting at Aling-Aling Waterfall leads to a series of other waterfalls, all with swimming areas and cliff-jump ledges. **Kroya Waterfall** has a 5-meter (16-foot) ledge and rock slide, **Kembar Waterfall** has a 10-meter (33-foot) ledge, and **Pucuk** a 15-meter (50-foot) ledge. At all falls, the water can get tumultuous, and wearing a life jacket (provided by the tour guide) is recommended.

If you plan simply to look at the waterfalls, you can pay the entrance fee only and walk along the trodden path to Aling-Aling Waterfall (10,000 Rp). However, if you plan to swim at Kroya, Kembar, and Pucuk Waterfall, local guides will pressure you to pay for their guiding services and will then tell you which areas are safe to enter the water.

★ SEKUMPUL WATERFALL
(Air Terjun Sekumpul)

Village of Sekumpul, 20 km (12 mi) inland from Singaraja; 125,000 Rp guide, 20,000 Rp admission, 2,000 Rp parking, village of Lemuki 15,000 Rp admission

Sekumpul Waterfall is not one single waterfall but rather a collection of separate waterfalls that flow from 80 meters (262 feet) above into a gorge below, with another set of falls, Fiji Waterfall, a 5-minute walk away. The roar of the water, the cool spray against your skin, vibrant rainbows in the mist, and the bright greenery overwhelm the senses. The waterfalls are at the bottom of a steep trail marked with stairs, and you follow the water downstream.

As the waterfalls have become more popular, scams have become more prevalent. Beware of fake registration stalls set up along the village of Sekumpul that request payment to see the waterfall. You will be prompted to pay again at the actual registration stand. The real registration stand has a "Sekumpul Waterfall" sign and is close to the trailhead. As of recently, locals will charge 125,000 Rp to swim near the falls with a private guide. To view the falls only, the price is 20,000 Rp. However, the prices are not standardized and tend to change depending on who is around.

GITGIT WATERFALL
(Air Terjun GitGit)

Jalan Raya Bedugul, 10 km (6 mi) inland from Singaraja; 20,000 Rp admission

Hundreds of steps with souvenir and food stands along the way lead down to a rocky valley that GitGit Waterfall flows into, where it pools into an area ideal for wading.

BANYUMALA TWIN WATERFALLS

Jalan Wanagiri, 30 km (18.5 mi) inland from Singaraja; 20,000 Rp admission

The Banyumala Twin Waterfalls are easier to get to than many other falls within the region, a 20-minute walk downstairs from the main parking lot. Two main falls with smaller cascades surrounding them flow down a rocky cliff ledge into a pool where you can wade and swim. It's so serene, the falls look like it's home to fairies, with tiny cascades that trickle down in between jungle plants.

FOOD
Indonesian
SINGARAJA FOOD MARKET

Jalan Durian; daily 5am-8pm daily; plates from 10,000 Rp

Singaraja Food Market is a traditional town market that's chaotic and cluttered with stalls selling fresh produce, snacks, tobacco, and a mix of handicrafts and jewelry. At night, the market transforms to sell cheap plates of fried noodles, soups, rice, and meat satay.

WARUNG BAMBU PEMARON

Jalan Puri Bagus Pemaron; tel. 362/31455; www. warung-bambu.mahanara.com; daily 11am-11pm; 40,000-70,000 Rp mains

Warung Bambu Pemaron is a restaurant built from bamboo and decorated with paintings made by local artists. The chef cooks traditional Indonesian fare and is happy to host cooking lessons where you can learn how to make each dish on the menu yourself. Cooking classes are themed for beginners, more advanced chefs, vegetarians, and those with a penchant for cooking sweet treats. If you are in a group, you can request a custom cooking class that allows you to choose six items on the Warung Bambu Pemaron menu. The class offers free transportation between Singaraja and Lovina.

INFORMATION AND SERVICES
RSU KERTHA USADHA HOSPITAL

Jalan Tekurkur; tel. 362/26277; www.rsukerthausada. com; open 24/7

A general hospital with an emergency room, ambulance service, and pharmacy. Rooms are clean and many staff members speak basic English.

BULELENG GENERAL HOSPITAL

Jalan Ngurah Rai No. 30; tel. 362/22573; open 24/7

This is the largest hospital in the region, with an emergency room and specialized care services.

GETTING THERE
By Bus and *Bemo*

Singaraja has three bus terminals outside of its city center: **Penarukan Terminal** (off Jalan WR Supratman—look for sign that says "Terminal" 3.5 km (2 mi) east of Yudha Mandala Tama Monument), **Banyuasri Terminal** (Jalan Samudra, the most central station), and **Suksada Terminal** (Jalan I Dewa Made Kaler, off of Jalan Jelantik Gingsir), all with connections that run between each other. *Bemos* cost 10,000-20,000 Rp, though drivers may ask for more if seats are not filled. Buses and *bemos* do not keep to a set timetable, and your best bet for finding a spot on one is by arriving in the morning, before 11am. Public transport around this region is largely unreliable.

By Car

Singaraja is best accessed with your own **private driver** from **Denpasar** (81 km/50 mi; 2 hours 15 minutes), **Kuta** (87 km/54 mi; 2.5 hours), **Amed** (80 km/50 mi; 2 hours), **Ubud** (70 km/43 mi; 2.5 hours), **Kintamani** (50 km/31 mi; 1.5 hours), **Lovina** (10 km/6 mi;

20 minutes), or **Pemuteran** (60 km/37 mi; 1 hour 45 minutes).

GETTING AROUND

There are no metered taxis in Singaraja, and there are limited places to reliably rent a motorbike. The best way to get around is with a **private driver** or with your own motorbike—so long as you are comfortable managing hectic traffic. While you can walk around the **harbor,** major sights in the Singaraja area are far apart.

Lovina Area

Lovina was founded as a holiday destination by the former raja of Buleleng, Anak Agung Panji Tisna, who called his beachfront home "Lovina," as a nickname for "Love Indonesia" in the mid-1950s (though this moniker is often disputed). A line of villages along the North Bali coastline merge to form what's colloquially referred to as Lovina. These include Tukad Mungga, Anturan, Kabukbuk, Kaliasem, and Temukus. Calm water, a long sandy beach, mid-range guesthouses, and a main road lined with little warungs make Lovina a laid-back destination to enjoy.

SIGHTS
Dolphin Monument

Jalan Binaria, Pantai Lovina; free

Lovina is most known for its resident dolphins who swim along the coastline each morning. The central marker of Pantai Lovina, the region's main beach, is a monument with a crowned dolphin on top and a handful of smaller dolphins riding a wave at its base.

Air Panas Banjar Hot Springs

Jalan Banjar, 10 km (6 mi) west of Lovina; tel. 362/92901; https://banjarhotspring.co.id; daily 8:30am-5:30pm; 20,000 Rp adult, 10,000 Rp child

Air Panas Banjar Hot Springs is a hot spring with one large swimming pool and a shallow children's pool, both with massage fountains and surrounded by gardens. Don't expect anything too fancy, but it's a nice way to spend a morning or soak after a day of hiking around waterfalls. Massage treatments are also available.

★ Brahmavihara-Arama

Gg. Sahadewa, 10 km (6 mi) west of Lovina; tel. 362/92954; daily 8am-6pm; 20,000 Rp admission, 5,000 Rp parking

Brahmavihara-Arama is the island's largest Buddhist monastery and hosts a miniature replica of Borobudur, the world's largest Buddhist temple found in Java. Built in 1970, the grounds of the temple are tranquil and often busy with practicing Buddhists meditating and praying among the lotus ponds, while the sound of chimes tinkle in the background. Visitors are welcome to make use of the meditation areas and admire the gold-plated Buddhas given to Bali as gifts from Thailand and Sri Lanka. As you walk through the grounds, note the blend of Balinese, Javanese, Thai, and Hindu influences that make up the Brahmavihara-Arama temple. The main meditation room is adorned with intricate paintings, the scent of incense, and a statue of Prince Siddhartha.

TOUR
★ RAMA LOVINA TOUR

tel. 82247752988; https://baliuncoveredtour. business.site; daily 7am-9pm; 600,000 Rp full day tour

Ketut, owner of Rama Lovina Tour, offers fullday and half-day tours that can be customized to suit your interests. Ketut can help plan waterfall treks, temple tours, and cultural trips. As a Lovina local, Ketut is very knowledgeable about the region and keen to share his favorite spots with guests.

Lovina

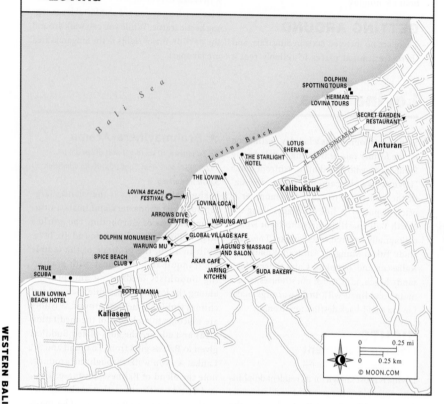

BEACH

LOVINA BEACH

(Pantai Lovina)

Access along Jalan Seririt-Singaraja; free

Pantai Lovina is Lovina's main beach made from dark sand and bordered by calm water, where you can sit and watch boats bob along the water. The beach stretches out from Kalibukbuk, Lovina's central village. Expect to be approached by local entrepreneurs in search of customers for the next day's snorkeling or dolphin watching tour.

WATER SPORTS

Diving and Snorkeling

While Pemuteran holds the reputation for being the region's best dive area, it's worth going on a boat dive or snorkeling tour around the waters of Lovina. Shore dives like Puri Jati, 10 km (6 mi) west of Lovina, are great for a chilled-out muck dive that's rarely crowded. The reef offshore of central Lovina Beach is a 5-minute ride in a *jukung* boat, where you're likely to see schools of tropical fish. Sadly, the reef is lackluster in parts due to damage from tourists stepping on coral, boat anchors, pollution, and a dark history of dynamite fishing. Farther offshore, the seabed deepens, and scuba divers will likely find carpets of anemones with their resident fish, nudibranchs,

1: Sekumpul Waterfall **2:** Brahmavihara-Arama **3:** Air Panas Banjar Hot Springs **4:** dolphin-watching at Pantai Lovina

Dolphin-Spotting Tours: Expectations vs. Reality

Every morning at sunrise, you'll hear the buzz of fishing boats loaded with tourists as they take to the waters off Lovina in search of resident dolphins. Most travelers expect a peaceful trip, where dwarf spinner dolphins are admired at a distance from the comforts of a quaint fishing boat. In the high season, more than 30 boats pursue the dolphins like hunters in search of prey, with each boat accelerating to be the one with the best view—it is more of a chase than a passive or peaceful experience. The long-term impact on the dolphins has not been well-studied, and it's unknown if and how the constant pursuit of boats and underwater noise has ill effects. If you do choose to participate in a dolphin-spotting tour, request that your boat driver follow the Dolphin SMART principles recommended by the U.S. National Oceanic and Atmospheric Administration.

- S: Stay at least 50 meters from the dolphins (pack a zoom camera lens or pair of binoculars for a close-up view).

- M: Move away slowly if the dolphins show signs of disturbance.

- A: Always put the vessel in neutral if dolphins are near.

- R: Refrain from feeding, touching, and swimming with wild dolphins.

- T: Teach others to be Dolphin SMART.

If tourists pressure boat captains to engage in dolphin-first behaviors, the experience may change into one that is more sustainable. Capping the number of boats that can go out, regulating boat speeds, and limiting the time spent with the dolphins are all acts that could improve the lives of Lovina's resident dolphins. Until these actions are in place, it's up to individual travelers to help morph the dolphin-spotting scene into one that is more ethical.

pygmy seahorses, lobsters, crabs, and Moray eels hiding among the coral bommies.

ARROWS DIVE CENTER

Jalan Mawar; tel. 362/41504; www.arrows-dive.com; daily 8am-9pm; 900,000 Rp local dives, 1,300,000 Rp Menjangan Island, 2 fun dives

Arrows Dive Center is a 5-Star PADI Dive Center that runs no-frills snorkeling tours and dive trips around the area. Courses range from open water to rescue. Local hotel pickup service is included with the cost of each dive. Most trips venture to Pemuteran, Menjangan Island, and Lovina Reef.

TRUE SCUBA

Jalan Seritit-Singaraja; tel. 8123833338; www. truescubabali.com; daily 7am-10pm; 700,000 Rp local dives, 1,100,000 Rp Menjangan Island, 2 fun dives

Most dives at True Scuba are led by Mangku,

the founder of the PADI Dive Center and a dive instructor who is passionate about marine conservation. The dive center hosts scuba courses ranging from discover to divemaster and runs trips to Lovina Reef, Menjangan Island, Pemuteran, and Tulamben.

OTHER SPORTS AND RECREATION

Dolphin Spotting Tours

HERMAN LOVINA TOURS

tel. 81915665544; www.lovinatours.com; daily 5:30am-6pm; 100,000 Rp per person shared boat, 300,000 Rp per person private boat

Herman Lovina Tours arranges dolphin-spotting tours, where you can see pods of dolphins swimming offshore of Lovina at sunrise. The tour agency can also help with transportation, day tours, and snorkeling excursions.

Yoga
LOTUS SHERAB
Jalan Raya Seririt; tel. 85339128680; classes Tues.-Sun. 9am-11am, 5pm-7pm, closed Mon.; 120,000 Rp class

Lotus Sherab is a small yoga studio that overlooks the water, where classes are taught on an open-air terrace. Groups are kept small, and the instructor, Yvonne, is happy to offer pose adaptations for beginner yogis.

Spas
AGUNG'S MASSAGE AND SALON
Jalan Damai; tel. 362/42018; www.agungs.com; daily 11am-7pm; 135,000 Rp 60-minute Balinese massage

Agung's Massage and Salon is a rustic spa offering massages, scrubs, manicures, pedicures, and waxing. Treatments take place in an outdoor garden where the sound of chickens clucking and scratching adds to the overall charm. Afterward, guests can shower outside and end their spa session with a hot cup of tea. Because the spa is somewhat hard to find, request pickup and drop-off if you're staying in the Lovina area.

ENTERTAINMENT AND EVENTS
KRISNA FUNTASTIC LAND
Jalan Raya Seririt; tel. 8113887709; www. krisnafuntasticland.com; daily 4pm-10pm; 76,000 Rp per person for unlimited rides, 10,000 Rp admission weekdays, 15,000 Rp admission weekends

Krisna Funtastic Land is a funky theme park where families can drive bumper cars, zoom down waterslides, climb around in an old Boeing 737 airplane, and take a ride on the Ferris wheel. At night, the park lights up. It's a bit small for teens and adults, but younger kids will likely love it.

★ LOVINA BEACH FESTIVAL
Pantai Lovina; Sept.; free

Plan your trip to Lovina during the Lovina Beach Festival, a three-day event held on Lovina's central beach where you can witness a parade, dance and music performances, puppet shows, art exhibitions, and live music.

Pop-up stands serving Balinese fare and cold drinks are also set up along the festival area.

FOOD
Markets
LOVINA NIGHT MARKET
Jalan Raya Lovina; daily 5pm-11pm; 20,000-40,000 Rp

After sunset, the Lovina Night Market comes to life with the smell of grilled meat and chili. It's an upbeat scene where you can sample many plates without putting a dent in your budget. Fresh produce is also sold here, sourced primarily from the Central Mountains.

Indonesian
WARUNG AYU
Jalan Mawar; tel. 82147555034; daily 8am-11pm; 15,000-60,000 Rp mains

Warung Ayu is a family-run warung that serves Balinese classics like *gado-gado, nasi campur, mie goreng,* and *nasi goreng,* with their seafood basket being one of the most popular picks. The warung also serves pizza and fries, though they're rightfully outshined by the local menu options.

JARING KITCHEN
Jalan Damai; tel. 82146580046; daily 11:30am-10pm; 30,000-60,000 Rp mains

Enjoy classic Balinese meals at Jaring Kitchen, an open-air warung built from bamboo and decorated with red tassled umbrellas. Cheerful staff match the vibe of the restaurant's simple yet silly menu that describes its veggie burger as a "veggiesaurus" and black rice pudding as "50 shades of black." If you're hungry for more, enroll in the restaurant's cooking class, where you can learn to create your favorite meals.

SECRET GARDEN
Jalan Pura Dalem Lovina Singaraja; tel. 8873321007; daily 5pm-10pm; 60,000-130,000 Rp mains

Secret Garden is a romantic restaurant that has an open seating area surrounded by well-kept gardens and accented with fresh flowers.

Private tables under a thatched umbrella make for a private anniversary or celebratory meal. Curries, fried rice, and satay skewers are the highlights of the menu, with chocolate cake, crepes, and *pisang goreng* (fried banana drizzled with syrup) tempting guests to order dessert.

European
★ BUDA BAKERY

Jalan Damai; tel. 8124691779; daily 8am-11pm; 40,000-70,000 Rp mains

Buda Bakery serves thoughtfully presented dishes in a casual dining room with red brick walls accented by local art pieces. It's set over two floors, with a downstairs bakery serving an array of pies, tarts, cakes, and fresh loaves of bread. Upstairs, the dining area overlooks the neighborhood and has a slightly fancier atmosphere. Mains include pork ribs, fresh fish, pork *rendang* (spicy stew), stuffed lobster, and duck served with cauliflower puree. The bakery also sells customized cakes made to order.

★ SPICE BEACH CLUB

Pantai Lovina; tel. 85100012666; www. spicebeachclubbali.com; daily 10am-midnight; 70,000-250,000 Rp mains

Head to Spice Beach Club for sunset. This upbeat beach club is known for its seafood platters and tuna steaks, though pizzas, pasta, ribs, and burgers are available as well. In the evenings, the venue often hosts live music along with Balinese dance performances on its seaside stage. Bamboo structures, driftwood decor, white paint, and lounge chairs keep the club loyal to its seaside aesthetic.

Vegan and Vegetarian
★ AKAR CAFÉ

Jalan Binaria; tel. 362/3435636; daily 7am-10pm; 30,000-60,000 Rp

The casual Akar Café serves a variety of vegan and vegetarian meals in a quirky all-green restaurant with green menus to match. Come in the morning for breakfast to have omelets, waffles, breakfast wraps, or granola.

At lunch, the menu switches to serve a range of Mediterranean and Asian meals like falafel and hummus, pasta with chili, chickpea and spinach curry, quiches, and salads. The dessert menu is worth a glance—especially the vegan crepe flavored with lemon zest and cinnamon brown sugar.

International
GLOBAL VILLAGE KAFE

Jalan Raya Lovina; tel. 362/41928; www. globalvillagefoundation.net; daily 8am-10pm; 20,000-70,000 Rp

Global Village Kafe is a restaurant where all profits go toward the Global Village Foundation, a charity that works toward providing healthcare and education for those in Bali's most impoverished areas. The restaurant is decorated with portaits of inspirational figures, sculptures, and motivational quotes, creating an inclusive atmosphere. The menu is extensive, with a long list of vegetarian, Indonesian, and European items—to an almost overwhelming degree. Jewelry, paintings, sculptures, and souvenirs are for sale onsite for a fair price.

BARS AND NIGHTLIFE

Lovina is a destination where travelers come to chill rather than to party, but there's still fun to be had once the sun goes down. As a general rule, if the spot has marketed itself as a bar, steer clear of their food. Bars in Lovina can draw a raucous crowd and serve good deals on drinks, despite their grubby exteriors.

WARUNG MU

Jalan Binaria; tel. 87762758222; daily 2pm-11pm; 15,000-40,000 Rp drinks, 20,000-60,000 Rp mains

Warung Mu is a funky reggae bar decorated with dream catchers and chimes made of driftwood, and doused in rasta colors. It's small and busy, and the owner is often around chatting with guests and offering local trip recommendations. Don't leave without adding your name to the wall.

PASHAA

Jalan Singaraja-Gilimanuk; tel. 87787017149; daily 7pm-late; 40,000-60,000 Rp drinks

Pashaa hosts Lovina's largest dance floor, where guests can work it until the early morning. The crowds can be hit or miss when it comes to the vibe, depending on who is playing. While it's rarely packed, it's worth taking a peek inside before venturing elsewhere for the night.

ACCOMMODATIONS
Under 1,000,000 Rp
★ LOVINA LOCA

Jalan Mas Lovina; tel. 817359993; 100,000 Rp dorm bed, 200,000 Rp double room

Lovina Loca is the type of place you'd create as a kid if someone were to ask you to draw a hotel with a box of crayons. This whimsical homestay has rooms where each wall is a different color, motivational signs hung up around the property, and furniture that looks almost as if it's built from pieces of wood found and then glued together. Somehow, it works. There are dorm rooms with single twin beds, as well as double and triple rooms on-site. All have private bathrooms and include breakfast. Both fan and air-conditioned rooms are available.

BOTTELMANIA

Jalan Krisna; 250,000 Rp double room

Bottelmania doesn't look like much from the outside. Once you wander inside, you'll find a well-stocked game room with a pool table, ping pong table, and Wii, as well as an indoor pool and Jacuzzi. Rooms are spacious, clean, and equipped with TVs, air-conditioning, and a private bathroom. A hearty breakfast is included with each stay, and the property is just a 5-minute walk from the beach.

THE STARLIGHT HOTEL

Jalan Starlight; 362/7005271; www.starlight-bali. com; 700,000 Rp double room

The Starlight Hotel hosts airy beachside bungalows and villas that can accommodate up to seven people. All come with a balcony, flat-screen TV, Wi-Fi access, private bathroom, mini-fridge, electric kettle, and a safe. Their beachside restaurant serves fresh seafood and cold drinks in an atmosphere that might tempt you to pass on the hotel's free shuttle service to central Lovina.

Over 1,000,000 Rp
LILIN LOVINA BEACH HOTEL

Jalan Singaraja; tel. 362/41670; https:// lilinlovinabeachhotel.com; 900,000-1,500,000 Rp double room

At Lilin Lovina Beach Hotel, shorefront bungalows have their own plunge pool. The one- and two-bedroom bungalows are designed with a beach chic aesthetic, all with a playful porch that's the perfect spot to laze with a book in hand. All units have air conditioning, Wi-Fi, a mini-fridge, and drinking water. When you're feeling hungry, follow the beach to the hotel's restaurant, which often hosts live music at sunset.

THE LOVINA

Jalan Mas Lovina; tel. 362/3435800; www. thelovinabali.com; 1,500,000 Rp double room

The Lovina might have been the classic hotel that Anak Agung Panji Tisna envisioned when he destined Lovina to be a holiday tourism hub. It attracts honeymooners, but all will love the range of suites and villas that are elegantly decorated with light wooden furniture and paintings crafted by local artists. Some villas and suites have sea views, while others look out to rice paddies behind the resort. Days are started with a buffet breakfast, and rooms are equipped with air-conditioning, a TV, minibar, safe, and Wi-Fi. It's easy to keep busy with the resort's complimentary use of kayaks, bicycles, snorkeling gear, and there's a shuttle bus that zips guests to and from central Lovina. The two resort pools, the beach bar, and the restaurant ensure that you don't spend too much time outside the hotel.

★ THE DAMAI

Jalan Damai; tel. 81338437703; www.thedamai.com; 1,500,000-3,000,000 Rp double room

Surrounded by dense vegetation, The Damai is an inland retreat with views that stretch out to the sea. Each villa is decorated with tasteful Indonesian artwork and furnished with dark wood. Some villas have garden or ocean views, and some have their own pool (or pools). Small details like open-air showers, floor-to-ceiling windows, and a private veranda add to the tropical luxe appeal. When you step outside your villa and into the restaurant, enjoy meals made from produce harvested from the resort's garden. The spa offers massage treatments, scrubs, manicures, and pedicures.

INFORMATION AND SERVICES
LOVINA GOVERNMENT TOURIST INFORMATION OFFICE

Jalan Singaraja-Gilimanuk; tel. 81936352377; www. dispar.bulelengkab.go.id; Mon.-Sat. 8am-8pm; closed Sun.

This simple tourist office has maps of the area and staff who can help arrange tours and activities for a fixed price. Their website has information on upcoming regional festivals and events.

GETTING THERE
By Bus and *Bemo*

To come from Bali's southern end, you will first need to make your way to **Singaraja.** *Bemos* run regularly from Singaraja's **Banyusari Terminal** to Lovina, dropping off passengers anywhere along Lovina's main road, **Jalan Seririt-Singaraja,** for 20,000 Rp. From Pemuteran, head to Singaraja and request to be dropped off earlier in Lovina to avoid backtracking.

The **Perama** shuttle bus (Jalan Seririt-Singaraja, 3.5 km/2 mi east of central Lovina Beach; tel. 362/41161; www.peramatour. com; daily 8am-6pm) services Lovina from **Bedugul** (1.5 hour; 75,000 Rp), **Candidasa**

(3.5 hours; 175,000 Rp), **Padangbai** (3 hours 45 minutes; 175,000 Rp), **Kuta** (3.5 hours; 125,000 Rp), **Sanur** (3 hours; 125,000 Rp), and **Ubud** (3.5 hours; 125,000 Rp). Travel times can vary widely.

By Car

Lovina is easily reached with your own set of wheels from **Denpasar** (81 km/50 mi; 2.5 hours), **Kuta** (87 km/54 mi; 2.5 hours), **Amed** (90 km/56 mi; 2.5 hours), **Ubud** (70 km/43 mi; 2.5 hours) **Kintamani** (60 km/37 mi; 2 hours), **Singaraja** (10 km/6 mi; 20 minutes), and **Pemuteran** (50 km/31 mi; 1 hour 15 minutes). From Kuta, Denpasar, and Ubud, it is best to drive directly north, following signs to Singaraja, connecting to Jalan Baturiti Bedugul. Take the main road that wraps over the northern shoreline of Danau Buyan and Danau Tamblingan, Jalan Raya Wanagiri. From there, turn right on Jalan Asah Gobleg and connect to Jalan Bangkiang Sidem, following roads north to Lovina. Road turnoffs are unmarked, so it's best to have a GPS or preloaded map on Maps.me to navigate through the area. From Kintimani, take Jalan Gn. Batur to the main coastal road, Jalan Raya Singaraja, and pass through Singaraja following the main coastal road to Lovina. From Amed, stay on the main coastal road 90 km (56 mi) west to Lovina. From Pemuteran, go via the coastal road, Jalan Singaraja-Gilimanuk, and it's 50 km (31 mi) east to Lovina.

Getting Around

Many activities, restaurants, and hotels offer **free transport** within the 8-km (5-mi) stretch of Lovina. You can easily **cycle** (30,000 Rp per day rental) along the main road of **Jalan Seritit-Singaraja** or **walk** within central Lovina (the town of **Kalibukbuk**). The road is also easily accessed by **motorbike** (50,000 Rp per day rental).

Pemuteran

Fishing was Pemuteran's largest industry until scuba divers peeked at the underwater world that spans from Pemuteran to Menjangan Island. Humble resorts dot the shoreline and have slowly crept inland to Pemuteran's village community, blending tourism and everyday life. All the while, temples like Pura Melanting, Pura Pulaki, and Pura Pabean guard the community from malevolent spirits and are often crowded with locals partaking in traditional ceremonies.

Pemuteran is somewhat of an enigma compared to Bali's other popular beach towns. You can lounge on the sand without the presence of those touting their goods and tours, and wander through the many streets and alleys that venture from the main road, Jalan Singaraja-Gilimanuk, without being disturbed. While you're here, it's worth exploring the world's largest bio reef project, an artificial coral reef that's teeming with sea life and best seen through the lens of a snorkel mask.

SIGHTS
Melanting Temple
(Pura Melanting)
Jalan Pura Melanting

A staircase leads to an arch marked by barong's open mouth at Pura Melanting, one of the trio of temples in Pemuteran. The temple is primarily used for local ceremonies, and rarely draws a crowd of outsiders. If you're intrepid, head here to watch the sunrise.

★ Pulaki Temple
(Pura Pulaki)
Jalan Singaraja-Gilimanuk; tel. 81337485388

Pura Pulaki is the most sacred temple in Pemuteran, built on a jagged coastal ledge. The temple opens out to the ocean and hosts a roadside shrine where many Balinese Hindus slow down to pay tribute—some drivers do it in the form of a horn honk. Legend states that the temple, as well as Pura Melanting

and Pura Pabean, are devoted to the daughter of Dang Hyang Nirartha, a Javanese Hindu priest who came to Bali to establish temples and start the Shaivite priesthood. Legend states that Pura Pulaki honors his daughter. Unfortunately, the original temple was destroyed in the 1979 earthquake and was rebuilt in 1980.

Pura Pulaki is spiritually guarded by monkeys and physically overrun with them to the point where many shrines have cages around them to stay protected from their handsy landlords. At low tide, the monkeys often scramble to the shoreline and search for food in the exposed rocks. If it's hot outside, you might even catch them doing cannonballs into deeper pools of water, swimming and splashing as they cool down.

Pabean Temple
(Pura Pabean)
Jalan Singaraja-Gilimanuk; tel. 8179790411

Stylistically, Pura Pabean is similar to its neighboring temples. Paying homage to Pura Pabean was thought to bring good fortune to traders who came by Bali's northern coast, usually from Java or China. Buddhist and Islamic influences are seen in the color choice and architecture of the temple, revealing its heritage.

Project Penyu Turtle Hatchery
Jalan Singaraja-Gilimanuk, at Reef Seen Divers; tel. 8123894051; https://reefseenbali.com; daily 9am-5pm, feeding daily at 4:30pm; 25,000 Rp entrance

The number of green sea turtles, native to the waters off Bali's coastline, has dwindled for decades. Overfishing, reef damage, and development in areas where turtles nest have caused undue stress to the population to the point where they are now endangered. Odds aren't in the favor of green sea turtles, as it

Pemuteran

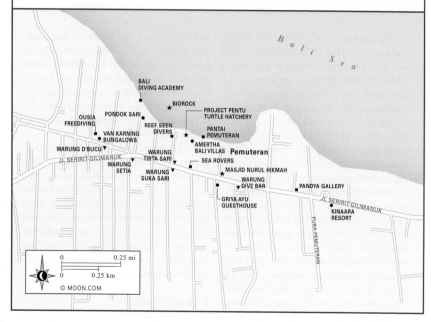

Bali Diving Academy
BIOROCK
PROJECT PENTU TURTLE HATCHERY
OUSIA FREEDIVING
PONDOK SARI
REEF SEEN DIVERS
PANTAI PEMUTERAN
VAN KARNING BUNGALOWS
AMERTHA BALI VILLAS
WARUNG D'BUCU
WARUNG TIRTA SARI
SEA ROVERS
Pemuteran
JL. SERIRIT-GILIMANUK
WARUNG SETIA
WARUNG SUKA SARI
MASJID NURUL HIKMAH
WARUNG DIVE BAR
PANDYA GALLERY
GRIYA AYU GUESTHOUSE
JL. SERIRIT-GILIMANUK
KINAARA RESORT
PURA PEMUTERAN

Bali Sea

0   0.25 mi
0   0.25 km
© MOON.COM

takes 15 years for turtles to breed and only one in a few hundred hatchlings survives to adulthood. Olive ridley and hawksbill turtles also lay eggs around the region.

At Project Penyu Turtle Hatchery, volunteers and staff provide incentives for locals to alert the project of turtle nests so that the eggs can hatch without the threat of being destroyed or eaten. Then, the conservationists take care of the hatchlings in a tank until they are large enough to be released into the wild. Guests can visit the turtle hatchery, donate, and sponsor a hatchling's release. Turtle release happens from 9am-10pm as needed.

Biorock

Pantai Pemuteran; www.biorock-indonesia.com;
sunrise-sunset; free, donation requested

The Pemuteran Biorock is a marine conservation program that works to stimulate coral growth and provide structures to protect

juvenile reef fish, with the goal of creating a healthy underwater environment. During a tumultuous economic climate in the late 1990s, fishermen used cyanide and dynamite along the coral reefs to kill hundreds of fish at a time, damaging coral reefs that took centuries to grow into their once-pristine form. Structures made of metal and cement are placed at the Biorock Project area, where you can snorkel or scuba dive in search of interesting sculptures. Bicycles, Buddhas, Hindu figures like Garuda and Vishnu, pyramids, and dozens of other oddities await.

Masjid Nurul Hikmah

Jalan Singaraja-Gilimanuk

Pemuteran's main mosque was recently renovated and is stunning with its colorful rooftops and pastel blue walls. Because of its proximity to Java, Pemuteran has a higher Muslim population compared to many of Bali's other coastal towns.

What Is Coral Gardening?

Biorock project

CORAL BASICS

Corals are small invertebrate animals called cnidaria, related to sea anemones and jellyfish. Each individual coral is a tiny polyp, and they grow on top of one another to form a colony. These colonies of coral polyps form the beautiful structures of a coral reef. Hard corals form a calcareous skeleton, which is what you see when you find a white piece of broken coral while walking along Pemuteran's shoreline.

Though corals are more than 200 million years old, they are fragile and can only thrive in very specific conditions. Coral reefs are an asset to healthy seas, as they provide food for sea turtles and a habitat for juvenile pelagic fish, reef fish, and small critters like nudibranchs and seahorses.

CORAL GARDENING

Coral gardening is when young corals are grown in a protected area until they reach a size where they have a chance to survive in the wild. Coral crags are gathered from the seabed and used to spur further coral growth. Structures in the Biorock project are built from steel and have low-voltage electricity running through them via cables that are buried on the beach. The current causes the creation of limestone around the steel structures, a prime base for coral growth. The project reports that the use of this method helps corals grow two to six times faster than they would without the help of coral gardening and Biorock's technology.

BEACHES
PEMUTERAN BEACH
(Pantai Pemuteran)
Accessed along small roads leading from Jalan Singaraja-Gilimanuk

Pantai Pemuteran is the main beach in town, with ash and tan colored sand. The water is generally calm, and there are coral bommies off the shoreline, making it a prime snorkeling destination. It's easy to find a spot to yourself. Beach resorts, restaurants, *jukung* boats, and dive centers line up against the sand.

★ SCUBA DIVING, SNORKELING AND FREEDIVING

Pemuteran hosts nearly 20 dive sites in the region and makes for an ideal base to explore

Menjangan Island. Sea turtles, whale sharks, eagle rays, and reef sharks are often the headline acts of local dives, though if you look closely you'll find an abundance of nudibranchs, sea sponges, and pygmy seahorses camouflaging themselves inside Gorgonian sea fans.

Depths of more than 100 meters (328 feet) are just a short boat ride away from the shoreline of Pemuteran. Warm, clear, and still water make it a freediver's playground.

REEF SEEN DIVERS

Jalan Singaraja-Gilimanuk; tel. 8123894051; https:// reefseenbali.com; daily 8am-6pm; 1,100,000 Rp local, 1,800,000 Rp Menjangan Island for 2 fun dives

Reef Seen Divers' Resort was the first dive resort in Pemuteran, and its divemasters were some of the first to name the dive sites in the area. The owner, Chris Brown, is passionate about conservation and developing projects within the community, like hosting a youth dance group, protecting turtle hatchlings through Project Penyu, and managing a coral garden in front of the dive center. Reef Seen offers PADI dive courses ranging from Discover Scuba to advanced open water. A restaurant and basic accommodation are available on-site as well.

SEA ROVERS

Jalan Singaraja-Gilimanuk; tel. 8113857118; https:// searovers.net; daily 8am-7:30pm; 1,100,000 Rp local, 1,800,000 Rp Menjangan Island for 2 fun dives, packages available

The owner of Sea Rovers, Paul, looks like he needs a peg leg and a hook to match his pirate-themed dive center. He has a penchant for keeping diving groups small. The dive center offers SSI and SDI dive courses, from Discover Scuba to Divemaster, with special courses on photography. Snorkelers are welcome onboard, and it's possible for mixed groups of scuba divers and snorkelers to venture on the same trip if requested in advance.

BALI DIVING ACADEMY

Jalan Singaraja-Gilimanuk; tel. 81339176652; https:// scubali.com; daily 7:30am-6pm; 1,000,000 Rp local, 1,600,000 Rp Menjangan Island for 2 fun dives

Bali Diving Academy is a PADI Dive Center set on the sandy shores of Pemuteran. The staff are friendly and efficient, running fun dives around the region and hosting scuba courses ranging from Discover Scuba to Divemaster.

OUSIA FREEDIVING

Jalan Raya Taman Sari; tel. 811907594; www. ousiafreediving.com; daily 7am-7pm; 1,250,000 Rp AIDA 1 course, 3,750,000 Rp AIDA 2 course

Founded by Yoshua Surjo, an accomplished Indonesian freediving instructor trainer, Ousia Freediving teaches AIDA freediving courses, ranging from beginner to instructor level. Coaching and training sessions complete with video analysis are also available. Yoshua's style of teaching is calm and methodical, complementing the relaxed mindset that's needed to succeed at the sport. Equipment rental is included with each course.

SHOPPING

PANDYA ART GALLERY

Jalan Singaraja-Gilimanuk; tel. 81338536318; www. tarunapemuteran.com; daily 8am-10pm

Pandya Art Gallery is a cluttered shop that sells handicrafts like stone and wood sculptures, masks, figurines, jewelry, clothing, scarves, and other souvenirs. Ground coffee is also available for purchase.

FOOD

Indonesian

WARUNG SUKA SARI

Jalan Singaraja-Gilimanuk; tel. 81338262829; www.sukasaricottages.com; daily 7:30am-10pm; 20,000-60,000 Rp

Warung Suka Sari is a family-run open-air warung that serves plates of Balinese fare in

---

1: Pura Pabean **2:** diving in Pemuteran **3:** Pantai Pemuteran **4:** Project Penyu Turtle Hatchery

a garden area. Food is fresh, and their *sambal* (chili sauce) is some of the best around—it's worth asking for a serving on the side no matter what main dish you order.

★ WARUNG TIRTA SARI

Jalan Singaraja-Gilimanuk; tel. 362/3361245; www. tirtasaribungalowandspa.com; daily 9am-10pm; 30,000-80,000 Rp

The hull of an old *jukung* boat is used as the welcome sign to Warung Tirta Sari, where you can dine on fresh Balinese dishes around a cute garden. Meals are presented thoughtfully, often with floral or banana leaf accents. Guests are presented with a platter displaying the catch of the day, which is then cooked on the grill. Everything pairs well with their refreshing ginger iced tea. During the high season, the restaurant regularly hosts dance performances and live music.

WARUNG SETIA

Jalan Singaraja-Gilimanuk; tel. 85238311212; daily 10am-10pm; tel. 40,000-60,000 Rp

Come hungry to Warung Setia, where heaped portions of well-spiced noodles, rice, curries, satay, and soups are served alongside its most popular option, the sashimi. Being on the main road, it's noisier and dustier than many restaurants set back from the road or along the beachfront, but those downsides are easy to forget once the food comes out.

★ WARUNG D'BUCU

Jalan Raya Gilimanuk-Seririk; tel. 85338096639; daily 11am-10pm; 50,000-80,000 Rp

Make a reservation in advance at Warung D'Bucu, a warung that seems unremarkable from the outside and is hidden off the main road. The family-run warung serves plates of fresh fish, green curry, tempeh, satay, and more. Some of the local spearfishermen take their catch to Warung D'Bucu for them to clean and grill. Warung D'Bucu also delivers meals to nearby hotels.

Bars
WARUNG DIVE BAR

Jalan Singaraja-Gilimanuk; tel. 85253792939; daily 11am-11pm; 30,000-60,000 Rp

Warung Dive Bar serves pizzas, cocktails, and cold beers, and regularly hosts live music. Pemuteran is a sleepy town where it's hard to find a crowd that's awake after 9pm. Cheeky signs that could offend those with fragile egos hang around the bar, adding to the casual and cool vibe.

ACCOMMODATIONS
Under 1,000,000 Rp
GRIYA AYU GUESTHOUSE

Jalan Raya Gilimanuk-Seririk, on a side road across from the mosque; tel. 82147171516; 350,000 Rp double room

Griya Ayu Guesthouse is a new guesthouse hosting a handful of spacious and spotless rooms with tile floors. Each room comes with air-conditioning, a king-sized bed, an outdoor bathroom, and Wi-Fi access. Breakfast is served on a private patio. Though Wi-Fi is advertised, it's a bit unreliable. The owners of the guesthouse also own the laundromat at the beginning of the road and are happy to wash dirty clothes for an added cost.

VAN KARNING BUNGALOW

Jalan Singaraja-Gilimanuk; tel. 82342025252; 700,000 Rp double room

Feel as though you're staying in Pemuteran's village at Van Karning Bungalows, where red-roofed rooms are set around an immaculately kept garden and grass lawn. Each room has a double bed, air-conditioning, and fast Wi-Fi, and breakfast is included with each stay. The quaint outdoor bathrooms are a highlight with their pebble floors and showerhead that pours from a ceramic pot. The guesthouse pool is a bonus—a rarity for guesthouses in the area.

Over 1,000,000
★ PONDOK SARI

Pantai Pemuteran; tel. 362/94738; www.pondoksari. com; 800,000-2,000,000 double room

Set on the shores of Pemuteran's main beach,

Pondok Sari is a peaceful hotel with paths that weave through a large tropical garden accented with lotus ponds and shaded with palm trees. Each accommodation is uniquely Balinese with its intricately carved wooden furniture and antique decor, thatched roofing, and Indonesian fabrics. Guests can swim in the large pool, relax in the shade of a *bale* (pavilion), and dine with their toes in the sand at the seaside restaurant. Pondok Sari can also arrange dive trips with Werner Lau Dive Center.

★ KINAARA RESORT

Jalan Singaraja-Gilimanuk; tel. 362/3437271; www. kinaararesort.com; 1,200,000 double room

Kinaara Resort has a tropical resort feel, offering a lagoon-style swimming pool with a pool bar, shaded lounge chairs, and palm trees. The resort has two types of accommodation options: *lumbung* (barn) bungalows built from weaved bamboo, or thatched-roof wooden bungalows. Both types have air-conditioning, a private patio, a mosquito net, safe, and outdoor bathroom. When you want a break from the pool, head to the red-brick spa for a massage. Their open-air restaurant serves seafood and Indonesian fare that can compete with some of the best restaurants in town.

AMERTHA BALI VILLAS

Jalan Singaraja-Gilimanuk; tel. 362/94831; www. amerthabalivillas.com; 2,500,000 Rp double room

Amertha Bali Villas welcomes guests in its 15 luxury rooms and one- to two-bedroom villas that are steps away from the sand and the sea. Each option has Wi-Fi, air-conditioning, a daybed, an outdoor bathroom, a mini bar, and access to private pools of varying sizes. Everyone can enjoy the seaside restaurant and spa. Snorkeling is great just off the shore. A large well-kept lawn in front of the property ensures that nobody feels cramped.

INFORMATION AND SERVICES

ATMs are finnicky in Pemuteran, and you might have to try a few. They're located along the main road of Jalan Singaraja-Gilimanuk.

GETTING THERE
By Bus and *Bemo*

Pemuteran does not have an official bus station, but you can hop off buses or *bemos* that are running between Gilimanuk and Singaraja.

There is a private shuttle service, Pemuteran Shuttle (tel. 81238937651), that runs a once-daily shuttle service to and from Munduk (1.5 hours; 150,000 Rp), Ubud (3.5-4 hours; 225,000 Rp), Kuta (4-4.5 hours; 225,000 Rp), and Sanur (4-4.5 hours; 225,000 Rp).

By Car or Private Driver

Expect to pay around 600,000-800,000 Rp to get to Pemuteran from South Bali or Ubud.

Pemuteran is reached via Denpasar (130 km/80 mi; 3.5 hours), Kuta (135 km/84 mi; 3.5 hours), Ubud (120 km/75 mi; 3 hours), Lovina (50 km/31 mi; 1 hour), or Gilimanuk (30 km/18.5 mi; 45 minutes). To reach Pemuteran from Kuta, Denpasar, and Ubud, you can drive directly north following signs to Gilimanuk. Roads heading through the Central Mountain region are often unmarked; using GPS or downloading a map through Maps.me is recommended. Driving from Bali's southern end west along the coastal road, Jalan Raya Denpasar-Gilimanuk to Jalan Singaraja-Gilimanuk adds an extra 30 km (18.5 mi) but is the simplest route. From Lovina, drive 45 km (28 mi) west along Jalan Singaraja-Gilimanuk. From Gilimanuk, drive 30 km (18.5 mi) east on Jalan Singaraja-Gilimanuk.

GETTING AROUND

Pemuteran is spread out on one 8-km (5-mi) strip. You can walk to most places in the area if you are based along Jalan Singaraja-Gilimanuk, though driving your own car or motorbike is much more convenient, and can be rented through your accommodation or from stands along Jalan Singaraja-Gilimanuk.

West Bali National Park

West Bali National Park (Taman Nasional Bali Barat) is the only national park on the island. It was declared a conservation sanctuary in 1941 after government officials noticed the sharp decline in indigenous bird populations, like the Bali starling. Other animals like Javanese *rusa* deer, muntjac (barking) deer, wild boar, *bateng* (a small species of cattle), monitor lizards, and macaque monkeys reside in the park. The park covers nearly 200 square km (77 square mi), with 580 km (223 mi) of largely uninhabited land to its east. The landscape ranges from arid scrublands to coastal savannah to forest to mangroves, making it an interesting area for wildlife watching. Extinct volcanoes dominate the skyline.

If you plan to scuba dive or go on a snorkeling trip within the park boundaries, it is more economical and convenient to arrange this in advance through dive shops based in Pemuteran—almost all of them offer tours to Menjangan Island.

SIGHTS

★ Menjangan Island
(Pulau Menjangan)

250,000-350,000 Rp admission fee does not include guide; guides available for 350,000 Rp for 2 people from the park headquarters in Bali Barat National Park Headquarters or Labaun Lalang

Menjangan Island is part of the West Bali National Park and was named after the small barking deer, called muntjac, that inhabit it. The reefs surrounding Menjangan Island are the healthiest in Bali, where you can snorkel and scuba dive to see reef walls thriving with corals, sea sponges, and sea fans that resemble lace. Sometimes the barking deer walk to the water's edge and can be seen by snorkelers.

There is one wreck dive site offshore of Menjangan Island called **Anchor Wreck,** thanks to its coral-encrusted anchor. Sea life, like sea turtles, pygmy seahorses, Moray eels, electric clams, anemone fish, mandarin fish,

batfish, barracuda, reef sharks, and more all make their home in the reef areas around Menjangan Island. Tours and equipment are best arranged from your accommodation on Menjangan Island or from dive companies based in Pemuteran. The island is only accessible by boat.

PURA GANESHA MENJANGAN
northeast point of Menjangan Island

A large white statue of Ganesha under an elaborate arch guards Menjangan Island from evil spirits. Many locals believe that those who visit Ganesha will be rewarded with inspiration and creativity. The view from the temple looks out to the shallow reef beyond its rocky shoreline.

HIKING

Multiple trails divide the park. Almost all are unmarked and a bit overgrown, though they offer opportunities to spot wildlife. All hikers must be accompanied by a **guide.** Bring **food** and **water** into the park with you, as there are no shops inside the park.

Expect to pay 300,000 Rp for a short trek of up to two hours, 350,000 Rp for up to three hours, and 400,000 Rp for any treks longer than four hours. The best time to trek is at sunrise from August to November, before the wet season starts. Treks are arranged through the park headquarters. Putu Suardila, a local guide, offers customized tours for snorkelers and trekkers, and is best reached on WhatsApp at tel. 628123957889.

TEGAL BLUNDER TRAIL
Hiking Distance: *8 km (5 mi) out-and-back*
Hiking Time: *2.5-3 hours*
Information and Maps: *Bali Barat Nasional Park Visitor's Center*

1: muntjac deer on Menjangan Island **2:** reef surrounding Menjangan Island

The Tegal Blunder trail is an easy 2-hour out-and-back that offers the highest chance of seeing a Bali starling, a rare bird known for its white feather mohawk and royal blue circles around its eyes—it looks like a rockstar of the bird world. It starts at the **Bali Starling Breeding Center** and runs west toward **Pantai Prapat Agung.**

COASTAL LOOP TRAIL
Hiking Distance: *18 km (11 mi) loop*
Hiking Time: *4.5-6 hours*
Information and Maps: *Bali Barat Nasional Park Visitor's Center*
The Coastal Loop Trail cuts through the middle of West Bali National Park's large peninsula and weaves through forests with banyan trees to the eastern edge of the park. It begins at the **Bali Starling Breeding Center** and ventures west.

ACCOMMODATIONS
MENJANGAN HILL
Jalan Jalak Putih; tel. 82146612343; https:// menjanganhill.com; 850,000 Rp double room
Menjangan Hill is a remote getaway with just four bungalows built from bamboo on its property. While you're here, lounge by the pool that overlooks Bali's northern coastline and enjoy a fresh meal from the Menjangan Hill's on-site warung. The family that runs the property can help arrange fairly priced treks and day trips to java. Or, wander around Pejarakan village to get a feel for local daily life.

★ MENJANGAN DYNASTY
Jalan Pasir Putih; tel. 362/3355000; www. themenjangan.com; 2,000,000-3,000,000 double room
Feel connected to nature while still having luxurious amenities at Menjangan Dynasty, a glamping resort where giant safari tents look out to the channel separating the resort from the national park. All guests have access to a beachside infinity pool and can dine in an architecturally impressive restaurant built from bamboo. Scuba dives around Menjangan

Gilimanuk Bay and Transfer to Java

If you're coming from Java, you may find yourself at the **Gilimanuk Ferry Terminal** (Jalan Raya Denpasar-Gilimanuk); the ride costs 6,000 Rp and takes 1.5 hours, running every half hour. Just a short walk away is Gilimanuk Bay, often called "Secret Bay" by locals. While it's probably not worth a stop on its own, it's a great place to lounge and enjoy the tended gardens before or after transferring to Java. If you bring a snorkel and cruise around, you'll likely find some interesting macro life hiding amid the nearby mangroves.

Island are easily arranged, as are massage treatments at the open-air spa. All tents have a TV, air-conditioning, Wi-Fi, and a balcony.

INFORMATION AND SERVICES
BALI BARAT NATIONAL PARK HEADQUARTERS
The intersection of Jalan Singaraja-Gilimanuk and Jalan Raya Cekik; tel. 365/61060; daily 7:30am-5pm
The Bali Barat National Park Headquarters is the best place to find a reliable guide—the closer to the headquarter office, the better. You can look at maps, learn about wildlife, and discuss trail routes.

BALI BARAT NATIONAL PARK VISITOR'S CENTER
Jalan Labaun Lalang (turn onto signs directing you from Jalan Singaraja-Gilimanuk); daily 7:30am-5pm
This office can arrange guided treks and snorkeling tours to Menjangan Island, though it's typically less hassle to arrange things through your hotel.

TRANSPORTATION
Getting There
Buses and *bemos* run to **Gilimanuk** from Denpasar (Ubung Terminal, 50,000 Rp) and Singaraja (30,000 Rp). Once you are in Gilimanuk or the outskirts, you will need

your own **car** or **motorbike** to get into West Bali National Park.

Getting Around
The West Bali National Park area is best seen on a guided tour or with your own vehicle. Many of the trails are open to hikers and cyclists only. Mountain bikes can be arranged through **West Bali Explorer** (tel. 82146612343; westbaliexplorer@gmail.com).

Jembrana Area

Life moves at a slow pace in Jembrana, a sparsely populated region with Negara as its single large town. Though most travelers stop at Negara only for a quick bite before continuing onward, it's worth driving around town to admire the Buginese architecture with the signature balconies—particularly along Jalan Gunung Agung—built by mercenaries who came by boat from Sulawesi to fight for Jembrana's royal family in the late 1600s. Off the road connecting Denpasar in the south to Gilimanuk in the north, you'll find dirt paths where children run around without abandon. Everything is quiet until the buffalo races are on. Then, the region comes alive.

The coastline of Jembrana hosts the neighborhood of Medewi, where surfers from all over the world come for their shot at riding the island's longest left.

BEACHES AND SURF BREAKS
Medewi Beach
(Pantai Medewi)
Jalan Pantai Medewi

A ribbon of gray sand and pebbles separates some of Bali's best waves from rice fields and palm trees. A shabby warung set up in front of Medewi's point break serves cheap snacks and cold Bintangs, the surfers' staples. At low tide, fishermen walk out along the rocks and cast their lines.

MEDEWI SURF BREAK
Paddle out from Pantai Medewi

If there's a swell, surfers from Bali's southern end will motorbike to Medewi before daybreak with the hopes of paddling out before the sunrise. Medewi is an iconic lefthander that is best surfed when it's a south-southwest 3- to 10-foot swell. Local surfers are notorious for being aggressive in Medewi, though some have mellowed out after the worst offenders were plastered on social media. Beginner-friendly beach breaks roll in along the shoreline in either direction of Medewi's main spot.

FOOD
WARUNG SRI TEN PANDAN
Pantai Yeh Sumbul; tel. 8111797006; daily 8am-10pm; 20,000-40,000 Rp

Warung Sri Ten Pandan is the ultimate spot for sunset where you can dine under a cluster of pandanus trees. Choose a fish for the grill or order a plate of their just-right spiced noodles. Beach lounge chairs shaded with umbrellas are available to all guests.

★ RASTA CAFÉ
tel. 85237020393; Sat.-Thurs. 11am-10pm, Fri. 5pm-10pm; 20,000-50,000 Rp

Bob Marley is well-represented at Rasta Café, a warung serving grilled fish, *nasi goreng, mie goreng, nasi campur,* and giant smoothie bowls in the midst of rice fields. Service can be slow, but that's easily forgotten once you have a coconut to sip on while you wait. The owners Dwi and her husband, "Rasta Man," are happy to chat about things to do in the area and where their penchant for reggae music came from.

KEDAI JUKUNG
tel. 87754917077; daily 11am-10pm; 20,000-60,000 Rp

Close to Medewi's surf break, Kedai Jukung

Bali's Buffalo Races

Buffalo racing in Bali, referred to as *makepung,* is a sport thought to have been brought over by Madurese farmers. Sunday mornings from August to November, farmers race their best buffaloes from a wooden chariot around a 4-km (2.5-mi) dirt track. The bull's horns are wrapped in intricate cloth and adorned with items that make them stand out. At many events, the races are followed by a bovine fashion parade. All throughout Jembrana, roads and sports fields are modified into training tracks. Each team of farmer-cum-jockey and buffalo, called *kerbau pepadu,* strives to win the regency's championship cup. It's a colorful clash of dirt and sweat. The air surrounding the races is thick with dust and excitement. The prizes for winning aren't grand, but the pride the racers take home to their village certainly is.

The life of a racing bull is somewhat more glamorous than that of an ordinary farm animal. Racing bulls are revered and are not typically used to plow fields. Many of them are fed *jamu,* a tonic that promotes good health. A ceremony takes place before each important race.

HOW TO SEE A RACE

Races start between 7:30 and 9am, so it's best to spend the night before in the region if you plan to watch one. Trips to watch the races can be arranged through a guide, Wayan Dodik Widnyana (tel. 8123972800; https://baikbaikbalitour.com).

makes for a great post-paddle meal. Burgers, chicken wings, fries, fish and chips, milkshakes, pizza, and pasta are all on offer at this nautical-themed restaurant with an aqua-blue exterior. Simple Indonesian dishes are available as well. The Oreo ice cream cake is a must on a hot day.

ACCOMMODATIONS

The best stays in the region are found in between the rice fields of Medewi. Mosques in the region host their call to prayer at all hours of the day. Light sleepers should pack earplugs.

DIKALOHA SURF CAMP

Jalan Pantai Yeh Sumbul No. 91; tel. 87862317208; https://dikalohamedewisurfcamp.com; 150,000 Rp double room

Surrounded by rice fields, Dikaloha Surf Camp is a laid-back surf retreat where terraces look out to the ocean. Guests can take surf lessons with Dika, the owner of the camp and a patient surf instructor. The five rooms at the guesthouse are clean and come with hot water showers. You can opt for a package that includes daily surf lessons, accommodation, airport transfers, breakfast, and local tours (including a visit to the buffalo races) for 710,000 Rp per day.

AGA LIVING VILLA

Jalan Gelogor Carik Gg. No. 3; tel. 365/4501878; www.agalivingvilla.com; 500,000 Rp double room

Aga Living Villa is a comfortable resort a short walk away from Medewi's main surf break. The grounds are well kept, with tropical flowers throughout the property, adding to the getaway feel. Their best rooms overlook the beach, which is often cluttered with colorful fishing boats on the sand. All rooms have air-conditioning, a TV, Wi-Fi access, and hot water showers. The friendly owner, Aga, and his staff work hard to make guests feel as though they're at home.

UMADEWI SURF AND SUITES

Jalan Pantai Medewi; tel. 85100700080; 1,000,000 Rp double room

Umadewi Surf and Suites is the spot to stay if you're keen to be the first surfer out in Medewi each morning. The newly renovated beach resort offers chic, minimally decorated rooms with air-conditioning, a TV, and balcony with a surfboard rack. The beachfront bungalows open out to the beach, and it's possible to watch the waves roll in from the comforts of your bed. Community areas like a book swap library, pool, and outdoor restaurant make it a place you might not leave the whole time you're in Medewi.

★ DAJUMA

Jalan Ngurah Rai; tel. 811388709; www.dajuma.com; 1,500,000 double room

Dajuma is a quirky eco resort that has 35 rooms around its large property, including suites, bungalows, and one- to three-bedroom villas. Each option is equipped with air-conditioning and a fan, a mini-fridge, a safe, Wi-Fi access, and a kettle. The higher-end options also have a kitchenette and satellite TV. Three kids' pools, one 60-meter lap pool with a slide, and two infinity pools tempt guests to stay out of the ocean, which is only steps away. Three restaurants and a handful of bars ensure that nobody stays hungry—or sober. There are plenty of things to do here, with games, cultural workshops, daily yoga classes, and spa treatments. Kids will love it here.

INFORMATION AND SERVICES

ATMs are available in Negara but are scarce in Medewi, where vendors typically prefer cash.

GETTING THERE

Expect delays and traffic jams in the Jembrana area. Trucks running between the north and south points of the island are often too big to let traffic pass on this region's narrow roads. The best way to get here is by **car.** Medewi is 20 km (12 mi) or 40 minutes south of Negara. Negara is accessible by car from **Denpasar** (100 km/62 mi; 3 hours) and **Gilimanuk** (33 km/20 mi; 45 minutes). Arriving to the region is easy by driving west along Jalan Raya Denpasar-Gilimanuk from Denpasar and driving east along Jalan Raya Denpasar-Gilimanuk from Gilimanuk.

By Bus and *Bemo*

You can catch a bus to Negara or Medewi on *bemos* running between **Denpasar** (Ubung Terminal) and **Gilimanuk.** Request to be dropped off along the way (50,000 Rp).

GETTING AROUND

The only efficient way to get around the region is with your own **car** or **motorbike.**

colorful fishing boat on the beach by Aga Living Villa

Negara Gamelans

Negara is famous around Indonesia for its music ensembles, or gamelans, that play *jegog* music, where musicians use 14 bamboo xylophones to create percussive rhythms. Traditional dancers perform wearing bold costumes with golden crowns and tassels, emphasizing hand and facial expressions to convey a feeling. The instruments are often painted in bright colors and adorned with images of Hindu deities—especially in music troupes that play regularly at Balinese ceremonies.

In Jembrana, it's common to see two gamelan orchestras participate in a *mebarung,* a battle where two teams play against one another to see who can capture the audience's heart. Musicians and their listeners often seem to fall into a trance while playing and listening to *jegog* music, and it can be a challenge to know when one song ends and another begins.

SEEING A PERFORMANCE

Ask your accommodation or local restaurant staff where you can listen to live performances. Restaurants, hotels, and cultural sites in Ubud often have gamelan performances with musicians trained in Negara.

Tabanan

Patchwork patterns of green make up Tabanan, a regency that's quilted in rice terraces. The *subak* system in Tabanan is a recognized UNESCO World Heritage method for emulating the *tri hita karana* philosophy that combines mankind, nature, and the spiritual world. Inland, Tabanan is predominantly a farming community that's staved off the encroachment of hotels from Bali's populous southern point. When you think of Tabanan, think of tranquility.

SIGHTS

★ Tanah Lot Temple
(Pura Tanah Lot)

Jalan Tanah Lot; tel. 361/880361; daily 7am-7pm; 60,000 Rp adult, 30,000 Rp child, 2,000-5,000 Rp parking

Tanah Lot ranks as one of the most-visited temples in Bali, and if you venture here during high season, the crowds certainly reflect this. Despite the throngs of tourists armed with selfie sticks, it's one of the best spots to watch the sunset. The temple is on a small island 100 meters offshore. At high tide, water swirls around the temple and spindrift lingers in the air for an ethereal look. At low tide, Balinese Hindus may enter the temple to worship. The temple was built at the command of Dang Hyang Niratha and honors the spirits that preside over the sea.

Taman Ayun Temple
(Pura Taman Ayun)

Jalan Ayodya No. 10; tel. 361/9009270; daily 8am-6pm; 20,000 Rp admission includes sarong rental

Fortressed by a moat, Pura Taman Ayun is a relic of the village of Mengwi's prominent past. In the 16th century, the kingdom of Mengwi was the strongest in Bali thanks to its great military power, with an influence that extended to eastern Java. The Mengwi kindom fell in 1891 after being sabotaged by its neighbors, leaving behind Pura Taman Ayun, built in 1634.

On one side of the temple, a series of *merus* form a row where each one is higher than the one before it. The highest *meru* has 11 tiers, signifying its importance on the island. Gardens, lotus ponds, and ceremonial areas are spread throughout the temple.

The Truth About *Kopi Luwak*

Kopi luwak is known for being the world's most expensive coffee, where just a kg (2.2 lbs) can cost upward of $150 USD. *Kopi luwak* is made from coffee beans that have been swallowed, digested, and excreted by a civet cat. It's thought that the enzymes from the civet cat's stomach create a better flavor than coffee beans processed using traditional methods. In the wild, civet cats would eat the coffee cherries as they pleased. Then, farmers would comb coffee plantations in search of their feces.

Today, however, most *kopi luwak* in Bali comes from cruel means. Civet cats are kept in cramped, squalid conditions. They're often force fed a diet of only coffee cherries rather than eating a range of foods as they would in the wild. The quality of life for a civet cat kept in a cage is low, and mortality rates are high. Because the industry is unregulated, many coffee shops that claim to source *kopi luwak* from wild civets are sadly misguiding their customers. Also, taste tests show that there is virtually no difference in a cup of regular coffee versus one that came from civet cat feces.

Coffee sampling is no doubt a must-do while in Bali. Sampling *kopi luwak,* however, is not.

Ogoh-Ogoh Bali Museum

Jalan Ayodya No. 1; tel. 81337951854; daily 9am-6pm; donation requested

Ogoh-ogoh masks are a bit of an onomatopoeia that are used as demon effigies intended to ward off evil spirits. The goal is to impersonate demons that are fiercer than the demons themselves. Each year on Pengrupukan, the day before Nyepi, the day that Bali shuts down, these *ogoh-ogoh* masks and monsters are paraded through the streets before being smothered in flames. At the Ogoh-Ogoh Bali Museum, you can grimace at the masks and statues that have bulging eyes, pendulous breasts, long tongues, gnashed teeth, strings of matted hair, and yellow nails that look like they're ready to harvest entrails.

Subak Museum

Jalan Gatot Subrato; tel. 361/810315; Mon.-Thurs. 8am-4pm, Fri.-Sat. 8am-noon, closed Sun.; 15,000 Rp adult, 10,000 Rp child

The *subak* system in Bali is a method of farming rice that is a philosophical and religious system just as much as it is an agricultural one. At the Subak Museum, learn about the different tools, methods, and beliefs that go into harvesting each grain of rice. Before water irrigates a rice field, it must flow through a temple. Then, the water feeds into the rice paddies through a series of terraces and canals.

Farmers tend to the rice, harvesting it only on sacred days. Next to the museum is a traditional home that explains the layout of most Balinese homes. Note the home's position in relation to Gunung Agung and the ocean.

BEACHES AND SURF BREAKS

Balian Beach
(Pantai Balian)

Access Jalan Pantai Balian

Pantai Balian is a mellow, wide, black sand beach with some tatty, and some cute warungs at the back, and they all serve cold beer. Balian straddles a rivermouth that can get polluted after a big storm, which is somewhat ironic as the beach was named Balian after balian, Bali's traditional healers. The river mouth was once thought to have healing properties, though it's not advisable to surf after it rains—you might get sick. Surf stands rent boards in all conditions, and the stand attendant is sure to know someone who can help repair any surfboard dings you accrue in the water.

BALIAN SURF BREAK

Paddle out from Pantai Balian

The main break at Balian peaks left and right at a rocky river mouth. You won't usually find a huge crowd unless it's flat on Bali's southern end. The wave is a swell magnet that works best from 3 to 10 feet and needs south-southwest swell.

FOOD

BALIAN NIGHT MARKET

Jalan Raya Denpasar-Gilimanuk; daily 6pm-10pm; mains from 15,000 Rp

Every day after sunset, the Balian Night Market comes alive with stands selling deep-fried vegetables and spring rolls, crepes, satay skewers, grilled fish, and fried bananas.

SUSHI SURF

Pantai Balian; tel. 81238045178; daily 7am-10pm; 20,000-130,000 Rp

Enjoy colorful sushi rolls, nigiri, soups, and salads at Sushi Surf, a casual open-air restaurant with tables that overlook the beach. Fresh juice and cocktails are also available, though the bartender has a light hand when it comes to pouring the spirits.

★ SIZZLEWRAPS

Jalan Tanah Lot; tel. 81239548265; daily 8am-11pm; 30,000-50,000 Rp

Sizzlewraps serves burritos, quesadillas, wraps, and salads all made fresh to order in front of you. Choose the fillings you like or opt for the "Burgeritto," which has all the trimmings of a hamburger wrapped inside of a tortilla and served with a side of fries. Gluten free, vegetarian, and vegan options are available.

ACCOMMODATIONS

OYO SEKAR ARUM GUESTHOUSE

Jalan Pantai Nyanyi; tel. 361/4790694; www.sekararumresort.com; 200,000 Rp double room

Oyo Sekar Arum Guesthouse is a no-frills but clean guesthouse a 10-minute drive away from Tanah Lot. Some stand-alone rooms are in newly built wooden bungalows, while others belong to the main block. All have a private bathroom, TV, and patio. The community pool is a nice bonus given the guesthouse's price.

SUN SANG ECO VILLAGE

Jalan Raya Denpasar-Gilimanuk; sunsangecovillage.com; 600,000 Rp double room

Sun Sang Eco Village is a resort surrounded by trees where each bungalow is built from bamboo with alang-alang (grass) roofs. Inside, the furnishings are made of wood or bamboo and beds are draped in mosquito nets. Staying here feels like you've moved into a treehouse. Sounds of singing birds, running water, and thrumming frogs hum in the background.

Pantai Balian

For breakfast, enjoy meals made with produce from the resort's permaculture garden.

DE MOKSHA

Jalan Benuo; tel. 361/4790790; www.villamoksha. com; 1,000,000 Rp double room

A retreat that's removed from any semblance of city life, De Moksha is a luxury boutique resort with rooms, as well as one-bedroom, and two-bedroom villas. The architecture is interesting—bordering on bizarre—with green leaf-shaped roofs with jutting rooftop gardens plopped on top of solid white walls. Somehow, it works. All guests have access to a pool (private or shared), and the stand-alone villas have kitchens. Outdoor bathrooms add to the novelty of the place. Yogis will enjoy classes at the yoga *shala* (studio). Fresh Balinese fare is served in a restaurant surrounded by rice fields and tropical plants.

★ WAKAGANGGA

Jalan Pantai Yeh Gangga; tel. 361/8469699; https:// wakahotelsandresorts.com; 2,500,000-3,500,000 Rp double room

At WakaGangga, guests can stay in luxurious one- to two-bedroom villas with conical roofs; many villas open out to a personal pool and gazebo. Each villa is spacious and timelessly decorated with Balinese textiles and wooden sculptures. Canopy-covered beds, large windows, a stand-alone bathtub, and a small wall dividing each villa creates an intimate and romantic feel. Outside, enjoy the beachside pool, lounge area, restaurant, and spa.

GETTING THERE

Tabanan itself isn't crowded, but it's very prone to traffic jams. Day-trippers venturing to **Tanah Lot,** improper planning, and big trucks rumbling through the narrow roads create long congo lines of cars and motorbikes.

By Bus or *Bemo*

Bemos running the **Gilimanuk-Denpasar** route pass through Tabanan, where you can get dropped off along the way (50,000 Rp). From there, you might be lucky to find an *ojek* or private driver—but you shouldn't depend on it.

By Private Driver

Tabanan is easily accessed by car from **Denpasar** (23 km/14 mi; 1 hour), **Kuta** (30 km/18.5 mi; 1 hour 15 minutes), **Ubud** (25 km/15.5 mi; 1 hour), and **Jembrana** (75 km/46.5; 2 hours). If you are coming from the south, budget extra time for travel.

GETTING AROUND

You will need a **motorbike** or **rental car** to easily get around Tabanan. Rideshare apps and taxis outside of Tanah Lot are uncommon.

The Gili Islands

No matter what type of beach life you're into,
you'll likely find it on the Gili Islands. These three little islands off Lombok's northwestern coastline, surrounded by coral reefs, make up one of the sea turtle capitals of the world. And who can blame these laid-back creatures for choosing the Gili Islands as their home? On land, the pace of life is slow, the drinks are cold, and you're never more than a 10-minute bike ride away from a sandy beach. It's the type of place where you can spend days enjoying the water world of scuba diving, snorkeling, freediving, surfing, and paddling, all before snoozing in a hammock or in a beanbag chair.

Each of the islands has its own appeal. For vibrant nightlife, an abundance of restaurants, and many dive centers to choose from,

Highlights

Look for ★ to find recommended sights, activities, dining, and lodging.

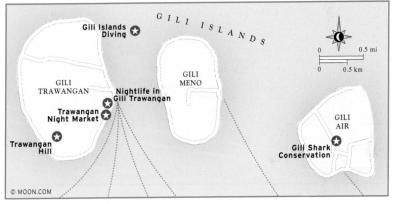

© MOON.COM

★ Trawangan Hill: Enjoy views of the islands, mainland Lombok, and Bali from the top of a modest hill (page 356).

★ Gili Islands Diving: Explore underwater to find out why these islands are known as the sea turtle capital of the world (page 360).

★ Trawangan Night Market: Sample traditional Sasak dishes, snacks, and produce at Gili Trawangan's most popular place to eat (page 361).

★ Nightlife in Gili Trawangan: Drink and dance to tropical beats on a pub crawl (page 364).

★ Gili Shark Conservation: Immerse yourself in local life during a two-week volunteer program where you gather data about sharks after learning to scuba dive (page 374).

Gili Islands

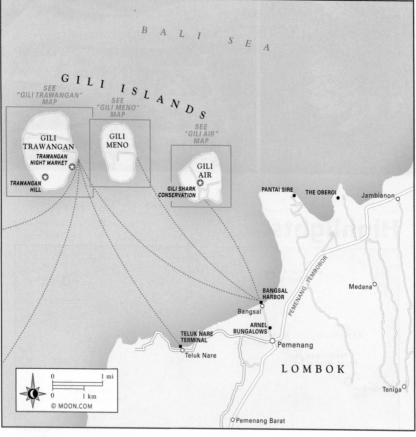

B A L I   S E A

G I L I   I S L A N D S

SEE
"GILI TRAWANGAN"
MAP

SEE
"GILI MENO"
MAP

SEE
"GILI AIR"
MAP

GILI
TRAWANGAN

TRAWANGAN
NIGHT MARKET

TRAWANGAN
HILL

GILI
MENO

GILI
AIR

GILI SHARK
CONSERVATION

PANTAI SIRE   THE OBEROI   Jambianon

PEMENANG - TEMBOBOR

Medana

BANGSAL
HARBOR

Bangsal

ARNEL
BUNGALOWS

TELUK NARE
TERMINAL

Teluk Nare

Pemenang

LOMBOK

Teniga

0   1 mi

0   1 km

© MOON.COM

Pemenang Barat

tell your boat driver to take you to Gili Trawangan. Gili Air is a mellow island, yet it has plenty of restaurants and a small taste of nightlife. Gili Meno is the least developed of the three islands and offers a sense of authenticity that will have you feeling nostalgic for days before the Gili Islands turned into one of Indonesia's most popular destinations. On all islands, you'll discover white sand beaches, intriguing coral reefs, and strong communities that unified and rebuilt themselves after the devastating 2018 earthquakes that brought down many of the islands' homes and buildings.

ORIENTATION

The Gili Islands are three tiny islands off the northwest coast of Lombok. Each takes less than two and a half hours to walk around. **Gili Trawangan,** the largest of the three Gili Islands, is the farthest offshore, about 5 km (3 mi) away from mainland Lombok. **Gili Air** is

Previous: Gili Meno boats; lionfish; Trawangan Night Market.

Top Restaurants

★ **Pituq:** This is the place to go to enjoy Indonesian classic meals made with mock meat. Bring all your friends, as plates are meant to be shared (page 362).

★ **Casa Vintage:** Dine on Caribbean cuisine and enjoy bonfires at the beach (page 362).

★ **Mahamaya:** This luxurious restaurant serves seafood in a romantic atmosphere (page 371).

★ **Waroeng Alam Damai:** Freshly cooked Indonesian fare is offered in an open-air restaurant built from bamboo (page 377).

★ **Mama Pizza:** Consider this the best seaside wood-fired pizza place on the Gili Islands (page 377).

the closest island to shore, less than 2 km (1.2 mi) from the shoreline. **Gili Meno** is sandwiched in between. **Bangsal,** on Lombok, is the main point of departure for public boats to the Gili Islands, though it's possible to come from a few ports on **Bali** as well. Coral reefs known for being home to sea turtles surround the white sandy beaches of the Gili Islands.

PLANNING YOUR TIME

The Gili Islands are the type of place where you intend to stay a week and end up staying for much longer. You can get a good feel of **Gili Meno** over two days, but **Gili Trawangan** and **Gili Air** command at least two to three nights. For nightlife, restaurants, and a vast choice in accommodations, opt for Gili Trawangan. If you seek a shoreline that is mellow and romantic, Gili Air is a top contender. Gili Meno is the least built-up of the trio and has stunning beaches alongside a traditional Sasak feel. **Dive centers** run dive trips around all three islands, so it doesn't matter which island you stay on, even if you have a particular dive site in mind.

Because each of the Gili Islands is so small, all are affected by the crowds of **high season.** The best accommodations are booked out at least a month in advance during December and early January, and from July to early

September. The **shoulder months** of March, April, October, and November will allow you to enjoy the Gili Islands in their prime, without the congestion of bicycles clogging the seaside paths.

Once you are on the Gili Islands, there is no form of motorized transportation. On every island, your destination is just a **walk** or bicycle ride **away.**

GETTING TO THE GILI ISLANDS

There are many ways to get to the Gili Islands. Each island has a port, and both public and private boats run between the islands regularly throughout the day. Weather conditions and strong swells can delay or cancel boats traveling between Lombok and Bali, and swimming between the islands is dangerous due to strong currents and boat traffic.

It's possible to take the public ferry from **Padangbai,** Bali to **Lembar Harbor,** Lombok for 46,000 Rp adult and 29,000 Rp child, but it's a 5-6.5-hour journey compared to an average of 1.5-2 hours on a fast boat. In addition, **Lembar Harbor,** mainland Lombok, is a 2-hour taxi ride from Bangsal Harbor, where public boats run regularly to the Gili Islands. The fast boat is likely a more practical option.

Top Accommodations

★ **Blu D'Amare:** Cozy *joglos* (traditional wooden houses) on the edge of Gili Trawangan's main drag have a rustic yet luxury feel (page 366).

★ **Pesona Beach Resort:** This bohemian hotel with an eco-friendly spirit has a restaurant, spa, dive center, and *shisha* (smoking) lounge on its beachside premises (page 366).

★ **Gili Treehouses:** Luxury meets deserted island as you sleep in a wooden treehouse that sits above a private pool (page 368).

★ **The Rabbit Tree:** You won't find a similar hostel anywhere in this whimsical place where ball pits, labyrinths, and mountains of plush pillows are the norm (page 371).

★ **Captain Coconuts:** You'll feel as though you've lucked out on a deserted isle in rooms built from reclaimed wood with solar-heated showers. Beds are suspended from the ceilings (page 378).

From Bangsal Harbor

Bangsal Harbor, located on mainland Lombok's northwest coast, is the closest harbor to the Gili Islands. **Gili Air** is about 10 minutes away from Bangsal Harbor. **Gili Meno** and **Gili Trawangan** are 5-10 minutes apart in succession (14,000 Rp Gili Air, 15,000-25,000 Rp Gili Meno, 20,000 Rp Gili Trawangan boat ticket). **Public boats** run regularly, leaving when full.

Bangsal Harbor has a reputation for being a stressful place where you must search for a true staff member among a crowd of imposters. Almost everyone who greets you will want a commission when helping you sell a ticket. When you already have one, hasslers may try to tell you that your ticket is no longer valid and pressure you to purchase another. Put your blinders on and walk straight to the **official ticket stations,** marked by large signs. Employees working for boat and transport companies usually wear a logoed shirt. Private boat drivers also offer their services. The going rate is typically 85k/person or 400k/per entire boat charter that can accommodate up to 10 people.

Bangsal is about 1.5-2 hours away from **Lombok International Airport** in **Praya** (60 km/37 mi), 30 minutes from **Senggigi Beach** (20 km/12 mi), and one hour from **Mataram** (30 km/18.5 mi) by car. Taxi fares typically range around 100,000 Rp to Senggigi, 100,000 Rp to Mataram, 250,000 Rp to Lombok International Airport, and 300,000 Rp to Kuta, Lombok.

Perama Shuttle Bus (tel. 361/751875; Peramatour.com) services Bangsal from **Mataram** (60,000 Rp), **Lombok International Airport** (175,000 Rp), and **Senggigi** (60,000 Rp). The bus needs at least two travelers to run.

Teluk Nare Terminal

Jalan Raya Senggigi; tel. 85274547993; open 24/7

Boats also arrive and depart from Teluk Nare Terminal, 5 km (3 mi) west of Bangsal Harbor. Teluk Nare Terminal is generally less crowded and ideal for chartering private boats to/from the Gili Islands (85,000 Rp per person or 350,000-500,000 Rp per boat for up to 10 people). Transfers can be arranged through **Feel Lombok** (tel. 85938380730; https://feel-lombok.com).

LOMBOK PRAYA INTERNATIONAL AIRPORT

Jalan By Pass Bil Praya; tel. 370/6157000; https:// Lombok-airport.co.id

Direct flights from Bali's **Ngurah Rai International Airport** to Lombok Praya

Stopover in Bangsal

Dreary compared to the Gili Islands, the port town of Bangsal is home to the main harbor for boats running between Lombok's mainland and the Gili Islands. If you need to stay in Bangsal itself, expect persistent touts for boat tickets and transport around the island. This aggressive pestering has unfortunately spoiled what could be a pleasant area. Once you enter Bangsal, you'll find quaint beaches and luxury resorts north and south of the harbor.

BEACHES

Pantai Sire (East of Bangsal Harbor, enter near Anema Resort) is a stretch of white sand and coral east of Bangsal Harbor that is popular with locals rather than tourists. There is a handful of warungs and hotels selling drinks or snacks, and offering access to beach lounges. The water is mellow and idyllic for swimming when the sea is clear.

Raw and undeveloped **Pantai Sejuk** (2 km/1.2 mi north of Bangsal Harbor) embodies Lombok's pre-tourism days. Palm trees line the sand, which is often speckled with bits of bleached coral and seaweed.

ACCOMMODATIONS

- **Arnel Bungalows** (Jalan New Bangsal; tel. 85205422220; 400,000 Rp double): Within walking distance of Bangsal Harbor, this no-frills guesthouse is run by a helpful family, offering useful suggestions of things to do and assistance with arranging transportation. This is a prime spot if you are arriving in Lombok late and want to make your way to the Gili Islands or elsewhere in Lombok in the morning. Rooms are clean and minimally furnished, and all have spotty Wi-Fi access.

- **The Oberoi** (Pantai Medana; tel. 370/6138444; www.oberoihotels.com; 8,000,000 Rp double): This is one of the best luxury resorts in Lombok, with five-star service across its 9-hectare (24-acre) property. Regal rooms and villas are furnished with dark wood, with windows opening out to the garden or ocean. Some villas have a private pool, though everyone is welcome at the resort's infinity pool. Snorkel and scuba dive with the on-site dive center. Then, return for a massage or scrub at the spa. Meals are served in an open-air restaurant every night, with traditional cultural performances happening regularly.

GETTING AROUND

Having your own **motorbike** or using a metered **Bluebird Taxi** (available through the My-Bluebird app) is best for getting around Bangsal.

International Airport are offered by Lion Air (www.lionair.co.id), AirAsia (www.airasia.com), NAM Air (www.flynamair.com), Sriwijaya Air (www.sriwijayaair.co.id), and Garuda Indonesia (www.garuda-indonesia.com). The flight time is about 20-30 minutes and costs around 400,000 Rp one way, though prices rise from June to August. The app and website Skyscanner (www.skyscanner.com) is one of the best ways to find cheap flights. Flying to Lombok is a good option if you plan to do some traveling around mainland Lombok before or after your time on the Gili Islands.

Lombok Praya International Airport is a 1.5-hour **drive** or **taxi ride** (250,000 Rp) from Bangsal Harbor. **Perama Shuttle Bus** also services Bangsal from the airport.

By Fast Boat from Bali

Several fast boat companies run between the Gili Islands and Bali. The crossing from **Padangbai** takes 1.5 to 2 hours and costs 350,000-700,000 Rp. Bad weather and rough seas can double these travel times. Some fast boats stop in Bali's Nusa Islands first, extending your journey to 4 hours. Listed prices are not always cheapest; it's worth trying to negotiate a better deal. Some boats stop at all Gili Islands and Bangsal Harbor. From **Benoa Harbor, Sanur,** and **Serangan Harbor,** the travel time is around 2.5 hours. Some companies to consider are:

- **Gili Gili Fast Boat:** Departs **Padangbai;** tel. 361/763306; www.giligilifastboat.com; 552,000 Rp adult one way
- **Blue Water Express:** Departs **Serangan** and **Padangbai;** tel. 361/8951111; https://bluewater-express.com; 870,000 Rp adult, 770,000 Rp child one way
- **Patagonia Xpress:** Departs **Benoa Harbor** and **Padangbai;** tel. 361/756666; www.patagonia-xpress.com; 550,000-650,000 adult one way
- **Scoot:** Departs **Sanur** and stops at **Nusa Lembongan;** tel. 361/271030; scootcruise.com; 750,000 Rp adult, 650,000 Rp child one way
- **Gili Getaway:** Departs **Serangan;** tel. 8113801717; https://giligetaway.com; 710,000 Rp adult, 560,000 Rp child one way

By Helicopter

Air Bali (tel. 81236598171; www.airbali.com) runs a helicopter service from **Benoa, Bali** (Jalan Raya Pelabuhan Benoa) to Gili Trawangan (45 minutes; from 15,000,000 Rp).

Itinerary Ideas

THREE DAYS ON THE GILI ISLANDS

Day 1: Gili Trawangan

1 Wake up before sunrise for a morning paddleboard session—or paddleboard yoga session—with **Fly Gili Water Sports and SUP Yoga.**

2 Shop for souvenirs along **Jalan Gili Trawangan,** near the boat landing area. Yin sells beautiful silver jewelry.

3 Have a healthy lunch at **Kayu Café.**

4 Walk to the top of **Trawangan Hill** for sunset to enjoy views of the islands and mainland Lombok.

5 Watch the sunset with dinner and a bonfire on the beach at **Casa Vintage** before bar-hopping until the last bar closes.

Day 2: Gili Meno

1 Spend the morning searching for sea turtles and admiring the **Nest Sculpture Garden** while snorkeling off Gili Meno's shoreline.

2 Stop for a drink at **Diana's Café.**

3 Head to inland Gili Meno for lunch at **Pojok No 5 Star.**

4 Cycle around Gili Meno with swim breaks in between, with a detour to **Gili Meno Lake.**

5 Finish with a romantic sunset dinner at **Mahamaya.**

Itinerary Ideas

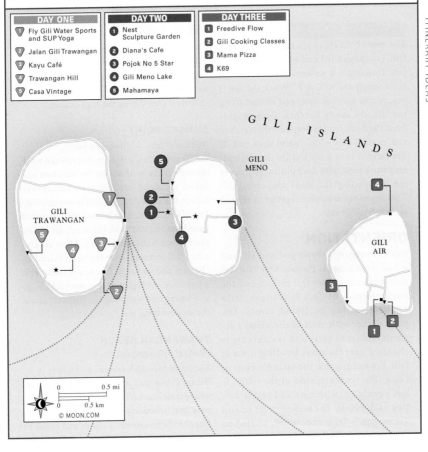

DAY ONE
1. Fly Gili Water Sports and SUP Yoga
2. Jalan Gili Trawangan
3. Kayu Café
4. Trawangan Hill
5. Casa Vintage

DAY TWO
1. Nest Sculpture Garden
2. Diana's Cafe
3. Pojok No 5 Star
4. Gili Meno Lake
5. Mahamaya

DAY THREE
1. Freedive Flow
2. Gili Cooking Classes
3. Mama Pizza
4. K69

GILI ISLANDS

GILI MENO

GILI TRAWANGAN

GILI AIR

0   0.5 mi

0   0.5 km
© MOON.COM

Day 3: Gili Air

1   Spend the morning taking a freediving course at **Freedive Flow.**

2   Learn to cook a local meal, and enjoy it after, at **Gili Cooking Classes.**

3   Walk around Gili Air, stopping for pizza and a beer at **Mama Pizza.**

4   Post-sunset, hang out at **K69,** where you can admire local artwork and chat with the owner.

Gili Trawangan

The most boisterous island of the bunch, Gili Trawangan is Lombok's unruly child. Gili Trawangan is its formal name, though most simply call it "Gili T." While the sun is out, people snorkel, dive, and lounge along the island's sandy beaches. Come nighttime, the main road is clogged with travelers and locals: Those who live and work on Gili Trawangan have a work ethic that embodies a work hard, play hard philosophy. After the 2018 earthquake, those who called Gili Trawangan home banded together to rebuild at an incredible rate.

ORIENTATION

Gili Trawangan is the largest and farthest island from Bangsal Harbor. One **coastal sidewalk** runs 6 km (3.7 mi) around the circumference of Gili Trawangan, with roads dissecting the island across. The main village with most of the island's accommodations, bars, and restaurants is clustered near the **boat landing area** of Gili Trawangan, on the island's eastern coast. The **western side** of the island is less populated, with bars and hotels dotting its shoreline. The highest point on Gili Trawangan is **Trawangan Hill,** located on the southern half of the island.

SIGHTS
★ Trawangan Hill

Trail starts next to Sunset Point from Jalan Gili Trawangan; free

At 60 meters (197 feet) above sea level, Trawangan Hill is the highest point on the island. There are two trailheads. One starts from Sunset Point, and the other starts from Jalan Sunset Road, near La Boheme. The walk takes about 15 minutes to complete and offers views of Lombok's mainland, Gili Air, and Gili Meno.

BEACHES

The coastline of Gili Trawangan is covered in white sand. Walk around the island and stop at whatever beach calls to you. The northwestern side of the island tends to be the least crowded, even during the high season.

SUNSET POINT

West side of Jalan Gili Trawangan; free

Gili Trawangan is unique in that you can wake up and see the sunrise over the water on one side of the island and admire the sunset over Bali on the same day. The southwestern coastline of Gili Trawangan is lined with bars that have beanbag chairs in the sand, an idyllic place to watch the sun go down. There are also a handful of swings over the water placed by the bars and warungs; free to use them with a purchase. At high tide, it's enjoyable to go snorkeling and watching the fish dart about the shallow coral reef.

TRAWANGAN BEACH (Pantai Trawangan)

East side of Jalan Gili Trawangan; boat landing

Pantai Trawangan is the island's main beach, where most boats arrive and depart. Warungs, bars, hotels, boutiques, and bike rental stands line the shore, crowding closer and closer to the water each year. This beach is fun for people watching and lounging, though it can be dangerous for swimming due to the boat traffic.

WATER SPORTS
Surfing and Stand-Up Paddling
BONGKAS REEF SURF BREAK

Paddle out from southwest point

Bongkas Reef Surf Break is a fast and hollow right-hander that needs a large southsouthwest swell to work. The currents are strong and the reef is sharp and shallow,

Gili Trawangan

making it a bit of a beast. Reef booties are recommended. There are small surf stands nearby that rent boards for about 50,000 Rp per hour.

FLY GILI WATER SPORTS AND SUP YOGA

Jalan Gili Trawangan; tel. 81907683924; daily 6am-5:00pm; 100,000 Rp 1-hour SUP rental, 750,000 Rp parasailing, 500,000 Rp wakeboarding, 300,000 Rp guided snorkeling tour, 250,000 Rp 75-minute SUP yoga

Fly Gili offers daily sunrise yoga classes taught on a stand-up paddleboard—a memorable start to the day. The shop also rents paddleboards, snorkeling gear, and transparent kayaks to explore the calm waters off Gili Trawangan. Wakeboarding, parasailing, and tube riding are available for thrill-seekers. For something different, take a ride on the subwing, a submersible wing that riders can use to feel like they're flying underwater. You may receive a 15 percent discount for booking multiple activities.

Rally to Rebuild: Aftermath of the 2018 Earthquakes

On July 29, 2018, a 6.4 magnitude earthquake struck on Lombok, a foreshock to the 6.9 earthquake that occurred a week later on August 5, 2019. The main earthquake and its aftershocks caused major damage to almost all of the structures in North Lombok, including the Gili Islands. Many of these buildings collapsed, killing 563 people and injuring thousands more. Landslides, power outages, and a shortage of resources followed for weeks to come. The 2018 earthquake is the strongest earthquake to hit Lombok in recorded history.

Chaos and panic occurred on the Gili Islands following the earthquakes, with tourists and locals desperate to leave the island and make it onto the mainland. Thousands of people fled to Trawangan Hill, fearing a tsunami. On Gili Air and Gili Meno, there was no higher ground to flee to.

Some chose to immediately set up an emergency medical clinic. Dive instructors trained in first aid and emergency response administered basic treatments to those who were injured. After the injured and the majority of the island evacuated, those who stayed behind formed makeshift task units to knock down unstable structures that could kill or injure someone in a future quake, cleared out rotting food to prevent infestations, locked up businesses, and moved their valuables to avoid looting—even if the business belonged to a competitor. Without the passion and quick response from those who stayed behind, the Gili Islands would no doubt have had a much longer recovery.

Scuba Diving, Snorkeling, and Freediving

BLUE MARLIN

Jalan Gili Trawangan; tel. 370/6132424; www. bluemarlindive.com; daily 8am-9pm; 540,000 Rp fun dive, 5,900,000 Rp open water course

Blue Marlin was the first dive center to set up shop on Gili Trawangan in 1992 and is now a renowned 5-Star PADI dive resort and TDI technical diving facility. Many of the sites were named by or after its founder, Simon Liddiard. Blue Marlin welcomes all, no matter if you're a first-time diver or looking to progress from your existing training. Every Monday night, Blue Marlin also hosts the best party on the island.

DIVE CENTRAL GILI

Jalan Gili Trawangan; tel. 370/6194839; www. divecentralgili.com; daily 8am-9pm; 540,000 Rp fun dive, 5,900,000 Rp open water course

Dive Central Gili is one of the newer 5-Star PADI dive resorts on Gili Trawangan, and a top choice for those who want the experience of a boutique dive center rather than one where you're more likely to get lost among the masses of students and divers. Courses range from Discover Scuba to Divemaster. Dive Central Gili's business is related to Blue Marlin, but the former has a more intimate atmosphere.

MANTA DIVE

Jalan Gili Trawangan; tel. 87865556914; https:// manta-dive.com; daily 8am-10pm; 540,000 Rp fun dive, 5,900,000 Rp open water course

Manta Dive is one of the largest dive centers on Gili Trawangan, offering SSI certifications from beginner scuba diver to Divemaster, with courses for technical divers available as well. At first, the sheer number of divers moving around the property can seem overwhelming, but friendly dive guides and instructors quickly lead you into your dive gear and out onto the water.

FREEDIVE GILI

Jalan Gili Trawangan; tel. 371/6197180; www. freedivegili.com; daily 9am-7pm; 4,250,000 Rp SSI Level 1

Learn to dive deep into the ocean on one breath at Freedive Gili, a freediving and yoga

1: surfing at Trawangan Beach 2: Blue Marlin boat

☆ The Gili Islands' Best Dive Sites

The reefs around the Gili Islands are a haven for sea turtles, reef sharks, rays, nudibranchs, and many more interesting creatures. Dive sites range from deep wrecks to mellow, shallow reefs, where there is always something new to explore, along with the **Gili Islands BioRock** project (www.gili-paradise.com/gilis-information/dive-the-gilis/dive-operator/biorock-project), where artificial reefs made from steel and stimulated with a low voltage current are becoming habitats for corals, sponges, and reef fish.

These are some of the best dive sites around the islands.

GILI TRAWANGAN

- **Deep Turbo:** This site looks somewhat otherworldly, with bizarre formations of coral bommies, sea mounds, and jagged ledges. Garden eels cover the seabed, disappearing if you get too close.

- **Halik:** With a mild current, Halik makes for an ideal drift dive where you can admire coral reefs and their residents. Sea turtles, reef sharks, and rays are often spotted here.

- **Shark Point:** Meet the island's toothy residents at Shark Point, where you can usually find white tip reef sharks tucked underneath the reef's ledge. Sea turtles, cuttlefish, bumphead parrotfish, rays, and eels also enjoy this spot.

GILI MENO

- **Simon's Reef:** An interesting array of corals await at this reef dive that gives way to a sandy seabed. Close looks might reveal interesting macro life while a peek under coral overhangs reveals hiding rays and reef sharks.

- **Turtle Heaven** (Beginner+, 10-30 meters/33-98 feet): Sea turtles steal the spotlight at Turtle Heaven, a dive site that's earned its name thanks to its resident green sea turtles, hawksbill turtles, and loggerheads. Dive alongside chilled out sea turtles as they laze around the reef.

---

center that has accommodation for trainees. Founded by national record holders Kate Middleton and Mike Board, the center is a hub for those who want to master the art of moving meditation. Yoga teacher trainings and advanced freediving workshops take place throughout the year. Yoga classes are offered for freedivers and non-freedivers multiple times per day (www.giliyoga.com; 120,000 Rp 60-minute class).

OTHER SPORTS AND RECREATION

Bicycles are available for rent along **Jalan Gili Trawangan,** especially near the **boat landing area,** for about 50,000 Rp per day. Most stands will request the name of your hotel and a local phone number if you're renting for multiple days.

Yoga
SUNSET YOGA

Jalan Gili Trawangan; www.villasunsetbeach.com; daily classes 8:30am and 4:30pm; 130,000 Rp 75-minute class including juice

Stretch to the sound of the sea at Sunset Yoga, where yoga classes are taught on a raised bamboo platform that overlooks the ocean. Classes are offered twice per day, with one class taking place just before sunset. A highlight is the Fly High yoga class, where yogis do inverted poses and stretch with the help of a swing. Each class includes a free juice from the juice bar below.

SORAYA YOGA

Jalan Gili Trawangan (The Pearl Beachfront); www.sorayayoga.com; classes Mon., Weds., Sat. 6:15am; 150,000 Rp 60-minute class

Welcome the day with sun salutations at

Bounty Wreck

- **Bounty Wreck** (Beginner+, 25 meters/82 feet): The Bounty is less of an eerie shipwreck and more an old pontoon that sprung a leak and sunk to the bottom of the reef. Reef fish, corals, and crabs have completely taken over.

GILI AIR

- **Blue Plains:** Some of the world's quirkiest creatures like box fish, pygmy seahorses, lionfish, nudibranchs, and frog fish hide at Blue Plains Reef.

Soraya Yoga's sunrise classes, which take place on the sand. Postures can be scaled down for beginners, and a steady flow ensures that more experienced yogis won't be bored. Private yoga classes, guided meditations, and other energy healing services are available on request.

SHOPPING

Fixed-price boutiques selling jewelry, clothes, and accessories can be found along **Jalan Gili Trawangan** near the boat harbor.

YIN
Jalan Gili Trawangan; tel. 81236403151; www. yinjewelryforthesoul.com; daily 10am-6pm; 350,000 Rp class

Beautiful silver jewelry is sold at Yin, where you can also try your hand at crafting a piece

for yourself during a silver-jewelry-making workshop.

GILI ECO TRUST
Jalan Ikan Hiu; tel. 81339600553; www.giliecotrust. com; Mon.-Sat. 9am-5pm, closed Sun.

Gili Eco Trust is a shop selling reusable items, local artwork and crafts, and other eco-friendly items. Staff can also help arrange volunteer placements and provide information on their many animal, community, and environmental campaigns taking place throughout the Gili Islands.

FOOD
Markets
★ TRAWANGAN NIGHT MARKET
Corner of Jalan Bintang Laut and Jalan Gili Trawangan; 6:30pm-1am; 10,000-30,000 Rp

Culture Clash on Gili Trawangan

Traditionally, Gili Trawangan was—and in some ways still is—a socially conservative island where most of its local inhabitants practice Islam. Many locals wear clothing that covers most of their body, including their head, and abstain from alcohol. Compare this to the influx of tourists who enter the island in search of cheap happy hours, cycle around the island wearing nothing but a swimsuit, and partake in public displays of affection with their longtime partner or lover of the night. To show respect toward local customs, here are a few things to consider when enjoying the island.

- **Plan your stay around the call to prayer:** Five times per day, the local mosque hosts a call to prayer that can be heard throughout the island. Practicing Muslims will take time to complete their prayers, which sometimes take place in the early hours of the morning. If you're a light sleeper, don't forget your earplugs, or stay somewhere away from the **mosque** near the boat harbor on the eastern side of Gili Trawangan. Complaining to staff about the "noise" is rude.

- **Dress modestly when away from the beaches:** On the beach, it's acceptable to wear swimwear. However, when walking around the inner part of the island, men and women should cover up with a T-shirt, long shorts, or a sarong. Topless sunbathing is not acceptable.

Every evening, the grills fire up at the Trawangan Night Market. Sample fresh produce, Indonesian dishes, and fresh juices for a fraction of what you'd pay elsewhere. Its cramped seating area is busy with locals and tourists alike.

Vegan/Vegetarian
KAYU CAFÉ
Jalan Gili Trawangan; tel. 81917496698; daily 7am-9pm; 30,000-60,000 Rp

For the health-conscious, Kayu Cafe serves fresh all-day breakfasts, bagels, wraps, paninis, smoothie bowls, kombucha, juices, and coffee. Their glass cake display will tempt anyone with a sweet tooth. Sit indoors to enjoy the air-conditioning or head to the rooftop to feel the breeze and people-watch the busy road below.

★ PITUQ
Jalan Villa Kelapa; tel. 81236775161; https://pituq. com; Sat.-Weds. 9am-10pm, Fri.-Sat. 3pm-10pm; 30,000-60,000 Rp

Pituq is a community warung serving vegan Indonesian dishes, where you can try a classic dish like beef *rendang* (spicy stew) made with mock vegan meat. Dishes are made to share and split among friends, so go with a

group and don't shy away from trying anything on the menu you might not have considered otherwise. Proceeds from Pituq go toward rebuilding communities that were heavily damaged in the 2018 earthquake.

★ CASA VINTAGE
Jalan Gili Trawangan; tel. 87704407271; www. casavintageliving.com; daily 8am-10pm; 40,000-90,000 Rp

Casa Vintage is a chic and stylish beachside restaurant where sunset bonfires are the highlight of every evening. Caribbean dishes are featured, including jerk chicken, fish stew, vegetable stew, and fried cassava, all with robust flavor. Enjoy your meal in a hammock, on a lounge chair, or at one of the beachside tables. All options are next to the sea. Though the dishes themselves seem somewhat upscale for a restaurant on Gili Trawangan, the atmosphere is strictly casual.

Indonesian
WARUNG DEWI
Jalan Gili Trawangan; tel. 81907633826; daily 8am-9pm; 20,000-35,000 Rp

A little warung hidden from Gili Trawangan's main drag, Warung Dewi serves plates of fresh *nasi campur*. Simply choose the dishes you

Cats of the Gili Islands

a Gili cat

The Gili Islands are home to hundreds of quirky cats, many of which have tails that are kinked, curly, bobbed, or no more than little stumps—all from a genetic mutation. The cats have a very full schedule, lazing around beaches, creeping through alleyways, and ensuring the islands' rat and pest communities don't spiral out of control.

The Gili Eco Trust (www.giliecotrust.com) and its affiliated partner, **Cats of Gili** (www.catsofgili.com), provide spay and neuter services, veterinary care, and food to the cats of the Gili Islands. Cats receive care at the kitty clinic at **Lutwala Dive** on Gili Trawangan. Tourists can donate supplies or volunteer at the "Trap, Neuter, Release" clinics that take place every few months. There is also a **Cats of Gili** charity shop on Jalan Nautilus where you can purchase feline-themed goods (proceeds go toward cats in need). Check the Cats of Gili Facebook page (@catsofgili) for updates on requested goods and dates for cat clinics.

like and enjoy with a heaped pile of cooked rice. The jackfruit curry, tempeh satay, beef *rendang* (spicy stew), fried fish, and coconut *sambal* (chili sauce) are usually the first plates to run out.

EXILE

Jalan Gili Trawangan; tel. 81907229053; www.theexilegilit.com; daily 8am-10pm; 20,000-70,000 Rp

If you're after a meal with a view, enjoy basic Indonesian meals like *gado-gado,* satay, grilled tuna, *mie goreng,* and *nasi goreng* at Exile. Watch the sky turn different shades of orange for sunset while live music plays in the background.

American
LE PETIT GILI

Jalan Gili Trawangan; tel. 87865855545; open 24/7; 30,000-40,000 Rp

After a late night out, travelers flock to Le Petit Gili for burgers, fries, burritos, and salads. Staff are friendly and excited to cook fresh food in an open kitchen after the original Le Petit Gili was destroyed in the 2018 earthquake.

Asian Fusion
JALI KITCHEN

Jalan Nautilus; tel. 8170005254; daily 7am-11pm; 60,000-80,000 Rp

Jali Kitchen is one of the more hidden

restaurants on Gili Trawangan, but it's popular among dive staff. Jali Kitchen serves a range of Thai, Indonesian, Indian, and Asian fusion dishes. Top choices include their spicy Thai panang curry with peanut sauce, pork stew with an apple cider base, and butter chicken. Seating is outdoors, with casual communal benches and basic decor. Portions are generous.

Cooking Schools
SWEET AND SPICY COOKING SCHOOL
Jalan Gili Trawangan; tel. 87865776429; https:// gilicookingschool.webs.com; 10am-10pm; 385,000 Rp per person per course

Master local dishes at Sweet and Spicy Cooking School, where local chefs teach two-hour courses on how to make chicken taliwang, steamed fish in banana leaves, sauces, and fried noodles in a beachside kitchen. Vegan and vegetarian cooking, as well as courses on specific dishes, can be taught if requested in advance. All abilities and ages are welcome at the school, and you'll leave with each recipe to re-create back home.

★ BARS AND NIGHTLIFE

If you've come to Gili Trawangan to experience the party scene, join the **Gili T Pub Crawl** (Starts at Tir Na Nog, Jalan Gili Trawangan; Tues., Fri., and Sun. 6:30pm; 250,000 Rp per person). Three nights a week, a crew of partiers gather at Tir Na Nog and bar-hop along Gili Trawangan's main road. Your admission fee includes shots, an island discount card, an exclusive drink special, and a shirt. Expect Joss shots, where a bit of sugary Joss energy powder is followed by a shot of hard alcohol.

CAPTAIN JACK BAR
Jalan Gili Trawangan; daily 11am-9pm; 20,000-60,000 Rp

Captain Jack Bar is one of the funkiest bars on the island, where just about everything that can be covered in paint is covered in paint. Silly hand-painted signs, fake palm trees

that belong in a Dr. Seuss book, and beanbag chairs are available for guests. The vibe is upbeat and friendly, thanks to regular live music and the bar's crew of happy-go-lucky staff.

EVOLUTION
Jalan Gili Trawangan; tel. 81917112209; daily 7pm-1am; 30,000-60,000 Rp

Evolution is one of Gili Trawangan's grittier bars and a first-stop party spot for evening newcomers onto the island, as it's based near the boat arrivals. Beer pong tables challenge travelers to test their hand-eye coordination—which no doubt gets worse the longer you stay at Evolution. Come on Sunday, when the bar hosts the evening's main party.

TIR NA NOG
Jalan Gili Trawangan; tel. 370/6139463; www. tirnanogbar.com; daily noon-1am, 30,000-70,000 Rp drinks

Tir Na Nog is a popular Irish pub known for getting rowdy and serving some of the island's best fish and chips. Their DJs play a mix of Top 40 hits and popular dance tunes. The bar hosts Gili Trawangan's Wednesday night party, and women get half off drinks each Sunday. The Gili Trawangan pub crawl starts at Tir Na Nog.

SAMA SAMA REGGAE BAR
Jalan Gili Trawangan; noon-1am daily; 30,000-80,000 Rp drinks

Sama Sama Reggae Bar is the place to go for live reggae music in an upbeat, Rasta influenced atmosphere. The cocktails are strong, the beer is cold, and Saturday is their busiest night.

JIGGY BOAT PARTY
Jalan Gili Trawangan; tel. 87765539803; www. jgyboatparty.com; daily 1pm-7pm; 455,000 per person

At Jiggy Boat Party, you can board a boat and cruise around the Gili Islands on a five-hour

---

1: Casa Vintage 2: Captain Jack Bar 3: Pesona Beach Resort 4: The Pearl of Trawangan

boat party. Rounds of shots and live music keep the festivities going until sunset, when it's time to head back to land. VIP tickets are available for reserved seating and bottles of spirits.

ACCOMMODATIONS
Under 1,000,000 Rp
THE BROKEN COMPASS HOSTEL
Jalan Ikan Hiu; tel. 85937005788; 550,000 Rp double, 170,000 Rp dorms

Part of Compass Divers, The Broken Compass is a clean and simple hostel with bright dorm rooms. Some rooms have an en suite bathroom, while others share a bathroom. Private double rooms are also available. Dorm beds have a locker and a curtain. All stays include breakfast, air-conditioning, Wi-Fi in lounge areas, and access to the on-site pool. After sunset, most guests get together to socialize with drinks.

MOANA GUESTHOUSE
Road inland from Buddha Dive; moanaguesthousegili@hotmail.com; 300,000 Rp double

Moana Guesthouse is a cheerful and welcoming guesthouse where everyone is greeted with a cookie and invited to hang out in a rainbow-colored lounge area with pillow puffs to sit on. It's ideal for social travelers looking to meet others and sing, snack, and chat in the communal area. Rooms are basic with double or twin beds, Wi-Fi, and air-conditioning.

1,000,000-2,000,000 Rp
★ BLU D'AMARE
Jalan Gili Trawangan; tel. 85888662490; 1,000,000 Rp double

Blu D'Amare is a tranquil retreat that features wooden *joglo* bungalows with a pool and beach access. Each room has a rustic, cozy feel with large patios, mosquito nets draped over the beds, air-conditioning, minibar, and in-room safe. The location is ideal for those who want easy access to Gili Trawangan's busy boat-landing area without the noise and the crowds. Friendly staff with high hospitality standards add to Blu D'Amare's appeal.

LA COCOTERAIE ECOLODGE
Jalan Villa Kelapa; tel. 81907976985; www. lacocoteraiegili.com; 1,400,000 Rp double

Sleep in luxury safari-style tents at La Cocoteraie Ecolodge, a boutique property with eight tents that blend in with the palm trees and garden surroundings. All tents have air-conditioning, a queen-sized bed with mosquito net, hot water shower, Wi-Fi access, and drinking water. Enjoy lounging in a poolside beanbag chair or exploring the island with your own bicycle. The on-site restaurant has a luxe yet casual vibe with open-air seating and a menu that features fresh juice and Indonesian fare.

GILI TEAK RESORT
Jalan Gili Trawangan; tel. 370/6197254; https:// giliteak.com; 2,000,000 Rp double

Set on the beachfront, Gili Teak Resort hosts eight stand-alone cottages built from teak wood and designed with chic and minimal decor. The grounds are kept tidy and simple, with a freshwater pool to use as a refreshing change from the sand and the salt. One of the highlights is an outdoor bathroom with dual showers, where you bathe next to a pond of fish. All cottages have air-conditioning, a TV, a safe, and fan. Request a room at the front of the property to relish ocean views.

★ PESONA BEACH RESORT
Jalan Gili Trawangan; tel. 81338088963; www. pesonaresort.com; 2,000,000 Rp double

This is not your average resort, with its affiliated *shisha* lounge and bar, spa, dive center, and restaurant. Rooms are decorated with bright and bohemian murals, curtains, and fish scale-tiled showers. All rooms have a TV, safe, air-conditioning, and hot water showers. The pick of the resort are the poolside rooms with a balcony swing set next to the grotto-like swimming pool. The staff are exceptionally helpful when it comes to recommending activities and sorting out any issues.

Cidomo Carriage Ponies: Should You Use Them?

cidomo carriage ponies

Because motorized vehicles are banned on the Gili Islands, ponies with colorful carriages, called cidomos, are used to transport scuba tanks, cases of Bintang, food, building supplies, and people. These working ponies were essential in rebuilding the islands so quickly after the recent earthquakes. Though they certainly look beautiful, there has been a history of cidomos being overworked, and they are susceptible to dehydration as they are often given brackish water. Alternative solutions like bicycles with carts, rentable wheelbarrows, or strict penalties for overloading a cart have yet to take hold. There is no way to visit the Gili Islands without tangibly supporting the strained cidomo industry.

After a handful of awareness campaigns by dedicated animal welfare activists, the cidomos have been receiving better treatment in recent years. Initiatives like **Gili Eco Trust** (www. giliecotrust.com) and **Horses of Gili** (http://horsesofgili.com/wordpress/index.php) work to provide fresh water, veterinary care, and education on how to care for the ponies.

It is best to enjoy the island by bicycle or on foot, to avoid adding any unnecessary trips for the ponies. If you do use one to move luggage, keep the load light by taking two, or walking or cycling, while cidomos carry solely the luggage. To help the ponies' working conditions, donate to Gili Eco Trust so that they can pay for medications, fresh water, feed, veterinary care, and properly fitted equipment.

Over 2,000,000 Rp
THE PEARL OF TRAWANGAN

Jalan Gili Trawangan; tel. 81337156999; www.
pearloftrawangan.com; 3,000,000 Rp double

The Pearl of Trawangan is an impressive hotel with a bamboo reception and lounge area at the front of the property, and a large pool with a swim-up bar in its interior. Choose between a one- or two-bedroom villa, *lumbung* cottage, or double room. Each is romantically decorated and has air-conditioning, a TV, and Wi-Fi access. The beach in front of the property has a range of shaded lounge chairs for guests to enjoy. One of the most underrated things about staying at The Pearl of Trawangan is its included breakfast with drinks, fresh fruit, and more than 10 a la carte dishes to choose from.

★ GILI TREEHOUSES

Jalan Villa Kelapa; tel. 85339389108; www. gilitreehouses.com; 3,500,000 Rp double

Tucked away from Gili Trawangan's party scene on the quieter side of the island, Gili Treehouses is a quirky hotel where guests can spend the night in a luxury treehouse villa perched above a private pool. Each room has a king-size bed, air-conditioning, seating area, and private bathroom. Below the treehouse, you can relax in the shaded lounge area with cushioned sofas, a table, and a hammock. Breakfast is included, and each guest is given a bicycle and snorkel set to use during their stay. Who knew that living like Tarzan could feel so extravagant?

INFORMATION AND SERVICES

There are multiple **ATMs** along Jalan Gili Trawangan, with most clustered near the boat harbor.

Major announcements come through a loudspeaker from Gili Trawangan's main **mosque,** located near the boat harbor.

Safety

Drug use is common on Gili Trawangan, despite being illegal in Indonesia. Penalties for drug use can be life-altering, with long prison sentences awaiting those who are caught. For years, Indonesian police turned a blind eye to the Gili Islands, as there was no official police posting. However, after the earthquakes, police presence in Gili Trawangan has increased.

Health and Medicine

There are no hospitals on the Gili Islands. However, you can find medical clinics that treat common issues, such as simple cuts, mosquito bites, infections, and dehydration.

Blue Island Clinic is open 24/7 and offers basic care as well as emergency evacuation services (Villa Ombok Hotel, tel. 81999705701; www.blueislandclinic.com). There is also **Trawangan Medical Clinic,** which offers basic services and emergency evacuation (Jalan Gili Trawangan, northwestern side of island; tel. 85338110348; www. gilimedservice.com).

GETTING THERE AND AROUND

Boats arrive on the western shoreline of Gili Trawangan. **Public boats** from the harbor on the eastern side of the island go between the three Gili Islands regularly, and cost about 15,000 Rp per trip.

Walking one lap around Gili Trawangan takes two to two and a half hours. **Jalan Villa Kelapa** cuts across the center.

By Bike

Bicycles are available for rent along **Jalan Gili Trawangan,** especially near the boat landing area, for about 50,000 Rp per day. Most stands will request the name of your hotel and a local phone number if you're renting for multiple days. Some paths are potholed or covered in sand, so expect to walk your bike in many areas; on the plus side, you'll return home with chiseled quads.

Gili Meno

Quiet and authentic, Gili Meno is where you can walk along without a resort, trendy restaurant, or dive shop in sight once you veer inland. This little island is a nostalgic reflection of what Gili Air and Gili Trawangan likely looked like before the Gili Islands became a popular destination for those in search of white sand beaches and clear, calm waters.

SIGHTS
Turtle Sanctuary
Jalan Pantai Gili Meno; tel. 81339599644; daily 9am-9pm; donation requested

The Gili Meno Turtle Sanctuary is essentially a one-man operation. The founder uses donations to harvest turtle eggs, care for hatchlings, and release them once they are ready. Tanks are small and clean. Note that there is no guarantee of seeing hatchlings at any given time.

Gili Meno Lake
west side of Gili Meno

Gili Meno Lake is one of the only inland bodies of water on the Gili Islands, made from saltwater. Mangroves line the lake, and it's an interesting spot to search for wildlife, though don't expect to swim. The lake's walking pier is a bit unstable; tread lightly and carefully if you choose to walk on it.

WATER SPORTS
Snorkeling and Scuba Diving
NEST SCULPTURE GARDEN
Swim out 200 meters (656 feet) from Diana's Café, near Bask Resort; free

Created by artist and sculptor Jason DeCaires Taylor, the Nest is a sculpture garden made from 48 statues depicting lovers embracing one another, with others laying at their feet. As time passes, fish and corals will use the sculpture garden as an artificial reef, helping the marine life populations thrive. The sculpture can be seen while snorkeling offshore of Gili Meno in front of Bask Resort.

BLUE MARLIN GILI MENO
Jalan Pantai Gili Meno; tel. 370/639980; www. bluemarlindive.com; daily 8am-7pm; 540,000 Rp fun dive, 5,900,000 Rp open water

Gili Meno Lake

Gili Meno

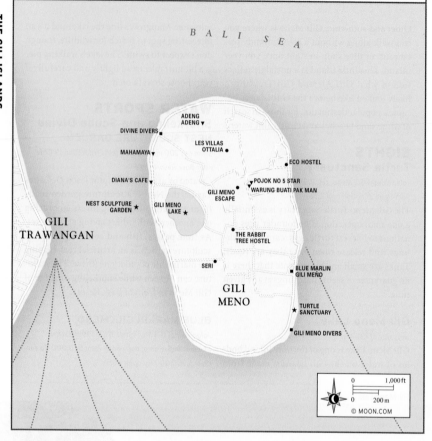

Blue Marlin is a quality dive shop located at Gili Meno Harbor that runs PADI dive courses from Discover Scuba to instructor and fun dives around the three Gili Islands. Small groups are able to request specific dive sites.

DIVINE DIVERS

Jalan Pantai Gili Meno; tel. 85240570777; www. divinedivers.com; daily 7:30am-7pm; 540,000 Rp fun dive, 5,900,000 Rp open water

Scuba divers can stay in one of Divine Divers' poolside bungalows, all with air-conditioning, a TV, a safe, and breakfast included. The dive center itself offers reputable PADI dive courses from Discover Scuba to Rescue Diver.

GILI MENO DIVERS

Jalan Pantai Gili Meno; tel. 87864095490; www. gilimenodivers.com; daily 8:30am-6pm; 540,000 Rp fun dive, 5,900,000 Rp open water

One of the most popular dive centers on Gili Meno, Gili Meno Divers teaches SSI scuba courses ranging from Introductory Scuba to Advanced Adventurer, while certified divers can hop on a fun diving trip. To explore without the confines of scuba gear, enroll in their SSI freediving course.

FOOD
WARUNG BUATI PAK MAN

GPS: -8.347755, 116.058183; daily 10am-8pm;
15,000-30,000 Rp

Run by a jovial family with a father who calls himself "Pak Man," Warung Buati serves generous portions of local dishes like *mie* and *nasi goreng,* chicken and vegetables, *gado-gado,* and meat and vegetables cooked in coconut milk. The concept is simple: Just write your order down and hand it to the staff. If the kids are around, it'll feel like you're dining inside a local home.

POJOK NO 5 STAR

tel. 82144488331; noon-10pm; 20,000-60,000 Rp

Pojok No 5 Star, run by a friendly couple, serves fresh quality food that must be ordered a few hours to a day in advance for some of their specialty meals, like fresh grilled fish served with pesto pasta, chicken cordon bleu, spring rolls, and burgers. The restaurant itself is cozy, with private dining tables.

DIANA'S CAFE

Jalan Pantai Gili Meno; daily 9am-10pm;
30,000-60,000 Rp

Decorated with driftwood and coral buntings, Diana's Bar and Café is the best place to go for sunset on Gili Meno. Enjoy sipping a cocktail from their treehouse platform, or dig your toes into the sand at a beachside table. You might find better food elsewhere, but the price and ambience make it worth a stop for a drink and a small meal.

★ MAHAMAYA

Jalan Pantai Gili Meno; tel. 8113905828; www.
mahamaya.com; daily 8am-10pm; 60,000-
150,000 Rp

The restaurant attached to the Mahamaya is one of the best on the island, serving romantic beachside dinners that feel opulent even under a thatched roof. Meals are cooked in an open kitchen, where plates of seafood, pizza, lamb shank, pasta, and local dishes are served. If notified in advance, staff can decorate tables with flower petals and candles to create an intimate atmosphere.

ADENG ADENG

North Gili Meno; tel. 81805341018; daily 10am-8pm;
70,000-150,000 Rp

A popular pizza joint that frequently plays live music, Adeng Adeng is the place to go for a casual meal. The new restaurant is somewhat hard to find; follow the signs that say "Pizza." The restaurant is still rebuilding, adding a wall or feature every few months. No matter—the pizzas and margaritas taste great regardless.

ACCOMMODATIONS
Under 1,000,000 Rp
ECO HOSTEL

Jalan Pantai Gili Meno; 100,000 Rp dorm, 200,000
Rp double

A ramshackle set of structures built from bamboo, Eco Hostel looks like it was built by a band of backpackers stranded on a desert island, with stilted and traditional bungalows to sleep in. Hammocks strewn around the property tempt guests to enjoy some midday lounging. The beach bar is a prime spot to make friends. The hostel is environmentally conscious, with mosquito nets, compost toilets in the shared bathrooms, and showers built from bamboo. Four-bed and six-bed dorm rooms, as well as private double rooms, are available.

★ THE RABBIT TREE

By Gili Meno Lake; tel. 81291491843; www.
therabbittree.com; 250,000 Rp double, 100,000
Rp dorm

There is no hostel quite like The Rabbit Tree, where rooms are the embodiment of a creative imagination. One room has a pit of colorful plastic balls. Another is built to look like a flying ship. Nap in a suspended net, attend a craft workshop where you can create artwork from recycled plastics, witness a fireshow, and relax inside the indoor movie theater. Dorm and twin rooms are available, all with

air-conditioning. Social activities take place each day, and if you don't connect with the other guests, you'll likely enjoy spending time with the friendly staff.

SERI

Jalan Pantai Gili Meno; tel. 82237596677; www.
seriresortgilimeno.com; 900,000 Rp double
On the beachfront, Seri is an elegant hotel that overlooks one of Gili Meno's best snorkeling spots. The best rooms open out to the sea and it's easy to spend the day moving between the beachside lounge chairs and the pool. Bungalows and suites are available, all with air-conditioning, Wi-Fi, a TV, and outdoor seating area. Stretch out at the on-site yoga studio or relax with a massage and pampering treatments at the spa.

Over 1,000,000 Rp
LES VILLAS OTTALIA
off Jalan Gili Meno; tel. 81932435700; www.
lesvillasottaliagili.com; 1,200,000 Rp double
In the center of Gili Meno, Les Villas Ottalia is a four-star resort with a pool, spacious bar area, and cozy rooms with a luxurious feel. All rooms come with air-conditioning, a mini fridge, TV, safe, and hot rainwater-style shower. Each bungalow is made from mostly natural materials like wood and bamboo, and rooms also have a private patio area.

GILI MENO ESCAPE
tel. 81936219413; www.gilimenoescape.com;
1,300,000 Rp double
Gili Meno Escape is a luxury boutique resort where tasteful bamboo bungalows with thatched roofing welcome guests into a peaceful environment. The property has a steep commitment to all things wood, with distressed wooden furniture, rattan baskets, and bamboo dining chairs, all accented with blue and aqua decor. Each bungalow has a TV, mini-fridge, Wi-Fi access, and air-conditioning. With just six rooms on-site, the small communal pool never feels too crowded.

INFORMATION AND SERVICES
There are multiple **ATMs** on Gili Meno, but they are not always in working order. It's best to bring **cash** to the island just in case (otherwise, you will likely have to boat over to Gili Air or Gili Trawangan for ATM access).

There are no hospitals on Gili Meno. **Blue Island Medical Clinic** offers basic medical care and evacuation (Jalan Gili Meno, near boat landing area; tel. 81999705702; www. blueislandclinic.com; open 24/7).

Getting There and Around
Public boats to Gili Meno from **Bangsal Harbor, Gili Air,** and **Gili Trawangan** arrive regularly, leaving when full. The cost is about 15,000 Rp each way per person. Boats depart on the eastern side of the island.

It takes about one hour to **walk** the circumference of Gili Meno, with multiple roads crossing through the island east to west and north to south.

Bicycles can be rented on Gili Meno for about 50,000 Rp per day. All areas of the island are accessible by bike, though much of it is covered in sand or damaged with holes—expect to walk it a fair bit.

Gili Air

If the Gili Islands were a Venn diagram, Gili Air would be the evenly blended intersection of Gili Trawangan and Gili Meno. Romantic walks are a given (partner not required), thanks to its winding pathways and unspoiled beaches. Gili Air has plenty of bars, restaurants, accommodations, and activities to keep you busy. When you want to escape, a spot to yourself is just a short walk away.

WATER SPORTS
Scuba Diving and Freediving
★ GILI SHARK CONSERVATION

sharks@gilisharkconservation.com; https:// gilisharkconservation.com; Tues.-Sat. 2pm-5pm; around 28,000,000 Rp for 2 weeks

Gili Shark Conservation is an initiative that collects data on the marine life, particularly sharks, living within the Gili Matra Marine Recreational Reserve. Volunteers can join Gili Shark Conservation as research assistants for a minimum of two weeks—no experience in scuba diving or marine biology needed. There are also campaigns to study sea turtles, coral reefs, plastic reduction education, and more. The program fees include open-water scuba certification, transportation, 15 meals per week, eight dives per week with rental equipment included, shared accommodation, and transport between Bali and Gili Air.

OCEANS 5

Jalan Pantai Gili Air; tel. 81338777144; www. oceans5dive.com; 540,000 Rp fun dive, 5,900,000 Rp open water course

Oceans 5 is a 5-Star PADI instructor development center dive resort and one of the largest dive centers within the Gili Islands. It has two training pools, multiple dive boats, an on-site restaurant, and bungalows for divers wanting to use Oceans 5 as a home base. Courses range from introductory to instructor level.

GILI AIR DIVERS

Jalan Pantai Gili Air (Grand Sunset Resort); tel. 87865367551; www.giliairdivers.com; 540,000 Rp fun dive, 5,900,000 open water course

Gili Air Divers is a SSI Dive Center running fun dives around the islands as well as a range of courses from Discover Scuba to Divemaster level. Trips and courses are well-organized and led by patient, friendly staff.

FREEDIVE FLOW

Jalan Mojo; tel. 8113981166; www.freediveflow.com; courses from 1,600,000

One of the main freediving schools in Asia, Freedive Flow is owned by Oli Christen, a renowned freediver who has advised on AIDA and Molchanov's course manuals. With a large lap pool and dedicated freediving boat, students can receive their AIDA, Molchanovs, or PADI freediving certifications. Certified freedivers hoping to progress can enroll in a coaching or training session to advance their skills safely and in the beautiful waters off of the Gilis.

OTHER SPORTS AND RECREATION
Yoga
FLOWERS AND FIRE

Jalan Mojo; tel. 87853920435; www.flowersandfire. yoga; daily 7:15am-7pm; 120,000 Rp class

Flowers and Fire is a boutique hotel and yoga studio in the middle of Gili Air with private rooms, ideal for a yoga retreat. Yoga classes take place multiple times per day in an upstairs bamboo open area with plenty of props to use to accommodate your practice. Flowers and Fire is decorated with tropical plants and murals, and its highlight is a gargantuan mango tree in the middle of the property. DIY salad bowls and fresh juices are served underneath the yoga studio next to the pool.

Gili Air

H2O YOGA AND MEDITATION

Jalan Budha Way; tel. 87761038836; www. h2oyogaandmeditation.com; daily 7:15am-7pm; 120,000 Rp class

Experience serenity at H2O Yoga and Meditation, a center that focuses on mindfulness and health. Yoga classes take place three times per day, as well as massages, workshops, and guided meditation sessions. Rooms on-site are basic and clean, and the restaurant, serving healthy vegetarian meals, is worth a visit whether you're a yogi or not.

Spas
SLOW SPA

Jalan Shady Lane (Slow Gili Air); tel. 87761702216; https://slowgiliair.com; daily 8:30am-8:30pm; 300,000 Rp 60-minute massage

Slow Spa is a minimally designed spa with bamboo walls, open windows, and comfortable spa beds. Spa therapists offer a range of massages, facials, hair baths, manicures, pedicures, waxing, and reflexology treatments. Their body scrub with sugar, ginger, and coconut oil helps revitalize your skin after a few

days spent in the saltwater and sunshine. Aloe vera treatments help soothe sunburns.

WAGWAN SPA

Jalan Pantai Gili Air (Scallywags Resort); tel. 87765344878; www.wagwanspa.com; daily 10am-10pm; 225,000 Rp 60-minute massage

Wagwan Spa is the ideal spot to receive pampering treatments like massages, facials, aromatherapy massages, manicures, pedicures, and hair treatments. They also have a range of products for sale like soaps, oils, and lotions. Treatment rooms are small and clean.

Cooking Classes

GILI COOKING CLASSES

Gili Air Harbor; tel. 87821570188; www. gilicookingclasses.com; daily 10am-10pm daily; 290,000-395,000 Rp class

Gili Cooking Classes teaches its students how to cook fresh, authentic Sasak meals. The school offers multiple classes ranging from 1 to 2.5 hours where students can learn how to cook *mie goreng,* peanut sauce, tempeh, chicken curry, *gado-gado,* and chicken *taliwang.* Vegetarians and vegans will learn traditional recipes replacing meat with tofu or tempeh. Classes take place at 11:30am, 4pm, and 7pm daily.

SHOPPING

RAINBOW SHOPS

Jalan Mojo; daily 9am-6pm

Jalan Mojo has a variety of boutiques, with a cluster of monochrome ones set facing one another. The pink shop sells only pink items, the blue shop sells only blue items, and so on. Look for jewelry, home decor, clothing, and souvenirs guaranteed to be in your favorite color.

LIZZY DARLING

Jalan Pantai Gili Air; daily 9am-6pm

For unique souvenirs you won't find elsewhere, check Lizzy Darling. The boutique sells silver jewelry, curated shoes, clothes,

accessories, and home decor—typically with an island theme. Many items are handmade.

FOOD

★ WAROENG ALAM DAMAI

tel. 85333685724; daily 8am-8pm; 20,000-50,000 Rp

Waroeng Alam Damai is unassuming from the outside: a bamboo warung with thatched roofing and strings of bleached coral suspended on fishing lines. Friendly staff and talented chefs serve thoughtfully plated local dishes like *mie goreng,* meat skewers, *urab-urab,* noodle soup, and yellow chicken soup. Wait times can be long when it's busy, but a cold drink helps pass the time.

GOGO'S SHAKES

corner of Coffee and Thyme near the boat harbor; 25,000-40,000 Rp drinks

After a lap around the island, quench your thirst at Gogo's Shakes, where you can sip fresh tropical juices and coffee blends out of a bamboo straw—yours to keep! Shakes and juices can be topped with grated coconut, chocolate, or caramel. This stand also sells eco-friendly items like reusable stainless-steel straws and compostable bamboo toothbrushes.

★ MAMA PIZZA

Jalan Pantai Gili Air; tel. 87821646371; daily noon-11:00pm; 40,000-90,000 Rp

Mama Pizza crafts the best wood-fired pizza on Gili Air, and you can enjoy it served on a beachside table alongside a cold Bintang or fresh juice. Get creative with your toppings or make it vegan by removing the cheese. It'll be a challenge, but be sure to leave some room for their tiramisu for dessert.

PACHAMAMA

Jalan Svea; tel. 82359075385; www. pachamamagiliair.com; daily 9am-10pm; 50,000-90,000 Rp

Pachamama caters to the health-conscious who don't mind giving in to a bit of sugar or alcohol. The café serves coffee, tea, wine,

---

1: Freedive Flow 2: food at Flowers and Fire yoga

smoothies, and home-brewed kombucha. Breakfasts of sweet or savory bowls and burritos are served all day, with burgers, spiced ground beef, and zucchini pasta tempting guests in the afternoon. The decor at Pachamama is trendy and beachy, appealing to those who keep photo food diaries.

COFFEE AND THYME

Jalan Pantai Gili Air; tel. 85338794046; www. coffeeandthyme.co; daily 7am-7pm daily; 50,000-100,000 Rp

The cute café of Coffee and Thyme welcomes you to Gili Air near the harbor entrance. Enjoy a cup of coffee made your way, though the crème brulee coffee is a nice hit of sugar and caffeine if you feel like trying something new. There are also sandwiches, salads, and fresh juices to dine on as you watch the boats come and go.

BARS AND NIGHTLIFE

LEGEND BAR

Jalan Pantai Gili Air; tel. 82247707722; daily 10am-midnight; 20,000-60,000 Rp drinks

Legend Bar is one of the most popular spots for hanging out in the evenings, with live music and a two-for-one happy hour. A bar area welcomes those looking to socialize, while shaded beanbag chairs invite those who want to chill undisturbed to take a seat. Enjoy the sunset view with a drink in hand.

POCKETS AND PINTS

Jalan Mojo; tel. 85339919897; daily 11am-midnight; 35,000-100,000 Rp

Pockets and Pints is a pub that serves woodfired pita pockets (choose from the menu or DIY), imported and local beers, ciders, and wine. Enjoy battling others in a board game or trying your hand at darts. For a bit of friendly competition, head over on Tuesdays to play beer pong.

K69

Jalan Pantai Gili Air

K69 is a funky art shack that serves curries, juices, and drinks next to the sea. The open-air bar is decorated with batik quilts, fluffy pillow pads, local artwork, and distressed wooden furniture. Their community library features books about permaculture and conservation.

ACCOMMODATIONS
Under 1,000,000 Rp
CASA BLANCA

off Jalan Sunset; tel. 81337511811; 350,000 Rp double room

If you love bright, open rooms, Casa Blanca is a small complex offering clean, all-white rooms. Each room has an outdoor bathroom with hot water shower, and a balcony that overlooks a simple garden. The rooms come with shelves, air-conditioning, Wi-Fi, a mini-desk, a hot water kettle, and a safe. A basic Indonesian breakfast is included with each stay.

★ CAPTAIN COCONUTS

Jalan Sunset; tel. 81237179083; www. captaincoconutshotel.com; 200,000 Rp dorm, 800,000 Rp double

Sleep in a cushy bed suspended from the ceiling at Captain Coconuts, a hip hotel with traditional Javanese *joglo* architecture. Choose between dorm rooms, private double rooms, or a two-bedroom villa. All stays include air-conditioning, Wi-Fi access, lockers, TV, a mini bar, and breakfast. The hotel is environmentally conscious; many of its structures were built from recycled timber, and rooms have solar-heated showers. The decor, pool, and thatched roof umbrellas around the garden create a carefree and tropical ambience.

VILLA NANGKA

from Jalan Gili Air up Budha Way, turn right at intersection; https://villanangkagiliair.com; 800,000 Rp double room, 1,800,000 Rp 2-bedroom villa

This hidden retreat has a one-bedroom *lumbung* bungalow and two-bedroom bamboo villa on its property, set alongside an 11-meter

1: Rainbow Shops 2: Legend Bar 3: K69 4: Pink Coco's resort boat

Conservation in the Gilis: Tips for an Eco-Friendly Stay

The Gili Islands have limited supplies, fresh water, and rubbish removal. Mass tourism puts a huge strain on the little islands' resources. Here are a few eco-friendly tips to help make your stay sustainable:

- **Bring a reusable water bottle and download the RefillMyBottle app:** There's a handful of places around the island where you can refill your water bottle for free, or cheaper than the cost of a single-use bottle. Speaking of beverages, skip the **straw** as well.

- **Wear reef-safe sunscreen:** Ingredients like oxybenzone, commonly used in sunscreen, can damage coral reefs. Instead, wear a rashguard and leggings with UPF 50 sun protection. Sunscreens with a non-nano base made from titanium oxide and zinc oxide are safest for reefs.

- **Participate in a cleanup:** Make friends while keeping the Gili Islands pristine. Many dive shops host weekly beach cleanups and underwater scuba dive cleanups, and **Trash Hero Gili Air** (tel. 87865358017; www.trashhero.org; usually run in the evenings; free) runs regular beach cleanups where you can make friends and keep Gili Air's beaches pristine. The cleanup schedule is found on their Facebook page (@trashherogiliair), and all volunteers receive a free small beer following the cleanup.

- **Look, don't touch:** Some snorkelers find it really tempting to touch the sea turtles who live around the Gili Islands. Do not swim above a sea turtle when it is coming up to breathe, and ensure that you're giving them their fair share of space. This also goes for touching corals and other underwater wildlife.

- **Skip the long showers:** The Gili Islands struggle when it comes to maintaining enough fresh water to host everyone. Embrace the island life with quick showers—you're going to be sweaty, salty, or wet again soon enough anyway.

(36-foot) swimming pool. All guests have access to the communal open-air kitchen equipped with modern appliances. Guests are welcome to snack on fresh fruit from the papaya, banana, and mango trees set around the garden. All villas have fresh hot water showers, air-conditioning, a safety deposit box, and semi-outdoor bathrooms. The owners, Rose and Andreas, are passionate about conservation and are happy to share their favorite things about Gili Air with their guests.

Over 1,000,000 Rp
BEL AIR RESORT

Jalan Pantai Gili Air; tel. 87862386677; www. belairresort-giliair.com; 1,000,000 Rp double room

With seaside views that look out to Gunung Rinjani, Bel Air Resort and Spa is a serene resort made even more so with its onsite spa. Each room and villa is modern, with Indonesian textiles and artwork on the walls.

All come with Wi-Fi access, a TV, a safety box, and air-conditioning. The highlight of the resort is its restaurant, built from a restored *joglo* decorated with an intricate mosaic floor. This contrasts with the futuristic dome-style villas and modern standard rooms.

PINK COCO

Jalan Pantai Gili Air; tel. 361/8957371; www. pnkhotels.com; 2,800,000 Rp double room

There's no place quite like Pink Coco, a bubblegum-colored hotel where even the resort's boat is bright pink. There are five types of feel-good rooms on the property, all with air-conditioning, a terrace, a TV, and quirky decorations. The hotel is directly on the beach, but guests also have the option of lounging in the resort's palm-surrounded swimming pool, complete with daybeds. Wear pink to the on-site restaurant to score a small discount on your order.

INFORMATION AND SERVICES

There are no hospitals on Gili Air. **Blue Island Medical Clinic** offers basic medical care and evacuation (Jalan Gili Air, near boat landing area; tel. 81999705703; www. blueislandclinic.com; open 24/7).

GETTING THERE AND AROUND

Boats arrive on the southern end of Gili Air. Public boats depart to the other **Gili Islands** and **Bangsal Harbor** (15,000 Rp), usually leaving once they've reached near capacity.

It takes one and a half to two hours to **walk** the circumference of Gili Air. Most restaurants and accommodations are clustered around its southern and eastern coastline.

Bicycles can be rented on Gili Air near the boat harbor for 50,000 Rp per day. Cycling paths are generally well-kept, though some parts are potholed or covered in sand.

Mataram and West Lombok

West Lombok, the area that connects the coast- line north of Senggigi to the tip of the island's southwestern peninsula, is a land of contrasts. Senggigi, Lombok's original tourist town, has some of the island's best restaurants and luxury resorts. The main beach itself is lively and often crowded, but a few kilometers in either direction you'll find beaches backed by coconut groves all to yourself. Many locals are still recovering from the 2018 earthquakes and are genuinely welcoming and appreciative of those who visit. Though Senggigi once had a reputation for being a sterile tourist town, it's on an upward climb.

In Mataram, you'll find the island's capital, where motorbikes dart around dusty markets and colorful mosques. Along the coastline north

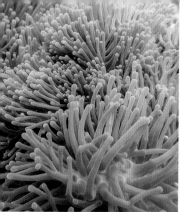

Highlights

Look for ★ to find recommended sights, activities, dining, and lodging.

★ **Beaches of Senggigi:** The area boasts bay after bay of sand, calm water, and palm trees (page 388).

★ **Ampenan Port:** A popular hangout spot for locals in search of good food and sunset views (page 395).

★ **Islamic Center Mosque:** The largest mosque on Lombok has a platform that looks out to the many other mosques of Mataram (page 397).

★ **Snorkeling the Southwest Gilis:** This cluster of islands surrounded by coral reefs teems with sea life (page 406).

★ **Desert Point Surf Break:** For experienced surfers only, this is often touted as the best left-hand barrel in the world (page 406).

© MOON.COM

Top Restaurants

★ **Coco Loco:** This laid-back beach restaurant serves fresh seafood, cold drinks, and sunset views (page 392).

★ **Square:** Sample Sasak classic dishes, served family style to share: a great way to find your favorite (page 392).

★ **Asmara:** A large garden and art boutique border this elegant restaurant, serving a mix of Indonesian and European fare (page 392).

★ **Quah:** Authentic Italian food is served on the shoreline of Senggigi (page 393).

★ **Roemah Langko:** Enjoy dinner inside an elegant colonial building that serves delicious Indonesian meals (page 401).

and south of Mataram, bays with untouched beaches are revealed after just about every turn. Explore the port town of Ampenan, a favorite hangout spot for locals. Tourists are largely an afterthought in terms of hotels and things to do, but if you spend time wandering through the neighborhoods from market to mosque, you're guaranteed to find someplace special. Some locals have taken to covering their streets and walls with rainbow splashes of paint, bringing new life into areas that were once lackluster.

South of Mataram, the Southwestern Peninsula is one of Lombok's best-kept secrets, with miniature islands all ringed with white sand and coral reefs just a short boat ride from the mainland. This sleepy coastline lacks electricity, with most accommodations only turning on their generators to provide light at night. If disconnection from stress and chaos is what you seek, this is your place. The westernmost point of the island, at the edge of Tanjung Desert, is a wave so powerful and perfect, surfers often camp in bare conditions just to catch a single ride.

ORIENTATION

Senggigi sits on the northwest coast of Lombok, with **Jalan Raya Senggigi**
connecting the beaches and peninsulas, many of which offer incredible views. Fifteen km (9 mi) south of Senggigi is **Mataram,** the capital of Lombok (pop. 400,000). Mataram comprises a handful of towns that have grown into one another: **Ampenan** is Mataram's port town, west of central Mataram. In central Mataram, you'll find the **Islamic Center Mosque** and **Epicentrum Mall.**

The Southwest Gili Islands begin at **Lembar Harbor,** a main port for boats shuttling to the islands and between Bali and Lombok. **Sekotong** is the main town, with the Southwestern Gili Islands close offshore. **Desert Point,** also known as **Bangko Bangko,** is the westernmost point of the Southwest Peninsula, a barren land with nothing but an iconic wave that trumps all others in the region.

PLANNING YOUR TIME

You can divide this region into three areas: **Senggigi, Mataram,** and the **Southwest Peninsula.** Senggigi itself can be seen in a day, though you might want to stretch it out longer, doing little else besides lounging on the beach and dining at the town's many worthwhile restaurants. You might find

---

Previous: fishing platform; anemone; Islamic Center Mosque.

Mataram and West Lombok

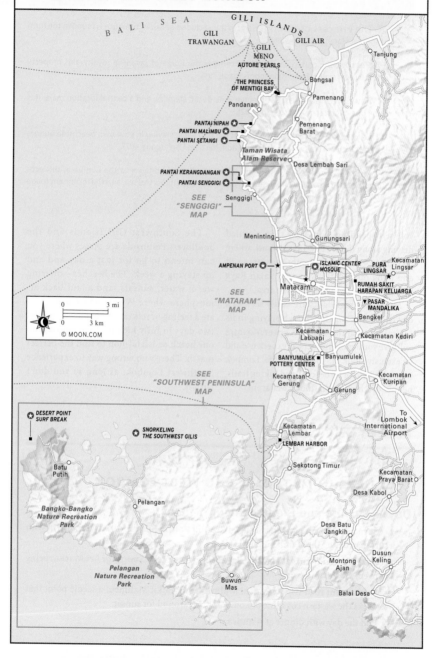

BALI SEA

GILI ISLANDS

GILI TRAWANGAN

GILI AIR

GILI MENO

AUTORE PEARLS

THE PRINCESS OF MENTIGI BAY

Tanjung

Bangsal

Pamenang

Pandanan

PANTAI NIPAH

PANTAI MALIMBU

PANTAI SETANGI

Pemenang Barat

Taman Wisata Alam Reserve

Desa Lembah Sari

PANTAI KERANGDANGAN

PANTAI SENGGIGI

Senggigi

SEE "SENGGIGI" MAP

Meninting

Gunungsari

AMPENAN PORT

ISLAMIC CENTER MOSQUE

PURA LINGSAR

Kecamatan Lingsar

Mataram

RUMAH SAKIT HARAPAN KELUARGA

SEE "MATARAM" MAP

PASAR MANDALIKA

Bengkel

Kecamatan Labuapi

Kecamatan Kediri

0   3 mi

0   3 km

© MOON.COM

BANYUMULEK POTTERY CENTER

Banyumulek

Kecamatan Gerung

Kecamatan Kuripan

Gerung

SEE "SOUTHWEST PENINSULA" MAP

To Lombok International Airport

DESERT POINT SURF BREAK

SNORKELING THE SOUTHWEST GILIS

Kecamatan Lembar

LEMBAR HARBOR

Batu Putih

Sekotong Timur

Kecamatan Praya Barat

Desa Kabol

Bangko-Bangko Nature Recreation Park

Pelangan

Pelangan Nature Recreation Park

Desa Batu Jangkih

Dusun Keling

Montong Ajan

Buwun Mas

Balai Desa

Top Accommodations

★ **The Princess of Mentigi Bay:** In this secluded getaway, romance is found in the form of spectacular views (page 394).

★ **Puri Mas Boutique Resort:** Formerly the home of Javanese royalty, this property offers a regal stay in beachside rooms (page 394).

★ **Favehotel Langko:** Bubblegum-pink decor, sparkles, and a central location make this hotel one of Mataram's best (page 402).

★ **Layar Beach Bungalow:** Get off the grid while staying in your own beachside bungalow. Electricity is limited, but the relaxation you'll feel isn't (page 407).

★ **Gili Asahan Eco Lodge:** End the day with a cold drink near the bonfire at this eco-friendly resort, where guests rotate between the yoga studio, the sea, and the restaurant (page 407).

yourself spending more time than planned driving along the area's **coastal road,** where incredible **viewpoints** tempt travelers to sit and hang out awhile. Stay near Jalan Raya Senggigi to make the most of the area.

Mataram's highlights are easily seen as a day trip from Senggigi, though staying in its central area near the **Islamic Center Mosque** will give you a more immersive experience and an exclusive look into Sasak city life. Lombok is best known for its beaches and hiking trails, neither of which you'll find in Mataram.

The Southwest Gili Islands and the Southwest Peninsula are places where you can intend to go for just a day and end up staying a week. The beaches—offering warm water, sunsets, and a laid-back atmosphere where Wi-Fi can't reach—create a feeling of relaxation that needs at least two days to fully kick in. Park yourself on one beach or island-hop to find the perfect match. There's no wrong way to experience Southwest Lombok, as long as you don't rush it.

Itinerary Ideas

TWO DAYS IN MATARAM AND WEST LOMBOK

Day 1: Surfing and Sightseeing in Senggigi

1 Spend the morning surfing Senggigi Reef, off **Pantai Senggigi,** on your own or with a surf instructor. Then, chill on the beach.

2 Browse for souvenirs along Jalan Raya Senggigi, with the **Senggigi Art Market** being a convenient starting point.

3 Take a mini road trip to **Pantai Malimbu** and Bukit Malimbu, a scenic point that overlooks the western coastline of Lombok. Stick around for sunset.

4 End the day with dinner at **Asmara.**

Itinerary Ideas

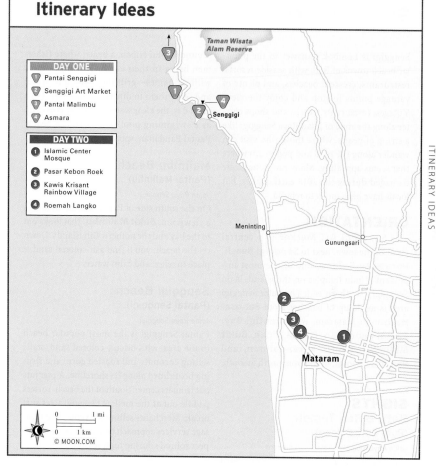

DAY ONE

1. Pantai Senggigi
2. Senggigi Art Market
3. Pantai Malimbu
4. Asmara

DAY TWO

1. Islamic Center Mosque
2. Pasar Kebon Roek
3. Kawis Krisant Rainbow Village
4. Roemah Langko

Taman Wisata Alam Reserve

Senggigi

Meninting

Gunungsari

Mataram

0   1 mi

0   1 km

© MOON.COM

Day 2: Make the Most of Mataram

1 Catch a ride to the **Islamic Center Mosque** to admire its striking exterior. Hire a tour guide to lead you to the top of the tower that awards 360-degree views of Mataram.

2 Then, drive to Ampenan, a port town with European architecture. Shop for fresh fruits at **Pasar Kebon Roek,** a traditional market.

3 Take a walk around the bright murals of **Kawis Krisant Rainbow Village.**

4 Finish with dinner at **Roemah Langko,** which serves top-notch Sasak dishes.

Senggigi Area

Senggigi is Lombok's answer to the popular beach towns of Bali, with seaside resorts, restaurants, crescent beaches, and plenty of vantage points to stop and enjoy the view. Villages, restaurants, hotels, and shops cluster along the road of Jalan Raya Senggigi like a string of pearls, where those who visit can wander along the road and pop in anywhere that seems appealing. Many properties were damaged during the 2018 earthquakes, but locals have been quick to rebuild.

ORIENTATION

The **Senggigi Art Market** is a central point of the town, next to **Senggigi Beach.** **Pura Batu Bolong,** one of the most important Hindu temples on the island, is on Senggigi's southern end. The outer Senggigi area is made up of beaches from **Bangsal Harbor** to Mataram, with **Mentigi Bay, Pantai Pandanan, Pantai Nipah, Bukit Malimbu, Pantai Kerandangan,** and **Pantai Senggigi,** found from north to south, respectively.

SIGHTS

Batu Bolon Temple
(Pura Batu Bolong)

Jalan Raya Senggigi; donation requested

The seaside Hindu temple of Pura Batu Bolong is almost hidden from the main road. Walk through its small entrance to see alters built from dark stone and platforms where ceremonies take place. An arch leads you from the temple out onto the neighboring beach.

★ BEACHES AND SURF BREAKS

Nipah Beach
(Pantai Nipah)

Jalan Raya Senggigi

The smell of freshly grilled seafood lingers around Pantai Nipah, a beach where fishermen bring in their catch. Warungs—most without names—grill the seafood in spices and serve them to diners on the shore. On a calm day, the clear water in the bay is as calm as a swimming pool. The northern beach, Pantai Pandanan, sports similar vibes.

Malimbu Beach
(Pantai Malimbu)

Jalan Raya Senggigi

On the south side of Pantai Malimbu, there's a viewpoint, **Bukit Malimbu,** that looks out to the bay and the nothern Gili Islands. Down on the beach, you'll find ash-colored sand, a place to relax, and calm water.

Senggigi Beach
(Pantai Senggigi)

Jalan Raya Senggigi

Pantai Senggigi is the most popular beach in the area, with biscuit-colored sand, stalls selling coconuts and roasted corn, and fishing boats lined along its shoreline. A pier juts out from its center. South of the beach, surfers paddle out at the mellow Senggigi Reef surf break. Merchants selling souvenirs and massage services approach constantly, so don't expect solitude during high season.

SENGGIGI REEF SURF BREAK

Offshore Pantai Senggigi

Senggigi Reef breaks left and right at mid to high tide, working best at a rising tide. Check for southwest swells and easterly winds for the best left conditions. The righthander, nicknamed "Baby Deserts," is more fickle and needs northerly winds. The left is mellow enough for beginner surfers, and locals in the lineup tend to be welcoming rather than aggressive.

1: Batu Bolon Temple 2: Malimbu Beach 3: Setangi Beach 4: lighthouse off Senggigi Beach

Senggigi

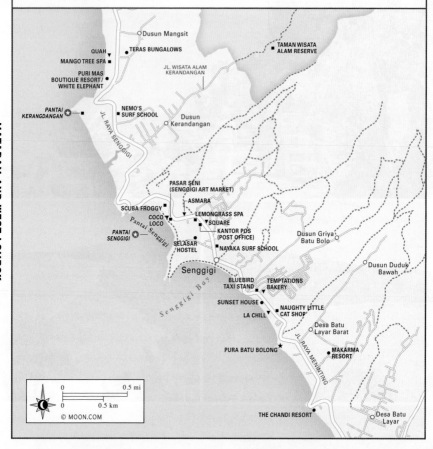

Kerangdangan Beach
(Pantai Kerangdangan)

Jalan Raya Senggigi

Pantai Kerangdangan is a rugged beach lined with palm trees on one side and a shallow reef on its other, making it a perfect spot to escape the crowd. However, it's less than ideal for swimming.

Setangi Beach
(Pantai Setangi)

Jalan Raya Senggigi

On Pantai Setangi's northern end, you'll find a cliffside building called the Haunted Villa *(Villa Hantu)*. Covered in graffiti, the abandoned villa overlooks Pantai Setangi and the ocean below. The beach of Pantai Setangi is covered in streaks of volcanic sand and is spacious enough to kick a ball around.

WATER SPORTS
Scuba Diving and Snorkeling
SCUBA FROGGY

Jalan Raya Senggigi; tel. 87865511090; www.scubafroggy.com; daily 8am-6pm; 1,300,000 Rp for 2 fun dives, 6,250,000 Rp open water

Scuba Froggy has two outposts in Senggigi, one on the main stretch of Jalan Raya Senggigi and another at the Sheraton. They host scuba dives and snorkel tours all throughout the region, as well as at their home dive sites.

Surfing
NAYAKA SURF SCHOOL
Jalan Raya Senggigi; tel. 370/693860; www. surfingsenggigi.com; daily 8am-5pm; 300,000 Rp group lesson, 500,000 Rp 2-hour private lesson

Nayaka Surf School has friendly instructors who are keen to teach kids and adults how to surf. Students will learn water safety, paddling technique, and how to pop up onto the board. Intermediate and experienced surfers can book a surf guiding trip to Lombok's heavier waves around the Southwest Peninsula. Surfboard rental is also available.

NEMO'S SURF SCHOOL
Jalan Raya Senggigi; tel. 87865592891; https:// nemossurfschool.com; 8am-5pm; 300,000 Rp group lesson, 350,000 Rp 3-hour private intro lesson

Nemo's Surf School has a reputation for its patient instructors, who teach beginner to advanced surf lessons for everyone. The instructors are usually armed with a waterproof camera to capture fun moments during the lesson. Those who know how to surf already can rent a board.

OTHER SPORTS AND RECREATION
Hiking
TAMAN WISATA ALAM RESERVE
Jalan Wisata Alam; 7,500 Rp admission

The Taman Wisata Alam Reserve is home to black monkeys, less commonly seen than the long-tailed macaques. Tropical trees, butterflies, and birds reside in the quiet park. Follow the loosely marked trail 1.5 km (0.9 mi) into the reserve to see **Goa Walet Waterfall**, a cascade that covers a cave. Another half km (0.3 mi) away is **Twin Princess Waterfall**, 2 waterfalls that mimic one another and a pool worthy of swimming

in. Shaded gazebos around the park make for prime picnicking spots.

Spas
Local masseuses trawl the beach offering massages for about 80,000-100,000 Rp per hour, or you can have one visit your hotel. Massage quality does not always correspond to the price or persistence of the masseuse.

MANGO TREE SPA
Jalan Raya Senggigi (Sudamala Resort); tel. 361/288555; www.sudamalaresorts.com; daily 9am-9pm; 509,000 Rp 60-minute Balinese massage

Book a pampering session at Mango Tree Spa, a luxury spa where you can enjoy traditional Balinese, aromatherapy, and reflexology massages in a tranquil atmosphere. For something different, try their warm seashell massage or their hot sand massage, where pouches of hot sand mixed with herbs are placed on your back to relieve tension. Body scrubs, wraps, nail treatments, and facial treatments are also available.

LEMONGRASS SPA
Jalan Raya Senggigi; tel. 370/693177; daily 10am-9pm; 85,000 Rp 60-minute Balinese massage

Lemongrass Spa is simply decorated, with wooden furniture and driftwood art pieces, welcoming those in search of traditional massages, reflexology treatments, scrubs, hot stone massages, and hair treatments. Rooms are clean and air-conditioned.

FESTIVALS AND EVENTS
SENGGIGI FESTIVAL
Jalan Raya Senggigi; July-Aug., 3-4 days; free

Senggigi Festival is a multiday celebration showcasing Lombok's traditional and unique costumes, music, artwork, and stick fighting performances. Extra stalls alongside Pasar Seni, Senggigi's art market, sell handcrafted goods and textiles to visitors. The main draw is the opening parade that marches along Jalan Raya Senggigi, where performers tell stories through music and movement.

SHOPPING

NAUGHTY LITTLE CAT SHOP

Jalan Raya Senggigi (Lombok Box); Tues.-Sun. 10am-5pm, closed Mon.

As its name suggests, Naughty Little Cat Shop is a quirky boutique selling cat-themed clothing, accessories, and pet items. It's a prime spot to whisk away something for your feline-loving friends.

PASAR SENI (SENGGIGI ART MARKET)

Jalan Raya Senggigi; daily 9am-5pm

If you're shopping for souvenirs, you'll have a good chance of finding them at Pasar Seni. This small market is colloquially called the Senggigi Art Market, and merchants sell goods crafted from all around the island. Wooden sculptures, jewelry, accessories, and paintings make up the bulk of the market. Bargaining is expected.

AUTORE PEARLS

Jalan Raya Senggigi (Teluk Nara); tel. 81339920020; https://autorepearls.com; daily 9am-5pm

Pearls farmed off Lombok's coastline are displayed at Autore Pearls, where guests can learn about how the pearls are seeded, grown, harvested, and rated. Loose and set pearls are available for purchase.

ANNA'S GIFT SHOP

Jalan Raya Senggigi; tel. 81917137308; annasgiftshoplombok@gmail.com; daily 9am-5pm

Anna's Gift Shop is a place where you can shop for souvenirs and handmade goods with the help of Anna, the friendly shopkeeper. Ceramics, clothing, scarves, jewelry, loose pearls, home decor, and sculptures are on offer. Anna is happy to help package and arrange international shipping for large orders. Prices are fixed.

FOOD

Indonesian

WHITE ELEPHANT

Jalan Raya Senggigi; tel. 370/693831; www. purimas-lombok.com; daily 8am-10pm

White Elephant is worth a visit for its furnishings and decor alone. White tile floors, dark wooden beams, and a high *joglo*-style (traditional Indonesian house) roof make up the restaurant, which is accented with Hindu figures, maroon and gold cushions, crystal chandeliers, and elephants on the walls. Indonesian dishes like chicken *taliwang,* where chicken is marinated in shrimp paste and palm sugar, served with a side of water spinach cooked in chili and garlic (*plecing kangkong*), grilled fish served with *sambal* (chili sauce), and other Sasak classics are well-spiced and authentic.

★ COCO LOCO

Jalan Raya Senggigi; tel. 85954411770; daily 10am-9pm; 20,000-60,000 Rp

The ultra-chill ambience at Coco Loco combined with friendly staff make this beachside warung a popular place to go among Senggigi regulars. Enjoy eating fried rice, curry, fried seafood served with noodles, fresh caught fish grilled in banana leaves, and other Indonesian dishes by the beach. Sit inside the open-air restaurant or request a table on the sand.

★ SQUARE

Jalan Raya Senggigi; tel. 370/693688; https:// squarelombok.com; daily 11:30am-11:30pm; 60,000-180,000 Rp

Square is one of the more upscale dining venues in Senggigi that serves Indonesian and international dishes. Their five-course set menu is recommended, as is their *begibung* menu where Sasak dishes are served family-style—an ideal experience for those who want to try a variety of traditional dishes. Soups, salads, steaks, and seafood are also on offer. On the first Friday of each month, Square hosts a buffet and free-flow wine dinner for 400,000 Rp per person.

★ ASMARA

Jalan Raya Senggigi; tel. 370/693619; www. asmara-group.com; daily 11am-11pm; 60,000-250,000 Rp

For more than two decades, Asmara has been one of Senggigi's most popular restaurants for a reason. The ambiance of the venue is distinctly Indonesian, decorated with artwork created from local artists, with tables set among plants and a well-kept garden. The menu is extensive with a range of Indonesian, Southeast Asian, and European fare. Asmara also has a boutique that sells a variety of Lombok-made artwork and goods at a fixed price. Free pickup and drop-off is available for those staying in the Senggigi area.

European
★ QUAH

Jalan Raya Senggigi No. 33; tel. 370/693800; www. quincivillas.com; daily 7am-11pm

Quah serves quality and authentic Italian fare in an open-air seating area or on the beach. Enjoy the romantic ambience, while dining on dishes like pasta, pizza, beef carpaccio, salads, and pistachio-crusted tuna, made even better with a glass of red wine. Though the restaurant serves food all day long, their dinner menu starting at 7pm each night is especially worth tasting.

LA CHILL

Jalan Raya Senggigi, Beachfront at Batu Bolong; tel. 370/693925; www.lachillbar.com; daily 8am-midnight; 30,000-70,000 Rp

There's always a good time to be had at La Chill, a beach bar with colorful beanbag chairs, Woodstock-worthy decor, and umbrellas to lounge under during the day. Enjoy burgers, sandwiches, pizzas, and local dishes. The drinks menu is the bar's highlight, with local and imported beers, spirits, cocktails, and wine. Come for happy hour 3pm-6pm daily. Live music plays on Saturday from 6pm until late.

Café
TEMPTATIONS BAKERY

Jalan Palm Raja No. 3; tel. 370/693463; www. temptations-lombok.com; daily 8am-9pm; 40,000-220,000 Rp

Temptations Bakery is a popular spot for breakfast, with highlights like eggs Benedict, pancakes, avocado toast, and hearty omelets.

Come for lunch or dinner to enjoy salads, sandwiches, soups, pasta, steaks, and Indonesian dishes like *nasi goreng* (fried rice), *mie goreng* (fried noodles), and *cap cay* (stir-fried vegetables). The café also has a small shop selling pastries, bread, and imported treats that are challenging to find elsewhere on the island.

ACCOMMODATIONS
Under 1,000,000 Rp
SELASAR HOSTEL

Jalan Lazuardi No. 88; tel. 87763027177; 250,000 Rp

A chic hostel with Scandinavian-style rooms, Selasar Hostel is central and lively, with eight four-bed dorm rooms and three double rooms, all clean and air-conditioned. Only the deluxe private room has its own bathroom. Otherwise, they're shared. Each guest has access to a private locker and Internet. Included breakfast is served at the patio restaurant.

MAKARMA RESORT

Batu Layar; tel. 81803600009; www.makarmaresort. com; 400,000 Rp

Bright colors, paintings of palm leaves, a pool, and a cheerful family welcome guests to stay at Makarma Resort. There are three types of rooms: basic block rooms, rustic wooden huts, and poolside bungalows. The poolside bungalows are the best of the bunch, with hammocks on the balcony, reliable Wi-Fi, a mosquito net over the bed, and a TV. The others are somewhat shabby and lack much-needed soundproofing.

SUNSET HOUSE

Jalan Raya Senggigi; tel. 370/692020; www. sunsethouse-lombok.com; 500,000 Rp

A tropical garden surrounds the 32 rooms at Sunset House, a beachfront resort with incredible views of Mount Agung and Nusa Penida in the distance. Each humbly decorated room is equipped with air-conditioning and a TV. Head to the rooftop bar that rewards those who visit with cold drinks, comfortable chairs, and spectacular colors should you come for sunset. The deluxe rooms are suitable for adults only and have access to a private pool.

TERAS BUNGALOWS

Mangsit; tel. 370/6199275; www.
teraslombokbungalow.com; 900,000 Rp

If you've ever wondered what Sasak life is like, stay at Teras Bungalows. Five cozy thatched-roof bungalows are situated in the village of Mangsit, where farm animals scamper across the road and locals go about their day. Friendly staff are happy to chat, especially over breakfast, which is included in each stay. The bungalows are quaint, with a small patio, air-conditioning, modern bathrooms, and Wi-Fi. All guests have access to the small pool in front of the property.

Over 1,000,000 Rp
★ THE PRINCESS OF MENTIGI BAY

Jalan Raya Senggigi, 15 km/9 mi north of
Senggigi Beach; tel. 81339906490; www.
princessofmentigibay.com; 2,400,000 Rp

The Princess of Mentigi Bay is a resort above Mentigi Bay with rooms that can sleep two to four people. The rooms are unique in that they're built from red brick, wooden floors, and traditional thatched roofs. All rooms have air-conditioning, a TV, coffee maker, and comfortable beds. The Princess of Mentigi Bay is a prime choice if you want to see both Senggigi and the Northern Gili Islands, as a shuttle service transports guests to Gili Trawangan daily. You might not be tempted to leave the 25-meter infinity pool, which offers views of the three Gili Islands.

THE CHANDI RESORT

Jalan Raya Senggigi; tel. 370/692198; www.
the-chandi.com; 3,500,000 Rp

The Chandi Resort is an intimate retreat for travelers looking for a beachside stay. Fifteen modest villas stand among uniform palm trees and large grass lawns. All have minimal furnishings, a semi-outdoor bathroom, TV, Wi-Fi access, minibar, and air-conditioning. The seaside pool invites guests to lounge awhile, with a top-notch beach bar and restaurant to satiate any cravings. An on-site spa offers massages, nail treatments, wraps, baths, and scrubs for further relaxation.

★ PURI MAS BOUTIQUE RESORT

Jalan Raya Senggigi; tel. 370/693831; www.
purimas-lombok.com; 4,000,000 Rp

Puri Mas Boutique Resort is one of the most elegant resorts in Senggigi, with ornate gates that welcome you onto the property. The owners of the resort descend from Javanese royalty, and the stylings certainly give off a sense of opulence. Rooms and villas are surrounded by statues and gardens, steps away from the shoreline, each adorned with elegant Indonesian decorations and equipped with a balcony, TV, air-conditioning, Wi-Fi, and private bathroom. Many have a bathtub, and the one- to four-bedroom villas host a private pool. The on-site restaurant and spa are some of the best in Senggigi, giving you little reason to leave the property. A small museum on site displays artwork and artifacts from around the region, collected by the royal family of Solo, Indonesia. Guests must be at least 12 years old to stay at the resort.

INFORMATION AND SERVICES

Kantor Pos (Jalan Raya Senggigi; tel. 370/693711) is a bare-bones post office that offers international shipping.

The main **police station** for the Senggigi area is located at Jalan Raya Senggigi (tel. 370/693267); many officers speak English.

GETTING THERE
By Bus and *Bemo*

Bemos connect Senggigi and **Mataram's Mandalika Terminal** (15,000 Rp), stopping in **Ampenan.** *Bemos* run between **Pemenang,** near **Bangsal Harbor,** and Senggigi (20,000 Rp).

Perama (tel. 361/751875; www.perama tour.com) offers shuttle bus transportation between Senggigi and **Bangsal** (45 minutes; 60,000 Rp), **Kuta** (2 hours; 125,000 Rp), **Lombok International Airport** (1.5 hours;

125,000 Rp), **Mataram** (1 hour; 35,000 Rp), **Padangbai, Bali** (4 hours; 125,000 Rp), and **Tetebatu** (2 hours; 125,000 Rp).

By Boat
Most boats from Bali arrive in **Bangsal Harbor** in the north or **Lembar Harbor** in the south.

Scoot (tel. 361/271030; www.scootcruise.com) connects Senggigi Harbor at Senggigi Beach to **Sanur, Bali** (3 hours; 750,000 Rp one way adult, 650,000 Rp one way child, 1,500,000 Rp return adult, 1,200,000 Rp return child), **Nusa Lembongan** (2.5 hours; 675,000 Rp one way adult, 550,000 Rp one way child, 1,300,000 Rp return adult, 1,100,000 Rp/return child), and **Gili Air, Gili Meno,** and **Gili Trawangan** (1.5-2 hours; 200,000 Rp one way adult/child, 400,000 Rp return adult/child).

By Car and Taxi
Roads leading to Senggigi are generally well-maintained; it's easily reached from **Mataram** (20 km/12 mi; 30 minutes), **Kuta** (65 km/40 mi; 1.5 hours), **Bangsal Harbor** (20 km/12 mi; 30 minutes), and **Tetebatu** (60 km/37 mi; 2 hours).

You'll find reliable, clean, and metered taxis to take you around the area at the **Bluebird Taxi Stand** (Jalan Palm Raja; tel. 370/627000).

Getting Around
Many shops, restaurants, and beaches are within **walking** distance of central Senggigi, near the **Senggigi Art Market.** Rideshare apps like **Grab, GoJek,** and **MyBluebird** are commonly used, with Bluebird taxis driving along **Jalan Raya Senggigi** regularly. **Motorbikes** can typically be rented from stands for 50,000-70,000 Rp per day. **Private drivers** will offer their services along the main road.

Mataram

The capital of Lombok, Mataram is a busy city where small neighborhoods blend together, connected by hundreds of colorful mosques. Crowing roosters, the call to prayer played over loudspeakers, and the hum of motorbikes are the background of daily city life. Wander from mosque to market, stroll along Ampenan's harbor front, and enjoy experiencing a place that's home to most of the island's population yet remains a stranger to most who visit.

Locals in Mataram tend to be more conservative than those residing in touristy areas like Kuta, Lombok, Senggigi, or the Gili Islands. Dress with your shoulders and knees covered when going out for the day.

ORIENTATION
Mataram encompasses not only Mataram itself, the city's center, but also smaller towns that have joined Mataram, with no clear border between them. **Ampenan** sits on the western coastline of Lombok, with a **seaside walkway** where many locals come for dinner and drinks just before sunset. Mataram's city center is marked by the **Islamic Center Mosque,** a short distance away from **Epicentrum Mall,** the most modern shopping center on the island. Inland, **Cakranegara** is considered the business district of Mataram; once the capital of the island when Lombok was under Balinese control, it features architecture influenced by Balinese culture and Hinduism.

SIGHTS
Ampenan Area
★ AMPENAN PORT
Jalan Pantai Ampenan
Stroll along the seaside walkway in Ampenan, a harbor town. At sunset, the edge is crowded with locals in search of a relaxed place to eat a cheap meal and watch the sun drift below the horizon. The town once hosted Mads

Mataram

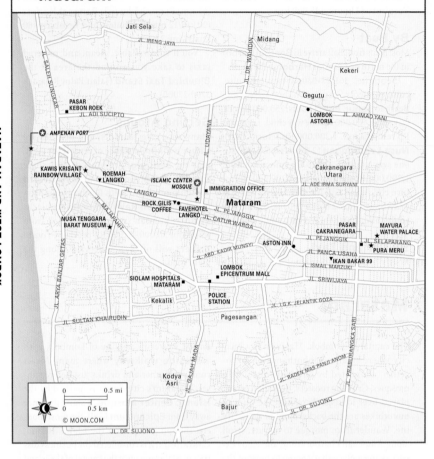

Jati Sela

JL. IRENG JAYA

Midang

Kekeri

Gegutu

PASAR
KEBON ROEK
JL. ADI SUCIPTO

LOMBOK
ASTORIA   JL. AHMAD YANI

AMPENAN PORT

Cakranegara
Utara

KAWIS KRISANT
RAINBOW VILLAGE   ROEMAH
LANGKO   ISLAMIC CENTER
MOSQUE   IMMIGRATION OFFICE   JL. ADE IRMA SURYANI

JL. LANGKO   Mataram

ROCK GILIS
COFFEE   FAVEHOTEL
LANGKO   JL. PEJANGGIK

NUSA TENGGARA   JL. CATUR WARGA
BARAT MUSEUM   PASAR
CAKRANEGARA   MAYURA
WATER PALACE

ASTON INN   JL. PEJANGGIK   JL. SELAPARANG

JL. ABD. KADIR MUNSYI   JL. PANCA USAHA   PURA MERU

IKAN BAKAR 99

JL. ISMAIL MARZUKI

SIOLAM HOSPITALS   LOMBOK   JL. SRIWIJAYA
MATARAM   EPICENTRUM MALL

Kekalik   POLICE
STATION   JL. I.G.K. JELANTIK GOZA

JL. SULTAN KHAIRUDIN   Pagesangan

Kodya
Asri

0   0.5 mi

0   0.5 km

Bajur   JL. DR. SUJONO

© MOON.COM

JL. DR. SUJONO

Lange, a Danish trader who took on the title of the "White Raja of Ampenan." He spent his time in Ampenan building alliances across enemy lines and trading weapons, opium, metals, rice, and textiles. Eventually, Lange was driven out of Ampenan after getting caught up in Lombok's civil war. Evidence of Ampenan's trade with China is seen in its small Chinatown, where a Buddhist temple is a highlight.

NUSA TENGGARA BARAT MUSEUM

Jalan Panji Tilar Negara No.6; tel. 62370632159; www.museumnegerintb.com; Sat.-Thurs. 8am-3pm, closed Fri.

The Nusa Tenggara Barat Museum is Lombok's main museum, housing more than 7,000 artworks and artifacts from around the region. The exhibits are a mishmash of textiles, costumes, and historical pieces, some with English descriptions.

Perang Topat: The Food Fight for Peace

Indonesia hosts a political and philosophical concept called **Pancasila,** five principles upon which the country is based. One of these principles is the belief in one God, which is why Balinese Hindus honor **Sang Hyang Widhi Wasa,** the ability for one god to manifest itself into many forms. In Indonesia, it is common to hear a sentiment that religions that honor one god are brothers to one another. In Mataram, there is a large Balinese Hindu population, as a Balinese king once ruled the city. The majority of Lombok, however, practices **Islam.**

Perang Topat is a festival in which Sasak Wetu Telu Muslims and Balinese Hindus come together to engage in a friendly battle that involves *ketupat,* sticky rice balls wrapped in weaved palm leaves as ammunition. This tradition was developed to signify unity after decades of violent clashes between the *rajas,* or kings, of Bali and Lombok. The rice is also used symbolically as a blessing for soil fertility and an abundant rice harvest. Groups line up along their respective sides of the temple, and a group of women carrying *ketupat* comes to the center and distributes the rice among the participants. Each side then throws rice at one another in jest. At the end of the celebration, many collect leftover rice to take home and plant among their own rice fields. This rice is thought to bring good fortune and a successful rice harvest.

Visitors can view and participate in ceremony themselves, which usually takes place between **November** and **December.**

KAWIS KRISANT RAINBOW VILLAGE

Jalan Leo and around

In Kawis Krisant Rainbow Village, murals, bright colors, and decorations are discovered all around the neighborhood. The color-movement started when Aisyah Odist, a local who is passionate about environmental conservation, decided to create artwork and practical items out of upcycled plastic. You can find her at Bank Sampah (Jalan Leo No. 26), crafting art objects and hosting village tours.

Central Mataram
★ ISLAMIC CENTER MOSQUE

Intersection of Jalan Langko and Jalan Udayana; https://islamiccenter.ntbprov.go.id; daily 9am-5pm, closed for certain ceremonies; tour with 10,000 Rp donation

The Islamic Center Mosque is the largest mosque in Lombok, and is eye-catching with its ivory, gold, and green adornments. At night, it lights up in bright colors. Muslims and non-Muslims can visit, though non-Muslims will be given a robe to cover up even if they are dressed modestly. A tour guide will take you to the top of a tower with a platform that reveals panoramic views of

Mataram—ideal for spotting hundreds of mosques in the distance.

Cakranegara
MAYURA WATER PALACE AND TEMPLE
(Pura Mayura)

Jalan Selaparang; daily 7am-8pm; 25,000 Rp admission

Mayura Water Palace is a murky lake with a pavilion in its center, built in 1744 during Balinese rule. A battle between the Dutch and Balinese rulers of Mataram took place at Mayura Water Palace, resulting in hundreds of casualties. Today, local families and couples like to come to the garden area to laze beneath a tree.

MERU TEMPLE
(Pura Meru)

Jalan Selaparang; daily 7am-8pm; free

Pura Meru is a Hindu temple that dates back to the early 1700s, when it was originally built under Balinese rule. It's the largest Hindu temple on the island with an 11-tiered *meru* (shrine) next to two nine-tiered *merus* on its center to honor Shiva, Brahma, and Vishnu. The grounds have certainly seen better days.

Lombok: The Island of 1,000 Mosques

No matter where you go on Lombok, a mosque is close by. The call to prayer is heard at all hours of the day, interspersed with general announcements coming from the mosque speaker. Some Sasak people of Lombok practice a unique, non-orthodox form of Islam called **Wetu Telu,** where the call to prayer is done three times per day rather than five. Wetu Telu also has elements of Hinduism and animism intertwined with the teachings of the Koran. Before Islam, **Sasak Boda** was the mainstay religion of Lombok, where believers worshipped ancestral spirits.

Islam became the widespread religion of Lombok after Balinese (Hindu) and Dutch (Christian) forces occupied the island, almost as a rebuttal. Sasak Muslims who practice **Watu Lima,** a form of Islam that prays five times per day, steadily clash against those who practice Wetu Telu. Tensions have resulted in many Watu Telu being confined to small villages in rural Lombok, while those in the island's more condensed areas practice Watu Lima.

Mosques of all sizes and colors decorate the island of Lombok, making it a top destination not just for Muslim tourists but also for those with an eye for interesting architecture.

Persistent locals requesting 20,000-50,000 Rp for entrance and another 50,000 Rp for guiding (they'll claim it's mandatory—it's not) taint the would-be serenity.

East Mataram
LINGSAR TEMPLE
(Pura Lingsar)
Jalan Raya Lingsar; daily 8am-6pm; donation requested

Built in 1714, Pura Lingsar is rare in that it is a symbol of religious harmony with dedicated worshipping areas for Balinese Hindus and for those practicing Wetu Telu, the Sasak form of Islam. A pond in the temple is home to resident albino eels, which are considered sacred and are fed boiled eggs by those who visit. Pura Lingsar hosts Perang Topat, a ceremony that bonds Hindus and Muslims through a good-spirited food fight.

FESTIVALS AND EVENTS
LEBARAN
After Ramadan

Following the month of Ramadan, Lebaran (also called Idul Fitri) is a holiday when families gather together and spend time with one another, wearing their finest clothes and enjoying their favorite foods. It's a time where forgiveness is extended for any wrongdoings in the past year. Parades complete with floats and decorations march through villages, typically starting and ending at mosques illuminated with lights. It's common for locals to invite tourists into their homes to dine.

PERESEAN STICK FIGHTING FESTIVAL

Peresean is a festival that involves luck, strength, and blood. Peresean is a challenge between two fighters, each holding a stick and a shield made from buffalo hide. To start, a referee chooses two men from the audience, who then must strike one another with the cane. Each strike accrues points, and the winner is chosen after five rounds or after one fighter surrenders. A hug signifies the end of the game. Many believe that the more blood is drawn, the more rain Lombok will have.

SHOPPING
LOMBOK CRAFTS AND TEXTILES CENTER
Jalan Kerajinan; daily 8am-6pm

Lombok Crafts and Textiles Center hosts an ensemble of worn-down shops selling jewelry, textiles, wooden sculptures, and ceramics created in the region. Bargaining is expected. Many shopkeepers are trying to meet a target;

1: Ampenan Port **2:** Kawis Krisant Rainbow Village **3:** Islamic Center Mosque **4:** market in Ampenan

try to add in an item rather than driving the price down for the best deal.

LOMBOK EPICENTRUM MALL

Jalan Sriwijaya No. 333; tel. 370 6172999; www. lombokepicentrum.com; 10am-10pm daily

Lombok Epicentrum Mall is an air-conditioned oasis in the heart of Mataram with a movie theater; grocery store; clothing shops like Levis, Billabong, Polo, and Ralph Lauren; and a food court.

BANYUMULEK POTTERY CENTER

Jalan Wisata Banyumulek; tel. 87864512371; daily 9am-5pm

The village of Banyumulek is known for its pottery, and homes often display ceramic pieces for sale along the street. At the Banyumulek Pottery Center, you can watch pottery creation in all its stages, as it is crafted from clay, decorated, glazed, and fired in a kiln.

PASAR CAKRANEGARA

Jalan Selaparang; daily 9am-4pm

Pasar Cakranegara (also called Pasar Cakra) is a multilevel market with stalls selling designer knockoffs, handicrafts, jewelry, textiles, and everyday goods. Part of the market sells raw meat, seafood, and produce. It's a fine spot to get clothing tailored, though you might have to communicate through an impromptu game of charades.

FOOD
Markets
PASAR MANDALIKA

Jalan Sandubaya No. 86; daily 7am-5pm

Pasar Mandalika is one of the largest markets in Mataram. Locals flock here for deals on produce and spices. It's a prime spot to visit if you're interested in Sasak daily life; the market is attached to the main bus station.

PASAR KEBON ROEK

Jalan Adi Sucipto; daily 6am-6pm

A busy market in Ampenan, Pasar Kebon Roek is a labyrinth where piles of fruits, vegetables, snacks, and meat spill onto the walkways.

Indonesian
IKAN BAKAR 99

Jalan Subak; tel. 81933138188; daily 1pm-10pm; 20,000-40,000 Rp

Ikan Bakar means "grilled fish" in Bahasa Indonesia. At Ikan Bakar 99, you simply choose whether you want fish, squid, shrimp,

---

Lombok Epicentrum Mall

Interesting Indonesian Fruits

If you walk through a market in Indonesia, you'll likely see fruits that look otherworldly. Textures that range from smooth to scaly to hairy make you question the sanity of the first person to take a bite. Fear not; despite their appearance, these are some delicious fruits to try in Indonesia.

- **Mangosteen** (*Manggis*): Mangosteen looks like a maroon or purple ball with a thick stem and bulbous leaves on top. Twist off the top, pinch the fruit, and you'll find white flesh in its center. The fruit is sweet, soft, and juicy. Take care when eating—the purple rind is often used as a permanent dye.

- **Snakefruit** (*Salak*): Snakefruit is shaped like a teardrop and covered in snakeskin-like scales. Inside, there's a hard, sectioned fruit that resembles a garlic clove and tastes like a mix of pineapple, apple, and pear. Pull off the pointy part of the fruit and peel back the skin to enjoy. Snakefruit trees are spiked; leave harvesting it to the professionals.

- **Rambutan:** Rambutan is nature's take on pom-poms. The tough skin covered in red and yellow long hairs has a soft jelly berry in its center. The taste is sweet and light, like a lychee.

- **Durian:** Durian might be one of the most polarizing fruits in the world. Its spiky yellow-green exterior opens to a creamy flesh that tastes like either crème brulee or feet, depending on your taste buds. Many hotels ban durian due to its pungent odor.

- **Jackfruit** (*Nangka*): Jackfruits are green and spiky and can easily grow to be bigger than a basketball. These large fruits have sectioned pieces of stringy flesh that taste somewhat sweet and are often used in place of chicken in Indonesian vegetarian recipes.

- **Banana** (*Pisang*): Bananas in Indonesia range from bright yellow to green to red and might be ripe at any of these colors. These bananas are creamy and sweet, often sweeter than their larger cousins. Sampling them deep-fried and drizzled in coconut syrup is a must.

- **Starfruit** (*Belimbing*): Starfruit got its name thanks to its five edges that reveal a star once it's sliced. The yellow, waxy skin is edible along with the flesh inside. Expect a mix of sweet and sour.

or crab. Next, ask for it grilled or fried. Then, request to have it served with soy sauce, sweet and sour sauce, oyster sauce, black pepper, butter, or chili sauce. Meals are eaten communally at long tables.

★ **ROEMAH LANGKO**

Jalan Langko No. 68; tel. 370/630080; https://puteralombok.com; daily 10am-10pm; 40,000-80,000 Rp

Roemah Langko, set in a unique Dutch-influenced building, serves Sasak dishes like chicken *taliwang,* cooked with chili, garlic, and shrimp paste, and then smothered in *sambal.* Other favorite dishes include fish soup, satay skewers, and *nasi goreng* made with red rice. Meals are spiced for local taste buds; ask

for chilis on the side if you're not used to the heat. While you wait, spend some time wandering around the building to admire the architecture and antique artworks on the walls.

Café
ROCK GILIS COFFEE

Jalan Langko No. 23; tel. 370/6170758; www.rockgilis. com; daily 8am-midnight; 30,000-50,000 Rp

Rock Gilis Coffee is a casual coffee shop with a simple menu serving pizzas, paninis, sandwiches, omelets, and desserts near the Islamic Center Mosque. Their drinks menu is extensive, including smoothies, coffee (hot or iced), and fresh juice. It's a popular spot for meetings and for those tapping away on their laptops.

ACCOMMODATIONS
★ FAVEHOTEL LANGKO

Jalan Langko No. 21; tel. 370/6170111; www.
favehotels.com; 500,000 Rp

Favehotel Langko stands out from the rest with its bright pink, sparkling decor. Expect clean rooms with fast Wi-Fi, air-conditioning, hot water showers, and a 24-hour reception. Favehotel Langko is one of the most centrally located properties in Mataram, a 15-minute walk from the Islamic Center Mosque and Epicentrum Mall, as well as many restaurants, convenience stores, and neighborhoods ideal for strolling. Be sure to book an in-room massage, a welcome treat after a long day of sightseeing.

ASTON INN

Jalan Panca Usaha No. 01; tel. 370/7505000; www.
astonhotelsinternational.com; 800,000 Rp

A sleek hotel with modern amenities, Aston Inn is where you'll find air-conditioned rooms outfitted with a TV, Wi-Fi access, en suite bathroom, and desk. The beds are exceptionally comfortable for the region. A filling breakfast at the on-site restaurant (included in the room rate) features an omelet bar, pastries, pancakes, and a selection of Indonesian dishes. The outdoor swimming pool is a refreshing retreat from Mataram's humidity and heat.

LOMBOK ASTORIA

Jalan Jend. Sudirman No. 40; tel. 370/6170999; www.
lombokastoriahotel.com; 1,500,000 Rp

Chic and sleek, the Lombok Astoria hotel is a modern hotel on the outskirts of Mataram, where rooms on the upper floors overlook rice fields. Wade in the infinity pool, relax in the restaurant, or take advantage of the hotel's on-site gym. Each room has a TV, safety deposit box, air-conditioning, and Wi-Fi access.

INFORMATION AND SERVICES

The **Mataram Immigration office** (Jalan Udayana; tel. 370/632520; Mon.-Fri. 8am-noon and 2pm-4pm, closed Sat.-Sun. and holidays) can handle visa extensions and fingerprinting. Travelers must be dressed modestly to enter the building, and there are cases when tourists have been refused entry. The **police station** (tel. 370/693110) is located at Jalan Gajah Mada No. 7.

Health and Medicine
RUMAH SAKIT HARAPAN KELUARGA

Jalan Ahmad Yani No. 9; tel. 370/670000; www.
harapankeluarga.co.id; open 24/7

Rumah Sakit Harapan Keluarga is a private hospital with basic medical care, ambulance and emergency services, and dental, outpatient, and inpatient care. There is also an on-site **pharmacy.**

SILOAM MATARAM

Jalan Majapahit No. 10; tel. 370/623999; https://
siloamhospitals.com; open 24/7

Siloam Mataram is a modern hospital with an emergency department, inpatient care, diagnostic services, and other specialized treatments. The hospital can also arrange an ambulance and medical evacuation services.

GETTING THERE
By Bus and *Bemo*

Buses and *bemos* arrive and depart at **Mandalika Terminal** (Jalan Raya Mataram) from **Kuta, Lombok** (1.5 hours; 60,000 Rp), Labuhan (2.5 hours, 35,000 Rp), **Lombok International Airport** in Praya (1 hour; 30,000 Rp), **Lembar** (45 minutes; 25,000 Rp), and **Senggigi** (1 hour; 15,000-40,000 Rp).

By Car and Motorbike

You can reach Mataram by car and motorbike from **Kuta** (50 km/31 mi; 1 hour), **Senggigi** (20 km/12 mi; 30 minutes), **Praya** (Lombok International Airport 40 km/25 mi; 45 minutes), and **Labuhan Lombok** (90 km/56 mi; 2.5 hours). **Bluebird taxis** can be taken from **Senggigi,** though they are less reliable outside of Mataram.

GETTING AROUND

Motorbikes are available for rent for around 50,000 Rp day, but be prepared for erratic and congested traffic inside Mataram. If you're not used to driving a motorbike, Mataram is not a safe place to learn.

Rideshare apps like **Grab** and **GoJek** are available, so you can have a local drive you to your destination. **Bluebird** taxis are also easy to catch and use, with many clustered around **Epicentrum Mall.** Bluebird taxis can also be hailed through the **MyBluebird App.**

Southwest Peninsula

The Southwest Peninsula of Lombok rewards those who venture outside of the island's tourist-heavy areas. Little islands called the "Secret Gili Islands," with rings of white sand and fringing coral reefs, beckon those who seek sunshine and solitude. On the tip of the Southwest Peninsula, one of the best waves in the Indonesian archipelago tempts surfers in search of barrels. Electricity is a precious and well-regulated commodity; the hum of a generator only revs up for dinnertime. This is where you fulfill your dream of being stranded on a desert isle.

ORIENTATION

The region of **Sekotong** covers the entire Southwest Peninsula, including most of the peninsula's offshore islands. **Jalan Raya Sekotong** runs along the northern part of the peninsula's shoreline, with boats to the Southwest Gili Islands leaving from its shoreline, many from the coastal village of **Tawun.** In Sekotong itself, you'll find small clusters of homes, warungs, mosques, and the odd convenience shop. The only **ATM** on the peninsula is found in town. Restaurants outside of your accommodation can be hard to find; those staying for more than a night or two might want to consider bringing extra food.

LEMBAR HARBOR

Lembar Harbor is the main harbor connecting Lombok's southwest coastline, where ferries run between **Bali** and **Lombok,** and from mainland Lombok to its outer islands. The harbor is 20 km (12 mi) south of **Mataram.**

You can reach Lembar Harbor from **Padangbai, Bali** by **public ferry** (46,000 Rp adult, 29,000 Rp child) that takes four to six hours, depending on the sea's conditions.

THE ISLANDS
Gili Gede

The largest of the Southwest Gili Islands, Gili Gede is dotted with quiet fishing villages, and its infrastructure consists of dirt roads and generators. Cows, goats, and chickens dart in between the odd motorbike humming around the island. Fishing boats are the preferred method of transportation. Beaches range from fine sand to bits of coral to rubbish-strewn.

Gili Sudak

Gili Sudak is a popular spot for day-trippers venturing around the Southwest Gili Islands, though few spend the night on the island. Beachside warungs serve plates of noodles, rice, and fish, and a lonely guesthouse welcomes those wanting to stay overnight. Great snorkeling sites are found just offshore. Finding a beach to yourself is guaranteed.

Gili Kedis

Gili Kedis is perhaps the cutest micro-island in the Southwest Gili Islands, with a shoreline that can be traversed in minutes. A shaded lounge area, swings, and a thriving reef will keep you occupied for a few hours.

Gili Tangkong

Untamed except for a grove of palm trees, Gili Tangkong is one of the least-visited islands. Like elsewhere, the beaches are idyllic for lounging and the reefs are teeming with

Southwest Peninsula

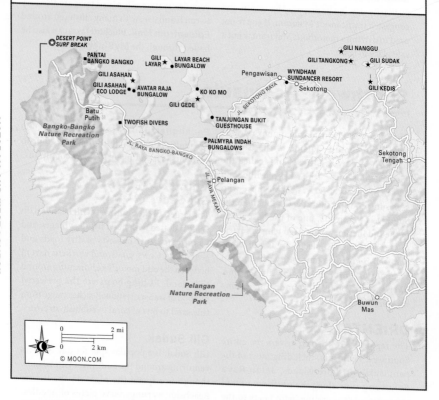

life. This island is not included in many day trips around, and may need to be requested as a side trip.

Gili Nanggu

Gili Nanggu is one of the best sites to snorkel in the Southwest Gili Islands, with an artificial reef that attracts corals, reef fish, sponges, and crustaceans. Coral reefs sweep around the island, giving way to a field of sea grass where you might spot pipefish and neon-colored sea urchins. Shaded platforms are available for those who need shelter from the sun.

Gili Asahan

You'll only need two hours to walk around the little island of Gili Asahan, which is home

to one of the best resorts in the region, **Gili Asahan Eco Lodge.** By day, explore the beaches, coral reefs, and miniature hills. At night, stargaze on the beach. The neighboring island of **Gili Goleng** is just a short kayak trip away.

Gili Layar

Gili Layar is the place to go when you don't want your regular life to follow. This island takes relaxation to the next level, with few things to do other than swim with the resident sea turtles. It's a popular spot among Lombok locals to visit, making it surprisingly crowded on the weekends or public holidays—though

1: Gili Kedis 2: Gili Sudak

☆ The Legendary Desert Point Surf Break

Only the intrepid tend to venture to Tanjung Desert, a desolate stretch of land with an unforgiving surf break. If you get barreled, it's unforgettable. Warungs, restaurants, and accommodations are scarce.

The beach, **Pantai Bangko Bangko** (Jalan Raya Sekotong), is prime for sunbathing and watching surfers dance along the face of the beach's iconic wave. As for the wave, it's a challenge to name a better lefthander in Southeast Asia than Desert Point. This fast and hollow wave breaks over shallow reef and needs a massive swell to break. It rewards those who are patient with 20+ second tube rides. The crowds can get entitled and nasty. Still, it's worth surfing if you have the skill. Watch for southwest swells and southeasterly winds; your best chance of having prime conditions is from May to October. Mid- to low tide is best for paddling out.

Basic accommodations can usually be found just by showing up to Desert Point/Bangko Bangko, where **cinderblock huts** have thin-mattress beds. Few accommodations have reliable phone or Internet connection to take bookings in advance. Expect to pay 80,000-100,000 Rp per room. Electricity is limited at best, and thefts are not unheard of.

You'll need your own **car** to get to Tanjung Desert. Follow **Jalan Raya Sekotong** to the end, where it then turns into dirt road. Some ride **motorbikes,** though the road conditions are prime for popping tires. If you run into trouble, it could be a while before you get help (especially if there is no surf).

you'll still find a quiet place to yourself. Head to the hill for sunset views.

★ SNORKELING AND SCUBA DIVING
MIMPI MANIS SNORKELING TOUR
Pickup Kuta Lombok or meet at Pantai Tawun, Sekotong; tel. 62818369950; www.mimpimanis.com; daily 7am-4pm; 450,000 Rp full day tour

See the tiny islands of Gili Nanggu, Gili Sudak, and Gili Kedis on a Mimpi Manis snorkeling tour that includes snorkeling gear, breakfast, and water (excludes lunch). Gemma, your guide, is knowledgeable about the area and will rattle off the names of any marine creatures you come across. She is an expert on knowing where to look for some of the islands' elusive residents. Groups are kept small, and a boat takes you from island to island, stopping midway through the day for a beachside lunch.

TWO FISH DIVERS
Jalan Raya Siung; tel. 81907852073; www. twofishdivers.com; daily 7am-8pm daily; 750,000 Rp fun dive, 5,900,000 Rp open water

Two Fish Divers is a 5-Star PADI dive resort offering fun dives around the Southwest Gili Islands, where divers are likely to see a variety of reef life, sea turtles, sardines, and reef sharks. New divers can get open water certified. Stay-and-dive packages are available for discounted dives and accommodation.

ACCOMMODATIONS
Under 1,000,000 Rp
PALMYRA INDAH BUNGALOWS
Sekotong; tel. 87760077714; www.palmyraindah.com; 90,000-150,000 Rp

Palmyra Indah Bungalows is a remote getaway with bungalows set around a grassy area, a short walk to a sandy beach. The double bungalows come with a private bathroom, large patio, fan, and queen-sized beds wrapped in mosquito nets. Spotty Wi-Fi is also included. There is also one larger bungalow that can host up to three guests. The on-site restaurant serves fresh salads, seafood, and Indonesian dishes. Fruit juices and a range of spirits are also available.

TANJUNGAN BUKIT GUESTHOUSE
Gili Gede; tel. 81805290314; 500,000 Rp

Run by a friendly Indonesian and French

couple, Tanjungan Bukit Guesthouse is a clean and quiet resort where you can enjoy the solitude of Gili Gede from a room or a bungalow tucked in between palm trees and an untamed garden. Bamboo furniture, beanbag chairs, tropical decor, and views that overlook the water create an oasis-like ambience. Even if you are not staying as a guest of Tanjungan Bukit Guesthouse, it's worth visiting the **restaurant** to enjoy a fusion of Indonesian and French cuisine.

★ LAYAR BEACH BUNGALOW

Gili Layar; tel. 81211111388; www.layarbeachbungalow. com; 375,000-850,000 Rp

It's a challenge to feel stressed at Layar Beach Bungalow, a beachside resort with thatched roof huts and beanbag chairs set under a bamboo lounge area. The five bungalows are rustic and quaint, built from natural materials and equipped with an outdoor bathroom with cold water showers. Only the larger bungalows have air-conditioning, while the others have fans. Expect to disconnect during the daytime, when electricity is limited to the communal area. For those who plan to spend their time in the water, there is a thriving reef, rife with sea life, in front of the resort.

★ GILI ASAHAN ECO LODGE

Gili Asahan; tel. 81339604779; www.giliasahan.com; 700,000-2,000,000 Rp

The secret's out about Gili Asahan Eco Lodge, an environmentally conscious resort that's often booked out during high season. The resort has luxurious bungalows built from wood, bamboo, and thatched roofs. Inside, crisp linens and driftwood furniture create a comfortable respite from the sand and the heat. Each evening, guests can enjoy the crackle of a bonfire and top-end Indonesian and Italian meals from the on-site restaurant. At high tide, the calm water and reef out in front of the resort make up for the property not having a pool.

AVATAR RAJA BUNGALOW

Gili Asahan; tel. 81803625093; www. avatarbungalow-giliasahan.blogspot.com; 750,000 Rp

If sleeping on a desert island is what you seek, head to Avatar Raja Bungalow. Three small bungalows backed against palm trees have a mini patio, basic furnishings, and cold-water showers. The host, Safari, serves breakfast on the beach and is happy to teach guests about coral restoration and things to do in the area.

Wyndham Sundancer Resort

Over 1,000,000 Rp
KO-KO-MO GILI GEDE

Gili Gede; tel. 81907325135; www.kokomogiligede.com; from 2,500,000 Rp

For some serious escapism, head to Ko-Ko-Mo, a luxury resort on the quiet island of Gili Gede. One- and two-bedroom villas have modern designs with tasteful decor; all are equipped with a seating area, Wi-Fi access, TV, and open-air bathrooms, and they are surrounded by immaculate gardens. The best picks of the property have private pools and views that look out to the ocean. You'll never be bored, with a gym, golf course, tennis court, spa, stand-up paddleboards, kayaks, snorkeling gear, bicycles, and a beachside pool surrounded by cushy lounge chairs to keep you entertained. Staff can help arrange snorkeling and fishing trips. The on-site restaurant has an extensive menu, including seafood and imported meat dishes.

WYNDHAM SUNDANCER RESORT

Sekotong; tel. 85337389497; www.wyndhamsundancerlombok.com; 3,000,000 Rp

Wyndham Sundancer Resort is relatively new, with spacious one- and two-bedroom suites. A king-sized bed, living room, porch or balcony, air-conditioning, TV, Wi-Fi, and large bathtub are found in all rooms. The full kitchen in each suite is a nice touch, though it is mostly for show when you consider the lack of shops nearby. Enjoy dining in the two on-site **restaurants,** one near the lagoon-style pool with swim-up bar, and the other on the beach, where you can dine at a wooden table or in your comfortable beach chair.

GETTING THERE AND AROUND

You will need your own set of wheels or a **private driver** to get to the South Gilis. Phone reception can be spotty, roads are pot-holed, and the few businesses around shutter early; it's best to **arrive during daylight.** To reach the Lembar from **Senggigi** (50 km/31 mi; 1.5 hours), take **Jalan Raya Senggigi** to **Mataram** (30 km/18.5 mi; 45 minutes) and follow **Jalan Raya Lembar** to Lembar. There is only one major road through the peninsula, **Jalan Raya Sekotong,** which runs 50 km (31 mi) along the coastline from Lembar to **Desert Point.**

A **boat** is needed to get to each of the Southwest Gili Islands. You hire one privately from fishermen on the shores of **Tawun** or make arrangements through your accommodation. A reliable boat driver with limited English, **Suhap,** can be reached at tel. 87765578665.

Gili Getaway (tel. 82144899502; https://giligetaway.com) offers transport services between **Gili Gede** and **Serangan, Bali** (2 hours; 710,000 Rp one-way, 1,320,000 Rp round-trip), **Nusa Lembongan, Bali** (1.5 hours; 650,000 Rp one way, 1,200,000 Rp round-trip), and **Nusa Penida, Bali** (1 hour 650,000 Rp one way, 1,200,000 Rp round-trip).

Kuta, Lombok

In the stillness of morning, just before sunrise, the local mosque blares its call to prayer. The sound of motorbikes driven by surfers chasing morning waves rev up, drowning out the voice of the imam and crowing roosters. This is Kuta, a small beach town and the hub for travelers yearning to explore Lombok's southern coastline.

Kuta once hosted only a handful of ramshackle guesthouses and rickety warungs to accommodate the backpackers who ventured here. Today, in the town center, there are boutique hotels and international restaurants serving food that can compete with the best in Bali. Major urban growth, in the form of the Mandalika Development Project, looms in Kuta's future—with plans for luxury villas, large hotels, a

Highlights

Look for ★ to find recommended sights, activities, dining, and lodging.

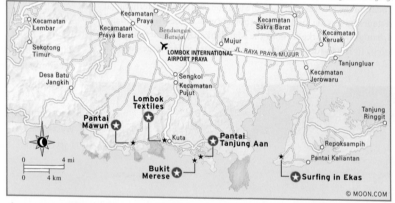

Kecamatan Lembar
Kecamatan Praya
Kecamatan Praya Barat
Bendungan Batujai
Kecamatan Sakra Barat
Kecamatan Keruak
Sekotong Timur
Mujur
LOMBOK INTERNATIONAL AIRPORT PRAYA
JL. RAYA PRAYA MUJUR
Tanjungluar
Desa Batu Jangkih
Sengkol
Kecamatan Pujut
Kecamatan Jerowaru
Lombok Textiles ★
Tanjung Ringgit
Pantai Mawun ★
Kuta
Pantai Tanjung Aan ★
Repoksampih
0   4 mi
0   4 km
Bukit Merese ★
Pantai Kaliantan
★ **Surfing in Ekas**

© MOON.COM

★ **Bukit Merese:** This is a romantic place to enjoy the beautiful beach of Tanjung Aan from above and a prime spot for sunset (page 414).

★ **Pantai Mawun:** Enjoy a stretch of sand to yourself at a beach that's worthy of being the front page of Lombok's travel brochure (page 416).

★ **Pantai Tanjung Aan:** A bay with white sand and turquoise water, this beach is what travel clichés are made of (page 418).

★ **Lombok Textiles:** Beautiful textiles crafted on a wooden loom are sold on the beaches of Kuta and inside Lombok's traditional villages (page 424).

★ **Surfing in Ekas:** There's a wave for everyone just east of Kuta, but you might need to venture down a dirt road to find it (page 434).

Top Restaurants

★ **Warung Flora:** Dine on plates of noodles and rice served fresh under a large thatched roof (page 423).

★ **Warung Turtle:** Enjoy Lombok's classic warung, on the shores of Pantai Tanjung Aan (page 423).

★ **El Bazar:** Meze plates and Mediterranean fare are doled out under ambient lighting (page 425).

★ **Terra:** All-vegan dishes are made with love, with healthy meals served alongside sweet treats (page 425).

★ **Milk Espresso:** This café built from shipping containers offers good coffee and a lively rooftop bar (page 425).

yacht marina, and golf course—but for now, Kuta is still relatively sleepy and laid-back. Women with bundles of colorful fabrics—handmade in one of the traditional villlages inland from Kuta—sell them on the beaches. It's the type of place where you can lose a day or two to the nearby beaches, run into the same handful of locals and travelers each day, and feel prematurely nostalgic knowing that Kuta might not remain how it is for much longer.

Outside Kuta, bay after bay awaits where those who visit will discover beaches with white sand, pink sand, and variations in between. Some are crowded with beach lounges while others are utterly deserted. Most are connected by one paved road that gives way to a pathway made from dirt and potholes. The journey is usually worth it. If you're looking for relaxation, you'll find it on the shores of Pantai Tanjung Aan, Pantai Mawun, Pantai Selong Belanak, and on the hilltop of Bukit Merese. If you've come to the island in search of thrills, you'll be challenged paddling out at the waves at Pantai Mawi, Gerupuk, and Ekas. Or, you can dive with hammerhead sharks in Belongas. No matter your style, a filling plate

of *nasi goreng* (fried rice) is just a short motorbike ride away.

ORIENTATION

Kuta and its neighboring beaches sit along Lombok's southern coastline, just 17 km (10.5 mi) south of the **Lombok International Airport.** The hub of Lombok's dry south, Kuta is a quirky beach town that sits in the near center of a string of beaches. Southern Lombok starts at the Southwest Peninsula, with **Pantai Belongas** being the westernmost beach featured in this area. Moving east, **Selong Belanak** is a 45-minute drive from Kuta, with the beaches of **Pantai Lancing** and **Pantai Tampah, Pantai Mawun,** and **Pantai Areguling** in between.

Driving east from Kuta, you'll pass the quiet beaches of **Pantai Serenting** and **Pantai Tanjung Aan. Gerupuk,** the legendary surf town, is where you'll find more accommodations. **Awang Bay** carves into the island with **Ekas** on the tip of its eastern peninsula—often best reached by boat.

The town of Kuta itself is easy to navigate, with just a few main roads throughout. **Jalan Raya Kuta** leads to the beach, with stalls of

Previous: Gerupuk sunrise; Pantai Mawun; surfing in Ekas.

Top Accommodations

★ **Bombora Bungalows:** Simple bamboo shacks with hammocks and lounge chairs are set around a dip-worthy pool (page 426).

★ **Lara Homestay:** This welcoming family-run guesthouse has clean rooms and delightful food (page 427).

★ **Mana:** You'll feel like you're sleeping in the middle of a jungle at this retreat where yoga classes and fresh juices are part of the daily routine (page 427).

★ **Charlie's Shack:** Here, you'll find friendly staff and a prime location for surfing Gerupuk's many waves (page 433).

★ **Ekas Surf Resort:** This is a surfer's retreat in a social setting, where boat rides to the nearby break are included with each stay (page 434).

textiles, hotels, and restaurants along its path. **Jalan Mawun,** also filled with accommodations and restaurants, leads west of Kuta to the western beaches, with **Ashtari** being the marker that signals you're heading out of town. **Jalan Pariwisata Pantai Kuta** is another popular road that leads to the beach, and wraps around the beachfront. Follow this to reach the western point of town that's marked by Novotel. To get to the coast's eastern beaches, drive along the bumpy road of **Jalan Sengkol** or head up to the better paved road of **Jalan Sengkol Mujul.** Kuta is a short drive from **Lombok International Airport** in the town of **Praya.**

PLANNING YOUR TIME

Lombok's southern coastline is drier than the rest of the island, making it an ideal place for a beach getaway, no matter the time of year. For surfers, swells are influenced by the two seasons of Lombok, dry season and wet season. Most of the waves are best during the dry season from **April** to **September,** though you'll find storm swells and glassy waves through the wet season, from **October** to **March.** If you want to learn how to surf here, consider enrolling in a **surf camp.** Some surf camps recommend a three-day commitment—just enough time to truly get the hang of surfing friendly waves.

If you're keen to see most of the beaches along Lombok's southern coastline, base yourself in **Kuta** for the most accommodation and restaurant options. The town is central to the beaches to the west and to the east. If you simply want to master a handful of waves, base yourself in **Gerupuk.** That way, you can catch a few more minutes of sleep and still beat the sunrise surf crowd to the breaks. If you want to beach-hop, you can easily spend two full days bouncing between Kuta's neighboring beaches. The most convenient way to get around the region is with a rental **motorbike** or **private driver,** arranged through your accommodation.

Itinerary Ideas

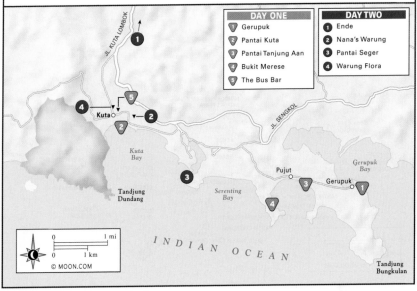

DAY ONE	DAY TWO
1 Gerupuk	1 Ende
2 Pantai Kuta	2 Nana's Warung
3 Pantai Tanjung Aan	3 Pantai Seger
4 Bukit Merese	4 Warung Flora
5 The Bus Bar	

Itinerary Ideas

TWO DAYS IN KUTA, LOMBOK

Day 1: Kuta and Around

1 Head to **Gerupuk** for a sunrise session at one of the surf spots breaking within the bay. Plan your trip with Hassan, a local surf guide.

2 Next, head to **Pantai Kuta** to shop for textiles from local vendors.

3 Enjoy **Pantai Tanjung Aan**, a beautiful beach with white sand and shaded lounge chairs that are free to use with a purchase of food or drink from a warung.

4 Walk up to **Bukit Merese** to enjoy a spectacular sunset.

5 Drive back to Kuta for dinner in town and drinks at **The Bus Bar.**

Day 2: Kuta Like a Local

1 Drive to **Ende,** a traditional village where women weave fabrics on a wooden loom.

2 Drive back to Kuta for lunch, stopping at **Nana's Warung** for fresh and delicious fare.

3 Walk or drive to **Pantai Seger** and admire views of Kuta from its headland, then walk down to the shoreline for a retreat.

4 For dinner, eat a fresh Indonesian meal at **Warung Flora.**

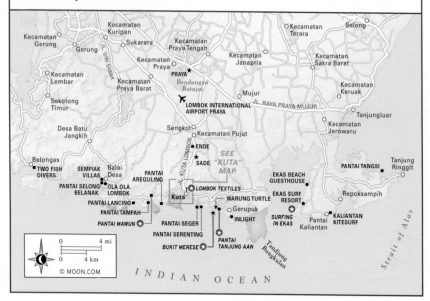

Kuta, Lombok

Sights

★ Bukit Merese

*Edge of Pantai Tanjung Aan; 10,000 Rp car, 5,000
Rp motorbike parking*

Bukit Merese has earned its reputation for being the best place to sit and watch the sunset in the region. A hilly peninsula juts out beyond Pantai Tanjung Aan, revealing clearwater coves and a jagged coastline. Livestock, locals, and travelers all share the grassy hill—though even in high season, you'll find a quiet place to yourself. Purchase a coconut or drink from the bottom of the trailhead and enjoy it once you reach the top. Walking to the top of Bukit Merese takes about 10 minutes at a leisurely pace. There are few better places to watch the sky change from blue to flame-colored hues. **Park** close to the Bukit Merese trailhead if you plan to stay after sunset.

Praya and Lombok International Airport

Home to the Lombok International Airport, Praya is a manicured town with flowerbeds on the sides of the roads and rice fields sprawling out from its surrounds. ATMs, warungs, small shops, and hotels catering to travelers catching early morning flights are found within its limits.

LOMBOK INTERNATIONAL AIRPORT

Lombok International Airport (LOP, Jalan Bypass Praya; tel. 370/615700; https://lombok-airport.co.id), also called **Zainuddin Abdul Madjid International Airport**, is the main airport on Lombok and the only airport offering international flights. **Batik Air** (www.batikair.com), **Citilink** (www.citilink.co.id), **AirAsia** (www.airasia.com), **Garuda Indonesia** (www.garuda-indonesia.com), **Lion Air** (www.lionair.co.id), **NAM Air** (flynamair.com), and **Silk Air** (www.silkair.com) all offer routes linking to the airport.

GETTING TO AND FROM THE AIRPORT

Taxis are available in front of the airport leading to Kuta (30 min; 150,000 Rp), Mataram (45 minutes; 200,000 Rp), and Senggigi (1.5 hours; 250,000 Rp); they charge about 50,000 Rp extra per trip for late arrivals. You can attempt to call a taxi through the MyBluebird app in advance, but drivers may refuse to pick up from the airport to avoid harassment from the airport taxi band. **DAMRI shuttle buses** to Mataram are available out front for those going to Mataram (45 minutes; 30,000 Rp) and Senggigi (1.5 hours; 40,000 Rp).

Many car rental companies will include a private driver with the rental price. Private drivers can be arranged through **Feel Lombok** (tel. 85938380730; https://feel-lombok.com; info@feel-lombok.com) for around 600,000 Rp per day. **Surya Rent Car** (tel. 81917048330; www.carrentallombok.com; info@carrentallombok.com) offers self-drive car rentals and is best arranged in advance of your arrival (300,000-500,000 Rp day).

To get to Lombok International Airport from **Senggigi** (50 km/31 mi; 1-1.5 hours), take Jalan Raya Senggigi 20 km (12 mi) south to **Mataram,** which is 30 km (18.5 mi; 30 minutes-1 hour) from the airport, best reached along Jalan By Pass Bandara Int. Lombok. From **Kuta** (20 km/12 mi; 30 minutes), take Jalan Kuta Lombok 10 km (6 mi) to Jalan Raya Tanak Awu for 4 km (2.5 mi) to a roundabout, and follow signs saying "Bandara Internasional Lombok" to the airport.

Beaches and Surf Breaks

Explore Lombok's southern coastline and you'll find one stunning beach after the next. While the main road leading along Southern Lombok is well maintained, many of the roads you'll use to reach the beaches themselves are made of dirt and rife with potholes. It's best to see the beaches with your own rental motorbike or private driver, taking care to drive carefully on roads in dire need of maintenance.

Kuta Beach
(Pantai Kuta)

Jalan Raya Kuta; 10,000 Rp car, 5,000 Rp motorbike parking

Pantai Kuta is the town's main beach, where locals from all around the island congregate. It's busy with fishermen and fishing boats, hawkers selling jewelry and blankets, kids at play, and tourists lounging on the sand. At the eastern side of the beach, monkeys scamper around a small grove of mangrove trees.

Kuta

Map labels:
- JL. RAYA KUTA
- JL. PARIWISATA
- JL. MAWUN
- ASHTARI
- HORIZON AT ASHTARI
- LOKA GYM
- LOMBOK INTERNATIONAL MEDICAL SERVICE
- MATCHA SPA
- RAYA KUTA
- KURA KURA SURF CAMP
- MANA
- WARUNG FLORA
- BURGER ZONE
- SCUBA FROGGY
- FLOW SURF STORE
- MILK ESPRESSO
- THE BUS BAR
- JL. SENGKOL
- BAMBA
- LARA HOMESTAY
- NALUA SURF
- COCO SURF
- EL BAZAR
- TERRA
- NANA'S WARUNG
- SASAK SOUL
- YOGI BAR
- Kuta
- LOTUS MANDALIKA
- JL. MAWUN
- RIVIERA
- BLUE MARLIN
- BOMBORA BUNGALOWS
- HARMONY VILLAS
- SURFERS BAR
- WHATSUP? LOMBOK
- PANTAI KUTA
- Kuta Bay
- Tanjung Tampa Nature Recreation Park
- 0   1,000 ft
- 0   200 m
- © MOON.COM

Tampah Beach and Lancing Beach
(Pantai Tampah and Pantai Lancing)

Jalan Mawun; 10,000 Rp car, 5,000 Rp motorbike parking

The neighboring beaches of Pantai Tampah and Pantai Lancing are slivers of white sand that weave along calm waters. Unless it's a holiday, you're likely to have most of it all to yourself. A handful of thatched roof-shaded areas offer a break from the sunshine.

★ Mawun Beach
(Pantai Mawun)

Jalan Mawun; 10,000 Rp car, 5,000 Rp motorbike parking

A relaxed beach with little to do but swim and lounge, Pantai Mawun is popular among locals rather than tourists. The elephant ear bay sweeps between jagged peninsulas. A handful of lonely shacks sell soft drinks and fresh coconuts.

1: Bukit Merese 2: Pantai Kuta 3: Pantai Mawun 4: Pantai Areguling

MAWUN SURF BREAK

Paddle out through channel at Pantai Mawun

Mawun Surf Break is a right-hand point break with glassy walls and long rides under the right conditions. It works best in 1-meter (4-foot) southeast to southwesterly swells and northwesterly winds. The vibe tends to be friendly, as long as you respect the lineup—though the locals might not.

Areguling Beach
(Pantai Areguling)

Jalan Pariwisata Areguling; 10,000 Rp car, 5,000 Rp motorbike parking

A spacious beach with an offshore island punctuating the water, Pantai Areguling requires an off-road ride along a dirt road to reach. Fishing boats, driftwood, and thatched-roof shacks clutter the shoreline. It's a local spot, where you're likely to sip a coconut in solitude.

AREGULING SURF BREAKS

Paddle out through the reef channel in the middle of the bay

Pantai Areguling (also called "Air Guling") hosts a lefthander and righthander in its bay. The righthander barrels with southeast/southwest swells and northerly winds, holding up to 3 meters (10 feet). The less-impressive lefthander breaks in the middle of the bay and works best with mid- to high tide.

Seger Beach
(Pantai Seger)

Follow road alongside Novotel, parking before bridge; 10,000 Rp car, 5,000 Rp motorbike parking

The appeal of Pantai Seger is not necessarily the beach itself but the viewpoints that surround it. In either direction, you can enjoy walking up a hill to admire the neighboring bays. On the beach, you'll find a thin sliver of coarse sand and a pack of stray dogs to keep you company. Snack shacks sell fresh fruit, coconuts, and simple meals, served on a shaded platform.

SEGER SURF BREAK

Paddle out at Pantai Seger; take care when paddling over shallow reef

The wave offshore of Pantai Seger is a friendly righthander with shifty peaks that welcomes an intermediate crowd at mid-tide. It breaks during small southern swells and works best with northeasterly winds. If the swell picks up, you might find strong currents and closeouts.

Serenting Beach
(Pantai Serenting)

Jalan Beach Walk; 10,000 Rp car, 5,000 Rp motorbike parking

Pantai Serenting is a mellow beach with a handful of shaded bamboo seating areas, though it is largely undeveloped. A long stretch of seaweed-speckled sand borders the shoreline. Mid- to high tide is best for swimming, while low tide reveals rock pools in the reef with sea life hidden in between the crags.

★ Tanjung Aan Beach
(Pantai Tanjung Aan)

Jalan Mandalika; 10,000 Rp car, 5,000 Rp motorbike parking

A sugar-white sand beach that wraps around a bright blue bay, Pantai Tanjung Aan is just what people imagine when they dream of lounging on one of Lombok's beaches. Sunset views are found on Bukit Merese to the west; another hill makes for a great lookout point to its east. Picturesque umbrellas and lounge chairs line the shoreline.

The Best Surf Spots in Southern Lombok

- **Outside Gerupuk** (Right): This fast swell magnet barrels under the right conditions and keeps experienced surfers on their toes (page 432).

- **Don Don:** Mellow rights and lefts offer long rides in relaxed conditions; it's a playground for beginners and intermediate surfers (page 432).

- **Mawi:** A fast and hollow left-hand barrel breaks inside a beautiful bay (page 431).

- **Inside Ekas:** This relaxed A-frame rewards surfers with an easy take off and 100-meter+ (328-foot) rides (page 434).

- **Outside Ekas:** Here you'll find a heavy righthander that barrels in the best conditions (page 434).

Water Sports

STAND-UP PADDLEBOARDING
WHATSUP? LOMBOK
Pantai Kuta; tel. 87865978701; www.whatsuplombok. com; daily 8am-8pm

The waters off of Lombok are your playground with Whatsup? Lombok. Here you can rent stand-up paddleboards, surfboards, kitesurf gear, and kayaks, and arrange a variety of ocean sports tours with partnered local businesses. For a unique adventure, join a nighttime stand-up paddleboard tour where you explore Pantai Kuta under the stars on a board outfitted with LED lights (380,000 per person).

SCUBA DIVING AND SNORKELING
SCUBA FROGGY
Jalan Raya Kuta and Novotel; tel. 87864541402; www.scubafroggy.com; daily 10am-8pm; 5,500,000 Rp open water, 600,000 Rp fun dive

Longtime operator Scuba Froggy offers PADI dive courses and fun dive trips around Kuta, Gerupuk, and Tampah, as well as to Belongas if you book in advance. The divemasters are knowledgeable about the ideal dive sites for each condition. Snorkeling tours are also available.

BLUE MARLIN
Jalan Raya Kuta; tel. 81237393491; www. bluemarlindive.com; daily 8am-6pm; 5,500,000 Rp open water, 540,000 Rp fun dive

Blue Marlin is a household name in Lombok, having been the first dive operation to set up on Gili Trawangan. They've recently expanded to Kuta, where dive guides and instructors offer PADI dive courses from open water to Divemaster, along with fun dive excursions around the region.

SURFING
NALUA SURF
Jalan Pariwisata; tel. 81907969162; www.naluasurf. com; 7,900,000 Rp per week (1 surf session per day plus room)

Nalua Surf has a small surf shop, modern fan or air-conditioned rooms, and a rooftop lounge where surfers enjoy breakfast and practice yoga. They offer a range of surf camp packages, with lessons and coaching for beginner or intermediate surfers, and guides for more experienced surfers. Daily surf lessons are available for those who don't want a package. Surf sessions, accommodation, surf analysis, board rental, day trips, and breakfast are included for those who stay a week or longer.

SASAK SOUL
Jalan Mawun No. 16; tel. 85337800970; https:// sasaksoul.com; daily 8:30am-8:30pm; 450,000 Rp lesson, 6,800,000 Rp per week surf camp (2 hours of surfing per day plus room)

Sasak Soul combines surfing with Sasak culture by offering surf camps, surf lessons, and cultural tours of the island. Those who teach at Sasak Soul are friendly, passionate, and patient. Surf camps include airport transfer, private or dorm room accommodation with air-conditioning, surf lessons, and surf photography with analysis. Daily surf lessons are also available for surfers staying elsewhere.

KURA KURA SURF CAMP
Jalan Mawun; tel. 81337226477; www. kurakurasurfcamp.com; sunrise-sunset; 7,500,000 Rp per week (2 lessons per day)

Kura Kura is a boutique surf camp where surfers stay in bungalows and enjoy two surf lessons per day. Camp packages include airport transfer, breakfast, surf photography with analysis, and surf equipment. Beginner camps start on Saturdays, though intermediate and advanced surfers may stay longer. Surf lessons are not available outside of the surf camp package, and the camp requires a minimum stay of five nights.

Other Sports and Recreation

YOGA
ASHTARI
Jalan Mawun; tel. 81236080862; www.ashtari.yoga; daily 7:15am-8:30pm; 120,000 Rp class

Taking a yoga class at Ashtari is worth doing simply for the view. The venue overlooks the valley below and spans to Kuta and the sea. Ashtanga classes take place Monday to Saturday, *hatha* and *yin* yoga classes take place daily. Their on-site restaurant makes for a great post-yoga place to eat, also offering incredible views. The yoga class schedule is updated on their website.

MANA
Jalan Baturiti I; tel. 85338628659; www. manalombok.com; daily 7:30am-7:30pm; 120,000 Rp class

Stay at Mana for a complete yoga retreat, or drop in to one of their four daily classes

Kura Kura Surf Camp

(schedule found online). A large open-air yoga room surrounded by tropical plants welcomes yogis to take part in a range of *yin, vinyasa,* meditation, *hatha,* and specialized classes. All classes can be adapted to suit beginners or advanced yogis, with all equipment provided.

SPAS
MATCHA SPA

Jalan Raya Kuta; tel. 82339050182; daily 10am-7:30pm; 180,000 Rp 60-minute traditional massage

Matcha Spa is a serene gym with private rooms offering massages, facials, scrubs, wraps, manicures, pedicures, and spa packages. Their sea salt and citrus scrub is one of the best after a long day of travel. Book your treatment 10am-noon to get a 10 percent discount.

Festivals and Events

BAU NYALE FESTIVAL

Pantai Kuta, Pantai Seger; Feb.; free
Bau Nyale Festival is a Sasak folk festival based on the legend of Princess Mandalika. Princess Mandalika was said to be so beautiful and charming, every prince on Lombok professed his love for her. Her father, the king, hosted competitions for princes to battle for her, leading to a period of turmoil. Princess Mandalika abhorred the violence and threw herself into the sea to stop the bloodshed. When locals went to look for her, they only found sea worms. The name of the festival, Bau Nyale, translates into "To catch worms."

Each year, locals flock to the shallow water in search of sea worms that are iridescent and range from green to pinkish-brown. These sea worms represent the reincarnation of Princess Mandalika and bring good fortune to those who catch them. At the Bau Nyale Festival, participants search for worms and then eat them raw or smoke them inside a banana leaf. Makeshift huts pop up on the shoreline to house locals who come from inland villages. Surf contests, games, live music, and traditional performances also take place during the festival.

Shopping

SURF SHOPS
FLOW

Jalan Raya Kuta; daily 8am-10pm
Flow is a surf shop that sells clothing, backpacks, surf accessories, sunscreen, and surfboards, and also rents out Channel Islands surfboards. It has a very east-coast Australia surf shop aesthetic.

COCO SURF

Jalan Pariwisata; tel. 85239100331; daily 8am-9pm
In addition to offering surf lessons, CoCo Surf has a shop with shirts, surf accessories, natural sunscreen, and surfboards for rent. The shop also does ding repairs and can arrange for a surf photographer to accompany you while you surf.

TEXTILES
JALAN RAYA KUTA
TEXTILE STREET

10am-8pm daily; 50,000-100,000 Rp sarong
Along Jalan Raya Kuta, stands selling Sasak textiles line the roads. You'll see full-sized blankets, sarongs, scarves, and home decor in various patterns and colors. Women carrying

bundles of textiles also comb the beaches. The towel-sized sarongs woven (not printed) from a wooden loom are often high-quality and durable. Decorative fabrics made from silk, however, should be treated with care. Bargaining is expected, and merchants are often happy to make a deal if you purchase multiple items.

Food

LOCAL
LOTUS MANDALIKA
Mandalika Bazaar; 81246522873; 10am-9pm daily; 20,000-40,000 Rp

Owned by Made, a local fisherman, and his family, the seafood at Lotus Mandalika is fresh and perfectly spiced. Guests can arrange to join Made on a six-hour fishing trip (1,200,000 Rp/2-person trip) and cook their catch back at the warung. The warung also serves classic Indonesian dishes and fresh juice.

NANA'S WARUNG
Jalan Mawun No. 16; tel. 81938219835; daily 11am-9pm; 20,000-60,000 Rp

Run by Nana and her family, Nana's Warung is a quaint and quiet warung that's somewhat unassuming from the outside. The spring rolls are a must, as is the coconut smoothie mixed with chocolate. Enjoy *gado-gado,* fish curry, *mie goreng, nasi goreng,* and more, all served in large portions. Keep a lookout for the shop front entrance with yellow and blue signs; the warung is easy to miss.

★ WARUNG FLORA
Jalan Raya Kuta; tel. 87865300009; daily 11am-10pm; 30,000-60,000 Rp

Warung Flora is a popular Indonesian restaurant serving heaping plates of curries, *gado-gado,* fried rice, and fried noodles—though they're known for their grilled fish cooked in banana leaves. Meals are spiced for a tourist's palate; request *sambal* on the side if you'd like a bit more heat.

★ WARUNG TURTLE
Pantai Tanjung Aan; tel. 85205182860; daily 11am-8pm; 30,000-70,000 Rp

Warung Turtle is a quirky beach restaurant serving Indonesian classic meals on the shoreline of Pantai Tanjung Aan. Being the original warung on the beach, it holds a sense of nostalgia for many who visit Lombok time and time again. Coconut crumbed fish, satay skewers, spring rolls, and plates of noodles are the mainstays of the menu. Be prepared to be approached by dogs in search of a stray morsel as you dine.

EUROPEAN
RIVIERA
Jalan Raya Kuta; tel. 8155736390; daily 5pm-11pm; 35,000-80,000 Rp

Riviera is a newly renovated restaurant serving some of the best pizzas and tapas in Kuta. The wine menu is extensive, featuring bottles imported from all over the globe. The cocktail section is worth a glance as well. On Thursday and Saturday nights, the restaurant hosts a party led by live DJs, and you'll often find the owner tearing up the dancefloor among the guests.

YOGI BAR
Jalan Pariwisata; tel. 370/6503518; daily 8:30am-10:30pm; 40,000-100,000 Rp

Yogi Bar is a café and restaurant that's sure to make both omnivores and vegans happy. For breakfast, enjoy smoothie bowls, coffee, and fresh juice. Later in the day, opt for the curries, pastas, salads, soups, or tapas—many with a French flair. Their drinks menu is sure to even out any health kick you get from their wholesome meals. The atmosphere is bright and boho chic, making this an easy place to sit and stay awhile.

☆ Lombok's Lovely Textiles

Lombok's textiles

Woven textiles handmade by Sasak women are essential parts of daily life and ceremonies in Lombok.

HOW THEY'RE MADE

The most common form of weaving is done on a wooden loom, where cotton thread dyed with natural materials is used to create *songket* or *ikat* textiles. Patterns of these fabrics range from intricate to simple, with one side of the fabric often differing from the other. Many times, one side is shown during the day while the other is donned at night. Simple patterns take around two weeks to make, while more intricate motifs may take months.

CULTURAL IMPORTANCE

Villages like Sade, Sukarara, and Pringgasela are famous for their textiles, as many women are taught the skill of weaving from a young age. Today, many weavers' livelihoods are at risk as machines take the place of handwoven fabrics.

Textiles in Lombok range from practical to symbolic. In villages like Bayan, believers of the *wetu telu* form of Islam integrate fabrics into ceremonies in a variety of ways. There is a belief that cloths can be sacred, with spirits intertwined within the threads. Cloths are often wrapped around precious or religious objects, protecting the item not only physically but also spiritually. Cloths play a large role in circumcision, hair cutting, and religious ceremonies.

WHERE TO BUY

To find a textile souvenir, visit the town of Kuta where colorful fabrics are sold along Jalan Raya Kuta and at the main beach of Pantai Kuta. These fabrics can also be purchased from shops at the village of Sade, a 10-minute drive from Kuta along Jalan Kuta Lombok. For the best price, bargain with the merchants at Pantai Kuta.

HORIZON AT ASHTARI

Jalan Mawun; tel. 8113884838; Mon.-Fri. noon-9pm,
Sat.-Sun. 8am-9pm; 60,000-130,000 Rp

It's hard to find a better view in Kuta than Horizon at Ashtari, a restaurant with seating that overlooks the town and the sea. Juices, coffee, cocktails, wine, and beer grace their drinks menu. A variety of pizzas, pasta dishes, salads, seafood, and grilled meat feature on the food menu. The restaurant often hosts all-you-can-eat pizza nights, Indonesian cooking classes (275,000 Rp per person), and live music each Sunday from 5pm to 9pm. Shuttle service is included for parties spending 300,000 Rp or more in the Kuta area.

AMERICAN

BURGER ZONE

Jalan Pariwisata; tel. 82147946648; daily noon-10pm;
40,000-70,000 Rp

Burger Zone has a simple menu of burgers and French fries, served in a casual open-air restaurant with bamboo furniture. Try their tempeh, fish, chicken, or classic beef burger with a cold soft drink, juice, or beer. If you'd rather eat at your hotel, Burger Zone also delivers.

MEDITERRANEAN

★ EL BAZAR

Jalan Raya Kuta; tel. 81999113026; www.
elbazarlombok.com; daily 7am-10pm;
50,000-175,000 Rp

El Bazar has quickly become a favorite restaurant among Kuta regulars, and it's easy to understand why. With ambient lighting, cozy tables, and mosaic decor, this restaurant makes you feel as though you've stepped into a café in a Moroccan village. The meze platter is a necessary starter: enjoy soft pita with ramekins of hummus, baba ghanoush, tabbouleh, feta, and more. Lamb and chicken tagine, beef skewers, and vegetarian kebabs make up the mains.

VEGETARIAN AND VEGAN

WARUNG SBY JAVA FOOD

Food cart usually parked on Jalan Raya Kuta; daily
noon-10pm; 20,000 Rp first plate, 15,000 Rp after

Warung SBY Java Food is a green food cart with two shelves of traditional street food. The bottom shelf is fully vegetarian, while chicken and eggs are often on the top shelf. The owner of the cart will happily point out the fully vegan items to those who ask. Simply grab a plate and take whatever you like; the meal costs 20,000 Rp. If you'd like to go back for more, second and third helpings are just 15,000 Rp. Meals vary depending on the day but are usually a mix of tempeh, curry, tofu, and vegetable dishes.

★ TERRA

Jalan Mawun; tel. 85936633130; Fri.-Weds.
8am-9pm, closed Thurs.; 50,000-90,000 Rp

Terra is a fully vegan plant-based café where all dishes are gluten-free. The dishes lovingly crafted by Chef Mamiko are colorful, fresh, and healthy, ranging from salads to curries to vegetable sushi rolls and creative takes on jackfruit wraps. Treats like warm waffles topped with ice cream and banoffee pie will quell any sugar cravings. For breakfast, enjoy smoothie bowls or a tofu omelet. Their drinks are just as healthy as the mains, with a mix of juices, kombucha, organic coffees, and smoothies. This is the place to recover from a long surf or a bender from the night before.

CAFÉS

★ MILK ESPRESSO

Jalan Raya Kuta; tel. 82266189838; daily
7am-midnight; 40,000-200,000 Rp

Milk Espresso epitomizes café culture with all-day breakfasts that include eggs all ways, pancakes, avocado toast, and more. Meanwhile, lunch and dinner feature salads, burgers, sandwiches, pastas, and platters. Live music takes place regularly, and Wednesday and Friday will have you getting tipsy on the cheap with half-priced cocktails 5pm-7pm. On Sunday, enjoy two-for-one pastas. Slate-colored shipping containers make up the building, and you can shop for clothes and accessories inside their boutique while you wait for your food.

The Kids of Kuta

Throughout Kuta you'll see motorbikes driven by kids who look young enough to still have their baby teeth. Sitting up to five to a motorbike, the kids of Kuta roll up to beaches and restaurants with planks wrapped in jewelry under their arms. Pulling at the heartstrings of potential customers, kids beg and plead for tourists to purchase the bracelets, often claiming that the money goes toward school fees. However, schooling in Lombok is free, and many of the children sell goods from shortly after the school day is over until late into the night.

TIPS FOR INTERACTING

It's a challenge to resist their charisma, charm, and knack for mimicking accents. However, purchasing products from children potentially puts them in harm's way, as they interact with strangers.

One answer to the kids who approach is, "I'm sorry, I do not buy things from children." Rather than purchasing goods from children, consider supporting adult-owned and -operated businesses within the area. Many of the children's parents own small shops that are worthy of patronage. Or, donate to **Pelita Foundation** (pelitafoundationlombok.org), an organization that hosts after-school educational programs.

Bars and Nightlife

WARUNG RASTA

Jalan Pariwisata; tel. 85333661049; daily 5pm-late; 30,000-50,000 Rp

Under a simple A-frame roof propped up by poles of bamboo with wooden benches underneath, Warung Rasta serves its own version of Mexican food during the day. At night, acoustic musicians or DJs come to play tunes. Come for sunset to enjoy picturesque views of the beach.

SURFERS BAR

Jalan Raya Kuta; tel. 85338497038; daily 3pm-late; 30,000-50,000 Rp

Surfers Bar was built and opened by one of the original surf guides of Kuta and has a distinctively salty vibe about it. The bar attracts a crowd on Friday, when live bands and DJs play a mix of classics, reggae, and house music.

THE BUS BAR

Jalan Pariwisata; tel. 82340897270; daily 6pm-late; 35,000-50,000 Rp

Dance parties center around The Bus Bar, where a converted Volkswagen Kombi serves cocktails and beer to anyone who wants one. Live DJs play a mix of house and techno music on Wednesday and Saturday nights.

Accommodations

At night, Kuta can be noisy. Dogs, roosters, parties, and calls from the mosque mean that it'll be a challenge to find completely soundproof accommodations. Pack a pair of earplugs if you're a light sleeper.

UNDER 1,000,000 RP

★ BOMBORA BUNGALOWS

Jalan Raya Kuta; tel. 370/6502571; 300,000 Rp double

Trendy bamboo bungalows surround a small

pool at Bombora Bungalows, a boutique hotel with a health-conscious café at its entrance. The bungalows have outdoor bathrooms with cold water showers, air-conditioning or fan cooling, and a spacious patio with a hammock to lounge in. The whole property has a very laid-back, away-from-it-all vibe to it.

★ LARA HOMESTAY

Alley from Jalan Raya Kuta; tel. 87763100315; www. larahomestay.com; 350,000-500,000 Rp double

Lara Homestay is like a home away from home, with spotless rooms and a location that's central but set back from the main road, making it one of the quieter places to stay. Lara, the owner, is a friendly host and skilled chef; the included daily breakfast is a treat. All rooms are equipped with hot water showers, air-conditioning, a TV, hair dryer, mini fridge, and a balcony. The third-floor deluxe rooms make you feel like you're sleeping amid the trees.

BAMBA

Jalan Raya Kuta; tel. 87860519009; www.bamba.id; 500,000 Rp double, 120,000 Rp dorm

There's no accommodation in the region quite like Bamba, a minimalistic hotel and restaurant with a day-club-style pool, rooftop bar, and grassy lounge area. Simply designed double rooms and futuristic dorm beds where you sleep inside of a pod are available. Each comes with air-conditioning, Wi-Fi, and a private bathroom. Live music at Bamba usually plays at the hotel on Monday, often accompanied by all-night happy hours.

★ MANA

Jalan Baturiti I; tel. 85338628659; https:// manalombok.com; 700,000 Rp-1,500,000 Rp double, 300,000 Rp dorm

Tropical plants envelop the rooms at Mana, a retreat that attracts yogis and health-conscious travelers. The property hosts yoga classes, yoga teacher trainings, movie nights, and spa treatments, and it has an on-site restaurant serving fresh food made from local ingredients. The rooms are airy and whimsical, with mosquito nets, local fabrics, and windows that open out to the garden area. Choose a bungalow, dorm bedroom, or a four-bedroom villa with a full kitchen and swimming pool. All room types include breakfast, Internet access, air-conditioning, and hot water showers.

OVER 1,000,000 RP

HARMONY VILLAS

Jalan Raya Kuta; tel. 87861772474; www. harmonyvillaslombok.com; 1,200,000 double

Harmony Villas is a boutique resort with five white villas set around a turquoise pool, bean-bag lounge chairs, and palm trees. Inside, the rooms are white with accents of blue, creating a setting of solitude. All rooms come with a balcony area, Wi-Fi access, a TV, and comfortable beds. Breakfast is delivered to your room each morning. The resort only accepts guests aged 16 and up.

Information and Services

TOURIST INFORMATION

There are **ATMs** along Jalan Raya Kuta. Many venues are cash-only.

The citizens of Kuta and Southern Lombok are traditionally conservative. Bathing suits are accepted on the beaches only, and tourists are expected to cover up when walking around town or driving along the road.

Safety

There is a history of robberies that have taken place on the road beyond Selong Belanak. When driving or riding as a passenger, it's best to store items inside the motorbike helmet compartment. Do not resist robbery attempts. Fortunately, these incidents have decreased in recent years.

HEALTH AND MEDICINE

LOMBOK INTERNATIONAL MEDICAL SERVICE

Jalan Raya Kuta; tel. 818353343; open 24/7

This medical clinic offers basic medical care; the staff members are familiar with treating road rash and reef cuts.

BLUE ISLAND MEDICAL CLINIC

Jalan Pariwisata; tel. 81999705700; www. blueislandclinic.com; open 24/7

Blue Island Medical Clinic provides emergency services, evacuation organization, and basic medical care.

Transportation

GETTING THERE AND AWAY

By Bus and *Bemo*

Despite Kuta's popularity among travelers and locals, there are few reliable public transportation options to get to Kuta. Shuttle buses from **Perama** (tel. 361/751875; www.peramatour. com) run between Kuta and **Mataram** (1-1.5 hours; 125,000 Rp), **Senggigi** (1.5-2 hours; 125,000 Rp), the **Lombok International Airport** (30 minutes; 60,000 Rp), and **Tetebatu** (1.5-2 hours; 150,000 Rp); minimum of two passengers is needed to run.

To leave Kuta, your best bet is to **book a driver through your accommodation** or join one of the shuttle buses departing around Lombok. Shuttle bus options are advertised along **Jalan Raya Kuta** and **Jalan Mawun;** your fare usually includes hotel pickup and drop-off.

By Car and Motorbike

Kuta is reached by car or motorbike from **Mataram** (50 km/31 mi; 1 hour), **Senggigi** (65 km/40 mi; 1.5 hours), **Tetebatu** (60 km/37 mi; 1.5 hours), and the **Lombok International Airport** (20 km/12 mi; 0.5 hour). The route connecting Kuta to Senggigi passes through Mataram and by the Lombok International Airport. From Senggigi, take **Jalan Raya Senggigi** 20 km (12 mi) south to Mataram. Take **Jalan By Pass Bandara Int. Lombok** 20 km (12 mi), which will pass by the Lombok International Airport. From Lombok International Airport, take Jalan Kuta Lombok to Kuta.

By Taxi

A taxi is the best way to get to Kuta from the **Lombok International Airport** (150,000 Rp), **Mataram** (150,000 Rp), and **Senggigi** (200,000 Rp). **Bluebird** is the most reliable service, with taxis easily hailed through the MyBluebird app.

GETTING AROUND

The town of Kuta itself is very **walkable.** The restaurants, accommodations, and shops sprawl out from Pantai Kuta. However, most locals and travelers end up renting a **motorbike** (50,000-70,000 Rp per day). In the past, Kuta was plagued by motorbike scams where those who rented out would often pressure travelers to pay for existing damage upon return. Fortunately, these scams seem to have dwindled. It's safest to arrange motorbike rental directly through your guesthouse or hotel; most accommodations have secure **parking.**

To rent a **driver,** expect to pay around 600,000 Rp per day. This is a great option if you're in a group and want to do day trips around the region's outer beaches.

The **parking fee** you pay to leave your motorbike in a beach parking lot is used to pay **security** to watch the bike. Many of these security guards will stay with the bike until you return; always ask how long they will be attending the bike if you plan to stay somewhere past sunset. Without clarifying, you might find your bike abandoned (and at risk of being stolen) or you might cause the security guard to miss dinner.

West of Kuta

Hop on a set of wheels and explore the many beaches that stretch beyond Kuta. A paved road leads through villages, with bumpy turn-offs to undisturbed stretches of sand. Here, you can hop onboard a small fishing boat and take a ride to world-class waves, stretch out on the sand where no one is around to disturb you, discover marine life hidden in between coral bommies, and watch intricate fabrics being woven firsthand.

BELONGAS

Known for little more than the hammerhead sharks that migrate just outside of its large bay, Belongas is a destination for divers seeking a thrill. There are multiple dive sites that are known for their challenging yet rewarding conditions—having more than 50-100 logged dives is mandatory for some sites during part of the year.

Scuba Diving
THE MAGNET
2 km (1.2 mi) offshore of western Belongas Bay
Out of the bay, the Magnet is the most famous dive site, known for the hammerhead sharks that make their way there from June to October. Mobula rays and eagle rays tend to pass through from late July to September. The coral pinnacle has a strong surge and attracts barracuda, tuna, giant trevally, and reef sharks, and is rife with smaller marine creatures taking refuge from the big fellas within its reef.

THE CATHEDRAL
1 km (0.6 mi) offshore of eastern Belongas Bay
Inside the bay and therefore often calmer, The Cathedral is another pinnacle dive site known for its sea snakes, and Gili Sarang is a playground for divers interested in rays or macro life; both are worth exploring.

TWO FISH DIVERS
Jalan Raya Sepi; tel. 81907852073; www. twofishdivers.com; 1,350,000 Rp for 2 fun dives
Two Fish Divers hosts scuba trips to Belongas Bay where you can dive at the Magnet (experienced divers only) or at other worthy sites in and around Belongas Bay. Their dive guides know the bay well—a necessity when diving in conditions notorious for strong currents and surge.

Getting There
The best way to get to Belongas is with a **private driver** (600,000 Rp per day) or with your own **motorbike** (50,000-70,000 Rp per day), best arranged through your accommodation. There are no reliable forms of public transport to this area. Belongas is 20 km (12 mi; 30 minutes) away from **Pantai Selong Belanak,** connected by **Jalan Selong Belanak.** Belongas is 47 km (29 mi; 1.5 hours) from **Kuta,** along **Jalan Mawun,** which turns into Jalan Selong Belanak.

SELONG BELANAK BEACH
(Pantai Selong Belanak)
Jalan Selong Belanak; 10,000 Rp parking
Selong Belanak is a spacious beach that's often busy with surfers, sunseekers, and warungs selling freshly grilled corn, soft drinks, snacks, and Sasak meals. The soft white sand is ideal for strolling along, stopping when you like for a swim among the sea's playful waves. As you venture from east to west along the shoreline, the beach becomes less crowded and more rural.

Surfing
SELONG BELANAK SURF SPOT
Paddle out along shoreline of Pantai Selong Belanak
Selong Belanak is one of the best places to

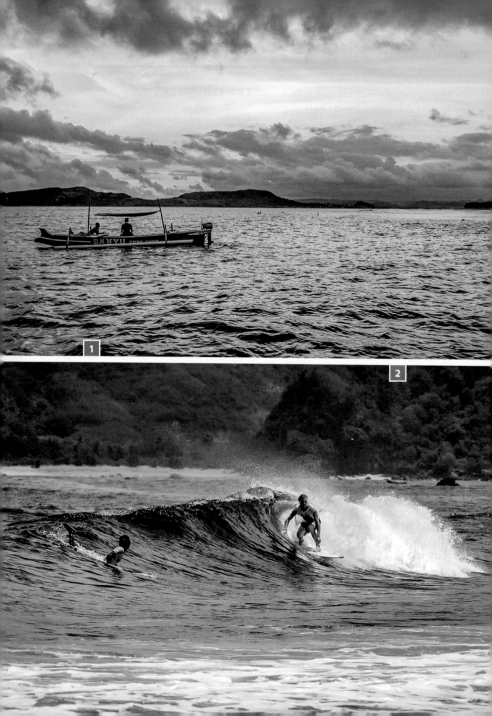

learn how to surf. Friendly beach breaks roll through along the beach; it's prime for catching waves in the whitewash with a sandy bottom beneath you. Soft-top boards are easily rented from the beach, where there are plenty of local surf guides also available to offer beginner lessons.

Accommodations
SEMPIAK VILLAS
Pantai Selong Belanak; tel. 82144303337; www. sempiakvillas.com; 1,500,000 Rp double

A romantic getaway near the shores of Selong Belanak, Sempiak Villas offers hillside villas with views of the sea. The resort welcomes guests 12 years old and older, and each villa has air-conditioning, a fridge, a safe, and a large balcony to laze the day away. No two villas are alike and there are options to accommodate from two to eight people. Because of the location, the villas feel as though they're in a hideaway despite being so close to the sea. One of the highlights of the property is its beachside restaurant with an elegant dining area that opens out to the ocean.

OLA OLA LOMBOK
Jalan Selong Belanak; tel. 85338134195; www. olaolalombok.com; 250,000-350,000 Rp double

Stay within a 10-minute walk of Pantai Selong Belanak at Ola Ola Lombok, a boutique hotel with nine basic but chic rooms. Three of the rooms are fan-cooled, while six come with air-conditioning and hot-water showers. Every guest has breakfast included, Wi-Fi, and access to the communal swimming pool. Turn your experience into a full-on retreat by bundling surf lessons and yoga classes into a package with your accommodation.

Getting There
You will need a **private driver** (600,000 Rp per day) or **motorbike** (50,000-70,000 Rp per day) to reach **Selong Belanak,** which can usually be arranged through your accommodation. Selong Belanak is best reached along **Jalan Mawun,** which turns into **Jalan Selong Belanak,** 23 km (14 mi) west of **Kuta** (30 minutes).

MAWI BEACH
(Pantai Mawi)
Turn off at Jalan Selong Belanak; 5,000 Rp motorbike parking

An unforgiving road leads to Pantai Mawi, a bay that looks like it could belong in a Jurassic Park film. A rickety warung serves carved pineapple, snacks, beers, and fresh coconuts to surfers and beachgoers who venture here. Walk to the beach's southern rocky point to watch surfers catch waves up close.

Surfing
MAWI SURF SPOT
Paddle out at channel of Pantai Mawi

During small southwest swells, Mawi breaks left and right over a shallow reef. As the size picks up, the right closes out but the left stays fast and hollow. Strong currents sweep through the bay once the waves pick up, making it a bad spot for beginners. Intermediate and experienced surfers might find it one of the best waves in the area.

Getting There
Like the other beaches in the area, you will need a **private driver** (600,000 Rp per day) or rental **motorbike** (50,000-70,000 Rp per day), hired through your accommodation. To get to Pantai Mawi, take **Jalan Mawun** 17 km (11 mi) west of **Kuta** until you see a road turn off marked by a green sign that says "Mawi." The 3-km (2-mi) road leading to Pantai Mawi is poorly maintained.

1: Gerupuk sunrise 2: Mawi Surf Spot

East of Kuta

There are no regular buses or *bemos* that lead to the destinations along Lombok's southern coastline. The main road connecting Kuta to the rest of Southern Lombok is hilly and well-paved, though roads leading to many of the beaches themselves are often made of corrugated dirt or marked with potholes. Sometimes, you can pay extra to have a **surf guide** drive with you as a pillion rider.

GERUPUK

Gerupuk is a quiet fishing village, where locals now use their fishing boats to shuttle surfers from break to break in Gerupuk Bay in between catching fish. Though there was once a sandy beach in Gerupuk, it was destroyed during a tsunami in 1977, as were most buildings within the village. In lieu of a beach, a seawall protects the village from future erosion and inundation. Around the bay, bamboo structures mark seaweed farms and lobster farms, two major sources of the village's income. Despite the development in Kuta and popularity of Gerupuk among travelers, water is trucked in daily and the road leading to Gerupuk is made of dirt.

Gerupuk at sunrise might have you surfing in the glassiest conditions, beating the morning-rush crowds. Fortunately, the crowds often dwindle around lunchtime—even in the high season. There are five different breaks in the bay. Surfers tend to scatter out based on their abilities, with beginner surfers learning at the bay's friendly waves and more experienced surfers paddling where they're sure to find a challenge.

A boat is needed to access all main breaks of Gerupuk. You can hire a boat from surf guides or fishermen gathered around Gerupuk Harbor at the end of Jalan Mandalika Resort Pantai Putri Nyale for 200,000 Rp per trip or 50,000 Rp per person if you're in a group of more than four surfers.

Surfing

KID'S POINT (PELAWANGAN)

On most days, you'll see kids and beginners catching waves on a usually mellow right-hand break. However, it occasionally picks up enough to barrel—with waves fast enough to turn boys into men.

INSIDE GERUPUK

Inside Gerupuk is a fun and playful right-hander that peels along a seaweed-padded reef. This is a popular spot among beginner surfers; it works best during southwest swells. The wave is mellow and slow, perfect for practicing turns. With so many surf camps flocking to the spot, expect drop-ins done out of ignorance rather than malice. You can usually find a wave that's surfable all year long.

OUTSIDE GERUPUK (RIGHT)

Outside Gerupuk is a wobbly but consistent righthander that works best with at least 1.2 meters (4 feet) of swell at mid- to high tide. It can wall up and break heavy; intermediate surfers will have fun on its shoulder.

OUTSIDE GERUPUK (LEFT)

The twin wave to Outside Gerupuk Right, this lefthander can get fast and hollow, attracting experienced surfers only.

DON DON

Don Don needs serious swell to pick up. Once it does, you'll find fun A-frames with peeling left and rights over seaweed-covered reef. It works best at an outgoing tide. Crowds flock here as soon as it gets good, so expect to be hosting many impromptu party waves as soon as you stand up.

SURF WITH HASSAN

Gerupuk Harbor; tel. 82341921192; www.facebook.com/ichsan.gerupuk; 150,000 Rp surf guide
Take a boat to Gerupuk's best surf spots with

From Shark Fishing to Snorkel Tours

Indonesia is the biggest exporter of shark fins. As sharks are apex predators and necessary for a healthy marine ecosystem, overfishing of sharks can have drastic consequences. One place that is notorious for selling juvenile sharks and rays is **Tanjung Luar Fish Market**, found on Lombok's southern coastline. Here, some Sasak fishermen fish for sharks, and many of these sharks are killed only for their fins. This is done to meet the lucrative demand of shark fins overseas in destinations like China, Hong Kong, Singapore, Russia, and Peru.

HOW TO HELP

As an alternative to shark fishing, some fishermen in Tanjung Luar, Lombok, use their boats to offer snorkeling tours around Lombok's southern coastline, where you'll discover small islands and reefs rarely seen by anyone else. These tours are in collaboration with **The Dorsal Effect** (http://thedorsaleffect.com; 14,000 Rp for half-day trip, extra for pickup in Kuta, Senggigi, or Mataram), an initiative that hopes to help shark conservation by replacing income made from shark fishing with tourism. Fishermen answer questions about sharks and about the reality behind shark fishing. The tour also stops at **Pantai Tangsi,** also known as Pink Beach thanks to its pastel pink sand. Some tours may also take you to other pink beaches in the region that are only accessible by boat.

Hassan, a friendly surf guide and instructor. Hassan's teaching demeanor is patient and kind, always willing to offer advice as needed. Beginners will enjoy having a dedicated instructor while those who want a guide will find his tips on where to sit on the lineup useful.

Accommodations
★ CHARLIE'S SHACK
Jalan Mandalika; tel. 85338625996; www. charliesshack.com; 300,000 Rp double
Gerupuk Homestay is inside Gerupuk's small village, where you can get a full night of sleep and still make it to the waves for sunrise. Rooms are tiny and tidy, set around a communal area complete with bean bag chairs, an entertainment system, and bar area. The rooms each have a private bathroom with a hot water shower, Wi-Fi access, and a choice between soft or firm pillows on the bed. The hosts of the guesthouse are Gerupuk locals, happy to teach guests about the history of Gerupuk and give insight on daily life within the village.

INLIGHT
Jalan Mandalika tel. 85338038280; www. inlightlombok.com; 1,000,000 Rp double
Inlight is a beachside getaway that can be turned into a DIY health and surf retreat. Guests can lounge by its infinity pool that overlooks Gerupuk Bay, practice yoga, surf with a guide, and dine at the on-site vegetarian restaurant. Rooms are minimally decorated with unique wooden furniture and local textiles, and the bathrooms come with a bathtub.

Getting There
To get to Gerupuk, you can pay a local about 50,000 Rp to give you an *ojek* (back of motorbike) ride to Gerupuk. Having your own **motorbike** is the best way to get there, arranged through your accommodation.

The beach town of Gerupuk is 11 km (6.8 mi; 25 minutes) east of **Kuta** along **Jalan Sengkol,** turning right toward Pantai Tanjung Aan and following the beach road to Gerupuk.

EKAS
A remote peninsula with a dusty fishing village on its point, Ekas hosts a handful of waves that beckon surfers from the most developed sides of the island. There's a convenient beginner-intermediate-expert setup when it comes to waves. Beginners will have fun in friendly

whitewash, and top-tier surfers will feel their hearts race when the set wave comes through. Ekas also has prime **kitesurfing** conditions with 15-25 knots blowing consistently from April to early October. The Wi-Fi signal is spotty and most facilities are basic, but that's easily forgotten once you get into the water.

★ Surfing and Kitesurfing
EKAS BEACH BREAK
This is a friendly beach break with mellow peaks that peel along the shoreline. Novice surfers can practice paddling out and their popups with sand below.

INSIDE EKAS
Inside Ekas gets moving when a decent southwest swell rolls through. When it's small, the wave is perfect for novice surfers who can cruise along its near-perfect wall, often barreling in 2-meter (6-foot+) conditions. Inside Ekas breaks left and right for over 100 meters (328 feet) during low to mid-tide. During high tide, the right teeters out and the left shines.

OUTSIDE EKAS
Outside Ekas is a powerful left best left to expert surfers only. Currents are strong, but the thrill of a steep drop in, multiple barrel

sections, and plenty of face to move around make it worth it. It works at all tides, southwest swells, and easterly winds.

KALIANTAN KITESURF
tel. 82237916767; www.kaliantankitesurf.com; 14,000 Rp 2-hour rental, 9,100,000 Rp beginner lesson
Kaliantan Kitesurf is a reputable school with IKO-certified kitesurfing instructors, who teach lessons or can simply watch for safety. Equipment rental is available for kite-surfers who are already capable of going upwind.

Accommodations
EKAS BEACH GUESTHOUSE
Pantai Ekas; tel. 82340839948; 150,000 Rp double
Run by Rumaji and his friendly family, Ekas Beach Guesthouse is a simple homestay with basic, funky colored rooms. Your stay comes with breakfast and a private bathroom. The real appeal of staying here is the proximity to local life and Rumaji's many activity options, where you can look at the family lobster farm, dine in a ramshackle floating restaurant, and enjoy a traditional massage.

★ EKAS SURF RESORT
Ekas Neighborhood; tel. 81246647522; www. ekassurfresort.com; 700,000-900,000 Rp double

Ekas Beach Break

Southern Lombok's Traditional Villages

textiles in Sade

Peek at traditional Sasak culture inside these villages located in Southern Lombok. You'll gain insight on how goods are made and the type of music Sasak people enjoy listening to, engage in friendly competitions, and admire local architecture.

SADE

Sade (6 km/3.7 mi north of Kuta; donation required) is one of the most-visited villages for witnessing textiles being created in Lombok. Here, you can try your hand at weaving on a wooden loom and look inside of traditional Sasak homes. Textiles and crafts are on display, and bargaining is expected. Tours often get to see traditional *peresean* stick fights, feel the vibrations from a musical troupe playing the drums and gongs, and be mesmerized by dance performances. The performances feel authentic—until someone pulls you away and demands a *mandatory* donation. For a less tourist-heavy experience, go past Sade and into **Rembitan,** another traditional village.

ENDE

Less known than the neighboring village of Sade, Ende (8 km/5 mi north of Kuta, donation requested) is a traditional village with Sasak architecture where you can admire *bali tani* structures built from bamboo, cow dung, and grass. Traditionally, men sleep outside while women and children rest inside. Persean stick fights often take place for visitors' entertainment, with weaving workshops also available.

SUKARARA

Sukarara (26 km/16 mi north of Kuta) is where you can witness fabrics being woven on a traditional backstrap loom, shop for products, and take pictures dressed up in Sasak ceremonial attire.

Ekas Surf Resort is a relaxed boutique resort with just a handful of air-conditioned rooms with twin or double beds, all with modern bathrooms, a fridge, Wi-Fi access, and a safety deposit box. The surprising highlight of the resort is its restaurant, where local dishes are made fresh. Free boat rides to Inside Ekas surf break are included with each stay, and staff can help arrange surf lessons and tours of the nearby beaches. A choice of board games, the little outdoor pool, the ping pong table, and the giant communal TV create a vibe that's ideal for making travel mates.

Getting There

To get to Ekas, you should have a **private driver** (600,000 Rp per day) or your own **motorbike** (50,000-70,000 Rp per day), best arranged through your accommodation. Ekas is located on the eastern side of **Awang Bay,** a 48-km (30-mi; 1.5-hour) drive from **Gerupuk.** If you are only planning to surf, not stay, at Ekas, drive 15 km (9 mi; 30 minutes) east along Jalan Sengkol to **Teluk Awang Harbor.** Charter a boat for 200,000-300,000 Rp to shuttle you out to the Ekas surf breaks.

PINK BEACH
(Pantai Tangsi)

Jalan Pantai Tangsi; 50,000 Rp parking

Pantai Tangsi, also called Pink Beach, is one of the most bizarre beaches on Lombok. Over time, pieces of red coral have been ground down into small fragments, mixing in with bits of white coral on Pantai Tangsi. This has created a pink hue. Most images of the beach online have been amped with color saturation to create a bubblegum glow; expect to see more of a pastel pink. It's best to visit the beach during full sunlight, as shadows dull the color. A hilltop lookout offers prime views of the beach from above. Small islands are seen offshore. Note that the road leading from the main road to Pantai Tangsi is made of dirt and marked with potholes.

As a side trip from Pantai Tangsi, venture down a dirt road to **Tanjung Ringgit.** This desert cape overlooks the ocean and offers spectacular views. Locals may offer *ojek* rides from Pantai Tangsi to Tanjung Ringgit for about 30,000 Rp round-trip.

Getting There

The road to Pantai Tangsi is not known for being well-kept. You should go with a **private driver** (600,000 Rp per day) or arrange a **motorbike** rental (50,000-70,000 Rp per day), both best reserved through your accommodation. Take Jalan Sengkol around Awang Bay toward Ekas. Turn right onto Jalan Serumbung-Ekas toward Pemongkong. Then, turn left onto Jalan Pantai Tangsi until you reach the northeastern point of the cape. The entire journey takes about 2 hours (54 km/34 mi).

Mount Rinjani and Northern Lombok

The sacred peak of Gunung Rinjani stands 3,726 meters (2.3 mi) above sea level, an important point in Balinese Hinduism and Sasak animist beliefs. Many locals believe that Gunung Rinjani is directly linked to a higher power, and they make pilgrimages and offerings in an effort to appease the being behind the holy volcano.

The volcano's large crater rim has a tranquil lake in its center and a smaller volcano in its base. Emerald valleys accented by lacey waterfalls and streams, Sasak villages, grasslands, and tropical wilderness stretch out from its slopes. Venture to Northern Lombok to experience traditional Sasak culture, hike to incredible vistas, and feel waterfalls cool your skin. It's a raw and lush place, where paths are often overgrown and there are few set itineraries to follow.

Highlights

Look for ★ to find recommended sights, activities, dining, and lodging.

★ **Air Terjun Tiu Kelep:** Hike to a waterfall enveloped by tropical foliage and wade in its cool pool (page 442).

★ **Bukit Pergasingan:** Trek through grasslands that lead up to the top of a hill, where you can camp and admire the patchwork quilt of farmlands below (page 445).

★ **Waterfalls of Tetebatu:** The small town of Tetebatu is surrounded by waterfalls that range from thin and tall to wide and drizzling (page 446).

★ **Shopping around Tetebatu:** The villages around Tetebatu are filled with artisans selling one-of-a-kind goods (page 448).

★ **Trekking Gunung Rinjani:** Spend the night on the crater rim of Lombok's most sacred volcano (page 451).

Top Accommodations

★ **Saifana Organic Farm:** Connect to nature by staying in a rustic bungalow set amid an organic farm (page 442).

★ **Rinjani Lodge:** Admire views of a jungle valley and rice terraces below from the edge of an infinity pool (page 444).

★ **Sembalun Kita Cottages:** A quiet family-run guesthouse where each balcony has its own hammock (page 445).

★ **Dream Catcher Camp:** Sleep in a treehouse or a mini hut at this bohemian forest camp where singing songs around the campfire is the norm (page 448).

★ **Satu Lingkung Bungalows:** Walk among rice terraces and admire the views from this quiet and quaint property's bamboo lookout tower (page 449).

In 2018, the region was battered by earthquakes that reduced some settlements to rubble. The resiliency of the local people plus the trickle of money coming in from tourists trekking Gunung Rinjani have helped communities rebuild. Don't let the lack of accommodations or restaurant options put you off seeing the region for yourself. Multiple trails leading to the crater rim of Gunung Rinjani have reopened, and the views from the top are as beautiful as ever. In the lush towns of Senaru and Sembulan, each passing week sees more warungs firing up their woks and guesthouses opening their doors. Tetebatu, on Gunung Rinjani's southern flank, is another town where you can walk among vivid gardens and relax to the melodies of songbirds.

ORIENTATION

Gunung Rinjani, Lombok's highest point, commands much of the northern coastline, with the town of **Senaru** in its northern foothills, **Sembalun Valley** 30 km (18.5 mi) east of Senaru. These towns are the main points of entry for trekking Gunung Rinjani, with trails that weave up the outer edge of the volcano's crater rim and into the caldera. A lake

and smaller volcanos sit inside the crater rim, extended from Gunung Rinjani, with the volcano's summit on the northeastern edge of the crater rim. The small farming town of **Tetebatu** sits on Gunung Rinjani's southern flank, 45 km (28 mi) northeast of **Mataram.** Along Lombok's eastern coastline, you'll find black sand beaches and tiny offshore islands with coral reefs ready to be explored.

PLANNING YOUR TIME

Before the 2018 earthquakes destroyed most of the buildings of Northern Lombok, the most accommodating towns for tourists were **Senaru** and **Sembalun Valley.** While Senaru has made some incredible progress and is re-establishing itself as a prime place to create a home base, Sembalun Valley still has some work to do before there are enough warungs and accommodations to make it a viable option for visitors to stay longer than a night or two. The town of **Tetebatu** has the most options when it comes to accommodations and restaurants, and the roads are better than those in the towns up north.

A visit to this area feels incomplete without summitting **Gunung Rinjani,** a **two-day**

Previous: summiting Gunung Rinjani; trekking Gunung Rinjani; Air Terjun Tiu Kelep.

Mount Rinjani

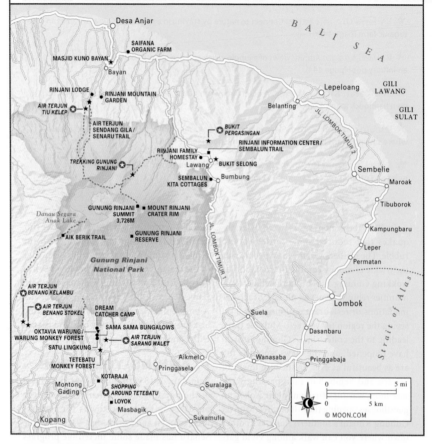

trek that can be arranged through a tour organizer of your choice. The hike allows you to see the crater's interior lake, the smaller volcano of Gunung Barujari, and the sunset, sunrise, and stars from the crater's interior rim. If you're not up for this intense hike, there are plenty of **shorter treks** to waterfalls to keep you busy.

If your plans revolve around trekking, especially Gunung Rinjani, it's best to visit Northern Lombok during **dry season.** The volcano trails are usually open from **April** to **November,** with the prime time to trek being from **May** to **October.** The park is currently issuing permits to enter to a set number of trekkers. You'll have the best chance of securing a permit for the Senaru and Sembalun trailheads if you **plan your trek during the week** and **book at least a few weeks in advance.** Permits are usually done by your trekking organizer through the Gunung Rinjani National Park website (www.tnrinjani.net). Most treks start early in the morning; you'll want to spend the night near the volcano the night before. The trek takes two days to complete if you plan to hike to the top of the crater rim. For other treks in the area, a full day is recommended.

2018 Earthquakes in Northern Lombok

On July 29, 2018, Sembalun Valley was at the epicenter of an earthquake that registered 6.4 on the Richter scale, causing landslides and trapping over 1,000 trekkers, porters, and guides on the slopes of Gunung Rinjani. Following the earthquake, the region was struck by a series of after-shocks, foreshocks, and a 6.9 earthquake on August 5, 2018. Almost all structures in Sembalun Valley were destroyed, with more than 560 people killed and thousands of people displaced throughout Lombok. Locals often call it the time that the earth felt like it was ending, and they wondered if the shaking would ever stop.

REBUILDING TODAY

Today, the rebuilding process is still ongoing, with locals eager to welcome travelers back to the foothills of Gunung Rinjani. The Sembalun trailhead leading to the crater of Gunung Rinjani is now open, with more accommodations, warungs, and trekking guides opening their doors each passing month.

Itinerary Idea

WALKING AMONG WATERFALLS

1 In the morning, drive to the entrance of **Tetebatu Monkey Forest** and walk among the wilderness in search of gray long-tailed macaques and black Javan lutung monkeys.

2 For lunch, enjoy a fresh plate of *gado-gado* at **Warung Monkey Forest.** If the owner is present, you might be able to tour the nearby farm where many ingredients are grown.

3 Drive one hour to the trailhead of **Air Terjun Benang Stokel,** twin waterfalls that often have a third flowing alongside them. Farther ahead is the incredible swimming area and mystical waterfall of Air Terjun Benang Kelambu.

4 Finish your day with a delicious meal at **Oktavia Warung.**

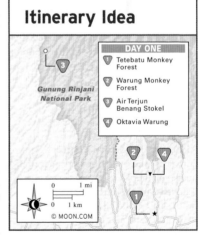

Senaru

A heavy, cool mist always seems to linger in the air of Senaru, a quiet village on the base of Gunung Rinjani. Along the main road, most warungs and guesthouses overlook rice fields, rivers, and dense jungle valleys below. Visit Senaru to see two of Lombok's best waterfalls, hike to the crater rim of Gunung Rinjani, and take part in the rebirth of one of the towns hit hardest by the 2018 earthquakes.

SIGHTS

Sendang Gile Waterfall
(Air Terjun Sendang Gile)

Trailhead at Jalan Pariwisata; 10,000 admission

Two tiers of a narrow cascade flow over jungle vines at Air Terjun Sendang Gile, a waterfall that crashes into a shallow stream. Monkeys swing from the treetops surrounding the waterfall, keeping an eye out for dropped morsels of food from locals picnicking at the waterfall. A steep and slippery staircase pathway leads directly to the waterfall.

★ Tiu Kelep Waterfall
(Air Terjun Tiu Kelep)

Trailhead at Jalan Pariwisata; 150,000 Rp guide
(includes Air Terjun Sendang Gile)

Air Terjun Tiu Kelep is a waterfall worthy of fairy tales, where wisps of water pour from a jungle cliff into a pool of water below. A main waterfall flows from an upper ledge, accented by the smaller waterfalls. It's possible to wade in the cool water near the waterfall's curtain, though currents can be rough if you get too close. The path to the waterfall is not clearly marked, as it has been rerouted from landslides; it is about a 45-minute trek beyond Air Terjung Sendang Gile. It's best to go with a local guide.

Masjid Kuno Bayan

Jalan Raya Bayan (outside of Senaru); Donation

Seven km (4 mi) outside of Senaru is Masjid Kuno Bayan, Lombok's oldest mosque. The interior is closed, but visitors can see the mosque's exterior, which was built from stone and tiered wood.

ACCOMMODATIONS

RINJANI MOUNTAIN GARDEN

Jalan Teres Genit; tel. 818569730; https://rinjani-mountain-garden.com; 300,000 Rp double

Rinjani Mountain Garden offers thatched-roof bungalows hidden among rice terraces marked with the hoofprints of roaming farm animals. There are multiple bungalow options available, including one- and two-bedroom units with en suite bathrooms and double-room bungalows that share a bathroom. Only the rooms with en suite bathrooms have hot water showers. Meals are served in an open-air dining area built from wood and bamboo, where guests can help themselves to the included breakfast of fresh fruit, bread, juice, and coffee.

★ SAIFANA ORGANIC FARM

Jalan Raya Bayan, 10 km (6 mi) from Senaru center; tel. 8113966689; www.saifana-lombok.com; 350,000 Rp double

Rich volcanic soil grows organic fruits, nuts, and vegetables at Saifana Organic Farm, where goats roam throughout the property and cashews are processed and then consumed by the handful. Relax on the bungalow's balcony, then head inside to sleep on a plush bed protected by mosquito netting. Bathrooms have cold water showers. The lack of Wi-Fi makes it easy to connect with the farmland and jungle surroundings. Guided walks and tours of the garden are a must.

1: Air Terjun Sendang Gile 2: Air Terjun Tiu Kelep 3: Lombok's coastline

Lombok's Black Sand Beaches

Eruptions from Gunung Rinjani have created a coastline with sparkling black and gray sand beaches.

- **Pantai Tebing** (Jalan Raya Bayan): A sliver of black sand backs up against small sandstone cliffs.

- **Pantai Ketapang Tampes** (Jalan Raya Bayan): For a midday meal, many locals in the area flock to Pantai Ketapang Tampes to eat at one of the handful of warungs on this little beach.

- **Pantai Dasan Krepuk** (Jalan Raya Bayan): At this spacious ash sand beach lined with fishing boats and palm trees, there's plenty of space to relax and watch boats arrive and depart.

- **Pantai Greneng** (Jalan Raya Bayan): Walk along a lonely black sand beach where you're likely to be the only one making footprints in the sand. A pier marks its eastern end.

Note that many of these beaches are in villages or areas where it's not common to see tourists lounging in swimwear. It's wise to wear a **rashguard** and **leggings** while swimming to discourage unwanted attention.

★ RINJANI LODGE

Jalan Parwisata; tel. 81907384944; www. rinjanilodge.com; 1,000,000 Rp double

Tropical plants and two infinity pools overlook the jungle valley below. Rinjani Lodge is one of Senaru's most iconic boutique hotels, with newly built modern rooms where wooden elements tie the lodge to its natural surroundings. Each room has air-conditioning, a fridge, spotty Wi-Fi access, a TV, and an entertainment system. The semi-outdoor bathroom is a highlight where you can soak sore post-hike muscles in a bathtub that sits alongside a miniature garden. A fresh breakfast served on your patio or at the popular open-air restaurant is included with each stay.

GETTING THERE AND AROUND

There is no direct or reliable transportation leading to Senaru. The best way to get to Senaru is with your own vehicle or a **private driver** from **Senggigi** (80 km/5.5 mi; 2 hours; 400,000 Rp), **Mataram** (85 km/53 mi; 2.5 hours; 400,000 Rp), Kuta (130 km/80 mi; 3 hours; 650,000 Rp), **Lombok International Airport** (120 km/75 mi; 3 hours; 500,000 Rp), or **Bangsal** (60km/37 mi; 1.5 hours; 400,000 Rp).

If you plan to trek Gunung Rinjani, many **trekking companies** based in Senaru offer pickup and drop-off included in the trekking price.

Motorbikes can be rented from most accommodations for 60,000 Rp per day.

Sembalun Valley

Sembalun Valley is made up of Sembalun Lawang and Sembalun Bumbung, two neighboring villages in the foothills of Gunung Rinjani. While most know Sembalun as the stepping-stone up to Rinjani's crater rim, it's also a breadbasket for the island of Lombok. Farms growing garlic, coffee, cocoa, garlic, vegetables, and fruits all form an interesting patchwork when seen from above. After being at the epicenter of a major earthquake that led to the devastation of 90 percent of the structures in Sembalun Valley, the community is slowly coming back. Spend your days taking farm tours and trekking around Gunung Rinjni, then recover with a sweet glass of fresh strawberry juice in town.

Bring cash to Sembalun, as there are no reliable ATMs available.

SIGHTS
Bukit Selong

Sembulan Lawang; 10,000 Rp admission when staffed
Walk to the top of Bukit Selong to admire a quilt made of farmlands in varying shades of green, spanning across Sembalun below. From a distance, the squares almost look like pixels on a screen. A precarious road leads to the base of the hill where it's a short and steep walk up to the top.

★ Bukit Pergasingan

Sembulan Lawang; 800,000 Rp 1-day trek, 1,400,000 Rp overnight trek, 50,000 Rp admission if trekking alone
An alternative to Gunung Rinjani, Bukit Pergasingan is one of the best places in Lombok to sit and admire the sunrise. To make the most of Bukit Pergasingan, embark on a sunrise trek with **Muji Trekker** (information below) that starts at 3am and leads three hours up a gentle incline through grasslands and forest to the top. From there, enjoy the view of Gunung Rinjani and the farmlands below. During springtime, the trail is often accented with wildflowers. Two-day, one-night treks are also available. It is possible to trek without a guide. Plan your hike during a weekday when you won't have to compete with local weekend tourists for a spot to sleep.

TREKKING
MUJI TREKKER

Pickup service; tel. 81917774082; www.mujitrekker. com; 2,000,000 Rp 2-day trek Gunung Rinjani; 800,000-1,400,000 Rp trek Bukit Pergasingan
Muji Trekker, based in Sembalun, is an experienced outfitter that offers customized treks within the area. Excursions can be themed toward waterfalls or wildflowers. Muji Trekker also offer trips to Gunung Rinjani and Bukit Pergasingan for overnight stays under the stars. Muji, the main guide, is personable and helps motivate those who need the extra push.

ACCOMMODATIONS

Most accommodations collapsed during the 2018 earthquakes and are in the process of rebuilding. There's a handful of warungs—many unnamed—around the area, though there is no solid restaurant scene. Plan to have many of your meals at your accommodation.

★ SEMBALUN KITA COTTAGES

Jalan Raya Sembalun Lawang; tel. 82339509934; 200,000 Rp double
Friendly hosts often cook up delicious strawberry pancakes for breakfast at Sembalun Kita Cottages. Small cottages with a hammock on the balcony are surrounded by rice fields, backed by Gunung Rinjani. The cottages have private bathrooms with warm water showers, though that's about where the amenities end. Staff can help arrange transport, treks, and tours of the area, providing insight into Sasak daily life.

RINJANI FAMILY HOMESTAY

Sembalun Lawang; tel. 87863478799; www. rinjanifamily.com; 300,000 Rp double

Run by a longtime Gunung Rinjani trekking guide, Armasih, and his family, Rinjani Family Homestay offers a local experience of life in Sembalun. The property is quiet, offering simple rooms with private bathrooms, surrounded by gardens and fruit trees, where fruit is often harvested and served as a midday snack or breakfast treat. Armasih and his staff are happy to help arrange tours, treks, and transportation around Lombok.

INFORMATION AND SERVICES

RINJANI INFORMATION CENTER

Jalan Raya Sembalun Lawang; tel. 81805791762; https://rinjanilombok.net; daily 6am-6pm

Rinjani Information Center provides weather updates and basic trekking information. This is where trekkers register their hike before embarking up the Sembalun route into Gunung Rinjani.

GETTING THERE AND AROUND

The road to Sembalun is badly damaged in some areas, and many **drivers** are hesitant to bring travelers to Sembalun for a low price. Expect to pay 600,000-700,000 Rp if you are coming from outside of the region, such as from **Senggigi** (100 km/62 mi; 3 hours), **Mataram** (85 km/53 mi; 2.5 hours), or **Kuta** (90 km/56 mi; 2.5 hours). **Senaru** is one hour away, and a ride between the two areas costs around 150,000 Rp.

Motorbikes can be rented for 50,000-70,000 Rp per day, but take care on the roads as they are not maintained.

Tetebatu and Around

Tetebatu is one of Lombok's best-kept secrets; it's a small town surrounded by rice terraces and plantations growing crops like nutmeg, cocoa, coffee, and vanilla. Each morning dewdrops defy gravity on tree leaves. Gunung Rinjani's jagged peak stands regally in the background. Wander down a dirt pathway and you're sure to find serenity in the form of waterfalls and wildlife. It's a place that could easily become a muse for a traveling artist.

SIGHTS

Tetebatu Monkey Forest

North Tetebatu; tel. 81999028098; daily 7am-5pm

Tetebatu Monkey Forest is lush and peaceful. That is, until a long-tailed macaque hears the rustle of a plastic bag. Boisterous monkeys hang out in the forest, getting their tiny hands on snacks, whether through charity or through force. More timid than their light gray forest mates, the rare Javan lutung monkeys with jet black hair tend to keep more distance.

★ Waterfalls

Waterfalls are the highlight of Tetebatu. It's best to visit during the end of rainy season and the beginning of dry season, March to June, when you're likely to have clear days and see the waterfalls at full flow.

SARANG WALET WATERFALL (Air Terjun Sarang Walet)

Central Tetebatu; 150,000 Rp guided trek

A trek along rice fields, through knee-deep water, and a short hand-over-foot scramble through a slippery path leads you to Air Terjun Sarang Walet. This waterfall flows into a cave from a crack in the rocks above. The path to get here can be challenging to follow, so a guide is recommended.

BENANG STOKEL WATERFALL (Air Terjun Benang Stokel)

Aik Berik Village, 1 hour west of Tetebatu; 30,000 Rp admission, 80,000 guided tour

A cool, shaded pathway leads to Air Terjun

Benang Stokel, twin narrow waterfalls that flow into a shallow pool. A third smaller fall often also appears after heavy rains. Jungle vines and large palm leaves split the falls, which flow into a small stream under a bridge and then turn into yet another waterfall. Locals often jump from a spot near the bridge into the pool below; however, this is probably not a smart move for those who don't know the area. Guides may push their services, but the path (with stairs) is well-marked and easy to complete on your own.

BENANG KELAMBU WATERFALL
(Air Terjun Benang Kelambu)

Aik Berik Village, 1 hour west of Tetebatu, shares trail with Air Terjun Benang Stokel 500 meters (1,640 feet) upstream; 30,000 Rp admission, 80,000 guided tour

Veering west from Air Terjun Benang Stokel, a 30-minute walk leads you along more waterfalls, ending at Air Terjun Benang Kelambu. The name Kelambu translates into curtain, and the fall got its moniker after its sheet-like appearance, created when water flows from four tiers of cracks and terraces. The best way to enjoy this fall is to walk back and admire the scene from a distance. The longer you look, the more streams of water you'll find appearing from the crags. Calm swimming

pools form at the base of the falls, so pack a change of clothes.

TREKKING AND TOURS

It is possible to trek to the crater rim of Gunung Rinjani from Air Berik, an hour from Tetebatu. Many of the best views in Tetebatu are on private property. Local guides like **Edi,** often found at **Warung Oktavia** (tel. 82339168368), and **Jonny** (tel. 85337415142) offer local tours of Tetebatu and around for 200,000 Rp for 4 hours.

JAYA TREKKER

tel. 85337920005; https://jayatrekker.com; 2,100,000-4,200,000 Rp per person, depending on group size

Jaya Trekker is a local company that offers treks and tours to waterfalls around Tetebatu, as well as treks to Gunung Rinjani's crater rim. The benefit of trekking to the crater rim from Tetebatu is the view you're offered of the lake and the summit from the vantage point of the crater.

JONNY TOUR GUIDE

tel. 85337415142; www.jonnytourguide.com; 450,000 Rp per person walking tour

A local with a passion for showing tourists

Tetebatu Monkey Forest

447

MOUNT RINJANI AND NORTHERN LOMBOK
TETEBATU AND AROUND

the best of Tetebatu, Jonny is a go-to guide for rice terrace walks, waterfall treks, and cycling tours of the region. Jonny is friendly, knowledgeable, and accommodating to families and those with special requests. River tubing along rice fields can also be arranged.

★ SHOPPING

While Tetebatu is known for its tobacco and spices, there are many villages famous for their handiwork on Tetebatu's outskirts. It's best to visit these villages with an English-speaking private driver, who can help navigate roads that could use extra signage and help translate any transactions. Bargaining is expected in the villages, and bulk orders are the best way to score a true deal. As a rule of thumb, you can often skim 30-40 percent off the original asking price.

Loyok

Loyok is a small village found 10 km (6.2 mi) south of Tetebatu that's famous for weaving bamboo, rattan, and grass baskets, and home decor. Shop here for woven goods and take a class on how to craft these woven baskets yourself.

Pringgasela

Some of the most intricate and interesting textiles come from Pringgasela, where women weave ceremonial attire, sarongs, and home decor on wooden looms. Shop for colorful textiles and learn how each fabric is made from start to finish.

Penka

Using local clay, artists shape pottery and design pieces with traditional patterns. Each family has its own style, often reflecting works made from the generations before them.

Kotaraja

Jalan Kotaraja; daily 7am-noon
Shop at a traditional market in the neighboring town of Kotaraja, where you can find produce, handmade goods, and snacks in a small market area crowded with cidomos, stalls, and motorbikes.

FOOD

WARUNG MONKEY FOREST

tel. 81999028098; daily 8am-9pm; 20,000-50,000 Rp
Warung Monkey Forest is a small warung known for fresh Sasak fare. The charismatic owner, Roon, is almost always around and is happy to offer itinerary suggestions and teach basic Sasak lessons. He also gives cooking lessons for those who want to take delicious *gado-gado* or curry recipes back home with them. If it's not crowded, Roon might also give an impromptu tour of his property.

OKTAVIA WARUNG

tel. 81229168368; daily 8am-9pm; 20,000-50,000 Rp
Edi, a friendly tour guide, and his wife, a skilled chef, own and run Oktavia Warung. Spend the day walking through the rice fields or traipsing under waterfalls before making it here for a prime plate of Sasak food. Curries, rice, satays, soups, and vegetables cooked in coconut milk are all available for hungry guests.

ACCOMMODATIONS

★ DREAM CATCHER CAMP

Near Tetebatu Monkey Forest; tel. 85237679747; dreamcatchercamp@yahoo.com; 100,000 Rp bed
Dream Catcher Camp is a taste of Woodstock in the countryside of Tetebatu. Hammocks, views of rice terraces, swings, painted acoustic guitars, communal bonfires, and group activities are just a few things to expect once you walk onto the property. The owner's little pack of friendly dogs wander from hut to hut in search of head pats and praise. The treehouses and huts are rustic and simple, and their cozy size combined with bathrooms that could use an extra scrub make you feel like you're camping rather than staying in a guesthouse.

SAMA SAMA BUNGALOWS

Tetebatu; tel. 82340296543; 150,000 Rp double

There are plenty of places to lounge around at Sama Sama Bungalows, a guesthouse with bungalows that have spacious balconies with hammocks strewn across, private bathrooms, Wi-Fi access, and included breakfast. Quirky, upbeat signs add to the welcoming atmosphere of the property, as does the smiling family that runs it. Live music occasionally plays at the property's bar and warung.

★ SATU LINGKUNG BUNGALOWS

Jalan Pariwisata Lingkung; https://satulingkung.com; 275,000 Rp double

Sleep in a gorgeous wooden bungalow with a thatched roof surrounded by gardens at Satu Lingkung Bungalows. Fall asleep to a chorus of frogs and wake up to the sound of songbirds. Some bungalows have a private veranda where you can sway in a hammock with a book in hand; all have en suite bathrooms. The family running the homestay is happy to lead guided walks to the nearby waterfall and rice terraces, teach cooking classes at the onsite warung, and host DIY tours of the area. A bamboo lookout tower on the property offers incredible sunset views.

GETTING THERE AND AROUND

Bemos leave from **Mandalika Terminal** in **Mataram** to **Pomotong,** a town 12 km (7.5 mi) south of Tetebatu. However, the most convenient way to get to Tetebatu is with a **private driver** or **arranged transport through your accommodation.** It's possible to drive to Tetubatu from **Senggigi** (60 km/37 mi; 2 hours), **Mataram** (45 km/28 mi; 1.5 hours), **Kuta** (55 km/34 mi; 1.5 hours), **Senaru** (85 km/53 mi; 2.5 hours), and **Sembalun** (55 km/34 mi; 2 hours). It's not recommended to do this without a reliable **GPS** navigator.

Perama (tel. 361/751875; www.peramatour.com) also offers shuttle buses from **Senggigi** (2-2.5 hours; 150,000 Rp), **Mataram** (1.5-2 hours; 125,000 Rp), and the **Lombok International Airport** (1.5-2 hours; 150,000 Rp).

To get around Tetebatu, it's best to use a **motorbike,** which can be rented for 60,000 Rp per day. Many roads around the region are unmarked and made of dirt. For some of the more remote waterfalls, sights, and trails, it's best to go with a **guide** who can provide a driver or *ojek* service.

Gunung Rinjani Reserve

Gunung Rinjani Reserve is home to its namesake volcano. The park also encompasses a holy lake, **Segara Anak,** and two smaller volcanoes in its center, **Gunung Rombongan** and **Gunung Barujari.** Gunung Rinjani is seen as one of the most spiritual places on the island. Many Sasak and Balinese Hindus embark on a pilgrimage to its crater rim and hot springs, which are thought to have healing properties.

In 2018, an earthquake triggered landslides within the Gunung Rinjani Reserve, rendering many trails impassable. While tourists cannot trek to the summit of the volcano, those who venture to the top of the volcano's

crater can admire views of steaming vents, a tranquil lake, a jagged rim, and clouds as they roll through the vibrant skyline.

GUIDES

Those wanting to trek Gunung Rinjani must do so with a guide. Only 500 trekkers can access the trails of Gunung Rinjani per day from Senaru (150 trekkers), Sembalun (150 trekkers), Aik Berik (100 trekkers), and Timbanuh (100 trekkers). All visitors must register themselves through eRinjani (www.erinjani.id) before their trek, though almost all trekking operators will do so for you.

Gunung Rinjani Trekking Tips

The trails leading to the crater rim of Gunung Rinjani are steep, and many visitors find the trek more difficult than they expected. To make the most of your trip, here are a few tips to keep in mind.

- **Pack as light as possible during your trek.** If you've booked a typical guided trek, your porter will carry your water, food, and camping gear. In addition to your hiking clothes, pack an extra layer of clothes to sleep in, a waterproof jacket, sunglass, a hat, sunscreen, a headlamp, and basic toiletries. Face wipes will also help you feel refreshed at the crater rim, as there are no shower facilities to use after a long day of hiking. Make sure the shoes you are wearing for the trek are already broken in.

- **June** and **July** are the driest months to trek Gunung Rinjani. The weekends often see domestic tourists coming to hike, and trail tickets for Senaru and Sembalun might be taken.

- **Prepare for the trek in advance** by strength training, hiking steep nearby hills, and jogging.

- **Not all trekking operators are equal.** Many provide worn-out tents, tattered sleeping bags, and punctured mats—these are often reflected in the company's price point and in their (lack of) emphasis on safety. Pay a little more for a low guide-to-hiker ratio, quality camping gear, and nutritious meals. Many trekking operators offer discounts to trekkers who collect rubbish, leaving the volcano better than they found it.

- Notify your trekking organizer in advance if you have any **dietary requests.** The porters will be bringing all meals and snacks up the mountain, and there is nowhere to get alternative supplies.

- **Book a trek directly with the trekking operator.** There are many faux representatives, combing through Lombok's tourist areas, who will book your tour with their preferred company (the one that kicks over the largest commission), rather than the one you've requested. Companies with prices that sound too good to be true might have you trekking with shoddy equipment and minimal food in large groups, and the guide might not be licensed or trained to lead groups.

GREEN RINJANI

Pickup Service; tel. 85237214385; www.greenrinjani. com; 5,400,000 Rp private, 2,700,000 Rp shared 2-day trek

A reputable and environmentally conscious trekking operator, Green Rinjani offers two-day, one-night trips to Gunung Rinjani's crater rim from Senaru and Sembalun. Choose between standard service, with basic camping provisions and a thin mattress, or the deluxe service, which comes with better meals and a thicker camping mattress. The deluxe service is worth the splurge. A challenging one-day trek that starts at midnight and goes from Senaru to the crater rim is also available.

RUDY TREKKER

Pickup Service; tel. 81803652874; www.rudytrekker. com; 2,700,000-3,500,000 Rp per person for 2-day trek

Rudy Trekker is one of the most well-known and experienced trekking companies offering trips to Gunung Rinjani. They host trips starting from Sembalun and Senaru, with all equipment included. Run by Rudy, the trekking guides are skilled at pointing out notable things about the trail and cooking meals that can compete with some of the best warungs, and porters go out of their way to ensure trash is removed from the slopes.

RINJANI TREK ADVENTURE

Pickup service/Jalan Parwisata; tel. 82340997161; rinjanitrekadventure.com; 1,750,000 Rp per person for group tour or 2,250,000 Rp per person for private 2-day trek

Friendly guides lead two-day trips to the crater rim. Choose between a private tour or a shared group tour with up to eight people per group. Porters and guides are attentive even with the larger groups. Equipment is clean and well-maintained, and meals are different each day.

★ TREKKING GUNUNG RINJANI

The trails to Gunung Rinjani are open from **April** until **December,** outside of rainy season. After the 2018 earthquakes, many parts of the trail and the summit of Gunung Rinjani were badly damaged. At the time of research, it is not possible to trek to the summit of Gunung Rinjani, but reserve rangers are hoping to repair the trail and reopen it soon.

There are four routes that lead through Gunung Rinjani. Most choose to trek from **Sembalun** and **Senaru,** the original popular trekking routes; therefore, these trails are well-trod and can be crowded. The Sembalun and Senaru trails are also the only treks that connect to Gunung Rinjani's summit. **Timbanuh** and **Aik Berik** trails lead to the crater rim. Senaru and Sembalun trails once connected to one another by going into the crater and along the lake, though this route is currently closed.

The trail from the crater rim to the summit is narrow and made of volcanic ash. At times, it can feel as though you are taking two steps forward and sliding one step back. The exposure to the sun and wind at this altitude can be intense; wear warm clothing and put on a layer of sunscreen, or pack it with you for the trek back down to the crater rim after sunrise. Starting in Senaru is less strenuous than starting in Sembalun, and it's the most popular route to hike. It's also possible to do this trek in three days and two nights, but the four-day trek is preferable, as you will have more time to rest, enjoy the views, and plan your timing around the weather.

SENARU TRAIL

Hiking Distance: *25 km (15.5) round-trip*
Hiking Time: *4 days, 3 nights*
Maps and Information: *Rinjani Information Center and mtrinjanitrek.com*

The Senaru Trail offers a mix of forest and exposed grasslands leading up to the crater rim, where you'll enjoy views of Gunung Rinjani's summit across the lake. You will start at the edge of the Gunung Rinjani reserve trailhead and hike up the crater rim on the first day, summit Gunung Rinjani on the first night, trek to the interior of the caldera on the second day, and camp by the lake or on the opposing crater rim. Then, you will trek down the exterior of the crater rim and end in Senaru.

SEMBALUN TRAIL

Hiking Distance: *20 km (12 mi) round-trip*
Hiking Time: *4 days, 3 nights*
Maps and Information: *Rinjani Information Center and mtrinjanitrek.com*

Sembalun Trail starts at the Rinjani Information Center and takes you through spacious grasslands and climbs up steep forest to the crater rim, on the same side as Gunung Rinjani's summit. This is one of the steeper trails with few switchbacks. This trail is simply the reverse of the Senaru.

TIMBANUH TRAIL

Hiking Distance: *22 km (13.5 mi) round-trip*
Hiking Time: *2 days, 1 night*
Maps and Information: *mtrinjanitrek.com*

The Timbanuh Trail, starting in the village of Timbanuh, is green and offers interesting views of Sumbawa.

AIK BERIK TRAIL

Hiking Distance: *20 km (12 mi) round-trip*
Hiking Time: *2 days, 1 night*
Maps and Information: *mtrinjanitrek.com*

The trailhead of Aik Berik Trail starts at the beautiful Benang Stokel waterfall. This trail is slightly easier than Senaru and Sembalun, offering a shaded and uncrowded route through Lombok's natural forests.

INFORMATION AND SERVICES

Balai Taman Nasional Gunung Rinjani releases official updates about trail openings and events in Gunung Rinjani Reserve (www. tnrinjani.net).

GETTING THERE AND AROUND

Most major trekking companies offer **pickup services** within mainland Lombok to the trailhead before your excursion. Within the reserve, almost all paths are dirt; **walking** is the only way forward.

1: hiking Sembalun Trail **2:** tents along Sembalun Trail

Background

The Landscape

GEOGRAPHY

Bali is a small island in Indonesia that measures about 5,780 square km (2,231 square miles). It is made up of the main island of Bali, as well as the three smaller islands of Nusa Lembongan, Nusa Ceningan, and Nusa Penida. Java is its neighbor 3.2 km (2 mi) to the east, while Lombok is 35 km (22 mi) to its west. The largest volcano on Bali, Gunung Agung, is active and stands at 3,031 meters (almost 10,000 feet) on Bali's eastern edge. In its center, Bali is mountainous, with Gunung Batur (1,717 meters/5,600 feet), Gunung Batukaru (2,276

meters/7,467 feet), and lakes like Danau Batur, Danau Beratan, Danau Buyan, and Danau Tamblingan. In this Central Mountain region, forests with gushing waterfalls, hot springs, and steep slopes and valleys are found. South of Bali's mountainous region, much of the land is used for rice cultivation. Ash and rainfall from the nearby volcanoes create soil that is fertile.

Moving south to Bali's Bukit Peninsula, land tends to be arid and many beaches are backed by sheer limestone cliffs. Along Bali's mainland shoreline, sand ranges from off-white to jet-black, with many of the world's best waves peeling along the coast.

Lombok is 4,725 square km (1,824 square mi). Its most striking feature, Gunung Rinjani (3,726 meters/12,000 feet high), is Indonesia's second-tallest volcano and is home to a turquoise crater lake in its center. The area surrounding Gunung Rinjani ranges from lush forest to sprawling grasslands; the change in landscape can be sudden and breathtaking. The southern half of Lombok is barren and arid; droughts are common. However, this southern region offers sandy beaches, peninsulas that jut out into the sea, and world-class waves, attracting surfers from all around the globe. Off mainland Lombok, there are dozens of tiny islands made from white sand and scrubland. The most famous are the islands of Gili Trawangan, Gili Meno, and Gili Air.

Both Bali and Lombok are in the Coral Triangle, a marine area named after the nearly 600 species of reef-building coral native to the area.

CLIMATE

Bali and Lombok have two seasons, dry and wet. The dry season spans April to September while the wet season lasts from October to March. Climates vary from region to region. As a general rule, the greener and higher you go through the island's central mountains, the cooler and rainier it tends to be.

ENVIRONMENTAL ISSUES

Bali and Lombok are islands located on what's commonly called the Ring of Fire, officially the Circum-Pacific Belt. This region is one of the most geologically active, with common volcanic eruptions and earthquakes. This activity also puts the region at risk of tsunami. In 2017, the Gunung Agung volcano on Bali became active, and its condition is monitored daily. In 2018, a series of earthquakes devastated Northern Lombok. Bali and Lombok are also at risk of suffering from regional droughts that can lead to water shortages and uncontrolled fires.

With no truly efficient waste management system, one of the largest problems that Bali and Lombok face today is the influx of single-use plastics. Plastic is often burned, releasing carcinogens into the air. Plastics are also frequently dumped in waterways; the plastic then flows inland to the ocean, where it gathers on beaches and harms marine life.

An explosion in building development has led to myriad environmental issues, like coastal erosion coupled with stress on reefs, thanks to dredging, sewage contamination, and tourists trampling over fragile corals. Water demands have lowered water tables, drying up local wells. Wildlife habitats have also been destroyed, causing the decline of Bali's native bird life.

PLANTS

If land is fertile on Bali and Lombok, it's likely been used for agriculture. When the islands are viewed from high above, they often look as though they're cloaked in a patchwork quilt. Rice has been cultivated on Bali for more than 2,000 years, and rice is a part of just about every aspect of daily life. Because of this, you'll find that native plants are mostly found in West Bali National Park (Taman Nasional Bali Barat) and on the slopes of the island's major mountains. On Lombok,

Average Temperatures and Rainfall

BALI (DENPASAR)

- **January:** 25-30°C (77-86°F); 345mm (13.5 in) rainfall
- **February:** 25-31°C (77-88°F); 275mm (10.8 in) rainfall
- **March:** 25-31°C (77-88°F); 235mm (9.25 in) rainfall
- **April:** 25-31°C (77-88°F); 88mm (3.5 in) rainfall
- **May:** 25-30°C (77-86°F); 93mm (3.6 in) rainfall
- **June:** 25-30°C (77-86°F); 53mm (2 in) rainfall
- **July:** 24-29°C (75-84°F); 55mm (2.1 in) rainfall
- **August:** 24-29°C (75-84°F); 25mm (1 in) rainfall
- **September:** 24-30°C (75-86°F); 47mm (1.85 in) rainfall
- **October:** 25-31°C (77-88°F); 63mm (2.5 in) rainfall
- **November:** 25-31°C (77-88°F); 179mm (7 in) rainfall
- **December:** 26-31°C (79-88°F); 276mm (10.8 in) rainfall

LOMBOK (MATARAM)

- **January:** 24-31°C (75-88°F); 317mm (12.5 in) rainfall
- **February:** 24-31°C (75-88°F); 254mm (10 in) rainfall
- **March:** 24-32°C (75-84°F); 206mm (8.1 in) rainfall
- **April:** 23-32°C (73-84°F); 105mm (4.1 in) rainfall
- **May:** 23-32°C (73-84°F); 101mm (4 in) rainfall
- **June:** 22-31°C (71-88°F); 51mm (2 in) rainfall
- **July:** 21-31°C (88-88°F); 48mm (1.9 in) rainfall
- **August:** 21-31°C (70-88°F); 34mm (1.3 in) rainfall
- **September:** 22-31°C (71-88°F); 36mm (1.4 in) rainfall
- **October:** 23-32°C (73-84°F); 95mm (3.7 in) rainfall
- **November:** 24-32°C (75-84°F); 150mm (5.9 in) rainfall
- **December:** 24-32°C (75-84°F); 219mm (8.6 in) rainfall

indigenous plants thrive on the slopes of Gunung Rinjani.

Trees

Because Balinese and Sasak people traditionally have animist beliefs, many trees are considered sacred on the islands. The most impressive is the *waringin* (banyan) tree, which symbolizes reincarnation as it can grow new life from the offshoot of a single branch. Vines reaching from its treetop intertwine down its trunk into the ground, making it a sight to behold.

Palms are one of the most vital plants

Pollution: How Tourists Can Help

When visiting Bali and Lombok, it's helpful to be conscious of the demand tourists place on resources like energy and water, and the amount of waste the tourism industry produces. Here are a few ways to travel more sustainably throughout the islands:

- **Cut down on single-use plastic:** Bring a water sterilizer like **LifeStraw** (www.lifestraw.com) to drink from the tap. Pack a reusable bottle and check the app **Refill My Bottle** (https://refillmybottle.com) to find free or cheap water-refill stations. Instead of ordering bottles of soda, stop at a warung for a fresh juice. When you throw something into a trash can, assume that it could end up in a nearby river or on a beach.

- **Take short showers:** Some regions that support tourists like the Gili Islands, the Bukit Peninsula, and Southern Lombok often have water shortages. Cut down your shower time as much as possible.

- **Eat local:** Bali and Lombok have a surplus of fresh produce and many restaurants are truly farm-to-table. Opt for local dishes over those made from imported ingredients.

- **Be energy conscious:** Turn off your air-conditioning when you leave your hotel room. Air dry your towels rather than requesting a fresh one after every swim.

- **Join clean-ups:** Beach clean-ups organized by **Trash Hero Indonesia** (https://trashhero.org) and other local businesses often host beach clean-ups where you can socialize while making the islands more pristine.

- **Reward those who go green:** Where money flows, trends follow. Support businesses taking eco-friendly initiatives over large polluters.

to the islands. Coconuts grown from palm trees provide kindling, sterile juice for drinking, and flesh, oil, and sugar for cooking. Bamboo is used to build homes, decorations, and kites, and is stripped to create weaving materials.

Flowers

If you visit a Balinese market in the morning, you'll see piles of colorful flowers used to create offerings. Flowers in colors from light blue to hot pink to sugar white are all welcome when it comes to crafting a gift to the gods. *Jepun* (plumeria/frangipani) trees drop soft and fragrant white flowers with yellow and pink accents that are used to adorn offerings. Women often collect fallen *jepun* flowers and press them for oil. Hibiscus, orchids, poinsettia, jasmine, lotus, magnolia, and laceleaf flowers all thrive throughout the region. On Bali, you'll find immaculate gardens on temple grounds, lining the outside of homes, and at any major palace or park.

ANIMALS
Mammals

Most animals you see scampering around Bali and Lombok are of the domestic variety. Chickens are kept as food, prized roosters are kept for cockfighting, and pigs run around compounds as the clean-up crew. Buffalo and cattle are used to plow fields. On Lombok, small ponies are used to cart locals and belongings. Almost every rice farmer has a flock of ducks who waddle through the rice paddies in search of pests, fertilizing the land as they go. Stray dogs are common on Bali. The Gili Islands wouldn't be the same without their resident cats, almost all of whom have wonky tails.

When it comes to wildlife, one of the cheekiest animals on the islands is no doubt the long-tailed macaque, a monkey who has learned to barter and steal to get what it wants. The black Javan lutung, a shy and reclusive monkey, can also be spotted swinging from the treetops of Bali and Lombok.

The Wallace Line

Sir Alfred Russel Wallace (1822-1913), a naturalist and biologist, noticed that there was a distinct difference between the flora and fauna of Asia and that of Australasia. He speculated that animals migrated along land east of Bali during an ice age, where crossing islands would be feasible on foot. However, once these animals—large mammals in particular—arrived at Bali's western end, they would be hindered by the deep Lombok Strait. Life on Lombok and islands west of Lombok developed in line with that in Australasia. The transition zone that blends Bali and Lombok together is often referred to as Wallacea.

Even rarer is the barking deer, the *muntjac,* which is found on Palau Menjangan. Civet cats, called *luwak,* roam through forests in search of fallen coffee cherries. Bats reside inside many caves, taking flight to look for food just after sunset.

Sea Life

There are thousands of species of fish and hundreds of species of corals native to the waters surrounding Bali and Lombok, which is in the Coral Triangle. Sea life like nudibranchs, pygmy seahorses, sea snakes, pipefish, peacock mantis shrimp, clown and other anemone fish, octopus, cuttlefish, crabs, scorpion fish, lionfish, reef sharks, and many more take refuge within the coral. Large lace-like gorgonian fans accent the reef.

Six of the world's seven sea turtle species live in the waters off Bali and Lombok. Snorkelers might see green, hawksbill, loggerhead, olive ridley, leatherback, and flatback sea turtles cruising over the coral reefs. In deeper waters, divers might spot thresher sharks, tuna, trevally, bull sharks, hammerhead sharks, whale sharks, manta rays, and the *mola-mola,* a fish that can weigh a whopping 1,000 kg (2,200 lbs).

Birds

Though hundreds of bird species thrive on Bali's variety of terrain, only one is native to the island. The Bali starling (*jalak),* a white bird with a beautiful blue mask over its eyes, is at risk of extinction. Commonly spotted birds include different species of egrets, herons, kingfishers, sandpipers, and swallows. Colorful birds, like the peafowl and cendrawasih, are thought to be connected to the spiritual realm. The black-crested cockatoo is found on Lombok, the farthest point west of Australia and a key indicator of the border between Asian wildlife and Australasian wildlife.

Reptiles and Amphibians

A *cecak,* an onomatopoeia derived from the sound that it makes, is a small lizard seen just about everywhere on the islands. These lizards linger around lightbulbs, hoping to snag a fly or mosquito as a tasty snack. Their larger cousin, the tokay gecko, can grow up to 30 cm in length and roam in humid, tropical habitats. Frogs and snakes are also found on the islands.

Insects and Arachnids

A visit to a botanical garden on Bali or Lombok is likely to reveal a variety of butterflies. Praying mantises, spiders, mosquitoes, flies, ants, and cockroaches are also found on both islands.

History

ANCIENT CIVILIZATIONS

The Indonesian archipelago was first populated by homo erectus, who traversed the islands during the ice ages. Nearly 50,000 years ago, homo sapiens crossed over from Java onto Bali, using rudimentary tools to survive. Around 10,000 BC, the landmass of Bali likely separated from Java. Seafaring Austronesians arrived 7,000 years later and settled around Bali's western end with knowledge of growing rice and domesticating animals. During the Bronze Age, Bali engaged in trade with outer islands, receiving a bronze-casted kettledrum called the Pejeng Moon, which is considered sacred. Few archaeological remains have been found on Lombok to determine their origin, though it's speculated the first people came from northwest India.

INDIANIZATION OF BALI

It is unknown exactly how or when Bali became Indianized. It was likely a gradual process heavily influenced by the royal powers at the time, who thought Indian religions to be compatible with their political beliefs. Java Indianized first and those communities and beliefs then influenced the beliefs of Bali, whose populace was already receptive to artwork, legends, and music of outside cultures, thanks to an established history of trade. There are no known written records of these accounts, so exact timelines are purely speculation. An artifact dated from the 9th century shows that by then, Bali held Hindu-Buddhist beliefs. Religious carvings made at Goa Gajah and Gunung Kawi prove that there was a local adoption of the religions rather than having just received religious items as part of a trade.

Airlangga (990-1049), one of Java's most successful rajas, united Bali and Lombok as a result of the marriage of his parents, the princess of East Java, Mahendradatta, and the raja of Bali, Udayana. Following Airlangga's

succession to the throne, Bali fought Java for centuries, winning and losing it at multiple points. Animosity toward Java grew, and in 1343, Bali was conquered by Gajah Mada, the leader of the Majapahit area of East Java. Gajah Mada then moved to Bali and established the caste system already implemented in Java. The Majapahit dynasty also overtook Lombok, though Lombok adhered to folk animist beliefs over Hindu ideology. Some Balinese rebuked his ideas and retreated into hard-to-find regions of Bali, isolating themselves as the Bali Aga. For centuries following, the Bali Aga remained apart and developed different customs from the rest of the island.

In 1515, the Majapahit dynasty was overtaken by Islamic forces. Javanese Hindus fled to Bali, taking their religious and cultural ideas with them. Conquerers of Java did not overtake Bali, allowing Bali to operate as a largely independent Hindu state. The ruling king of Bali was established in Gegel. In 1546, a Javanese Hindu Priest, Nirartha, arrived as a counselor to the Gegel king and established a Shaivite form of Hinduism. The king, under advisement of Niratha, issued the building of major Shaivite temples throughout the island.

THE GEGEL GOLDEN AGE AND FALL

During the 16th century, Bali entered the Gegel Golden Age after the Dewa Agung (King of Bali) united all of Bali's regencies and conquered East Java, Lombok, and Sumbawa. Bali had a cultural renaissance as it tried to form its own identity. The Dewa Agung's successors were inept at ruling and promptly lost East Java, Lombok, and Bali. Rajas from other regencies sensed weakness and began to take more power. Feeling as though they've been cursed, the Gegel royal family moved their palace to Klungklung in 1710. By 1750, they'd lost their spot as supreme rulers of Bali.

Historical Timeline

1 million-500,000 BC	Homo erectus exist on Java, fossils of "Java Man" found in 1891.
48,000 BC	Earliest homo sapiens reach Bali and leave traces of crude tools.
10,000 BC	Bali separates from Java and becomes its own island.
3,000 BC	Austronesians arrive in Bali.
1,000 BC	Bali engages in trade with the outside world.
9th Century	A pillar with an inscription is made in Sanur as proof of Bali's acceptance of Hindu-Buddhist beliefs.
1019	Airlangga rules East Java and conquers Bali, uniting the two islands.
1343	Bali is overtaken by Gajah Mada and establishes the Majapahit Dynasty.
1515	The Majapahit Dynasty falls, Javanese Hindus flee to Bali.
1546	Nirartha, a Shaivite priest, arrives and issues the building of new temples.
1550	The Gegel Golden Age transpires—Bali conquers East Java, Lombok, and Sumbawa.
1585	A Portuguese shipwreck occurs off the Bukit Peninsula.

LOMBOK HAPPENINGS

In the late 16th century, Lombok was conquered by the Balinese. All the while, Muslim traders influenced Sasak tribes, who took hold of Islamic ideology. Balinese Hindus on Lombok frequently clashed with Sasak Muslims, leading to increased tension. Until the 19th century, Bali lost and regained control over Lombok—particularly its western region, which was at risk of conquering thanks to its valuable port in Ampenan. In 1830, the Dutch stationed themselves on the island of Lombok as a strategic post for trade and battle. Tensions between Balinese and Sasak kingdoms continued until 1891, when Sasak forces burned the Balinese palace on Lombok, overthrowing Balinese rule.

EUROPEAN CONTACT

In the 1500s, many European trade ships spotted Bali but did not come ashore. In 1585, a Portuguese ship crashed on the reef offshore of the Bukit Peninsula. Five survivors were welcomed ashore but were not allowed to return home. In 1597, a Dutch fleet led by an unsavory captain, Cornelis de Houtman, arrived. De Houtman facilitated a trade relationship between Bali and the Netherlands. The Dutch established a trading port on the neighboring island of Java. From the 1600s to the 1700s, Bali traded slaves in exchange for opium and other goods. Balinese rajas enslaved anyone deemed to be a burden on the kingdom, like orphans, criminals, and debtors. The Dutch recruited Balinese slaves to fight in their colonial army and act as servants on Java.

1597	Dutch fleet led by Cornelis de Houtman arrive and establish a trade relationship between the Netherlands and Bali.
1750	The Gegel Golden Age ends as other rajas around Bali take more power.
1839	Mads Lange frequently acts as a mediator to prevent Dutch-Lombok-Balinese violence.
1906-1908	Dutch battles on Bali lead to ritual suicide called *puputan*.
1942	Japanese land on Balinese shores as a base for WWII, driving Balinese deeper into poverty.
1945-1949	Sukarno declares Indonesian independence; Dutch forces leave by 1949.
1963	Gunung Agung erupts, displacing 100,000 Balinese.
1965	Coup triggers anti-communist killings on Bali and Lombok.
1972	Movie *Morning on Earth* shows Bali as a premier surf destination; tourists arrive in droves.
1997	Asian Financial Crisis hits Indonesia; Suharto resigns under pressure.
2002 and 2005	Islamic terrorist group detonates bombs in Kuta and Bali, killing hundreds.

DUTCH CONQUEST

In the early 1800s, the Dutch worked to establish relationships with Balinese rajas that would help them succeed in wars with other European colonizers. Success varied, and tensions rose throughout the 1830s over reef rites after a series of Dutch shipwrecks and Balinese plunders. Tension increased over the next few decades. In 1906, the Dutch stormed Denpasar. Princes of the kingdom realized that they couldn't beat the Dutch and engaged in *puputan,* a ritual form of suicide. The royal family and surrounding members donned their finest jewels and attire before driving *krises* (daggers) into their own hearts. This happened again in 1908 with the noble family of Klungkung.

In 1942, the Japanese stationed themselves on Bali as an outpost for World War II. Japanese soldiers drained the island of resources, and did not free the Balinese from Dutch rule as they had implied.

INDEPENDENCE

In 1945, a pro-nationalist leader by the name of Sukarno (1901-1970) led a movement to assert Indonesia's independence from Dutch rule, officially declaring it on August 17, 1945. A prominent Balinese war hero, I Gusti Ngurah Rai (1917-1946), led troops against Dutch forces in 1946. I Gusti Ngurah Rai and his men were overpowered and committed suicide, known as *puputan*. Engaged in battles elsewhere, Dutch resources were spread thin and they struggled to regain power of the archipelago, officially ceding control of Indonesia in 1949.

Mads Lange: The White Raja

In 1833 Mads Lange and his three younger brothers sailed from Denmark to Hong Kong. Mads Lange continued to Bali and Lombok in search of entrepreneurial adventure, settling in Ampenan, Lombok. He set up a trading company, exporting rice and spices and importing weapons and textiles.

His business grew to be so lucrative, he became informally known as the White Raja of Ampenan and allied with the Raja of Karangasem, who held power over West Lombok. A clash between the northern raja of Lombok and Karangasem led to Karangasem ceding Lombok to the raja on Lombok. Mads Lange fled to Bali, where he settled in Kuta and established a profitable trade company. While living on Bali, Mads Lange formed friendships with the Balinese royal families and acted as a mediator between Dutch troops and Balinese rajas. Because of his diplomacy, truces were signed (some under dubious circumstances) and violent confrontation was often avoided.

His reign came to the end after a Dutch blockade and constant warring between the Netherlands and Bali caused his exports to decline. Just before he was set to return to Denmark after 18 years spent on Bali, Mads Lange suddenly died. Those who were closest to him suspect he was poisoned.

Though Sukarno inspired rebellion and led a successful campaign against Dutch forces, his leadership over Indonesia proved to be problematic as he moved from a democratic leader to a dictator. A coup in 1965 instigated by Indonesia's communist party damaged Sukarno's regime and sparked violence within Bali and Lombok. Those perceived to be communist were killed by traditionalists, with more than 50,000 suspected communists killed on Bali and 10,000 killed on Lombok. These acts followed the 1963 volcanic eruption of Gunung Agung, a disaster that was seen as a curse from the gods and misplaced over 100,000 people.

After years of unrest, Suharto (1921-2008) became the second president of Indonesia in 1968 and established what he called the New Order. Indonesia flourished with economic prosperity as foreign investors pumped money into the country. However, much of this was merely a facade built on corruption, and the good fortune came at the cost of personal liberties like freedom of speech and political opposition. In 1997, Indonesia was badly damaged during the Asian financial crisis. Inflation soared to unsustainable rates, sinking Indonesia's economy and leading to nationwide riots. Crumbling from the pressure, Suharto stepped down after more than 30 years in power.

CONTEMPORARY TIMES

Following the fall of Suharto, Indonesia embarked on a reform era that established term limits and set up a more organized democratic system. Being a Hindu minority, Bali continued to look at its Muslim neighbors with skepticism. Religious tension was a constant undercurrent following the Bali Bombings of 2002 and 2005, carried out by Islamic terrorist group Jemaah Islamiah. Bali was targeted due to its relationship with the West, as one of the premier destinations for Australian, European, and American tourists. The president of Indonesia (2014-present), Jokowi (born 1961), has recently been re-elected. Time will tell as to whether or not his leadership will unite the islands or divide them.

Reef Rites

Surrounded by treacherous coral reefs, Bali became notorious among traders as an island that was ruthless when it came to aiding **shipwrecks.** The Balinese believed that the sea belonged to the gods. Ships that wrecked along the island's coastline were considered a gift and were plundered. Stranded sailors were often taken as slaves. Because of this, Bali was often marked with a **skull and crossbones** on maps and would-be traders or invaders sailed past the island in search of friendlier waters. Reef rites were a source of conflict between the Balinese and the Dutch for years.

Government and Economy

ORGANIZATION

The Indonesian government is divided into the executive branch, legislative branch, and judicial branch. It is led by a democratically elected president, who heads the executive branch. The Indonesian constitution, developed in 1945, gives most authority to the president, who appoints ministers to his or her cabinet. Indonesia also has what's called the Pancasila, five philosophical principles that govern the country. The Pancasila includes: (1) The belief in one God; (2) Honest and civilized humanism; (3) Unity; (4) Democratic citizenship and wise representation; (5) Social justice for all citizens. The country of Indonesia has 34 provinces, with Jakarta as its capital. These provinces are then divided into smaller regencies and cities, each with locally elected governors who hold five-year terms.

Bali is its own province, with eight regencies and one capital city of Denpasar. Lombok is part of the West Nusa Tenggara province that also includes the island of Sumbawa. It has eight regencies and two cities, with Mataram as its capital. These regencies' borders are the remnants of former kingdoms. The regencies and cities also have their own form of local governments. Neighborhoods form unofficial governments that regulate rules within their community.

POLITICAL PARTIES

There are 10 major political parties represented in the Indonesian legislature. They are typically divided into secular parties and Islamic parties, though many secular parties have Muslim leaders. The largest party is the Indonesian Democratic Party of Struggle (PDI-P), which is a populist, secular, and nationalist party that stemmed from Sukarno's Indonesian Democratic Party, with many of its supporters in Java. The next-largest party is the Great Indonesia Movement Part (Gerindra), a secular party with undefined political stances as it is pinned to its leader, Prabowo Subianto, who was a presidential candidate in 2014 and 2019. The third-largest party is Golkar, which is the oldest party in Indonesia and holds tightly to Suharto's political ideologies, though it has grown to become a populist party appealing to those in rural areas.

Because Bali is a minority when it comes to religion and representation, most Balinese vote for secular parties. Lombok is a Muslim-majority island, so Sasak voters tend to vote for Islamic-leaning secular parties or Islamic parties.

ELECTIONS

Indonesian citizens directly elect the president and vice president to hold five-year terms in office. Citizens also elect their representatives in the legislative branch (made up of the 575-member People's Representative Council and 136-member Regional Representative Council) through constituencies. Governors are elected by their province citizens and hold five-year terms.

Because Indonesia has a multiparty system, it is rare for one party to gain an outright majority in the legislative branch. Political parties often form coalition governments to press laws in their best interest. To vote, citizens must be 17 or older.

The current president of Indonesia is Joko Widodo, commonly known as Jokowi and a member of the Indonesian Democratic Party of Struggle (PDI-P), who secured his office with 55.5 percent of the vote in April 2019. The election had an 82 percent voter turnout. Following election results, protestors claimed that the election had been fraudulent, after 569 of the 7 million election workers died during the counting process from poor working conditions. Riots resulting from the protests killed eight people and injured 600.

AGRICULTURE

Agriculture is one of the key drivers of Bali and Lombok's economy. Almost all viable land on Bali and Lombok is used for growing crops like rice, cloves, cinnamon, cocoa, coffee, vanilla, nutmeg, cassava, coconut, tea, and tobacco. Currently, the islands struggle to retain young farmers, as many young workers opt for jobs in tourism, tech, science, art, and government.

INDUSTRY AND TOURISM

Prior to the 1970s, agriculture was Bali's largest industry. During the past 50 years, tourism has become the largest industry on the island and Bali is the biggest tourism destination in Indonesia when it comes to foreign visitors. Those who venture to the island expect to experience the unique culture that Bali holds. While some say that tourism has impacted Bali's culture in a negative way through the rise of sterile cafés, hotels, and alcohol-fueled debauchery, tourism dollars also fund temple maintenance and cultural performances, and contribute to the preservation of Bali's unique culture, as it is the thing that draws tourists to the island in the first place. In 2018, more than 6 million foreign tourists touched down on Bali, a 6 percent increase from 2017. Despite the rise in tourists visiting Bali, the quality of life for many locals has not grown proportionally in rural areas that do not receive many tourists.

On Lombok, many locals live as subsistence farmers. Agriculture, fishing, and tourism are the main money-makers for the island. Most visitors trickle over from Bali, and Lombok's success is closely linked to that of its popular neighbor. The Indonesian government has established the Mandalika Resort Development Project in Kuta, Lombok, that is planned to host hotels, beach clubs, a golf course, a theme park, and a Formula One circuit. However, many locals are skeptical of its success, as many tourists come to Lombok in search of solitude and unspoiled beaches.

In 2018, Lombok received one million foreign tourists, though the aftermath of the 2018 earthquakes has hindered the upward trend seen over the past few decades. The impact of this increase in tourism has been felt culturally and through the rapid development of Lombok's once-unspoiled landscape. Tension arises when bikini-clad or shirtless tourists walk with a beer in hand in public. Some locals are resistant to development, having seen the large hotel eyesores arrive, and there is resentment of foreign corporations owning land that once belonged to locals. Many tourists who visit Lombok are domestic Muslims, as the island is known for its mosques and halal-friendly restaurants and accommodations.

DISTRIBUTION OF WEALTH

Despite the boom of tourism on Bali, there is still a high level of income inequality. While many locals residing in tourism-heavy regions like the Bukit Peninsula, Kuta, Denpasar, Ubud, and Lovina have risen to middle-class, those in rural areas struggle to earn a livable wage. The sense of inequality is widened as the government invests in income-generating regions more so than regions that may need resources the most. This is coupled with the fact that many tourism businesses are foreign-owned, funneling money off the island while raising the cost of living for locals. The wealth discrepancy has also caused tension among Balinese and non-Balinese Indonesians, many of whom have migrated to Bali from Java or outer islands in search of lucrative jobs.

On Lombok, most locals earn a low income or live as subsistence farmers. Lombok is part of one of the poorer provinces in Indonesia, with the World Bank classifying 1.2 million of its residents living in absolute poverty. Wages are expected to rise with the development of new tourism projects, and with direct flights from Australia to Lombok being added to upcoming flight schedules and incentivizing tourists to visit the region.

People and Culture

DEMOGRAPHY AND DIVERSITY

The island of Bali is home to 4.2 million people. According to a 2014 census, 90 percent of these are Balinese, 7 percent are Javanese, and 1 percent are Madurese. Most residents are Hindu (83.5 percent), followed by Muslim (13.4 percent), Christian (2.5 percent), and Buddhist (0.5 percent). There are around 30,000 expats living on the island as well.

On Lombok, there are 3.4 million residents. More than 85 percent of the citizens are Sasak, 10 percent are Balinese, and the rest of Lombok's residents hail from Java, Sumatra, Sumbawa, and other Indonesian islands. Most of Lombok's residents are Muslim, though most Balinese residents are devout Balinese Hindus.

INDIGENOUS CULTURES

Balinese and Sasak people are defined more by their cultural and historical identity rather than racial identity. Not much is known about the first people to arrive on either Bali or Lombok, who were Austronesian. Everything from dress, religion, rituals, language, and food can change greatly from region to region.

Bali Aga (Bali)

There are small subsets of indigenous communities called the Bali Aga, who claim to be the first people of Bali. It is disputed as to whether they are genetically different from Balinese. As they have been isolated from most of the major cultural and political events of the last few centuries, Bali Aga tend to practice a form of animism mixed with folk Hinduism; they do not follow a caste system, and they have their own form of architecture. Marrying outside of the community leads to banishment, which is how the subculture has maintained its own identity for generations.

RELIGION

Balinese Hinduism

Multiple times per day, Balinese Hindus place an offering made of flowers and incense as a way of honoring the spiritual and physical realms. Traffic comes to a halt as a parade of hundreds of people dressed in immaculate clothes walk through carrying baskets of food and crafts to the temples. The religion clings tightly to mystical and animistic beliefs not found in other Hindu-dominated cultures.

How did Bali become Hindu? It's a question that has left scholars scratching their heads. Most believe that the island was Indianized through political powers. Artifacts from the 8th and 9th centuries reveal a Hindu-Buddhist Bali, with both religions intermingling with one another at the time. Transition to the Hindu religion was likely slow, which is why many traditional animist beliefs coexisted with Indian Hinduism. In the 1940s, Balinese Hinduism had to break from its polytheistic roots and become monotheistic in order to be accepted as a religion by the Indonesian government. This led to the belief in Sang Hyand

Widhi Wasa, the supreme god who can manifest into all Hindu gods. The three main gods worshipped are Shiva, the god of destruction; Vishnu, the god of preservation; and Brahma, the god of creation. There are also gods related to almost every aspect of life including crops, water, weather, and death. Demons are also ever-present and must be appeased or scared away through rituals and offerings. Balinese Hindus believe in karma through the forces of good and evil, as well as reincarnation. As many as 10 percent of Balinese couples are in plural marriages, as men can legally have up to four wives.

There is a community of Balinese Hindus on Lombok, descendants from when the Balinese Karangasem kingdom ruled over western Lombok.

Islam

Most of Lombok's Sasak people are Muslim. Islamification on Lombok was a slow process until recent times, which is why many Sasak communities still hold onto animist beliefs. Religious scholars believe that the religion was introduced to the island sometime in the 13th century, likely from merchants from already-Islamic islands. Today, mosques around the island attract halal tourists who've come to see why Lombok is known as the Land of 1,000 Mosques.

Most Sasak Muslims follow the traditional five pillars of Islam. This includes being loyal to the Muslim faith, praying five times per day, contributing to charity, fasting during Ramadan, and making a pilgrimage to Mecca. The call to prayer is played five times per day from the local mosque. While some women cover their hair, not all do. Some Sasak communities practice polygamy, where men can have up to four wives. There is a movement toward following a more traditional form of Islam, largely influenced by the political happenings and media influence coming from Java.

Wetu Telu

Wetu Telu translates into "Three Times," a reference to how many times per day Wetu Telu Muslims pray. These prayers are typically not signaled by the call to prayer from a mosque but rather when the believer feels it is a good time. There is a designated corner facing mecca in all buildings to do so. Though those who follow Wetu Telu accept Muhammad as Allah's prophet, they also hold to folk animist and vaguely Hindu beliefs. In addition, they only observe three days of fasting rather than a full month during Ramadan. This form of Islam, believed to have come from the village of Bayan, was once commonly practiced throughout Lombok and its participants adhered to a four-tiered caste system. However, in recent times, Wetu Telu has ceded to the more stringent form of Islam.

LANGUAGE

Many Indonesians are bilingual or trilingual. On Bali, locals speak Balinese (also called Basa Bali). On Lombok, Sasak is spoken. The common language is Bahasa Indonesia, which is taught in school.

VISUAL ARTS

Much of Bali's best artwork is used for everyday items and ceremonies. Each morning, women craft beautiful offerings from flowers and palm leaves. Effigies are built and burned as a symbol of life's cycle of creation, preservation, and destruction. Even temples are built from stone and grass known to wear down and disintegrate, ensuring that future generations will have reason to visit and tend to the sacred sites in the future.

On Lombok, villages are known for their art pieces that double as practical items. It's common to see women crafting technicolor fabrics on wooden looms or creating vases made from clay. Artistic techniques on Bali, Lombok, and their neighboring islands have jumped from one village to the next, adapting to suit the supplies and interests of wherever the technique lands.

Kris

Though the *kris* originated on Java, it has

Balinese Hindu Rituals and Ceremonies

- **Reincarnation:** When a child is born, he or she is taken to a local priest who will tell the family what ancestral spirit the child holds. All people are thought to be reincarnations of their ancestors. The spirit will go through a cycle of reincarnation until it is pure and united with the spiritual world.

- **A baby's first year:** An infant is considered sacred and is carried above the ground among family members for the first 105 days of life, because it is deemed too holy to touch the earth. At the *nyabutan* ceremony, a priest and family members gather to welcome the baby into the earthly realm and the child takes its name. At the end of the infant's first year (210 days), a ceremony blessing the child takes place inside the local temple.

- **Teeth filing ceremony:** One of the most important rites of passage is the Balinese teeth filing ceremony, called *metatah*. Long incisor and canine teeth are associated with demons and demon-like human traits, called *sad ripu*, that include greed, lust, wrath, envy, ego, and addiction. Once puberty begins, the adolescent is adorned in ceremonial attire and the points of his or her teeth are filed flat.

- **Marriage:** Marriage is an important milestone for Balinese as it allows men to become members of the *banjar*, their local informal government. Couples often elope or partake in a tradition where the man kidnaps the woman in jest, returning with her to her family as a married couple. Of course, ceremonies take place no matter how it is done.

- **Death and cremation:** The largest ceremony to take place is typically cremation. The entire community attends, often attracting people from nearby villages as well. They are elaborate affairs where no expense is spared. Additionally, the cremation must take place on a sacred date. Because of this, many bodies are buried and unearthed years later for cremation. Families often combine resources for joint cremations when possible. The body is placed in a tiered pyre. Sometimes, the sarcophagus is preceded by a parade carrying a sacred cow effigy. It may take dozens of men to hold the coffin. Every so often, the coffin spins in circles to confuse the spirit so that it moves to the spiritual realm and abandons its corpse. The body is burned while music plays in the background. The ashes are then scattered into the sea. Outsiders are welcome and the ceremony is often regarded as a joyous rather than somber occasion, with music and cheering.

- **Yadnya:** The concept of *yadnya* is selfless sacrifice. This includes cleaning up a public area, donating a meal to someone less fortunate, or helping an animal in need. *Yadnya* is the root of many ceremonies that revolve around paying tribute to the gods.

- **Melasti pilgrimage:** Before Nyepi, Balinese take temple belongings to the sea and cleanse them in a purification ritual.

- **Black magic:** Seemingly tranquil and beautiful places are often abandoned due to dark spirits or curses that Balinese Hindus can feel when they enter the area. Ailments, misfortune, and death are often blamed on black magic curses. When someone becomes a victim of a curse, they see a spiritual healer called a *balian* to remove it.

been a symbol of status and power throughout the Indonesian archipelago. A *kris* has a wavy blade made from metal and a hilt made of horn, wood, and metal. It is placed in a sheath that is often made from wood and embossed with gold. The rajas of Bali often decorated the hilt with gemstones, gold, and silver. Symbolically the *kris* is important as it was used to commit ritual suicide, or *puputan*, as a final act of surrender. Today, a *kris* is considered an heirloom or work of art more than a weapon. Many have been passed down for generations.

Paintings

Prior to the influx of foreign artists in the

early 1900s, paintings were typically commissioned by priests or royal families to adorn temples and palaces. Paintings almost always depicted intricate Hindu legends or portrayed stories that could be passed from one royal member to another. Classical paintings can be read almost like a page in a book, with one scene leading into the next.

When German artist Walter Spies (1895-1942) and Dutch artist Rudolph Bonnet (1895-1978) came to Bali and began painting dreamlike scenes of Balinese daily life, it sparked a renaissance among local artists. More than 100 artists formed what was called the Pita Maha, quickly becoming one of the most influential art scenes on the island. Many Balinese artists took the classical style of storytelling through painting, depicting many scenes in a single canvas and telling stories close to them rather than Hindu legends. This style of painting is known as *batuan*. During this time, one of Bali's most influential artists, I Gusti Nyoman Lempad (1862-1978), sculpted and designed many of the temples and features seen around Ubud today, such as Pura Saraswati. Lempad was also a skilled painter whose work is on display for tourists to see at his former home in Ubud.

Following World War II, an art scene known as the Young Artists sprung up when Dutch painter Arie Smit (1916-2016) handed a paintbrush and paint to the future leader of the Young Artists art scene, I Nyoman Cakra. This style is colorful and whimsical, and portrays everyday activities.

Contemporary artists still tend to stick to folk themes depicting daily life, but the influx of outside artists onto Bali has spurred artists to break away from traditional norms. Galleries featuring the work of local artists are found nearly everywhere on Bali.

Sculpture

Stone carving and wood carving are skills handed down from generation to generation. Sculptors are kept busy crafting Hindu statues for temples and meeting a newfound demand for artwork from foreign markets.

These sculptures protect temples from malevolent spirits, tell stories, and pay tribute to Hindu deities and legends. Artists in the villages of Karang and Batubalan are considered some of the island's best. Woodworkers craft everything from small souvenirs to furniture to tiered sculptures and ornate doors fixed to simple homes, all with a unique sense of style. The village of Mas is rightfully the go-to place to find incredible pieces. Wooden masks are distinctly Balinese; they are used in *topeng* dance performances to tell tales of gods and demons. Many masks are custom-made to suit an individual dancer.

Jewelry

Balinese silversmiths are experts at crafting interesting pieces by hand. Silver is mined from northern Bali and sent to silversmith towns like Celuk. Styles range from minimalistic and modern to traditional and highly detailed. Many of the island's jewelry makers now sell silver by the gram and offer classes on how to design and create a piece yourself.

Textiles

Colorful flashes of woven fabric and lace are seen throughout the islands of Bali and Lombok. Fabrics are used to adorn statues, craft ceremonial attire, and decorate homes. Many fabrics have two sides to denote formal and informal events or are flipped, depending on whether it is day or night. Many techniques have been adapted from neighboring islands, especially Java. Batik fabrics are designed using wax and dye. First, a design is placed on the fabric with wax. The fabric is then dyed, soaked in boiling water to remove the wax, then dyed again. *Ikat,* which means to tie, is named after the technique used to create the patterns on an *ikat* fabric. Threads are bound into bundles and dyed. Once the colors are in the threads, it is woven into a fabric. One signature feature of *ikat* is an illusion of blurriness to a fabric as it is very challenging to create a pattern that is sharp and crisp. For formal occasions, *songket* fabrics are made by intertwining gold or silver threads into the piece. This creates a sense of opulence, and *songket* fabrics are typically used for ceremonies and major events, especially among Sasak communities.

Weaving

Using natural materials like grasses, rattan, palm leaves, and bamboo, artisans craft mats, baskets, furniture, and decor. The skill of the craftsperson is often seen in the tightness of the weave and the shape of the item. Masters will have virtually no gaps; their designs are symmetrical with smooth edges.

Ceramics

Pottery that ranges from purely decorative to functional is crafted with care in some villages of Bali and Lombok. Lombok's villages of Banyumulek and Penujak are famous for their well-crafted pottery. Traditionally, women sculpt the piece by hand, creating a smooth surface with a paddle or stone. Men then fire the ceramic piece and children decorate it. Decorative statues are primarily sold for souvenirs, while pots and vases of various sizes are used for cooking, storing, and rituals. Rattan is often used as an overlay to decorate and protect the piece.

MUSIC
Gamelen

Stick to the main tourism drag on Bali, and you'll undoubtedly hear the same handful of soothing songs playing in every spa, hotel reception, and restaurant. However, if you venture to a live music performance, you'll hear the trance-like chimes of an ensemble called a gamelan, made up of musicians playing bamboo and bronze xylophones (*gangsa*), drums (*kendang*), gongs (*kempli*), chimes, flutes, and other percussive instruments. At major ceremonies or performances, there can be more than 50 musicians in a single troupe. Most musicians learn by ear, and pieces are passed from generation to generation. Gamelans often play at restaurants, hotels, ceremonies, and dance performances; ask around and you're sure to find one.

Gendang Beleq

Gendang beleq is a drum performance that was once used to motivate troops heading to, or returning from, battle. There has been a revival in *gendang beleq* performances, as locals introduce it into ceremonies and events. The ensemble is made up of two drums built from wood and goat hide. The drummers lead the ensemble, followed by musicians playing cymbals, a flute, and gongs.

THEATER AND DANCE

On Bali, theater and dance have long been a part of storytelling and culture. Balinese dancers must be adept at using facial expressions, as well as precise finger and wrist movements, and match the tone of the music, which can jump in pace without warning. Those who portray demons in a storytelling dance need to take utmost care when dancing and handling costumes, so as not to allow the demon to jump from the costume and into the person's spirit. In *topeng* dances, up to 30 masked dancers embody the character of their mask in a performance.

The *kecak* dance comprises men dressed in black and white checkered *kains* (sarongs), chanting to a trancelike beat. Dancers portray the legend of *Ramayana,* a love story that involves Prince Raya, Princess Sita, and a white monkey. Fittingly, one of the best places to witness the *kecak* dance is at Pura Uluwatu, a temple overrun by long-tailed macaques.

Another Hindu legend is told through the tale of good versus evil in a Barong and Rangda performance. Barong is a benevolent panther-like spirit who defends all things good in the world. Statues of him are often placed at the entrance of temples to ward off evil spirits. Rangda, a witch and leader of evil spirits, is forever Barong's arch nemesis. The dance moves to the beat of a gamelan orchestra and involves a curse where the good performers are drawn to commit suicide at the hand of their own *krises*. In the end, good triumphs and Rangda retreats.

Legong performances are some of the most popular on Bali, thanks to their golden costumes, gracefulness, and emphasis on facial expressions. Three young female dancers tell the story of a woman named Rangkesari, who is kidnapped by an evil raja. A bird appears to the raja, telling him to release Rangkesari. When the raja refuses, he is killed by Rangkesari's brother in battle. There are no tell-tale signs of the plotline without knowing the dance's background, but the *legong* is entertaining to watch nonetheless. Like the *legong*, a *baris* dance is a war story performed by a male dancer who must use small gestures and facial expressions to tell the tale.

Wayang Kulit

Wayang kulit is a shadow puppet performance that uses puppets backlit by an oil lamp to tell stories and legends. On Bali, the puppet theater has a history of being one of the many ways royal families communicated stories, philosophies, and political ideologies to their people. More recently, contemporary artists have crafted modern tales of love and war through traditional Hindu legends like the tale of *Ramayana*. On Lombok, shadow puppet performances are called *wayang sasak,* and typically relay poems written by Muslim poets.

ARCHITECTURE
Bali

From modest homes to the island's largest temples, every structure built on Bali is painstakingly planned and designed. At first, it can be a challenge to navigate the many sections of a home, compound, or temple, but there is order in it all. No matter if a building is built from bamboo, cement, or stone, Balinese are deeply connected to the structures they spend time in.

All homes and temples are built in accordance to two directions, *kaja* and *kelod*. *Kaja* refers to the direction of the island's most scared mountain, Gunung Agung. *Kelod* faces the sea. Many properties are comprised of multiple *bale*: open-air pavilions that can simply be large enough for one or two people

to lay down for a nap, or for the resident to cook a meal or host a community meeting.

Balinese Homes and Villages

Most Balinese families live on a compound made up of multiple buildings rather than one single structure. The compound typically comprises multiple pavilions for sleeping, a dedicated kitchen, a *bale* to receive and entertain guests, shrines dedicated to various guardian spirits, and most importantly, a family temple to honor Brahma, Vishnu, and Shiva. Entrances to the compound often have an *aling-aling,* a wall set back from the compound entrance to ensure privacy and keep evil spirits from entering. Modest homes that may not have multiple rooms within the property will almost always have shrines and a small temple.

Balinese Hindu Temples

There are many ranks of shrines and temples on Bali and in Balinese Hindu communities of Lombok. Small temples and shrines protect areas that are perceived to be dangerous, such as road intersections, riverbanks, and the sea. In every village, there are multiple temples dedicated to the village citizens, ancestors, and founders. These are also built in accordance with the location of Gunung Agung. Outside of these main temples, there are temples dedicated to the gods of the sea, agriculture, water, fertility, and many other Hindu figures. Temples link around Bali's coastline, guarding the land entirely. The mother temple, Pura Besakih, is thought to be holiest of all.

Temples vary in design and size, and they are not always correlated to the temple's importance. One key symbol of a temple's importance is the number of tiers it has stacked in a *meru*. *Merus* are pagoda-like towers that feature an odd number of tiers, with 11 tiers being the highest. Temples also often feature impressive *candi bentar,* temple gateways that mark each temple's entrance. Shrines, statues, courtyards, and *bale* make up the temple's interior. Many temples close off their most sacred areas to non-Hindus in order to perform ceremonies without interruption from outsiders.

Sasak Architecture

Sasak homes are traditionally built using locally sourced wood and natural materials, though stone and cement structures are becoming increasingly common. Key features include a *bale* for resting and gathering, the family pavilion that typically sleeps women and children if the men cannot fit, and a raised *lumbung* that is used to store rice and other dry goods. The *lumbung* rice barn is often used as a practical building, where people gather underneath for shade and food is kept high, away from water and pests.

Essentials

Transportation

GETTING THERE

The best airport to fly into for Bali is **Ngurah Rai International Airport** in Denpasar (DPS; Jalan Raya Gusti Ngurah Rai; tel. 361/9351011). For Lombok, fly into **Lombok International Airport,** which is also called **Zainuddin Abdul Madjid International Airport** (LOP; Jalan By Pass Bil Praya; tel. 370/6157000).

Arriving in Ngurah Rai International Airport can be an overwhelming experience for some. Taxi drivers line the arrivals area and will relentlessly tout their services. Expect to pay above market rate if booking

a taxi at the airport. If you are walking to meet a driver arranged in advance, firmly decline and ignore those who approach you. ATMs, money changing services, and overpriced SIM cards are available in arrivals. To have someone assist with luggage, pay 10,000 Rp per bag. The airport has free Wi-Fi.

Lombok International Airport is a small airport with very few amenities. Taxi drivers tend to be less aggressive than in Bali, though a bit of hassle is not unheard of. Wi-Fi, ATMs, and money-changing services are available at the airport.

From North America

There are no direct flights from North America to Bali or Lombok. If you're coming from the West Coast, most flights will stop over in Asia, with the most common layover points being Taiwan, China, Hong Kong, or the Philippines. Airlines like EVA Air, Philippine Airlines, China Airlines, Cathay Pacific, and Singapore Airlines tend to offer the best fares. Total flight time ranges between 20-30 hours, including a layover. Expect to pay around $600-$900 USD return in the low season, $800-$1200 USD return in the high season.

From Europe

There are direct flights from Istanbul, Turkey (13.5 hours) and Moscow, Russia (13.5 hours), to Bali. Otherwise, all other routes from Europe will require a layover. One of the best ways to get to Bali and Lombok is via Singapore, flying on Singapore Airlines and Scoot, which has direct flights from Singapore to England, France, Spain, Germany, Italy, Switzerland, Sweden, Denmark, and the Netherlands (10-13 hours). From Singapore, Bali is a 2.5-hour flight and Lombok is a 3-hour flight. Flying to Bali via Doha on Qatar Airlines (18 hours) is also worth considering.

From Australia and New Zealand

Getting to Bali and Lombok from Australia and New Zealand is economical and easy, as there are many airlines servicing major cities. If you're coming from Australia to Bali, there are direct flights from Perth (3.5-4 hours), Adelaide (5 hours), Melbourne (6 hours), Sydney (6 hours), Brisbane (6 hours), Cairns (4.5 hours), and Darwin (2.5 hours). From New Zealand, there are direct flights from Auckland to Bali (8 hours). The most common airlines offering these routes are Jetstar, AirAsia, Garuda Indonesia, Scoot, Qantas, and Virgin Australia.

From South Africa

There are no direct flights from Bali and Lombok to South Africa. Finding flights with a single stopover can be a challenge, as most cheap fares will have you hopping on three flights to reach Bali, and another one to get to Lombok. Emirates offers flights from Cape Town to Ngurah Rai International Airport, changing planes in Dubai (25 hours). Cathay Pacific serves flights with a layover in Hong Kong (23 hours); Qatar Airways will change planes in Doha (23 hours). Flying from Johannesburg cuts down your travel time dramatically, as you can fly via Singapore with Singapore Airlines (14 hours).

GETTING AROUND

The best method of transportation depends on the season and the region where you are traveling. Some areas of Bali and Lombok have very limited options where it may be challenging to find a metered taxi driver or bus. Other areas are well-connected by all forms of transportation. No matter where you are, you can expect to share the road with chickens, cows, stray dogs, children, patches of gravel, potholes, ceremonial precessions, and more. Overall, Bali and Lombok are best

---

Previous: flower petals at the Jimbaran Market

covered with a private driver, or your own rental car or motorbike.

By Air

Bali and Lombok's international airports are connected by direct flights (30 minutes) from Garuda Indonesia, AirAsia, NAM Air, Lion Air, and Sriwijaya Air. This is the quickest and usually the most economical way to travel between Bali and Lombok.

By Ferry and Fast Boat

Ferries and fast boats connect Bali (Sanur, Serangan, Padangbai, Nusa Lembongan, Nusa Penida) to Lombok (Lembar, Gili Gede, Bangsal, Gili Trawangan, Gili Meno, Gili Air, and other smaller ports). The most popular routes run from Padangbai (Bali) to the Bangsal and the Gili Islands (Lombok; 58 km/37 mi); Sanur (Bali) and Nusa Lembongan (Bali; 18 km/11 mi); Sanur (Bali) and Lembar Harbor (Lombok; 87 km/55 mi). Fast boat companies offering multiple route options include Scoot (scootcruise.com; tel. 361/271030), Bluewater Express (https://bluewater-express.com; tel. 361/8951111), and Gili Getaway (https://giligetaway.com; tel. 8113801717).

Indonesia does not hold a strong safety record when it comes to boat safety. Boats have caught fire and sunk while traversing the channel between Lombok and Bali. When deciding to choose a boat company, opt for one with reputable and recent online reviews. When you board the boat, check for life jackets and you can request to be seated next to them. Be flexible when it comes to travel dates, so that you don't feel pressured to hop onboard the only boat leaving to the next island when all other boats are grounded thanks to tumultuous ocean conditions—and check conditions on a website like Magic Seaweed (magicseaweed.com) before booking. In general, the larger the boat, the sturdier it is.

By Bus

There are a variety of buses and minibuses called *bemos* that serve Bali and Lombok. The Bukit Peninsula is well-connected with affordable tourist buses that go around the peninsula and to Ubud. Outside of these areas, buses and *bemos* are unreliable and may only leave when full. Rates typically will not be posted, and drivers may try to charge tourists higher rates than they charge locals. As a rule of thumb, expect to pay 10,000 Rp per 10 minutes of driving, and never more than 50,000 Rp per ride, no matter how long the ride is. Some buses, usually a large van, cater to tourists; you can find price information and departure times for these walking along the main roads of most major tourist areas.

Private shuttle buses catering to tourists also offer rides around Bali and Lombok. This can be one of the most economical and direct ways to travel. **Perama** (tel. 361/750808; www.peramatour.com) offers the most reliable service and the most common routes, with tickets ranging from 30,000 to 200,000 Rp, depending on how far you're going. **Kura Kura** (tel. 361/757070; www.kura2bus.com) connects locations in Bali's southern end—like Kuta, Seminyak, Jimbaran, Sanur, Denpasar, and Uluwatu—with Ubud; they're easily recognizable for their lime-green buses. Single-ride tickets (20,000-80,000 Rp) and day passes are available (100,000 Rp 1 day, 150,000 Rp 3 days, 250,000 Rp 7 days).

By Car and Motorbike

Having your own set of wheels to explore Bali and Lombok can give you a sense of freedom not found anywhere else. That is, until you find yourself stuck in the middle of traffic or behind a truck stacked sky-high with logs in its bed. Traffic is heavy in the Denpasar region and around Ubud in Bali. In Mataram, Lombok, roads can also get hectic.

It is not advised to drive a motorbike if you are unfamiliar with driving one and/or if you do not already know the road conditions.

INTERNATIONAL DRIVER'S LICENSES

To rent a car, tourists must have an international driver's license. However, this is rarely checked or enforced. It is relevant, however, for many travel insurance companies, who will not cover you should you get in an accident while driving with an incorrect license. The same goes for driving a motorbike. Technically, all visitors should have an international motorcycle license, but few tourists do. The fine for driving without a valid license is around 2,000,000 Rp, though a cop will happily take a 50,000-100,000 Rp bribe in lieu of enforcing this fee.

To get an Indonesian driver's license, visit **Polresta Station** in Denpasar (Jalan Gunung Sanghyang No. 110; tel. 361/8448902; www.polrestadenpasar.org) with your passport, a passport picture, your home driver's license, a copy of your passport, and 300,000 Rp. You will be instructed to take a driver's test in English. If you pass, you'll receive a permit.

CAR AND MOTORBIKE RENTAL

Cars are usually rented for 200,000-300,000 per day. Motorbikes can be rented for 50,000-70,000 Rp per day, including a helmet. The best place to rent a car is at the **Ngurah Rai International Airport** through **Avis** (www.avis.com), **Eazy** (www.eazyrent. co.id), or **TRAC Astra** (www.trac.astra. co.id). For convenience purposes, opt for the meet-and-greet service at the airport, where you are led directly to your car. On Lombok, it is best to hire a car at the Lombok International Airport through Surya Rent Car (tel. 81917048330; www.carrentallombok.com; info@carrentallombok.com).

Take pictures of the motorbike or car that you hire, especially any dents or scratches to avoid being blamed (and charged) for any damage that you did not cause. It is best to hire your motorbike directly through your accommodation or an associated rental agency of your accommodation. This offers peace of mind for the owner and the driver, as the accommodation will almost always have a safe place to park the motorbike and is less likely to rip you off.

Petrol is sold for around 8,000 Rp per liter if purchased at a petrol station. Petrol stations are typically only found along major roads and in major towns. However, if you drive along any road—even in rural areas—you'll likely find petrol sold for 10,000 Rp per liter out of vodka bottles. Fill up the gas tank regularly, as motorbike petrol gauges are often broken, and it may be a while before you reach the next petrol stop.

NAVIGATION

While many roads in the main cities and tourist areas are paved and well-marked, those leading inland or to more rural destinations often lack clear signs and are pocked with potholes. Roads do not always have one consistent name, but rather change names as they move through a main area. To help clarify this, some roads are named after their start and end point. For example, Jalan Singaraja-Gilimanuk connects the towns of Singaraja and Gilimanuk. However, this road also passes through the town of Lovina and will take on the name of Jalan Raya Lovina. The word "raya" in a road name denotes that it is a main road.

Many locals will tell directions in terms of north, south, east, and west rather than instruct you to go left, right, or straight. Locals might also have routes memorized by landmarks rather than road names. Instead of having a local write or tell directions, it's best to look at a **map** together and mark major turn points. You can download offline maps of Bali and Lombok through **Maps.Me** or **Google Maps.**

By Private Driver

Going around Bali and Lombok with the help of a private driver is the best way to see the islands. A driver often knows the best routes, local hangouts, and itineraries, and can help with any translation issues you may have. Private drivers in tourist areas often advertise themselves by holding up signs or saying, "Yes? Transport?" at a mind-numbingly regular rate. It's a good idea to get recommendations from other travelers before committing to a driver. Drivers tend to cost

Driving and Safety Tips

Here are some rules of thumb to observe while you're on the road in Bali.

- **Drive on the left.** In Bali, cars drive on the same side of the road as in the U.K. (on the left), which is the opposite of how traffic flows in the U.S.

- **Be generous with horn honks.** It's the primary way of letting others know you're there.

- **Drive predictably.** Traffic can be chaotic in Indonesia's city centers. Go with the flow and know that you are responsible for keeping a fair distance from those in front of you—including those who have haphazardly swerved into your lane or have pulled blindly out of a driveway.

- **Do not drive during dawn and dusk.** Roads are not well lit, and there are likely to be people and animals crossing the roads at all hours.

- **Keep a decoy wallet with small notes on you when you're driving.** If you are pulled over by police, they'll likely be looking for a bribe after telling you your mistake and flipping through your registration papers. Many will claim that you owe an on-the-spot fine (for which no receipt will be issued). Open your wallet to show you only have a 50,000 Rp note or two.

- On a motorbike, always wear a **helmet.** Keep your purse or flashy belongings inside of the bike or somewhere inconspicuous to avoid **bag snatchings.** Stay clear of the motorbike's **exhaust pipe** to avoid getting burned.

600,000-800,000 Rp for up to 8 hours, including petrol. After 8 hours, most charge 50,000 per hour. You can typically book a driver through your accommodation.

By Taxi and *Ojek*

Taxis are regularly available in Kuta, Seminyak, Sanur, and Denpasar on Bali. On Lombok, you'll find them in Mataram and Senggigi.

Bluebird is the most reputable taxi company with metered taxis—to a point where there's an entire industry of Bluebird imposters. You can hail Bluebird taxis with the MyBluebird app (tel. 361/701111; www.bluebirdgroup.com). It's also possible to get rides via **Grab** (www.grab.com) and **GoJek** (www.gojek.com), where your fare is predetermined through an app. Tension is high between traditional taxi drivers and Grab/GoJek drivers, and there have been violent clashes between the groups. Many *banjar,*

or neighborhoods, have banned the use of Grab and GoJek. If you do use Grab or GoJek, do not make it obvious to others. Keep your phone hidden and tell anyone enquiring—usually nosy taxi drivers—that you're waiting for a private driver whom you met earlier.

Some locals double as *ojeks,* or motorbike taxis, and will offer their seat on the back of a motorbike. *Ojeks* are especially popular in the less touristy areas of Lombok. Rides are about 15,000-30,000 Rp per 10-minute trip.

By Cidomo

Cidomos are carts pulled by a pony, often seen on Lombok. They are the only major form of transportation (aside from bicycles) on the Gili Islands. Unfortunately, neglect is common among owners of these ponies, and there is no regulation on their working conditions. We do not recommend them as a form of transport.

Visas and Officialdom

PASSPORT REQUIREMENTS

Your passport must be valid for six months from the date you intend to leave Indonesia. Your passport also must have two blank passport pages. You must also have **proof of onward travel** before you will be allowed to board the aircraft, though this is inconsistently enforced. Some airlines will not allow you to board the flight without proof of onward travel. If you are unsure of your departure details, it's best to arrive early at the airport and prepare to book a flexible or refundable flight out of Indonesia.

Note that your visa date includes the date of your arrival and the date of your departure. For example, if you receive a 30-day visa on October 20, it is valid until November 18. Many tourists make the mistake of overstaying their visa by one or two days. The penalty of overstaying is 1,000,000 Rp per day.

VISAS

A free 30-day visa-on-arrival is available for **Australian, Canadian, U.S., South African, European,** and **U.K.** travelers. For visits over 30 days, you can purchase a **30-day extension** for 491,000 Rp. This extension must be purchased at the time of your arrival. If you get the first free 30 days without purchasing the 30-day extension, you will not be able to extend your stay beyond the initial first 30 days. For other visa information, visit www.imigrasi.go.id.

Other visas are available for those who want to stay long-term or wish to enter multiple times throughout the year. To see relevant options, go to www.imigrasi.go.id. Click on the "Public Services" dropdown menu to select visas available under the "Foreign Citizen" section. These following visas will need an application letter, guarantee letter, copy of passport with 6 months' validity for the Visit Visa and 18 months' validity for the Multiple Visit Visa, a copy of your bank account records, and proof of onward travel.

Visit Visa: Visitors can enter Indonesia for up to 60 days and apply for up to five 30-day extensions.

Multiple Visit Visa: Visitors can enter Indonesia multiple times for one year; each visit is valid for 60 days and cannot be extended.

EMBASSIES AND CONSULATES

Most embassies and consulates are found in **Jakarta** though some embassies have consulates in **Denpasar, Bali.** For Indonesian embassies and consulates outside of Indonesia, locations can be found on the **Indonesia Ministry of Foreign Affairs website** (https://kemlu.go.id). Australia, the United Kingdom, and the United States of America have consulates in Denpasar.

Clearing Customs with Ease

Clearing customs in Bali and Lombok is relatively easy so long as you follow a few key rules.

- **Fill out your Passenger Arrival Card before entering the customs counter.** Declare all items that the card prompts you to.

- **Stick to duty limits:** 1 liter of alcohol; 200 cigarettes or 50 cigars or 100 grams of tobacco; a reasonable amount of perfume per adult (a vague description, but if you are bringing more than a few bottles, take them out of their packaging to avoid looking as though you plan to sell them).

- **Don't transport items that are prohibited:** Firearms, illegal drugs, pornography, and politically sensitive materials are prohibited from entering Indonesia. If you are bringing medication, ensure that you have your prescription or a statement from your doctor in English or Indonesian. Videotapes/CDs/DVDs may be taken out and played for examination.

- **Indonesia has very strict antidrug-trafficking laws.** If you are coming from a destination where marijuana is legal, comb through your belongings to make sure that there are no remnants. Label all medications clearly with brand and generic names.

Recreation

With beaches, mountains, rivers, and coral reefs, Bali and Lombok are playgrounds for those who love to spend time outside.

BEACHES AND WATER SPORTS
Surfing

It's easy to see how Bali developed as a surfer's paradise, with world-class waves breaking along its southern shoreline. Near-perfect waves like Padang Padang, Uluwatu, and Keramas attract expert surfers as soon as a swell rolls in. Beginner and intermediate surfers won't be left dry, either. Balian, Medewi, Kuta, Seminyak, Sanur, Nusa Lembongan, and the Bukit Peninsula all host a variety of surf spots. Lombok is home to incredible waves for all experience levels, with Desert Point reigning as the island's crown jewel. It might just be one of the best left-hand barrels in the world. If that's too heavy, check out the waves around Gerupuk, Ekas, Mawi, Mawun, Kuta, and Selong Belanak.

Stand-Up Paddleboarding

Stand-up paddle over tranquil bays, catch waves, and circumnavigate tiny islands with a board under your feet. Perfect your balance by participating in a stand-up paddleboard yoga class on the Gili Islands, or rent one and get creative. Nusa Lembongan, Sanur, and Kuta, Lombok all have rental shops with stand-up paddleboards.

Windsurfing and Kitesurfing

With consistent onshore tradewinds blowing along Bali and Lombok's coastline, you can harness the power of the wind to take advantage of flat water and surf spots long after the surfers have paddled back to shore. You'll spot kites in the air at Sanur and Bali, and along Lombok's southern coastline near Ekas and Kuta.

Scuba Diving, Freediving, and Snorkeling

With diverse marine life and vibrant coral reefs, the warm waters around Bali and Lombok are sure to fascinate visitors. Reef sharks, manta rays, *mola-mola*, sea turtles, and hammerhead sharks attract those in search of Indonesia's larger creatures.

Meanwhile, nudibranchs, pygmy seahorses, crabs, reef fish, and eels reward those who take the time to slow down and look closely. Whether you dive with a tank or without one, there's sure to be a dive site you'll want to visit again and again. Explore the shipwreck of Tulamben, train with some of the world's best freedivers in Amed, glide along with manta rays around Nusa Penida and Nusa Lembongan, and snorkel among the sea turtles of the Gili Islands. For offbeat spots, check out Lombok's southwestern Gilis. Experienced divers can search for hammerhead sharks in Belongas Bay.

YOGA AND WELLNESS

Bali and Lombok have a siren song for health-conscious travelers looking to relax in tropical paradise. Travelers can sip fresh coconuts and alkaline water on the beach, get pampered at one of the many spas, take vegan cooking classes, stretch out at a yoga retreat, join guided meditations, and be blessed by a traditional healer. Ubud is the hub for all things healthy in Bali, but you'll find spas and yoga classes almost everywhere else. Getting a soothing Balinese massage should be a regular occurrence while on the island. After all, Bali has one of the highest spa-per-capita ratios in the world.

HIKING

Have you ever wanted to watch the sunrise from the top of a volcano? Wander through rice terraces that seem to extend forever? Or, feel sweat run down your back as you trek to a cool waterfall with a pool perfect for swimming? Bali's Central Mountains offer unlimited hiking opportunities. You can trek to the top of Gunung Batur and Gunung Batukaru. On Lombok, sleep on the rim of the caldera at Gunung Rinjani. Bali and Lombok are islands where you can go for a gentle birdwatching stroll one day and climb hand over foot up the slope of a volcano the next.

CYCLING

Experience Bali and Lombok from the view of a bicycle saddle as you peddle from one village to the next, weaving in between rice paddies as you go. One of the best routes to take is a scenic one that links Sanur to Ubud. Or, explore the villages around Danau Batur on a two-wheel cultural tour. Whether you want to cycle as part of a tour or embark on your own adventure, you'll become part of the scenery rather than just zip by it in a motorized blur.

Festivals and Events

BALI

There's a sentiment among Balinese people that whenever they are not participating in a ceremony, they are saving money and planning one. Local ceremonies, festivals, and events are a regular part of Balinese life, taking place regularly throughout the year. No matter when you visit, you're sure to see a precession of locals dressed in their finest clothes carrying piles of immaculately crafted offerings and food. Because Bali has two traditional calendars, the *saka* calendar that spans 354-356 days and the *pawukon* calendar, which runs 210 days and is based on the lunar cycle, holiday dates can change drastically from year to year. To see something outside of the norm, these are Bali's most important holidays and festivals:

GALUNGAN AND KUNINGAN

Galungan and Kuningan is Bali's largest holiday of the year, commemorating the triumph of good over evil. On Galungan, at the beginning of the holiday, ancestral spirits come to visit and are greeted with offerings, food, and decorations. Curved bamboo poles with elaborate trimmings, called *penjor,* line the sides of roads and adorn the fronts of homes.

On Kuningan, the last day of the celebration, ancestors return to the spirit world. The holiday takes place at the end of every *pawukon* year. You can check holiday dates online at https://balithisweek.com under the "Bali Info" section.

January-March
NYEPI

Nyepi is Bali's Day of Silence, which precedes the Hindu New Year, typically at the end of March or early April. Ceremonies with *ogohogohs*, an effigy of a demon, take place before Nyepi and all can enjoy and attend. On the day of Nyepi, everyone quietly stays inside in hopes of convincing the demons that Bali has been deserted. After a day of no entertainment, activity, or travel, ceremonies begin again.

BALI SPIRIT FESTIVAL

www.balispiritfestival.com

Cultures collide in this festival, celebrating music, yoga, and dance. There are well-being workshops, yoga classes, vegan culinary courses, and more set between the rice terraces of Ubud for a week in March or April.

April-June
BALI ARTS FESTIVAL

https://disbud.baliprov.go.id/pesta-kesenian-bali

This cultural art festival runs from mid-June to mid-July at Denpasar's Taman Werdhi Budaya Arts Centre in Denpasar. It's a colorful month of traditional performances with gamelan music, plays, dances, fragrant food, and artwork.

July-September
BALI KITES FESTIVAL

Every year at the beginning of the windy season, usually in July, thousands of kites ranging from traditional to modern shapes are launched into the sky above Sanur Beach.

SANUR VILLAGE FESTIVAL

www.sanurvillagefestival.com

This multiday event in August typically celebrates a theme like rice or bamboo. You can watch dance performances, fly kites, take part in parades, and listen to live music at Sanur Beach.

INDONESIAN INDEPENDENCE DAY

On August 17, Indonesians adorn themselves, and just about everything else, with red and white flags to celebrate Indonesian Independence, which was declared in 1945.

MAKEPUNG BUFFALO RACES

Dozens of buffaloes and jockeys race at circuits in West Bali from August to November while pulling wooden ploughs. The most impressive buffaloes are paraded through the streets for all to admire.

October-December
UBUD READERS AND WRITERS FESTIVAL

www.ubudwritersfestival.com

Creative minds gather in Ubud, the cultural center of Bali, for a few days of collaboration, workshops, and readings for a week in October or November. Stay for a few days afterward to enjoy Ubud's Food Festival, a sister festival featuring Bali's best cuisine.

LOMBOK

While Hindus on Lombok celebrate similar holidays as the Hindus on Bali, Sasak locals on Lombok also host their own folk, religious, and cultural events. Whenever one takes place, many flock to their local beach and set up a makeshift shelter on the sand to celebrate the holiday by swimming, trading goods, and enjoying time together. Here are a few of the major festivals and events:

GENDANG BELEQ

Sasak musicians perform using large drums and percussive instruments, often donning simple costumes made from vibrant fabrics. Performances take place throughout the year, often at major events and local ceremonies. For your best shot at experiencing this for yourself, ask hotel and restaurant staff.

January-March
BAU NYALE FESTIVAL

Every year, technicolor *nyale* sea worms wash ashore on Lombok's southern beaches. The worms are thought to be the reincarnation of Princess Mandalika, a Sasak princess who disappeared into the sea. The worms bring vitality, fertility, and beauty to those who eat them. It falls during the 10th month of the Sasak calendar, typically in February or March.

April-June
IDUL FITRI WEEK AND TAKBIR PARADE

This weeklong celebration and parade in Mataram marks the end of Ramadan (May).

July-September
SENGGIGI FESTIVAL

This week of art exhibitions, cultural performances, textile weaving workshops, and food takes place for three days in September along the main road of Jalan Raya Senggigi. Those who visit will also witness stick fighting, called *peresean,* which is a form of martial arts that uses sticks to take down an opponent.

October-December
MULANG PEKELEM

At the end of the dry season, typically in October, Balinese Hindus in Lombok make a pilgrimage to Segara Anak, the lake inside Rinjani's crater, and make offerings to the gods in a plea for rain and fertility.

PERANG TOPAT

Balinese Hindus and Muslims come together to celebrate unity at Pura Lingsar, a temple where all are welcome to worship. Participants throw sticky rice at one another in a lighthearted food fight during November or December.

Food and Drink

Indonesia is one of the most diverse countries in the world, with more than 300 ethnic groups spread over thousands of islands. Many of the most fragrant and delicious dishes have hopped across the islands and the best are served in Bali and Lombok. In many places, you'll find that no two restaurants cook the same meal alike.

Most meals are made with a base of rice, one of the most sacred food items on the islands, as well as meat and vegetables. Occasionally, dishes will be made with noodles. Nearly all noodle and rice dishes taste great with a heaping spoonful of *sambal,* a spicy condiment made from freshly chopped chilis.

Chefs on Bali and Lombok strive to serve dishes that contain the six flavors thought to promote vitality (spicy, sweet, salty, bitter, umami, and tart). This is done by being heavy-handed on spices and ingredients like ginger, coconut, sugar, chili, tamarind, and fish sauce.

EATING IN

Most locals cook only in the morning, and the food will be served at lunch and dinner. Meals are crafted from in-season produce and fresh meat, and are almost always served with rice. Ingredients are sourced from the morning market, where shoppers are bound to find the best items just after sunrise, when most markets open.

Instead of enjoying a full meal for breakfast, Balinese people snack on sweet treats like glutinous rice cakes, rice balls with a sweet center wrapped in banana leaves, and boiled bananas rolled in shredded coconut and drizzled in syrup. Coffee is a must. On Lombok, breakfast is usually a simple affair—if it is eaten at all. It typically consists of leftovers from the day before. Snacks are reserved for ceremonies, guests, or special occasions.

On Bali and Lombok, families or the neighborhood warung cooks once per day, and the same meal is served for both lunch and

The Role of Rice

Rice is arguably the most important crop grown on Bali and Lombok. Rice is a staple for all major meals, a lucrative export, with a part of local religious ceremonies. On Bali, local rice farmers form communities and honor the *subak* system of growing rice, where water irrigating rice must be holy and pass through a temple. Harvests must occur solely on auspicious days, determined by local religious authorities. **Dewi Sri**, the goddess of rice in Balinese Hinduism, symbolizes fertility and life. On Lombok, **Inang Sariti** is a significant figure in Sasak tradition as the goddess of rice.

Because the islands have a history of experiencing droughts and famines, many farmers store dried rice in a granary, called a *lumbung*. These *lumbungs* are placed on stilts to protect the harvest from pests and mold. The granaries are social meeting areas and are used as markers for a farmer's social status. There are nuances when it comes to who can ration the rice, how much should be stored for future use, and how much rice can be doled out for ceremonial events.

dinner. Locals tend to have their largest meal of the day at lunch, when the food is hot and fresh. Meals are eaten with the right hand, whenever the person is hungry rather than at a set time. Washing your hands before and after you eat is considered polite, no matter if you're using utensils or not. However, eating habits are changing in areas where locals and tourists often dine together.

If you plan to cook your own meals, do as the locals do and venture to the market early in the morning for fresh produce, meat, and rice. However, you'll likely find that it's economical and tastier to dine from a roadside stand or warung—look for places where the locals are eating.

EATING OUT

No matter where you go on Bali and Lombok, you'll find **warungs,** small restaurants serving plates of local fare for no more than 30,000 Rp per meal. Most of the time, you'll be given *nasi campur* (rice served with a variety of dishes). *Nasi campur* is also often served from carts with glass windows displaying the different foods inside. In the morning, rice treats served with sweet coconut and pineapple syrup act as a quick snack for locals on the way to work. At larger warungs, the cuisine tends to be pan-Indonesian with plates of *gado-gado* (vegetables with peanut dressing), *mie goreng* (fried noodles), and *nasi goreng*

(fried rice). In rural areas, do not expect servers and chefs to speak English. It's a good idea to have a few dishes in mind before ordering just in case you cannot understand the menu.

Try to eat at warungs or food carts that are popular with locals. If the dish is premade, assume it was cooked in the morning and has been left at room temperature throughout the day.

International restaurants that range from casual stops to fine dining experiences have already taken hold of destinations like Kuta, Seminyak, Sanur, and Ubud on Bali, as well as Senggigi, Kuta, and the Gili Islands on Lombok. The foodie scene on the islands has placed immense pressure on restaurants in these areas to serve food that's innovative and on-trend. These restaurants will likely have menus in both Indonesian and in English.

Some of the mid-range to higher-end restaurants will add a 10 percent tax and 5 percent service charge to the final bill. **Tipping** is not expected but always appreciated.

SPECIALTIES

It can be a challenge to distinguish dishes that are solely Balinese or Sasak from dishes that have hopped throughout the Indonesian archipelago. Many meals started on one Indonesian island and have been slightly adapted to suit the taste buds of their neighboring island. No matter, it's all tasty.

Pan-Indonesia
MIE GORENG/NASI GORENG
This dish consists of fried noodles (*mie*) or rice (*nasi*) served with meat and vegetables. It tends to be tangy, sweet, and salty thanks to a concoction of sweet soy sauce, chili, and shrimp paste.

RIJSTTAFEL
The name itself, which means "rice table," is a remnant of Dutch occupation in Indonesia. This plate is made from rice and an array of side dishes that are traditionally West Sumatran.

GADO-GADO
At almost every warung, you'll find this sweet and salty salad of boiled vegetables served with peanut sauce.

NASI CAMPUR
This is the go-to dish for locals, made from a scoop of rice with four or five smaller foods on the side. The dishes can be smoked meat, cooked vegetables, shrimp crackers, tempeh, tofu, or egg. The dish varies from warung to warung.

Bali
BABI GULING
Anthony Bourdain helped make this Bali's most famous dish internationally. *Babi guling* is a pig stuffed with a concoction of spices, and spit-roasted over smoldering coconut husks.

BEBEK BETUTU
Ducks are usually raised on Bali's rice paddies, tending to the fields as pest control. As such, many of Bali's best dishes are made from duck marinated in a sauce of chili, garlic, and coconut oil, then steamed in palm tree bark. *Ayam betutu* is made with chicken in lieu of poultry.

Lombok
PELECING KANGKONG
Lombok's most popular vegetable dish is made from blanched spinach and served cold with a heaping spoonful of *sambal*. It's often accompanied by a side of string beans and grated coconut.

ARES
If you attend a Lombok cultural event or ceremony, you'll likely see *ares* as a side dish. Ares is made with meat (typically beef or chicken) and young bananas, and cooked with coconut milk, spices, and chilis.

AYAM TALIWANG
This dish consists of chicken that is half-grilled and then tenderized and spiced with garlic, shrimp paste, and chili before being fried or grilled. The chicken is served with a generous portion of *sambal*.

Accommodations

Guesthouse/Homestay
The most popular forms of budget accommodation are usually marketed as guesthouses, homestays, or *losmen*. These are usually simple rooms with a double bed and private bathroom. These tend to be family-owned, with the family living on-site. Most guesthouses will be hotel-style rooms where you simply enter from outside and into your room, rather than going in the main entrance of someone's home. Shared kitchens are not common. Most stays include a simple breakfast of pancakes, eggs, toast, and/or fruit. Without air-conditioning, Wi-Fi, and hot water, rooms typically range from 150,000 to 300,000 Rp. With air-conditioning, Wi-Fi, and hot water, expect to pay 300,000-600,000 Rp, depending on the area. Sometimes guesthouses are built from concrete blocks, while others offer bungalow-style stand-alone rooms built from bamboo.

Hostel

Hostels are becoming increasingly more common in areas like the Kuta, Seminyak, Sanur, Amed, and Bali's Bukit Peninsula. On Lombok, you can find them on the Gili Islands, Senggigi, and Kuta. While these are ideal for budget travelers looking to make friends, guesthouses often offer better value for what you get. A single bed in a hostel starts at around 60,000 Rp per person per night.

Retreat

If you've come to surf, dive, or practice yoga, you can check into a retreat-style lodging where your activities, transportation, meals, and accommodation are all included. Prices depend on your length of stay, the activities you do, and where the retreat is located. You'll find yoga and wellness retreats in Ubud, surf camps in Kuta and Lombok as well as Bali's Bukit Peninsula, and dive packages on the Gili Islands.

Hotel

Hotels range from quirky boutique stays to soulless monoliths all throughout Bali and Lombok. Fortunately, it's easy to find a room that's clean, charming, and good value no matter where you go. Many hotels cater to wellness seekers, luxury travelers, surfers, families, honeymooners, and backpackers wanting nothing more than a simple place to spend the night. Prices start at 300,000-400,000 Rp and can climb into the millions.

Villa

Bali and Lombok have exceptional villas, where groups and families can enjoy the freedom of having a private pool, kitchen, and a cleaning service. For an extra fee and advance notice, villas can also offer a cooking service where a chef pepares meals in-house.

Conduct and Customs

On both Bali and Lombok, locals are very forgiving when it comes to tourists making unintentional cultural faux pas. Here are a few cultural behaviors to keep in mind as you travel.

In Indonesia, aggressive confrontation is considered embarrassing for all involved. This relates to a concept called *malu*, or avoiding any behaviors or interactions that appear shameful. Whenever possible, it's best to try to resolve conflict in a calm and direct way rather than displaying anger or frustration.

You might find that Balinese and Sasak locals ask a series of questions like "Are you married?" "How old are you?" and "How many children do you have?" This can also lead to, "Why aren't you married?" and "Why don't you have children?" These questions are not seen as invasive but are rather the local way of participating in small talk. It's okay to ask the same questions back to those who you meet.

Dress

Dress modestly whenever you are not inside a resort or on a beach that is popular with tourists. Never go shirtless or walk around in swimming attire while visiting any village. Throwing a T-shirt and sarong or shorts over your swimwear will go a long way when it comes to showing respect. This goes for both men and women.

Remove your shoes when entering a home or place of worship. On Lombok, you might see women wearing long sleeves, skirts, and head scarves. Many women swim in full attire. In remote beach areas, female travelers might feel more comfortable swimming, surfing, and scuba diving in a rashguard and leggings.

Gesture and Behavior

Don't point or wave people over. If you need to beckon someone, wave your hand in a downward motion with the palm facing the ground.

Point with your whole hand rather than your index finger. Similarly, do not point your feet or show the bottom of your feet to others.

When passing or taking an item to someone, use your right hand. The left hand is considered dirty as it is used for personal hygiene. It's polite to receive and take with both hands.

Do not touch anyone on the head, as the head is considered sacred.

Religious Etiquette
There are many beautiful temples throughout Bali. When entering the temple grounds, cover your shoulders and wrap a sarong around your legs. Many temples will not let you participate in a ceremony if you are not dressed in full temple attire. People are asked not to enter a temple if they are menstruating or have any open wounds. Speak quietly and stick to the outer edge of ceremonies. Many temples popular with tourists will rent out clothing if you forget to bring your own. Walk behind, not in front, of anyone praying. Crouch while walking to ensure that your head never stands higher than a priest's or higher than a temple.

When walking anywhere in Bali or through Balinese communities on Lombok, be careful to avoid stepping on or knocking over *canang sari,* small offerings that are placed on the ground and around the property.

The call to prayer is broadcast from the local mosques on Lombok multiple times per day—sometimes during early morning or late at night. It is rude to complain publicly about or talk over the call to prayer. If you don't want to be disturbed, choose hotels that are far away from the local mosque and pack ear plugs.

During Ramadan, do not walk around while eating in public. Instead, eat meals inside your hotel or at indoor restaurants.

Health and Safety

COMMUNICABLE DISEASES
Rabies exists on Bali, spread through the saliva of infected animals like dogs and monkeys. Do not taunt animals or encourage monkeys to climb onto you, as many tourists do in places like Ubud and Uluwatu. Monkey bites are one of the most common injuries tourists get while traveling through the region.

Mosquitoes carry diseases like dengue fever, Japanese encephalitis, malaria, and Zika virus in certain regions of Bali and Lombok. Pack a few pairs of lightweight, mosquito-proof clothes and mosquito repellent. Take extra precautions at sunset, when mosquitos are most active. Avoid scratching mosquito bites to prevent them from becoming infected.

FOOD AND WATER
Tourists often suffer from travelers' diarrhea (dubbed "Bali belly") in Indonesia, especially within the first few days of arrival. This can be caused by bacteria or a change in diet. Most cases last between one to three days. There are medical clinics throughout Bali and Lombok. Over-the-counter medications such as Imodium and Loperamide may help, and they are available at most pharmacies. Activated charcoal can be purchased at mini-marts, petrol stations, or supermarkets. To help avoid getting Bali belly, drink only bottled or filtered water and avoid eating unwashed produce.

Arak is the Indonesian equivalent to moonshine made from palm sap, coconut, or sugarcane. It is very dangerous to drink homemade or unregulated arak because it is often contaminated with methanol. Methanol is colorless, odorless, and tasteless in alcoholic drinks. It can cause blindness, paralysis, and death. Arak is most likely to be present in areas with lively nightlife like Kuta, Seminyak, and Gili Trawangan. Free drinks and cheap cocktails are sometimes made with arak. When in doubt, order beer, wine, or hard liquor bottles purchased from duty free shops at the airport.

BEACH, OCEAN, AND WATER SPORT SAFETY

The seas surrounding Bali and Lombok range from flat, calm water over sandy beaches to strong currents that rip over reefs. If you're unfamiliar with ocean conditions, only swim at tourist beaches with a lifeguard present. Ask your hotel for safe swimming area suggestions and swim with a buddy. Surf tourists should watch a few sets and know where the safest entry and exit points are before paddling out. If you cut yourself on the reef, be vigilant at disinfecting and covering the wound to avoid infection.

For **scuba diving-related illnesses**, contact Divers Alert Network (tel. 919/6849111; www.diversalertnetwork.org for emergency hotline) to be directed to the nearest functioning hyperbaric chamber. Sanglah Hospital Denpasar (Jalan Diponegoro; tel. 361/227911; www.sanglahhospitalbali.com) hosts the hyperbaric chamber on Bali. On Lombok, it is found at Rumah Sakit Harapan Keluarga (Jalan Ahmad Yani No. 9; tel. 370/6177000; harapankeluarga.co.id).

Bali and Lombok tend to be hot and humid. Protect yourself against **sunburn and heat stroke exhaustion** by wearing a hat, applying sunscreen, and drinking water throughout the day. If it's a very sunny day, duck into the shade between the hours of 11am and 2pm, when the sun tends to be strongest.

NATURAL DISASTERS

Bali and Lombok are prone to natural disasters like volcanic eruptions, earthquakes, tsunami, and tropical cyclones. Obey any evacuation orders and call your travel insurance company for advice at the first sign of an incident. For natural disaster information and warnings, download the **BMKG app** (www.bmkg.go.id), which provides earthquake information and tsunami warnings.

RESOURCES AND TREATMENT

Stay up to date on tourist advice for travel around Indonesia through government websites like **Smartraveller.gov.au** (Australia), **Travel.state.gov** (U.S.), **Gov.uk** (U.K.), **Travel.gc.ca** (Canada), and **Safetravel. govt.nz** (New Zealand). Note that these websites often lump Bali and Lombok under happenings with the whole of Indonesia, and advice may not be relevant. Before traveling to Indonesia, purchase **travel insurance** with coverage for emergency evacuation in the case of serious illnesses or injury.

Emergency phone numbers:

- **All emergency services:** 112
- **Police:** 110
- **Fire:** 113
- **Ambulance:** 118
- **Tourist police phone number for Bali:** 361/7540599 or 361/224111
- **Tourist police phone number for Lombok:** 370/632733

Vaccinations

Consult a travel doctor to see what vaccinations are recommended before your trip to Bali and Lombok. Though none are legally required to enter Indonesia, the following inoculations are recommended: Measles-Mumps-Rubella (MMR), Polio, Hepatitis A and B, Typhoid, Japanese Encephalitis if staying for longer than one month and/or staying in rural areas, Rabies if at risk of exposure to animals, Tetanus, and Yellow Fever.

Clinics and Hospitals

If serious treatment is needed, it is best to go to the nearest major hospital listed in the destination chapters. The largest clinics and the ones most likely to have English-speaking staff are in Denpasar and Kuta, Bali. Some clinics offer ambulance and emergency evacuation services. In rural areas, take care when receiving treatment from a traditional healer such as a *balian*. Many times, unsterilized items are placed in a wound and can cause serious infection. For major ailments, seek professional and clinical treatment.

CRIMES AND SCAMS

Most crime in Bali and Lombok is related to petty theft and scams. Criminals tend to target drunk tourists around Kuta, Bali, and other tourist-heavy areas of Lombok like the Gili Islands. Avoid wearing obviously expensive jewelry, and keep belongings close in a cross-body bag or tucked into a sturdy backpack.

At many major tourist attractions, a local may claim that a tour guide is required, and they may accompany you as you browse through the attraction. At the end of your excursion, they'll demand money. If you aren't interested in a tour guide, firmly decline from the beginning. Touts pressuring you to purchase an item or book transportation are similarly persistent.

Indonesia is not the destination to dabble with illicit substances. Aside from the potential health consequences, drug possession and trafficking are crimes punishable by heavy fines, long jail sentences, and death.

Avoid visiting "orphanages," which are often not true orphanages but may be simply a money-making scheme. Supporting orphanage tourism also puts children at risk of being in contact with unvetted visitors and can create unhealthy attachments.

Islamic extremist groups have threatened many areas of Indonesia and have targeted tourist destinations in the past (such as the Bali bombings of 2002 and 2005). Though security has increased in the most populated areas of Bali, it's best to avoid political demonstrations or large religious gatherings. Stay updated on any news warnings or developments. If you're not sure where to look, check local or Australian media outlets.

Travel Tips

WHAT TO PACK

There are major shopping malls in Kuta, Bali, and Mataram, Lombok, should you forget any major item. Convenience stores sell toiletries and there are plenty of pharmacies selling basic over-the-counter medication. Pack on the lighter side, as laundry services are commonly available and affordable in hotels. One-day turnaround service costs only about 20,000 Rp per kg (2 lbs) of clothes.

MONEY

Bali and Lombok use the **Indonesian Rupiah** (Rp or IDR) as currency. Because the currency is so inflated ($1 USD is about 14,000 Rp), it's easy to miss a zero when handing out change or exchanging money. For simplicity, many businesses shave off the last three zeros of their price tag—200,000 becomes 200. Coins come in 50 Rp, 100 Rp, 200 Rp, 500 Rp, and 1,000 Rp. Notes are available in 1,000 Rp,

2,000 Rp, 5,000 Rp, 10,000 Rp, 20,000 Rp, 50,000 Rp, and 100,000 Rp denominations. Many tourists make the mistake of handing over a red 100,000 Rp note rather than a purple 10,000 Rp note when paying for items. **Cash** is king on the islands, and it's practical to expect to pay for almost everything, aside from mid-range to luxury accommodation, in cash.

Credit cards are accepted in areas like Kuta, Seminyak, Denpasar, Ubud, Senggigi, and Mataram, where it's common to pay a 2-3 percent charge for card payments. Outside of these major areas, many businesses will not accept card payment.

ATMs and Money Exchange

ATMs are available in most major towns and cities of Bali and Lombok. On smaller islands, like Nusa Penida, Nusa Lembongan, and the Gili Islands, ATMs may run out of

Packing List

CLOTHING

- Swimwear
- Rashguard with UPF 50+ sun protection
- Hiking shoes
- Underwear, socks
- Sturdy sandals
- T-shirts
- Shorts, trousers, skirt, yoga pants
- Dress/collared shirt
- Sarong (can be purchased during trip)
- Jacket/sweater
- Sunglasses
- Lightweight long-sleeved shirt with UPF 50+ sun protection (often found in fishing section of sporting goods store)

TOILETRIES

- Shampoo, conditioner, soap, brush
- Toothbrush, toothpaste, floss
- Glasses, contact solution, contacts
- Makeup
- Medication
- Reef-safe sunscreen
- Mosquito repellent

GEAR

- Day bag or backpack (a dry bag backpack is useful to keep items dry during rainy days)
- Lightweight rain jacket if visiting during wet season
- Reef booties if surfing

ELECTRONICS

- Camera, memory card
- Phone
- Laptop, tablet, e-reader
- Travel power adapter
- Power bank

DOCUMENTS

It's best also to have a backup of these documents stored online.

- Copy of passport
- International driver's license
- Proof of onward travel (flight tickets)
- Insurance
- Doctor's note explaining medications if entering with many different types
- It's best to have a backup of each doctor's note and prescription stored online

cash. This often happens if departing boats have been canceled due to weather and new boats have trouble entering the island. Always keep a small amount of cash hidden as backup should you enter a small town or small island. ATMs usually give money in 50,000 Rp or 100,000 Rp denominations. Holding 50,000 Rp notes will prove to be more useful. Most ATMs allow you to withdraw around 1,500,000-2,500,000 Rp at a time.

Card skimming is common. Try to pull money out at a bank itself or an ATM with security. Pull lightly on the card reader before inserting your card. If a card skimmer is attached, it will often come off with a simple tug.

Money changers are also available to exchange cash. If you see a sign advertising a great exchange rate, be cautious. Some money changers have quick hands that could rival the most talented Las Vegas magicians. The scam happens when the money changer hands the money to you. They often slip a few notes back to themselves. They create a distraction by asking you for a different note or pointing at something to divert your gaze. Pull cash out of ATMs or exchange at official money changers. Don't be tempted by run-down stalls offering alluring exchange rates. U.S. dollars and Australian dollars are the easiest currencies to exchange.

Shopping

When it comes to shopping, assume that many prices are not fixed. Bargaining is common in Bali and Lombok, and it can be fun for all parties with the right attitude. While being cheap or stingy is rude, there's no harm in bargaining if you do so with a smile. However, many tourists treat bargaining as a sport where they try to drive a price down to a point where it is barely profitable for the merchant. This is considered rude.

COMMUNICATIONS
Cell Phones

Bring an unlocked phone that accepts **SIM cards** into Indonesia. Data costs about 50,000 Rp for 5 GB. You can purchase SIM cards from informal street vendors, but new regulations claim that SIM card users must register their passport number to the SIM card. If you purchase from a street vendor, there's a chance your SIM card may suddenly stop working. Instead, it's best to go directly to an official communications shop, where they will take a photo of your passport and register the SIM to your passport number. You will need to clarify if you want your SIM card to work on both Bali and Lombok.

Telkomsel (www.telkomsel.com) is the largest provider in Indonesia and has reliable coverage. **XL** (www.xl.co.id) is a reliable alternative.

- **Indonesia country code:** 62
- **International access codes:** 001/008/017

Many locals use **WhatsApp** to communicate rather than direct texting or calling. When adding a phone number into WhatsApp, do not forget the +62 country code.

Wi-Fi

Wi-Fi is available in many cafés and hotels throughout Bali and Lombok. In more rural areas, it is not common for cafés to have Wi-Fi. The reliability and speed of available Wi-Fi vary from venue to venue. If you need a stable connection, it is best to get a **SIM card** with data and use your phone as a mobile hotspot.

Shipping and Postal Service

If you need to ship an item, look for shops that say *kantor pos.* They typically have bright orange shop fronts and branding. The major post offices with the most services are known as the Kantor Pos Wilayah or Regional Post Office.

You can send letters and postcards from any post office. If you're sending anything internationally, delivery can take up to a month.

Most post offices can send packages internationally, but your parcel may not come with tracking information, and it may not arrive. If you are sending anything of value or a large item, it's best to go through a private delivery service with tracking. **DHL** (www.dhl.com), **FedEx** (www.fedex.com), and **UPS** (www.ups.com) have a few branches throughout Bali and offer reliable international delivery and door-to-door service when receiving goods. Do not seal your package before your transaction, as security often comes over to check and confirm the contents.

Public Holidays

Many public and religious holidays are linked to their respective calendars; dates may vary from year to year.

- **New Year's Day:** January 1
- **Chinese New Year:** January/February
- **Nyepi (Bali only):** March
- **Good Friday:** April
- **Labor Day:** May 1
- **Hari Waisak (Buddhist holiday):** May
- **Ascension of Christ:** May

Why Does the Indonesian Rupiah Have So Many Zeros?

When you're handed a stack of 100,000 Rp bills, it's easy to feel like a millionaire. Unfortunately, 1,000,000 Rp is only about $71 U.S. dollars. To understand the trail of zeros that create Indonesia's currency, it's important to look at the country's history.

In 1945, Indonesia gained independence from the Dutch and began to establish a uniform independent currency, which was not in place until 1949, under Sukarno as president. From 1959 to 1970, Indonesia struggled with inflation and currency devaluation, leading to the printing of 1,000 Rp and 10,000 Rp notes. In 1967, Sukarno was ousted by Suharto. In 1975, sub-100 Rp notes were removed from circulation. By 1992, the rupiah had inflated to a point where 20,000 Rp notes needed to be issued. In 1996, $1 USD was worth about 2,500 Rp.

Then came the Asian Financial Crisis of 1997-1998, when Indonesia's currency plummeted by 80 percent. In 1998, Indonesian students at Trisakti University protested corruption of Sukarno's regime. Four students were killed, and dozens of others were injured by police forces. This event, coupled with the devaluation of the Indonesian currency, let to nationwide riots and civil unrest, triggering Suharto's resignation. By June 1998, $1 USD was worth 16,800 Rp. In 1999, the 100,000 Rp note entered circulation. Today, the 100,000 Rp note is worth a little over $7 USD. Though there have been plans and proposals to redenominate the Indonesian rupiah by removing the last three zeros from each note, many locals are hesitant for this to happen until the currency stabilizes. Until then, tourists will have to double-count the zeros when handing over a bill to ensure they're not paying 100,000 Rp for a 10,000 Rp treat.

- **Independence Day:** August 17
- **Christmas:** December 25

OTHER ISLAMIC HOLIDAYS (DATES VARY)

- **Ascension of Prophet Muhammad**
- **Islamic New Year**
- **Ramadan**
- **Idul Fitri**
- **Idul Adha**
- **Birthday of the Prophet Muhammad**

WEIGHTS AND MEASURES

Indonesia uses the **metric system:** Distance is measured in meters and kilometers, mass/weight is measured in grams and kilograms, and volume is measured in liters.

TOURIST INFORMATION
Tourist Offices

Tourist offices around Bali and Lombok are not always helpful with practicalities. Oftentimes, the staff at a tour company or large hotel will be more adept at helping travelers with information and crafting itineraries than the tourism offices are. On Lombok, many tourist offices are simply places to find brochures.

DENPASAR
Bali Tourism Board (Jalan Raya Puputan No. 41; tel. 361/235600; https://balitourismboard. or.id; Mon.-Sat. 9am-5pm, closed Sun.) is the main tourism board office of Bali.

UBUD
Fabulous Ubud (Jalan Raya Ubud; tel. 361/973285; www.fabulousubud.com; daily 8am-9pm) is one of the more helpful offices on Bali, and understandably has an Ubud-heavy focus. It's an ideal place to source maps.

Maps
Periplus Travel has detailed maps of Bali and Lombok (sold separately). If you're driving, it's worth investing in the Periplus *Bali Street Atlas*. Because road conditions change constantly, it is also ideal to back up paper maps with offline digital maps through **Maps.Me** or **Google Maps.**

Budgeting

To help you budget for your trip, here's what you can expect to pay for common necessities.

- **Coffee:** 15,000 Rp
- **Beer:** 30,000-40,000 Rp
- **Cocktail:** 50,000-80,000 Rp
- **Sandwich:** 20,000 Rp
- **Lunch:** 30,000-50,000 Rp
- **Dinner:** 50,000-100,000 Rp
- **Guesthouse accommodation:** 300,000 Rp per night
- **Surfboard rental:** 50,000 Rp per hour
- **Yoga class:** 120,000 Rp per one-hour class
- **Guided hike:** 100,000-150,000 Rp per person per hour of hiking
- **Car rental (with driver):** 500,000-800,000 Rp per day
- **One-way bus fare:** 20,000-50,000 Rp
- **Taxi:** 100,000 Rp per hour

Traveler Advice

OPPORTUNITIES FOR STUDY AND EMPLOYMENT

Study

Udayana University (Denpasar), Warmadewa University (Denpasar), Undiknas University (Denpasar), and Mataram University (Mataram) offer coursework for international students.

Employment

It can be a challenge to gain full-time employment on Bali and Lombok, as companies prefer to give jobs to qualified locals. All foreign workers must obtain a work permit, referred to as IMTA (Ijin Mempekerjakan Tenaga Kerja Asing, which translates into "Foreign Worker Permit"). When you are granted an IMTA, you are also issued a KITAS (Kartu Izin Tinggal Sementara, which translates into "Temporary Stay Permit"). This permit is valid from six to 12 months. Colloquially, KITAS is used to talk about a work permit as well. To obtain the IMTA/KITAS permits, a company must sponsor your job and work in conjunction with you to secure all relevant permits. This process typically takes two to three months. Jobs are commonly found in hospitality and tourism, the dive industry, and teaching. Many foreigners work on Bali and Lombok illegally; if caught, the foreign worker is likely to be deported and fined.

Retirement

Foreigners over the age of 55 can apply for a **KITAS retirement permit** that allows non-Indonesians to stay inside Indonesia for consecutive years without any entry or exit restrictions. To secure the permit, you must have a licensed emigration agency sponsor your application. Working is forbidden under this permit.

Volunteering

There are multiple community programs on Bali and Lombok that often need volunteers and contributions.

Amicorp Community Center (www.amicorp.com) focuses on developing Balinese cultural programs in Les, Bali.

BAWA (https://bawabali.com) is a charity program that works toward controlling the stray dog population on Bali through spay and neuter programs.

Friends of the National Parks Foundation (www.fnpf.org) hosts a volunteer program geared toward environmental conservation on Nusa Penida.

Pelita Foundation (www.pelita foundationlombok.org) holds free after-school classes in Lombok to teach children English. It also offers a scholarship program for continuing education, and provides earthquake damage relief.

R.O.L.E. Foundation (www.role foundation.org) works on sustainability programs and waste management.

Yayasan Rama Sesana (www.yrsbali.org) helps upskill local women and provides family-planning services.

TRAVELING WITH CHILDREN

Bali and Lombok are destinations that stimulate a child's imagination and innate sense of exploration. Outside of school hours, local children are engaged in community events and activities, so kids are both seen and heard by visitors. Indonesians tend to have a warm demeanor toward children, and it's common for hotel and restaurant staff to engage them in a quick game or conversation.

Not all of Bali and Lombok's areas are family-friendly, however. Strong currents, rickety staircases leading down cliffs, unmarked trails, and heavy traffic can make a visit feel stressful rather than relaxing for families. Here are some practicalities to consider when traveling with your little ones:

Don't expect to be able to walk comfortably around Bali or Lombok with a stroller thanks to potholes, open drains, sand, and other obstacles. A baby carrier might be a more convenient option.

Do not rely on public transportation when traveling with young children. Bus and *bemo* wait times can be long and drivers may not follow the route you expect. Instead, it's best to hire a private driver and provide your own car seat.

Most venues do not have baby-changing facilities. Many restaurants, especially in rural areas, have squat toilets that young children may need assistance using.

Many families love to bring children to places known for their monkeys, such as Sacred Monkey Forest in Ubud and Pura Uluwatu in Uluwatu. However, take care while visiting. Monkeys are known to bite and scratch when startled by a laugh or a scream. They are also known to steal items from unsuspecting people. It might be best to watch from a distance.

ACCESS FOR TRAVELERS WITH DISABILITIES

Some regions on Bali and Lombok are more accessible for wheelchair users than others; planning and creativity can go a long way. One of the best things about Balinese and Sasak culture is that people tend to adapt and think of creative solutions to include others. This is largely thanks to the heavy emphasis on ceremonies where all community members, regardless of their abilities, are obliged to attend.

Bali and Lombok are not known for their immaculate sidewalks and roads. Open drains, potholes, objects in the roads, and high curbs can make navigating a challenge. It's not uncommon for a sidewalk suddenly to have a meter-wide hole that drops into a drain.

Note that ferries and boats often do not arrive at a pier or a jetty. Rather, they require using a ladder and may require passengers to wade into the water.

Bali Access Travel (tel. 361/8519902; www.baliaccesstravel.com; info@baliaccess

Opening Hours

- **Restaurants:** 8am-8pm daily in rural areas; 8am-10pm in tourist areas
- **Shops:** 9am-6pm in rural areas; 9am-10pm in tourist areas
- **Markets:** 6am-3pm
- **Banks:** Mon.-Thurs. 8am-2pm, Fri. 8am-noon, Sat. 8am-11am, closed Sun.
- **Government offices and post offices:** Mon.-Thurs. 8am-2pm, Fri. 8am-11am, Sat. 8am-1pm, closed Sun.

travel.com) is the go-to tour planner for arranging transportation, dive and snorkel trips, temple tours, hotel room care, and custom itineraries. They also offer equipment like wheelchairs, hoists, shower chairs, walkers, and portable ramps. **Bali Beach Wheels** (tel. 87765085812; www.balibeachwheels.com; info@balibeachwheels.com) offers Hippocampe wheelchairs for rent for 500,000 Rp per day or 3,000,000 Rp per week. **Accessible Indonesia** (www.accessibleindonesia.org; info@accessibleindonesia.org) is a premier tour company with multiday trips that are ideal for those with disabilities.

Best wheelchair-accessible beaches: Sanur and Nusa Dua have hotels that can accommodate a wheelchair. Sanur's easy beachfront access and road make it one of the most accessible places on the island. Seminyak, Legian, and Kuta also have hotels with ramps and beach access.

Best temples and cultural sites: Pura Uluwatu, Pura Tirta Gangga, Pura Ulun Danu Beratan, and Pura Tanah Lot have ramp access.

WOMEN TRAVELING ALONE

Women who are traveling alone on Bali and Lombok will likely feel safe and comfortable if they take regular precautions: It's best not to walk late at night or wander down unknown paths. Never leave a drink unattended or accept a drink from a stranger; drink spiking does happen. Sometimes, drivers and tour guides can become overly friendly—to the point of discomfort—toward women traveling alone. In some areas, local men hold a stereotype that foreign women are promiscuous. This is especially the case in areas of Lombok like Senggigi, Kuta, and the Gili Islands, as well as in major tourist areas of Bali.

It's best to avoid revealing that you're traveling alone if someone is making you uncomfortable. A claim that you are meeting a friend later or are waiting for your partner often deters would-be pests from hanging around. Some men, dubbed as "Kuta Cowboys," actively seek single women to latch onto in hopes of having their time together bankrolled by the woman. Of course, many locals also find solo women more approachable than other travelers and may simply be curious about who you are and what your time on the islands is like.

Women might feel more comfortable dressing conservatively in areas like Lombok and rural areas of Bali. Cover your shoulders and thighs while out, and only wear resort clothes and bathing suits in popular tourist beaches or around your hotel. Local women on Lombok tend to dress modestly. On Bali it depends on the region, but to attempt to mitigate stares and unwanted approaches, it's best to cover up with a sarong and T-shirt.

LGBTQ TRAVELERS

Bali is a hub for LGBTQ tourists, and its out local and expat community is growing

Bali's Most Family-Friendly Destinations

BEST BEACHES
Sanur, Lovina, Amed, the **Gili Islands, Nusa Lembongan,** and **Nusa Dua** all have calm-water spots with mellow waves. Kuta, Lombok, is also worth visiting for the laid-back beach of Pantai Tanjung Aan.

BEST SURFING
Seminyak and **Legian** have white-water waves where young kids can catch their first ride. Hotels often have large pools, splash pads, and programs tailored for children.

BEST ENTERTAINMENT
Ubud hosts regular cultural performances and dance classes, and has a colorful community of monkeys who swing from the treetops to the telephone poles.

BEST SNORKELING
Observe sea turtles off **Gili Meno, Gili Air,** and **Gili Trawangan;** spot Nemo in his anemone at **Gili Nanggu;** and go for a total adventure to the island of **Palau Menjangan.**

BEST ADVENTURES
Waterbom Bali is Bali's biggest and best water park, and it is a major hit with children of all ages. Kids will also love zooming above the sky on a zipline adventure course at the **Bali Treetop Adventure Park.**

---

steadily. However, in rural areas, both Bali and Lombok are generally intolerant of homosexual couples when it comes to their own family members. Those in the Balinese and Sasak community often seek partners from other islands or nations to hide their orientations. Public displays of affection are discouraged among all couples—homosexual and heterosexual. If same-sex couples are seen holding hands, many locals will assume that the pair are simply friends. This is partly because showing affection among friends is somewhat common and partly because it is the norm to maintain a semblance of harmony.

It might be a challenge to find open LGBTQ communities on Lombok. However, Bali has pockets where openly homosexual couples are embraced; Bali hosts one of the largest gay scenes in Indonesia. **Yayasan Gaya Dewata** organization (www.gayadewata. com) is a great resource for sourcing contraception and health screenings. Large hotels tend to be welcoming of same-sex couples.

Treatment at guesthouses can vary, though it's rare for any local to say anything directly.

In Seminyak there is an array of gay bars along Jalan Camplung Tanduk Arcade. Drag shows, go-go dancers, celebrity impersonators, and pole dancing are part of regularly scheduled entertainment.

As the Indonesian government inches toward more anti-LGBTQ legislation, many LGBTQ events have gone defunct or underground. Openly gay hotel and restaurant owners are quietly removing their listings from LGBTQ directories and websites as an act of protection. Word of mouth and apps like Grindr are the best way to find out about upcoming events.

TRAVELERS OF COLOR
The main tourist areas of Bali, such as Kuta, Seminyak, Ubud, and the Bukit Peninsula, receive visitors from all around the world. In these areas, locals are typically used to interacting with travelers of color. In rural areas, Balinese and Sasak communities tend to be

homogenous in terms of appearance. Travelers of color may find locals pointing, staring, or taking pictures of anyone who looks different from the norm. Locals may ask invasive questions or make blunt observations about physical features. Many toiletry products and beauty products contain skin whitening agents, especially in lotions and deodorants, and it may be a challenge to find products for natural hair.

TRAVELING WITH A PARTNER

All public displays of affection between lovers are discouraged on both Bali and Lombok. Handholding is generally accepted in tourist areas, but anything further will prompt telepathic messages from locals urging you to get a room.

Some locals and regular visitors to Indonesia are concerned about a recent law proposal that would nudge Indonesia in a more conservative direction. There are laws proposing that straight couples traveling together must provide proof of marriage before renting a room together. Same-sex couples would be banned from renting a room altogether. This proposal has been picked up and promptly dubbed the "Bali Bonk Ban" by media outlets. Other bans include showing contraception to a minor, spreading communist ideology, insulting the government, and promoting fake news. The law also aims to criminalize abortion and limit access to healthcare after rape or other medical emergencies.

At the time of research, these laws have not been enacted. It is worth speculating that even if passed, these laws may take years to implement and may not even be enforced. Indonesia is currently trying to develop major tourism areas around the country, and these laws would likely impact this in a negative way.

Resources

Glossary

A

adat: traditional laws and cultural customs

air: water

alang-alang: Imperata cylindrica; grass used to create thatched roofing

aling-aling: a wall built to guard a property against malevolent spirits

arak: local liquor made from coconut palm sap, sugarcane, lontar, or coconut

B

bale banjar: open-air community or neighborhood building

bale bengong: open-air gazebo used for resting, typically found in front of homes

balian: traditional healer with connections to the spiritual realm

banjar: neighborhood or community made up of a council of local married men to enact and enforce local rules

Barong: a deity who fights against evil spirits, the enemy of Rangda; often the character in a Barong mask show; can take on multiple animal forms depending on the region—lion and panther are most common

batik: fabric with designs made from wax applications and wax-resistant dye

bemo: public minivan or minibus

Brahma: Hindu god of creation, part of the holy trinity with Shiva and Vishnu

bukit: hill

C D

canang sari: Hindu offering typically made from flowers, incense, and money placed in a small woven basket

candi: entrance to a temple, often an arch

candi bentar: split temple gates

cidomo: pony and carriage (usually found on Lombok)

danau: lake

desa: village

dewa/dewi: God/goddess of the Sang Hyang Widi Wasa

G

Galungan: Balinese holiday when ancestral spirits visit their families

gamelan: orchestra of percussive instruments often made from bamboo

gang: alley

Ganesh: Hindu deity of the arts and remover of obstacles; usually depicted with an elephant head

Garuda: Hindu bird-like creature who carries Vishnu

gedong: shrine where holy objects may be kept

gili: island

goa: cave

gunung: mountain

I J

ikat: fabric that is dyed before weaving and crafted to make an intricate pattern

jalan: road

jepun: plumeria or frangipani flower

joglo: traditional Javanese home with distinctive roof

jukung: wooden outrigger canoe typically used for fishing

K

kain: fabric

kain poleng: black and white checkered fabric wrapped around sacred objects; sometimes worn during cultural performances

kaja: Balinese directional term that dictates how a temple or home will be built; toward the mountains; north; opposite of kelod

kantor: office

kecak: Hindu dance performance that portrays the story of Ramayana and the legend of the white monkey

kelod: Balinese directional term that dictates how a temple or home will be built; toward the sea; south; opposite of kaja

kota: city

kris: a dagger or sword with a wavy blade; often intricately made and a royal heirloom

Kuningan: the end of the Galungan holiday, when Balinese ancestors return to their spiritual homes

L M N O

legong: traditional Balinese dance with elaborate costumes and stories told through movement, song, and facial expression

leyak: a demon made of a head and entrails that follows the commands of Rangda

lontar: manuscripts crafted from inscribed palm leaves

lumbung: an elevated structure used to store rice

makepung: bull race

meru: a pagoda-like Hindu shrine made of odd-numbered tiered roofs

nusa: island

Nyepi: Start of the Saka New Year; day of silence to ward evil spirits off the island

ogoh-ogoh: statue to represent evil spirits used during parades before Nyepi; burnt to mark new beginnings and purification

ojek: motorbike taxi

P

padi: rice paddy

pantai: beach

pasar: market

pawukon: Balinese 210-day calendar

pondok: cottage

propinsi: province of Indonesia

pulau: island

puputan: mass ritual suicide during a time of war as a form of surrender

pura: Hindu temple

pura dalem: temple for those who have died

pura desa: village temple

puri: palace

pusit kota: city center

R

raja: king or prince

Ramadan: Islamic month of fasting, self-reflection, and prayer; the ninth month of the Islamic calendar

Ramayana: Hindu epic that narrates the life of a prince, Rama

Rangda: a demon-witch who leads evil spirits

raya: main; often denotes a major road

S

saka: Balinese lunar calendar used alongside pawukon calendar and Gregorian calendar; Nyepi marks start of new year

Sanghyang Widhi Wasa: the unification of all Hindu gods; symbolized at shrines as an empty chair

sarong: piece of fabric wrapped around the waist

sate: meat satay

sawah: rice fields

sepeda motor: motorbike, motorcycle

Shiva: Hindu god of destruction, part of the holy trinity with Brahma and Vishnu

songket: hand-woven textiles with intricate patterns, often features metallic elements

subak: community of rice farmers who adhere to strict religious and farming codes

T V W

tanjung: cape

tirta: water

toko: store

trimurti: the trio of the three main Hindu gods of Brahma, Shiva, and Vishnu

Vishnu: Hindu god of preservation, part of the holy trinity with Brahma and Shiva

warung: small restaurant

wayang kulit: shadow puppet play

Phrasebook

Though Indonesian, also called Bahasa Indonesia, is the language of the country, most Indonesians speak a handful of languages. On Bali, the mother tongue is Balinese. On Lombok, most locals speak Sasak. Many Indonesians speak the languages of their neighboring islands in addition to their mother tongue and Indonesian. Outside of areas where tourists are common, English is seldom spoken. Occasionally, you will see Dutch remnants in local spellings (waroeng vs. warung).

Balinese and Sasak have different forms of language, depending on who is speaking. The language changes whether you are speaking upward, downward, or on an even level as you when it comes to social standing, priesthood, and authority. The language is also largely regional. It can be a challenge to know how to address someone in Balinese or Sasak, which is why Indonesian or English is the preferred language when speaking to a stranger.

For the sake of simplicity, the Essential Phrases are in Indonesian.

PRONUNCIATION

Pronouncing Indonesian words is fortunately very simple. The phonetic spelling is very consistent, though inflection and intonation come with practice and immersion. When it comes to stressing syllables, two-syllable words usually have equal emphasis. In words longer than three syllables, the emphasis is on the second-to-last syllable.

Vowels

a   like *a* in *call*
e   like *e* in *pet*
i   like *i* in *lip*
o   like *o* in *rob*
u   like *u* in *put*

Consonants

B, d, f, g, j, k, l, m, n, p, s, t, and w are pronounced the same as they are in English. Other letters like q, v, x, and z usually appear in words taken from other languages.

c   like *ch* in *chomp*
kh   like *k*, as in *loch*
r   often pronounced with a rolled *r* sound
sy   like *sh* in *sharp*
ng   like *ng* in *singer*
ngg slightly different, as in *anger*

One example of a word that is commonly mispronounced is the town of Canggu (Chang-gu).

Split Words

After being in Indonesia for a while, you might notice that when some people write, they split a word in two; this is especially common in numbers and places. Examples include Padang Bai vs. Padangbai, Candi Dasa vs. Candidasa, Are Guling vs. Areguling. If you are having trouble finding a location on a map, try splitting the word or combining multiple words into one.

ESSENTIAL PHRASES

Bad Buruk

Beautiful Cantik

Can you help me? Bisakah kamu membantu saya?

Can you please speak slowly? Bisakah kamu berbicara lebih pelan?

Can you take my/our photo? Bisakah Anda mengambil foto saya/kami?

Do you speak English? Apakah kama bisa bahasa Inggris?

Excuse me Permisi

Good Baik

Good-bye Salamat tinggal

Hello Halo/Salam

Hi Hai

How are you? Bagaimana kabarmu?

How do you say...? Begaimana anda mengatakan...?

I do not speak Indonesian Saya tidak bisa bahasa Indonesia

I do not understand Saya tidak mengerti

Maybe Mungkin
My name is… Nama saya adalah…
Mrs./Mr./Miss Ibu/Bapak/Nona
Nice to meet you Senang bertemu denganmu
No Tidak
Please Silahkan
See you later Sampai nanti
Sorry Maaf
Sweet dreams Mimpi manis
Take care Hati hati
Thank you Terima kasih
Welcome Selamat datang
What's your name? Siapa namamu?
Where are the restrooms/toilets? Di manakah kamar mandinya?
You're welcome Sama sama

Transportation/Directions

Can I walk there? Bisakah saya jalan ke sana?
Does this bus go to…? Apakah bus ini pergi ke…?
East Timur
How far is…? Seberapa jauh…?
I am looking for the hotel/hospital/bank Saya mencari hotel/rumah sakit/bank
I would like to look at the schedule Saya ingin melihat jadwal
I would like to purchase a ticket to… Bisakah saya membeli tiket ke…
I would like to reserve a ticket Saya ingin memesan tiket
Is it far/close? Apakah itu jauh?/Apakah sudah dekat?
Is there a bus to…? Apakah ada bus ke…?
North Utara
South Selatan
Straight? Lurus?
To the left? Ke kiri?
To the right? Ke kanan?
West Barat
What time does the bus leave/arrive? Pukul berapa bus ke berangkat/tiba?
Where can I buy a ticket? Di mana saya bisa membeli tiket?

Where can I get petrol? Di mana saya bisa mendapatkan bensin?
Where can I rent a car/motorbike? Di mana saya bisa menyewa mobil/sepeda motor?
Where do I get off? Di mana saya turun?
Where is…? Di mana…?
Where is a good restaurant? Di mana restoran yang bagus?
Where is the beach/city center? Di mana pantainya/pusat kota?
Where is the bus station? Di mana terminal busnya?

Hotels

Air-conditioning AC
Balcony Balkon
Bathroom Kamar mandi
Breakfast Sarapan
How much does it cost per night? Berapa biayanya semalam?
I would like a single/double room Saya mau kamar single/dobel
I would like to cancel my reservation Saya ingin membatalkan reservasi saya
Parking Parkir
Sea view Pemandangan laut
What time is check out? Jam berapa check out?

Shopping

Cash Tunai
Closed Tutup
Do you take credit cards? Apakah kamu menerima kartu kredit?
How much does it cost? Berapa harganya?
I'm just looking Saya hanya melihat
It's too expensive/cheap Itu terlalu mahal / murah
Money Uang
Open Buka
Where are the shops? Di mana toko-toko?

Restaurants

beef daging sapi
beer bir

bottled water air botol
bread roti
breakfast makan pagi
cake kue
Can I have the bill, please? Bisakah saya minta tagihannya?
chicken ayam
coffee kopi
Could you show me the menu? Bisakah kamu menunjukkan menunya?
dinner makan malam
Do you have a menu in English? Apakah Anda memiliki menu dalam bahasa Inggris?
duck bebek
egg telur
fish ikan
fruit buah
I do not eat... Saya tidak mau makan...
I would like a coffee Saya mau kopi
I would like some water Saya mau air
I would like to order... Saya ingin memesan...
ice cubes es batu
I'm a vegan Saya vegan
I'm a vegetarian Saya vegetarian
juice jus
lamb daging anak domba
lunch makan siang
milk susu
noodles mie
pork daging babi
restaurant warung
rice nasi
salad salad
salsa sambal
shrimp udang
snack camilan
soup sop
soy sauce kecap
tap water air ledeng
tea the
vegetable sayur-mayur
What is the daily special? Apa yang special hari ini?
wine anggur

Health
antibiotic antibiotika

burn membakar
cramp kejang
fever demam
headache sakit kepala
I am allergic to penicillin/ cortisone Saya alergi terhadap penisilin/ kortison
I am diabetic Saya kena diabetes
I am pregnant Saya hamil
I feel a lot of pain here... Saya merasa kesakitan...
I need to go to the hospital Saya harus pergi ke rumah sakit
I need to see a doctor Saya perlu ke dokter
Is there a doctor who speaks English? Adakah dokter yang berbahasa Inggris?
medicine obat
My blood type is...positive / negative Golong darah saya ... positif/ negatif
nausea mual
pain rasa sakit
pharmacy farmasi/apotek
pill/tablet pil/tablet
Please call an ambulance Tolong panggilkan ambulans
She/he has been stung/bitten Dia disengat/digigit
stomachache sakit perut
toothache sakit gigi
vomiting muntah

Numbers
0 nol
1 satu
2 dua
3 tiga
4 empat
5 lima
6 enam
7 tujuh
8 delapan
9 sembilan
10 sepuluh
11 sebelas
12 dua belas

13 tiga belas
14 empat belas
15 lima belas
16 enam belas
17 tujuh belas
18 delapan belas
19 sembilan belas
20 dua puluh
30 tiga puluh
40 empat puluh
50 lima puluh
60 enam puluh
70 tujuh puluh
80 delapan puluh
90 sembilan puluh
100 seratus
101 seratus satu
200 dua ratus
500 lima ratus
1,000 seribu
10,000 sepuluh ribu
100,000 seratus ribu
1,000,000 satu juta

Time

afternoon sore
evening petang
It's three/seven o'clock Jam tiga/tujuh
midday tengah hari
midnight tengah malam
morning pagi
night malam
today hari ini
tomorrow besok
What time is it? Jam berapa sekarang?
yesterday kemarin

Days and Months

day hari
week minggu
month bulan
year tahun
Monday Senin
Tuesday Selasa
Wednesday Rabu
Thursday Kamis
Friday Jumat
Saturday Sabtu
Sunday Minggu
January Januari
February Februari
March Maret
April April
May Mei
June Juni
July Juli
August Agustus
September September
October Oktober
November Nopember
December Desember

Verbs

There is no distinction between masculine and feminine when paired with verbs. The word for both he and she is *dia*.

to arrive / I arrive / he/she arrives / they arrive untuk tiba / saya tiba / dia tiba / mereka tiba
to be / I am / he/she is / they are menjadi / saya / dia adalah / mereka
to buy / I buy / he/she buys / they buy untuk membeli / saya membeli / dia membeli / mereka membela
to come / I come / he/she comes / they come datang / saya datang / dia datang / mereka datang
to eat / I eat / he/she eats / they eat untuk makan / saya makan / dia makan / mereka makan
to drink / I drink / he/she drinks / they drink untuk minum / saya minum / dia minum / mereka minum
to give / I give / he/she gives / they give untuk memberi / saya memberi / dia memberi / mereka memberi
to go / I go / he/she goes / they go untuk pergi / aku pergi / dia pergi / mereka pergi
to look at / I look at / he/she looks at / they look at untuk melihat / saya melihat / dia melihat / mereka melihat
to look for / I look for / he/she looks for / they look for untuk mencari / saya mencari / dia mencari / mereka mencari
to stop / I stop / he/she stops / they

stop untuk berhenti / saya berhenti / dia berhenti / mereka berhenti

to want / I want / he/she wants / they want untuk ingin / saya ingin / dia ingin / mereka ingin

to write / I write / he/she writes / they write untuk menulis / saya menulis / dia menulis / mereka menulis

Asking Questions

How? Bagaimana?

What? Apa?

When? Kapan?

Where? Di mana?

Which? Yang mana?

Who? Siapa?

Why? Kenapa?

Basic Balinese Phrases

Bali's caste system is reflected in its language. When speaking with a low-caste (Sudra) person, *Ia* Balinese is spoken. When speaking with a stranger or a person on a higher social ranking, *Ipun* is spoken. When talking to royalty or a higher caste (Brahman, Wesia, or Satriya cate), the highest form of Balinese, *Ida*, is spoken.

Good morning/afternoon/evening/night Rahajeng semeng/sanja/peteng/wengi

Hello Om swastiastu

How are you? Kenken kebara?

I am from… Tiang uli negara…

I'm sorry Ampura

My name is… Tiang…

Thank you Matur suksma (formal) / Suksma (informal)

What do you call this in Balinese? Ne ape adane di Bali?

What is your name? Sira wastene?

Where are you from? Uli dija?

Basic Sasak Phrases

The Sasak language is an oral language, and regional dialects can vary greatly. Sasak changes formality depending on who is being addressed.

Hello Helo

How are you? Berembe kabar?

I am from… Deri…

I'm sorry Ampure

My name is… Arankah aku…

Thank you Tampak asih

What do you call this in Sasak? Ape aran sak iyak elek bahase Sasek?

What is your name? Saik aranm side?

Where are you from? Deri mana?

Suggested Reading

HISTORY

Bonella, Kathryn. *Hotel Kerobokan.* 2009. An inside look at Bali's notorious Kerobokan Prison.

Bonella, Kathryn. *Snowing in Bali.* 2012. Depicts the underground drug trade of Southeast Asia, with Bali in its center.

Copeland, Jonathan and Ni Wayan Murni. *Secrets of Bali: Fresh Light on the Morning of the World.* 2010. A dive into the history, religion, and cultural nuances of Bali.

Forbes, Cameron. *Under the Volcano: The Story of Bali.* 2007. A vivid history of Bali told through the stories of colorful characters.

Hanna, William. *A Brief History of Bali: Piracy, Slavery, Opium and Guns.* 2016. A superficial history of Bali and some aspects of Lombok.

Pringle, Robert. *A Short History of Bali.* 2004. Covers the history of Bali in a way that's easy to follow and understand.

Vickers, Adrian. *Bali: A Paradise Created.* 1997. Insight into how Bali became the popular tourism hub that it is today—and how its visitors have impacted the island.

Wallace, Alfred Russel. *The Malay Archipelago.* 1869. A naturalist travels throughout the archipelago, including to Bali and Lombok, documenting the natural environment with descriptions of places and creatures that no longer exist.

ARTS AND CULTURE

Dibia, I. Wayan and Rucina Ballinger. *Balinese Dance, Drama, and Music: A Guide to the Performing Arts of Bali.* 2011. A beautifully written book about Balinese dance and music.

Eiseman Jr., Fred B. *Bali: Sekala and Niskala.* 1990. Essays on Balinese religion, art, and rituals.

Keeny, Bratford. *Balians: Traditional Healers of Bali.* 2004. Interviews with Balinese traditional healers, and including illustrations to ward off evil spirits.

McAlaney, Clare and Trish McNeill. *Bali Soul Journal.* 2013. Captivating photographs and interviews with the locals who call Bali home.

McKinnon, Jean. *Vessels of Life: Lombok Earthenware.* 1996. Photographs and descriptions featuring Sasak pottery and insight into its meaning.

McPhee, Colin. *A House in Bali.* 1946. A captivating account of the Balinese music and dance scene of the 1930s.

TRAVELOGUES AND MEMOIRS

Covarrubias, Miguel. *Island of Bali.* 1937. A depiction of daily life in Bali through the eyes of an expat artist.

De Neefe, Janet. *In Fragrant Rice: My continuing Love Affair With Bali.* 2004. A lighthearted memoir and cookbook centered around the author's move to Bali, finding love, and features Balinese recipes.

Gilbert, Elizabeth. *Eat, Pray, Love.* 2006. A memoir about the author's spiritual and romantic journey around the world; highlights Ubud and spurred its popularity.

Ingram, William. *A Little Bit One O'Clock: Living With a Balinese Family.* 1998. An earnest story of joining a Balinese family as an outsider.

Wheeler, Cat. *Bali Daze: Freefall off the Tourist Trail.* 2011. Humorous and honest short stories about living as an expat in Ubud.

Wicks, Becky. *Balilicious: The Bali Diaries.* 2012. A fun-loving traveler goes on a spiritual journey to find herself in Bali, chaos ensues.

FICTION

Baum, Vicki. *Love and Death in Bali.* 2011. First published in 1937 using notes that relied heavily on Walter Spies, this story tells about Dutch occupation and the tragic ritual of *puputan* (mass suicide).

Internet Resources and Apps

TRAVEL RESOURCES AND PLANNING

AGODA
Agoda.com
Hotel booking platform, often includes dorms and guesthouses.

THE BALI BIBLE
TheBaliBible.com
Travel planning and news.

CHANTAE WAS HERE
Chantae.com
First-person stories and recommendations on Bali and Lombok.

HONEYCOMBERS
TheHoneycombers.com
Lifestyle and travel content about Bali.

THE LOMBOK GUIDE
TheLombokGuide.com
Lombok-related tourism magazine; online issues available.

FOOD AND DRINK

HAPPY COW
HappyCow.net
App and website used to find vegan and vegetarian-friendly restaurants.

REFILLMYBOTTLE
RefillMyBottle.com
Website and app used to find free or cheap water bottle refill stations.

WEATHER AND NAVIGATION

AGENCY FOR METEOROLOGY CLIMATOLOGY AND GEOPHYSICS
rtsp.bmkg.go.id
Website and app used to update natural disaster warnings.

ALLTRAILS
AllTrails.com
App and website used with GPS-mapped hiking routes.

GOJEK
GoJek.com
Similar to Grab, app used to find rides.

GRAB
Grab.com
App used to find local rides.

MAPS.ME
Maps.Me
Download offline maps for GPS navigation.

COMMUNICATION

BASABALI WIKI
dictionary.basabali.org
An online free Balinese dictionary.

NEWS AND CULTURE

THE BALI TIMES
TheBaliTimes.com
Bali-related news and relevant tourism-related articles.

COCONUTS
Coconuts.co
News and lifestyle articles about Bali.

THE JAKARTA POST
TheJakartaPost.com
Relevant news around Indonesia.

SEMINYAK TIMES
SeminyakTimes.com
Bali-related news targeted toward the expat community.

Index

INDEX

List of Maps

Photo Credits

Embark on an epic journey along the historic Camino de Santiago, stroll the top European cities, or chase Norway's northern lights with Moon Travel Guides!

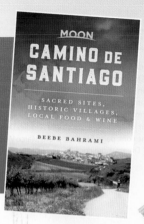

MOON

CAMINO DE SANTIAGO

SACRED SITES, HISTORIC VILLAGES, LOCAL FOOD & WINE

BEEBE BAHRAMI

MOON

AMALFI COAST

With Capri, Naples & Pompeii

LAURA THAYER

MOON

BARCELONA & MADRID

JESSICA JONES

MOON

CROATIA & SLOVENIA

SHANN FOUNTAIN ALIPOUR

MOON

EDINBURGH, GLASGOW & THE ISLE OF SKYE

MOON

FRENCH RIVIERA: NICE, CANNES, MONACO & ST-TROPEZ

JON BRYANT

MOON

ICELAND

MOON

IRELAND

CAMILLE DI ANGELIS

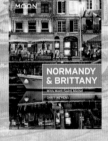

MOON

NORMANDY & BRITTANY

With Mont-Saint-Michel

CHRIS NEWENS

MOON

NORWAY

DAVID NIKEL

MOON

PORTUGAL

CARRIE-MARIE BRATLEY

MOON

PRAGUE, VIENNA & BUDAPEST

MOON

PROVENCE

MOON

ROME, FLORENCE & VENICE

ALEXEI J. COHEN

GO BIG AND GO BEYOND!

These savvy city guides include strategies to help you see the top sights and find adventure beyond the tourist crowds.

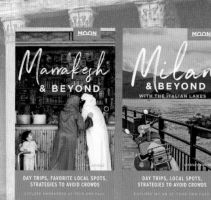

OR TAKE THINGS ONE STEP AT A TIME

ROAD TRIPS AND DRIVE & HIKE GUIDES

MOON
Drive & Hike
APPALACHIAN TRAIL
THE BEST TRAIL TOWNS, DAY HIKES, AND ROAD TRIPS IN BETWEEN
TIMOTHY MALCOLM

MOON
BLUE RIDGE PARKWAY
Road Trip
INCLUDING SHENANDOAH & GREAT SMOKY MOUNTAINS NATIONAL PARKS
JASON FRYE

MOON
CALIFORNIA
Road Trip
SAN FRANCISCO, YOSEMITE, LAS VEGAS, GRAND CANYON, LOS ANGELES, & THE PACIFIC COAST HIGHWAY
STUART THORNTON

MOON
NASHVILLE TO NEW ORLEANS
Road Trip
NATCHEZ TRACE PARKWAY · MEMPHIS · TUPELO · MISSISSIPPI BLUES TRAIL
MARGARET LITTMAN

MOON
NEW ENGLAND
Road Trip
BOSTON, ACADIA NATIONAL PARK, WHITE MOUNTAINS, BERKSHIRES, NEWPORT, AND CAPE COD
JEN ROSE SMITH

MOON
NORTHERN CALIFORNIA
Road Trip
SAN FRANCISCO, WINE COUNTRY, SONOMA, REDWOODS, LAKE TAHOE, SHASTA, LASSEN, YOSEMITE, BIG SUR
STUART THORNTON & KAYLA ANDERSON

MOON
PACIFIC COAST HIGHWAY
CALIFORNIA, OREGON & WASHINGTON
IAN ANDERSON

MOON
Drive & Hike
PACIFIC CREST TRAIL
THE BEST TRAIL TOWNS, DAY HIKES, AND ROAD TRIPS IN BETWEEN
CAROLINE HINCHLIFF

MOON
PACIFIC NORTHWEST
Road Trip
SEATTLE, VANCOUVER, VICTORIA, THE OLYMPIC PENINSULA, PORTLAND, THE OREGON COAST & MOUNT RAINIER
ALLISON WILLIAMS

MOON.COM | ROADTRIPUSA.COM

MOON

ROUTE 66
Road Trip

JESSICA DUNHAM

MOON

SOUTH FLORIDA & THE KEYS
Road Trip

WITH MIAMI, WALT DISNEY WORLD, TAMPA & THE EVERGLADES

JASON FERGUSON

MOON

SOUTHERN CALIFORNIA
Road Trip

DRIVES ALONG THE BEACHES, MOUNTAINS, AND DESERTS WITH THE BEST STOPS ALONG THE WAY

IAN ANDERSON

MOON

SOUTHWEST
Road Trip

LAS VEGAS, ZION & BRYCE, MONUMENT VALLEY, SANTA FE & TAOS, AND THE GRAND CANYON

TIM HULL

MOON

VANCOUVER & CANADIAN ROCKIES
Road Trip

VICTORIA, BANFF, JASPER, CALGARY, THE OKANAGAN, WHISTLER & THE SEA-TO-SKY HIGHWAY

CAROLYN B. HELLER

MOON

YELLOWSTONE TO GLACIER NATIONAL PARK
Road Trip

JACKSON HOLE, CODY, THE GRAND TETONS & THE ROCKY MOUNTAIN FRONT

CARTER G. WALKER

Road Trip USA

Covering more than 35,000 miles of blacktop stretching from east to west and north to south, *Road Trip USA* takes you deep into the heart of America.

This colorful guide covers the top road trips including historic Route 66 and is packed with maps, photos, illustrations, mile-by-mile highlights, and more!

MOON

Road Trip USA

CROSS-COUNTRY ADVENTURES ON AMERICA'S TWO-LANE HIGHWAYS

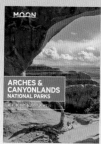

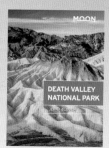

MOON ACADIA NATIONAL PARK — HILARY NANGLE

MOON ARCHES & CANYONLANDS NATIONAL PARKS

MOON BANFF NATIONAL PARK — HIKE · CAMP · KAYAK — ANDREW HEMPSTEAD

MOON DEATH VALLEY NATIONAL PARK

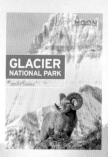

MOON GLACIER NATIONAL PARK

MOON GRAND CANYON — KATHLEEN BRYANT

MOON GREAT SMOKY MOUNTAINS NATIONAL PARK — HIKE · BIKE · CAMP — JASON FRYE

MOON MOUNT RUSHMORE & THE BLACK HILLS — LAURA A. BISWELL

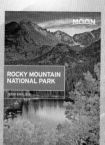

MOON ROCKY MOUNTAIN NATIONAL PARK — ERIN ENGLISH

MOON YELLOWSTONE & GRAND TETON — HIKE · CAMP · SEE WILDLIFE — BECKY LOMAX

MOON YOSEMITE SEQUOIA & KINGS CANYON — ANN MARIE BROWN

MOON ZION & BRYCE

In these books:

- Full coverage of gateway cities and towns
- Itineraries from one day to multiple weeks
- Advice on where to stay (or camp) in and around the parks

Get inspired for your next adventure

Follow **@moonguides** on Instagram or subscribe to our newsletter at **moon.com**

MAP SYMBOLS

═════ Expressway	○ City/Town	ⓘ Information Center	▲ Park
═════ Primary Road	◉ State Capital	🅿 Parking Area	⌣ Golf Course
═════ Secondary Road	⊛ National Capital	♠ Church	✛ Unique Feature
▪▪▪▪▪ Unpaved Road	✪ Highlight	🍇 Winery/Vineyard	🖉 Waterfall
────── Trail	★ Point of Interest	🆃🅷 Trailhead	Λ Camping
────── Ferry	● Accommodation	🚇 Train Station	▲ Mountain
━━━━━ Railroad	▾ Restaurant/Bar	✈ Airport	🎿 Ski Area
▦▦▦▦ Pedestrian Walkway	■ Other Location	✈ Airfield	⬯ Glacier
▨▨▨▨ Stairs			

CONVERSION TABLES

°C = (°F - 32) / 1.8
°F = (°C x 1.8) + 32
1 inch = 2.54 centimeters (cm)
1 foot = 0.304 meters (m)
1 yard = 0.914 meters
1 mile = 1.6093 kilometers (km)
1 km = 0.6214 miles
1 fathom = 1.8288 m
1 chain = 20.1168 m
1 furlong = 201.168 m
1 acre = 0.4047 hectares
1 sq km = 100 hectares
1 sq mile = 2.59 square km
1 ounce = 28.35 grams
1 pound = 0.4536 kilograms
1 short ton = 0.90718 metric ton
1 short ton = 2,000 pounds
1 long ton = 1.016 metric tons
1 long ton = 2,240 pounds
1 metric ton = 1,000 kilograms
1 quart = 0.94635 liters
1 US gallon = 3.7854 liters
1 Imperial gallon = 4.5459 liters
1 nautical mile = 1.852 km

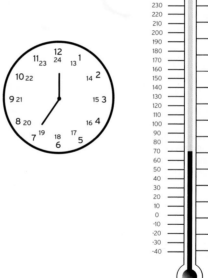

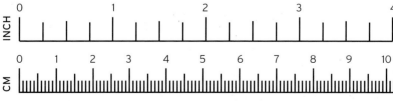

MOON BALI & LOMBOK

Avalon Travel
Hachette Book Group
1700 Fourth Street
Berkeley, CA 94710, USA
www.moon.com

Editor: Megan Anderluh
Managing Editor: Hannah Brezack
Copy Editor: Barbara Schultz
Graphics and Production Coordinator: Darren Alessi
Cover Design: Faceout Studio, Charles Brock
Interior Design: Domini Dragoone
Moon Logo: Tim McGrath
Map Editor: Albert Angulo
Cartographers: Moon Street Cartography (Durango, Co), Karin Dahl, and Andrew Dolan
Proofreader: Lina Carmona
Indexer: Sam Arnold-Boyd

ISBN-13: 978-1-64049-107-6

Printing History
1st Edition — June 2020
5 4 3 2 1

Front cover photo: Tegalalang Rice Terraces near Ubud © Richard Taylor / Sime / eStock Photo
Back cover photo: Beratan Lake in Bali © Ruengrit | Dreamstime.com

Printed in China by RR Donnelley